CATENA AUREA

A.M.D.G.

CATENA AUREA

COMMENTARY

ON THE

FOUR GOSPELS

COLLECTED OUT OF THE

WORKS OF THE FATHERS

BY

ST. THOMAS AQUINAS

Volume IV
St. John

Translation edited by the
Venerable John Henry Cardinal Newman of the Oratory

The Saint Austin Press
296 Brockley Road, London SE4 2RA
MCMXCIX

First published in English by John Henry Parker, Oxford, 1841.

This edition first published in 1997 by

The Saint Austin Press
296 Brockley Road
London SE4 2RA

Telephone: (0181) 692 6009
Facsimile: (0181) 469 3609
Electronic mail: books@saintaustin.org

Second impression, 1999.

The publisher gratefully acknowledges the support of those who subscribed to the republication of this work. Their names appear at the end of Volume II.

ISBN 1 901157 40 7
(4 volume set, not for sale separately)

[ISBN for this volume only: 1 901157 44 X]

A catalogue record for this book is available from the British Library.

Printed in Great Britain by Polestar Wheatons, Exeter.

COMMENTARY

ON THE GOSPEL ACCORDING TO

ST. JOHN.

CHAP. I.

Ver. 1. In the beginning was the Word,

CHRYS. While all the other Evangelists begin with the Chrys. Hom.iv. [iii.] in Joan. Incarnation, John, passing over the Conception, Nativity, education, and growth, speaks immediately of the Eternal Generation, saying, *In the beginning was the Word.* AUG. Aug.lib. lxxxiii. Quæst. q. 63. The Greek word "logos" signifies both Word and Reason. But in this passage it is better to interpret it Word; as referring not only to the Father, but to the creation of things by the operative power of the Word; whereas Reason, though it produce nothing, is still rightly called Reason. AUG. Words Aug. Tract. super Joan. i. c. 8. by their daily use, sound, and passage out of us, have become common things. But there is a word which remaineth inward, in the very man himself; distinct from the sound which proceedeth out of the mouth. There is a word, which is truly and spiritually that, which you understand by the sound, not being the actual sound. Now whoever can conceive the de Trin. l. xv. c.19.(x.) notion of word, as existing not only before its sound, but even before the idea of its sound is formed, may see enigmatically, and as it were in a glass, some similitude of that Word of Which it is said, *In the beginning was the Word.* For when we give expression to something which we know, the word used is necessarily derived from the knowledge thus retained in the memory, and must be of the same quality with that knowledge. For a word is a thought formed from a thing which we know; which word is spoken in the heart, being neither Greek nor Latin, nor of any language, though, when we want to communicate it to others, some sign is assumed

Ibid. cap. 20. (xi.) by which to express it. . . . Wherefore the word which sounds externally, is a sign of the word which lies hid within, to which the name of word more truly appertains. For that which is uttered by the mouth of our flesh, is the voice of the word; and is in fact called word, with reference to that from which it is taken, when it is developed externally. BASIL; This Word Basil. Hom. in princ. Joan. is not a human word. For how was there a human word in the beginning, when man received his being last of all? There was not then any word of man in the beginning, nor yet of Angels; for every creature is within the limits of time, having its beginning of existence from the Creator. But what says the Gospel? It calls the Only-Begotten Himself the Word. CHRYS. But why omitting the Father, does he Chrys. Hom. in Joan. ii. [i.] §. 4. proceed at once to speak of the Son? Because the Father was known to all; though not as the Father, yet as God; whereas the Only-Begotten was not known. As was meet then, he endeavours first of all to inculcate the knowledge of the Son on those who knew Him not; though neither in discoursing on Him, is he altogether silent on the Father. And inasmuch as he was about to teach that the Word was the Only-Begotten Son of God, that no one might think this παθητὴν a possible generation, he makes mention of the Word in the first place, in order to destroy the dangerous suspicion, and shew that the Son was from God impassibly. And a second John15, 15. reason is, that He was to declare unto us the things of the Father. But he does not speak of the Word simply, but with the addition of the article, in order to distinguish It from other words. For Scripture calls God's laws and commandments words; but this Word is a certain Substance, or Person, an Essence, coming forth impassibly from the Father Himself. Basil. Hom. in princ. Joan. c. 3. BASIL; Wherefore then Word? Because born impassibly, the Image of Him that begat, manifesting all the Father in Himself; abstracting from Him nothing, but existing perfect in Himself. AUG. As our knowledge differs from God's, so Aug. xv. de Trin. c. 22. (xiii.) does our word, which arises from our knowledge, differ from that Word of God, which is born of the Father's essence; we might say, from the Father's knowledge, the Father's wisdom, or, more correctly, the Father Who is Knowledge, the Father Who is Wisdom. The Word of God then, the c. 23. (xiv.) Only-Begotten Son of the Father, is in all things like and

equal to the Father; being altogether what the Father is, yet
not the Father; because the one is the Son, the other the
Father.   And thereby He knoweth all things which the
Father knoweth; yet His knowledge is from the Father, even
as is His being: for knowing and being are the same with
Him; and so as the Father's being is not from the Son, so
neither is His knowing.   Wherefore the Father begat the
Word equal to Himself in all things as uttering forth Himself.   For had there been more or less in His Word than in
Himself, He would not have uttered Himself fully and perfectly.   With respect however to our own inner word, which
we find, in whatever sense, to be like the Word, let us not
object to see how very unlike it is also.   A word is a forma- cap. 25.
tion of our mind going to take place, but not yet made, and (xv.)
something in our mind which we toss to and fro in a slippery
circuitous way, as one thing and another is discovered, or
occurs to our thoughts.   When this, which we toss to and
fro, has reached the subject of our knowledge, and been
formed therefrom, when it has assumed the most exact likeness to it, and the conception has quite answered to the
thing; then we have a true word.   Who may not see how
great the difference is here from that Word of God, which
exists in the Form of God in such wise, that It could not
have been first going to be formed, and afterwards formed,
nor can ever have been unformed, being a Form absolute,
and absolutely equal to Him from Whom It is.   Wherefore
in speaking of the Word of God here nothing is said about
thought in God; lest we should think there was any thing
revolving in God, which might first receive form in order to
be a Word, and afterwards lose it, and be carried round
and round again in an unformed state.   AUG. Now the Word Aug. de
of God is a Form, not a formation, but the Form of all Verb.
Dom.
forms, a Form unchangeable, removed from accident, from Serm.
failure, from time, from space, surpassing all things, and 38.
existing in all things as a kind of foundation underneath,
and summit above them.   BASIL; Yet has our outward Basil.
word some similarity to the Divine Word. For our word Hom. in
princ.
declares the whole conception of the mind; since what we Joan.
conceive in the mind we bring out in word.   Indeed our c. 3.
heart is as it were the source, and the uttered word the

Chrys.
Hom. i.

stream which flows therefrom. CHRYS. Observe the spiritual wisdom of the Evangelist. He knew that men honoured most what was most ancient, and that honouring what is before every thing else, they conceived of it as God. On this account he mentions first the beginning, saying, *In the beginning*

Orig.
tom. i.
in Joan.
c. 16.
et sq.
Prov.
16.
Vulg.
Job 40,
19.
1 chief
of, F.T.
princi-
pium,
Vulg.
Col. 1,
18.

was the Word. ORIGEN; There are many significations of this word *beginning.* For there is a beginning of a journey, and beginning of a length, according to Proverbs, *The beginning of the right path is to do justice.* There is a beginning too of a creation, according to Job, *He is the beginning* [1] *of the ways of God.* Nor would it be incorrect to say, that God is the Beginning of all things. The preexistent material again, where supposed to be original, out of which any thing is produced, is considered as the beginning. There is a beginning also in respect of form : as where Christ is the beginning of those who are made according to the image of God. And there is a beginning

Heb. 5,
12.

of doctrine, according to Hebrews; *When for the time ye ought to be teachers, ye have need that one teach you again which be the first principles of the oracles of God.* For there are two kinds of beginning of doctrine: one in itself, the other relative to us; as if we should say that Christ, in that He is the Wisdom and Word of God, was in Himself the beginning of wisdom, but to us, in that He was the Word incarnate.

c. 22.

There being so many significations then of the word, we may take it as the Beginning through Whom, i. e. the Maker; for Christ is Creator as The Beginning, in that He is Wisdom; so that the Word is in the beginning, i. e. in Wisdom; the Saviour being all these excellences at once. As life then is in the Word, so the Word is in the Beginning, that is to say, in Wisdom. Consider then if it be possible according to this signification to understand the Beginning, as meaning that all things are made according to Wisdom, and the patterns contained therein ; or, inasmuch as the Beginning of the Son is the Father, the Beginning of all creatures and existencies, to understand by the text, *In the beginning*

Aug. de
Trin. vi.
c. 3. (ii)
Basil.
Hom. in
princ.
Joan.

was the Word, that the Son, the Word, was in the Beginning, that is, in the Father. AUG. Or, *In the beginning,* as if it were said, before all things. BASIL; The Holy Ghost foresaw that men would arise, who should envy

the glory of the Only-Begotten, subverting their hearers by
sophistry; as if because He were begotten, He was not; and
before He was begotten, He was not. That none might presume then to babble such things, the Holy Ghost saith, *In
the beginning was the Word.* HILARY; Years, centuries, Hilar.
ages, are passed over, place what beginning thou wilt in thy Trin.
imagining, thou graspest it not in time, for He, from Whom it c. 13.
is derived, still *was.* CHRYS. As then when our ship is near Chrys.
shore, cities and port pass in survey before us, which on the Hom. i.
open sea vanish, and leave nothing whereon to fix the eye;
so the Evangelist here, taking us with him in his flight above
the created world, leaves the eye to gaze in vacancy on an
illimitable expanse. For the words, *was in the beginning,*
are significative of eternal and infinite essence. AUG. They Aug. de
say, however, if He is the Son, He was born. We allow it. verb.
They rejoin: if the Son was born to the Father, the Father Serm.
was, before the Son was born to Him. This the Faith [117.]
rejects. Then they say, explain to us how the Son could §. 6.
be born from the Father, and yet be coeval with Him from
whom He is born: for sons are born after their fathers, to
succeed them on their death. They adduce analogies from
nature; and we must endeavour likewise to do the same for
our doctrine. But how can we find in nature a coeternal,
when we cannot find an eternal? However, if a thing
generating and a thing generated can be found any where
coeval, it will be a help to forming a notion of coeternals.
Now Wisdom herself is called in the Scriptures, the bright- Wisd. 7,
ness of Everlasting Light, the image of the Father. Hence 26.
then let us take our comparison, and from coevals form a
notion of coeternals. Now no one doubts that brightness
proceeds from fire: fire then we may consider the father
of the brightness. Presently, when I light a candle, at
the same instant with the fire, brightness ariseth. Give
me the fire without the brightness, and I will with thee
believe that the Father was without the Son. An image
is produced by a mirror. The image exists as soon as
the beholder appears; yet the beholder existed before he
came to the mirror. Let us suppose then a twig, or a blade
of grass which has grown up by the water side. Is it not born
with its image? If there had always been the twig, there

would always have been the image proceeding from the twig.
And whatever is from another thing, is born. So then that
which generates may be coexistent from eternity with that
which is generated from it. But some one will say perhaps,
Well, I understand now the eternal Father, the coeternal Son:
yet the Son is like the emitted brightness, which is less bril-
liant than the fire, or the reflected image, which is less real than
the twig. Not so: there is complete equality between Father
and Son. I do not believe, he says; for thou hast found
nothing whereto to liken it. However, perhaps we can find
something in nature by which we may understand that the
Son is both coeternal with the Father, and in no respect
inferior also: though we cannot find any one material of comparison that will be sufficient singly, and must therefore join
together two, one of which has been employed by our adversaries, the other by ourselves. For they have drawn their
comparison from things which are preceded in time by the
things which they spring from, man, for example, from man.
Nevertheless, man is of the same substance with man. We
have then in that nativity an equality of nature; an equality
of time is wanting. But in the comparison which we have
drawn from the brightness of fire, and the reflexion of a twig,
an equality of nature thou dost not find, of time thou dost.
In the Godhead then there is found as a whole, what
here exists in single and separate parts; and that which
is in the creation, existing in a manner suitable to the
Gest.
Conc.
Eph.   Creator. Ex Gestis Concilii Ephesini; Wherefore in one
place divine Scripture calls Him the Son, in another the
Word, in another the Brightness of the Father; names
severally meant to guard against blasphemy. For, forasmuch as thy son is of the same nature with thyself, the
Scripture wishing to shew that the Substance of the Father
and the Son is one, sets forth the Son of the Father, born of
the Father, the Only-Begotten. Next, since the terms birth
and son, convey the idea of passibleness, therefore it calls
the Son the Word, declaring by that name the impassibility
of His Nativity. But inasmuch as a father with us is necessarily older than his son, lest thou shouldest think that this
applied to the Divine nature as well, it calls the Only-Begotten
the Brightness of the Father; for brightness, though arising

from the sun, is not posterior to it. Understand then that *Brightness,* as revealing the coeternity of the Son with the Father; *Word* as proving the impassibility of His birth, and *Son* as conveying His consubstantiality. CHRYS. But they ^{Chrys.} say that *In the beginning* does not absolutely express eternity: for that the same is said of the heaven and the earth: *In the beginning God made the heaven and the earth.* But are not *made* and *was,* altogether different? For in like manner as the word *is,* when spoken of man, signifies the present only, but when applied to God, that which always and eternally is ; so too *was,* predicated of our nature, signifies the past, but predicated of God, eternity. ORIGEN; The verb *to be,* has a double signification, sometimes expressing the motions which take place in time, as other verbs do; sometimes the substance of that one thing of which it is predicated, without reference to time. Hence it is also called a substantive verb. HILARY; Consider then the world, understand what is written of it. *In the beginning God made the heaven and the earth.* Whatever therefore is created is made in the beginning, and thou wouldest contain in time, what, as being to be made, is contained in the beginning. But, lo, for me, an illiterate unlearned fisherman is independent of time, unconfined by ages, advanceth beyond all beginnings. For the Word was, what it is, and is not bounded by any time, nor commenced therein, seeing It was not *made* in the beginning, but *was.* ALCUIN; To refute those who inferred from Christ's Birth in time, that He had not been from everlasting, the Evangelist begins with the eternity of the Word, saying, *In the beginning was the Word.*

Margin notes: Chrys. Hom. in Joan. iii. [ii.] §. 2. Gen. 1, 1. / Orig. Hom. ii. divers. loc. / Hilar. ii. de Trin. c. xiii. / *meus piscator* (Hil.)

And the Word was with God.

CHRYS. Because it is an especial attribute of God, to be eternal and without a beginning, he laid this down first : then, lest any one on hearing *in the beginning was the Word,* should suppose the Word Unbegotten, he instantly guarded against this ; saying, *And the Word was with God.* HILARY ; From the beginning He is with God : and though inde-

Margin notes: Chrys. Hom.iii. [ii.] 3. / Hilar. ii. de Trin.

Basil.
Hom.in
princ.
Joan.
§. 4.
pendent of time, is not independent of an Author. BASIL;
Again he repeats this, *was*, because of men blasphemously
saying, that there was a time when He was not. Where
then was the Word? Illimitable things are not contained
in space. Where was He then? With God. For neither
is the Father bounded by place, nor the Son by aught

Orig.
Hom. ii.
in Joan.
c. 1.
[1] *factum*
Vulg.
came
E. T.
circumscribing. ORIGEN; It is worth while noting, that,
whereas the Word is said to come[1] [be made] to some, as to
Hosea, Isaiah, Jeremiah, with God it is not made, as though
it were not with Him before. But, the Word having been
always with Him, it is said, *and the Word was with God:*
for from the beginning it was not separate from the Father.

Chrys.
Hom.iii.
CHRYS. He has not said, was *in* God, but was *with* God:
exhibiting to us that eternity which He had in accordance

Theoph.
in loco.
with His Person. THEOPHYL. Sabellius is overthrown by
this text. For he asserts that the Father, Son, and Holy
Ghost are one Person, Who sometimes appeared as the
Father, sometimes as the Son, sometimes as the Holy Ghost.
But he is manifestly confounded by this text, *and the Word
was with God;* for here the Evangelist declares that the Son
is one Person, God the Father another.

And the Word was God.

Hilar.ii.
de Trin.
c. 15.
HILARY; Thou wilt say, that a word is the sound of the voice,
the enunciation of a thing, the expression of a thought:.this
Word was in the beginning with God, because the utterance
of thought is eternal, when He who thinketh is eternal. But
how was that in the beginning, which exists no time either
before, or after, I doubt even whether *in* time at all? For
speech is neither in existence before one speaks, nor after; in
the very act of speaking it vanishes; for by the time a
speech is ended, that from which it began does not exist.
But even if the first sentence, *in the beginning was the Word*,
was through thy inattention lost upon thee, why disputest
thou about the next; *and the Word was with God?* Didst
thou hear it said, " *In* God," so that thou shouldest understand this Word to be only the expression of hidden
thoughts? Or did John say *with* by mistake, and was not

aware of the distinction between being *in*, and being *with*,
when he said, that what was in the beginning, was not
in God, but *with* God? Hear then the nature and name of
the Word; *and the Word was God.* No more then of the
sound of the voice, of the expression of the thought. The
Word here is a Substance, not a sound; a Nature, not an
expression; God, not a nonentity. HILARY; But the title is Hilar.
absolute, and free from the offence of an extraneous subject. Trin. c.
To Moses it is said, *I have given*[1] *thee for a god to* 9,10,11.
Pharaoh: but is not the reason for the name added, when it 1.
is said, *to Pharaoh?* Moses is given for a god to Pharaoh, [1]*datusest* Vulg.
when he is feared, when he is entreated, when he punishes, *made*,
when he heals. And it is one thing to be *given* for a God, Eng. Tr.
another thing to *be* God. I remember too another application of the name in the Psalms, *I have said, ye are gods.* Ps. 82.
But there too it is implied that the title was but bestowed;
and the introduction of, *I said*, makes it rather the phrase
of the Speaker, than the name of the thing. But when I
hear *the Word was God*, I not only hear the Word said to
be, but perceive It proved to be, God. BASIL; Thus cutting Basil.
off the cavils of blasphemers, and those who ask what the Hom. i. in princ.
Word is, he replies, *and the Word was God.* THEOPHYL. Or Joan. c. 4.
combine it thus. From the Word being with God, it follows
plainly that there are two Persons. But these two are of
one Nature; and therefore it proceeds, *In the Word was
God:* to shew that Father and Son are of One Nature, being
of One Godhead. ORIGEN; We must add too, that the Orig.
Word illuminates the Prophets with Divine wisdom, in that tom. ii. in Joan.
He *cometh* to them; but that with God He ever is, because in princ.
He is God[a]. For which reason he placed *and the Word was
with God*, before *and the Word was God.* CHRYS. Not assert- Chrys.
ing, as Plato does, one to be intelligence[1], the other soul[2]; for Hom. ii. [i.] §. 4.
the Divine Nature is very different from this. . . . . But you [1] τοῦς
say, the Father is called God with the addition of the article, [2] ψυχὴ iv. [iii.]
the Son without it. What say you then, when the Apostle [3].

---

[a] The Greek has, πρὸς δὲ τὸν Θεὸν ὁ
Θεὸς ἐστὶ τυγχάνων, ἀπὸ τοῦ εἶναι πρὸς
αὐτόν. lit. but with God, God is present
at all times, because He is with Him,
i. e. τυγχάνειν and εἶναι are one with
God. The Word, as God, is always
equally present with God. S. Thomas
avoids the apparent tautology in the
original by substituting " apud Deum
vero est Verbum obtinere ab eo quod
sit Deus."

Tit. 2,
13.
Rom. 9,
5.
Rom. 1,
7.
writes, *The great God and our Saviour Jesus Christ;* and again, *Who is over all, God;* and *Grace be unto you and peace from God our Father;* without the article? Besides, too, it were superfluous here, to affix what had been affixed just before. So that it does not follow, though the article is not affixed to the Son, that He is therefore an inferior God.

2. The same was in the beginning with God.

Hilar.
ii. de
Trin. c.
16.
HILARY; Whereas he had said, *the Word was God,* the fearfulness, and strangeness of the speech disturbed me; the prophets having declared that God was One. But, to quiet my apprehensions, the fisherman reveals the scheme of this so great mystery, and refers all to one, without dishonour, without obliterating [the Person], without reference to time [b], saying, *The Same was in the beginning with God;* with One Unbegotten God, from whom He is, the One Only-begotten God. THEOPHYL. Again, to stop any diabolical suspicion, that the Word, because He was God, might have rebelled against His Father, as certain Gentiles fable, or, being separate, have become the antagonist of the Father Himself, he says, *The Same was in the beginning with God;* that is to say, this Word of God never existed separate from God.
Chrys.
Hom.iv.
[iii.] §.
1.
CHRYS. Or, lest hearing that *In the beginning was the Word,* you should regard It as eternal, but yet understand the Father's Life to have some degree of priority, he has introduced the words, *The Same was in the beginning with God.* For God was never solitary, apart from Him, but
ibid. 3.
always God with God. Or forasmuch as he said, *the Word was God,* that no one might think the Divinity of the Son inferior, he immediately subjoins the marks of proper
τὸ δημι-
ουργικὸν
Divinity, in that he both again mentions Eternity, *The Same was in the beginning with God;* and adds His attribute of Creator, *All things were made by Him.* ORIGEN; Or thus,
Orig.
tom. ii.
in Joan.
c. 4.
the Evangelist having begun with those propositions, reunites them into one, saying, *The Same was in the beginning with*

---

[b] Since He was 1) " in the beginning," and 2) " God," and 3) " with God," He was 1) not " in time," nor 2) a word, but The Word, (see p. 8.) nor 3) in existing *in* God only, so as to confound or destroy the Personality. [from S. Hil. l. c.]

God. For in the first of the three we learnt *in what* the Word was, that *it was in the beginning;* in the second, *with whom, with God;* in the third *who* the Word was, *God.* Having, then, by the term, The Same, set before us in a manner God the Word of Whom he had spoken, he collects all into the fourth proposition, viz. *In the beginning was the Word, and the Word was with God, and the Word was God;* into, *the Same was in the beginning with God.* It may be asked, however, why it is not said, In the beginning was the Word of God, and the Word of God was with God, and the Word of God was God? Now whoever will admit that truth is one, must needs admit also that the demonstration of truth, that is wisdom, is one. But if truth is one, and wisdom is one, the Word which enuntiates truth and developes wisdom in those who are capable of receiving it, must be One also. And therefore it would have been out of place here to have said, the Word of God, as if there were other words besides that of God, a word of angels, word of men, and so on. We do not say this, to deny that It is the Word of God, but to shew the use of omitting the word God. John himself too in the Apocalypse says, *And his Name is called the Word of God.* Rev. 19, ALCUIN; Wherefore does he use the substantive verb, *was?* [13.] That you might understand that the Word, Which is co-eternal with God the Father, was before all time.

3. All things were made by him.

ALCUIN; After speaking of the nature of the Son, he proceeds to His operations, saying, *All things were made by him,* i. e. every thing whether substance, or property. HILARY; Hilar. Or thus: [It is said], the Word indeed was in the beginning, ii. de but it may be that He was not before the beginning. But Trin. what saith he; *All things were made by him.* He is infinite c. 17. by Whom every thing, which is, was made: and since all things were made by Him, time is likewise[c]. CHRYS. Moses Chrys. indeed, in the beginning of the Old Testament, speaks to Hom. v. us in much detail of the natural world, saying, *In the* [iv.] 1.

[c] That is to say, The text, *All things were made by Him,* makes up for the words, *in the beginning,* should these appear to fall short of eternity. For He Who made all things, made time, and so must have existed before time, i. e. from eternity.

beginning God made the heaven and the earth; and then relates how that the light, and the firmament, and the stars, and the various kinds of animals were created. But the Evangelist sums up the whole of this in a word, as familiar to his hearers; and hastens to loftier matter, making the whole of his book to bear not on the works, but on the Maker. AUG. Since *all things were made by him,* it is evident that light was also, when God said, *Let there be light.* And in like manner the rest. But if so, that which God said, viz. *Let there be light,* is eternal. For the Word of God, God with God, is coeternal with the Father, though the world created by Him be temporal. For whereas our *when* and *sometimes* are words of time, in the Word of God, on the contrary, when a thing ought to be made, is eternal; and the thing is then made, when in that Word it is that it ought to be made, which Word hath in It neither *when,* or at *sometime,* since It is all eternal. AUG. How then can the Word of God be *made,* when God by the Word made all things? For if the Word Itself were made, by what other Word was It made? If you say it was the Word of the Word by Which That was made, *that* Word I call the Only-Begotten Son of God. But if thou dost not call It the Word of the Word [1], then grant that that Word was not made, by which all things were made. AUG. And if It is not made, It is not a creature; but if It is not a creature, It is of the same Substance with the Father. For every substance which is not God is a creature; and what is not a creature is God. THEOPHYL. The Arians are wont to say, that all things are spoken of as made by the Son, in the sense in which we say a door is made by a saw, viz. as an instrument; not that He was Himself the Maker. And so they talk of the Son as a thing made, as if He were made for this purpose, that all things might be made by Him. Now we to the inventors of this lie reply simply: If, as ye say, the Father had created the Son, in order to make use of Him as an instrument, it would appear that the Son were less honourable than the things made, just as things made by a saw are more noble than the saw itself; the saw having been made for their sake. In like way do they speak of the Father creating the Son for the sake of the things made, as if, had He thought good to create the universe, neither would He have produced

Marginal notes:
Aug. 1. de Gen. ad lit. cap. 2.

Aug. in Joan. tract. i. c. 11.

[1] Verbum Verbi ed. Ben.

Aug. de Trin. i. c.9.(vi.)

Theoph. in loc.

the Son. What can be more insane than such language?
They argue, however, why was it not said that the Word
made all things, instead of the preposition *by*[1] being used? [διὰ]
For this reason, that thou mightest not understand an Un-
begotten and Unoriginate Son, a rival God[d]. CHRYS. If the preposition *by* perplex thee, and thou wouldest learn from Scripture that the Word *Itself* made all things, hear David, *Thou, Lord, in the beginning hast laid the foundation of the earth, and the heavens are the work of Thy hands.* That he spoke this of the Only-Begotten, you learn from the Apostle, who in the Epistle to the Hebrews applies these words to the Son. CHRYS. But if you say that the prophet spoke this of the Father, and that Paul applied it to the Son, it comes to the same thing. For he would not have mentioned that as applicable to the Son, unless he fully considered that the Father and the Son were of equal dignity. If again thou dream that in the preposition *by* any subjection is implied, why does Paul use t of the Father? as, *God is faithful, by Whom ye were called into the fellowship of His Son;* and again, *Paul an Apostle by the will of God.* ORIGEN; Here too Valentinus errs, saying, that the Word supplied to the Creator the cause of the creation of the world[e]. If this interpretation is true, it should have been written that all things had their existence from the Word through the Creator, not contrariwise, through the Word from the Creator.

Chrys.
Hom. in
Joan. v.
[iv.]c.2.
Ps. 101.

Chrys.
Hom. v.
c. 2. 3.

1 Cor. 1,
9.
2 Cor. 1,
1.
Orig.
tom. ii.
c. 8.

And without him was not any thing made.

CHRYS. That you may not suppose, when he says, *All things were made by Him,* that he meant only the things Moses had spoken of, he seasonably brings in, *And without Him was not any thing made,* nothing, that is, cognizable either by the senses, or the understanding. Or thus; Lest you should suspect the sentence, *All things were made by Him,* to refer to the miracles which the other Evangelists had related, he adds, *and without Him was not any thing made.* HILARY; Or thus; That *all things were made by him,* is pronouncing

Chrys.
Hom. v.
in princ.

Hilar.
lib. ii.
de Trin.
c. 18.

---

[d] The text of Aug. has et Dei con-
ditorem, perhaps it should be, et Deo
contrarium, (as before Patri contrarium.)
Theoph. has ἀντίθιον.

[e] τὸν τὴν αἴτιην παρέχοντα τῆς γινίσιως
τοῦ κοσμοῦ τῷ δημιουργῷ. Origen is
speaking of Heracleon, a disciple of
Valentinus.

too much, it may be said. There is an Unbegotten Who is made of none, and there is the Son Himself begotten from Him Who is Unbegotten. The Evangelist however again implies the Author, when he speaks of Him as Associated; saying, *without Him was not any thing made.* This, that nothing was made without Him, I understand to mean the Son's not being alone, for ' by whom' is one thing, ' not with-out whom' another. ORIGEN: Or thus, that thou mightest not think that the things made by the Word had a separate existence, and were not contained in the Word, he says, *and without Him was not any thing made:* that is, not any thing was made externally of Him; for He encircles all things, as the Preserver of all things. AUG. Or, by saying, *without Him was not any thing made,* he tells us not to suspect Him in any sense to be a thing made. For how can He be a thing made, when God, it is said, made nothing without Him? ORIGEN; If all things were made by the Word, and in the number of all things is wickedness, and the whole influx of sin, these too were made by the Word; which is false. Now ' nothing' and ' a thing which is not,' mean the same. And the Apostle seems to call wicked things, things which are not, *God calleth those things which be not, as though they were.* All wickedness then is called *nothing,* forasmuch as it is made *without* the Word. Those who say however that the devil is not a creature of God, err. In so far as he is the devil, he is not a creature of God; but he, whose character it is to be the devil, is a creature of God. It is as if we should say a murderer is not a creature of God, when, so far as he is a man, he *is* a creature of God. AUG. For sin was not made by Him; for it is manifest that sin is nothing, and that men become nothing when they sin. Nor was an idol made by the Word. It has indeed a sort of form of man, and man himself was made by the Word; but the form of man in an idol was not made by the Word: for it is written, *we know that an idol is nothing.* These then were not made by the Word; but whatever things were made naturally, the whole universe, were; every creature from an angel to a worm. ORIGEN; Valentinus excludes from the things made by the Word, all that were made in the ages which he believes to have existed before the Word. This is plainly false; inasmuch

Orig. Hom.iii. in div. loc.

Aug. Quæst. Test. N. V. qu. 97.

Orig. in Joh. tom. ii. c. 7.

Rom. 4, 17.

Aug. in Joh. tract. i. c. 13.

1 Cor. 8, 4.

Orig. tom. ii. c. 8.

as the things which he accounts divine are thus excluded from the "all things," and what he deems wholly corrupt are properly ' all things!' AUG. The folly of those men is not to be listened to, who think *nothing* is to be understood here as *something*, because it is placed at the end of the sentence[1] : as if it made any difference whether it was said, without Him nothing was made, or, without Him was made nothing. ORIGEN ; If ' the word' be taken for that which is in each man, inasmuch as it was implanted in each by *the Word*, which *was in the beginning*, then also, we commit nothing without this ' word' [reason] taking this word ' nothing' in a popular sense. For the Apostle says that sin was dead without the law, but when the commandment came, sin revived ; for sin is not imputed when there is no law. But neither was there sin, when there was no Word, for our Lord says, *If I had not come and spoken to them, they had not had sin.* For every excuse is withdrawn from the sinner, if, with the Word present, and enjoining what is to be done, he refuses to obey Him. Nor is the Word to be blamed on this account; any more than a master, whose discipline leaves no excuse open to a delinquent pupil on the ground of ignorance. All things then were made by the Word, not only the natural world, but also whatever is done by those acting without reason.

Aug. de Natura boni, c. 25.
[1] Vulgate
Orig. tom. ii. c. 9.
John 15, 22.

4. In him was life.

Vulg. quod factum est in ipso vita erat.

BEDE ; The Evangelist having said that every creature was made by the Word, lest perchance any one might think that His will was changeable, as though He willed on a sudden to make a creature, which from eternity he had not made; he took care to shew that, though a creature was made in time, in the Wisdom of the Creator it had been from eternity arranged what and when He should create. AUG. The passage can be read thus: *What was made in Him was life*[1]. Therefore the whole universe is life: for what was there not made in Him? He is the Wisdom of God, as is said, *In Wisdom hast Thou made them all.* All things therefore are made *in* Him, even as they are by Him. But, if whatever was made in Him is life, the earth is life, a stone is life. We must not interpret it so unsoundly, lest the sect of the

Bede in 1 Joh.
Aug. in Joh. tr. i. c. 16, 17.
[1] Vulg. Ps. 104.

Manicheans creep in upon us, and say, that a stone has life, and that a wall has life; for they do insanely assert so, and when reprehended or refuted, appeal as though to Scripture, and ask, why was it said, *That which was made in Him was life?* Read the passage then thus: make the stop after *What was made,* and then proceed, *In Him was life.* The earth was made; but, the earth itself which was made is not life. In the Wisdom of God however there is spiritually a certain Reason after which the earth is made. This is Life[f]. A chest in workmanship is not life, a chest in art is, inasmuch as the mind of the workman lives wherein that original pattern exists. And in this sense the Wisdom of God, by Which all things are made, containeth in art ' all things which are made, according to that art.' And therefore whatever is made, is not in itself life, but is life in Him.

Origen. Hom. ii. in div. loc. ante med.   ORIGEN; It may also be divided thus: *That which was made in him;* and then, *was life;* the sense being, that all things that were made by Him and in Him, are life in Him, and are one in Him. They *were,* that is, in Him; they exist as the cause, before they exist in themselves as effects. If thou ask how and in what manner all things which were made by the Word subsist in Him vitally, immutably, causally, take some examples from the created world. See how that all things within the arch of the world of sense have their causes simultaneously and harmoniously subsisting in that sun which is the greatest luminary of the world: how multitudinous crops of herbs and fruits are contained in single seeds: how the most complex variety of rules, in the art of the artificer, and the mind of the director, are a living unit, how an infinite number of lines coexist in one point. Contemplate these several instances, and thou wilt be able as it were on the wings of physical science, to penetrate with thy intellectual eye the secrets of the Word, and as far as is allowed to a human understanding, to see how all things

---

[f] The passage continues thus in the Tract. " I will explain my meaning. A workman makes a chest. He first has that chest in his art; for otherwise he could not make it. The chest however does not exist in his art, as a visible chest; it exists there invisibly, and is then brought into visible existence by workmanship. The chest is then first in workmanship; but does it cease to be in art? there it remains still, and there it will continue, the pattern of other chests, when the first visible one has rotted. Mark the distinction between a chest in art, and a chest in workmanship. A chest," &c.

which were made by the Word, live in Him, and were made in Him. HILARY; Or it can be understood thus. In that he had said, *without Him was not any thing made*, one might have been perplexed, and have asked, Was then any thing made by another, which yet was not made without Him? if so, then though nothing is made *without*, all things are not made *by* Him: it being one thing to make, another to be with the maker. On this account the Evangelist declares what it was which was not made without Him, viz. what was made in Him. This then it was which was not made without Him, viz. what was made in Him. And that which was made in Him, was also made by Him. For all things were created in Him and by Him. Now things were made *in* Him, because He was born God the Creator. And for this reason also things that were made in Him, were not made without Him, viz. that God, in that He was born, *was life*, and He who *was life*, was not made life after being born. Nothing then which was made in Him, was made without Him, because He was life, in Whom they were made; because God Who was born of God was God, not after, but in that He was born[h]. CHRYS. Or to give an-other explanation. We will not put the stop at *without Him was not any thing made*, as the heretics do. For they wishing to prove the Holy Ghost a creature, read, *That which was made in Him, was life.* But this cannot be so understood. For first, this was not the place for making mention of the Holy Ghost. But let us suppose it was; let us take the passage for the present according to their reading, we shall see that it leads to a difficulty. For when it is said, *That which was made in Him, was life;* they say the life spoken of is the Holy Ghost. But this life is also light; for the Evangelist proceeds, *The life was the light of men.* Wherefore according to them, he calls the Holy Ghost the light of all men. But the Word mentioned above, is what he here calls consecutively, God, and Life, and Light. Now *the Word was made flesh.* It follows that the Holy Ghost is in-carnate, not the Son. Dismissing then this reading, we adopt a more suitable one, with the following meaning: *All things*

Chrys. Hom. v. [iv.] in Joan. c. 1, 2.

---

[h] i. e. the Son ever being what He is, in that He is, " Living of Living, Perfect of Perfect," not [as man] re-ceiving subsequently, He was the Creator, in that He was, and always the Creator, and so of all things, because what He was, He was always, in that He was.

were made by Him, and without Him was not any thing made which was made : there we make a stop, and begin a fresh sentence : *In Him was life. Without Him was not* γιꞓντὸν *any thing made which was made ;* i. e. which could be made. You see how by this short addition, he removes any difficulty which might follow. For by introducing *without Him was not any thing made,* and adding, *which was made,* he includes all things invisible, and excepts the Holy Spirit : for δημιουρ- the Spirit cannot be made. To the mention of creation, γίας succeeds that of providence. *In Him was life*[1]. As a fountain which produces vast depths of water, and yet is nothing diminished at the fountain head ; so worketh the Only-Begotten. How great soever His creations be, He Himself is none the less for them. By the word *life* here is meant not only creation, but that providence by which the things created are preserved. But when you are told that *in Him was life,* do John 5, not suppose Him compounded ; for, *as the Father hath life* 26. *in Himself, so hath He given to the Son to have life in Himself.* As then you would not call the Father compounded, so Orig. neither should you the Son. ORIGEN; Or thus: Our Saviour t.ii.c.12, 13. is said to be some things not for Himself, but for others ; others again, both for Himself and others. When it is said then, *That which was made in Him was life;* we must enquire whether the life is for Himself and others, or for others only ; and if for others, for whom ? Now the Life and the Light are both the same Person: He is the light of men : He is therefore their life. The Saviour is called Life here, not to Himself, but to others; whose Light He also is. This life is inseparable from the Word, from the time it is added on to it. For Reason or the Word must exist before in the soul, cleansing it from sin, till it is pure enough to receive the life, which is thus ingrafted or inborn in every one who renders himself fit to receive the Word of God. Hence observe, that though the Word itself in the beginning was not made, the Beginning never having been without the Word; yet the life of men was not always in the Word. This life of men was *made,* in that It was the light of men; and

---

[1] τὸν περὶ τῆς προνοίας λόγον. *Life,* he says. The Hom. continues: Life, the Evangelist says, in order that we might not be incredulous as to so many things having come from Him. For as, &c.

this light of men could not be before man was; the light of
men being understood relatively to men [k]. And therefore he
says, That which was made in the Word was life; not That
which *was* in the Word was life. Some copies read, not
amiss, " That which *was made, in Him is life.*" If we understand the life in the Word, to be He who says below,
' I *am* the life,' we shall confess that none who believe not
in Christ live, and that all who live not in God, are dead. John 11, 25; 14, 6.

And the life was the light of men.

THEOPHYL. He had said, *In him was life*, that you might Theoph. in loc.
not suppose that the Word was without life. Now he shews
that that life is spiritual, and the light of all reasonable
creatures. *And the life was the light of men:* i. e. not
sensible, but intellectual light, illuminating the very soul.
AUG. Life of itself gives illumination to men, but to cattle Aug. in Joh. tr. l. c. 18.
not: for they have not rational souls, by which to discern
wisdom: whereas man, being made in the image of God, has
a rational soul, by which he can discern wisdom. Hence that
life, by which all things are made, is light, not however of all
animals whatsoever, but of men. THEOPHYL. He saith not,
the Light of the Jews only, but of all men: for all of us, in so
far as we have received intellect and reason, from that Word
which created us, are said to be illuminated by Him. For
the reason which is given to us, and which constitutes us the
reasonable beings we are, is a light directing us what to do,
and what not to do. ORIGEN; We must not omit to notice, Orig. non occ.
that he puts the *life* before *the light of men.* For it would
be a contradiction to suppose a being without life to be
illuminated; as if life were an addition to illumination. But tom. ii. c. 16.
to proceed: if *the life was the light of men*, meaning men
only, Christ is the light and the life of men only; an
heretical supposition. It does not follow then, when a thing is
predicated of any, that it is predicated of those only; for of
God it is written, that He is the God of Abraham, Isaac, and
Jacob; and yet He is not the God of those fathers only. In
the same way, the *light of men* is not excluded from being
the light of others as well. Some moreover contend from c. 17.

[k] *τοῦ φῶτος τῶν ἀνθρώπων κατὰ τὴν πρὸς ἀνθρώποις σχέσιν νοουμένου.*

Gen. 1,
26. Genesis, *Let us make man after our image,* that man means whatever is made after the image and similitude of God. If so, the light of men is the light of any rational creature whatever.

5. And the light shineth in darkness.

Aug. tr.
1. c. 19. AUG. Whereas that life is the light of men, but foolish hearts cannot receive that light, being so incumbered with sins that they cannot see it; for this cause lest any should think there is no light near them, because they cannot see it, he continues: *And the light shineth in darkness, and the darkness comprehended it not.* For suppose a blind man standing in the sun, the sun is present to him, but he is absent from the sun. In like manner every fool is blind, and wisdom is present to him; but, though present, absent from his sight, forasmuch as sight is gone: the truth being, not that she is absent from him, but that he is absent from her.

Orig. in
Joan. t.
ii. c. 14.
Eph. 5,
8. ORIGEN; This kind of darkness however is not in men by nature, according to the text in the Ephesians, *Ye were sometime darkness, but now are ye light in the Lord*[1]. ORIGEN;

Orig.
Hom. ii.
in div.
loc. Or thus, The light shineth in the darkness of faithful souls,

[1] Nicolai, for this passage which is incorrectly given, substitutes the following. (Origen, Tom. ii. c. 13. in Joh.) Now if the life is one with the light of men, none who in darkness lives, and none who lives is in darkness; since every one who lives is also in light, and conversely, whoever is in light, also lives. Again, as in thus discoursing on contraries, we may understand the contraries to them which are omitted, and life, and the light of men, are the subjects of our discourse; and the contrary of life is death, and the contrary of the light of men is the darkness of men: we may perceive, that whoever is in darkness, is also in death, and he who does the works of death, is certainly in darkness; whereas he who does the things which are of the light, that is, he whose works shine before men, and who is mindful of God, is not in death, as we read in Ps. vi. He is not in death who remembereth thee. [Vulg. Quoniam non est in morte qui memor sit tui. Eng. T. In death no man remembereth thee.] But whether men's darkness and death are so by nature or not, is another consideration. *We were*

sometime darkness, but now light in the Lord; although we be in some degree holy and spiritual. Whosoever was sometime darkness, did, as Paul, become darkness, although being capable and framed such as to be made light in the Lord. And again, The light of men is our Lord Jesus Christ, Who manifested Himself in human nature to every rational and intelligent creature, and opened to the hearts of the faithful the mysteries of His Divinity, in Which He is equal to the Father; according to the Apostle's saying, (Eph. 5, 8.) Ye were sometime darkness, but now are ye light in the Lord. Hence the light shineth in darkness, because the whole human race, not by nature but as the desert of original sin, was in the darkness of ignorance of the truth; but after His Birth of the Virgin, Christ shineth in the hearts of those who discern Him. But because there are some who still abide in the most profound darkness of impiety and deceit, the Evangelist adds, And the darkness comprehended it not; as though he would say, The Light, &c.

beginning from faith, and drawing onwards to hope; but the deceit and ignorance of undisciplined souls did not comprehend the light of the Word of God shining in the flesh. That however is an ethical meaning. The metaphysical signification of the words is as follows. Human nature, even though it sinned not, could not shine by its own strength simply; for it is not naturally light, but only a recipient of it; it is capable of containing wisdom, but is not wisdom itself. As the air, of itself, shineth not, but is called by the name of darkness, even so is our nature, considered in itself, a dark substance, which however admits of and is made partaker of the light of wisdom. And as when the air receives the sun's rays, it is not said to shine of itself, but the sun's radiance to be apparent in it; so the reasonable part of our nature, while possessing the presence of the Word of God, does not of itself understand God, and intellectual things, but by means of the divine light implanted in it. Thus, *The light shineth in darkness:* for the Word of God, the life and the light of men, ceaseth not to shine in our nature; though regarded in itself, that nature is without form and darkness. And forasmuch as pure light cannot be comprehended by any creature, hence the text: *The darkness comprehended it not.*

CHRYS. Or thus: throughout the whole foregoing passage he had been speaking of creation; then he mentions the spiritual benefits which the Word brought with it: *and the life was the light of men.* He saith not, the light of Jews, but of all men without exception; for not the Jews only, but the Gentiles also have come to this knowledge. The Angels he omits, for he is speaking of human nature, to whom the Word came bringing glad tidings. ORIGEN; But they ask, why is not the Word Itself called the light of men, instead of the life which is in the Word? We reply, that the life here spoken of is not that which rational and irrational animals have in common, but that which is annexed to the Word which is within us through participation of the primæval Word. For we must distinguish the external and false life, from the desirable and true. We are first made partakers of life: and this life with some is light potentially only, not in act; with those, viz. who are not eager to search out the things which appertain to knowledge: with others it is actual light, those who, as the

Chrys.
Hom. v.
[iv.]c.3.

Orig.
tom. ii.
in Joan.
c. 19.

1 Cor.
12, 31.
c. 14. Apostle saith, covet earnestly the best gifts, that is to say, the word of wisdom. (If[k] the life and the light of men are the same, whoso is in darkness is proved not to live, and none Chrys.
Hom. v.
[iv.]c.3. who liveth abideth in darkness. CHRYS[l]. Life having come to us, the empire of death is dissolved; a light having shone upon us, there is darkness no longer: but there remaineth ever a life which death, a light which darkness cannot overcome. Whence he continues, *And the light shineth in darkness:* by darkness meaning death and error, for sensible light does not shine in darkness, but darkness must be removed first; whereas the preaching of Christ shone forth amidst the reign of error, and caused it to disappear, and Christ by dying changed death into life, so overcoming it, that, those who were already in its grasp, were brought back again. Forasmuch then as neither death nor error hath overcome his light, which is every where conspicuous, shining forth by its own strength; therefore he adds, *And* Orig.
tom. ii.
c. 20. *the darkness comprehended it not*[m]. ORIGEN; As the light of men is a word expressing two spiritual things, so is darkness also. To one who possesses the light, we attribute both the doing the deeds of the light, and also true understanding, inasmuch as he is illuminated by the light of knowledge: and, on the other hand, the term darkness we apply both to unlawful acts, and also to that knowledge, which seems such, but is not. Now as the Father is light, and in Him is no darkness at all, so is the Saviour also. Yet, inasmuch as he underwent the similitude of our sinful flesh, it is not incorrectly said of Him, that in Him there was some darkness; for He took our darkness upon Himself, in order that He might dissipate it. This Light therefore, which was made the life of man, shines in the darkness of our hearts, when the prince of this darkness wars with the human race. This Light the darkness persecuted, as is clear from what our Saviour and His children suffer; the darkness fighting against

---

[k] Nicolai omits this clause, as not being Origen's, nor fitting in with what precedes and substitutes, "which is afterwards followed by the word of knowledge, &c."

[l] Nicolai inserts from S. Chrys., in order to make the connection clear, "The word 'life' means here not only that life which is received by creation, but that perpetual and immortal life which is prepared for us by the Providence of God." Life having, &c.

[m] i. e. could not *get hold* of it; for Chrysostom adds, it is too strong to be contended with.

the children of light. But, forasmuch as God takes up the
cause, they do not prevail; nor do they apprehend the light, for
they are either of too slow a nature to overtake the light's quick
course, or, waiting for it to come up to them, they are put to
flight at its approach. We should bear in mind, however,
that darkness is not always used in a bad sense, but
sometimes in a good, as in Psalm xvii. *He made darkness His* Ps. 18,
secret place : the things of God being unknown and incompre-¹¹·
hensible. This darkness then I will call praiseworthy, since
it tends toward light, and lays hold on it: for, though it
were darkness before, while it was not known, yet it is
turned to light and knowledge in him who has learned.
AUG. A certain Platonist once said, that the beginning of this Aug. de
Gospel ought to be copied in letters of gold, and placed Dei, l.x.
in the most conspicuous place in every church. BEDE; c. 29.
The other Evangelists describe Christ as born in time ; Bede,
John witnesseth that He was in the beginning, saying, in loc.
In the beginning was the Word. The others describe His
sudden appearance among men ; he witnesseth that He was
ever with God, saying, *And the Word was with God.* The
others prove Him very man ; he very God, saying, *And the
Word was God.* The others exhibit Him as man conversing
with men for a season ; he pronounces Him God abiding with
God in the beginning, saying, *The Same was in the beginning
with God.* The others relate the great deeds which He did
amongst men ; he that God the Father made every creature
through Him, saying, *All things were made by Him, and
without Him was not any thing made.*

6. There was a man sent from God, whose name
was John.

7. The same came for a witness, to bear witness of
the Light, that all men through him might believe.

8. He was not that Light, but was sent to bear
witness of that Light.

AUG. What is said above, refers to the Divinity of Christ. Aug.
He came to us in the form of man, but man in such sense, as Tr. ii.
that the Godhead was concealed within Him. And therefore c. 2.

there was sent before a great man, to declare by his witness
that He was more than man. And who was this? He was
a man. THEOPHYL. Not an Angel, as many have held.
The Evangelist here refutes such a notion. AUG. And how
could he declare the truth concerning God, unless he were
sent from God. CHRYS. After this esteem nothing that he
says as human; for he speaketh not his own, but his that
sent him. And therefore the Prophet calls him a messenger,
I send My messenger, for it is the excellence of a messenger,
to say nothing of his own. But the expression, *was sent,* does
not mean his entrance into life, but to his office. As Esaias was
sent on his commission, not from any place out of the world,
but from where he saw the Lord sitting upon His high and
lofty throne; in like manner John was sent from the desert
to baptize; for he says, *He that sent me to baptize with water,*
the same said unto me, Upon Whom thou shalt see the Spirit
descending, and remaining on Him, the same is He which
baptizeth with the Holy Ghost. AUG. What was he called?
whose name was John? ALCUIN. That is, the grace of God, or
one in whom is grace, who by his testimony first made
known to the world the grace of the New Testament, that is,
Christ. Or John may be taken to mean, to whom it is given:
because that through the grace of God, to him it was given,
not only to herald, but also to baptize the King of kings.
AUG. Wherefore came he? *The same came for a witness, to*
bear witness of the Light. ORIGEN; Some try to undo the
testimonies of the Prophets to Christ, by saying that the Son
of God had no need of such witnesses; the wholesome words
which He uttered and His miraculous acts being sufficient to
produce belief; just as Moses deserved belief for his speech
and goodness, and wanted no previous witnesses. To this
we may reply, that, where there are a number of reasons to
make people believe, persons are often impressed by one
kind of proof, and not by another, and God, Who for the
sake of all men became man, can give them many reasons
for belief in Him. And with respect to the doctrine of
the Incarnation, certain it is that some have been forced
by the Prophetical writings into an admiration of Christ
by the fact of so many prophets having, before His advent,
fixed the place of His nativity; and by other proofs of the

same kind. It is to be remembered too, that, though the display of miraculous powers might stimulate the faith of those who lived in the same age with Christ, they might, in the lapse of time, fail to do so; as some of them might even get to be regarded as fabulous. Prophecy and miracles together are more convincing than simply past miracles by themselves. We must recollect too that men receive honour themselves from the witness which they bear to God. He deprives the Prophetical choir of immeasurable honour, whoever denies that it was their office to bear witness to Christ. John when he comes to bear witness to the light, follows in the train of those who went before him. CHRYS. Not because the light wanted the testimony, but for the reason which John himself gives, viz. *that all might believe on Him.* For as He put on flesh to save all men from death; so He sent before Him a human preacher, that the sound of a voice like their own, might the readier draw men to Him. BEDE; He saith not, that all men should believe *in* him; for, *cursed be the man that trusteth in man;* but, *that all men through him might believe;* i. e. by his testimony believe in the Light. THEOPHYL. Though some however might not believe, he is not accountable for them. When a man shuts himself up in a dark room, so as to receive no light from the sun's rays, he is the cause of the deprivation, not the sun. In like manner John was sent, that all men might believe; but if no such result followed, he is not the cause of the failure. CHRYS. Forasmuch however as with us, the one who witnesses, is commonly a more important, a more trustworthy person, than the one to whom he bears witness, to do away with any such notion in the present case the Evangelist proceeds; *He was not that Light, but was sent to bear witness of that Light.* If this were not his intention, in repeating the words, *to bear witness of the Light,* the addition would be superfluous, and rather a verbal repetition, than the explanation of a truth. THEOPHYL. But it will be said, that we do not allow John or any of the saints to be or ever to have been light. The difference is this: If we call any of the saints light, we put light without the article. So if asked whether John is light, without the article, thou mayest allow without hesitation that he is: if with the article, thou allow it not. For he is not

Chrys. Hom. vi. [v.] in Joh. c. 1.

Bed. in loc. Jer. 17, 5.

Chrys. Hom. vi. in Joh. c. 1.

very, original, light, but is only called so, on account of his partaking of the light, which cometh from the true Light.

9. That was the true Light which lighteth every man that cometh into the world.

Aug. in Joan. Tr. ii. AUG. What Light it is to which John bears witness, he shews himself, saying, *That was the true Light.* CHRYS. Or

Chrys. Hom. in Joan. vii. [vi.] 1. thus; Having said above that John had come, and was sent, to bear witness of the Light, lest any from the recent coming of the witness, should infer the same of Him who is witnessed to, the Evangelist takes us back to that existence which is

Aug. Tract.ii. in Joh.§. 7. beyond all beginning, saying, *That was the true Light.* AUG. Wherefore is there added, *true?* Because man enlightened is called light, but the true Light is that which lightens. For our eyes are called lights, and yet, without a lamp at night, or the sun by day, these lights are open to no purpose. Wherefore he adds: *which lighteneth every man:* but if every man, then John himself. He Himself then enlightened the person, by whom He wished Himself to be pointed out. And just as we may often, from the reflexion of the sun's rays on some object, know the sun to be risen, though we cannot look at the sun itself; as even feeble eyes can look at an illuminated wall, or some object of that kind: even so, those to whom Christ came, being too weak to behold Him, He threw His rays upon John; John confessed the illumination, and so the Illuminator Himself was discovered. It is said, *that cometh into the world.* Had man not departed from Him, he had not had to be enlightened; but therefore is he to be here enlightened, because he departed thence, when

Theoph. in loc. he might have been enlightened. THEOPHYL. Let the Manichean blush, who pronounces us the creatures of a dark and malignant creator: for we should never be enlightened, were

Chrys. Hom. viii. c. 2. we not the children of the true Light. CHRYS. Where are those too, who deny Him to be very God? We see here that He is called very Light. But if He lighteneth every man that cometh into the world, how is it that so many have gone on without light? For all have not known the worship of Christ. The answer is: He only enlighteneth every man, so far as pertains to Him. If men shut their eyes, and will not

receive the rays of this light, their darkness arises not from
the fault of the light, but from their own wickedness, inasmuch as they voluntarily deprive themselves of the gift of
grace. For grace is poured out upon all; and they, who
will not enjoy the gift, may impute it to their own blindness.
AUG. Or the words, *lighteneth every man*, may be under- Aug.
stood to mean, not that there is no one who is not enlightened, de Pecc.
but that no one is enlightened except by Him. BEDE; In- et Remiss.
cluding both natural and divine wisdom; for as no one can i.c.xxv.
exist of himself, so no one can be wise of himself. ORIGEN; Orig.
Or thus: We must not understand the words, *lighteneth every* Hom. 2,
in div.
man that cometh into the world, of the growth from hidden loc.
seeds to organized bodies, but of the entrance into the invisible world, by the spiritual regeneration and grace, which is
given in Baptism. Those then the true Light lighteneth,
who come into the world of goodness, not those who rush
into the world of sin. THEOPHYL. Or thus: The intellect Theoph.
which is given in us for our direction, and which is called in loc.
natural reason, is said here to be a light given us by God. But
some by the ill use of their reason have darkened themselves.

**10. He was in the world, and the world was made
by him, and the world knew him not.**

AUG. The Light which lighteneth every man that cometh Aug.
into the world, came here in the flesh; because while He Tr. in
Joan. ii.
was here in His Divinity alone, the foolish, blind, and un- c. 8.
righteous could not discern Him; those of whom it is said
above, *The darkness comprehended it not.* Hence the text;
He was in the world. ORIGEN; For as, when a person Orig.
leaves off speaking, his voice ceases to be, and vanishes; so Hom. 2
in div.
if the Heavenly Father should cease to speak His Word, the loc.
effect of that Word, i. e. the universe which is created in the
Word, shall cease to exist. AUG. You must not suppose, Aug.
however, that He was in the world in the same sense in which Tr. ii.
c. 10.
the earth, cattle, men, are in the world; but in the sense in
which an artificer controls his own work; whence the text,
And the world was made by Him. Nor again did He make
it after the manner of an artificer; for whereas an artificer is

external to what he fabricates, God pervades the world, carrying on the work of creation in every part, and never absent from any part: by the presence of His Majesty He both makes and controls what is made. Thus *He was in the world,* as He by Whom the world was made. Chrys. And again, because He was in the world, but not coeval with the world, for this cause he introduced the words, *and the world was made by Him:* thus taking you back again to the eternal existence of the Only-Begotten. For when we are told that the whole of creation was made by Him, we must be very dull not to acknowledge that the Maker existed before the work. Theophyl. Here he overthrows at once the insane notion of the Manichæan[o], who says that the world is the work of a malignant creature, and the opinion of the Arian, that the Son of God is a creature. Aug. But what meaneth this, *The world was made by Him?* The earth, sky, and sea, and all that are therein, are called the world. But in another sense, the lovers of the world are called the world, of whom he says, *And the world knew Him not.* For did the sky, or Angels, not know their Creator, Whom the very devils confess, Whom the whole universe has borne witness to? Who then did not know Him? Those who, from their love of the world, are called the world; for such live in heart in the world, while those who do not love it, have their body in the world, but their heart in heaven; as saith the Apostle, *our conversation is in heaven.* By their love of the world, such men merit being called by the name of the place where they live. And just as in speaking of a bad house, or good house, we do not mean praise or blame to the walls, but to the inhabitants; so when we talk of the world, we mean those who live there in the love of it. Chrys. But they who were the friends of God, knew Him even before His presence in the body; whence Christ saith below, *Your father Abraham rejoiced to see My day.* When the Gentiles then interrupt us with the question, Why has He come in these last times to work our salvation, having neglected us so long? we reply, that *He was in the world before,* superintending what He had made, and was known to all who were worthy of Him; and that, if the world knew Him not, those of whom the world

Chrys. Hom. in Joan. viii. c. 1.

Theoph. in loc.

Aug. Tr. in Joan. ii. c. 11.

Phil. 3, 20.

Chrys. Hom. viii. c. 8. 56.

---

[o] So Theoph. Other copies have "of Marcion."

was not worthy knew Him. The reason follows, why *the world knew Him not.* The Evangelist calls those men the world, who are tied to the world, and savour of worldly things ; for there is nothing that disturbs the mind so much, as this melting with the love of present things.

11. He came unto his own, and his own received him not.

12. But as many as received him, to them gave he power to become the sons of God, even to them that believe on his name :

13. Which were born, not of blood, nor of the will of the flesh, nor of the will of man, but of God.

CHRYS. When He said that the world knew Him not, he referred to the times of the old dispensation, but what follows has reference to the time of his preaching; *He came unto his own.* AUG. Because all things were made by Him. THEO-PHYL. By *his own*, understand either the world, or Judæa, which He had chosen for His inheritance. CHRYS. He came then unto His own, not for His own good, but for the good of others. But whence did He Who fills all things, and is every where present, come? He came out of condescension to us, though in reality He had been in the world all along. But the world not seeing Him, because it knew Him not, He deigned to put on flesh. And this manifestation and condescension is called His advent. But the merciful God so contrives His dispensations, that we may shine forth in proportion to our goodness, and therefore He will not compel, but invites men, by persuasion and kindness, to come of their own accord : and so, when He came, some received Him, and others received Him not. He desires not an unwilling and forced service; for no one who comes unwillingly devotes himself wholly to Him. Whence what follows, *And his own received him not.* He here calls the Jews His own, as being his peculiar people; as indeed are all men in some sense, being made by Him. And as above, to the shame of our common nature, he said, that the world which was made by Him, knew not its Maker: so here again, indignant at the in-

Chrys.
Hom. in
Joan.
ix. 1.

Aug.
in Joan.
Tr. i.

Chrys.
Hom.
x.[ix.]2.

Hom.ix.
[viii.] 1.

gratitude of the Jews, he brings a heavier charge, viz. that *His*
Aug.Tr. *own received Him not.* AUG. But if none at all received,
in Joan.
ii. 12. none will be saved. For no one will be saved, but he who
received Christ at His coming; and therefore he adds, *As*
Chrys. *many as received Him.* CHRYS. Whether they be bond or
Hom.
in Joan. free, Greek or Barbarian, wise or unwise, women or men, the
x. [ix.] young or the aged, all are made meet for the honour, which
2.
the Evangelist now proceeds to mention. *To them gave He*
Aug. *power to become the sons of God.* AUG. O amazing goodness!
Tr.ii.13.
He was born the Only Son, yet would not remain so; but
grudged not to admit joint heirs to His inheritance. Nor was
Chrys. this narrowed by many partaking of it. CHRYS. He saith not
Hom.
x. [ix.] that He made them the sons of God, but gave them power to
2. become the sons of God: shewing that there is need of
much care, to preserve the image, which is formed by our
adoption in Baptism, untarnished: and shewing at the same
time also that no one can take this power from us, except we
rob ourselves of it. Now, if the delegates of worldly governments have often nearly as much power as those governments
themselves, much more is this the case with us, who derive
our dignity from God. But at the same time the Evangelist
wishes to shew that this grace comes to us of our own will
and endeavour: that, in short, the operation of grace being
supposed, it is in the power of our free will to make us the
sons of God. THEOPHYL. Or the meaning is, that the most
perfect sonship will only be attained at the resurrection, as
Rom. 8, saith the Apostle, *Waiting for the adoption, to wit, the*
23. *redemption of our body.* He therefore gave us the power to
become the sons of God, i. e. the power of obtaining this
Chrys. grace at some future time. CHRYS. And because in the
Hom. x.
2. matter of these ineffable benefits, the giving of grace belongs
to God, but the extending of faith to man, He subjoins,
even to those who believe on his name. Why then declarest
thou not, John, the punishment of those who received Him
not? Is it because there is no greater punishment than that,
when the power of becoming the sons of God is offered to
men, they should not become such, but voluntarily deprive
themselves of the dignity? But besides this, inextinguishable
Aug.Tr. fire awaits all such, as will appear clearly farther on. AUG.
ii. 14. To be made then the sons of God, and brothers of Christ,

they must of course be born; for if they are not born, how
can they be sons? Now the sons of men are born of flesh
and blood, and the will of man, and the embrace of wedlock;
but how *these* are born, the next words declare: *Not of
bloods*[1]; that is, the male's and the female's. Bloods is not ᴵˣ *αἱμα-*
correct Latin, but as it is plural in the Greek, the translator ᵗῶν
preferred to put it so, though it be not strictly grammatical,
at the same time explaining the word in order not to offend
the weakness of one's hearers. BEDE; It should be understood
that in holy Scripture, blood in the plural number, has the
signification of sin: thus in the Psalms, *Deliver me from blood-* Ps. 51,
guiltiness[p]. AUG. In that which follows, *Nor of the will of* Aug.
the flesh, nor of the will of man, the flesh is put for the Tr.ii.14.
female; because, when she was made out of the rib, Adam
said, *This is now bone of my bone, and flesh of my flesh.* Gen.2,
The flesh therefore is put for the wife, as the spirit some- 23.
times is for the husband; because that the one ought to
govern, the other to obey. For what is there worse than an
house, where the woman hath rule over the man? But these
that we speak of are born neither of the will of the flesh,
nor the will of man, *but of God.* BEDE; The carnal birth
of men derives its origin from the embrace of wedlock, but
the spiritual is dispensed by the grace of the Holy Spirit.
CHRYS. The Evangelist makes this declaration, that being Chrys.
taught the vileness and inferiority of our former birth, which Hom. x.
is through blood, and the will of the flesh, and understanding [ix.] 3.
the loftiness and nobleness of the second, which is through
grace, we might hence receive great knowledge, worthy of
being bestowed by him who begat us, and after this shew
forth much zeal.

14. And the Word was made flesh, and dwelt among us.

AUG. Having said, *Born of God;* to prevent surprise and Aug.
trepidation at so great, so apparently incredible a grace, Tr.ii.15.
as that men should be born of God; to assure us, he says,
And the Word was made flesh. Why marvellest thou then
that men are born of God? Know that God Himself
was born of man. CHRYS. Or thus, After saying that they Chrys.
Hom.
xi. [x.]
P Plur. in the Vulg. as in the Heb.   1.

were born of God, who received Him, he sets forth the cause
of this honour, viz. the Word being made flesh, God's own
Son was made the son of man, that he might make the sons
of men the sons of God.   Now when thou hearest that
the Word was made flesh, be not disturbed, for He did not
change His substance into flesh, which it were indeed
impious to suppose; but remaining what He was, took upon
Him the form of a servant.   But as there are some who say,
that the whole of the incarnation was only in appearance,
to refute such a blasphemy, he used the expression, *was
made,* meaning to represent not a conversion of substance,
but an assumption of real flesh.   But if they say, God is
omnipotent; why then could He not be changed into flesh?
we reply, that a change from an unchangeable nature is

Aug.
de Trin.
xv. c.20.
(xi.)
a contradiction.   AUG. As our word[q] becomes the bodily
voice, by its assumption of that voice, as a means of developing
itself externally; so the Word of God was made flesh, by
assuming flesh, as a means of manifesting Itself to the world.
And as our word is made voice, yet is not turned into voice;
so the Word of God was made flesh, but never turned into
flesh.   It is by *assuming* another nature, not by *consuming*
themselves in it, that our word is made voice, and the Word,

P. iii.
Hom.
Theod.
Ancyr.
de Nat.
Dom.
flesh.   EX GESTIS CONC. EPH. The discourse which we utter,
which we use in conversation with each other, is incorporeal,
imperceptible, impalpable; but clothed in letters and characters, it becomes material, perceptible, tangible.   So too the
Word of God, which was naturally invisible, becomes visible,
and that comes before us in tangible form, which was by nature

in Joan.
1, 1.
incorporeal.   ALCUIN. When we think how the incorporeal
soul is joined to the body, so as that of two is made one
man, we too shall the more easily receive the notion of the
incorporeal Divine substance being joined to the soul in the
body, in unity of person; so as that the Word is not turned
into flesh, nor the flesh into the Word; just as the soul is
not turned into body, nor the body into soul.

Theoph.
in loc.
THEOPHYL. Apollinarius of Laodicea raised a heresy upon
this text; saying, that Christ had flesh only, not a rational

Aug.
con.
Serm.
Arian.
c. 7. (9.)
soul; in the place of which His divinity directed and con-
trolled His body.   AUG. If men are disturbed however by its

                    [q] See above, p. 1—3.

being said that *the Word was made flesh*, without mention
of a soul; let them know that the flesh is put for the whole
man, the part for the whole, by a figure of speech; as
in the Psalms, *Unto thee shall all flesh come;* and again Ps.65,2.
in Romans, *By the deeds of the law there shall no flesh be* Rom. 3,
justified. In the same sense it is said here that *the Word* 20.
was made flesh; meaning that the Word was made man.
THEOPHYL. The Evangelist intends by making mention of Theoph.
the flesh, to shew the unspeakable condescension of God, in loc.
and lead us to admire His compassion, in assuming for our
salvation, what was so opposite and incongenial to His nature,
as the flesh: for the *soul* has some propinquity to God. If
the Word, however, was made flesh, and assumed not at the
same time a human soul, our souls, it would follow, would not
be yet restored: for what He did not assume, He could not
sanctify. What a mockery then, when the soul first sinned,
to assume and sanctify the flesh only, leaving the weakest part
untouched! This text overthrows Nestorius, who asserted
that it was not the very Word, even God, Who the Self-same
was made man, being conceived of the sacred blood of the
Virgin: but that the Virgin brought forth a man endowed
with every kind of virtue, and that the Word of God was united
to him: thus making out two sons, one born of the Virgin,
i. e. man, the other born of God, that is, the Son of God,
united to that man by grace, and relation, and love[r]. In
opposition to him the Evangelist declares, that the very
Word was made Man, not that the Word fixing upon a
righteous man united Himself to him. CYRIL; The Word Cyril.ad
uniting to Himself a body of flesh animated with a rational Nes.Ep. 8.
soul, substantially, was ineffably and incomprehensibly made
Man, and called the Son of man, and that not according to
the will only, or good-pleasure, nor again by the assumption
of the Person alone. The natures are different indeed which
are brought into true union, but He Who is of both,
Christ the Son, is One; the difference of the natures, on the

---

[r] The union of the two Natures in
our Lord, κατὰ σχίσιν, or σχιτικὴ συνά-
φεια, in the Nestorian heresy, stands
opposed to the belief of their "natural"
ἕνωσις φυσικὴ in one Person. σχίσις is used
for "relation, cognateness, affection,
conjunction," to describe a "nearness"
of the Manhood, as united *externally*,
by dignity, or likeness of honour, or
unity of will, or good-pleasure, or love,
or affection, or power, instead of being
"taken into God." See Petav. de
Incarn. iii. 3.

other hand, not being destroyed in consequence of this coa-

Theoph. in v. 14. lition. THEOPHYL. From the text, *The Word was made flesh*, we learn this farther, that the Word Itself is man, and being the Son of God was made the Son of a woman, who is rightly called the Mother of God, as having given birth to God in the

Hil. x. de Trin. c. 21,22. flesh. HILARY; Some, however, who think God the Only-Begotten, God the Word, Who was in the beginning with God, not to be God substantially, but a Word sent forth, the Son being to God the Father, what a word is to one who utters it, these men, in order to disprove that the Word, being substantially God, and abiding in the form of God, was born the Man Christ, argue subtilly, that, whereas that Man (they say) derived His life rather from human origin than from the mystery of a spiritual conception, God the Word did not make Himself Man of the womb of the Virgin ; but that the Word of God was in Jesus, as the spirit of prophecy in the Prophets. And they are accustomed to charge us with holding, that Christ was born a Man, not [s] of our body and soul; whereas we preach the Word made flesh, and after our likeness born Man, so that He Who is truly Son of God, was truly born Son of man; and that, as by His own act He took upon Him a body of the Virgin, so of Himself He took a soul also, which in no case is derived from man by mere parental origin. And seeing He, The Self-same, is the Son of man, how absurd were it, besides the Son of God, Who is the Word, to make Him another person besides, a sort of prophet, inspired by the Word of God; whereas our Lord Jesus Christ

Chrys. Hom. in Joan. xi. [x.] 2. is both the Son of God, and the Son of man. CHRYS. Lest from it being said, however, that *the Word was made flesh*, you should infer improperly a change of His incorruptible nature, he subjoins, *And dwelt among us.* For that which inhabits is not the same, but different from the habitation: different, I say, in nature; though as to union and conjunction, God the Word and the flesh are one, without confusion or extinction of substance. ALCUIN ; Or, *dwelt among us*, means, lived amongst men.

14. And we saw his glory, the glory as of the only begotten of the Father, full of grace and truth.

---

^s non is omitted in some Mss ; but S. Hilary in writing against the Arians, throughout guards against Sabellianism. Ben.

CHRYS. Having said that we are made the sons of God, and in no other way than because *the Word was made flesh;* he mentions another gift, *And we saw His glory.* Which glory we should not have seen, had He not, by His alliance with humanity, become visible to us. For if they could not endure to look on the glorified face of Moses, but there was need of a veil, how could soiled and earthly creatures, like ourselves, have borne the sight of undisguised Divinity, which is not vouchsafed even to the higher powers themselves. AUG. Or thus; in that *the Word was made flesh and dwelt among us,* His birth became a kind of ointment to anoint the eyes of our heart, that we might through His humanity discern His majesty; and therefore it follows, *And we saw His glory.* No one could see His glory, who was not healed by the humility of the flesh.   For there had flown upon man's eye as it were dust from the earth: the eye had been diseased, and earth was sent to heal it again; the flesh had blinded thee, the flesh restores thee.   The soul by consenting to carnal affections had become carnal; hence the eye of the mind had been blinded: then the physician made for thee ointment.   He came in such wise, as that by the flesh He destroyed the corruption of the flesh.   And thus *the Word was made flesh,* that thou mightest be able to say, *We saw His glory.*   CHRYS. He subjoins, *As of the Only-Begotten of the Father:* for many prophets, as Moses, Elijah, and others, workers of miracles, had been glorified, and Angels also who appeared unto men, shining with the brightness belonging to their nature; Cherubim and Seraphim too, who were seen in glorious array by the prophets.   But the Evangelist withdrawing our minds from these, and raising them above all nature, and every preeminence of fellow servants, leads us up to the summit Himself; as if he said, Not of prophet, or of any other man, or of Angel, or Archangel, or any of the higher powers, is the glory which we beheld; but as that of the very Lord, very King, very and true Only-Begotten Son. GREG. In Scripture language *as,* and *as it were,* are sometimes put not for likeness but reality; whence the expression, *As of the Only-Begotten of the Father.*   CHRYS. As if he said : We saw His glory, such as it was becoming and proper for the Only-Begotten and true Son to have.   We have a

Chrys. Hom. xii.[xi.] l.

Aug. in Joan. Tr. ii. c. 16.

Chrys. Hom. in Joan. xii.[xi.] l.

Greg. lxviii. Moral. c.6.(12.)

Chrys. Hom. xii.[xi.] l.

form of speech, like it, derived from our seeing kings always
splendidly robed. When the dignity of a man's carriage is
beyond description, we say, *In short, he went as a king.*
So too John says, *We saw His glory, the glory as of the Only
Begotten of the Father.* For Angels, when they appeared,
did every thing as servants who had a Lord, but He as
the Lord appearing in humble form. Yet did all creatures
recognise their Lord, the star calling the Magi, the Angels
the shepherds, the child leaping in the womb acknowledged
Him : yea the Father bore witness to Him from heaven, and
the Paraclete descending upon Him : and the very universe
itself shouted louder than any trumpet, that the King of
heaven had come. For devils fled, diseases were healed, the
graves gave up the dead, and souls were brought out of
wickedness, to the utmost height of virtue. What shall
one say of the wisdom of precepts, of the virtue of heavenly
laws, of the excellent institution of the angelical life?
Origen. ORIGEN; *Full of grace and truth.* Of this the meaning is two-
Hom. 2. fold. For it may be understood of the Humanity, and the
Divinity of the Incarnate Word, so that the fulness of grace
has reference to the Humanity, according to which Christ is
the Head of the Church, and the first-born of every creature:
for the greatest and original example of grace, by which
man, with no preceding merits, is made God, is manifested
primarily in Him. The fulness of the grace of Christ may
also be understood of the Holy Spirit, whose sevenfold
Is.11,2. operation filled Christ's Humanity. The fulness of truth
applies to the Divinity.........But if you had rather understand the fulness of grace and truth of the New Testament,
you may with propriety pronounce the fulness of the grace of
the New Testament to be given by Christ, and the truth of
Theoph. the legal types to have been fulfilled in Him. THEOPHYL.
hoc loc. Or, *full of grace,* inasmuch as His word was gracious, as saith
Ps.45,3. David, *Full of grace are thy lips; and truth,* because what
Moses and the Prophets spoke or did in figure, Christ did in
reality.

15. John bare witness of him, and cried, saying,
This was he of whom I spake, He that cometh after
me is preferred before me, for he was before me.

ALCUIN ; He had said before that there was a man sent to bear witness; now he gives definitely the forerunner's own testimony, which plainly declared the excellence of His Human Nature and the Eternity of His Godhead. *John bare witness of Him.* CHRYS. Or he introduces this, as Chrys. if to say, Do not suppose that we bear witness to this out Hom. of gratitude, because we were with Him a long time, and in Joan. partook of His table; for John who had never seen Him before, [xii.] 1, nor tarried with Him, bare witness to Him. The Evangelist 2, 3. repeats John's testimony many times here and there, because he was held in such admiration by the Jews. Other Evangelists refer to the old prophets, and say, *This was done that it might be fulfilled which was spoken by the prophet.* But he introduces a loftier, and later witness, not intending to make the servant vouch for the master, but only condescending to the weakness of his hearers. For as Christ would not have been so readily received, had He not taken upon Him the form of a servant ; so if he had not excited the attention of servants by the voice of a fellow-servant beforehand, there would not have been many Jews embracing the word of Christ. It follows, *And cried;* that is, preached with openness, with freedom, without reservation. He did not however begin with asserting that this one was the natural only-begotten Son of God, but cried, saying, *This was He of whom I spake, He that cometh after me is preferred before me, for He was before me.* For as birds do not teach their young all at once to fly, but first draw them outside the nest, and afterwards try them with a quicker motion; so John did not immediately lead the Jews to high things, but began with lesser flights, saying, that Christ was better than he; which in the mean time was no little advance. And observe how prudently he introduces his testimony ; he not only points to Christ when He appears, but preaches Him beforehand; as, *This is He of whom I spake.* This would prepare men's minds for Christ's coming: so that when He did come, the humility of His garb would be no impediment to His being received. For Christ adopted so humble and common an appearance, that if men had seen Him without first hearing John's testimony to His greatness, none of the things spoken of Him would have had any effect. THEOPHYL. He saith,

Who cometh after me, that is, as to the time of His birth. John was six months before Christ, according to His humanity. CHRYS. Or this does not refer to the birth from Mary; for Christ was born, when this was said by John; but to His coming for the work of preaching. He then saith, *is made*[a] *before me;* that is, is more illustrious, more honourable; as if he said, Do not suppose me greater than He, because I came first to preach. THEOPHYL. The Arians infer from this word[1], that the Son of God is not begotten of the Father, but made like any other creature. AUG. It does not mean—He was made before I was made; but He is preferred to me. CHRYS. If the words, *made before me,* referred to His coming into being, it was superfluous to add, *For He was before me.* For who would be so foolish as not to know, that if He was *made* before him, He *was* before him. It would have been more correct to say, He was before me, because He was made before me. The expression then, *He was made before me,* must be taken in the sense of honour: only that which was to take place, he speaks of as having taken place already, after the style of the old Prophets, who commonly talk of the future as the past.

Chrys. Hom. xiii. [xii.] 3.

Theoph. in loc.
1 γίγονιν

Aug. in Joan. Tr. 3.

Chrys. Hom. xiii. [xii.] 3.

16. And of his fulness have all we received, and grace for grace.

17. For the law was given by Moses, but grace and truth came by Jesus Christ.

ORIGEN; This is to be considered a continuation of the Baptist's testimony to Christ, a point which has escaped the attention of many, who think that from this to, *He hath declared Him,* St. John the Apostle is speaking. But the idea that on a sudden, and, as it would seem, unseasonably, the discourse of the Baptist should be interrupted by a speech of the disciple's, is inadmissible. And any one, able to follow the passage, will discern a very obvious connexion here. For having said, *He is preferred before me, for He was before me,* he proceeds, From this I know that He is before me, because I and the Prophets who preceded me

Orig. in Joan. t. vi. 3.
v. 18.

---

a γίγονιν. Vulg. *factus.* Eng. T. *preferred.*

have received of His fulness, and grace for grace, (the second grace for the first.) For they too by the Spirit penetrated beyond the figure to the contemplation of the truth. And hence receiving, as we have done, of his fulness, we judge that the law was given by Moses, but that grace and truth were made[1], by Jesus Christ—made, not given: the Father ¹ἐγένετο: gave the law by Moses, but made grace and truth by Jesus. facta Vulg. But if it is Jesus who says below, *I am the Truth,* how is E. T. truth made by Jesus? We must understand however that came. John14, the very substantial Truth[2], from which First Truth and Its 6. Image many truths are engraven on those who treat of the ²αὐτο-αλήθεια truth, was not made through Jesus Christ, or through any one; but only the truth which is in individuals, such as in Paul, e. g. or the other Apostles, was made through Jesus Christ. CHRYS. Or thus; John the Evangelist here adds Chrys. his testimony to that of John the Baptist, saying, *And* in Joan. Hom. *of his fulness have we all received.* These are not the xiv. [xiii.] 1. words of the forerunner, but of the disciple; as if he meant to say, We also the twelve, and the whole body of the faithful, both present and to come, have received of His fulness. AUG. But what have ye received? *Grace for grace.* Aug. So that we are to understand that we have received a certain in Joan. Tr. iii. something from His fulness, and over and above this, *grace for* c. 8. *grace;* that we have first received of His fulness, first grace; et seq. and again, we have received grace for grace. What grace did we first receive? Faith: which is called grace, because it is given freely[3]. This is the first grace then which the ³ gratis sinner receives, the remission of his sins. Again, we have grace for grace; i. e. in stead of that grace in which we live by faith, we are to receive another, viz. life eternal: for life eternal is as it were the wages of faith. And thus as faith itself is a good grace, so life eternal is grace for grace. There was not grace in the Old Testament; for the law threatened, but assisted not, commanded, but healed not, shewed our weakness, but relieved it not. It prepared the way however for a Physician who was about to come, with the gifts of grace and truth: whence the sentence which follows: *For the law was given by Moses, but grace and truth were made by Jesus Christ.* The death of thy Lord hath destroyed death, both temporal and eternal; that is the grace which was promised, but not contained, in the law. CHRYS. Or we have received grace for grace; that is, the new in the place of the old. For as there is a justice and a justice besides, an adoption and another adoption, a circumcision and another circumcision; so is there a grace and another grace: only the one being a type, the other a reality. He brings in the words to shew that the Jews as well as ourselves are saved by grace: it being of mercy and grace that they received the law. Next, after he has said, *Grace for grace*, he adds something to shew the magnitude of the gift; *For the law was given by Moses, but grace and truth were made by Jesus Christ*. John when comparing himself with Christ above had said, *He is preferred before me*: but the Evangelist draws a comparison between Christ, and one much more in admiration with the Jews than John, viz. Moses. And observe his wisdom. He does not draw the comparison between the persons, but the things, contrasting grace and truth to the law: the latter of which he says *was given*, a word only applying to an administrator; the former *made*, as we should speak of a king, who does every thing by his power: though in this King it would be with grace also, because that with power He remitted all sins. Now His grace is shewn in His gift of Baptism, and our adoption by the Holy Spirit, and many other things; but to have a better insight into what the truth is, we should study the figures of the old law: for what was to be accomplished in the New Testament, is prefigured in the Old, Christ at His Coming filling up the figure. Thus was the figure given by Moses, but the truth made by Christ. AUG. Or, we may refer grace to knowledge, truth to wisdom. Amongst the events of time the highest grace is the uniting of man to God in One Person; in the eternal world the highest truth pertains to God the Word.

18. No man hath seen God at any time; the only begotten Son, which is in the bosom of the Father, he hath declared him.

ORIGEN; Heracleon asserts, that this is a declaration of the disciple, not of the Baptist: an unreasonable supposition;

for if the words, *Of His fulness have we all received,* are the
Baptist's, does not the connexion run naturally, that he
receiving of the grace of Christ, the second in the place of
the first grace, and confessing that the law was given by Moses,
but grace and truth came by Jesus Christ; understood here
that no man had seen God at any time, and that the Only
Begotten, who was in the bosom of the Father, had committed
this declaration of Himself to John, and all who with him
had received of His fulness? For John was not the first
who declared Him; for He Himself who was before Abraham,
tells us, that Abraham rejoiced to see His glory. CHRYS. Or
thus; the Evangelist after shewing the great superiority of
Christ's gifts, compared with those dispensed by Moses,
wishes in the next place to supply an adequate reason for
the difference. The one being a servant was made a minister
of a lesser dispensation: but the other Who was Lord, and Son
of the King, brought us far higher things, being ever coexistent
with the Father, and *beholding* Him. Then follows, *No man
hath seen God at any time, &c.* AUG. What is that then
which Jacob said, *I have seen God face to face;* and that
which is written of Moses, *he talked with God face to face;*
and that which the prophet Isaiah saith of himself, *I saw the
Lord sitting upon a throne?* GREG. It is plainly given us to
understand here, that while we are in this mortal state, we
can see God only through the medium of certain images, not
in the reality of His own nature. A soul influenced by the grace
of the Spirit may see God through certain figures, but cannot
penetrate into his absolute essence. And hence it is that Jacob,
who testifies that he saw God, saw nothing but an Angel: and
that Moses, who talked with God face to face, says, *Shew me
Thy way, that I may know Thee:* meaning that he ardently
desired to see in the brightness of His own infinite Nature, Him
Whom he had only as yet seen reflected in images. CHRYS.
If the old fathers had seen That very Nature, they would
not have contemplated It so variously, for It is in Itself simple
and without shape; It sits not, It walks not; these are the
qualities of bodies. Whence he saith through the Prophet,
*I have multiplied visions, and used similitudes, by the
ministry of the Prophets:* i. e. I have condescended to them,
I appeared that which I was not. For inasmuch as the Son

Chrys.
in Joan.
Hom.
xiv.
[xiii.] 1.

Aug.
Ep. to
Paulina
(Ep.
147.
[112.]
c. 5.)
Gen. 32.
Ex. 33.
Isa. 6.
Greg.
Moral.
c. 54.
(88.)
rec. 28.

Exod.
33, 13.

Chrys.
Hom.
xv.
[xiv.]

Hosea
12, 10.

of God was about to manifest Himself to us in actual flesh,
men were at first raised to the sight of God, in such ways as
allowed of their seeing Him. AUG. Now it is said, *Blessed are*
the pure in heart, for they shall see God; and again, *When*
He shall appear, we shall be like unto Him, for we shall see
Him as He is. What is the meaning then of the words here :
No man hath seen God at any time? The reply is easy: those
passages speak of God, as to be seen, not as already seen.
They shall see God, it is said, not, they *have* seen Him:
nor is it, we *have* seen Him, but, *we shall see Him as*
He is. For, *No man hath seen God at any time,* neither in
this life, nor yet in the Angelic, as He is ; in the same way
in which sensible things are perceived by the bodily vision.
GREG. If however any, while inhabiting this corruptible flesh,
can advance to such an immeasurable height of virtue, as to
be able to discern by the contemplative vision, the eternal
brightness of God, their case affects not what we say. For
whoever seeth wisdom, that is, God, is dead wholly to this
life, being no longer occupied by the love of it. AUG. For
unless any in some sense die to this life, either by leaving the
body altogether, or by being so withdrawn and alienated from
carnal perceptions, that he may well not know, as the Apostle
says, *whether he be in the body or out of the body,* he
cannot be carried away, and borne aloft to that vision. GREG.
Some hold that in the place of bliss, God is visible in His
brightness, but not in His *nature.* This is to indulge in over
much subtlety. For in that simple and unchangeable essence,
no division can be made between the nature and the brightness. AUG. If we say, that the text, *No one* [d] *hath seen God*
at any time, applies only to men ; so that, as the Apostle
more plainly interprets it, *Whom no man hath seen nor can*
see, no one is to be understood here to mean, no one *of men :*
the question may be solved in a way not to contradict what
our Lord says, *Their Angels do always behold the face of My*
Father ; so that we must believe that Angels see, what no
one, i. e. of men, hath ever seen. GREG. Some however
there are who conceive that not even the Angels see God.
CHRYS. That very existence which is God, neither Pro-

Aug.
Ep. to
Paulina
sparsim.
Matt. 5,
8.
1 John
3, 2.

Greg.
xviii.
Moral.

Aug. xii.
on Gen.
ad litte-
ram c.
27.

2 Cor.
12, 2.
Greg.
xviii.
Moral.
c. 54. 90.
vet.
xxxviii.

Aug.
to Paul.
c. iv.
1 Tim.
6, 16.

Mat. 18,
10.
Greg.
xviii.
Moral.
c. 54.
(91.) vet.
xxxviii.
Chrys.
Hom.
xv.
(xiv.) 1.

d *ἰδὼν* : Vulg. nemo : E. T. no man.

phets, nor even Angels, nor yet Archangels, have seen.
For enquire of the Angels; they say nothing concerning His
Substance; but sing, *Glory to God in the highest*, and *Peace* Luke 2,
on earth to men of good will. Nay, ask even Cherubim and ^{1.}
Seraphim; thou wilt hear only in reply the mystic melody of
devotion, and that heaven and earth are full of His glory. Is. 6, 3.
AUG. Which indeed is true so far, that no bodily or even Aug. to
mental vision of man hath ever embraced the fulness of Paulina
God; for it is one thing to see, another to embrace the whole c. 7.
of what thou seest. A thing is seen, if only the sight of it be
caught; but we only see a thing fully, when we have no
part of it unseen, when we see round its extreme limits.
CHRYS. In this complete sense only the Son and the Holy Chrys.
Ghost see the Father. For how can created nature see that in Joan.
which is uncreated? So then no man knoweth the Father as xv.
the Son knoweth Him: and hence what follows, *The Only-* [xiv.] 1.
*Begotten Son, Who is in the bosom of the Father, He hath
declared Him.* That we might not be led by the identity of
the name, to confound Him with the sons made so by grace,
the article is annexed in the first place; and then, to put
an end to all doubt, the name *Only-Begotten* is introduced. HILARY; The Truth of His Nature did not seem Hil. de
sufficiently explained by the name of Son, unless, in ad- Trin.
dition, its peculiar force as proper to Him were expressed, vi. 39.
so signifying its distinctness from all beside. For in that,
besides *Son,* he calleth Him also *the Only-Begotten,* he cut
off altogether all suspicion of adoption, the Nature of *the
Only-Begotten* guaranteeing the truth of the name. CHRYS. Chrys.
He adds, *Which is in the bosom of the Father.* To dwell Hom.
in the bosom is much more than simply to see. For he who [xiv.] 2.
sees simply, hath not the knowledge thoroughly of that which
he sees; but he who dwells in the bosom, knoweth every
thing. When you hear then that no one knoweth the
Father save the Son, do not by any means suppose that he
only knows the Father more than any other, and does not
know Him fully. For the Evangelist sets forth His residing
in the bosom of the Father on this very account: viz. to
shew us the intimate converse of the Only-Begotten, and His Aug.
coeternity with the Father. AUG. In the bosom of the Father, in Joan.
i. e. in the secret Presence[1] of the Father: for God hath not Tr. iii.
c. 17.

¹ secreto

the fold[e] on the bosom, as we have; nor must be imagined to sit, as we do; nor is He bound with a girdle, so as to have a fold: but from the fact of our bosom being placed innermost, the secret Presence of the Father is called the bosom of the Father. He then who, in the secret Presence of the Father, knew the Father, the same hath declared what He saw.

Chrys. Hom. xv. [xiv.] 3. CHRYS. But what hath He declared? That God is one. But this the rest of the Prophets and Moses proclaim: what else have we learnt from the Son Who was in the bosom of the Father? In the first place, that those very truths, which the others declared, were declared through the operation of the Only Begotten: in the next place, we *have* received a far greater doctrine from the Only Begotten; viz. that God is a Spirit, and those who worship Him must worship Him in spirit and in truth; and that God is the Father of the Only Begotten.

Bede in loc. BEDE; Farther, if the word *declared* have reference to the past, it must be considered that He, being made man, declared the doctrine of the Trinity in unity, and how, and by what acts we should prepare ourselves for the contemplation of it. If it have reference to the future, then it means that He will declare Him, when He shall introduce His elect to the vision of His brightness.

Aug. Tr. iii. c. 18. AUG. Yet have there been men, who, deceived by the vanity of their hearts, maintained that the Father is invisible, the Son visible. Now if they call the Son visible, with respect to His connexion with the flesh, we object not; it is the Catholic doctrine. But it is madness in them to say He was so before His incarnation; i. e. if it be true that Christ is the Wisdom of God, and the Power of God. The Wisdom of God cannot be seen by the eye. If the human word cannot be seen by the eye, how can the

Chrys. Hom. xvi. [xv.] 1. Word of God? CHRYS. The text then, *No man hath seen God at any time,* applies not to the Father only, but also to the Son: for He, as Paul saith, is the Image of the invisible God; but He who is the Image of the Invisible, must Himself also be invisible.

19. And this is the record of John, when the Jews sent priests and Levites from Jerusalem to ask him, Who art thou?

---

[e] κολπὸς, sinus, bosom, mean often, fold of the garment on the bosom.

20. And he confessed, and denied not; but confessed, I am not the Christ.

21. And they asked him, What then? Art thou Elias? And he saith, I am not. Art thou that prophet? And he answered, No.

22. Then said they unto him, Who art thou? that we may give an answer to them that sent us. What sayest thou of thyself?

23. He said, I am the voice of one crying in the wilderness, Make straight the way of the Lord, as said the prophet Esaias.

ORIGEN; This is the second testimony of John the Baptist to Christ, the first began with, *This is He of Whom I spake;* and ended with, *He hath declared Him.* THEOPHYL. Or, after the introduction above of John's testimony to Christ, *is preferred before me,* the Evangelist now adds when the above testimony was given, *And this is the record of John, when the Jews sent priests and Levites from Jerusalem.* ORIGEN; The Jews of Jerusalem, as being of kin to the Baptist, who was of the priestly stock, send Priests and Levites to ask him who he is; that is, men considered to hold a superior rank to the rest of their order, by God's election, and coming from that favoured above all cities, Jerusalem. Such is the reverential way in which they interrogate John. We read of no such proceeding towards Christ: but what the Jews did to John, John in turn does to Christ, when he asks Him, through His disciples, *Art thou He that should come, or look we for another?* CHRYS. Such confidence had they in John, that they were ready to believe him on his own words: witness how it is said, *To ask him, Who art thou?* AUG. They would not have sent, unless they had been impressed by his lofty exercise of authority, in daring to baptize. ORIGEN; John, as it appears, saw from the question, that the Priests and Levites had doubts whether it might not be the Christ, who was baptizing; which doubts however they were afraid to profess openly, for fear of incurring the charge of credulity. He wisely determines therefore first to correct their mistake, and then to proclaim the truth. Accordingly, he first of all

Orig.
in Joan.
tom. ii.
c. 29.
Theoph.
in loc.

Orig.
t. vi.
c. 4.

c. 6.

Luke 7,
20.
Chrys.
in Joan.
Hom.
xvi.
[xv.]
Aug.Tr.
4. c. 3.
Orig.
in Joh.
tom. vi.
c. 6.

shews that he is not the Christ: *And he confessed, and denied not; but confessed, I am not the Christ.* We may add here, that at this time the people had already begun to be impressed with the idea that Christ's advent was at hand, in consequence of the interpretations which the lawyers had collected out of the sacred writings to that effect. Thus Theudas had been enabled to collect together a considerable body, on the strength of his pretending to be the Christ; and after him Judas, in the days of the taxation, had done Acts 5. the same. Such being the strong expectation of Christ's advent then prevalent, the Jews send to John, intending by the question, *Who art thou?* to extract from him whether Greg. he were the Christ. GREG. He denied directly being what Hom. vii. in he was not, but he did not deny what he was: thus, by his Evang. c. 1. speaking truth, becoming a true member of Him Whose Chrys. name he had not dishonestly usurped. CHRYS. Or take this Hom. xvi. explanation: The Jews were influenced by a kind of human [xv.] 1, sympathy for John, whom they were reluctant to see made 2. subordinate to Christ, on account of the many marks of greatness about him; his illustrious descent in the first place, he being the son of a chief priest; in the next, his hard training, and his contempt of the world. Whereas in Christ the contrary were apparent; a humble birth, for which they Mat. 13, reproach Him; *Is not this the carpenter's son?* an ordinary 55. way of living; a dress such as every one else wore. As John then was constantly sending to Christ, they send to him, with the view of having him for their master, and thinking to induce him, by blandishments, to confess himself Christ. They do not therefore send inferior persons to him, ministers and Herodians, as they did to Christ, but Priests and Levites; and not of these an indiscriminate party, but those of Jerusalem, i. e. the more honourable ones; but they send them with this question, to ask, *Who art thou?* not from a wish to be informed, but in order to induce him to do what I have said. John replies then to their intention, not to their interrogation: *And he confessed, and denied not; but confessed, I am not the Christ.* And observe the wisdom of the Evangelist: he repeats the same thing three times, to shew John's virtue, and the malice and madness of the Jews. For it is the character of a devoted servant, not only to forbear taking to himself

his lord's glory, but even, when numbers offer it to him, to
reject it.   The multitude indeed believed from ignorance
that John was the Christ, but in these it was malice; and in
this spirit they put the question to him, thinking, by their
blandishments to bring him over to their wishes.   For unless
this had been their design, when he replied, *I am not the
Christ,* they would have said, We did not suspect this; we
did not come to ask this.   When caught, however, and discovered in their purpose, they proceed to another question:
And they asked him, What then? Art thou Elias? AUG. Aug.
For they knew that Elias was to preach Christ; the name of in Joan.
Christ not being unknown to any among the Jews; but they c. 4.
did not think that *He* our Lord was the Christ: and yet did
not altogether imagine that there was no Christ about to come.
In this way, while looking forward to the future, they mistook
at the present.

　　And he said, I am not. GREG. These words gave rise to Greg.
a very different question.   In another place, our Lord, when Hom.
asked by His disciples concerning the coming of Elias, vii. c. 1.
replied, *If ye will receive it, this is Elias.* But John says, Mat.11,
I am not Elias.   How is he then a preacher of the truth, if [14.]
he agrees not with what that very Truth declares? ORIGEN; Orig.
Some one will say that John was ignorant that he was Elias; in Joan.
as those say, who maintain, from this passage the doctrine c. 7.
of a second incorporation, as though the soul took up a new
body, after leaving its old one.   For the Jews, it is said,
asking John by the Levites and priests, whether he is Elias,
suppose the doctrine of a second body to be already certain;
as though it rested upon tradition, and were part of their
secret system.   To which question, however, John replies,
I am not Elias: not being acquainted with his own prior
existence.   But how is it reasonable to imagine, if John
were a prophet enlightened by the Spirit, and had revealed
so much concerning the Father, and the Only-Begotten, that
he could be so in the dark as to himself, as not to know
that his own soul had once belonged to Elias? GREG. But Greg.
if we examine the truth accurately, that which sounds incon- Hom.
sistent, will be found not really so.   The Angel told Zacha- vii. in
rias concerning John, *He shall go before Him in the spirit* c. 1.
and power of Elias. As Elias then will preach the second [17.]

advent of our Lord, so John preached His first ; as the former will come as the precursor of the Judge, so the latter was made the precursor of the Redeemer. John was Elias in spirit, not in person : and what our Lord affirms of the spirit, John denies of the Person : there being a kind of propriety in this; viz. that our Lord to His disciples should speak spiritually of John, and that John, in answering the carnal multitude,

Orig.
in Joan.
tom. vi.
c. 7. should speak of his body, not of his spirit. ORIGEN ; He answers then the Levites and Priests, *I am not*, conjecturing what their question meant : for the purport of their examination was to discover, not whether the spirit in both was the same, but whether John was that very Elias, who was taken up, now appearing again, as the Jews expected, without another birth[i]. But he whom we mentioned above as holding this doctrine of a reincorporation, will say that it is not consistent that the Priests and Levites should be ignorant of the birth of the son of so dignified a priest as Zacharias, who was born too in his father's old age, and contrary to all human

Luke 1,
65. probabilities : especially when Luke declares, that *fear came on all that dwelt round about them.* But perhaps, since Elias was expected to appear before the coming of Christ near the end, they may seem to put the question figuratively, Art thou he who announcest the coming of Christ at the end of the world? to which he answers, *I am not.* But there is in fact nothing strange in supposing that John's birth might not have been known to all. For as in the case of our Saviour many knew Him to be born of Mary, and yet some wrongly imagined that He was John the Baptist, or Elias, or one of the Prophets ; so in the case of John, some were not unacquainted with the fact of his being son of Zacharias, and yet some may have been in doubt whether he were not the Elias who was expected. Again, inasmuch as many prophets had arisen in Israel, but one was especially looked forward to, of whom Moses had prophesied,

Deut.
18, 15. *The Lord thy God will raise up unto thee a Prophet from the midst of thee, of thy brethren, like unto me ; unto Him shall ye hearken :* they ask him in the third place, not

---

[i] Origen argues again against the re-incorporation from this same passage, in Matt. l. vii. and xiii. §. 1. see Pamph.

Apol. pro Orig. c. 10. p. 45. 46. ed. de la Rue.

simply whether he is a prophet, but with the article prefixed, *Art thou that Prophet?* For every one of the prophets in succession had signified to the people of Israel that he was not the one whom Moses had prophesied of; who, like Moses, was to stand in the midst between God and man, and deliver a testament, sent from God to His disciples. They did not however apply this name to Christ, but thought that He was to be a different person; whereas John knew that Christ was that Prophet, and therefore to this question, *he answered, No.* AUG. Or because John was more than a prophet: for that the prophets announced Him afar off, but John pointed Him out actually present. <sub/>Aug. in Joan. Tr. iv. c. 8.

Then said they unto him, Who art thou? that we may give an answer to them that sent us. What sayest thou of thyself? CHRYS. You see them here pressing him still more strongly with their questions, while he on the other hand quietly puts down their suspicions, where they are untrue, and establishes the truth in their place : saying, *I am the voice of one crying in the wilderness.* AUG. So spoke Esaias : the prophecy was fulfilled in John the Baptist. GREG. Ye know that the only-begotten Son is called the Word of the Father. Now we know, in the case of our own utterance, the voice first sounds, and then the word is heard. Thus John declares himself to be the voice, i. e. because he precedes the Word, and, through his ministry, the Word of the Father is heard by man. ORIGEN; Heracleon, in his discussion on John and the Prophets, infers that because the Saviour was the Word, and John the voice, therefore the whole of the prophetic order was only sound. To which we reply, that, if the trumpet gives an uncertain sound, who shall prepare himself for the battle? If the voice of prophecy is nothing but sound, why does the Saviour send us to it, saying, *Search the Scriptures?* But John calls himself the voice, not that crieth, but *of one that crieth* in the wilderness; viz. of Him Who stood and cried, *If any man thirst, let him come unto Me and drink.* He *cries,* in order that those at a distance may hear him, and understand from the loudness of the sound, the vastness of the thing spoken of. THEOPHYL. Or because he declared the truth plainly, while all who were under the law spoke obscurely. GREG. John crieth *in the* Chrys. Hom. xvi. [xv.] 2.

Aug.Tr. iv. c. 7. Greg. Hom. vii. c. 2.

Orig. in Joan. tom. vi. c. 12.

John 5, 39.

John 7, 37.

in loc. Greg. Hom. vii. in Ev. c. 2.

E

wilderness, because it is to forsaken and destitute Judæa
that he bears the consolatory tidings of a Redeemer.

Orig.
tom. vi.
c. 10.11.

ORIGEN; There is need of the voice *crying in the wilderness,*
that the soul, forsaken by God, may be recalled to making
straight the way of the Lord, following no more the crooked
paths of the serpent. This has reference both to the contemplative life, as enlightened by truth, without mixture of
falsehood, and to the practical, as following up the correct
perception by the suitable action. Wherefore he adds,
Make straight the way of the Lord, as saith the prophet

Greg.
Hom.
vii. in
Evang.
c. 2.

Esaias. GREG. The way of the Lord is made straight to the
heart, when the word of truth is heard with humility; the
way of the Lord is made straight to the heart, when the life
is formed upon the precept.

24. And they which were sent were of the Pharisees.

25. And they asked him, and said unto him, Why
baptizest thou then, if thou be not that Christ, nor
Elias, neither that prophet?

26. John answered them, saying, I baptize with
water: but there standeth one among you, whom ye
know not;

27. He it is, who coming after me is preferred before
me, whose shoe's latchet I am not worthy to unloose.

28. These things were done in Bethabara beyond
Jordan, where John was baptizing.

Orig.
in Joan.
tom. vi.
c. 13.

ORIGEN; The questions of the priests and Levites being
answered, another mission comes from the Pharisees: *And
they that were sent were of the Pharisees.* So far as it is
allowable to form a conjecture from the discourse itself here,
I should say that it was the third occasion of John's giving
his witness. Observe the mildness of the former question, so
befitting the priestly and levitical character, *Who art thou?*
There is nothing arrogant or disrespectful, but only what
becomes true ministers of God. The Pharisees however,
being a sectarian body, as their name implies, address the
Baptist in an importunate and contumelious way. *And they
said, Why baptizest thou then, if thou be not that Christ,*

neither Elias, neither that Prophet? not caring about information, but only wishing to prevent him baptizing. Yet the very next thing they did, was to come to John's baptism. The solution of this is, that they came not in faith, but hypocritically, because they feared the people. CHRYS. Or, those very same priests and Levites were of the Pharisees, and, because they could not undermine him by blandishments, began accusing, after they had compelled him to say what he was not. And they asked him, saying, *Why baptizest thou then, if thou art not the Christ, neither Elias, neither that Prophet?* As if it were an act of audacity in him to baptize, when he was neither the Christ, nor His precursor, nor His proclaimer, i. e. *that Prophet.* GREG. A saint, even when perversely questioned, is never diverted from the pursuit of goodness. Thus John to the words of envy opposes the words of life : *John answered them, saying, I indeed baptize with water.* ORIGEN ; For how would the question, *Why then baptizest thou,* be replied to in any other way, than by setting forth the carnal nature of his own baptism ? GREG. John baptizeth not with the Spirit, but with water ; not being able to remit sins, he washes the bodies of the baptized with water, but not their souls with pardon. Why then doth he baptize, when he doth not remit sins by baptism ? To maintain his character of forerunner. As his birth preceded our Lord's, so doth his baptism precede our Lord's baptism. And he who was the forerunner of Christ in His preaching, is forerunner also in His baptism, which was the imitation of that Sacrament. And withal he announces the mystery of our redemption, saying that He, the Redeemer, is standing in the midst of men, and they know it not : *There standeth one among you, whom ye know not :* for our Lord, when He appeared in the flesh, was visible in body, but in majesty invisible. CHRYS. *One among you.* It was fitting that Christ should mix with the people, and be one of the many, shewing every where His humility. *Whom ye know not;* i. e. not, in the most absolute and certain sense; not, who He is, and whence He is. AUG. In His low estate He was not seen; and therefore the candle was lighted. THEOPHYL. Or it was, that our Lord was in the midst of the Pharisees; and they not knowing Him. For

Chrys.
Hom.
xvi. (al.
xv.) 2.

Greg.
Hom.
vii. in
Evang.
c. 3.

Orig.
in Joan.
tom. vi.
c. 15.

Greg.
Hom.
vii. in
Evang.
c. 3.

Chrys.
xvi. 3.

Aug.
Tr. iv.
c. 9.

in loc.

they thought that they knew the Scriptures, and therefore, inasmuch as our Lord was pointed out there, He was in the midst of them, i. e. in their hearts. But they knew Him not, inasmuch as they understood not the Scriptures. Or take another interpretation. He was in the midst of them, as mediator between God and man, wishing to bring them, the Pharisees, to God. But they knew Him not. ORIGEN;

Orig. in Joan. tom. vi. c. 15.

Or thus; Having said, *I indeed baptize with water*, in answer to the question, *Why baptizest thou then?*—to the next, *If thou be not Christ?* he replies by declaring the preexistent substance of Christ; that it was of such virtue, that though His Godhead was invisible, He was present to every one, and pervaded the whole world; as is conveyed in the words; *There standeth one among you.* For He it is, Who hath diffused Himself through the whole system of nature, insomuch that every thing which is created, is created by Him; *All things were made by Him.* Whence it is evident that even those who enquired of John, *Why baptizest thou then?* had Him among them. Or, the words, *There standeth one among you*, are to be understood of mankind generally. For, from our character as rational beings, it follows that the word [s] exists in the centre of us, because the heart, which is the spring of motion within us, is situated in the centre of the body. Those then who carry the word within them, but are ignorant of its nature, and the source and beginning and the way in which it resides in them; these, hearing the word within them, know it not. But John recognised Him, and reproached the Pharisees, saying, *Whom ye know not.* For, though expecting Christ's coming, the Pharisees had formed no lofty conception of Him, but supposed that He would only be a holy man: wherefore he briefly refutes their ignorance, and the false ideas that they had of His excellence. He saith, *standeth;* for as the Father standeth, i. e. exists without variation or change, so standeth the Word ever in the work of salvation, though It assume flesh, though It be in the midst of men, though It stand invisible. Lest any one however should think that the invisible One Who cometh to all men, and to

---

[s] i. e. the λόγος ἐν ἀνθρώποις, reason; the word which is the image of *the* Word.

the universal world, is different from Him Who was made
man, and appeared on the earth, he adds, *He that cometh
after me,* i. e. Who will appear after me. The *after* however
here has not the same meaning that it has, when Christ
calls us *after* Him; for there we are told to follow after
Him, that by treading in His steps, we may attain to the
Father; but here the word is used to intimate what should
follow upon John's teaching; for he came that all may
believe, having by his ministry been fitted gradually by
lesser things, for the reception of the perfect Word. Therefore he saith, *He it is Who cometh after me.* CHRYS. As Chrys.
if he said, Do not think that every thing is contained in my Hom.
baptism; for if my baptism were perfect, another would not xvi. (al.
come after me with another baptism. This baptism of mine xv.) 3.
is but an introduction to the other, and will soon pass away,
like a shadow, or an image. There is One coming after me
to establish the truth: and therefore this is not a perfect
baptism; for, if it were, there would be no room for a
second: and therefore he adds, *Who is made before me:*
i. e. is more honourable, more lofty. GREG. *Made before* Greg.
me, i. e. preferred before me. He comes after me, that is, Hom.
He is born after me; He is made before me, that is, He vii. in
is preferred to me. CHRYS. But lest thou shouldest think Chrys.
this to be the result of comparison, he immediately shews it Hom.
to be a superiority beyond all comparison; *Whose shoe's* xv.) 3.
latchet I am not worthy to unloose: as if He said, He is so
much before me, that I am unworthy to be numbered among
the lowest of His attendants: the unloosing of the sandal
being the very lowest kind of service. AUG. To have Aug.
pronounced himself worthy even of unloosing His shoe's Tr. iv.
latchet, he would have been thinking too much of himself.
GREG. Or thus: It was a law of the old dispensation, that, Greg.
if a man refused to take the woman, who of right came to Hom.
him, to wife, he who by right of relationship came next to Ev. c. 3.
be the husband, should unloose his shoe. Now in what
character did Christ appear in the world, but as Spouse of
the Holy Church? John then very properly pronounced John 3,
himself unworthy to unloose this shoe's latchet: as if he said, 29.
I cannot uncover the feet of the Redeemer, for I claim not the
title of spouse, which I have no right to. Or the passage

may be explained in another way. We know that shoes are
made out of dead animals. Our Lord then, when He came
in the flesh, put on, as it were, shoes; because in His
Divinity He took the flesh of our corruption, wherein we had
of ourselves perished. And the latchet of the shoe, is the
seal upon the mystery. John is not able to unloose the shoe's
latchet; i. e. even he cannot penetrate into the mystery of
the Incarnation. So he seems to say: What wonder that
He is preferred before me, Whom, being born after me, I
contemplate, yet the mystery of Whose birth I comprehend
not. ORIG. The place has been understood not amiss thus
by a certain person [1]; I am not of such importance, as that
for my sake He should descend from this high abode, and
take flesh upon Him, as it were a shoe. CHRYS. John
having preached the thing concerning Christ publicly and
with becoming liberty, the Evangelist mentions the place
of His preaching: *These things were done in Bethany
beyond Jordan, where John was baptizing.* For it was in
no house or corner that John preached Christ, but beyond
Jordan, in the midst of a multitude, and in the presence of
all whom He had baptized. Some copies read more correctly Bethabara: for Bethany was not beyond Jordan, or in
the desert, but near Jerusalem. GLOSS; Or we must suppose
two Bethanies; one over Jordan, the other on this side, not
far from Jerusalem, the Bethany where Lazarus was raised
from the dead. CHRYS. He mentions this too for another
reason, viz. that as He was relating events which had only
recently happened, He might, by a reference to the place,
appeal to the testimony of those who were present and saw
them. ALCUIN. The meaning of Bethany is, house of
obedience; by which it is intimated to us, that all must
approach to baptism, through the obedience of faith. ORIG.
Bethabara means house of preparation; which agreeth with
the baptism of Him, who was making ready a people prepared for the Lord. Jordan, again, means, " their descent."
Now what is this river but our Saviour, through Whom
coming into this earth all must be cleansed, in that He came
down not for His own sake, but for theirs. This river it is
which separateth the lots given by Moses, from those given
by Jesus; its streams make glad the city of God. As the

Orig.
tom. vi.
in Joan.
[1] Hera-
cleon.
Chrys.
Hom.
xvii.(al.
xvi.) l.
in Joan.

Chrys.
Hom.
xvii.

Orig.
tom. vi.
c. 24.

c. 25.
et seq.

c. 29.

serpent lies hid in the Egyptian river, so doth God in this; for the Father is in the Son. Wherefore whosoever go thither to wash themselves, lay aside the reproach of Egypt, are made meet to receive the inheritance, are cleansed from leprosy, are made capable of a double portion of grace, and ready to receive the Holy Spirit; nor doth the spiritual dove light upon any other river. John again baptizes *beyond* Jordan, as the precursor of Him Who came not to call the righteous, but sinners to repentance. ^{Joshua 5, 9.} ^{2 Kings 5, 14.} ^{2 Kings 2, 9.}

29. The next day John seeth Jesus coming to him, and saith, Behold the Lamb of God, which taketh away the sin of the world.

30. This is he of whom I said, After me cometh a man which is preferred before me: for he was before me.

31. And I knew him not: but that he should be made manifest to Israel, therefore am I come baptizing with water.

ORIGEN; After this testimony, Jesus is seen coming to John, not only persevering in his confession, but also advanced in goodness: as is intimated by the second day. Wherefore it is said, *The next day John seeth Jesus coming to him.* Long before this, the Mother of Jesus, as soon as she had conceived Him, went to see the mother of John then pregnant; and as soon as the sound of Mary's salutation reached the ears of Elisabeth, John leaped in the womb: but now the Baptist himself after his testimony seeth Jesus coming. Men are first prepared by hearing from others, and then see with their own eyes. The example of Mary going to see Elisabeth her inferior, and the Son of God going to see the Baptist, should teach us modesty and fervent charity to our inferiors. What place the Saviour came from when He came to the Baptist we are not told here; but we find it in Matthew, *Then cometh Jesus from Galilee to Jordan unto John to be baptized of him.* CHRYS. Or; Matthew relates directly Christ's coming to His baptism, John His coming a second time subsequent to His baptism, as appears from what follows: *I saw the Spirit descending, &c.* The Evangelists ^{Orig. tom. vi. c. 30.} ^{Matt. 3, 13. Chrys.} ^{Hom. xvii. (al. xvi.)}

have divided the periods of the history between them; Matthew passing over the part before John's imprisonment, and hastening to that event; John chiefly dwelling on what took place before the imprisonment. Thus he says, *The next day John seeth Jesus coming to him.* But why did He come to him the next day after His baptism? Having been baptized with the multitude, He wished to prevent any from thinking that He came to John for the same reason that others did, viz. to confess His sins, and be washed in the river unto repentance. He comes therefore to give John an opportunity of correcting this mistake; which John accordingly did correct; viz. by those words, *Behold the Lamb of God, which taketh away the sin of the world.* For He Who was so pure, as to be able to absolve other men's sins, evidently could not have come thither for the sake of confessing His own; but only to give John an opportunity of speaking of Him. He came too the next day, that those who had heard the former testimonies of John, might hear them again more plainly; and other besides. For he saith, *Behold the Lamb of God*, signifying that He was the one of old sought after, and reminding them of the prophecy of Isaiah, and of the shadows of the Mosaic law, in order that through the figure he might the easier lead them to the substance. Aug.

Aug. Tr. iv. c. 10.

If the Lamb of God is innocent, and John is the lamb, must he not be innocent? But all men come of that stock

Ps. 51, 5.

of which David sings sorrowing, *Behold, I was conceived in wickedness.* He then alone was the Lamb, who was not thus conceived; for He was not conceived in wickedness, nor in sin did His mother bear Him in her womb, Whom a virgin conceived, a virgin brought forth, because that in faith

Orig. tom. vi. c. 32. et seq.

she conceived, and in faith received. ORIGEN; But whereas five kinds of animals are offered in the temple, three beasts of the field, a calf, a sheep, and a goat; and two fowls of the air, a turtle dove and a pigeon; and of the sheep kind three are introduced, the ram, the ewe, the lamb; of these three he mentions only the lamb; the lamb, as we know, being offered in the daily sacrifice, one in the morning, and one in the evening. But what other daily offering can there be, that can be meant to be offered by a reasonable nature, except the perfect Word, typically called the Lamb? This

sacrifice, which is offered up as soon as the soul begins to
be enlightened, shall be accounted as a morning sacrifice,
referring to the frequent exercise of the mind in divine
things; for the soul cannot continually apply to the highest
objects because of its union with an earthly and gross body.
By this Word too, Which is Christ the Lamb, we shall be able
to reason on many things, and shall in a manner attain to
Him in the evening, while engaged with things of the body[t].
But He Who offered the lamb for a sacrifice, was God hid
in human form, the great Priest, He who saith below, *No John 10,
man taketh it (My life) from Me, but I lay it down of* [18.]
Myself: whence this name, *the Lamb of God:* for He
carrying our sorrows, and taking away the sins of the whole Isaiah
world, hath undergone death, as it were baptism.   For God 53, 4.
suffers no fault to pass uncorrected; but punishes it by the 1 Pet. 2,
sharpest discipline.   THEOPHYL. He is called the Lamb of 24.
God, because God the Father accepted His death for our salva- Luke 2,
tion, or, in other words, because He delivered Him up to death 50.
for our sakes.   For just as we say, This is the offering of such in loc.
a man, meaning the offering made by him; in the same sense
Christ is called the Lamb of God Who gave His Son to die
for our salvation.   And whereas that typical lamb did not
take away any man's sin, this one hath taken away the sin
of the whole world, rescuing it from the danger it was in
from the wrath of God.   Behold Him[1] *Who taketh away the* [1] Vulg.
sin of the world: he saith not, who *will* take, but, *Who* Ecce re-
taketh away the sin of the world; as if He were always peated
doing this.   For He did not then only take it away when He
suffered, but from that time to the present, He taketh it
away; not by being always crucified, for He made one
sacrifice for sins, but by ever washing it by means of that
sacrifice.   GREG. But then only will sin be entirely taken Greg.
Moral.

---

[t] Christ the Word is our real daily
sacrifice. He carries on within us what
is outwardly typified by the Mosaic
ritual. As in the Jewish temple the
day began with the one continual sacrifice which was carried on by others in
their turn through the day, (vid. Orig. vi.
c. 34.) till at last the evening sacrifice
put a close to all sacred services: so in
our minds a sacrifice is offered up to God
when the Word (from Whom *our* word,
i. e. reason, is derived) lights up spiritual thoughts, and this is still con- viii. c.
tinued in the Christian, even although 32.
by reason of the infirmity of the flesh,
he cannot always abide in meditation on
the Divinest things, yet is, in Christ,
engaged on many useful things, and so
also when He comes even to the things
of the body, in themselves a sort of
evening and night to the soul, still
doing them also in Christ, he closes all
in Christ.

away from the human race, when our corruption has been turned to a glorious incorruption. We cannot be free from sin, so long as we are held in the death of the body. THEO-

Theoph. PHYL. Why does he say *the sin* of the world, not sins?
in loc.
Because he wished to express sin universally: just as we say commonly, that man was cast out of paradise; meaning the whole human race. GLOSS; Or by the sin of the world is meant original sin, which is common to the whole world: which original sin, as well as the sins of every one individually,

Aug. Christ by His grace remits. AUG. For He Who took not sin
Tr. iv. c.
10, 11. from our nature, He it is Who taketh away our sin. Some say, We take away the sins of men, *because* we are holy; for if he, who baptizes, is not holy, how can he take away the other's sin, seeing he himself is full of sin? Against these reasoners let us point to the text; *Behold Him Who taketh away the sin of the world;* in order to do away with such

Orig. presumption in man towards man. ORIGEN; As there was
tom. vi.
c. 36. a connexion between the other sacrifices of the law, and the daily sacrifice of the lamb, in the same way the sacrifice of this Lamb has its reflexion in the pouring out of the blood of the Martyrs, by whose patience, confession, and zeal for goodness, the machinations of the ungodly are frustrated.

Theoph. THEOPHYL. John having said above to those who came from
in loc.
the Pharisees, that there stood one among them whom they knew not, he here points Him out to the persons thus ignorant: *This is He of whom I said, After me cometh a man which is preferred before me.* Our Lord is called *a man,* in reference to His mature age, being thirty years old when He was baptized: or in a spiritual sense, as the Spouse of

2 Cor. the Church; in which sense St. Paul speaks, *I have espoused
11, 2.
you to one husband, that I may present you as a chaste virgin to Christ.* AUG. He *cometh after me,* because he was

Aug.
Tr. iv.
born after me: He *is made before me,* because He is preferred

Greg. to me. GREG. He explains the reason of this superiority, in
Hom.
vii. in what follows: *For He was before me;* as if his meaning was;

Ev. c. 3. And this is the reason of His being superior to me, though born after me, viz. that He is not circumscribed by the time of His nativity. He Who was born of His mother in time,

Theoph. was begotten of His Father out of time. THEOPHYL. Attend,
in loc.
O Arius. He saith not, He was created before me, but *He*

was before me. Let the false sect of Paul of Samosata attend. They will see that He did not derive His original existence from Mary; for if He derived the beginning of His being from the Virgin, how could He have been before His precursor? it being evident that the precursor preceded Christ by six months, according to the human birth. CHRYS. Chrys.
That He might not seem however to give His testimony from Hom. xvii.(al. any motive of friendship or kindred, in consequence of his being xvi.) 2. related to our Lord according to the flesh, he says, *I knew Him not.* John could not of course know Him, having lived in the desert. And the miraculous events of Christ's childhood, the journey of the Magi, and such like, were now a long time past; John having been quite an infant, when they happened. And throughout the whole of the interval, He had been absolutely unknown: insomuch that John proceeds, *But that He should be made manifest to Israel, therefore am I come baptizing with water.* (And hence it is clear that the miracles said to have been performed by Christ in His childhood, are false and fictitious. For if Jesus had performed miracles at this early age, he would not have been unknown to John, nor would the multitude have wanted a teacher to point Him out.) Christ Himself then did not want baptism; nor was that washing for any other reason, than to give a sign beforehand of faith in Christ. For John saith not, in order to change men, and deliver from sin, but, *that he should be made manifest in Israel,* have I come baptizing. But would it not have been lawful for him to preach, and bring crowds together, without baptizing? Yes: but this was the easier way, for he would not have collected such numbers, had he preached without baptizing. AUG. Aug.
Now when our Lord became known, it was unnecessary to Tr. iv. c. 12,13. prepare a way for Him; for to those who knew Him, He became His own way. And therefore John's baptism did not last long, but only so long as to shew our Lord's humility. Our Lord received baptism from a servant, in Tr. v. order to give us such a lesson of humility as might prepare c. 5. us for receiving the grace of baptism, And that the servant's baptism might not be set before the Lord's, others were baptized with it; who after receiving it, had to receive our Lord's baptism: whereas those who first received our Lord's baptism, did not receive the servant's after.

32. And John bare record, saying, I saw the Spirit descending from heaven like a dove, and it abode upon him.

33. And I knew him not: but he that sent me to baptize with water, the same said unto me, Upon whom thou shalt see the Spirit descending, and remaining on him, the same is he which baptizeth with the Holy Ghost.

34. And I saw, and bare record that this is the Son of God.

Chrys.
Hom.
xvii.(al.
xvi.) 2.

CHRYS. John having made a declaration, so astonishing to all his hearers, viz. that He, whom he pointed out, did of Himself take away the sins of the world, confirms it by a reference to the Father and the Holy Spirit. For John might be asked, how did you know Him? Wherefore he replies beforehand, by the descent of the Holy Spirit: *And John bare record, saying, I saw the Spirit descending from heaven like a dove, and it abode upon him.*

Aug. de
Trin.xv.
c. 46.
(6.)

AUG. This was not however the first occasion of Christ's receiving the unction of the Holy Spirit: viz. Its descent upon Him at His baptism; wherein He condescended to prefigure His body, the Church, wherein those who are baptized receive preeminently the Holy Spirit. For it would be absurd to suppose that at thirty years old, (which was His age, when He was baptized by John,) He received for the first time the Holy Spirit: and that, when He came to that baptism, as He was without sin, so was He without the Holy Spirit. For if even of His servant and forerunner John it is written, *He shall be filled with the Holy Ghost, even from His mother's womb;* if He, though sprung from His father's seed, yet received the Holy Ghost, when as yet He was only formed in the womb; what ought we to think and believe of Christ, whose very flesh had not a carnal but spiritual conception?

Aug.
deAgon.
Chris-
tiano, c.
24.(22.)

AUG. We do not attribute to Christ only the possession of a real body, and say that the Holy Spirit assumed a false appearance to men's eyes: for the Holy Spirit could no more, in consistency with His nature, deceive men, than could the Son of God. The Almighty God, Who made every creature out of nothing, could as easily form a real body of

a dove, without the instrumentality of other doves, as He
made a real body in the womb of the Virgin, without the
seed of the male. AUG. The Holy Ghost was made to Aug.
appear visibly in two ways: as a dove, upon our Lord at His in Joan.
baptism; and as a flame upon His disciples, when they were sparsim
met together: the former shape denoting simplicity, the
latter fervency. The dove intimates that souls sanctified
by the Spirit should have no guile; the fire, that in that
simplicity there should not be coldness. Nor let it disturb
thee, that the tongues are cloven; fear no division; unity is
assured to us in the dove. It was meet then that the Holy
Spirit should be thus manifested descending upon our Lord;
in order that every one who had the Spirit might know, that
he ought to be simple as a dove, and be in sincere peace
with the brethren. The kisses of doves represent this peace.
Ravens kiss, but they tear also; but the nature of the dove is
most alien to tearing. Ravens feed on the dead, but the
dove eats nothing but the fruits of the earth. If doves
moan in their love, marvel not that He Who appeared in the
likeness of a dove, the Holy Spirit, *maketh intercession for* Rom. 8,
us with groanings that cannot be uttered. The Holy Spirit 26.
however groaneth not in Himself, but in us: He maketh us
to groan. And he who groaneth, as knowing that, so long
as He is under the burden of this mortality, he is absent from
the Lord, groaneth well: it is the Spirit that hath taught him
to groan. But many groan because of earthly calamities;
because of losses which disquiet them, or bodily sickness
which weigh heavily on them: they groan not, as doth the
dove. What then could more fitly represent the Holy
Spirit, the Spirit of unity, than the dove? as He saith
Himself to His reconciled Church, *My dove is one.* What Cant. 6,
could better express humility, than the simplicity and 9.
moaning of a dove? Wherefore on this occasion it was
that there appeared the very most Holy Trinity, the Father
in the voice which said, *Thou art My beloved Son;* the
Holy Spirit in the likeness of the dove. In that Trinity the Matt.
Apostles were sent to baptize, i. e. in the name of the Father, 28, 19.
and of the Son, and of the Holy Ghost. GREG. He saith, Greg.
Abode upon Him: for the Holy Spirit visits all the faithful; liv. (90.)
but on the Mediator alone does He abide for ever in a

peculiar manner; never leaving the Son's Humanity, even as He proceeds Himself from the Son's Divinity. But when the disciples are told of the same Spirit, He shall dwell with you, how is the abiding of the Spirit a peculiar sign of Christ? This will appear if we distinguish between the different gifts of the Spirit. As regards those gifts which are necessary for attaining to life, the Holy Spirit ever abides in all the elect; such are gentleness, humility, faith, hope, charity: but with respect to those, which have for their object, not our own salvation, but that of others, he does not always abide, but sometimes withdraws, and ceases to exhibit them; that men may be more humble in the possession of His gifts. But Christ had all the gifts of the Spirit, uninterruptedly always. CHRYS. Should any however think that Christ really wanted the Holy Spirit, in the way that we do, he corrects this notion also, by informing us that the descent of the Holy Ghost took place only for the purpose of manifesting Christ: *And I knew Him not: but He that sent me to baptize with water, the same said unto me, Upon whom thou shalt see the Spirit descending, and remaining on Him, the same is He which baptizeth with the Holy Ghost.* AUG. But who sent John? If we say the Father, we say true; if we say the Son, we say true. But it would be truer to say, the Father and the Son. How then knew he not Him, by Whom he was sent? For if he knew not Him, by Whom he wished to be baptized, it was rash in him to say, *I have need to be baptized by Thee.* So then he knew Him; and why saith he, *I knew Him not?* CHRYS. When he saith, *I knew Him not,* he is speaking of time past, not of the time of his baptism, when he forbad Him, saying, *I have need to be baptized of Thee.* AUG. Let us turn to the other Evangelists, who relate the matter more clearly, and we shall find most satisfactorily, that the dove descended when our Lord ascended from the water. If then the dove descended after baptism, but John said before the baptism, *I have need to be baptized of Thee,* he knew Him before His baptism also. How then said he, *I knew him not, but He which sent me to baptize?* Was this the first revelation made to John of Christ's person, or was it not rather a fuller disclosure of what had been already revealed? John knew the Lord to be the Son

John 14, 17.

Chrys. Hom. xvii (al. xvi.) 2. in Joan.

Aug. Tr. v. c. i.

Chrys. Hom. xvii. (al. xvi.)c.3. in Joan.

Aug. Tr. iv.v. and vi. sparsim.

of God, knew that He would baptize with the Holy Ghost:
for before Christ came to the river, many having come
together to hear John, he said unto them, *He that cometh* Matt. 3,
after me is mightier than I: He shall baptize you with the [11.]
Holy Ghost and with fire. What then? He did not know
that our Lord (lest Paul or Peter might say, my baptism, as
we find Paul did say, my Gospel,) would have and retain to
Himself the power of baptism, the ministering of it however
passing to good and bad indiscriminately. What hindrance
is the badness of the minister, when the Lord is good? So
then we baptize again after John's baptism; after a homicide's
we baptize not: because John gave his own baptism, the
homicide gives Christ's; which is so holy a sacrament, that
not even a homicide's ministration can pollute it. Our Lord
could, had He so willed, have given power to any servant of
His to give baptism as it were in His own stead; and to the
baptism, thus transferred to the servant, have imparted the
same power, that it would have had, when given by Himself.
But this He did not choose to do; that the hope of the baptized
might be directed to Him, Who had baptized them; He
wished not the servant to place hope in the servant. And
again, had He given this power to servants, there would
have been as many baptisms as servants; as there had been
the baptism of John, so should we have had the baptism of
Paul and of Peter. It is by this power then, which Christ
retains in His own possession exclusively, that the unity of
the Church is established; of which it is said, *My dove is one.* Cant. 6,
A man may have a baptism besides the dove; but that any [9.]
besides the dove should profit, is impossible. CHRYS. The Chrys.
Father having sent forth a voice proclaiming the Son, the Holy Hom.
Spirit came besides, bringing the voice upon the head of Christ, xvii. (al.
in order that no one present might think that what was said of xvi.) 3.
Christ, was said of John. But it will be asked: How was it
that the Jews believed not, if they saw the Spirit? Such sights
however require the mental vision, rather than the bodily.
If those who saw Christ working miracles were so drunken
with malice, that they denied what their own eyes had seen,
how could the appearance of the Holy Spirit in the form of a
dove overcome their incredulity? Some say however that the
sight was not visible to all, but only to John, and the more

devotional part. But even if the descent of the Spirit, as
a dove, was visible to the outward eye, it does not follow
that because all saw it, all understood it. Zacharias himself,
Daniel, Ezechiel, and Moses saw many things, appearing to
their senses, which no one else saw: and therefore John
adds, *And I saw and bare record that this is the Son of
God.* He had called Him the Lamb before, and said that
He would baptize with the Spirit; but he had no where

Aug.
Tr. vii.
in Joan. called Him the Son before. Aug. It was necessary that the
Only Son of God should baptize, not an adopted son.
Adopted sons are ministers of the Only Son: but though
they have the ministration, the Only one alone has the
power.

35. Again the next day after John stood, and two
of his disciples;

36. And looking upon Jesus as he walked, he saith,
Behold the Lamb of God!

Chrys.
Hom.
xviii.(al.
xvii.) 1. CHRYS. Many not having attended to John's words at
first, he rouses them a second time: *Again the next day
after John stood, and two of his disciples.* BEDE; John

Bede.
Hom. in
Vigil.
S. And. *stood,* because he had ascended that citadel of all excellences, from which no temptations could cast him down: his
disciples stood with him, as stout-hearted followers of their

Chrys.
Hom.
xviii.(al.
xvii.) c.
2. master. CHRYS. But wherefore went he not all about,
preaching in every place of Judæa; instead of standing near
the river, waiting for His coming, that he might point Him
out? Because he wished this to be done by the works of
Christ Himself. And observe how much greater an effort was
produced; He struck a small spark, and suddenly it rose into
a flame. Again, if John had gone about and preached, it
would have seemed like human partiality, and great suspicion
would have been excited. Now the Prophets and Apostles
all preached Christ absent; the former before His appearance
in the flesh, the latter after His assumption. But He was to
be pointed out by the eye, not by the voice only; and
therefore it follows: *And looking upon Jesus as He walked,
he saith, Behold the Lamb of God!* THEOPHYL. Looking

he saith, as if signifying by his looks his love and admiration for Christ. AUG. John was the friend of the Bridegroom; *Aug. Tr. vii. c. 8.* he sought not his own glory, but bare witness to the truth. And therefore he wished not his disciples to remain with him, to the hindrance of their duty to follow the Lord; but rather shewed them whom they should follow, saying, *Behold the Lamb of God.* CHRYS. He makes not a long discourse, *Chrys. Hom. xviii. 1. in Joan.* having only one object before him, to bring them and join them to Christ; knowing that they would not any further need his witness. John does not however speak to his *c. 2.* disciples alone, but publicly in the presence of all. And so, undertaking to follow Christ, through this instruction common to all, they remained thenceforth firm, following Christ for their own advantage, not as an act of favour to their master[x]. John does not exhort: he simply gazes in admiration on Christ, pointing out the gift[y] He came to bestow, the cleansing from sin: and the mode in which this would be accomplished: both of which the word *Lamb* testifies to. *Lamb* has the article affixed to it, as a sign of preeminence. AUG. For He alone and singly *Aug. Tr. vii. c. 5.* is the Lamb without spot, without sin; not because His spots are wiped off, but because He never had a spot. He alone is the Lamb of God, for by His blood alone can men be redeemed. This is the Lamb whom the wolves fear; *c. 6.* even the slain Lamb, by whom the lion was slain. BEDE. *Bede. Hom. 1.* The Lamb therefore he calls Him; for that He was about to give us freely His fleece, that we might make of it a wedding garment; i. e. would leave us an example of life, by which we should be warmed into love. ALCUIN. John *stands* in a mystical sense, the Law having ceased, and Jesus comes, bringing the grace of the Gospel, to which that same Law bears testimony. Jesus *walks*, to collect disciples. BEDE. *Bede. Hom. in Vigil.* The *walking* of Jesus has a reference to the economy of the Incarnation, by means of which He has condescended to *S. And.* come to us, and give us a pattern of life.

37. And the two disciples heard him speak, and they followed Jesus.

---

[x] τὸν διδάσκαλον, i. e. John. In the Cat. is substituted "propter gratiam Christi."

[y] τὴν δωριὰν ἐφ᾽ ἧν συνήγινετο καὶ τὸν

τρόπον τοῦ καθαρμοῦ. The Cat. has "præparationem propter quam venit et modum preparationis." Perhaps it should be "purgationis."

F

38. Then Jesus turned, and saw them following, and saith unto them, What seek ye? They said unto Him, Rabbi, (which is to say, being interpreted, Master,) where dwellest thou?

39. He saith unto them, Come and see. They came and saw where he dwelt, and abode with him that day: for it was about the tenth hour.

40. One of the two which heard John speak, and followed him, was Andrew, Simon Peter's brother.

ALCUIN. John having borne witness that Jesus was the Lamb of God, the disciples who had been hitherto with him, in obedience to his command, followed Jesus: *And the two disciples heard him speak, and they followed Jesus.* CHRYS.

Chrys.
Hom.
xviii.
1 et sq.

Observe; when he said, *He that cometh after me is made before me,* and, *Whose shoe's latchet I am not worthy to unloose,* he gained over none; but when he made mention of the economy, and gave his discourse a humbler turn, saying, *Behold the Lamb of God,* then his disciples followed Christ. For many persons are less influenced by the thoughts of God's greatness and majesty, than when they hear of His being man's Helper and Friend; or any thing pertaining to the salvation of men. Observe too, when John says, *Behold the Lamb of God,* Christ says nothing. The Bridegroom stands by in silence; others introduce Him, and deliver the Bride into His hands; He receives her, and so treats her that she no longer remembers those who gave her in marriage. Thus Christ came to unite to Himself the Church; He said nothing Himself; but John, the friend of the Bridegroom, came forth, and put the Bride's right hand in His; i. e. by his preaching delivered into His hands men's souls, whom receiving He so disposed of, that they returned no more to John. And observe farther; As at a marriage the maiden goes not to meet the bridegroom, (even though it be a king's son who weds a humble handmaid,) but he hastens to her; so is it here. For human nature ascended not into heaven, but the Son of God came down to human nature, and took her to His Father's house. Again; There were disciples of John who not only did not follow Christ, but were even

enviously disposed toward Him ; but the better part heard,
and followed ; not from contempt of their former master, but
by his persuasion ; because he promised them that Christ
would baptize with the Holy Ghost. And see with what
modesty their zeal was accompanied. They did not straightway go and interrogate Jesus on great and necessary doctrines, nor in public, but sought private converse with Him;
for we are told that *Jesus turned, and saw them following,
and saith unto them, What seek ye?* Hence we learn, that
when we once begin to form good resolutions, God gives us
opportunities enough of improvement. Christ asks the
question, not because He needed to be told, but in order to
encourage familiarity and confidence, and shew that He
thought them worthy of His instructions. THEOPHYL. Observe then, that it was upon those who followed Him, that
our Lord turned His face and looked upon them. Unless
thou by thy good works follow Him, thou shalt never be
permitted to see His face, or enter into His dwelling.
ALCUIN. The disciples followed behind His back, in order to
see Him, and did not see His face. So He turns round, and,
as it were, lowers His majesty, that they might be enabled to
behold His face. ORIGEN. Perhaps it is not without a
reason, that after six testimonies John ceases to bear witness,
and Jesus asks seventhly, *What seek ye?* CHRYS. And
besides following Him, their questions shewed their love for
Christ; *They said unto Him, Rabbi, (which is, being interpreted, Master,) where dwellest Thou?* They call Him,
Master, before they have learnt any thing from Him ; thus
encouraging themselves in their resolution to become disciples, and to shew the reason why they followed. ORIGEN.
An avowal, befitting persons who came from hearing John's
testimony. They put themselves under Christ's teaching,
and express their desire to see the dwelling of the Son of
God. ALCUIN. They do not wish to be under His teaching
for a time only, but enquire where He abides; wishing an
immediate initiation in the secrets of His word, and afterwards meaning often to visit Him, and obtain fuller instruction. And, in a mystical sense too, they wish to know in
whom Christ dwells, that profiting by their example they
may themselves become fit to be His dwelling. Or, their

Margin notes: in loc. / Orig. tom. ii. c. 29. / Chrys. Hom. xviii. in Joan. sparsim

seeing Jesus walking, and straightway enquiring where He resides, is an intimation to us, that we should, remembering His Incarnation, earnestly entreat Him to shew us our eternal habitation. The request being so good a one, Christ promises a free and full disclosure. *He saith unto them, Come and see:* that is to say, My dwelling is not to be understood by words, but by works; *come,* therefore, by believing and working, and then *see* by understanding. ORIGEN. Or perhaps *come,* is an invitation to action; *see,* to contemplation. CHRYS. Christ does not describe His house and situation, but brings them after Him, shewing that he had already accepted them as His own. He says not, It is not the time now, to-morrow ye shall hear if ye wish to learn; but addresses them familiarly, as friends who had lived with him a long time. But how is it that He saith in another place, *The Son of man hath not where to lay His head?* when here He says, *Come and see* where I live? His not having where to lay His head, could only have meant that He had no dwelling of His own, not that He did not live in a house at all: for the next words are, *They came and saw where He dwelt, and abode with Him that day.* Why they stayed the Evangelist does not say: it being obviously for the sake of His teaching. AUG. What a blessed day and night was that! Let us too build up in our hearts within, and make Him an house, whither He may come and teach us. THEOPHYL. *And it was about the tenth hour.* The Evangelist mentions the time of day purposely, as a hint both to teachers and learners, not to let time interfere with their work. CHRYS. It shewed a strong desire to hear Him, since even at sunset they did not turn from Him. To sensual persons the time after meals is unsuitable for any grave employment, their bodies being overloaded with food. But John, whose disciples these were, was not such an one. His evening was a more abstemious one than our mornings. AUG. The number here signifies the law, which was composed of ten commandments. The time had come when the law was to be fulfilled by love, the Jews, who acted from fear, having been unable to fulfil it, and therefore was it at the tenth hour that our Lord heard Himself called, *Rabbi;* none but the giver of the law is the teacher[1] of the law.

Orig. tom. ii. c. 29.

Chrys. Hom. xviii. (al.xvii.) 3.

Matt. 8, 20.

Aug. Tr. vii. c. 9.

Chrys. Hom. xviii. 3.

Aug. Tr. vii. c. 10.

[1] magister

CHRYS. One of the two which *heard John speak and followed* Chrys.
Him was Andrew, Simon Peter's brother. Why is the other $\frac{\text{Hom.}}{\text{xviii. 3.}}$
name left out? Some say, because this Evangelist himself was
that other. Others, that it was a disciple of no eminence,
and that there was no use in telling his name any more than
those of the seventy-two, which are omitted. ALCUIN. Or it
would seem that the two disciples who followed Jesus were
Andrew and Philip.

41. He first findeth his own brother Simon, and
saith unto him, We have found the Messias, which is,
being interpreted, the Christ.

42. And he brought him to Jesus. And when Jesus
beheld him, he said, Thou art Simon the son of Jona:
thou shalt be called Cephas, which is by interpretation,
A stone.

CHRYS. Andrew kept not our Lord's words to himself; but Chrys.
ran in haste to his brother, to report the good tidings: *He* $\frac{\text{Hom.}}{\text{xix. 1.}}$
*first findeth his own brother Simon, and saith unto him, We
have found the Messias, which is, being interpreted, the
Christ.* BEDE. This is truly to find the Lord; viz. to have Bede.
fervent love for Him, together with a care for our brother's $\frac{\text{Hom. in}}{\text{Vig. St.}}$
salvation. CHRYS. The Evangelist does not mention what Andr.
Christ said to those who followed Him; but we may infer it $\frac{\text{Chrys.}}{\text{Hom.}}$
from what follows. Andrew declares in few words what he xix. (al.
had learnt, discloses the power of that Master Who had $^{\text{xviii.})1.}$
persuaded them, and his own previous longings after Him.
For this exclamation, *We have found*, expresses a longing for
His coming, turned to exultation, now that He was really
come. AUG. Messias in Hebrew, Christus in Greek, Unctus Aug.
in Latin. Chrism is unction, and He had a special unction, $\frac{\text{Tr. vii.}}{\text{c. 13.}}$
which from Him extended to all Christians, as appears in the
Psalm, *God, even Thy God, hath anointed Thee with the oil of* Ps. 44,
gladness above Thy fellows[1]. All holy persons are partakers $\frac{(45.)}{\text{partici-}}$
with Him; but He is specially the Holy of Holies, specially pibus
anointed. CHRYS. And therefore he said not Messias, but Chrys.
the Messias. Mark the obedience of Peter from the $\frac{\text{Hom.}}{\text{xix.1, 2.}}$
very first; he went immediately without delay, as appears

from the next words: *And he brought him to Jesus.*
Nor let us blame him as too yielding, because he did not
ask many questions, before he received the word. It is
reasonable to suppose that his brother had told him all,
and sufficiently fully; but the Evangelists often make omissions
for the sake of brevity. But, besides this, it is not absolutely
said that he did believe, but only, *He took him to Jesus;*
i. e. to learn from the mouth of Jesus Himself, what Andrew
had reported. Our Lord begins now Himself to reveal the things
of His Divinity, and to exhibit them gradually by prophecy.
For prophecies are no less persuasive than miracles; inasmuch as they are preeminently God's work, and are beyond
the power of devils to imitate, while miracles may be
phantasy or appearance: the foretelling future events with
certainty is an attribute of the incorruptible nature
alone: *And when Jesus beheld him, He said, Thou art
Simon the son of Jonas; thou shalt be called Cephas, which
is by interpretation, A stone.* BEDE. He beheld him not
with His natural eye only, but by the insight of His Godhead
discerned from eternity the simplicity and greatness of his
soul, for which he was to be elevated above the whole
Church. In the word Peter, we must not look for any
additional meaning, as though it were of Hebrew or Syriac
derivation; for the Greek and Latin word Peter, has the
same meaning as Cephas; being in both languages derived
from petra. He is called Peter on account of the firmness of
his faith, in cleaving to that Rock, of which the Apostle
speaks, *And that Rock was Christ;* which secures those
who trust in it from the snares of the enemy, and dispenses
streams of spiritual gifts. AUG. There was nothing very
great in our Lord saying whose son he was, for our Lord
knew the names of all His saints, having predestinated them
before the foundation of the world. But it was a great thing
for our Lord to change his name from Simon to Peter.
Peter is from petra, rock, which rock is the Church: so that the
name of Peter represents the Church. And who is safe,
unless he build upon a rock? Our Lord here rouses
our attention: for had he been called Peter before, we
should not have seen the mystery of the Rock, and should
have thought that he was called so by chance, and not pro-

Bede.
Hom. i.
Temp.
Hier. in
Vig. S.
Andr.

1 Cor.
10, 4.

Aug.
Tr. vii.
c. 14.

videntially. God therefore made him to be called by another name before, that the change of that name might give vividness to the mystery. CHRYS. He changed the name too to shew that He was the same who done so before in the Old Testament; who had called Abram Abraham, Sarai Sarah, Jacob Israel. Many He had named from their birth, as Isaac and Samson; others again after being named by their parents, as were Peter, and the sons of Zebedee. Those whose virtue was to be eminent from the first, have names given them from the first; those who were to be exalted afterwards, are named afterwards. AUG. The account here of the two disciples on the Jordan, who follow Christ (before he had gone into Galilee) in obedience to John's testimony; viz. of Andrew bringing his brother Simon to Jesus, who gave him, on this occasion, the name of Peter; disagrees considerably with the account of the other Evangelists, viz. that our Lord found these two, Simon and Andrew, fishing in Galilee, and then bid them follow Him: unless we understand that they did not regularly join our Lord when they saw Him on the Jordan; but only discovered who He was, and full of wonder, then returned to their occupations. Nor must we think that Peter first received his name on the occasion mentioned in Matthew, when our Lord says, *Thou art Peter, and upon this rock will I build My Church;* but rather when our Lord says, *Thou shalt be called Cephas, which is by interpretation, A stone.* ALCUIN. Or perhaps He does not actually give him the name now, but only fixes beforehand what He afterwards gave him when He said, *Thou art Peter, and upon this rock will I build My Church.* And while about to change his name, Christ wishes to shew that even that which his parents had given him, was not without a meaning. For Simon signifies obedience, Joanna grace, Jona a dove: as if the meaning was; Thou art an obedient son of grace, or of the dove, i. e. the Holy Spirit; for thou hast received of the Holy Spirit the humility, to desire, at Andrew's call, to see Me. The elder disdained not to follow the younger; for where there is meritorious faith, there is no order of seniority.

Chrys. Hom. xix. (al. xviii.2.)

Aug. de Con. Evang. l. ii. c. 17.

Mat.16, 18.

43. The day following Jesus would go forth into

Galilee, and findeth Philip, and saith unto him, Follow me.

44. Now Philip was of Bethsaida, the city of Andrew and Peter.

45. Philip findeth Nathanael, and saith unto him, We have found him, of whom Moses in the law, and the prophets, did write, Jesus of Nazareth, the son of Joseph.

46. And Nathanael said unto him, Can there any good thing come out of Nazareth? Philip saith unto him, Come and see.

Chrys. Hom. xix. CHRYS. After gaining these disciples, Christ proceeded to convert others, viz. Philip and Nathanael: *The day follow-ing, Jesus would go forth into Galilee.* ALCUIN. Leaving, that is, Judæa, where John was baptizing, out of respect to the Baptist, and not to appear to lower his office, so long as it continued. He was going too to call a disciple, and wished to *go forth into Galilee,* i. e. to a place of " transition" or " revelation," that is to say, that as He Himself increased in wisdom or stature, and in favour with God and man, and as He suffered and rose again, and entered into His glory: so He would teach His followers to *go forth,* and increase in virtue, and pass through suffering to joy. He *findeth Philip, and saith unto him, Follow Me.* Every one follows Jesus who imitates His humility and suffering, in order to be partaker of His resurrection and ascension. CHRYS. Observe, Chrys. Hom. xx. 1. He did not call them, before some had of their own accord joined Him: for had He invited them, before any had joined Him, perhaps they would have started back : but now having determined to follow of their own free choice, they remain firm ever after. He calls Philip, however, because he would be known to him, from living in Galilee. But what made Philip follow Christ? Andrew heard from John the Baptist, and Peter from Andrew ; he had heard from no one ; and yet on Christ saying, *Follow Me,* was persuaded instantly. It is not improbable that Philip may have heard John : and yet it may have been the mere voice of Christ which pro-duced this effect. THEOPHYL. For the voice of Christ sounded not like a common voice to some, that is, the faithful, but kindled in their inmost soul the love of Him. Philip having been continually meditating on Christ, and reading the books of Moses, so confidently expected Him, that the instant he saw, he believed. Perhaps too he had heard of Him from Andrew and Peter, coming from the same district; an explanation which the Evangelist seems to hint at, when he adds, *Now Philip was of Bethsaida, the city of Andrew and Peter.* CHRYS. The power of Christ appears by His gathering fruit out of a barren country. For from that Galilee, out of which there ariseth no prophet, He takes His most distinguished disciples. ALCUIN. Bethsaida means house of hunters. The Evangelist introduces the name of this place by way of allusion to the characters of Philip, Peter, and Andrew, and their future office, i. e. catching and saving souls. CHRYS. Philip is not persuaded himself, but begins preaching to others: *Philip findeth Nathanael, and saith unto him, We have found Him of whom Moses in the Law, and the Prophets, did write, Jesus of Nazareth, the Son of Joseph.* See how zealous he is, and how constantly he is meditating on the books of Moses, and looking for Christ's coming. That Christ was coming he had known before; but he did not know that this was the Christ, *of whom Moses and the Prophets did write:* He says this to give credibility to his preaching, and to shew his zeal for the Law and the Prophets, and how that he had examined them attentively. Be not disturbed at his calling our Lord the Son of Joseph; this was what He was supposed to be. AUG. The person to whom our Lord's mother had been betrothed. The Christians know from the Gospel, that He was conceived and born of an undefiled mother. He adds the place too, *of Nazareth.* THEOPHYL. He was bred up there: the place of His birth could not have been known generally, but all knew that He was bred up in Nazareth.

And Nathanael said unto him, Can there any good thing come out of Nazareth. AUG. However you may understand these words, Philip's answer will suit. You may read it either as affirmatory, *Something good can come out of Nazareth;* to which the other says, *Come and see:* or you may read it as a question, implying doubt on Nathanael's

Margin notes:
Chrys. Hom. xx. 1.

Chrys. Hom. xx. 1.

Aug. Tr. vii. c. 15.

Aug. Tr. vii. c. 15, 16, 17.

part, *Can any good thing come out of Nazareth? Come
and see.* Since either way of reading agrees equally with what
follows, we must inquire the meaning of the passage.
Nathanael was well read in the Law, and therefore the word
Nazareth (Philip having said that he had found Jesus of
Nazareth) immediately raises his hopes, and he exclaims,
Something good can come out of Nazareth. He had searched
the Scriptures, and knew, what the Scribes and Pharisees
could not, that the Saviour was to be expected thence.
ALCUIN. He who alone is absolutely holy, harmless, unde-
Isaiah
11, 1. filed; of whom the prophet saith, *There shall come forth
a rod out of the stem of Jesse, and a branch (Nazaræus) shall
grow out of his roots.* Or the words may be taken as ex-
Chrys.
Hom.
xx. 1, 2.
Micah
5, 2. pressing doubt, and asking the question. CHRYS. Nathanael
knew from the Scriptures, that Christ was to come from
Bethlehem, according to the prophecy of Micah, *And thou,
Bethlehem, in the land of Judah,—out of thee shall come a
Governor, that shall rule my people Israel.* On hearing of
Nazareth, then, he doubted, and was not able to reconcile
Philip's tidings with prophecy. For the Prophets call Him a
Nazarene, only in reference to His education and mode of
life. Observe, however, the discretion and gentleness with
which he communicates his doubts. He does not say, Thou
deceivest me, Philip; but simply asks the question, *Can any
good thing come out of Nazareth?* Philip too in turn is
equally discrete. He is not confounded by the question, but
dwells upon it, and lingers in the hope of bringing him to
Christ: *Philip saith unto him, Come and see.* He takes
him to Christ, knowing that when he had once tasted of
His words and doctrine, he will make no more resistance.

47. Jesus saw Nathanael coming to him, and saith
of him, Behold an Israelite indeed, in whom is no
guile!

48. Nathanael saith unto him, Whence knowest
thou me? Jesus answered and said unto him, Before
that Philip called thee, when thou wast under the fig
tree, I saw thee.

49. Nathanael answered and saith unto him, Rabbi, thou art the Son of God; thou art the King of Israel.

50. Jesus answered and said unto him, Because I said unto thee, I saw thee under the fig tree, believest thou? thou shalt see greater things than these.

51. And he saith unto him, Verily, verily, I say unto you, Hereafter ye shall see heaven open, and the angels of God ascending and descending upon the Son of man.

CHRYS. Nathanael, in difficulty as to Christ coming out of Nazareth, shewed the care with which he had read the Scriptures: his not rejecting the tidings when brought him, shewed his strong desire for Christ's coming. He thought that Philip might be mistaken as to the place. It follows, *Jesus saw Nathanael coming to Him, and saith of him, Behold an Israelite indeed, in whom is no guile!* There was no fault to be found with him, though he had spoken like one who did not believe, because he was more deeply read in the Prophets than Philip. He calls him *guileless*, because he had said nothing to gain favour, or gratify malice. AUG. What meaneth this, *In whom is no guile?* Had he no sin? Was no physician necessary for him? Far from it. No one was ever born, of a temper not to need the Physician. It is guile, when we say one thing, and think another. How then was there no guile in him? Because, if he was a sinner, he confessed his sin; whereas if a man, being a sinner, pretends to be righteous, there is guile in his mouth. Our Lord then commended the confession of sin in Nathanael; He did not pronounce him not a sinner. THEOPHYL. Nathanael however, notwithstanding this praise, does not acquiesce immediately, but waits for further evidence, and asks, *Whence knowest Thou me?* CHRYS. He asks as man, Jesus answers as God: *Jesus answered and said unto him, Before that Philip called thee, when thou wast under the fig tree, I saw thee:* not having beheld him as man, but as God discerning him from above. *I saw thee*, He says, that is, the character of thy life, *when thou wast under the fig tree:* where the two, Philip and Nathanael, had been talking to-

Chrys. Hom. xix.

Aug. Tr. vii. c. 19.

Chrys. Hom. xx.

gether alone, nobody seeing them; and on this account it is said, that on seeing him a long way off, He said, *Behold an Israelite indeed;* whence it appears that this speech was before Philip came near, so that no suspicion could attach to Christ's testimony. Christ would not say, I am not of Nazareth, as Philip told you, but of Bethlehem; in order to αμφισ- βησησι- μον λό- γον. avoid an argument: and because it would not have been sufficient proof, had He mentioned it, of His being the Christ. He preferred rather proving this by His having Aug. Tr. vii. c. 21. been present at their conversation. AUG. Has this fig tree any meaning? We read of one fig tree which was cursed, because it had only leaves, and no fruit. Again, at the creation, Adam and Eve, after sinning, made themselves aprons of fig leaves. Fig leaves then signify sins; and Nathanael, when he was under the fig tree, was under the shadow of death: so that our Lord seemeth to say, O Israel, whoever of you is without guile, O people of the Jewish faith, before that I called thee by My Apostles, when thou wert as yet under the shadow of death, and sawest Me not, I Greg. xviii. Mor. c. xxxviii. (59.) saw thee. GREG. When thou wast under the fig tree, I saw thee; i. e. when thou wast yet under the shade of the law, I chose thee. AUG. Nathanael remembered that he had been Aug. Serm. 40. (122.) under the fig tree, where Christ was not present corporeally, but only by His spiritual knowledge. Hence, knowing that he had been alone, he recognised our Lord's Divinity. CHRYS. Chrys. Hom. xx. That our Lord then had this knowledge, had penetrated into his mind, had not blamed but praised his hesitation, proved to Nathanael that He was the true Christ: *Nathanael answered and saith unto Him, Rabbi, Thou art the Son of God, Thou art the King of Israel:* as if he said, Thou art He who was expected, thou art He who was sought for. Sure proof being obtained, he proceeds to make confession; herein shewing his devotion, as his former hesitation had Hom. xxi. (al. xx.) 1. shewn his diligence. ID. Many when they read this passage, are perplexed at finding that, whereas Peter was pronounced blessed for having, *after* our Lord's miracles and teaching, confessed Him to be the Son of God, Nathanael, who makes the same confession *before,* has no such benediction. The reason is this. Peter and Nathanael both used the same words, but not in the same meaning. Peter confessed our

Lord to be the Son of God, in the sense of very God; the latter in the sense of mere man; for after saying, *Thou art the Son of God,* he adds, *Thou art the King of Israel;* whereas the Son of God was not the King of Israel only, but of the whole world. This is manifest from what follows. For in the case of Peter Christ added nothing, but, as if his faith were perfect, said, that he would build the Church upon his confession; whereas Nathanael, as if his confession were very deficient, is led up to higher things: *Jesus answered and said unto him, Because I said unto thee, I saw thee under the fig tree, believest thou? Thou shalt see greater things than these.* As if He said, What I have just said has appeared a great matter to thee, and thou hast confessed Me to be King of Israel; what wilt thou say when thou seest greater things than these? What that greater thing is He proceeds to shew: *And He saith unto him, Verily, verily, I say unto you, Hereafter ye shall see heaven open, and the angels of God ascending and descending upon the Son of man.* See how He raises him from earth for a while, and forces him to think that Christ is not a mere man: for how could He be a mere man, whom angels ministered to? It was, as it were, saying, that He was Lord of the Angels; for He must be the King's own Son, on whom the servants of the King descended and ascended; descended at His crucifixion, ascended at His resurrection and ascension. Angels too before this *came and ministered unto Him,* and angels brought the glad tidings of His birth. Our Lord made the present a proof of the future. After the powers He had already shewn, Nathanael would readily believe that much more would follow. AUG. Let us recollect the Old Aug. in Testament account. Jacob saw in a dream a ladder $\begin{smallmatrix} \text{Verb.} \\ \text{Dom.} \end{smallmatrix}$ reaching from earth to heaven; the Lord resting upon it, and the angels ascending and descending upon it. Lastly, Jacob himself understanding what the vision meant, set Gen. 28, up a stone, and poured oil upon it. When he anointed the $^{12.}$ stone, did he make an idol? No: he only set up a symbol, not an object of worship. Thou seest here the anointing; see the Anointed also. He is the stone which the builders refused. If Jacob, who was named Israel, saw the ladder, and Nathanael was an Israelite indeed, there was a fitness in our Lord telling him Jacob's dream; as if he said, Whose name thou art called by, his dream hath appeared unto thee: for thou shalt *see the heaven open, and the angels of God ascending and descending upon the Son of man.* If they descend upon Him, and ascend to Him, then He is both up above and here below at the same time; above in Himself, below in His members. AUG. Good preachers, however, who preach Christ, are as angels of God; i. e. they ascend and descend upon the Son of man; as Paul, who ascended to the third heaven, and descended so far even as to give milk to babes. He saith, *We shall see greater things than these:* because it is a greater thing that our Lord has justified us, whom He hath called, than that He saw us lying under the shadow of death. For had we remained where He saw us, what profit would it have been? It is asked why Nathanael, to whom our Lord bears such testimony, is not found among the twelve Apostles. We may believe, however, that it was because he was so learned, and versed in the law, that our Lord had not put him among the disciples. He chose the foolish, to confound the world. Intending to break the neck of the proud, He sought not to gain the fisherman through the orator, but by the fisherman the emperor. The great Cyprian was an orator; but Peter was a fisherman before him; and through him not only the orator, but the emperor, believed.

Aug.
Tr. vii.
in Joan.
c. 23.

2 Cor.
12, 2.
1 Cor.
3, 2.

c. 17.

CHAP. II.

1. And the third day there was a marriage in Cana of Galilee; and the mother of Jesus was there:

2. And both Jesus was called, and his disciples, to the marriage.

3. And when they wanted wine, the mother of Jesus saith unto him, They have no wine.

4. Jesus saith unto her, Woman, what have I to do with thee? mine hour is not yet come.

CHRYS. Our Lord being known in Galilee, they invite Him to a marriage: *And the third day there was a marriage in Cana of Galilee.* ALCUIN. Galilee is a province; Cana a village in it. CHRYS. They invite our Lord to the marriage, not as a great person, but merely as one they knew, one of the many; for which reason the Evangelist says, *And the mother of Jesus was there.* As they invited the mother, so they invited the Son: and therefore, *Jesus was called, and His disciples to the marriage:* and He came, as caring more for our good, than His own dignity. He who disdained not to take upon Him the form of a servant, disdained not to come to the marriage of servants. AUG. Let the proud man blush to see the humility of God. Lo, among other things, the Son of the Virgin comes to a marriage; He who, when He was with the Father, instituted marriage. BEDE. His condescension in coming to the marriage, and the miracle He wrought there, are, even considering them in the letter only, a strong confirmation of the faith. Therein too are condemned the errors of Tatian, Marcion, and others who detract from the honour of marriage. For if the undefiled bed, and the marriage celebrated with due chastity, partook at all of sin, our Lord would never have

[margin notes:]
Chrys.
Hom.
xxi. (al.
xx.) 1.

Chrys.
Hom.
xxi. 1.

Aug.
In Verb.
Dom.
Serm.
xli.

Bede.
Hom.
2d Sund.
after
Epiph.

come to one. Whereas now, conjugal chastity being good, the continence of widows better, the perfection of the virgin state best, to sanction all these degrees, but distinguish the merit of each, He deigned to be born of the pure womb of the Virgin; was blessed after birth by the prophetic voice of the widow Anna; and now invited in manhood to attend the celebration of a marriage, honours that also by the presence of His goodness. Aug. What marvel, if He went to that house to a marriage, Who came into this world to a marriage. For here He has His spouse whom He redeemed with His own blood, to whom He gave the pledge of the Spirit, and whom He united to Himself in the womb of the Virgin. For the Word is the Bridegroom, and human flesh the bride, and both together are one Son of God and Son of man. That womb of the Virgin Mary is His chamber, from which he went forth *as a bridegroom.* Bede. Nor is it without some mysterious allusion, that the marriage is related as taking place on the third day. The first age of the world, before the giving of the Law, was enlightened by the example of the Patriarchs; the second, under the Law, by the writings of the Prophets; the third, under grace, by the preaching of the Evangelists, as if by the light of the third day; for our Lord had now appeared in the flesh. The name of the place too where the marriage was held, Cana of Galilee, which means, desire of migrating, has a typical signification, viz. that those are most worthy of Christ, who burn with devotional desires, and have known the passage from vice to virtue, from earthly to eternal things. The wine was made to fail, to give our Lord the opportunity of making better; that so the glory of God in man might be brought out of its hiding place : *And when they wanted wine, the mother of Jesus saith unto Him, They have no wine.* Chrys. But how came it into the mother's mind to expect so great a thing from her Son? for he had done no miracle as yet: as we read afterwards, *This beginning of miracles did Jesus.* His real nature, however, was beginning now to be revealed by John, and His own conversations with His disciples; besides that His conception, and the circumstances of His birth, had from the first given rise to high expectations in her mind: as Luke tells us, *His mother kept all these sayings in her*

Aug. Tr. viii. c. 4.

Ps.19,5. Bede. in loc.

Chrys. Hom. xxi. 1,2.

Luke 2, 51.

heart. Why then did she never ask Him to work a miracle before? Because the time had now come that He should be made known. Before He had lived so much like an ordinary person, that she had not had the confidence to ask Him. But now that she heard that John had borne witness to Him, and that He had disciples, she asks Him confidently. ALCUIN. She represents here the Synagogue, which challenges Christ to perform a miracle. It was customary with the Jews to ask for miracles.

Jesus saith unto her, Woman, what have I to do with thee? AUG. Some who derogate from the Gospel, and say ^{Aug.} that Jesus was not born of the Virgin Mary, try to draw an ^{Tr. viii.} ^{c. 5.} argument for their error from this place; for, how, say they, could she be His mother to whom He said, *What have I to do with thee?* Now who is it who gives this account, and on whose authority do we believe it? The Evangelist John. But he himself says, *The mother of Jesus was there.* Why should He say it, unless both were true. But did He therefore come to the marriage to teach men to despise their mother? CHRYS. That He greatly venerated His mother, we ^{Chrys.} know from St. Luke, who tells us that He was subject unto His ^{Hom.} ^{xxi. (al.} parents. For where parents throw no obstacle in the way of ^{xx.) 2.} God's commands, it is our duty to be subject to them; but when they demand any thing at an unseasonable time, or cut us off from spiritual things, we should not be deceived into compliance. AUG. To mark a distinction between His Godhead ^{Aug. de} and manhood, that according to His manhood He was ^{Symbolo} ^{Serm. ii.} inferior and subject, but according to His Godhead supreme, ^{c. 14.} He saith, *Woman, what have I to do with thee?* CHRYS. ^(5.) ^{Chrys.} And for another reason, viz. to prevent any suspicion attach- ^{Hom.} ing to His miracles: for these it was proper should be asked ^{xxi. (al.} ^{xx.) 2.} for by those who wanted them, not by His mother. He wished to shew them that He would perform all in their proper time, not all at once, to prevent confusion; for He saith, *Mine hour is not yet come;* i. e. I am not yet known to ^{xxii.(al.} ^{xxi.) 1.} the persons present; nay, they know not that the wine hath failed; let them find out that first; he who perceives not his want beforehand, will not perceive when his want is ^{Aug.} supplied. AUG. Or it was because our Lord as God had not ^{Tr. viii.} ^{c. 9. et} a mother, though as man He had, and the miracle He was ^{seq.} ^{sparsim}

about to work was the act of His Divinity, not of human infirmity. When therefore His mother demanded a miracle, He, as though not acknowledging a human birth, when about to perform a divine work, said, *Woman, what have I to do with thee?* As if He said, Thou didst not beget that in Me, which works the miracle, My Divinity. (She is called woman, with reference to the female sex, not to any injury of her virginity.) But because thou broughtest forth My infirmity, I will acknowledge thee then, when that very infirmity shall hang on the cross. And therefore He adds, *Mine hour is not yet come:* as if to say, I will acknowledge thee when the infirmity, of which thou art the mother, shall hang from the cross. He commended His mother to the disciple, when about to die, and to rise again, before her death. But note; just as the Manicheans have found an occasion of error and pretext for their faithlessness in our Lord's word, *What have I to do with thee?* in the same way the astrologers support theirs from the words, *Mine hour is not yet come.* For, say they, if Christ had not been under the power of fate, He would never have said this. But let them believe what God says below, *I have power to lay it* (my life) *down, and I have power to take it again:* and then let them ask, why He says, *Mine hour is not yet come:* nor let them on such a ground subject the Creator of heaven to fate; seeing that, even were there a fatality in the stars, the Maker of the stars could not be under the dominion of the stars. And not only had Christ nothing to do with fate, as ye call it; but neither hast thou, or any other man. Wherefore said He then, *Mine hour is not yet come?* Because He had the power to die when He pleased, but did not think it expedient yet to exert the power. He was to call the disciples, to proclaim the Kingdom of heaven, to do marvellous works, to approve His divinity by miracles, His humility by partaking of the sufferings of our mortal state. And when He had done all, then the hour was come, not of destiny, but of will, not of obligation, but of power.

John 10, 18.

5. His mother saith unto the servants, Whatsoever he saith unto you, do it.

6. And there were set there six waterpots of stone,

after the manner of the purifying of the Jews, containing two or three firkins apiece.

7. Jesus saith unto them, Fill the waterpots with
water.　And they filled them up to the brim.

8. And he saith unto them, Draw out now, and
bear unto the governor of the feast.　And they bare
it.

9. When the ruler of the feast had tasted the water
that was made wine, and knew not whence it was:
(but the servants which drew the water knew;)　the
governor of the feast called the bridegroom,

10. And saith unto him, Every man at the beginning doth set forth good wine; and when men have
well drunk, then that which is worse: but thou hast
kept the good wine until now.

11. This beginning of miracles did Jesus in Cana
of Galilee, and manifested forth his glory; and his
disciples believed on him.

CHRYS. Although He had said, *Mine hour is not yet come,* He afterwards did what His mother told Him, in order to shew plainly, that He was not under subjection to the hour. For if He was, how could He have done this miracle before the hour appointed for it?　In the next place, He wished to shew honour to His mother, and make it appear that He did not go counter to her eventually.　He would not put her to shame in the presence of so many; especially as she had sent the servants to Him, that the petition might come from a number, and not from herself only; *His mother saith unto the servants, Whatsoever He saith unto you, do it.* BEDE; As if she said, Though He appear to refuse, He will do it nevertheless.　She knew His pity and mercifulness. *And there were set there six waterpots of stone, after the manner of the purifying of the Jews, containing two or three firkins apiece.*　Hydriæ[1] are vessels to hold water: hydor being the Greek for water.　ALCUIN. Vessels to hold water were there, after the manner of the purifying of Jews. Among other traditions of the Pharisees, they observed fre-

Marginal notes: Chrys. Hom. xxii. (al. xxi.) 1. — Bede. in loc. — 1 ὑδρίαι.

Chrys. Hom. xxii.(al. xxi.) 2. quent washings. CHRYS. Palestine being a dry country, with few fountains or wells, they used to fill waterpots with water, to prevent the necessity of going to the river, if they were unclean, and to have materials for washing at hand. To prevent any unbeliever from suspecting that a very thin wine was made by the dregs having been left in the vessels, and water poured in upon them, He says expressly, *According to the manner of the purifying of the Jews:* which shews that those vessels were never used to hold wine. AUG. A

Aug. Tr. ix. c. 7. firkin is a certain measure; as urn, amphora, and the like.

[1] μιτρη-ταὶ, 'fir-kins.' Metron is the Greek for measure: whence metretæ[1]. *Two or three*, is not to be taken to mean some holding two, others three, but the same vessels holding two or three.

Jesus saith unto them, Fill the waterpots with water. And

Chrys. Hom. xxii. 2. *they filled them up to the brim.* CHRYS. But why did He not work the miracle before they had filled the waterpots, which would have been much more wonderful; inasmuch as it is one thing to change the quality of some existing substance, another to make it that substance out of nothing? The latter miracle would be the more wonderful, but the former would be the more easy of belief. And this principle often acts as a check, to moderate the greatness of our Lord's miracles: He wishes to make them more credible, therefore He makes them less marvellous; a refutation this of the perverse doctrine of some, that He was a different Being from the Maker of the world. For we see He performs most of His miracles upon subject-matter already existing, whereas were He contrary to the Creator of the world, He would not use a material thus alien, to demonstrate His own power. He did not draw out the water Himself which He made wine, but ordered the servants to do so. This was for the sake of having witnesses of the miracle; *And He saith unto them, Draw out now, and bear unto the governor of the feast.* ALCUIN. The Triclinium is a circle of three couches, *cline* signifying couch: the ancients used to recline upon couches. And the Architriclinus is the one at the head of the Triclinium, i. e. the chief of the guests. Some say that among the Jews, He was a priest, and attended the marriage in order to instruct in the duties of the married state.

Chrys. Hom. xxii. 2. CHRYS. Or thus; It might be said that the guests were drunken, and could not, in the confusion of their senses, tell whether it were water or wine.   But this objection could not be brought against the attendants, who must have been sober, being occupied wholly in performing the duties of their service gracefully and in order.   Our Lord therefore bid the attendants *bear unto the governor of the feast;* who again would of course be perfectly sober.   He did not say, Give to the guests to drink.   HILARY;   Water is poured into the waterpots; wine is drawn out into the chalices; the senses of the drawer out agree not with the knowledge of the pourer in.   The pourer in thinks that water is drawn out; the drawer out thinks that wine was poured in.   *When the ruler of the feast had tasted the water that was made wine, and knew not whence it was, (but the servants who drew the water knew,) the governor of the feast called the bridegroom.* It was not a mixture, but a creation : the simple nature of water vanished, and the flavour of wine was produced; not that a weak dilution was obtained, by means of some strong infusion, but that which was, was annihilated; and that which was not, came to be.   CHRYS. Our Lord wished the power of His miracles to be seen gradually; and therefore He did not reveal what He had done Himself, nor did the ruler of the feast call upon the servants to do so; (for no credit would have been given to such testimony concerning a mere man, as our Lord was supposed to be,) but He *called the bridegroom,* who was best able to see what was done. Christ moreover did not only make wine, but the best wine. *And (the ruler of the feast) saith unto him, Every man at the beginning doth set forth good wine, and when men have well drunk, then that which is worse; but thou hast kept the good wine until now.*   The effects of the miracles of Christ are more beautiful and better than the productions of nature.   So then that the water was made wine, the servants could testify; that it was made good wine, the ruler of the feast and the bridegroom.   It is probable that the bridegroom made some answer; but the Evangelist omits it, only mentioning what it was necessary for us to know, viz. the water being made wine.   He adds, *This beginning of miracles did Jesus in Cana of Galilee.*   It was very ne-cessary to work miracles just then, when His devoted

Hilar.
iii. de
Trin.
c. 5.

Chrys.
Hom.
xxii. 2,
3.

Hom.
xxiii. 1.

disciples were all collected, and present at the place,
attending to what was going on. ID. Should any say that
there is not sufficient proof of this being the beginning of
miracles, because it is added, *in Cana of Galilee*, as if some
had been preferred elsewhere: we answer, as we did before,
that John says below, *That He might be made manifest
to Israel, therefore have I come baptizing.* Now if He
had performed miracles in the earlier part of His life, the
Jews would not have wanted another person to point Him
out. If our Lord in a short time became so distinguished
for the number of His miracles, that His Name was known
to every one, would He not have been much more so, had
He worked miracles from His earliest years? for the things
themselves would have been the more extraordinary, being performed by a Child, and in so long a time must have become
notorious. It was fit and proper however that He should not
begin to work miracles at so early an age : for men would have
thought the Incarnation a phantasy, and in the extremity of
envy would have delivered Him to be crucified before the
appointed time. AUG. This miracle of our Lord's, turning
the water into wine, is no miracle to those who know that
God worked it. For the Same that day made wine in the
waterpots, Who every year makes wine in the vine: only
the latter is no longer wonderful, because it happens uniformly. And therefore it is that God keeps some extraordinary
acts in store for certain occasions, to rouse men out of their
lethargy, and make them worship Him. Thus it follows,
He manifested forth His glory. ALCUIN: He was the King
of glory, and changed the elements because He was their
Lord. CHRYS. He manifests His glory, as far as related to
His own act; and if at the time many knew it not, yet was
it afterwards to be heard and known of all. *And His
disciples believed on Him.* It was probable that these
would believe more readily, and give more attention to what
went on. AUG. If now for the first time they believed on Him,
they were not His disciples when they came to the marriage.
This however is a form of speech, such as saying that the
Apostle Paul was born in Tarsus of Cilicia; not meaning by
this that he was an Apostle then. In the same way when
we hear of Christ's disciples being invited to the marriage,

Margin notes:
Hom. xx.

c. 1.
Hom. xxi. 2.

Aug. Tr. ix.

Chrys. Hom. xxiii. 1.

Aug. de Cons. Evang. l. ii. c. xvii. (38.)

we should understand not disciples already, but who were to be disciples. AUG. But see the mysteries which lie hid in that miracle of our Lord. It was necessary that all things should be fulfilled in Christ which were written of Him: those Scriptures were the water. He made the water wine when He opened unto them the meaning of these things, and expounded the Scriptures; for thus that came to have a taste which before had none, and that inebriated, which did not inebriate before. BEDE; At the time of our Lord's appearing in the flesh, the sweet vinous taste of the law had been weakened by the carnal interpretations of the Pharisees. AUG. Now if He ordered the water to be poured out, and then introduced the wine from the hidden recesses[1] of creation, He would seem to have rejected the Old Testament. But converting, as He did, the water into wine, He shewed us that the Old Testament was from Himself, for it was by His order that the waterpots were filled. But those Scriptures have no meaning, if Christ be not understood there. Now we know from what time the law dates, viz. from the foundation of the world. From that time to this are six ages; the first, reckoning from Adam to Noah; the second, from Noah to Abraham; the third, from Abraham to David; the fourth, from David to the carrying away into Babylon; the fifth, from that time to John the Baptist; the sixth, from John the Baptist to the end of the world. The six waterpots then denote these six ages of prophecy. The prophecies are fulfilled; the waterpots are full. But what is the meaning of their holding two or three firkins apiece? Had He said three only, our minds would have run immediately to the mystery of the Trinity. Nor perhaps can we reject it, even though it is said, *two or three:* for the Father and the Son being named, the Holy Ghost may be understood by consequence; inasmuch as it is the love between the Father and the Son, which is the Holy Ghost. Nor should we pass over another interpretation, which makes the two firkins alluded to the two races of men, the Jews and the Greeks; and the three to the three sons of Noah. ALCUIN. The servants are the doctors of the New Testament, who interpret the holy Scripture to others spiritually; the ruler of the feast is some lawyer, as Nicodemus, Gamaliel, or Saul.

Aug.
Tr. ix.
c. 5.

Bede. in
v. l.

Aug.
Tr. ix.
5. et sq.
[1] sinibus

c. 17.

When to the former then is committed the word of the Gospel, hid under the letter of the law, it is the water made wine, being set before the ruler of the feast.   And the three rows [1] of guests at table in the house of the marriage are properly mentioned; the Church consisting of three orders of believers, the married, the continent, and the doctors. Christ has kept the good wine until now, i. e. He has deferred the Gospel till this, the sixth age.

[1] Tricli-nium, three couches, see p. 84.

12. After this he went down to Capernaum, he, and his mother, and his brethren, and his disciples: and they continued there not many days.

13. And the Jews' passover was at hand, and Jesus went up to Jerusalem.

Chrys. Hom. xxiii.

CHRYS. Our Lord being about shortly to go up to Jerusalem, proceeded to Capernaum, that He might not take His mother and brethren every where about with Him: *After this he went down to Capernaum, He, and His mother, and His brethren, and His disciples, and they continued there not many days.*   AUG. The Lord our God is He, high, that He might create us; low, that He might create us anew; walking among men, suffering what was human, hiding what was divine.   So He hath a mother, hath brethren, hath disciples: whence He hath a mother, thence hath He brethren.   Scripture frequently gives the name of brethren, not to those only who are born of the same womb, or the same father, but to those of the same generation, cousins by the father's or mother's side.   Those who are unacquainted with this way of speaking, ask, Whence hath our Lord brothers?   Did Mary bring forth again?   That could not be: with her commenced the dignity of the virgin state.   Abraham was uncle of Lot, and Jacob was nephew to Laban the Syrian.   Yet Abraham and Lot are called brethren; and likewise Jacob and Laban. ALCUIN. Our Lord's brethren are the relations of Mary and Joseph, not the sons of Mary and Joseph.   For not only the blessed Virgin, but Joseph also, the witness of her chastity, abstained from all conjugal intercourse. A UG. *And His disciples;* it is uncertain whether Peter and Andrew and the sons of

Aug. Tr. x. in Joan. 1, 2.

Aug. de Cons. Ev. c. ii. c. xvii. (39.)

Zebedee, were of their number or not at this time. For Matthew first relates that our Lord came and dwelt at Capernaum, and afterwards that He called those disciples from their boats, as they were fishing. Is Matthew perhaps supplying what he had omitted? For without any mention that it was at a subsequent time, he says, *Jesus walking by the sea of Galilee saw two brethren.* Or is it better to suppose that these were other disciples? For the writings of the Evangelists and Apostles, call not the twelve only, but all who believing in God were prepared for the kingdom of heaven by our Lord's teaching, disciples[a]. How is it too that our Lord's journey to Galilee is placed here before John the Baptist's imprisonment[b], when Matthew says, *Now when Jesus had heard that John was cast into prison, he departed into Galilee:* and Mark the same? Luke too, though he says nothing of John's imprisonment, yet places Christ's visit to Galilee after His temptation and baptism[c], as the two former do. We should understand then that the three Evangelists are not opposed to John, but pass over our Lord's first coming into Galilee after his baptism ; at which time it was that He converted the water into wine. EUSEB. When copies of the three Gospels had come to the Evangelist John, he is reported, while he confirmed their fidelity and correctness, to have at the same time noticed some omissions, especially at the opening of our Lord's ministry. Certain it is that the first three Gospels seem only to contain the events of the year in which John the Baptist was imprisoned, and put to death. And therefore John, it is said, was asked to write down those acts of our Saviour's before the apprehension of the Baptist, which the former Evangelists had passed over. Any one then, by attending, will

Marginal notes: Matt. 4, 18. — id. cap. 18. — Euseb. Eccl. Hist. l. iii. c. 24.

---

[a] This supposition agrees best with what follows, which makes out the visit to Galilee, in St. Matthew, St. Mark, and St. Luke, to be the *second* visit. For they all mention the calling of the Apostles as taking place in this visit ; which calling therefore had not taken place at the time of this first visit, which St. John is relating now. And it is difficult to imagine that in all three this mention is parenthetical and out of the order of time.

[b] John 3, 23. 24. And John also was baptizing in Enon, near to Salim, because there was much water there : and they came and were baptized. For John was not yet cast into prison."

[c] Comparing Matt. 4, 12. Mark 1, 14. Luke 4, 13. 14. it is evident that the order of events in the three is exactly the same; excepting that St. Luke omits the mention of John the Baptist's imprisonment. The visit to Galilee in St. Luke is meant to be after John's imprisonment, though that event has not been mentioned.

find that the Gospels do not disagree, but that John is relating the events of a different date, from that which the others refer to. CHRYS. He did not perform any miracle at Capernaum, the inhabitants of which city were in a very corrupt state, and not well disposed to Him; He went there however, and stayed some time out of respect to His mother[d]. BEDE; He did not stay many days there, on account of the Passover, which was approaching: *And the Jews' passover was at hand.* ORIGEN; But what need of saying, *of the Jews,* when no other nation had the rite of the Passover? Perhaps[e] because there are two sorts of Passover, one human, which is celebrated in a way very different from the design of Scripture; another the true and Divine, which is kept in spirit and in truth. To distinguish it then from the Divine, it is said, *of the Jews.*

ALCUIN. *And He went up to Jerusalem.* The Gospels mention two journeys of our Lord to Jerusalem, one in the first year of His preaching, before John was sent to prison, which is the journey now spoken of; the other in the year of His Passion. Our Lord has set us here an example of careful obedience to the Divine commands. For if the Son of God fulfilled the injunctions of His own law, by keeping the festivals, like the rest, with what holy zeal should we servants prepare for and celebrate them? ORIGEN; In a mystical sense, it was meet that after the marriage in Cana of Galilee, and the banquet and wine, our Lord should take His mother, brethren, and disciples to the land of consolation (as Capernaum signifies[f]) to console, by the fruits that were to spring up and by abundance of fields, those who

Marginal notes:
Chrys. Hom. xxiii. 1.

Orig. tom. x. in Joan. c. 14.

Orig. tom. x. c. 6, 7.

---

[d] Whom, St. Chrys. adds, He was about to leave behind when He went to Jerusalem.

[e] Origen literally, It is called the *Jews',* as opposed to the *Lord's* Passover. For as the Jews had made His Father's house an house of merchandize, not sanctifying it, so had they made the Lord's passover a human, a Jewish passover, choosing that which was low and carnal.

[f] Origen literally, that He might console His disciples, and the soul that conceived Him of the Holy Ghost, or them who were there benefited with the fruits that were to spring up in their full [replenished] land. And

why is it, went down, and not went up? Perhaps his 'brethren' are here to be understood of those powers who went down with Him, not being called to the marriage, according to the interpretation we have mentioned, but receiving lower and inferior benefit from them; and of another sort from those called the disciples of Christ. For if His mother be invited, there are some bearing fruit, whom our Lord Himself goes down to help with the ministers of the Word, and His disciples; His mother too accompanying.—The interpretation to which Origen refers is lost.

received His discipline, and the mind which had conceived
Him by the Holy Ghost; and who were there to be holpen.
For some there are bearing fruit, to whom our Lord Himself
comes down with the ministers of His word and disciples,
helping such, His mother being present. Those however
who are called to Capernaum, do not seem capable of His
presence long: that is, a land which admitteth lower consolation, is not able to take in the enlightenment from many
doctrines; being capable to receive few only. ALCUIN. Or
Capernaum, we may interpret " a most beautiful village," and
so it signifies the world, to which the Word of the Father came
down. BEDE; But He continued there only a few days,
because he lived with men in this world only a short time.
ORIGEN; Jerusalem, as our Saviour Himself saith, is the city Orig.
of the great King, into which none of those who remain on tom. x.
in Joan.
earth ascend, or enter. Only the soul which has a certain c. 16.
natural loftiness, and clear insight into things invisible, is the
inhabitant of that city. Jesus alone goes up thither[g]. But His
disciples seem to have been present afterwards. *The zeal of
Thine house hath eaten me up.* But it is as though in every
one of the disciples who went up, it was Jesus who went up.

14. And found in the temple those that sold oxen
and sheep and doves, and the changers of money
sitting :

15. And when he had made a scourge of small
cords, he drove them all out of the temple, and the
sheep, and the oxen; and poured out the changers'
money, and overthrew the tables;

16. And said unto them that sold doves, Take these
things hence; make not my Father's house an house
of merchandise.

17. And his disciples remembered that it was
written, The zeal of thine house hath eaten me up.

BEDE; Our Lord on coming to Jerusalem, immediately

---

[g] He, and His mother, and disciples,
went to the marriage : He, and His
mother, and brethren, and disciples,
went down to Capernaum. Here Jesus
alone is mentioned.—Orig. in loc.

entered the temple to pray; giving us an example that, Mat.21. wheresoever we go, our first visit should be to the house of God to pray. And He found *in the temple those that sold oxen, and sheep, and doves, and the changers of money sitting.* Aug. Such sacrifices were prescribed to the people, in condescension to their carnal minds; to prevent them from turning aside to idols. They sacrificed sheep, and oxen, and doves. BEDE; Those however, who came from a distance, being unable to bring with them the animals required for sacrifice, brought the money instead. For their convenience the Scribes and Pharisees ordered animals to be sold in the temple, in order that, when the people had bought and offered them afterwards, they might sell them again, and thus make great profits. *And changers of money sitting;* changers of money sat at the table to supply change to buyers and sellers. But our Lord disapproving of any worldly business in His house, especially one of so questionable a kind, drove out all engaged in it. Aug. He who was to be scourged by them, was first of all the scourger; *And when He had made a scourge of small cords, He drove them all out of the temple.* THEOPHYL. Nor did He cast out only those who bought and sold, but their goods also: *The sheep, and the oxen, and poured out the changers' money, and overthrew the tables,* i. e. of the money changers, which were coffers of pence. ORIGEN; Should it appear something out of the order of things, that the Son of God should make a scourge of small cords, to drive them out of the temple? We have one answer in which some take refuge, viz. the divine power of Jesus, Who, when He pleased, could extinguish the wrath of His enemies however innumerable, and quiet the tumult of their minds: *The Lord bringeth the counsel of the heathen to nought.* This act indeed exhibits no less power, than His more positive miracles; nay rather, more than the miracle by which water was converted into wine: in that there the subject-matter was inanimate, here, the minds of so many thousands of men are overcome. Aug. It is evident that this was done on two several occasions; the first mentioned by John, the last by the other three. ORIGEN; John says here that He drove out the sellers from the temple; Matthew, the sellers and buyers. The number of buyers was

Margin notes:
Aug.
Tr. x.
c. 4.

Aug.
Tr. x.
c. 5.

Orig.
tom. x.
in Joan.
c. 16.

Ps. 32,
33, 10.

Aug.
de Cons.
Ev. l. ii.
c. 67.
Orig.
tom. x.
in Joan.
c. 17.

much greater than of the sellers: and therefore to drive them out was beyond the power of the carpenter's Son, as He was supposed to be, had He not by His divine power put all things under Him, as it is said.   BEDE; The Evangelist sets before us both natures of Christ: the human in that His mother accompanied Him to Capernaum; the divine, in that He said, *Make not My Father's house an house of merchandize.*   CHRYS. Lo, He speaks of God as His Father, and they are not angry, for they think He means it in a common sense.   But afterwards when He spoke more openly, and shewed that He meant equality, they were enraged.   In Matthew's account too, on driving them out, He says, *Ye have made it (My Father's house) a den of thieves.* This was just before His Passion, and therefore He uses severer language. But the former being at the beginning of His miracles, His answer is milder and more indulgent.   AUG. So that temple was still a figure only, and our Lord cast out of it all who came to it as a market.   And what did they sell? Things that were necessary for the sacrifice of that time.   What if He had found men drunken? If the house of God ought not to be a house of merchandize, ought it to be a house of drunkenness?   CHRYS. But why did Christ use such violence? He was about to heal on the Sabbath day, and to do many things which appeared to them transgressions of the Law. That He might not appear therefore to be acting contrary to God, He did this at His own peril; and thus gave them to understand, that He who exposed Himself to such peril to defend the decency of the house, did not despise the Lord of that house.   For the same reason, to shew His agreement with God, He said not, the Holy house, but, *My Father's house.*   It follows, *And His disciples remembered what was written; The zeal of thine house hath eaten me up.*   BEDE; His disciples seeing this most fervent zeal in Him, remembered that it was from zeal for His Father's house that our Saviour drove the ungodly from the temple.   ALCUIN. Zeal, taken in a good sense, is a certain fervour of the Spirit, by which the mind, all human fears forgotten, is stirred up to the defence of the truth.   AUG. He then is eaten up with zeal for God's house, who desires to correct all that he sees wrong there; and, if he cannot correct, endures and

Marginal notes: Chrys. Hom. xxiii. in Joan. c. 2. — c. xxi. — xxii. 13. — Aug. Tr. x. in Joan. c. 4. — Chrys. Hom. xxiii. 2. — in loc. — Aug. Tr. x. c. 9.

mourns. In thine house thou busiest thyself to prevent
matters going wrong; in the house of God, where salvation
is offered, oughtest thou to be indifferent? Hast thou a
friend? admonish him gently; a wife? coerce her severely;
a maid-servant? even compel her with stripes. Do what
thou art able, according to thy station. ALCUIN. To take
the passage mystically, God enters His Church spiritually
every day, and marks each one's behaviour there. Let us be
careful then, when we are in God's Church, that we indulge
not in stories, or jokes, or hatreds, or lusts, lest on a sudden
He come and scourge us, and drive us out of His Church.

Orig. tom. x. in Joan. c. 16. ORIGEN; It is possible even for the dweller in Jerusalem to
incur guilt, and even the most richly endowed may stray.
And unless these repent speedily, they lose the capacity
wherewith they were endued. He finds them in the temple,
i. e. in sacred places, or in the office of enunciating the
Church's truths, some who make His Father's house an
house of merchandize; i. e. who expose to sale the oxen
whom they ought to reserve for the plough, lest by turning
back they should become unfit for the kingdom of God:
also who prefer the unrighteous mammon to the sheep, from
which they have the material of ornament; also who for
miserable gain abandon the watchful care of them who are
called metaphorically doves, without all gall or bitterness[h].
Our Saviour finding these in the holy house, maketh a scourge
of small cords, and driveth them out, together with the sheep
and oxen exposed for sale, scatters the heaps of money,
as unbeseeming in the house of God, and overthrows the
tables set up in the minds of the covetous, forbidding them
to sell doves in the house of God any longer. I think too
that He meant the above, as a mystical intimation that
whatsoever[i] was to be performed with regard to that sacred
oblation by the priests, was not to be performed after the
manner of material oblations, and that the law was not to be
observed as the carnal Jews wished. For our Lord, by
driving away the sheep and oxen, and ordering away the doves,

---

[h] Solertiam columbarum privata qui-
libet amaritudine vilipendent. The text
is not grammatically correct, but solertiam is plainly the reading of ἰσμίλιαν,
and privata &c. of ἰστερημένου πάσης πι-

χρότητος which applies to the dove.
[i] Orig. literally, " that the Divine
service relating to that temple was no
longer to be performed," &c.

which were the most common offerings among the Jews, and
by overthrowing the tables of material coins, which in a
figure only, not in truth, bore the Divine stamp, (i. e. what according to the letter of the _aw seemed good,) and when with His
own hand He scourged the people, He as much as declared that
the dispensation was to be broken up and destroyed, and the
kingdom translated to the believing from among the Gentiles.
Aug. Or, those who sell in the Church, are those who seek Aug.
their own, not the things of Jesus Christ.   They who will Tr. x.
c. 6.
not be bought, think they may sell earthly things.   Thus
Simon wished to buy the Spirit, that he might sell Him :
for he was one of those who sell doves. (The Holy Spirit
appeared in the form of a dove.)   The dove however is not
sold, but is given of free grace [1]; for it is called grace.   BEDE ; [1] gratis
Bede.
They then are the sellers of doves, who, after receiving the in loc.
free grace of the Holy Spirit, do not dispense it freely [2], as [2] gratis
they are commanded, but at a price : who confer the laying
on of hands, by which the Holy Spirit is received, if not for
money, at least for the sake of getting favour with the people,
who bestow Holy Orders not according to merit, but favour.
Aug. By the oxen may be understood the Apostles and Aug.
Prophets, who have dispensed to us the holy Scriptures. Tr. x.
c. 7.
Those who by these very Scriptures deceive the people,
from whom they seek honour, sell the oxen ; and they sell
the sheep too, i. e. the people themselves ; and to whom do
they sell them, but to the devil ?   For that which is cut off
from the one Church, who taketh away, except the roaring 1 Pet.
lion, who goeth about every where, and seeketh whom he may 5, 8.
devour ?   BEDE ;   Or, the sheep are works of purity and Bede.
piety, and they sell the sheep, who do works of piety to gain in loc.
the praise of men.   They exchange money in the temple,
who, in the Church, openly devote themselves to secular
business.   And besides those who seek for money, or praise,
or honour from Holy Orders, those too make the Lord's
house a house of merchandize, who do not employ the rank,
or spiritual grace, which they have received in the Church at
the Lord's hands, with singleness of mind, but with an eye
to human recompense.   Aug. Our Lord intended a meaning Aug.
to be seen in His making a scourge of small cords, and then Tr. x.
c. 5.
scourging those who were carrying on the merchandize in

the temple. Every one by his sins twists for himself a cord, in that he goes on adding sin to sin. So then when men suffer for their iniquities, let them be sure that it is the Lord making a scourge of small cords, and admonishing them to change their lives : which if they fail to do, they will hear

Mat. 23.
Bede.
in loco.
at the last, *Bind him hand and foot.* BEDE ; With a scourge then made of small cords, He cast them out of the temple ; for from the part and lot of the saints are cast out all, who, thrown externally among the Saints, do good works hypocritically, or bad openly. The sheep and the oxen too He cast out, to shew that the life and the doctrine of such were alike reprobate. And He overthrew the change heaps of the money-changers and their tables, as a sign that, at the final condemnation of the wicked, He will take away the form even of those things which they loved. The sale of doves He ordered to be removed out of the temple, because the grace of the Spirit, being freely received, should be freely

Orig.
tom. x.
in Joan.
c. 16.
given. ORIGEN ; By the temple we may understand too the soul wherein the Word of God dwelleth ; in which, before the teaching of Christ, earthly and bestial affections had prevailed. The ox being the tiller of the soil, is the symbol of earthly affections: the sheep, being the most irrational of all animals, of dull ones ; the dove is the type of light and volatile thoughts ; and money, of earthly good things ; which money Christ cast out by the Word of His doctrine, that His Father's house might be no longer a market.

18. Then answered the Jews and said unto him, What sign shewest thou unto us, seeing that thou doest these things?

19. Jesus answered and said unto them, Destroy this temple, and in three days I will raise it up.

20. Then said the Jews, Forty and six years was this temple in building, and wilt thou rear it up in three days?

21. But he spake of the temple of his body.

22. When therefore he was risen from the dead, his disciples remembered that he had said this unto

them: and they believed the Scripture, and the word
which Jesus had said.

THEOPHYL. The Jews seeing Jesus thus acting with power, hoc loco.
and having heard Him say, *Make not My Father's house an*
house of merchandize, ask of Him a sign; *Then answered*
the Jews and said unto Him, What sign shewest Thou unto
us, seeing that Thou doest these things? CHRYS. But were Chrys.
signs necessary for His putting a stop to evil practices? Was xxiii. 2.
not the having such zeal for the house of God, the greatest
sign of His virtue? They did not however remember the
prophecy, but asked for a sign; at once irritated at the loss
of their base gains, and wishing to prevent Him from going
further. For this dilemma, they thought, would oblige Him
either to work miracles, or give up His present course. But
He refuses to give them the sign, as He did on a like
occasion, when He answers, *An evil and adulterous gene-* Mat.12,
ration seeketh after a sign, and there shall no sign be given 39.
it, but the sign of Jonas the prophet; only the answer is
more open there than here. He however who even anticipated
men's wishes, and gave signs when He was not asked, would
not have rejected here a positive request, had He not seen a
crafty design in it. As it was, *Jesus answered and said*
unto them, Destroy this temple, and in three days I will
raise it up. BEDE; For inasmuch as they sought a sign
from our Lord of His right to eject the customary merchandize from the temple, He replied, that that temple signified
the temple of His Body, in which was no spot of sin; as if
He said, As by My power I purify your inanimate temple
from your merchandize and wickedness; so the temple of
My Body, of which that is the figure, destroyed by your
hands, on the third day I will raise again. THEOPHYL. He
does not however provoke them to commit murder, by saying,
Destroy; but only shews that their intentions were not hidden
from Him. Let the Arians observe how our Lord, as the
destroyer of death, says, *I will raise it up;* that is to say, by
My own power. AUG. The Father also raised Him up again; Aug.
to Whom He says, *Raise Thou me up, and I shall reward* Tr. x. in
them. But what did the Father do without the Word? As Joan.
then the Father raised Him up, so did the Son also: even as Ps. 41,
                                                              10.

John 10, 30. He saith below, *I and My Father are one.* CHRYS. But
Chrys. why does He give them the sign of His resurrection? Because
Tract. xxiii. 3. this was the greatest proof that He was not a mere man;
shewing, as it did, that He could triumph over death, and in
Orig. tom. x. in Joan. c. 20. a moment overthrow its long tyranny. ORIGEN. Both those,
i. e. both the Body of Jesus and the temple, seem to me to
be a type of the Church, which with lively stones is built up
into a spiritual house, into an holy priesthood; according to
1 Cor. 12, 27. St. Paul, *Ye are the body of Christ, and members in
particular.* And though the structure of stones seem to be
broken up, and all the bones of Christ scattered by adversities
and tribulations, yet shall the temple be restored, and raised up
again in three days, and stablished in the new heaven and the
new earth. For as that sensible body of Christ was crucified
and buried, and afterward rose again; so the whole body of
Christ's saints was crucified with Christ, (each glorying in
that cross, by which He Himself too was crucified to the
world,) and, after being buried with Christ, hath also risen
with Him, walking in newness of life. Yet have we not
risen yet in the power of the blessed resurrection, which is
still going on, and is yet to be completed. Whence it is not
said, On the third day *I will build it up,* but, *in three days;*
for the erection is being in process throughout the whole of
the three days. THEOPHYL. The Jews, supposing that He
spoke of the material temple, scoffed: *Then said the Jews,
Forty and six years was this temple in building, and wilt
Thou rear it up in three days?* ALCUIN. Note, that they
allude here not to the first temple under Solomon, which was
finished in seven years, but to the one rebuilt under Zoro-
Ezra 4, 5. babel. This was forty-six years building, in consequence of
Orig. tom. x. c. 22. the hindrance raised by the enemies of the work. ORIGEN.
Or some will reckon perhaps the forty and six years from the
time that David consulted Nathan the Prophet on the building of the temple. David from that time was busy in
collecting materials. But perhaps the number forty may
with reference to the four corners of the temple allude to the
four elements of the world, and the number six, to the creation
Aug. iv. de Trin. c. 9. (v.) of man on the sixth day. AUG. Or it may be that this
number fits in with the perfection of the Lord's Body. For
six times forty-six are two hundred and seventy-six days,

which make up nine months and six days, the time that our
Lord's Body was forming in the womb; as we know by
authoritative traditions handed down from our fathers, and
preserved by the Church.   He was, according to general
belief, conceived on the eighth of the Kalends of April, the March
day on which He suffered, and born on the eighth of the 24.
Kalends of January[1].   The intervening time contains two Dec. 25.
hundred and seventy-six days, i. e. six multiplied by forty-
six.   Aug. The process of human conception is said to be Aug. b.
this.   The first six days produce a substance like milk, which lxxxiii.
in the following nine is converted into blood; in twelve more Quæst.
is consolidated, in eighteen more is formed into a perfect set 2. 5. f.
of limbs, the growth and enlargement of which fills up the
rest of the time till the birth.   For six, and nine, and twelve,
and eighteen, added together are forty-five, and with the
addition of one (which[1] stands for the summing up, all these [1] added
numbers being collected into one) forty-six. This multiplied from
by the number six, which stands at the head of this calcula- S. Aug.
tion[2], makes two hundred and seventy-six, i. e. nine months [2] hujus
and six days.   It is no unmeaning information then that the ordina-
temple was forty and six years building; for the temple pre- tionis
figured His Body, and as many years as the temple was in caput
building, so many days was the Lord's Body in forming. tenet.
Aug. Or thus, if you take the four Greek words, anatole, the Aug.
east; dysis, the west; arctos, the north; and mesembria, the in Joan.
south; the first letters of these words make Adam. And our Tr. x.
Lord says that He will gather together His saints from the c. 12.
four winds, when He comes to judgment.   Now these letters
of the word Adam, make up, according to Greek figuring, the
number of the years during which the temple was building.
For in Adam we have alpha, one; delta, four; alpha again,
one; and mi, forty; making up together forty-six.   The
temple then signifies the body derived from Adam; which
body our Lord did not take in its sinful state, but renewed
it, in that after the Jews had destroyed it, He raised it again
the third day.   The Jews however, being carnal, understood
carnally; He spoke spiritually. He tells us, by the Evangelist,
what temple He means; *But He spake of the temple of His
Body*.   THEOPHYL. From this Apollinarius draws an heretical Theoph.
inference: and attempts to shew that Christ's flesh was ad loc.
fin.

H 2

inanimate, because the temple was inanimate. In this way you will prove the flesh of Christ to be wood and stone, because the temple is composed of these materials.

John 12, 27.
ib. 10, 18.
Luke 23, 46.
Now if you refuse to allow what is said, *Now is My soul troubled;* and, *I have power to lay it* (My life) *down,* to be said of the rational soul, still how will you interpret, *Into Thy hands, O Lord, I commend My spirit?* you cannot understand this of an irrational soul: or again, the passage,

Ps. 16, 11.
Orig. tom. x. in Joan. c. 23.
Thou shalt not leave My soul in hell. ORIGEN. Our Lord's Body is called the temple, because as the temple contained the glory of God dwelling therein, so the Body of Christ, which represents the Church, contains the Only-Begotten,

Chrys. Hom. xxiii. in Joan. 3.
Who is the image and glory of God. CHRYS. Two things there were in the mean time very far removed from the comprehension of the disciples: one, the resurrection of our Lord's Body: the other, and the greater mystery, that it was God who dwelt in that Body: as our Lord declares by saying, *Destroy this temple, and in three days I will raise it up.* And thus it follows, *When therefore He had risen from the dead, His disciples remembered that He had said this unto them: and they believed the Scripture, and the word which Jesus had said.* ALCUIN. For before the resurrection they did not understand the Scriptures, because they

John 7, 39.
had not yet received the Holy Ghost, *Who was not yet given, because Jesus was not yet glorified.* But on the day of the resurrection our Lord appeared and opened their meaning to His disciples; that they might understand what was said of Him in the Law and the Prophets. And then they believed the prediction of the Prophets that Christ would rise the third day, and the word which Jesus had spoken to them:

Orig. Tr. x. c. 27.
Destroy this temple, &c. ORIGEN. But (in the mystical interpretation) we shall attain to the full measure of faith, at the great resurrection of the whole body of Jesus, i. e. His Church; inasmuch as the faith which is from sight, is very different from that which seeth as through a glass darkly.

23. Now when he was in Jerusalem at the passover, in the feast day, many believed in his name, when they saw the miracles which he did.

24. But Jesus did not commit himself unto them, because he knew all men.

25. And needed not that any should testify of man : for he knew what was in man.

BEDE. The Evangelist has related above what our Lord Bede. did on his way to Jerusalem ; now He relates how others *in loc.* were affected towards Him at Jerusalem ; *Now when He was in Jerusalem at the Passover, in the feast day, many believed in His Name, when they saw the miracles which He did.* ORIGEN. But how was it that many believed on Him from Orig. seeing His miracles ? for he seems to have performed no *tom. x.* supernatural works at Jerusalem, except we suppose Scrip- *c. 30.* ture to have passed them over. May not however the act of His making a scourge of small cords, and driving all out of the temple, be reckoned a miracle ? CHRYS. Those had been Chrys. wiser disciples, however, who were brought to Christ not by *Hom.* His miracles, but by His doctrine. For it is the duller sort *xxiv. 1.* who are attracted by miracles ; the more rational are con- vinced by prophecy, or doctrine. And therefore it follows, *But Jesus did not commit Himself unto them.* AUG. What Aug. meaneth this, *Many believed in His Name—but Jesus did not* Tr. xi. *commit Himself unto them ?* Was it that they did not believe in Joan. in Him, but only pretended that they did ? In that case the *c. 2. ?.* Evangelist would not have said, *Many believed in His Name.* Wonderful this, and strange, that men should trust Christ, and Christ trusts not Himself to men ; especially considering that He was the Son of God, and suffered voluntarily, or else need not have suffered at all. Yet such are all catechumens. If we say to a catechumen, Believest thou in Christ? he answers, I do believe, and crosses himself. If we ask him, Dost thou eat the flesh of the Son of man ? he knows not what we say[k], for Jesus has not committed Himself to him. ORIGEN. Or, it was those who believed *in His Name*, not Orig. *on Him*, to whom Jesus would not commit Himself. They *tom. x.* believe *on Him*, who follow the narrow way which leadeth unto *c. 28.* life ; they believe *in His Name*, who only believe the miracles. CHRYS. Or it means that He did not place confidence in them, Chrys.
Hom.
xxv. 1.

[k] Catechumens in the early Church not being taught the mystery of the Eucharist. Nic.

as perfect disciples, and did not, as if they were brethren of
confirmed faith, commit to them all His doctrines, for He
did not attend to their outward words, but entered into their
hearts, and well knew how short-lived was their zeal[1]. *Because
He knew all men, and needed not that any should testify of
man, for He knew what was in man.* To know what is in
man's heart, is in the power of God alone, who fashioned
the heart. He does not want witnesses, to inform Him of
that mind, which was of His own fashioning. AUG. The
Maker knew better what was in His own work, than the work
knew what was in itself. Peter knew not what was in himself
when he said, *I will go with Thee unto death ;* but our Lord's
answer shewed that He knew what was in man ; *Before the
cock crow, thou shalt thrice deny Me.* BEDE. An admonition
to us not to be confident of ourselves, but ever anxious and
mistrustful ; knowing that what escapes our own knowledge,
cannot escape the eternal Judge.

Aug.
Tr. xi.
c. 2.

Luke22,
33.
ver. 61.

---

[1] εἰδὼς τὴν πρόσκαιρον αὐτῶν θερμότητα. Aq. tempus opportunum manifestè sciens.

CHAP. III.

1. There was a man of the Pharisees, named Nicodemus, a ruler of the Jews:

2. The same came to Jesus by night, and said unto him, Rabbi, we know that thou art a teacher come from God: for no man can do these miracles that thou doest, except God be with him.

3. Jesus answered and said unto him, Verily, verily, I say unto thee, Except a man be born again, he cannot see the kingdom of God.

AUG. He had said above that, *when He was at Jerusalem*—*many believed in His Name, when they saw the miracles which He did.* Of this number was Nicodemus, of whom we are told; *There was a man of the Pharisees, Nicodemus, a ruler of the Jews.* BEDE. His rank is given, *A ruler of the Jews;* and then what he did, *This man came to Jesus by night:* hoping, that is, by so secret an interview, to learn more of the mysteries of the faith; the late public miracles having given him an elementary knowledge of them. CHRYS. As yet however he was withheld by Jewish infirmity: and therefore he came in the night, being afraid to come in the day. Of such the Evangelist speaks elsewhere, *Nevertheless, among the chief rulers also many believed on Him; but because of the Pharisees they did not confess Him, lest they should be put out of the synagogue.* AUG. Nicodemus was one of the number who believed, but were not as yet born again. Wherefore he came to Jesus by night. Whereas those who are born of water and the Holy Ghost, are addressed by the Apostle, *Ye were sometimes darkness, but now are ye light in the Lord.* HAYMO. Or, well may it be said that he came in the night, enveloped, as he was, in the

Aug.
Tr. xi.

Chrys.
Hom.
xxiv. 1.

John 12,
42.

Aug.
Tr. xi.
c. 3, 4.

Eph. 5,
8.

Haymo.
Hom.
in Oct.
Pent.

darkness of ignorance, and not yet come to the light, i. e. the belief that our Lord was very God. Night in the language of Holy Writ is put for ignorance. *And said unto him, Rabbi, we know that Thou art a teacher come from God.* The Hebrew Rabbi, has the meaning of Magister in Latin. He calls him, we see, a Master, but not God: he does not hint at that; he believes Him to be sent from God, but does not see that He is God. AUG. What the ground of his belief was, is plain from what immediately follows: *For no one can do these miracles that Thou doest, except God be with him.* Nicodemus then was one of the many who *believed in His Name, when they saw the signs that He did.* CHRYS. He did not however conceive any great idea of them from His miracles; and attributed to Him as yet only a human character, speaking of Him as a Prophet, sent to execute a commission, and standing in need of assistance to do His work; whereas the Father had begotten Him perfect, selfsufficient, and free from all defect. It being Christ's design however for the present not so much to reveal His dignity, as to prove that He did nothing contrary to the Father; in words He is often humble, while His acts ever testify His power. And therefore to Nicodemus on this occasion He says nothing expressly to magnify Himself; but He imperceptibly corrects his low views of Him, and teaches him that He was Himself all-sufficient, and independent in His miraculous works. Hence He answers, *Verily, verily, I say unto you, Except a man be born again, he cannot see the kingdom of God.* AUG. Those then are the persons to whom Jesus commits Himself, those born again, who come not in the night to Jesus, as Nicodemus did. Such persons immediately make professsion. CHRYS. He says therefore, *Except a man be born again, he cannot see the kingdom of God:* as if He said, Thou art not yet born again, i. e. of God, by a spiritual begetting; and therefore thy knowledge of Me is not spiritual, but carnal and human. But I say unto thee, that neither thou, nor any one, except he be born again of God, shall be able to see the glory which is around me, but shall be out of the kingdom: for it is the begetting by baptism, which enlightens the mind. Or the meaning is, Except thou art born from above, and

Aug. Tr. xi. c. 3.

Chrys. Hom. xxiv. 2. in Joan.

Aug. Tr. xi. c. 4.

Chrys. Hom. xxiv. 2.

hast received the certainty of my doctrines, thou wanderest out of the way, and art far from the kingdom of heaven. By which words our Lord discloses His nature, shewing that He is more than what He appears to the outward eye. The expression, *From above*[a], means, according to some, from heaven, according to others, from the beginning. Had the Jews heard it, they would have left Him in scorn; but Nicodemus shews the love of a disciple, by staying to ask more questions.

4. Nicodemus saith unto him, How can a man be born when he is old? can he enter the second time into his mother's womb, and be born?

5. Jesus answered, Verily, verily, I say unto thee, Except a man be born of water and of the Spirit, he cannot enter into the kingdom of God.

6. That which is born of the flesh is flesh; and that which is born of the Spirit is spirit.

7. Marvel not that I said unto thee, Ye must be born again.

8. The wind bloweth where it listeth, and thou hearest the sound thereof, but canst not tell whence it cometh, and whither it goeth; so is every one that is born of the Spirit.

CHRYS. Nicodemus coming to Jesus, as to a man, is Chrys. startled on learning greater things than man could utter, things too lofty for him. His mind is darkened, and he Hom. xxiv. 3. does not stand firm, but reels like one on the point of falling away from the faith. Therefore he objects to the doctrine as being impossible, in order to call forth a fuller explanation. Two things there are which astonish him, such a birth, and such a kingdom; neither yet heard of among the Jews. First he urges the former difficulty, as being the greatest marvel. *Nicodemus saith unto him, How can a man be born when he is old? can he enter a second time into his mother's womb, and be born?* BEDE. The question Bede. in loc.

---

[a] Desuper Aq. denuo Vulg. see Tr. 67 on Holy Baptism, p. 45 note.

put thus sounds as if a boy *might* enter a second time into his mother's womb and be born. But Nicodemus, we must remember, was an old man, and took his instance from himself; as if he said, I am an old man, and seek my salvation; how can I enter again into my mother's womb, and be born?

Chrys. Hom. xxiv. 2.

CHRYS. Thou callest Him Rabbi, and sayest that He comes from God, and yet receivest not His sayings, but usest to thy master a word which brings in endless confusion; for that *how*, is the enquiry of a man who has no strong belief; and many who have so enquired, have fallen from the faith; some asking, how God became incarnate? others, how He was born [b]? Nicodemus here asks from anxiety. But observe when a man trusts spiritual things to reasonings of his own,

Aug. Tr. xi. c. 6.

how ridiculously he talks. AUG. It is the Spirit that speaketh, whereas he understandeth carnally; he knew of no birth save one, that from Adam and Eve; from God and the Church he knows of none. But do thou so understand the birth of the Spirit, as Nicodemus did the birth of the flesh; for as the entrance into the womb cannot be repeated,

Chrys. Hom. xxiv. 3.

so neither can baptism. CHRYS. While Nicodemus stumbles, dwelling upon our birth here, Christ reveals more clearly the manner of our spiritual birth; Jesus answered, *Verily, verily, I say unto you, Except a man be born of water and of the*

Aug. Tr. xii. c. 5.

Spirit, he cannot enter into the kingdom of God. AUG. As if He said, Thou understandest me to speak of a carnal birth; but a man must be born of water and of the Spirit, if he is to enter into the kingdom of God. If to obtain the temporal inheritance of his human father, a man must be born of the womb of his mother; to obtain the eternal inheritance of his heavenly Father, he must be born of the womb of the Church. And since man consists of two parts, body and soul, the mode even of this latter birth is twofold; water the visible part cleansing the body; the Spirit by His

Chrys. Hom. xxv. 1.

invisible cooperation, changing the invisible soul. CHRYS. If any one asks how a man is born of water, I ask in return, how Adam was born from the ground. For as in the beginning though the element of earth was the subject-matter, the man was the work of the fashioner; so now too, though the element of water is the subject-matter, the whole work is

[b] So S. Chrys. and how He remained impassible. Aq.

done by the Spirit of grace. He then gave Paradise for a place to dwell in; now He hath opened heaven to us. But what need is there of water, to those who receive the Holy c. 2. Ghost? It carries out the divine symbols of burial, mortification, resurrection, and life. For by the immersion of our heads in the water, the old man disappears and is buried as it were in a sepulchre, whence he ascends a new man. Thus shouldest thou learn, that the virtue of the Father, and of the Son, and of the Holy Ghost, filleth all things. For which reason also Christ lay three days in the grave before His resurrection. That then which the Hom. womb is to the offspring, water is to the believer; he is xxvi. l. fashioned and formed in the water. But that which is fashioned in the womb needeth time; whereas the water all is done in an instant. For the nature of the body is such as to require time for its completion; but spiritual creations are perfect from the beginning. From the time that our Lord ascended out of the Jordan, water produces no longer reptiles, i. e. living souls; but souls rational and endued with the Spirit. Aug. Because He does not say, Except Aug. a man be born again[1] of water and of the Spirit, he shall lib. i. not have salvation, or eternal life; but, *he shall not enter* per. de Bapt. *into the kingdom of God;* from this, some infer that children c. 30. are to be baptized in order to be with Christ in the kingdom 1 Vulg. of God, where they would not be, were they not baptized; but that they will obtain salvation and eternal life even if they die without baptism, not being bound with any chain of sin. But why is a man born again, except to be changed from his old into a new state? Or why doth the image of God not enter into the kingdom of God, if it be not by reason of sin? HAYMO. But Nicodemus being unable to Haymo. take in so great and deep mysteries, our Lord helps him by Hom. the analogy of our carnal birth, saying, *That which is born* Pent. *of the flesh is flesh, and that which is born of the Spirit is spirit.* For as flesh generates flesh, so also doth spirit spirit. CHRYS. Do not look then for any material pro- Chrys. duction, or think that the Spirit generates flesh; for even the Hom. Lord's flesh is generated not by the Spirit only, but also by xxvi. in the flesh. That which is born of the Spirit is spiritual. Joan. 1. The birth here spoken of takes place not according to our

substance, but according to honour and grace. But the
birth of the Son of God is otherwise; for else what would
He have been more than all who are born again? And He
would be proved too inferior to the Spirit, inasmuch as His
birth would be by the grace of the Spirit. How does this
differ from the Jewish doctrine?—But mark next the part
c. 1, 13. of the Holy Spirit, in the divine work. For whereas above
some are said to be *born of God*, here, we find, the Spirit
generates them.—The wonder of Nicodemus being roused
again by the words, *He who is born of the Spirit is spirit,*
Christ meets him again with an instance from nature;
Marvel not that I said unto thee, Ye must be born again.
The expression, *Marvel not*, shews that Nicodemus was
surprised at His doctrine. He takes for this instance some
thing, not of the grossness of other bodily things, but still
removed from the incorporeal nature, the wind; *The wind
bloweth where it listeth, and thou hearest the sound thereof,
but canst not tell whence it cometh, and whither it goeth: so
is every one that is born of the Spirit.* That is to say, if no
one can restrain the wind from going where it will; much
less can the laws of nature, whether the condition of our
natural birth, or any other, restrain the action of the Spirit.
That He speaks of the wind here is plain, from His saying,
Thou hearest the sound thereof, i. e. its noise when it strikes
objects. He would not in talking to an unbeliever and
ignorant person, so describe the action of the Spirit. He
says, *Bloweth where it listeth[c];* not meaning any power of
choice in the wind, but only its natural movements, in their
uncontrolled power. *But canst not tell whence it cometh or
whither it goeth;* i. e. If thou canst not explain the action of
this wind which comes under the cognizance both of thy
feeling and hearing, why examine into the operation of the
Divine Spirit? He adds, *So is every one that is born of the
Spirit.* Aug. But who of us does not see, for example, that
Aug. Tr. xii. c. 7. the south wind blows from south to north, another wind from
the east, another from the west? And how then do we not

---

[c] S. Chrys. adds §. 2. that the whole
applies à fortiori to the Holy Spirit;
"It bloweth where It listeth" is spoken
also to express the power of the Spirit.
If no one restraineth the wind, but it is
borne whither it will, much more shall
not the laws of nature or the rules of
earthly birth, or any thing of this sort,
hold the might of the Spirit.

know whence the wind cometh, and whither it goeth? BEDE. Bede.
It is the Holy Spirit therefore, Who bloweth where He listeth. in Hom. in part.
It is in His own power to choose, whose heart to visit with Invent.
His enlightening grace. *And thou hearest the sound thereof.* S. Cruc. Ed.Nic.
When one filled with the Holy Spirit is present with thee
and speaks to thee. AUG. The Psalm soundeth, the Gospel Aug.
soundeth, the Divine Word soundeth; it is the sound of the Tr. xii. c. 5.
Spirit. This means that the Holy Spirit is invisibly present
in the Word and Sacrament, to accomplish our birth. ALCUIN.
Therefore, *Thou knowest not whence it cometh, or whither it
goeth;* for, although the Spirit should possess a person in
thy presence at a particular time, it could not be seen how
He entered into him, or how He went away again, because
He is invisible. HAYMO. Or, *Thou canst not tell whence it* Haymo.
cometh; i. e. thou knowest not how He brings believers to Hom. in Oct.
the faith; *or whither it goeth,* i. e. how He directs the Pent.
faithful to their hope. And *so is every one that is born
of the Spirit;* as if He said, The Holy Spirit is an invisible
Spirit; and in like manner, every one who is born of the
Spirit is born invisibly. AUG. Or thus: If thou art born of Aug.
the Spirit, thou wilt be such, that he, who is not yet born of Tr. xii. c. 5.
the Spirit, will not know whence thou comest, or whither
thou goest. For·it follows, *So is every one that is born of
the Spirit.* THEOPHYL. This completely refutes Macedonius in loc.
the impugner of the Spirit, who asserted that the Holy Ghost
was a servant. The Holy Ghost, we find, works by His
own power, where He will, and what He will.

9. Nicodemus answered and said unto him, How
can these things be?

10. Jesus answered and said unto him, Art thou a
master of Israel, and knowest not these things?

11. Verily, verily, I say unto thee, We speak that
we do know, and testify that we have seen; and ye receive not our witness.

12. If I have told you earthly things, and ye believe
not, how shall ye believe, if I tell you of heavenly
things.

HAYMO. Nicodemus cannot take in the mysteries of the Divine Majesty, which our Lord reveals, and therefore asks how it is, not denying the fact, not meaning any censure, but wishing to be informed: *Nicodemus answered and said unto* Chrys. *Him, How can these things be?* CHRYS. Forasmuch then as
Hom.
xxvi. 2. he still remains a Jew, and, after such clear evidence, persists in a low and carnal system, Christ addresses him henceforth with greater severity: *Jesus answered and said unto him, Art thou a master in Israel, and knowest not these*
Aug.   *things?* AUG. What think we? that our Lord wished to
Tr. xii.
c. 6.   insult this master in Israel? He wished him to be born of the Spirit: and no one is born of the Spirit except he is made humble; for this very humility it is, which makes us to be born of the Spirit. He however was inflated with his eminence as a master, and thought himself of importance because he was a doctor of the Jews. Our Lord then casts down his pride, in order that he may be born of the Spirit.
Chrys. CHRYS. Nevertheless He does not charge the man with
Hom.
xxvi. 2. wickedness, but only with want of wisdom, and enlightenment. But some one will say, What connexion hath this birth, of which Christ speaks, with Jewish doctrines? Thus much. The first man that was made, the woman that was made out of his rib, the barren that bare, the miracles which were worked by means of water, I mean, Elijah's bringing up the iron from the river, the passage of the Red Sea, and Naaman the Syrian's purification in the Jordan, were all types and figures of the spiritual birth, and of the purification which was to take place thereby. Many passages in the Prophets too have a hidden reference
Ps. 102, to this birth: as that in the Psalms, *Making thee young*
5.
Ps. 31, *and lusty as an eagle:* and, *Blessed is he whose unrighteous-*
1.   *ness is forgiven.* And again, Isaac was a type of this birth. Referring to these passages, our Lord says, *Art thou a master in Israel, and knowest not these things?* A second time however He condescends to his infirmity, and makes use of a common argument to render what He has said
ver. 11. credible: *Verily, verily, I say unto thee, We speak that we do know, and testify that we have seen, and ye receive not our testimony.* Sight we consider the most certain of all the senses; so that when we say, we saw such a thing with our

eyes, we seem to compel men to believe us. In like manner
Christ, speaking after the manner of men, does not indeed
say that he has seen actually, i. e. with the bodily eye, the
mysteries He reveals; but it is clear that He means it of the
most certain absolute knowledge. This then, viz. *That we
do know*, he asserts of Himself alone. HAYMO. Why, it is Haymo.
asked, does He speak in the plural number, *We speak that* Oct.
we do know? Because the speaker being the Only-Begotten Pent.
Son of God, He would shew that the Father was in the Son,
and the Son in the Father, and the Holy Ghost from both,
proceeding indivisibly. ALCUIN. Or, the plural number may
have this meaning; I, and they who are born again of the
Spirit, alone understand what we speak ; and having seen the
Father in secret, this we testify openly to the world; and ye,
who are carnal and proud, receive not our testimony. THEO-
PHYL. This is not said of Nicodemus, but of the Jewish race,
who to the very last persisted in unbelief. CHRYS. They are Chrys.
words of gentleness, not of anger; a lesson to us, when we Hom.
argue and cannot converse, not by sore and angry words, but xxvi. 3.
by the absence of anger and clamour, (for clamour is the
material of anger,) to prove the soundness of our views. Jesus
in entering upon high doctrines, ever checks Himself in
compassion to the weakness of His hearer: and does not
dwell continuously on the most important truths, but turns
to others more humble. Whence it follows: *If I have told
you earthly things, and ye believe not, how shall ye believe
if I tell you of heavenly things.* AUG. That is: If ye do not Aug.
believe that I can raise up a temple, which you have thrown Tr. xii.
down, how can ye believe that men can be regenerated by the c. 7.
Holy Ghost? CHRYS. Or thus: Be not surprised at His calling Chrys.
Baptism earthly. It is performed upon earth, and is com- Hom.
pared with that stupendous birth, which is of the substance xxvii. 1.
of the Father, an earthly birth being one of mere grace.
And well hath He said, not, Ye understand not, but, Ye
believe not: for when the understanding cannot take in
certain truths, we attribute it to natural deficiency or
ignorance: but where that is not received which it belongs
to faith only to receive, the fault is not deficiency, but unbelief. These truths, however, were revealed that posterity

might believe and benefit by them, though the people of that age did not.

13. And no man hath ascended up to heaven, but he that came down from heaven, even the Son of man which is in heaven.

Aug. After taking notice of this lack of knowledge in a person, who, on the strength of his magisterial station, set himself above others, and blaming the unbelief of such men, our Lord says, that if such as these do not believe, others will: *No one hath ascended into heaven, but He that came down from heaven, even the Son of man who is in heaven.* This may be rendered: The spiritual birth shall be of such sort, as that men from being earthly shall become heavenly: which will not be possible, except they are made members of Me; so that he who ascends, becomes one with Him who descended. Our Lord accounts His body, i. e. His Church, as Himself. **Greg.** Forasmuch as we are made one with Him, to the place from which He came alone in Himself, thither He returns alone in us; and He who is ever in heaven, daily ascendeth to heaven. **Aug.** Although He was made the Son of man upon earth, yet His Divinity with which, remaining in heaven, He descended to earth, He hath declared not to disagree with the title of Son of man, as He hath thought His flesh worthy the name of Son of God. For through the Unity of person, by which both substances are one Christ, He walked upon earth, being Son of God; and remained in heaven, being Son of man. And the belief of the greater, involves belief in the less. If then the Divine substance, which is so far more removed from us, and could for our sake take up the substance of man so as to unite them in one person; how much more easily may we believe, that the Saints united with the man Christ, become with Him one Christ; so that while it is true of all, that they ascend by grace, it is at the same time true, that He alone ascends to heaven, Who came down from heaven. **Chrys.** Or thus: Nicodemus having said, *We know that Thou art a teacher sent from God;* our Lord says, *And no man hath*

Aug. DePecc. mer. et remiss. c. xxxi.

Greg. xxvii. Mor.c.8. al. 11.

Aug. ut sup.

Chrys. Hom. xxvii. 1.

ascended, &c. in that He might not appear to be a teacher only like one of the Prophets. THEOPHYL. But when thou in loc. hearest that the Son of man came down from heaven, think not that His flesh came down from heaven; for this is the doctrine of those heretics, who held that Christ took His Body from heaven, and only passed through the Virgin. CHRYS. Chrys. By the title Son of man here, He does not mean His flesh, Hom. but Himself altogether; the lesser part of His nature being xxvii. 1. put to express the whole. It is not uncommon with Him to name Himself wholly from His humanity, or wholly from His divinity. BEDE; If a man of set purpose descend naked to the valley, and there providing himself with clothes and armour, ascend the mountain again, he who ascended may be said to be the same with him who descended. HILARY; Hilar. Or, His descending from heaven is the source of His origin de Trin. as conceived by the Spirit: Mary gave not His body its c. 16. origin, though the natural qualities of her sex contributed its birth and increase. That He is the Son of man is from the birth of the flesh which was conceived in the Virgin. That He is in heaven is from the power of His everlasting nature, which did not contract the power of the Word of God, which is infinite, within the sphere of a finite body. Our Lord remaining in the form of a servant, far from the whole circle, inner and outer, of heaven and the world, yet as Lord of heaven and the world, was not absent therefrom. So then He came down from heaven because He was the Son of man; and He was in heaven, because the Word, which was made flesh, had not ceased to be the Word. AUG. But thou wonderest that He was at once here, and in Aug. heaven. Yet such power hath He given to His disciples. Tr. xii. Hear Paul, *Our conversation is in heaven.* If the man Paul Phil. 3, walked upon earth, and had his conversation in heaven; 20. shall not the God of heaven and earth be able to be in heaven and earth? CHRYS. That too which seemeth very lofty is Chrys. still unworthy of His vastness. For He is not in heaven only, Hom. but every where, and filleth all things. But for the present xxvii. 1. He accommodates Himself to the weakness of His hearer, that by degrees He may convert him.

14. And as Moses lifted up the serpent in the wilderness, even so must the Son of man be lifted up:

15. That whosoever believeth in him should not perish, but have eternal life.

Chrys. Hom. xxvii. 1. CHRYS. Having made mention of the gift of baptism, He proceeds to the source of it, i. e. the cross: *And as Moses lifted up the serpent in the wilderness, even so must the Son of man be lifted up.* BEDE; He introduces the teacher of the Mosaic law, to the spiritual sense of that law; by a passage from the Old Testament history, which was intended Aug. de Pecc. mer. et remiss. c. xxxii. to be a figure of His Passion, and of man's salvation. AUG. Many dying in the wilderness from the attack of the serpents, Moses, by commandment of the Lord, lifted up a brazen serpent: and those who looked upon it were immediately healed. The lifting up of the serpent is the death of Christ; the cause, by a certain mode of construction, being put for the effect. The serpent was the cause of death, inasmuch as he persuaded man into that sin, by which he merited death. Our Lord, however, did not transfer sin, i. e. the poison of the serpent, to his flesh, but death; in order that in the likeness of sinful flesh, there might be punishment without sin, by virtue of which sinful flesh might be delivered in loc. both from punishment and from sin. THEOPHYL. See then the aptness of the figure. The figure of the serpent has the appearance of the beast, but not its poison: in the same way Christ came in the likeness of sinful flesh, being free from sin. By Christ's being *lifted up*, understand His being suspended on high, by which suspension He sanctified the air, even as He had sanctified the earth by walking upon it. Herein too is typified the glory of Christ: for the height of the cross was made His glory: for in that He submitted to be judged, He judged the prince of this world; for Adam died justly, because he sinned; our Lord unjustly, because He did no sin. So He overcame him, who delivered Him over to death, and thus delivered Adam from death. And in this the devil found himself vanquished, that he could not upon the cross torment our Lord into hating His murderers: but only made Him love and pray for them the more. In this way the cross of Christ was made His lifting up, and glory. Chrys. Hom. xxvii. 2. CHRYS. Wherefore He does not say, ' The Son of man must be suspended, but *lifted up*, a more honourable term, but

coming near the figure. He uses the figure to shew that the
old dispensation is akin to the new, and to shew on His
hearers' account that He suffered voluntarily; and that His
death issued in life. AUG. As then formerly he who looked Aug.
to the serpent that was lifted up, was healed of its poison, c. 11.
and saved from death; so now he who is conformed to the
likeness of Christ's death by faith and the grace of baptism,
is delivered both from sin by justification, and from death by
the resurrection: as He Himself saith; *That whosoever
believeth on Him should not perish, but have everlasting
life.* What need then is there that the child should be conformed by baptism to the death of Christ, if he be not
altogether tainted by the poisonous bite of the serpent?
CHRYS. Observe; He alludes to the Passion obscurely, in Chrys.
consideration to His hearer; but the fruit of the Passion He xxvii.2.
unfolds plainly; viz. that they who believe in the Crucified
One should not perish. And if they who believe in the
Crucified live, much more shall the Crucified One Himself.
AUG. But there is this difference between the figure and the Aug.
reality, that the one recovered from temporal death, the other c. 11.
from eternal.

16. For God so loved the world, that he gave his
only begotten Son, that whosoever believeth in him
should not perish, but have everlasting life.

17 For God sent not his Son into the world to
condemn the world; but that the world through him
might be saved.

18. He that believeth on him is not condemned:
but he that believeth not is condemned already, because
he hath not believed in the name of the only begotten
Son of God.

CHRYS. Having said, *Even so must the Son of man be lifted
up,* alluding to His death; lest His hearer should be cast down 1 ἀπω-
by His words, forming some human notion of Him, and ρατξίαν,
thinking of His death as an evil[1], He corrects this by saying, tion,
that He who was given up to death was the Son of God, and Nicolai,
that His death would be the source of life eternal; *So God* lutarem.

loved the world, that He gave His only begotten Son, that whosoever believeth in Him should not perish, but have everlasting life; as if He said, Marvel not that I must be lifted up, that you may be saved: for so it seemeth good to the Father, who hath so loved you, that He hath given His Son to suffer for ungrateful and careless servants. The text, *God so loved the world,* shews intensity of love. For great indeed and infinite is the distance between the two. He who is without end, or beginning of existence, Infinite Greatness, loved those who were of earth and ashes, creatures laden with sins innumerable. And the act which springs from the love is equally indicative of its vastness. For God gave not a servant, or an Angel, or an Archangel, but His Son. Again, had He had many sons, and given one, this would have been a very great gift; but now He hath given His Only Begotten Son. HILARY; If it were only a creature given up for the sake of a creature, such a poor and insignificant loss were no great evidence of love. They must be precious things which prove our love, great things must evidence its greatness. God, in love to the world, gave His Son, not an adopted Son, but His own, even His Only Begotten. Here is proper Sonship, birth, truth: no creation, no adoption, no lie: here is the test of love and charity, that God sent His own and only begotten Son to save the world. THEOPHYL. As He said above, that the Son of man came down from heaven, not meaning that His flesh did come down from heaven, on account of the unity of person in Christ, attributing to man what belonged to God: so now conversely what belongs to man, he assigns to God the Word. The Son of God was impassible; but being one in respect of person with man, who was passible, the Son is said to be given up to death; inasmuch as He truly suffered, not in His own nature, but in His own flesh. From this death follows an exceeding great and incomprehensible benefit: viz. that *whosoever believeth in Him should not perish, but have everlasting life.* The Old Testament promised to those who obeyed it, length of days: the Gospel promises life eternal, and imperishable. BEDE[1]; Note here, that the same which he before said of the Son of man, lifted up on the cross, he repeats of the only begotten Son of God: viz. *That whosoever believeth in*

Hilar. vi. de Trin. c. 40.

n loc.

1 Ed. Nicolai.

Him, &c. For the same our Maker and Redeemer, who was
Son of God before the world was, was made at the end of the
world the Son of man ; so that He who by the power of His
Godhead had created us to enjoy the happiness of an endless
life, the same restored us to the life we have lost by taking
our human frailty upon Him. ALCUIN. Truly through the Son
of God shall the world have life; for for no other cause came
He into the world, except to save the world. *God sent not
His Son into the world to condemn the world, but that the
world through Him might be saved.* AUG. For why is He Aug.
called the Saviour of the world, but because He saves the ^{Tr. xii.} c. 12.
world? The physician, so far as his will is concerned, heals
the sick. If the sick despises or will not observe the directions of the physician, he destroys himself. CHRYS. Because Chrys.
however He says this, slothful men in the multitude of their ^{Hom.} xxviii.1.
sins, and excess of carelessness, abuse God's mercy, and say,
There is no hell, no punishment; God remits us all our sins.
But let us remember, that there are two advents of Christ;
one past, the other to come. The former was, not to judge
but to pardon us: the latter will be, not to pardon but to
judge us. It is of the former that He says, I have not come
to judge the world. Because He is merciful, instead of
judgment, He grants an internal remission of all sins by
baptism ; and even after baptism opens to us the door of
repentance, which had He not done all had been lost ; *for* Rom. 3,
all have sinned, and come short of the glory of God. After- ^{23.}
wards, however, there follows something about the punish-
ment of unbelievers, to warn us against flattering ourselves
that we can sin with impunity. Of the unbeliever He says,
' he is judged already.'—But first He says, *He that believeth
on Him is not judged.* He who believeth, He says, not who
enquires. But what if his life be impure? Paul very strongly
declares that such are not believers: *They confess*, he says, Tit. 1,
that they know God, but in works deny Him. That is to ^{16.}
say, Such will not be judged for their belief, but will receive
a heavy punishment for their works, though unbelief will not
be charged against them. ALCUIN. He who believes on Him,
and cleaves to Him as a member to the head, will not be
condemned. AUG. What didst thou expect Him to say of ^{Aug.} Tr. xii.
him who believed not, except that he is condemned. Yet _{c. 12.}

mark His words: *He that believeth not is condemned already.*
The Judgment hath not appeared, but it is already given.
For the Lord knows who are His; who are awaiting the
crown, and who the fire. CHRYS. Or the meaning is, that
disbelief itself is the punishment of the impenitent: inasmuch
as that is to be without light, and to be without light is of
itself the greatest punishment. Or He is announcing what is
to be. Though a murderer be not yet sentenced by the
Judge, still his crime has already condemned him. In like
manner he who believes not, is dead, even as Adam, on the
day that he ate of the tree, died. GREG. Or thus: In the
last judgment some perish without being judged, of whom it
is here said, *He that believeth not is condemned already.*
For the day of judgment does not try those who for unbelief
are already banished from the sight of a discerning judge,
are under sentence of damnation; but those, who retaining
the profession of faith, have no works to shew suitable to that
profession. For those who have not kept even the sacraments
of faith, do not even hear the curse of the Judge at the last
trial. They have already, in the darkness of their unbelief,
received their sentence, and are not thought worthy of being
convicted by the rebuke of Him whom they had despised
Again; For an earthly sovereign, in the government of his state,
has a different rule of punishment, in the case of the dis-
affected subject, and the foreign rebel. In the former case,
he consults the civil law; but against the enemy he proceeds
at once to war, and repays his malice with the punishment it
deserves, without regard to law, inasmuch as he who never
submitted to law, has no claim to suffer by the law. ALCUIN.
He then gives the reason why he who believeth not is
condemned, viz. *because he believeth not in the name of the
only begotten Son of God.* For in this name alone is there
salvation. God hath not many sons who can save; He by
whom He saves is the Only Begotten. AUG. Where then
do we place baptized children? Amongst those who believe?
This is acquired for them by the virtue of the Sacrament, and
the pledges of the sponsors. And by this same rule we
reckon those who are not baptized, among those who believe
not.

Chrys.
Hom.
xxviii.1.

Greg.
l. xxvi.
Mor. c.
xxvii.
(50.)

Aug. de
Pecc.
mer. et
Rem.
l.1.c. 33.

19. And this is the condemnation, that light is come into the world, and men loved darkness rather than light, because their deeds were evil.

20. For every one that doeth evil hateth the light, neither cometh to the light, lest his deeds should be reproved.

21. But he that doeth truth cometh to the light, that his deeds may be made manifest, that they are wrought in God.

ALCUIN. Here is the reason why men believed not, and why they are justly condemned ; *This is the condemnation, that light is come into the world.* CHRYS. As if He said, So far from their having sought for it, or laboured to find it, light itself hath come to them, and they have refused to admit it ; *Men loved darkness rather than light.* Thus He leaves them no excuse. He came to rescue them from darkness, and bring them to light ; who can pity him who does not choose to approach the light when it comes unto him? BEDE. He calls *Himself* the light, whereof the Evangelist speaks, *That was the true light;* whereas sin He calls darkness. CHRYS. Then because it seemed incredible that man should prefer light to darkness, he gives the reason of the infatuation, viz. that *their deeds were evil.* And indeed had He come to Judgment, there had been some reason for not receiving Him ; for he who is conscious of his crimes, naturally avoids the judge. But criminals are glad to meet one who brings them pardon. And therefore it might have been expected that men conscious of their sins would have gone to meet Christ, as many indeed did ; for the publicans and sinners came and sat down with Jesus. But the greater part being too cowardly to undergo the toils of virtue for righteousness' sake, persisted in their wickedness to the last; of whom our Lord says, *Every one that doeth evil, hateth the light.* He speaks of those who choose to remain in their wickedness. ALCUIN. *Every one that doeth evil, hateth the light;* i. e. he who is resolved to sin, who delights in sin, hateth the light, which detects his sin. AUG. Because they dislike being deceived, and like to deceive, they love light for discovering

Chrys. Hom. xxviii.2.

Bede. in loc. c. 1.

Chrys. Hom. xxviii.2.

Aug. Conf. c. xxiii.

(34.)

herself, and hate her for discovering them. Wherefore it
shall be their punishment, that she shall manifest them
against their will, and herself not be manifest unto them.
They love the brightness of truth, they hate her discrimina-
tion; and therefore it follows, *Neither cometh to the light, that*
his deeds should be reproved. CHRYS. No one reproves a
Pagan, because his own practice agrees with the character
of his gods; his life is in accordance with his doctrines.
But a Christian who lives in wickedness all must condemn.
If there are any Gentiles whose life is good, I know them
not. But are there not Gentiles? it may be asked. For
do not tell me of the naturally amiable and honest; this
is not virtue. But shew me one who has strong passions,
and lives with wisdom. You cannot. For if the announcement of a kingdom, and the threats of hell, and other
inducements, hardly keep men virtuous when they are so,
such calls will hardly rouse them to the attainment of virtue
in the first instance. Pagans, if they do produce any thing
which looks well, do it for vain-glory's sake, and will therefore
at the same time, if they can escape notice, gratify their evil
desires as well. And what profit is a man's sobriety and
decency of conduct, if he is the slave of vain-glory? The
slave of vain-glory is no less a sinner than a fornicator; nay,
sins even oftener, and more grievously. However, even
supposing there are some few Gentiles of good lives, the
exceptions so rare do not affect my argument. BEDE; Mo-
rally too they love darkness rather than light, who when their
preachers tell them their duty, assail them with calumny.

But he that doeth truth cometh to the light, that
his deeds may be made manifest, that they are wrought
in God. CHRYS. He does not say this of those who are
brought up under the Gospel, but of those who are converted
to the true faith from Paganism or Judaism. He shews that
no one will leave a false religion for the true faith, till he
first resolve to follow a right course of life. AUG. He calls
the works of him who comes to the light, *wrought in God;*
meaning that his justification is attributable not to his own
merits, but to God's grace. AUG. But if God hath discovered all men's works to be evil, how is it that any have
done the truth, and come to the light, i. e. to Christ? Now

Margin notes:
Chrys. Hom. xxvii. 2.
Chrys. Hom. xxviii. 3.
Aug. de Pecc. mer. et Remiss. l.i. c. 53.
Aug. Tr. xii. 13, 14.

what He saith is, that *they loved darkness rather than light;*
He lays the stress upon that.   Many have loved their sins,
many have confessed them.   God accuseth thy sins; if thou
accuse them too, thou art joined to God.   Thou must hate
thine own work, and love the work of God in thee.   The
beginning of good works, is the confession of evil works,
and then thou doest the truth: not soothing, not flattering
thyself.   And thou art come to the light, because this very
sin in thee, which displeaseth thee, would not displease thee,
did not God shine upon thee, and His truth shew it unto
thee.   And let those even who have sinned only by word
or thought, or who have only exceeded in things allowable,
do the truth, by making confession, and come to the light
by performing good works.   For little sins, if suffered to
accumulate, become mortal.   Little drops swell the river:
little grains of sand become an heap, which presses and
weighs down.   The sea coming in by little and little, unless
it be pumped out, sinks the vessel.   And what is to pump
out, but by good works, mourning, fasting, giving and
forgiving, to provide against our sins overwhelming us?

22. After these things came Jesus and his disciples
into the land of Judæa; and there he tarried with them,
and baptized.

23. And John also was baptizing in Ænon near to
Salim, because there was much water there : and they
came, and were baptized.

24. For John was not yet cast into prison.

25. Then there arose a question between some
of John's disciples and the Jews about purifying.

26. And they came unto John, and said unto him,
Rabbi, he that was with thee beyond Jordan, to whom
thou barest witness, behold, the same baptizeth, and
all men come to him.

CHRYS. Nothing is more open than truth, nothing bolder; Chrys.
it neither seeks concealment, or avoids danger, or fears the Hom.
xxix. 1.
snare, or cares for popularity.   It is subject to no human
weakness.   Our Lord went up to Jerusalem at the feasts, not

from ostentation or love of honour, but to teach the people His doctrines, and shew miracles of mercy. After the festival He visited the crowds who were collected at the Jordan. *After these things came Jesus and His disciples into the land of Judæa ; and there he tarried with them, and baptized.* BEDE ; *After these things,* is not immediately after His dispute with Nicodemus, which took place at Jerusalem ; but on His return to Jerusalem after some time spent in Galilee. ALCUIN. By Judæa are meant those who confess, whom Christ visits ; for wherever there is confession of sins, or the praise of God, thither cometh Christ and His disciples, i. e. His doctrine and enlightenment ; and there He is known by His cleansing men from sin : *And there He tarried with them, and baptized.* CHRYS. As the Evangelist says afterwards, that Jesus baptized not but His disciples, it is evident that he means the same here, i. e. that the disciples only baptized. AUG. Our Lord did not baptize with the baptism wherewith He had been baptized ; for He was baptized by a servant, as a lesson of humility to us, and in order to bring us to the Lord's baptism, i. e. His own ; for Jesus baptized, as the Lord, the Son of God. BEDE ; John still continues bap ʾzing, though Christ has begun ; for the shadow remains sti. , nor must the forerunner cease, till the truth is manifested. *And John also was baptizing in Ænon, near to Salim.* Ænon is Hebrew for water ; so that the Evangelist gives, as it were, the derivation of the name, when he adds, *For there was much water there.* Salim is a town on the Jordan, where Melchisedec once reigned. JEROME ; It matters not whether it is called Salem, or Salim ; since the Jews very rarely use vowels in the middle of words ; and the same words are pronounced with different vowels and accents, by different readers, and in different places.

And they came, and were baptized. BEDE ; The same kind of benefit which catechumens receive from instruction before they are baptized, the same did John's baptism convey before Christ's. As John preached repentance, announced Christ's baptism, and drew all men to the knowledge of the truth now made manifest to the world : so the ministers of the Church first instruct those who come

Marginal notes:
Chrys. Hom. xxix. 1.
Aug. Tr. xiii. c. 4.
Hierom. Ep. c. xxiii. ad Evag.

to the faith, then reprove their sins; and lastly, drawing them
to the knowledge and love of the truth, offer them remission
by Christ's baptism. CHRYS. Notwithstanding the disciples Chrys.
of Jesus baptized, John did not leave off till his imprison-^{Hom.}_{xxix. 1.}
ment; as the Evangelist's language intimates, *For John was
not yet cast into prison*. BEDE; He evidently here is
relating what Christ did before John's imprisonment; a
part which has been passed over by the rest, who commence
after John's imprisonment. AUG. But why did John baptize? Aug.
Because it was necessary that our Lord should be baptized. ^{Tr. xiii.}_{c. 6.}
And why was it necessary that our Lord should be baptized?
That no one might ever think himself at liberty to despise
baptism. CHRYS. But why did he go on baptizing now? Chrys.
Because, had he left off, it might have been attributed to ^{Hom.}_{xx. 1.}
envy or anger: whereas, continuing to baptize, he got no
glory for himself, but sent hearers to Christ. And he was
better able to do this service, than were Christ's own
disciples; his testimony being so free from suspicion, and
his reputation with the people so much higher than theirs.
He therefore continued to baptize, that he might not increase the envy felt by his disciples against our Lord's
baptism.   Indeed, the reason, I think, why John's death was
permitted, and, in his room, Christ made the great preacher,
was, that the people might transfer their affections wholly
to Christ, and no longer be divided between the two.   For
the disciples of John did become so envious of Christ's
disciples, and even of Christ Himself, that when they saw
the latter baptizing, they threw contempt upon their baptism, as being inferior to that of John's; *And there arose
a question from some of John's disciples with the Jews
about purifying*.   That it was they who began the dispute,
and not the Jews, the Evangelist implies by saying, that
there arose a question from John's disciples, whereas he
might have said, The Jews put forth a question. AUG. The Aug.
Jews then asserted Christ to be the greater person, and His ^{Tr. xiii.}_{c. 8.}
baptism necessary to be received.   But John's disciples did
not understand so much, and defended John's baptism.
At last they come to John, to solve the question: *And they
came unto John, and said unto him, Rabbi, He that was with
thee beyond Jordan, behold, the Same baptizeth.* CHRYS. ^{Chrys.}_{Hom.}_{xxix. 2.}

Meaning, He, Whom thou baptizedst, baptizeth. They did not say expressly, Whom thou baptizedst, for they did not wish to be reminded of the voice from heaven, but, *He Who was with thee,* i. e. Who was in the situation of a disciple, who was nothing more than any of us, He now separateth Himself from thee, and baptizeth. They add, *To Whom thou barest witness;* as if to say, Whom thou shewedst to the world, Whom thou madest renowned, He now dares to do as thou dost. *Behold, the Same baptizeth.* And in addition to this, they urge the probability that John's doctrines would fall into discredit. *All men come to Him.* ALCUIN. Meaning, Passing by thee, all men run to the baptism of Him Whom thou baptizedst.

27. John answered and said, A man can receive nothing, except it be given him from heaven.

28. Ye yourselves bear me witness, that I said, I am not the Christ, but that I am sent before him.

29. He that hath the bride is the bridegroom; but the friend of the bridegroom, which standeth and heareth him, rejoiceth greatly because of the bridegroom's voice: this my joy therefore is fulfilled.

30. He must increase, but I must decrease.

Chrys.
Hom.
xxix. 2.
CHRYS. John, on this question being raised, does not rebuke his disciples, for fear they might separate, and turn to some other school, but replies gently, *John answered and said, A man can receive nothing, except it be given him from heaven;* as if he said, No wonder that Christ does such excellent works, and that all men come to Him; when He Who doeth it all is God. Human efforts are easily seen through, are feeble, and short-lived. These are not such: they are not therefore of human, but of divine originating. He seems however to speak somewhat humbly [k] of Christ, which will not surprise us, when we consider that it was not fitting to tell the whole truth, to minds prepossessed with such a passion as envy. He only tries for the present to alarm

---

[k] Referring to, " *A man* can receive nothing," &c. ver. 27.

them, by shewing that they are attempting impossible things, and fighting against God. AUG. Or perhaps John is speaking Aug. Tr. xiii. c. 9. here of himself: I am a mere man, and have received all from heaven, and therefore think not that, because it has been given me to be somewhat, I am so foolish as to speak against the truth. CHRYS. And see; the very argument Chrys. Hom. xxix. 2. by which they thought to have overthrown Christ, *To whom thou barest witness,* he turns against them; *Ye yourselves bear me witness, that I said, I am not the Christ;* as if he said, If ye think my witness true, ye must acknowledge Him more worthy of honour than myself. He adds, *But that I was sent before Him;* that is to say, I am a servant, and perform the commission of the Father which sent me; my witness is not from favour or partiality; I say that which was given me to say. BEDE; Who art thou then, since thou art not the Christ, and who is He to Whom thou bearest witness? John replies, He is the Bridegroom; I am the friend of the Bridegroom, sent to prepare the Bride for His approach: *He that hath the Bride, is the Bridegroom.* By the Bride he means the Church, gathered from amongst all nations; a Virgin in purity of heart, in perfection of love, in the bond of peace, in chastity of mind and body; in the unity of the Catholic faith; for in vain is she a virgin in body, who continueth not a virgin in mind. This Bride hath Christ joined unto Himself in marriage, and redeemed with the price of His own Blood. THEOPHYL. Christ is the spouse of every soul; the wedlock, wherein they are joined, is baptism; the place of that wedlock is the Church; the pledge of it, remission of sins, and the fellowship of the Holy Ghost; the consummation, eternal life; which those who are worthy shall receive. Christ alone is the Bridegroom: all other teachers are but the friends of the Bridegroom, as was the forerunner. The Lord is the *giver* of good; the rest are the despisers of His gifts. BEDE; His Bride therefore our Lord committed to His friend, i. e. the order of preachers, who should be jealous of her, not for themselves, but for Christ; *The friend of the Bridegroom which standeth and heareth Him, rejoiceth greatly because of the Bridegroom's voice.* AUG. As if He said, She is not My spouse. But dost thou Aug. Tr. xiii. c. 12. therefore not rejoice in the marriage? Yea, I rejoice, he

Chrys. Hom. xxviii.2.

saith, because I am the friend of the Bridegroom. CHRYS. But how doth he who said above, *Whose shoe's latchet I am not worthy to unloose,* call himself a friend? As an expression not of equality, but of excess of joy: (for the friend of the Bridegroom is always more rejoiced than the servant,) and also, as a condescension to the weakness of his disciples, who thought that he was pained at Christ's ascendancy. For he hereby assures them, that so far from being pained, he was right glad that the Bride recognised her Spouse.

Aug. Tr. xiii.

AUG. But wherefore doth he stand? Because he falleth not, by reason of his humility. A sure ground this to stand upon, *Whose shoe's latchet I am not worthy to unloose.* Again; He standeth, and heareth Him. So then if he falleth, he heareth Him not. Therefore the friend of the Bridegroom ought to stand and hear, i. e. to abide in the grace which he hath received, and to hear the voice in which he rejoiceth. I rejoice not, he saith, because of my own voice, but because of the Bridegroom's voice. I rejoice; I in hearing, He in speaking; I am the ear, He the Word. For he who guards the bride or wife of his friend, takes care that she love none else; if he wish to be loved himself in the stead of his friend, and to enjoy her who was entrusted to him, how detestable doth he appear to the whole world? Yet many are the adulterers I see, who would fain possess themselves of the spouse who was bought at so great a price, and who aim by their words at being loved themselves instead of

Chrys. Hom. xxix. 3.

the Bridegroom. CHRYS. Or thus; The expression, *which standeth,* is not without meaning, but indicates that his part is now over, and that for the future he must stand and listen. This is a transition from the parable to the real subject. For having introduced the figure of a bride and bridegroom, he shews how the marriage is consummated, viz. by word and

Rom. 10, 17.

doctrine. *Faith cometh by hearing, and hearing by the word of God.* And since the things he had hoped for had come to pass, he adds, *This my joy therefore is fulfilled;* i. e. The work which I had to do is finished, and nothing more is left, that I can do. THEOPHYL. For which cause I rejoice now, that all men follow Him. For had the bride, i. e.

Aug. Tr. xiv. c. 3.

the people, not come forth to meet the Bridegroom, then I, as the friend of the Bridegroom, should have grieved. AUG.

Or thus; *This my joy is fulfilled*, i. e. my joy at hearing the Bridegroom's voice. I have my gift; I claim no more, lest I lose that which I have received. He who would rejoice in himself, hath sorrow; but he who would rejoice in the Lord, shall ever rejoice, because God is everlasting. BEDE; He rejoiceth at hearing the Bridegroom's voice, who knows that he should not rejoice in his own wisdom, but in the wisdom which God giveth him. Whoever in his good works seeketh not his own glory, or praise, or earthly gain, but hath his affections set on heavenly things; this man is the friend of the Bridegroom. CHRYS. He next dis- Chrys. misses the motions of envy, not only as regards the present, Hom. xxix. 3. but also the future, saying, *He must increase, but I must decrease:* as if he said, My office hath ceased, and is ended; but His advanceth. AUG. What meaneth this, *He must in-* Aug. *crease?* God neither increases, nor decreases. And John Tr. xxv. c. 4, 5. and Jesus, according to the flesh, were of the same age: for the six months' difference between them is of no consequence. This is a great mystery. Before our Lord came, men gloried in themselves; He came in no man's nature, that the glory of man might be diminished, and the glory of God exalted. For He came to remit sins upon man's confession: a man's confession, a man's humility, is God's pity, God's exaltation. This truth Christ and John proved, even by their modes of suffering: John was beheaded, Christ was lifted up on the cross. Then Christ was born, when the days begin to lengthen; John, when they begin to shorten. Let God's glory then increase in us, and our own decrease, that ours also may increase in God. But it is because thou understandest God more and more, that He seemeth to increase in thee: for in His own nature He increaseth not, but is ever* perfect: even as to a man cured of blindness, who beginneth to see a little, and daily seeth more, the light seemeth to increase, whereas it is in reality always at the full, whether he seeth it or not. In like manner the inner man maketh advancement in God, and it seemeth as if God were increasing in Him; but it is He Himself that decreaseth, falling from the height of His own glory, and rising in the glory of God. THEOPHYL. Or thus; As, on the sun rising, the light of the other heavenly bodies seems to be extinguished, though in reality it is only obscured by the greater light: thus the forerunner is said to decrease; as if he were a star hidden by the sun. Christ increases in proportion as he gradually discloses Himself by miracles; not in the sense of increase, or advancement in virtue, (the opinion of Nestorius,) but only as regards the manifestation of His divinity.

31. He that cometh from above is above all: he that is of the earth is earthly, and speaketh of the earth: he that cometh from heaven is above all.

32. And what he hath seen and heard, that he testifieth;

Chrys.
Hom.
xxx. 1.

CHRYS. As the worm gnaws wood, and rusts iron, so vain-glory destroys the soul that cherishes it. But it is a most obstinate fault. John with all his arguments can hardly subdue it in his disciples: for after what he has said above, he saith yet again, *He that cometh from above is above all:* meaning, Ye extol my testimony, and say that the witness is more worthy to be believed, than He to whom he bears witness. Know this, that He who cometh from heaven, cannot be accredited by an earthly witness. He *is above all;* being perfect in Himself, and above comparison. THEOPHYL. Christ cometh from above, as descending from the Father; and is above all, as being elected in preference to all. ALCUIN. Or, *cometh from above;* i. e. from the height of that human nature which was before the sin of the first man. For it was that human nature which the Word of God assumed: He did not take upon Him man's sin, as He did his punishment.

He that is of the earth is of the earth; i. e. is earthly,
Chrys.
Hom.
xxx. 1.
and *speaketh of the earth,* speaketh earthly things. CHRYS. And yet he was not altogether of the earth; for he had a soul, and partook of a spirit, which was not of the earth. What means he then by saying that he is of the earth? Only to express his own worthlessness, that he is one born on the earth, creeping on the ground, and not to be compared with Christ, Who cometh from above. *Speaketh of the*

earth, does not mean that he spoke from his own understanding; but that, in comparison with Christ's doctrine, he
spoke of the earth: as if he said, My doctrine is mean and
humble, compared with Christ's; as becometh an earthly
teacher, compared with Him, in Whom are hid all the Col.2,3.
treasures of wisdom and knowledge. AUG. Or, *speaketh of* Aug.
the earth, he saith of the man, i. e. of himself, so far as he $_{c.~6.}^{Tr.~xiv.}$
speaks merely humanly. If he says ought divine, he is
enlightened by God to say it: as saith the Apostle; *Yet not* 1 Cor.
I, but the grace of God which was with me. John then, so $_{15,~10.}$
far as pertains to John, *is of the earth,* and *speaketh of the
earth:* if ye hear ought divine from him, attribute it to
the Enlightener, not to him who hath received the light.
CHRYS. Having corrected the bad feeling of his disciples, Chrys.
he comes to discourse more deeply upon Christ. Before $_{xxx.~1.}^{Hom.}$
this it would have been useless to reveal the truths which
could not yet gain a place in their minds. It follows therefore, *He that cometh from heaven.* GLOSS. That is, from
the Father. He is above all in two ways; first, in respect of
His humanity, which was that of man before he sinned:
secondly, in respect of the loftiness of the Father, to whom
He is equal. CHRYS. But after this high and solemn men- Chrys.
tion of Christ, his tone lowers: *And what he hath seen and* Hom.
heard, that he testifieth. As our senses are our surest $^{xxx.~1.}$
channels of knowledge, and teachers are most depended on
who have apprehended by sight or hearing what they teach,
John adds this argument in favour of Christ, that, *what he
hath seen and heard, that he testifieth:* meaning that every
thing which He saith is true. I want, saith John, to hear
what things He, Who cometh from above, hath seen and
heard, i. e. what He, and He alone, knows with certainty.
THEOPHYL. When ye hear then, that Christ speaketh what
He saw and heard from the Father, do not suppose that He
needs to be taught by the Father; but only that that knowledge, which He has naturally, is from the Father. For this
reason He is said to have heard, whatever He knows, from
the Father. AUG. But what is it, which the Son hath heard Aug.
from the Father? Hath He heard the word of the Father? $_{c.~7.}^{Tr.~xiv.}$
Yea, but He *is* the Word of the Father. When thou con-
ceivest a word, wherewith to name a thing, the very con-

K

ception of that thing in the mind is a word. Just then as thou hast in thy mind and with thee thy spoken word; even so God uttered the Word, i. e. begat the Son. Since then the Son is the Word of God, and the Son hath spoken the Word of God to us, He hath spoken to us the Father's word. What John said is therefore true.

32. —and no man receiveth his testimony.

33. He that hath received his testimony hath set to his seal that God is true.

34. For he whom God hath sent speaketh the words of God: for God giveth not the Spirit by measure unto him.

35. The Father loveth the Son, and hath given all things into his hand.

36. He that believeth on the Son hath everlasting life: and he that believeth not the Son shall not see life; but the wrath of God abideth on him.

Chrys.
Hom.
xxx. 1. CHRYS. Having said, *And what he hath seen and heard, that he testifieth,* to prevent any from supposing, that what he said was false, because only a few for the present believed, he adds, *And no man receiveth his testimony;* i. e. only a few; for he had disciples who received his testimony. John is alluding to the unbelief of his own disciples, and to the insensibility of the Jews, of whom we read in the beginning of the Gospel, *He came unto His own, and His own received Him not.* Aug.
Tr. xiv.
c. 8. AUG. Or thus; There is a people reserved for the wrath of God, and to be condemned with the devil; of whom none receiveth the testimony of Christ. And others there are ordained to eternal life. Mark how mankind are divided spiritually, though as human beings they are mixed up together: and John separated them by the thoughts of their heart, though as yet they were not divided in respect of place, and looked on them as two classes, the unbelievers, and the believers. Looking to the unbelievers, he saith, *No man receiveth his testimony.* Then turning to those on the right hand he saith, *He that hath received his testimony,*

hath set to his seal. CHRYS. i. e. hath shewn *that God is* true. This is to alarm them: for it is as much as saying, no one can disbelieve Christ without convicting God, Who sent Him, of falsehood: inasmuch as He speaks nothing but what is of the Father. *For He,* it follows, *Whom God hath sent, speaketh the words of God.* ALCUIN. Or, *Hath put to his seal,* i. e. hath put a seal on his heart, for a singular and special token, that this is the true God, Who suffered for the salvation of mankind. AUG. What is it, *that God is true,* except that God is true, and every man a liar? For no man can say what truth is, till he is enlightened by Him who cannot lie. God then is true, and Christ is God. Wouldest thou have proof? Hear His testimony, and thou wilt find it so. But if thou dost not yet understand God, thou hast not yet received His testimony. Christ then Himself is God the true, and God hath sent Him; God hath sent God, join both together; they are One God. For John saith, *Whom God hath sent,* to distinguish Christ from himself. What then, was not John himself sent by God? Yes; but mark what follows, *For God giveth not the Spirit by measure unto Him.* To men He giveth by measure, to His only Son He giveth not by measure. To one man is given by the Spirit the word of wisdom, to another the word of knowledge: one has one thing, another another; for *measure* implies a kind of division of gifts. But Christ did not receive by measure, though He gave by measure. CHRYS. By Spirit here is meant the operation of the Holy Spirit. He wishes to shew that all of us have received the operation of the Spirit by measure, but that Christ contains within Himself the whole operation of the Spirit. How then shall He be suspected, Who saith nothing, but what is from God, and the Spirit? For He makes no mention yet of God the Word, but rests His doctrine on the authority of the Father and the Spirit. For men knew that there was God, and knew that there was the Spirit, (although they had not right belief about His nature;) but that there was the Son they did not know. AUG. Having said of the Son, *God giveth not the Spirit by mea-sure unto Him;* he adds, *The Father loveth the Son,* and farther adds, *and hath given all things into His hand;*

Marginal notes: Chrys. Hom. xxx. 2. Aug. Tr. xiv. c. 8. Chrys. Hom. xxx. 2. Aug. Tr. xiv. c. 11.

in order to shew that *the Father loveth the Son*, in a peculiar sense. For the Father loveth John, and Paul, and yet
hath not given all things into their hands. But *the Father
loveth the Son*, as the Son, not as a master his servant:
as an only, not as an adopted, Son. Wherefore He
hath given all things into His hand ; so that, as great as
the Father is, so great is the Son; let us not think then
that, because He hath deigned to send the Son, any one
inferior to the Father has been sent. THEOPHYL. The
Father then hath given all things to the Son in respect of
His divinity ; of right, not of grace. Or; He *hath given
all things into His hand,* in respect of His humanity : inasmuch as He is made Lord of all things that are in heaven,
and that are in earth. ALCUIN. And because all things are
in His hand, the life everlasting is too: and therefore it
follows, *He that believeth on the Son hath everlasting life.*
BEDE. We must understand here not a faith in words only,
but a faith which is developed in works. CHRYS. He means
not here, that to believe on the Son is sufficient to gain
everlasting life, for elsewhere He says, *Not every one that
saith unto Me, Lord, Lord, shall enter into the kingdom of
heaven.* And the blasphemy against the Holy Ghost is of
itself sufficient to send into hell. But we must not think
that even a right belief on Father, Son, and Holy Ghost, is
sufficient for salvation ; for we have need of a good life
and conversation. Knowing then that the greater part are
not moved so much by the promise of good, as by the threat
of punishment, he concludes, *But He that believeth not the
Son, shall not see life; but the wrath of God abideth on
him.* See how He refers to the Father again, when He
speaketh of punishment. He saith not, the wrath of the
Son, though the Son is judge; but maketh the Father the
judge, in order to alarm men more. And He does not say,
in Him, but *on Him*, meaning that it will never depart from
Him ; and for the same reason He says, *shall not see life,*
i. e. to shew that He did not mean only a temporary death.
AUG. Nor does He say, *The wrath of God cometh·to him,*
but, *abideth on him.* For all who are born, are under the
wrath of God, which the first Adam incurred. The Son
of God came without sin, and was clothed with mortality :

Chrys.
Hom.
xxxi. 1.
Matt. 7.

Aug.
Tr. xiv.
c. 13.

He died that thou mightest live.   Whosoever then will not believe on the Son, on him abideth the wrath of God, of which the Apostle speaks, *We were by nature the children* Eph. 2, *of wrath.* 3.

CHAP. IV.

1. When therefore the Lord knew how the Pharisees had heard that Jesus made and baptized more disciples than John,

2. (Though Jesus himself baptized not, but his disciples,)

3. He left Judæa, and departed again into Galilee.

4. And he must needs go through Samaria.

5. Then cometh he to a city of Samaria, which is called Sychar, near to the parcel of ground that Jacob gave to his son Joseph.

6. Now Jacob's well was there. Jesus therefore, being wearied with his journey, sat thus on the well: and it was about the sixth hour.

[1] The nearest passage is one of S. Cyril. (Nic.)

Aug. Tr. xv. c. 2.

Chrys. Hom. xxxi. 1.

GLOSS.[1] The Evangelist, after relating how John checked the envy of his disciples, on the success of Christ's teaching, comes next to the envy of the Pharisees, and Christ's retreat from them. *When therefore the Lord knew that the Pharisees had heard, &c.* AUG. Truly had the Pharisees' knowledge that our Lord was making more disciples, and baptizing more than John, been such as to lead them heartily to follow Him, He would not have left Judæa, but would have remained for their sake: but seeing, as He did, that this knowledge of Him was coupled with envy, and made them not followers, but persecutors, He departed thence. He could too, had He pleased, have stayed amongst them, and escaped their hands; but He wished to shew His own example to believers in time to come, that it was no sin for a servant of God to fly from the fury of persecutors. He did it like a good teacher, not out of fear for Himself, but for our instruction. CHRYS. He did it too to pacify the envy of men, and perhaps to avoid bringing the dispensation of the incarnation into suspicion. For had he been taken and

escaped, the reality of His flesh would have been doubted.
AUG. It may perplex you, perhaps, to be told that Jesus *Aug.* *baptized more than John,* and then immediately after, *Though* *Jesus Himself baptized not.* What? Is there a mistake made, and then corrected? CHRYS. Christ Himself did not *Chrys.* baptize, but those who reported the fact, in order to raise the *Hom.* envy of their hearers, so represented it as to appear that Christ Himself baptized. The reason why He baptized not *non occ.* Himself, had been already declared by John, *He shall* *Luke 3,* *baptize you with the Holy Ghost and with fire.* Now He had not yet given the Holy Spirit: it was therefore fitting that He should not baptize. But His disciples baptized, as an efficacious mode of instruction; better than gathering up believers here and there, as had been done in the case of Simon and his brother. Their baptism, however, had no more virtue than the baptism of John; both being without the grace of the Spirit, and both having one object, viz. that of bringing men to Christ. AUG. Or, both are true; *Aug.* for Jesus both baptized, and baptized not. He baptized, *Tr. xv.* *c. 3.* in that He cleansed: He baptized not, in that He dipped not. The disciples supplied the ministry of the body, He the aid of that Majesty of which it was said, *The Same is* *ver. 33.* *He which baptizeth.* ALCUIN. The question is often asked, whether the Holy Ghost was given by the baptism of the disciples; when below it is said, *The Holy Ghost was not* *c. 7.* *yet given, because Jesus was not yet glorified.* We reply, that the Spirit was given, though not in so manifest a way as he was after the Ascension, in the shape of fiery tongues. For, as Christ Himself in His human nature ever possessed the Spirit, and yet afterwards at His baptism the Spirit descended visibly upon Him in the form of a dove; so before the manifest and visible coming of the Holy Spirit, all saints might possess the Spirit secretly. AUG. But we must *Aug.* believe that the disciples of Christ were already baptized *Ad Se-* *leuciam* themselves, either with John's baptism, or, as is more *Ep.xviii.* probable, with Christ's. For He who had stooped to the humble service of washing His disciples' feet, had not failed to administer baptism to His servants, who would thus be enabled in their turn to baptize others. CHRYS. Christ on *Chrys.* withdrawing from Judæa, joined those whom He was with *Hom.* *xxxi. 2.*

before, as we read next, *And departed again into Galilee.*
As the Apostles, when they were expelled by the Jews, went
to the Gentiles, so Christ goes to the Samaritans. But, to
deprive the Jews of all excuse, He does not go to stay there,
but only takes it on His road, as the Evangelist implies by
saying, *And he must needs go through Samaria.* Samaria receives its name from Somer, a mountain there, so called from
the name of a former possessor of it. The inhabitants of the
country were formerly not Samaritans, but Israelites. But
in process of time they fell under God's wrath, and the king
of Assyria transplanted them to Babylon and Media; placing
Gentiles from various parts in Samaria in their room. God
however, to shew that it was not for want of power on His
part that He delivered up the Jews, but for the sins of the
people themselves, sent lions to afflict the barbarians. This
was told the king, and he sent a priest to instruct them in
God's law. But not even then did they wholly cease from
their iniquity, but only half changed. For in process of
time they turned to idols again, though they still worshipped God, calling themselves after the mountain,
Samaritans. BEDE. He must needs pass through Samaria;
because that country lay between Judea and Galilee.
Samaria was the principal city of a province of Palestine, and
gave its name to the whole district connected with it. The
particular place to which our Lord went is next given: *Then
cometh He to a city of Samaria which is called Sychar.*
CHRYS. It was the place where Simeon and Levi made a
great slaughter for Dinah. THEOPHYL. But after the sons
of Jacob had desolated the city, by the slaughter of the
Sychemites, Jacob annexed it to the portion of his son Joseph,
as we read in Genesis, *I have given to thee one portion above
thy brethren, which I took out of the hand of the Amorite
with my sword, and with my bow.* This is referred to in
what follows, *Near to the place of ground which Jacob gave
to his son Joseph.*

Now Jacob's well was there. AUG. It was a well. Every
well is a spring, but every spring is not a well. Any water
that rises from the ground, and can be drawn for use, is a
spring: but where it is ready at hand, and on the surface, it
is called a spring only; where it is deep and low down, it is

Chrys. Hom. xxxi. 2.

Gen. 48, 22.

Aug. Tr. xv. c. 5.

called a well, not a spring. THEOPHYL. But why does the
Evangelist make mention of the parcel of ground, and the
well? First, to explain what the woman says, *Our father
Jacob gave us this well:* secondly, to remind you that what
the Patriarchs obtained by their faith in God, the Jews had lost
by their impiety. They had been supplanted to make room
for Gentiles. And therefore there is nothing new in what
has now taken place, i. e. in the Gentiles succeeding to the
kingdom of heaven in the place of the Jews. CHRYS. Christ
prefers labour and exercise to ease and luxury, and therefore
travels to Samaria, not in a carriage but on foot; until at
last the exertion of the journey fatigues Him; a lesson to us,
that so far from indulging in superfluities, we should often
even deprive ourselves of necessaries: *Jesus therefore being
wearied with His journey, &c.* AUG. Jesus, we see, is strong
and weak: strong, because *in the beginning was the Word;*
weak, because *the Word was made flesh.* Jesus thus weak,
being wearied with his journey, sat on the well. CHRYS. As
if to say, not on a seat, or a couch, but on the first place He saw
—upon the ground. He sat down because He was wearied, and
to wait for the disciples. The coolness of the well would be
refreshing in the midday heat: *And it was about the sixth
hour.* THEOPHYL. He mentions our Lord's sitting and
resting from His journey, that none might blame Him for
going to Samaria Himself, after He had forbidden the
disciples going. ALCUIN. Our Lord left Judæa also mystically, i. e. He left the unbelief of those who condemned
Him, and by His Apostles, went into Galilee, i. e. into the
fickleness[a] of the world; thus teaching His disciples to pass
from vices to virtues. The parcel of ground I conceive to
have been left not so much to Joseph, as to Christ, of whom
Joseph was a type; whom the sun, and moon, and all the
stars truly adore. To this parcel of ground our Lord came,
that the Samaritans, who claimed to be inheritors of the
Patriarch Israel, might recognise Him, and be converted to
Christ, the legal heir of the Patriarch. AUG. His journey
is His assumption of the flesh for our sake. For whither
doth He go, Who is every where present? What is this,

Chrys.
Hom.
xxxi. 3.

Aug.
Tr. xv,
c. 6.

Chrys.
Hom.
xxx. 3.

Aug.
Tr. xv.
c. 7.

---

[a] The Heb. root signifying to roll, revolve, &c. as applied to idols, it is a
term of shame.

except that it was necessary for Him, in order to come to us, to take upon Him visibly a form of flesh? So then His being wearied with His journey, what meaneth it, but that He is wearied with the flesh? And wherefore is it the sixth hour? Because it is the sixth age of the world. Reckon severally as hours, the first age from Adam to Noah, the second from Noah to Abraham, the third from Abraham to David, the fourth from David unto the carrying away into Babylon, the fifth from thence to the baptism of John; on this calculation the present age is the sixth hour. Aug. At the sixth hour then our Lord comes to the well. The black abyss of the well, methinks, represents the lowest parts of this universe, i. e. the earth, to which Jesus came at the sixth hour, that is, in the sixth age of mankind, the old age, as it were, of the old man, which we are bidden to put off, that we may put on the new. For so do we reckon the different ages of man's life: the first age is infancy, the second childhood, the third boyhood, the fourth youth, the fifth manhood, the sixth old age. Again, the sixth hour, being the middle of the day, the time at which the sun begins to descend, signifies that we, who are called by Christ, are to check our pleasure in visible things, that by the love of things invisible refreshing the inner man, we may be restored to the inward light which never fails. By His sitting is signified His humility, or perhaps His magisterial character; teachers being accustomed to sit.

Aug. l. lxxxiii. Quæst. qu. 64.

Col. 3,9.

7. There cometh a woman of Samaria to draw water: Jesus saith unto her, Give me to drink.

8. (For his disciples were gone away unto the city to buy meat.)

9. Then saith the woman of Samaria unto him, How is it that thou, being a Jew, askest drink of me, which am a woman of Samaria? for the Jews have no dealings with the Samaritans.

10. Jesus answered and said unto her, If thou knewest the gift of God, and who it is that saith to thee, Give me to drink; thou wouldest have asked of him, and he would have given thee living water.

11. The woman saith unto him, Sir, thou hast nothing to draw with, and the well is deep: from whence then hast thou that living water?

12. Art thou greater than our father Jacob, which gave us the well, and drank thereof himself, and his children, and his cattle?

CHRYS. That this conversation might not appear a violation of His own injunctions against talking to the Samaritans, the Evangelist explains how it arose; viz. for He did not come with the intention beforehand of talking with the woman, but only would not send the woman away, when she had come. *There came a woman of Samaria to draw water.* Observe, she comes quite by chance. AUG. The woman here is the type of the Church, not yet justified, but just about to be. And it is a part of the resemblance, that she comes from a foreign people. The Samaritans were foreigners, though they were neighbours; and in like manner the Church was to come from the Gentiles, and to be alien from the Jewish race. THEOPHYL. The argument with the woman arises naturally from the occasion: *Jesus saith unto her, Give me to drink.* As man, the labour and heat He had undergone had made Him thirsty. AUG. Jesus also thirsted after that woman's faith? He thirsteth for their faith, for whom He shed His blood. CHRYS. This shews us too not only our Lord's strength and endurance as a traveller, but also his carelessness about food; for His disciples did not carry about food with them, since it follows, *His disciples were gone away into the city to buy food.* Herein is shewn the humility of Christ; He is left alone. It was in His power, had He pleased, not to send away all, or, on their going away, to leave others in their place to wait on Him. But He did not choose to have it so: for in this way He accustomed His disciples to trample upon pride of every kind. However some one will say, Is humility in fishermen and tent-makers so great a matter? But these very men were all on a sudden raised to the most lofty situation upon earth, that of friends and followers of the Lord of the whole earth. And men of humble origin, when they arrive at dignity, are on this very account more liable

Chrys.
Hom.
xxxi. 4.

Aug.
Tract.
xv. c.
19.

Aug. l.
lxxxiii.
Quæst.
qu. 64.
Chrys.
Hom.
xxxi. 3.

than others to be lifted up with pride; the honour being so
new to them. Our Lord therefore to keep His disciples
humble, taught them in all things to subdue themselves.
The woman on being told, *Give Me to drink,* very naturally
asks, *How is it that Thou, being a Jew, askest drink of me,
who am a woman of Samaria?* She knew Him to be a Jew
from His figure and speech. Here observe her simpleness.
For even had our Lord been bound to abstain from dealing
with her, that was His concern, not hers; the Evangelist
saying not that the Samaritans would have no dealings with
the Jews, but that *the Jews have no dealings with the
Samaritans.* The woman however, though not in fault herself, wished to correct what she thought a fault in another.
The Jews after their return from the captivity entertained
a jealousy of the Samaritans, whom they regarded as aliens,
and enemies; and the Samaritans did not use all the Scriptures, but only the writings of Moses, and made little of the
Prophets. They claimed to be of Jewish origin, but the Jews
considered them Gentiles, and hated them, as they did the
rest of the Gentile world. AUG. The Jews would not even
use their vessels. So it would astonish the woman to hear
a Jew ask to drink out of her vessel; a thing so contrary to
Jewish rule. CHRYS. But why did Christ ask what the
law allowed not? It is no answer to say that He knew she
would not give it, for in that case, He clearly ought not
to have asked for it. Rather His very reason for asking,
was to shew His indifference to such observances, and to
abolish them for the future. AUG. He who asked to drink,
however, out of the woman's vessel, thirsted for the woman's
faith: *Jesus answered and said unto her, If thou knewest
the gift of God, or Who it is that saith to thee, Give Me to
drink, thou wouldest have asked of Him, and He would have
given thee living water.* ORIGEN. For it is as it were a doctrine, that no one receives a divine gift, who seeks not for it.
Even the Saviour Himself is commanded by the Father to
ask, that He may give it Him, as we read, *Require of
Me, and I will give Thee the heathen for Thine inheritance.*
And our Saviour Himself says, *Ask, and it shall be given
you.* Wherefore He says here emphatically, *Thou wouldest
have asked of Him, and He would have given thee.* AUG.

Aug.
Tract.
xiii.

Aug.
Tract.
xv.

Origen.
tom.xiv.
in Joan.

Ps.2,8.

Luke11,
9.

He lets her know that it was not the water, which she meant, ^{Aug. l.} that He asked for; but that knowing her faith, He wished ^{lxxxiii. Quæst.} to satisfy her thirst, by giving her the Holy Spirit. For so ^{qu. 64.} must we interpret the living water, which is the gift of God; as He saith, *If thou knewest the gift of God.* AUG. Living ^{Aug. Tr. xv.} water is that which comes out of a spring, in distinction to what is collected in ponds and cisterns from the rain. If spring water too becomes stagnant, i. e. collects into some spot, where it is quite separated from its fountain head, it ceases to be living water. CHRYS. In Scripture the grace of ^{Chrys. Hom. xxxii.} the Holy Spirit is sometimes called fire, sometimes water, which shews that these words are expressive not of its substance, but of its action. The metaphor of fire conveys the lively and sin-consuming property of grace; that of water the cleansing of the Spirit, and the refreshing of the souls who receive Him. THEOPHYL. The grace of the Holy Spirit then He calls living water; i. e. lifegiving, refreshing, stirring. For the grace of the Holy Spirit is ever stirring him who does good works, directing the risings of his heart. CHRYS. These words raised the woman's ^{Chrys. Hom. xxxi. 4.} notions of our Lord, and make her think Him no common person. She addresses Him reverentially by the title of Lord; *The woman saith unto Him, Lord, Thou hast nothing to draw with, and the well is deep: from whence then hast Thou that living water?* AUG. She understands the living ^{Aug. Tr. xv. c. 13.} water to be the water in the well; and therefore says, Thou wishest to give me living water; but Thou hast nothing to draw with as I have: Thou canst not then give me this living water; *Art Thou greater than our father Jacob, who gave us the well, and drank thereof himself, and his children, and his cattle?* CHRYS. As if she said, Thou canst not say that ^{Chrys. Hom. xxxi. 4.} Jacob gave us this spring, and used another himself; for he and they that were with him drank thereof, which would not have been done, had he had another better one. Thou canst not then give me of this spring; and Thou hast not another better spring, unless Thou confess Thyself greater than Jacob. Whence then hast Thou the water, which Thou promisest to give us? THEOPHYL. The addition, *and his cattle,* shews the abundance of the water; as if she said, Not only is the water sweet, so that Jacob and his sons drank of it,

but so abundant, that it satisfied the vast multitude of the
Chrys.
Hom.
xxxi. 4. Patriarchs' cattle. CHRYS. See how she thrusts herself upon
the Jewish stock. The Samaritans claimed Abraham as their
ancestor, on the ground of his having come from Chaldea;
and called Jacob their father, as being Abraham's grandson.
BEDE. Or she calls Jacob their father, because she lived
under the Mosaic law, and possessed the farm which Jacob
Orig.
t. xiii. 6. gave to his son Joseph. ORIGEN. In the mystical sense,
Jacob's well is the Scriptures. The learned then drink
like Jacob and his sons; the simple and uneducated, like
Jacob's cattle.

13. Jesus answered and said unto her, Whosoever
drinketh of this water shall thirst again :

14. But whosoever drinketh of the water that I shall
give him shall never thirst; but the water that I
shall give him shall be in him a well of water springing
up into everlasting life.

15. The woman saith unto him, Sir, give me this
water, that I thirst not, neither come hither to draw.

16. Jesus saith unto her, Go, call thy husband, and
come hither.

17. The woman answered and said, I have no husband. Jesus said unto her, Thou hast well said, I
have no husband :

18. For thou hast had five husbands; and he whom
thou now hast is not thy husband : in that saidst thou
truly.

Chrys.
Hom.
xxxii. 1. CHRYS. To the woman's question, *Art Thou greater than
our father Jacob ?* He does not reply, I am greater, lest He
should seem to boast; but His answer implies it; *Jesus
answered and said to her, Whosoever drinketh of this water
shall thirst again : but whosoever drinketh of the water that
I shall give him shall never thirst;* as if He said, If Jacob
is to be honoured because he gave you this water, what wilt
thou say, if I give thee far better than this ? He makes the
comparison however not to depreciate Jacob, but to exalt

Himself. For He does not say, that this water is vile and
counterfeit, but asserts a simple fact of nature, viz. that
whosoever drinketh of this water shall thirst again. AUG. Aug.
Which is true indeed both of material water, and of that of $_{c.\ 16.}^{Tr.\ xv.}$
which it is the type. For the water in the well is the
pleasure of the world, that abode of darkness. Men draw
it with the waterpot of their lusts; pleasure is not relished,
except it be preceded by lust. And when a man has en-
joyed this pleasure, i. e. drunk of the water, he thirsts again;
but if he have received water from Me, he shall never thirst.
For how shall they thirst, who are drunken with the
abundance of the house of God? But He promised this Ps.36,8.
fulness of the Holy Spirit. CHRYS. The excellence of this Chrys.
water, viz. that he that drinketh of it never thirsts, He ex- $_{xxxii.\ 1.}^{Hom.}$
plains in what follows, *But the water that I shall give him
shall be in him a well of water springing up into everlasting
life.* As a man who had a spring within him, would never
feel thirst, so will not he who has this water which I shall
give him. THEOPHYL. For the water which I give him is
ever multiplying. The saints receive through grace the
seed and principle of good; but they themselves make it
grow by their own cultivation. CHRYS. See how the woman Chrys.
is led by degrees to the highest doctrine. First, she thought $_{xxxii.1.}^{Hom.}$
He was some lax Jew. Then hearing of the living water,
she thought it meant material water. Afterwards she understands it as spoken spiritually, and believes that it can
take away thirst, but she does not yet know what it is, only
understands that it was superior to material things: *The
woman saith unto Him, Sir, give me this water, that I thirst
not, neither come hither to draw.* Observe, she prefers Him
to the patriarch Jacob, for whom she had such veneration.
AUG. Or thus; The woman as yet understands Him of the Aug.
flesh only. She is delighted to be relieved for ever from $_{c.15-18.}^{Tr.\ xv.}$
thirst, and takes this promise of our Lord's in a carnal sense.
For God had once granted to His servant Elijah, that he
should neither hunger nor thirst for forty days; and if He
could grant this for forty days, why not for ever? Eager to
possess such a gift, she asks Him for the living water; *The
woman saith unto Him, Sir, give me this water, that I thirst
not, neither come hither to draw.* Her poverty obliged her

to labour more than her strength could well bear; would that she could hear, *Come unto Me, all that labour and are heavy laden, and I will refresh you.* Jesus had said this very thing, i. e. that she need not labour any longer; but she did not understand Him. At last our Lord was resolved that she should understand : *Jesus saith unto her, Go call thy husband, and come hither.* What meaneth this? Did He wish to give her the water through her husband? Or, because she did not understand, did He wish to teach her by means of her husband? The Apostle indeed saith of women, *If they will learn any thing, let them ask their husbands at home.* But this applies only where Jesus is not present. Our Lord Himself was present here; what need then that He should speak to her through her husband? Was it through her husband that He spoke to Mary, who sat at His feet? CHRYS. The woman then being urgent in asking for the promised water, *Jesus saith unto her, Go call thy husband;* to shew that he too ought to have a share in these things. But she was in a hurry to receive the gift, and wished to conceal her guilt, (for she still imagined she was speaking to a man :) *The woman answered and said, I have no husband.* Christ answers her with a seasonable reproof; exposing her as to former husbands, and as to her present one, whom she had concealed ; *Jesus said unto her, Thou hast well said, I have no husband.* AUG. Understand, that the woman had not a lawful husband, but had formed an irregular connexion with some one. He tells her, *Thou hast had five husbands,* in order to shew her His miraculous knowledge. ORIGEN. May not Jacob's well signify mystically the letter of Scripture; the water of Jesus, that which is above the letter, which all are not allowed to penetrate into? That which is written was dictated by men, whereas the things which the eye hath not seen, nor ear heard, neither have entered into the heart of man, cannot be reduced to writing, but are from the fountain of water, that springeth up unto everlasting life, i. e. the Holy Ghost. These truths are unfolded to such as carrying no longer a human heart within them, are able to say with the Apostle, *We have the mind of Christ.* Human wisdom indeed discovers truths, which are handed down to posterity; but the teaching of the Spirit is

Mat. 11, 28.

1 Cor. 14, 35.

Chrys. Hom. xxxii. 2.

Aug. Tr. xv. c. 20.

Orig. tom. xiii. in Joan. c. 5, 6.

1 Cor. 11, 16.

a well of water which springeth up into everlasting life. The woman wished to attain, like the angels, to angelic and super-human truth without the use of Jacob's water. For the angels have a well of water within them, springing from the Word of God Himself. She says therefore, *Sir, give me this water.* But it is impossible here to have the water which is given by the Word, without that which is drawn from Jacob's well; and therefore Jesus seems to tell the woman that He cannot supply her with it from any other source than Jacob's well; If we are thirsty, we must first drink from Jacob's well. *Jesus saith unto her, Go, call thy husband, and come hither.* According to the Apostle, the Law is the husband of the soul. AUG. The five husbands some interpret to be the five books which were given by Moses. And the words, *He whom thou now hast is not thy husband,* they understand as spoken by our Lord of Himself; as if He said, Thou hast served the five books of Moses, as five husbands; but now *he whom thou hast,* i. e. whom thou hearest, *is not thy husband;* for thou dost not yet believe in him. But if she did not believe in Christ, she was still united to those five husbands, i. e. five books, and therefore why is it said, *Thou hast had five husbands,* as if she no longer had them? And how do we understand that a man must have these five books, in order to pass over to Christ, when he who believes in Christ, so far from forsaking these books, embraces them in this spiritual meaning the more strongly? Let us turn to another interpretation. AUG. Jesus seeing that the woman did not understand, and wishing to enlighten her, says, *Call thy husband;* i. e. apply thine understanding. For when the life is well ordered, the understanding governs the soul itself, pertaining to the soul. For though it is indeed nothing else than the soul, it is at the same time a certain part of the soul. And this very part of the soul which is called the understanding and the intellect, is itself illuminated by a light superior to itself. Such a Light was talking with the woman; but in her there was not understanding to be enlightened. Our Lord then, as it were, says, I wish to enlighten, and there is not one to be enlightened; *Call thy husband,* i. e. apply thine understanding, through which thou must be

Rom. 7,
1.
Aug. lib.
lxxxiii.
Quæst.
qu. 64.

Aug.
Tr. xv.
c. 19.

L.

taught, by which governed. The five former husbands may be explained as the five senses, thus : a man before he has the use of his reason, is entirely under the government of his bodily senses. Then reason comes into action; and from that time forward he is capable of entertaining ideas, and is either under the influence of truth or error. The woman had been under the influence of error, which error was not her lawful husband, but an adulterer. Wherefore our Lord says, Put away that adulterer which corrupts thee, and call thy husband, that thou mayest understand Me.

Origen. tom.xiii. c. 8. ORIGEN. And what more proper place than Jacob's well, for exposing the unlawful husband, i. e. the perverse law? For the Samaritan woman is meant to figure to us a soul, that has subjected itself to a kind of law of its own, not the divine law. And our Saviour wishes to marry her to a lawful husband, i. e. Himself; the Word of truth which was to rise from the dead, and never again to die.

19. The woman saith unto him, Sir, I perceive that thou art a prophet.

20. Our fathers worshipped in this mountain; and ye say, that in Jerusalem is the place where men ought to worship.

21. Jesus saith unto her, Woman, believe me, the hour cometh, when ye shall neither in this mountain, nor yet at Jerusalem, worship the Father.

22. Ye worship ye know not what: we know what we worship: for salvation is of the Jews.

23. But the hour cometh, and now is, when the true worshippers shall worship the Father in spirit and in truth: for the Father seeketh such to worship him.

24. God is a Spirit: and they that worship him must worship him in spirit and in truth.

Chrys. Hom. xxxii.2. CHRYS. The woman is not offended at Christ's rebuke. She does not leave Him, and go away. Far from it: her admiration for Him is raised: *The woman saith unto Him, Sir, I perceive that Thou art a Prophet:* as if she said, Thy knowledge of me is unaccountable, Thou must be a prophet.

AUG. The husband was beginning to come to her, though He had not yet fully come. She thought our Lord a prophet, and He was a prophet: for He says of Himself, *A prophet is not without honour, save in his own country.* CHRYS. And having come to this belief she asks no questions relating to this life, the health or sickness of the body: she is not troubled about thirst, she is eager for doctrine. AUG. And she begins enquiries on a subject that perplexed her; *Our fathers worshipped in this mountain; and ye say that in Jerusalem is the place where men ought to worship.* This was a great dispute between the Samaritans and the Jews. The Jews worshipped in the temple built by Solomon, and made this a ground of boasting over the Samaritans. The Samaritans replied, Why boast ye, because ye have a temple which we have not? Did our fathers, who pleased God, worship in that temple? Is it not better to pray to God in this mountain, where our fathers worshipped? CHRYS. By, *our fathers,* she means Abraham, who is said to have offered up Isaac here. ORIGEN. Or thus; The Samaritans regarded Mount Gerizim, near which Jacob dwelt, as sacred, and worshipped upon it; while the sacred place of the Jews was Mount Sion, God's own choice. The Jews being the people from whom salvation came, are the type of true believers; the Samaritans of heretics. Gerizim, which signifies division, becomes the Samaritans; Sion, which signifies watch-tower, becomes the Jews. CHRYS. Christ however does not solve this question immediately, but leads the woman to higher things, of which He had not spoken till she acknowledged Him to be a prophet, and therefore listened with a more full belief: *Jesus saith unto her, Woman, believe Me, the hour cometh, when ye shall neither in this mountain, nor yet at Jerusalem, worship the Father.* He says, *Believe me,* because we have need of faith, the mother of all good, the medicine of salvation, in order to obtain any real good. They who endeavour without it, are like men who venture on the sea without a boat, and, being able to swim only a little way, are drowned. AUG. *Believe Me,* our Lord says with fitness, as the husband is now present. For now there is one in thee that believes, thou hast begun to be present in the understanding; but *if ye will not believe, surely ye shall not be established.*

Aug. Tr. xv. c. 23.

Mat.13, 57.

Chrys. Hom. xxxii.2.

Aug. Tr. xv. c. 23.

Chrys. Hom. xxxii.2.

Origen. tom.xiii. c. 13.

Chrys. Hom. xxxii.3.

Aug. Tr. xv. c. 24.

Isa. 7, 9.

L 2

ALCUIN. In saying, *the hour cometh*, He refers to the Gospel dispensation, which was now approaching; under which the shadows of types were to withdraw, and the pure light of

Chrys.
Hom.
xxxiii.
1.

truth was to enlighten the minds of believers. CHRYS. There was no necessity for Christ to shew why the fathers worshipped in the mountain, and the Jews in Jerusalem. He therefore was silent on that question; but nevertheless asserted the religious superiority of the Jews on another ground, the ground not of place, but of knowledge; *Ye worship ye know not what, we know what we worship; for*

Orig.
tom.xiii.
c. 17.

salvation is of the Jews. ORIGEN. *Ye*, literally refers to the Samaritans, but mystically, to all who understand the Scriptures in an heretical sense. *We* again literally means the Jews, but mystically, I the Word, and all who conformed to My Image, obtain salvation from the Jewish Scriptures.

Chrys.
Hom.
xxxiii.1.

CHRYS. The Samaritans worshipped they knew not what, a local, a partial God, as they imagined, of whom they had the same notion that they had of their idols. And therefore they mingled the worship of God with the worship of idols. But the Jews were free from this superstition: indeed they knew God to be the God of the whole world; wherefore He says, *We worship what we know.* He reckons Himself among the Jews, in condescension to the woman's idea of Him; and says as if He were a Jewish prophet, *We worship,* though it is certain that He is the Being who is worshipped by all. The words, *For salvation is of the Jews*, mean that every thing calculated to save and amend the world, the knowledge of God, the abhorrence of idols, and all other doctrines of that nature, and even the very origin of our religion, comes originally from the Jews. In salvation too He includes His own presence, which He says is of the

Rom. 9,
5.

Jews, as we are told by the Apostle, *Of whom as concerning the flesh Christ came.* See how He exalts the Old Testament, which He shews to be the root of every thing good; thus proving in every way that He Himself is not opposed to

Aug.
in Joan.
Tr. xv.
c. 26.

the Law. AUG. It is saying much for the Jews, to declare in their name, *We worship what we know.* But He does not speak for the reprobate Jews, but for that party from whom the Apostles and the Prophets came. Such were all those saints who laid the prices of their possessions at the Apostle's feet.

CHRYS. The Jewish worship then was far higher than the Samaritan; but even it shall be abolished; *The hour cometh, and now is, when the true worshippers shall worship the Father in spirit and in truth.* He says, *and now is,* to shew that this was not a prediction, like those of the ancient Prophets, to be fulfilled in the course of ages. The event, He says, is now at hand, it is approaching your very doors. The words, *true worshippers,* are by way of distinction: for there are false worshippers who pray for temporal and frail benefits, or whose actions are ever contradicting their prayers. CHRYS. Or by saying, *true,* he excludes the Jews together with the Samaritans. For the Jews, though better than the Samaritans, were yet as much inferior to those who were to succeed them, as the type is to the reality. The true worshippers do not confine the worship of God to place, but worship in the spirit; as Paul saith, *Whom I serve with my spirit.* ORIGEN. Twice it is said, *The hour cometh,* and the first time without the addition, *and now is.* The first seems to allude to that purely spiritual worship which is suited only to a state of perfection; the second to earthly worship, perfected as far as is consistent with human nature. When that hour cometh, which our Lord speaks of, the mountain of the Samaritans must be avoided, and God must be worshipped in Sion, where is Jerusalem, which is called by Christ the city of the Great King. And this is the Church, where sacred oblations and spiritual victims are offered up by those who understand the spiritual law. So that when the fulness of time shall have come, the true worship, we must suppose, will no longer be attached to Jerusalem, i. e. to the present Church: for the Angels do not worship the Father at Jerusalem: and thus those who have obtained the likeness of the Jews, worship the Father better than they who are at Jerusalem. And when this hour is come, we shall be accounted by the Father as sons. Wherefore it is not said, Worship God, but, *Worship the Father.* But for the present the true worshippers worship the Father in spirit and in truth[a]. CHRYS. He speaks here

Chrys. Hom. xxxiii.1.

Chrys. Hom. xxiii. 2.

Rom. 1, 9. Origen. tom.xiii. c. 14.

Chrys. Hom. xxxiii.2.

---

[a] Origen literally. The words *the hour cometh* are repeated; the second time with the addition *and now is.* I think that the first expression signifies the most perfect worship that human nature is capable of in this life. So until the hour shall have come which the Lord speaks of, the mountain of the Samaritans (who represent those who separate themselves from the Church) is to be

of the Church; wherein there is true worship, and such as becometh God; and therefore adds, *For the Father seeketh such to worship Him.* For though formerly He willed that mankind should linger under a dispensation of types and figures, this was only done in condescension to human frailty, and to prepare men for the reception of the truth. ORIGEN. But if the Father seeks, He seeks through Jesus, Who came to seek and to save that which was lost, and to teach men what true worship was. *God is a Spirit;* i. e. He constitutes our real life, just as our breath (spirit) constitutes our bodily life. CHRYS. Or it signifies that God is incorporeal; and that therefore He ought to be worshipped not with the body, but with the soul, by the offering up a pure mind, i. e. that *they who worship Him, must worship Him in spirit and in truth.* The Jews neglected the soul, but paid great attention to the body, and had various kinds of purification. Our Lord seems here to refer to this, and to say, not by cleansing of the body, but by the incorporeal nature within us, i. e. the understanding, which He calls the spirit, that we must worship the incorporeal God. HILARY. Or, by saying that God being a Spirit ought to be worshipped in spirit, He indicates the freedom and knowledge of the worshippers, and the uncircumscribed nature of the worship: according to the saying of the Apostle, *Where the Spirit of the Lord is, there is liberty.* CHRYS. And that we are to worship in truth, means that whereas the former ordinances were typical; that is to say, circumcision, burnt offerings, and sacrifices; now, on the contrary, every thing is real. THEOPHYL. Or, because many think that they worship God in the spirit, i, e. with the mind, who yet held heretical doctrines concerning Him, for this reason He adds, *and in truth.* May not the words too refer to the two kinds of philosophy among us, i. e. active and contemplative; the spirit standing for action, according to the Apostle, *As many*

Origen. tom.xiii. c. 20.

Chrys. Hom. xxxii.2.

Hilar. ii. de Trin. c. 31.

2 Cor. 3, 17.
Chrys. Hom. xxxii.2.

Rom. 8, 14.

avoided and God must be worshipped in Sion at Jerusalem, which Christ calls the city of the Great King. What is this but the Church where the holy offerings of spiritual victims are presented by men of spiritual minds? But when the fulness of time shall have come, the true worship will no longer be performed in Jerusalem, that is, in the present Church. For the Angels do not worship the Father at Jerusalem: and so those who are like them worship the Father better than those who are in Jerusalem, even though for the sake of the latter they abide with them, and become Jews to the Jews, that they may gain the Jews. And when &c. Nicolai has missed the meaning of the last sentence.

as are led by the Spirit of God; truth, on the other hand, for contemplation. Or, (to take another view,) as the Samaritans thought that God was confined to a certain place, and ought to be worshipped in that place; in opposition to this notion, our Lord may mean to teach them here, that the true worshippers worship not locally, but spiritually. Or again, all being a type and shadow in the Jewish system, the meaning may be that the true worshippers will worship not in type, but in truth. God being a Spirit, seeketh for spiritual worshippers; being the truth, for true ones. Aug. O for a mountain to pray on, thou criest, high and inaccessible, that I may be nearer to God, and God may hear me better, for He dwelleth on high. Yes, God dwelleth on high, but He hath respect unto the humble. Wherefore descend that thou mayest ascend. " Ways on high are in their heart," it is said, " passing in the valley of tears," and in " tears" is humility. Wouldest thou pray in the temple? pray in thyself; but first do thou become the temple of God. Aug. Tr. xv. c. 25. Ps.74,7.

25. The woman saith unto him, I know that Messias cometh, which is called Christ: when he is come, he will tell us all things.

26. Jesus saith unto her, I that speak unto thee am he.

Chrys. The woman was struck with astonishment at the loftiness of His teaching, as her words shew: *The woman saith unto Him, I know that Messias cometh, which is called Christ.* Aug. Unctus in Latin, Christ in Greek, in the Hebrew Messias. She knew then who *could* teach her, but did not know Who *was* teaching her. *When He is come, He will tell us all things:* as if she said, The Jews now contend for the temple, we for the mountain; but He, when He comes, will level the mountain, overthrow the temple, and teach us how to pray in spirit and in truth. Chrys. But what reason had the Samaritans for expecting Christ's coming? They acknowledged the books of Moses, which foretold it. Jacob prophesies of Christ, *The sceptre shall not depart from Judah, nor a lawgiver from beneath his feet, until Shiloh come.* And Moses says, *The Lord thy God shall raise up a Prophet from the* Chrys. Hom. xxxii. 2. Aug. Tr. xv. c. 27. Chrys. Hom. xxxii. 2. Gen.49, 10. Deut.18, 15.

Orig. tom.xiii. c. 27. *midst of thee, of thy brethren.* ORIGEN. It should be known, that as Christ rose out of the Jews, not only declaring but proving Himself to be Christ; so among the Samaritans there arose one Dositheus by name, who asserted that he Aug.lib. lxxxiii. Quæst. qu. 64. was the Christ prophesied of. AUG. It is a confirmation to discerning minds that the five senses were what were signified by the five husbands, to find the woman making five carnal Chrys. Hom. xxxiii.2. answers, and then mentioning the name of Christ. CHRYS. Christ now reveals Himself to the woman: *Jesus saith unto her, I that speak unto thee am He.* Had He told the woman this to begin with, it would have appeared vanity. Now, having gradually awakened her to the thought of Christ, His disclosure of Himself is perfectly opportune. He is not John 10, 24. equally open to the Jews, who ask Him, *If Thou be the Christ, tell us plainly;* for this reason, that they did not ask in order to learn, but to do Him injury; whereas she spoke in the simplicity of her heart.

27. And upon this came his disciples, and marvelled that he talked with the woman: yet no man said, What seekest thou? or, Why talkest thou with her?

28. The woman then left her waterpot, and went her way into the city, and saith to the men,

29. Come, see a man, which told me all things that ever I did: is not this the Christ?

30. Then they went out of the city, and came unto him.

Chrys. Hom. xxxiii. 2, 3. CHRYS. The disciples arrive opportunely, and when the teaching is finished: *And upon this came His disciples, and marvelled that He talked with the woman.* They marvelled at the exceeding kindness and humility of Christ, in condescending to converse with a poor woman, and a Samaritan. Aug. Tr. xv. c. 29. AUG. He who came to seek that which was lost, sought the lost one. This was what they marvelled at: they Chrys. Hom. xxxiii.3. marvelled at His goodness; they did not suspect evil. CHRYS. But notwithstanding their wonder, they asked Him no questions, *No man said, What seekest Thou? or, Why talkest Thou with her?* So careful were they to observe the rank of disciples, so great was their awe and veneration for Him.

On subjects indeed which concerned themselves, they did
not hesitate to ask Him questions. But this was not one.
ORIGEN. The woman is almost turned into an Apostle. So Orig.
forcible are His words, that she leaves her waterpot to go to ^{tom.xiii.}_{in Joan.}
the city, and tell her townsmen of them. *The woman then* c. 28.
left her waterpot, i. e. gave up low bodily cares, for the sake
of benefitting others. Let us do the same. Let us leave off
caring for things of the body, and impart to others of our
own. AUG. Hydria answers to our word aquarium; hydor Aug.
being Greek for water. CHRYS. As the Apostles, on being ^{Tr. xv.}_{c. 30.}
called, left their nets, so does she leave her waterpot, to do Chrys.
the work of an Evangelist, by calling not one person, but a ^{Hom.}_{xxxiv.1.}
whole city: *She went her way into the city, and saith to the*
men, Come, see a man which told me all things that ever I
did: is not this the Christ? ORIGEN. She calls them Orig.
together to see a man, whose words were deeper than man's. ^{tom.xiii.}_{in Joan.}
She had had five husbands, and then was living with the c. 29.
sixth, not a lawful husband. But now she gives him up for
a seventh, and she leaving her waterpot, is converted to
chastity. CHRYS. She was not prevented by shame-faced- Chrys.
ness from spreading about what had been said to her. ^{Hom.}_{xxxiv.1.}
For the soul, when it is once kindled by the divine flame,
regards neither glory, nor shame, nor any other earthly thing,
only the flame which consumes it. But she did not wish
them to trust to her own report only, but to come and judge
of Christ for themselves. *Come, see a man,* she says. She
does not say, Come and believe, but, *Come and see;* which
is an easier matter. For well she knew that if they only
tasted of that well, they would feel as she did. ALCUIN. It
is only by degrees, however, that she comes to the preaching
of Christ. First she calls Him *a man,* not Christ; for fear
those who heard her might be angry, and refuse to come.
CHRYS. She then neither openly preaches Christ, nor wholly Chrys.
omits Him, but says, *Is not this the Christ?* This wakened ^{Hom.}_{xxxiv.1.}
their attention, *Then they went out of the city, and came*
unto Him. AUG. The circumstance of the woman's leaving
her waterpot on going away, must not be overlooked. For
the waterpot signifies the love of this world, i. e. concupiscence,
by which men from the dark depth, of which the well is the
image, i. e. from an earthly conversation, draw up pleasure.

It was right then for one who believed in Christ to renounce the world, and, by leaving her waterpot, to shew that she had parted with worldly desires. AUG. She cast away therefore concupiscence, and hastened to proclaim the truth. Let those who wish to preach the Gospel, learn, that they should first leave their waterpots at the well. ORIGEN. The woman having become a vessel of wholesome discipline, lays aside as contemptible her former tastes and desires.

*Aug.
Tr. xv.
c. 30.*

*Orig.
tom.xiii.
c. 29.*

31. In the mean while his disciples prayed him, saying, Master, eat.

32. But he said unto them, I have meat to eat that ye know not of.

33. Therefore said the disciples one to another, Hath any man brought him ought to eat?

34. Jesus saith unto them, My meat is to do the will of him that sent me, and to finish his work.

AUG. His disciples had gone to buy food, and had returned. They offered Christ some: *In the mean while His disciples prayed Him, saying, Master, eat.* CHRYS. They all ask Him at once, Him so fatigued with the journey and heat. This is not impatience in them, but simply love, and tenderness to their Master. ORIGEN. They think the present time convenient for dining; it being after the departure of the woman to the city, and before the coming of the Samaritans; so that they sit at meat by themselves. This explains, *In the mean while.* THEOPHYL. Our Lord, knowing that the woman of Samaria was bringing the whole town out to Him, tells His disciples, *I have meat that ye know not of.* CHRYS. The salvation of men He calls His food, shewing His great desire that we should be saved. As food is an object of desire to us, so was the salvation of men to Him. Observe, He does not express Himself directly, but figuratively; which makes some trouble necessary for His hearers, in order to comprehend His meaning, and thus gives a greater importance to that meaning when it is understood. THEOPHYL. *That ye know not of,* i. e. know not that I call the salvation of men food; or, know not that

*Aug.
Tr. xv.
c. 31.*

*Orig.
tom.xiii.
c. 31.*

*Chrys.
Hom.
xxxiv.1.*

the Samaritans are about to believe and be saved. The
disciples however were in perplexity : *Therefore said the
disciples one to another, Hath any man brought Him ought
to eat ?* AUG. What wonder that the woman did not under- Aug.
stand about the water ? Lo, the disciples do not under- Tr. xv.
stand about the meat. CHRYS. They shew, as usual, the Chrys.
honour and reverence in which they hold their Master, by Hom.
talking among themselves, and not presuming to question l.
Him. THEOPHYL. From the question of the disciples, *Hath
any man brought Him ought to eat,* we may infer that our
Lord was accustomed to receive food from others, when it
was offered Him : not that He who giveth food to all flesh, Ps. 146.
needed any assistance ; but He received it, that they who
gave it might obtain their reward, and that poverty thenceforth might not blush, nor the support of others be esteemed
a disgrace. It is proper and necessary that teachers should
depend on others to provide them with food, in order that,
being free from all other cares, they may attend the more
to the ministry of the word. AUG. Our Lord heard His Aug.
doubting disciples, and answered them as disciples, i. e. Tr. xv.
plainly and expressly, not circuitously, as He answered the c. 31.
women; *Jesus saith unto them, My meat is to do the will of
Him that sent Me.* ORIGEN. Fit meat for the Son of God, Orig.
who was so obedient to the Father, that in Him was the tom. xiii.
same will that was in the Father : not two wills, but one will c. 6.
in both. The Son is capable of first acccomplishing the
whole will of the Father. Other saints do nothing against
the Father's will ; He does that will. That is His meat in
an especial sense. And what means, *To finish His work ?*
It would seem easy to say, that a work was what was ordered
by him who set it ; as where men are set to build or dig.
But some who go deeper ask whether a work being finished
does not imply that it was before incomplete ; and whether
God could originally have made an incomplete work ? The
completing of the work, is the completing of a rational
creature : for it was to complete this work, which was as
yet imperfect, that the Word made flesh come. THEOPHYL.
He finished the work of God, i. e. man, He, the Son of God,
finished it by exhibiting our nature in Himself without sin,
perfect and uncorrupt. He finished also the work of God,

Rom.
10, 4.

Orig.
tom.xiii.
c. 31.
i. e. the Law, (for Christ is the end of the Law,) by abolish-
ing it, when every thing in it had been fulfilled, and changing a carnal into a spiritual worship. ORIGEN. The matter
of spiritual drink and living water being explained, the subject of meat follows. Jesus had asked the woman of Samaria,
and she could give Him none good enough. Then came the
disciples, having procured some humble food among the
people of the country, and offered it Him, beseeching Him
to eat. They fear perhaps lest the Word of God, deprived
of His own proper nourishment, fail within them; and
therefore with such as they have found, immediately propose
to feed Him, that being confirmed and strengthened, He
may abide with His nourishers. Souls require food as well
as bodies. And as bodies require different kinds of it, and
in different quantities, so is it in things which are above the

Heb. 5,
12.
body. Souls differ in capacity, and one needs more nourishment, another less. So too in point of quality, the same
nourishment of words and thoughts does not suit all.
Infants just born need the milk of the word; the grown up,
solid meat. Our Lord says, *I have meat to eat.* For one
who is over the weak who cannot behold the same things
with the stronger, may always speak thus[b].

35. Say not ye, There are yet four months, and
then cometh harvest? behold, I say unto you, Lift up
your eyes, and look on the fields; for they are white
already to harvest.

36. And he that reapeth receiveth wages, and
gathereth fruit unto life eternal: that both he that
soweth and he that reapeth may rejoice together.

37. And herein is that saying true, One soweth,
and another reapeth.

38. I sent you to reap that whereon ye bestowed
no labour: other men laboured, and ye are entered
into their labours.

---

[b] i. e. those of weak faith cannot
understand the spiritual gifts and nourishment of the strong. It is " meat
they know not of." So S. Aug., when
unconverted, of S. Ambrose, " What
comfort he had in adversities, and what
sweet joys Thy Bread had for the
hidden mouth of his spirit—I neither
could conjecture nor had experienced."
Conf. vi. 3.

CHRYS. What is the will of the Father He now proceeds Chrys.
to explain: *Say ye not, There are yet four months, and* ^{Hom.} xxxiv.1.
then cometh harvest? THEOPHYL. Now ye are expecting a
material harvest. But I say unto you, that a spiritual harvest is at hand: *Lift up your eyes, and look on the fields;
for they are white already to harvest.* He alludes to the
Samaritans who are approaching. CHRYS. He leads them, Chrys.
as his custom is, from low things to high. *Fields* and *har-* ^{Hom.} xxxiv.2.
vest here express the great number of souls, which are ready
to receive the word. The *eyes* are both spiritual, and
bodily ones, for they saw a great multitude of Samaritans
now approaching. This expectant crowd he calls very suitably
white fields. For as the corn, when it grows white, is ready
for the harvest; so were these ready for salvation. But why
does He not say this in direct language? Because by making
use in this way of the objects around them, he gave greater
vividness and power to His words, and brought the truth
home to them; and also that His discourse might be more
pleasant, and might sink deeper into their memories. AUG. Aug.
He was intent now on beginning the work, and hastened to ^{Tr. xv. c. 32.}
send labourers: *And he that reapeth receiveth wages, and
gathereth fruit unto life eternal, that both he that soweth
and he that reapeth may rejoice together.* CHRYS. Again, Chrys.
He distinguishes earthly from heavenly things, for as above ^{Hom.} xxxiv.2.
He said of the water, that he who drank of it should never
thirst, so here He says, *He that reapeth gathereth fruit
unto life eternal;* adding, *that both he that soweth and he
that reapeth may rejoice together.* The Prophets sowed,
the Apostles reaped, yet are not the former deprived of their
reward. For here a new thing is promised; viz. that both
sowers and reapers shall rejoice together. How different
this from what we see here. Now he that soweth grieveth
because he soweth for others, and he only that reapeth
rejoiceth. But in the new state, the sower and reaper share
the same wages. AUG. The Apostles and Prophets had Aug.
different labours, corresponding to the difference of times; ^{Tr. xv. c. 32.}
but both will attain to like joy, and receive together their
wages, even eternal life. CHRYS. He confirms what He Chrys.
says by a proverb, *And herein is that saying true, one* ^{Hom.} xxxiv.2.
soweth and another reapeth, i. e. one party has the labour,

and another reaps the fruit. The saying is especially applicable here, for the Prophets had laboured, and the disciples reaped the fruits of their labours: *I sent you to reap that whereon ye bestowed no labour.* AUG. So then He sent reapers, no sowers. The reapers went where the Prophets had preached. Read the account of their labours: they all contain prophecy of Christ. And the harvest was gathered on that occasion when so many thousands brought the prices of their possessions, and laid them at the Apostles' feet; relieving their shoulders from earthly burdens, that they might follow Christ. Yea verily, and from that harvest were a few grains scattered, which filled the whole world. And now ariseth another harvest, which will be reaped at the end of the world, not by Apostles, but by Angels. *The reapers,* He says, *are the Angels.* CHRYS. *I sent you to reap that whereon ye bestowed no labour,* i. e. I have reserved you for a favourable time, in which the labour is less, the enjoyment greater. The more laborious part of the work was laid on the Prophets, viz. the sowing of the seed: *Other men laboured, and ye are entered into their labours.* Christ here throws light on the meaning of the old prophecies. He shews that both the Law and the Prophets, if rightly interpreted, led men to Him; and that the Prophets were sent in fact by Himself. Thus the intimate connexion is established between the Old Testament and the New. ORIGEN. How can we consistently give an allegorical meaning to the words, *Lift up your eyes, &c.* and only a literal one to the words, *There are yet four months, and then cometh harvest?* The same principle of interpretation surely must be applied to the latter, that is to the former. The four months represent the four elements, i. e. our natural life; the harvest, the end of the world, when all conflict shall have ceased, and truth shall prevail. The disciples then regard the truth as incomprehensible in our natural state, and look forward to the end of the world for attaining the knowledge of it. But this idea our Lord condemns: *Say not ye, there are four months, and then cometh harvest? Behold, I say unto you, Lift up your eyes.* In many places of Holy Scripture, we are commanded in the same way to raise the thoughts of our minds, which cling so obstinately to earth. A difficult task this for one who

Margin notes:
Aug. Tr. xv. c. 32.

Mat. 13.

Chrys. Hom. xxxiv. 2.

Orig. tom. xv. in Joan. c. 39–49.

indulges his passions, and lives carnally. Such an one will not see if the fields be white to the harvest. For when are the fields white to the harvest? When the Word of God comes to light up and make fruitful the fields of Scripture. Indeed, all sensible things are as it were fields made white for the harvest, if only reason be at hand to interpret them. We lift up our eyes, and behold the whole universe overspread with the brightness of truth. And he that reapeth those harvests, has a double reward of his reaping; first, his wages; *And he that reapeth receiveth wages;* meaning his reward in the life to come; secondly, a certain good state of the understanding, which is the fruit of contemplation, *And gathereth fruit unto life eternal.* The man who thinks out the first principles of any science, is as it were the sower in that science; others taking them up, pursuing them to their results, and engrafting fresh matter upon them, strike out new discoveries, from which posterity reaps a plentiful harvest. And how much more may we perceive this in the art of arts? The seed there is the whole dispensation of the mystery, now revealed, but formerly hidden in darkness; for while men were unfit for the advent of the Word, the fields were not yet white to their eyes, i. e. the legal and prophetical Scriptures were shut up. Moses and the Pro- phets, who preceded the coming of Christ, were the sowers of this seed; the Apostles who came after Christ and saw His glory were the reapers. They reaped and gathered into barns the deep meaning which lay hid under the prophetic writings; and did in short what those do who succeed to a scientific system which others have discovered, and who with less trouble attain to clearer results than they who originally sowed the seed. But they that sowed and they that reaped shall rejoice together in another world, in which all sorrow and mourning shall be done away. Nay, and have they not rejoiced already? Did not Moses and Elias, the sowers, rejoice with the reapers Peter, James, and John, when they saw the glory of the Son of God at the Transfiguration? Perhaps in, *one soweth and another reapeth, one and another* may refer simply to those who live under the Law, and those who live under the Gospel. For these may both rejoice

together, inasmuch as the same end is laid up for them by one
God, through one Christ, in one Holy Spirit.

39. And many of the Samaritans of that city believed
on him for the saying of the woman, which testified,
He told me all that ever I did.   .

40. So when the Samaritans were come unto him,
they besought him that he would tarry with them : and
he abode there two days.

41. And many more believed because of his own
word ;

42. And said unto the woman, Now we believe,
not because of thy saying : for we have heard him
ourselves, and know that this is indeed the Christ, the
Saviour of the world.

Orig.   ORIGEN. After this conversation with the disciples, Scripture
tom.xiii. returns to those who had believed on the testimony of the
in Joan.
c. 50.   woman, and were come to see Jesus. CHRYS. It is now, as
Chrys.
Hom.   it were, harvest time, when the corn is gathered, and a whole
xxxiv.2. floor soon covered with sheaves ; *And many of the Samaritans
*of that city believed on Him, for the saying of the woman
which testified, He told me all that ever I did.* They considered that the woman would never of her own accord have
conceived such admiration for one Who had reproved her
offences, unless He were really some great and wonderful
Hom.   person. And thus relying solely on the testimony of the
xxxv.1. woman, without any other evidence, they went out to beseech
Christ to stay with them : *So when the Samaritans were
come to Him, they besought Him that He would tarry with
them.* The Jews when they saw His miracles, so far from
begging Him to stay, tried in every way to get rid of His
presence. Such is the power of malice, and envy, and vain-
glory, that obstinate vice which poisons even goodness itself.
Though the Samaritans however wished to keep Him with
them, He would not consent, but only *tarried there two days.*
Orig.   ORIGEN. It is natural to ask, why our Saviour stays with the
tom.xiii. Samaritans, when He had given a command to His disciples
c. 51.

not to enter into any city of the Samaritans. But we must
explain this mystically. To go the way of the Gentiles, is
to be imbued with Gentile doctrine ; to go into a city of the
Samaritans, is to admit the doctrines of those who believe
the Scriptures, but interpret them heretically. But when
men have given up their own doctrines, and come to Jesus,
it is lawful to stay with them. Chrys. The Jews disbelieved Chrys.
in spite of miracles, while these exhibited great faith, be- Hom.
fore even a miracle was wrought, and when they had only xxxv. 1.
heard our Lord's words. *And many more believed because of*
His own word. Why then do not the Evangelists give these
words ? To shew that they omit many important things, and
because the result shews what they were; the result being
that the whole city was convinced. On the other hand,
when the hearers are not convinced, the Evangelists are
obliged to give our Lord's words, that the failure may be
seen to be owing to the indifference of the hearers, not to
any defect in the preacher. And now, having become
Christ's disciples, they dismiss their first instructor; *And*
they said unto the woman, Now we believe not because of
thy saying : for we have heard Him ourselves, and know
that this is indeed the Christ, the Saviour of the world.
How soon they understand that He was come for the
deliverance of the whole world, and could not therefore
confine His purposes to the Jews, but must sow the Word
every where. Their saying too, *The Saviour of the world,*
implies that they looked on this world as miserable and
lost; and that, whereas Prophets and Angels had come
to save it, this was the only real Saviour, the Author not
only of temporal but eternal salvation. And, observe,
whereas the woman had spoken doubtfully, *Is not this the*
Christ ? they do not say, we suspect, but *we know,* know,
that this is indeed the Saviour of the world, not one Christ
out of many. Though they had only heard His words, they
said as much as they could have done, had they seen ever
so many and great miracles. Origen. With the aid of our Orig.
former observations on Jacob's well, and the water, it will tom.xvii.
not be difficult to see, why, when they find the true word, c. 50.
they leave other doctrines, i. e. the city, for a sound faith. c. 51.
Observe, they did not ask our Saviour only to enter Samaria,

St. John particularly remarks, or enter that city, but to tarry there. Jesus tarries with those who ask Him, and especially with those who go out of the city to Him. ORIGEN. They were not ready yet for the third day; having no anxiety to see a miracle, as those had who supped with Jesus in Cana of Galilee. (This supper was after He had been in Cana three days.) The woman's report was the ground of their belief. The enlightening power of the Word itself was not yet visible to them. AUG. So then they knew Christ first by report of another, afterwards by His own presence; which is still the case of those that are without the fold, and not yet Christians. Christ is announced to them by some charitable Christians, by the report of the woman, i. e. the Church; they come to Christ, they believe on Him, through the instrumentality of that woman; He stays withthem two days, i. e. gives them two precepts of charity. And thenceforth their belief is stronger. They believe that He is indeed the Saviour of the world. ORIGEN. For it is impossible that the same impression should be produced by hearing from one who has seen, and seeing one's self; walking by sight is different from walking by faith. The Samaritans now do not believe only from testimony, but from really seeing the truth.

Orig. tom.xiii. c. 53.

Aug. Tr. xv. c. 33.

Orig. tom.xiii. c. 52.

43. Now after two days he departed thence, and went into Galilee.

44. For Jesus himself testified, that a prophet hath no honour in his own country.

45. Then when he was come into Galilee, the Galilæans received him, having seen all the things that he did at Jerusalem at the feast: for they also went unto the feast.

Aug. Tr. xvi.

AUG. After staying two days in Samaria, He departed into Galilee, where He resided: *Now after two days He departed thence, and went into Galilee.* AUG. Why then does the Evangelist say immediately, *For Jesus Himself testified, that a prophet hath no honour in his own country.* For He would seem to have testified more to the truth, had He remained in Samaria, and not gone into Galilee. Not so:

He stayed two days in Samaria, and the Samaritans believed on Him: He stayed the same time in Galilee, and the Galileans did not believe on Him, and therefore He said, that *a prophet hath no honour in his own country.* CHRYS. Or consider this the reason that He went, not to Capernaum, but to Galilee and Cana, as appears below, His country being, I think, Capernaum. As He did not obtain honour there, hear what He says; *And thou, Capernaum, which art exalted unto heaven, shalt be brought down to hell.* He calls it His own country, because He had most resided here. THEOPHYL. Or thus: Our Lord on leaving Samaria for Galilee, explains why He was not always in Galilee: viz. because of the little honour He received there. *A prophet hath no honour in his own country.* ORIGEN. The country of the prophets was Judæa, and every one knows how little honour they received from the Jews, as we read, *Whom of the prophets have not your fathers persecuted?* One cannot but wonder at the truth of this saying, exemplified not only in the contempt cast upon the holy prophets and our Lord Himself, but also in the case of other teachers of wisdom who have been despised by their fellow-citizens and put to death[c]. CHRYS. But do we not see many held in admiration by their own people? We do; but we cannot argue from a few instances. If some are honoured in their own country, many more are honoured out of it, and familiarity generally subjects men to contempt. The Galileans however received our Lord: *Then when He was come into Galilee, the Galileans received Him.* Observe how those who are spoken ill of, are always the first to come to Christ. Of the Galileans we find it said below, *Search and look, for out of Galilee ariseth no prophet.* And He is reproached with being a Samaritan, *Thou art a Samaritan, and hast a devil.* And yet the Samaritans and Galileans believe, to the condemnation of the Jews. The Galileans however are superior to the Samaritans; for the latter believed from hearing the woman's words, the former from seeing the signs which He did: *Having seen all the things that He did at Jerusalem at the feast.* ORIGEN. Our Lord by ejecting those who sold sheep and oxen from the temple, had impressed the Galileans with a strong idea of His

Chrys. Hom. xxxv. 1.

Mat.11, 23.

Orig. tom.xvii. c. 54.

Mat.23.

Chrys. Hom. xxxv. 2.

Orig. tom.xvii. c. 55.

[c] In allusion to the persecution of some Greek philosophers.

Majesty, and they received Him. His power was shewn no less in this act, than in making the blind to see, and the deaf to hear. But probably He had performed some other miracles as well. BEDE. They had seen Him at Jerusalem, *For they also went unto the feast.* Our Lord's return has a mystical meaning, viz. that, when the Gentiles have been confirmed in the faith by the two precepts of love, i. e. at the end of the world, He will return to His country, i. e. Judæa. ORIGEN. The Galilæans were allowed to keep the feast at Jerusalem, where they had seen Jesus. Thus they were prepared to receive Him, when He came: otherwise they would either have rejected Him; or He, knowing their unprepared state, would not have gone near them.

Orig.
tom.xiii.
c. 55.

46. So Jesus came again into Cana of Galilee, where he made the water wine. And there was a certain nobleman, whose son was sick at Capernaum.

47. When he heard that Jesus was come out of Judæa into Galilee, he went unto him, and besought him that he would come down, and heal his son: for he was at the point of death.

48. Then said Jesus unto him, Except ye see signs and wonders, ye will not believe.

49. The nobleman saith unto him, Sir, come down ere my child die.

50. Jesus saith unto him, Go thy way; thy son liveth. And the man believed the word that Jesus had spoken unto him, and he went his way.

51. And as he was now going down, his servants met him, and told him, saying, Thy son liveth.

52. Then enquired he of them the hour when he began to amend. And they said unto him, Yesterday at the seventh hour the fever left him.

53. So the father knew that it was at the same hour, in the which Jesus said unto him, Thy son liveth: and himself believed, and his whole house.

54. This is again the second miracle that Jesus did, when he was come out of Judæa into Galilee.

CHRYS. On a former occasion our Lord attended a Chrys. Hom. xxxv. 2. marriage in Cana of Galilee, now He goes there to convert the people, and confirm by His presence the faith which His miracle had produced. He goes there in preference to His own country. AUG. There, we are told, *His disciples* Aug. Tr. xvi. c. 3. *believed on Him.* Though the house was crowded with guests, the only persons who believed in consequence of this great miracle, were His disciples. He therefore visits the city again, in order to try a second time to convert them. THEO-PHYL. The Evangelist reminds us of the miracle in order to express the praise due to the Samaritans [d]. For the Galileans in receiving Him were influenced as well by the miracle He had wrought with them, as by those they had seen at Jerusalem. The nobleman certainly believed in consequence of the miracle performed at Cana, though he did not yet understand Christ's full greatness ; *And there was a certain nobleman whose son was sick at Capernaum.* ORIGEN. Orig. tom.xvii. c. 57. Some think that this was an officer of King Herod's ; others, that he was one of Cæsar's household, then employed on some commission in Judæa. It is not said that He was a Jew. AUG. He is called a nobleman, either as being of the βασιλι- κὸς royal family, or as having some office of government. CHRYS. Chrys. Hom. xxxv.2. Some think that he is the same centurion, who is mentioned in Matthew. But that he is a different person is clear from Matt. 8, 5. this ; that the latter, when Christ wished to come to his house, entreated Him not ; whereas the former brought Christ to his house, though he had received no promise of a cure. And the latter met Jesus on His way from the mountain to Capernaum ; whereas the former came to Jesus in Cana. And the latter servant was laid up with the palsy, the former's son with a fever. Of this nobleman then we read, *When he heard that Jesus was come out of Judæa into Galilee, he went unto Him, and besought Him that He would heal his son : for he was at the point of death* AUG. Aug. Tr. xvi. c. 3. Did not he who made this request believe ? Mark what our Lord says ; *Then said Jesus unto him, Except ye see*

[d] διὰ τὸ αὐξῆσαι Σαμαριτῶν τὸ ἰγκώμιον. But in the Lat. it is, ut augeret Christi præconium.

signs and wonders, ye will not believe. This is to charge the man either with lukewarmness, or coldness of faith, or with want of faith altogether: as if his only object was to put Christ's power to the test, and see who and what kind of person Christ was, and what He could do. The word *prodigy* (wonder) signifies something *far off*, in futurity. AUG. Our Lord would have the mind of the believer so raised above all mutable things, as not to seek even for miracles. For miracles, though sent from heaven, are, in their subject matter, mutable. GREG. Remember what He asked for, and you will plainly see that he doubted. He asked Him to come down and see his son: *The nobleman saith unto him, Sir, come down, ere my child die.* His faith was deficient; in that he thought that our Lord could not save, except He were personally present. CHRYS. And mark his earthly mind, shewn in hurrying Christ along with him; as if our Lord could not raise his son after death. Indeed it is very possible that he may have asked in unbelief. For fathers often are so carried away by their affection, as to consult not only those they depend upon, but even those they do not depend upon at all: not wishing to leave any means untried, which might save their children. But had he had any strong reliance upon Christ, he would have gone to Him in Judæa. GREG. Our Lord in His answer implies that He is in a certain sense where He is invited present, even when He is absent from a place. He saves by His command simply, even as by His will He created all things: *Jesus saith unto him, Go thy way, thy son liveth.* Here is a blow to that pride which honours human wealth and greatness, and not that nature which is made after the image of God. Our Redeemer, to shew that things made much of among men, were to be despised by Saints, and things despised made much of, did not go to the nobleman's son, but was ready to go to the centurion's servant. CHRYS. Or thus; In the centurion there was confirmed faith and true devotion, and therefore our Lord was ready to go. But the nobleman's faith was still imperfect, as he thought our Lord could not heal in the absence of the sick person. But Christ's answer enlightened him. *And the man believed the word which Jesus had spoken to him, and went his way.* He did not believe, however, wholly or completely. ORIGEN. His

Margin notes:

Greg. Hom. in Evang. xxviii. 1.

Chrys. Hom. xxxv. 2.

Greg. Hom. in Evang. xxviii. 1, 2.

Chrys. Hom. xxxv. 2.

rank appears in the fact of his servants meeting him: *And as he was now going down, his servants met him, and told him, saying, Thy son liveth.* CHRYS. They met him, to announce what had happened, and prevent Christ from coming, as He was no longer wanted. That the nobleman did not fully believe, is shewn by what follows: *Then enquired he of them at what hour he began to amend.* He wished to find out whether the recovery was accidental, or owing to our Lord's word. *And they said unto him, Yesterday at the seventh hour the fever left him.* How obvious is the miracle? His recovery did not take place in an ordinary way, but all at once; in order that it might be seen to be Christ's doing, and not the result of nature: *So the father knew that it was at the same hour, in the which Jesus said unto him, Thy son liveth; and himself believed, and his whole house.* AUG. If he only believed when he was told that his son was well again, and had compared the hour according to his servant's account, with the hour predicted by Christ, he did not believe when he first made the petition. BEDE. So, we see, faith, like the other virtues, is formed gradually, and has its beginning, growth, and maturity. His faith had its beginning, when he asked for his son's recovery; its growth, when he believed our Lord's words, *Thy son liveth;* its maturity, after the announcement of the fact by his servants. AUG. The Samaritans believed on the strength of His words only: that whole house believed on the strength of the miracle which had been brought in it. The Evangelist adds, *This is again the second miracle which Jesus did, when He was come out of Judæa into Galilee.* CHRYS. *The second miracle,* he says markedly. The Jews had not come to the more perfect faith of the Samaritans, who saw no miracle. ORIGEN. The sentence is ambiguous. Taken one way, it means that Jesus after coming to Galilee, performed two miracles, of which that of healing the nobleman's son was the second: taken another, it means, that of the two miracles which Jesus performed in Galilee, the second was done after coming from Judæa into Galilee. The latter is the true and received meaning. Mystically, the two journeys of Christ into Galilee signify His two advents; at the first of which He makes us His guest at supper, and

Chrys. Hom. xxxv.3.

Aug. Tr. xvi. c. 3.

Aug. Tr. xvi. c. 3.

Chrys. Hom. xxxvi.1.

Orig. tom·xvii. c. 60.

c. 56.

gives us wine to drink; at the second, He raises up the
nobleman's son who was at the point of death, i. e. the
Jewish people, who, after the fulness of the Gentiles, attain
themselves to salvation. For, as the great King of
Kings is He, whom God hath seated upon His holy hill of
Sion, so the lesser king is he, who saw his day, and was
glad, i. e. Abraham[e]. And therefore his sick son is the
Jewish people fallen from the true religion, and thrown into
a fever in consequence by the fiery darts of the enemy. And
we know that the saints of old, even when they had put off
the covering of the flesh, made the people the object of
their care: for we read in Maccabees, after the death of
Jeremiah, *This is Jeremias the prophet of the Lord, who
prayeth much for the people.* Abraham therefore prays to
our Saviour to succour his diseased people. Again, the word
of power, *Thy son liveth,* comes forth from Cana, i. e. the work
of the Word, the healing of the nobleman's son, is done in
Capernaum, i. e. the land of consolation. The nobleman's
son signifies the class of believers who though diseased are yet
not altogether destitute of fruits. The words, *Except ye
see signs and wonders, ye will not believe,* are spoken of the
Jewish people in general, or perhaps of the nobleman, i. e.
Abraham himself, in a certain sense. For as John waited
for a sign; *on Whom thou shalt see the Spirit descending;*
so too the Saints who died before the coming of Christ in the
flesh, expected Him to manifest Himself by signs and wonders. And this nobleman too had servants as well as a son;
which servants stand for the lower and weaker class of
believers. Nor is it chance that the fever leaves the son at
the *seventh hour;* for seven is the number of rest. ALCUIN.
Or it was the seventh hour, because all remission of sins is
through the sevenfold Spirit; for the number seven divided
into three and four, signifies the Holy Trinity, in the four
seasons of the world, in the four elements. ORIGEN. There
may be an allusion in the two journeys to the two advents
of Christ in the soul, the first supplying a spiritual banquet of
wine, the second taking away all remains of weakness and
death. THEOPHYL. The little king stands for man generally;
man not only deriving his soul from the King of the

Marginal notes:
2 Macc. 12.

Orig.
t. xviii.
c. 56.

---

[e] The same word as nobleman: a more literal translation.

universe, but having Himself dominion over all things.   His
son, i. e. his mind, labours under a fever of evil passion
and desires.   He goes to Jesus and entreats Him to come
down; i. e. to exercise the condescension of His pity, and
pardon his sins, before it is too late.   Our Lord answers;
Go thy way, i. e. advance in holiness, and then thy son will
live; but if thou stop short in thy course, thou wilt destroy
the power of understanding and doing right.

CHAP. V.

1. After this there was a feast of the Jews; and Jesus went up to Jerusalem.

2. Now there is at Jerusalem by the sheep market a pool, which is called in the Hebrew tongue Bethesda, having five porches.

3. In these lay a great multitude of impotent folk, of blind, halt, withered, waiting for the moving of the water.

4. For an angel went down at a certain season into the pool, and troubled the water: whosoever then first after the troubling of the water stepped in, was made whole of whatsoever disease he had.

5. And a certain man was there, which had an infirmity thirty and eight years.

6. When Jesus saw him lie, and knew that he had been now a long time in that case, he saith unto him, Wilt thou be made whole?

7. The impotent man answered him, Sir, I have no man, when the water is troubled, to put me into the pool: but while I am coming, another steppeth down before me.

8. Jesus saith unto him, Rise, take up thy bed, and walk.

9. And immediately the man was made whole, and took up his bed, and walked: and on the same day was the sabbath.

10. The Jews therefore said unto him that was cured, It is the sabbath day: it is not lawful for thee to carry thy bed.

11. He answered them, He that made me whole, the same said unto me, Take up thy bed, and walk.

12. Then asked they him, What man is that which said unto thee, Take up thy bed, and walk?

13. And he that was healed wist not who it was: for Jesus had conveyed himself away, a multitude being in that place.

AUG. After the miracle in Galilee, He returns to Jerusalem: *After this there was a feast of the Jews, and Jesus went up to Jerusalem.* CHRYS. The feast of Pentecost. Jesus always went up to Jerusalem at the time of the feasts, that it might be seen that He was not an enemy to, but an observer of, the Law. And it gave Him the opportunity of impressing the simple multitude by miracles and teaching: as great numbers used then to collect from the neighbouring towns.

Now there is at Jerusalem by the sheep-market a pool, which is called in the Hebrew tongue Bethesda, having five porches. ALCUIN. The pool by the sheep-market, is the place where the priest washed the animals that were going to be sacrificed. CHRYS. This pool was one among many types of that baptism, which was to purge away sin. First God enjoined water for the cleansing from the filth of the body, and from those defilements, which were not real, but legal, e. g. those from death, or leprosy, and the like. Afterwards infirmities were healed by water, as we read: *In these* (the porches) *lay a great multitude of impotent folk, of blind, halt, withered, waiting for the moving of the water.* This was a nearer approximation to the gift of baptism, when not only defilements are cleansed, but sicknesses healed. Types are of various ranks, just as in a court, some officers are nearer to the prince, others farther off. The water, however, did not heal by virtue of its own natural properties, (for if so the effect would have followed uniformly,) but by the descent of an Angel: *For an Angel went down at a certain season into the pool, and troubled the water.* In the same way, in Baptism, water does not act simply as water, but receives first the grace of the Holy Spirit, by means of which it cleanses us from all our sins. And the Angel troubled the

Aug. de Con. Evang.

Chrys. Hom. xxxvi.1.

Chrys. Hom. xxxvi.1.

water, and imparted a healing virtue to it, in order to prefigure to the Jews that far greater power of the Lord of the
Angels, of healing the diseases of the soul.   But then their
infirmities prevented their applying the cure; for it follows, .
*Whosoever then first after the troubling of the water stepped
in, was made whole of whatsoever disease he had.*   But now
every one may attain this blessing, for it is not an Angel
which troubleth the water, but the Lord of Angels, which
worketh every where.   Though the whole world come, grace
fails not, but remains as full as ever; like the sun's rays
which give light all day, and every day, and yet are not
spent.   The sun's light is not diminished by this bountiful
expenditure: no more is the influence of the Holy Spirit by
the largeness of its outpourings.   Not more than one could be
cured at the pool; God's design being to put before men's
minds, and oblige them to dwell upon, the healing power of
water; that from the effect of water on the body, they might
believe more readily its power on the soul.   AUG. It was a
greater act in Christ, to heal the diseases of the soul, than
the sicknesses of the perishable body.   But as the soul itself
did not know its Restorer, as it had eyes in the flesh to
discern visible things, but not in the heart wherewith to
know God; our Lord performed cures which could be seen,
that He might afterwards work cures which could not be
seen.   He went to the place, where lay a multitude of sick,
out of whom He chose one to heal: *And a certain man was
there, which had an infirmity thirty and eight years.*   CHRYS.
He did not, however, proceed immediately to heal him, but
first tried by conversation to bring him into a believing
state of mind.   Not that He required faith in the first
instance, as He did from the blind man, saying, *Believe ye
that I am able to do this?* for the lame man could not well
know who He was.   Persons who in different ways had had
the means of knowing Him, were asked this question, and
properly so.   But there were some who did not and could
not know Him yet, but would be made to know Him by His
miracles afterwards.   And in their case the demand for faith
is reserved till after those miracles have taken place: *When
Jesus saw him lie, and knew that he had been a long time
in that case, He saith unto him, Wilt thou be made whole?*

Aug.
Tr. xvii.
c. 1.

Chrys.
Hom.
xxxiii.
1, 2.

Matt. 9,
28.

He does not ask this question for His own information, (this were unnecessary,) but to bring to light the great patience of the man, who for thirty and eight years had sat year after year by the place, in the hope of being cured; which sufficiently explains why Christ passed by the others, and went to him.   And He does not say, Dost thou wish Me to heal thee? for the man had not as yet any idea that He was so great a Person.   Nor on the other hand did the lame man suspect any mockery in the question, to make him take offence, and say, Hast thou come to vex me, by asking me if I would be made whole; but he answered mildly, *Sir, I have no man, when the water is troubled, to put me into the pool; but while I am coming, another steppeth down before me.* He had no idea as yet that the Person who put this question to him would heal him, but thought that Christ might probably be of use in putting him into the water.   But Christ's word is sufficient, *Jesus saith unto him, Rise, take up thy bed, and walk.*   AUG. Three distinct biddings. *Rise*, however, is not a command, but the conferring of the cure.   Two commands were given upon his cure, *take up thy bed, and walk.* CHRYS. Behold the richness of the Divine Wisdom. He not only heals, but bids him carry his bed also.   This was to shew the cure was really miraculous, and not a mere effect of the imagination; for the man's limbs must have become quite sound and compact, to allow him to take up his bed. The impotent man again did not deride and say, The Angel cometh down, and troubleth the water, and he only cureth one each time; dost Thou, who art a mere man, think that Thou canst do more than an Angel?   On the contrary, he heard, believed Him who bade him, and was made whole: *And immediately the man was made whole, and took up his bed, and walked.*   BEDE; There is a wide difference between our Lord's mode of healing, and a physician's.   He acts by His word, and acts immediately: the other's requires a long time for its completion.   CHRYS. This was wonderful, but what follows more so.   As yet he had no opposition to face. It is made more wonderful when we see him obeying Christ afterwards in spite of the rage and railing of the Jews: *And on the same day was the sabbath.   The Jews therefore said unto him that was cured, It is the sabbath day, it is not*

Aug. Tr. xvii. c. 7.

Chrys. Hom. xxxvi. 1, 2.

Chrys. Hom. xxxvii. 2.

Aug.
Tr. xvii.
c. 10. *lawful for thee to carry thy bed.* AUG. They did not charge our Lord with healing on the sabbath, for He would have replied that if an ox or an ass of theirs had fallen into a pit, would not they have taken it out on the sabbath day: but they addressed the man as he was carrying his bed, as if to say, Even if the healing could not be delayed, why enjoin the work? He shields himself under the authority of his Healer: *He that made me whole, the Same said unto me, Take up thy bed, and walk:* meaning, Why should not I Chrys.
Hom.
xxxvii.
2. receive a command, if I received a cure from Him? CHRYS. Had he been inclined to deal treacherously, he might have said, If it is a crime, accuse Him Who commanded it, and I will lay down my bed. And he would have concealed his cure, knowing, as he did, that their real cause of offence was not the breaking of the Sabbath, but the miracle. But he neither concealed it, nor asked for pardon, but boldly confessed the cure. They then ask spitefully; *What man is that who said unto thee, Take up thy bed, and walk.* They do not say, Who is it, who made thee whole? but only mention the offence. It follows, *And he that was healed wist not who it was, for Jesus had conveyed Himself away, a multitude being in that place.* This He had done first, because the man who had been made whole, was the best witness of the cure, and could give his testimony with less suspicion in our Lord's absence; and secondly, that the fury of men might not be excited more than was necessary. For the mere sight of the object of envy, is no small incentive to envy. For these reasons He departed, and left them to examine the fact for themselves. Some are of opinion, that this is the same with the one who had the palsy, whom Matthew mentions. But he is not. For the latter had many to wait upon, and carry him, whereas this man had none. And the place where the miracle was performed, is different. Aug.
Tr. xvii.
c. 1. AUG. Judging on low and human notions of this miracle, it is not at all a striking display of power, and only a moderate one of goodness. Of so many, who lay sick, only one was healed; though, had He chosen, He could have restored them all by a single word. How must we account for this? By supposing that His power and goodness were asserted more for imparting a knowledge of eternal salvation to the

soul, than working a temporal cure on the body. That which received the temporal cure was certain to decay at last, when death arrived : whereas the soul which believed passed into life eternal. The pool and the water seem to me to signify the Jewish people: for John in the Apocalypse obviously uses water to express people. BEDE. It is fitly described as a sheep pool. By sheep are meant people, according to the passage, *We are Thy people, and the sheep of Thy pasture.* AUG. The water then, i. e. the people, was enclosed within five porches, i. e. the five books of Moses. But those books only betrayed the impotent, and did not recover them; that is to say, the Law convicted the sinner, but did not absolve him. BEDE. Lastly, many kinds of impotent folk lay near the pool : the blind, i. e. those who are without the light of knowledge; the lame, i. e. those who have not strength to do what they are commanded; the withered, i. e. those who have not the marrow of heavenly love. AUG. So then Christ came to the Jewish people, and by means of mighty works, and profitable lessons, troubled the sinners, i. e. the water, and the stirring continued till He brought on His own passion. But He troubled the water, unknown to the world. *For had they known Him, they would not have crucified the Lord of glory.* But the troubling of the water came on all at once, and it was not seen who troubled it. Again, to go down into the troubled water, is to believe humbly on our Lord's passion. Only one was healed, to signify the unity of the Church: whoever came afterwards was not healed, to signify that whoever is out of this unity cannot be healed. Wo to them who hate unity, and raise sects. Again, he who was healed had had his infirmity thirty and eight years : this being a number which belongs to sickness, rather than to health. The number forty has a sacred character with us, and is significative of perfection. For the Law was given in Ten Commandments, and was to be preached throughout the whole world, which consists of four parts; and four multiplied into ten, make up the number forty. And the Law too is fulfilled by the Gospel, which is written in four books. So then if the number forty possesses the perfectness of the Law, and nothing fulfils the Law, except the twofold precept of love, why

Rev. 17, 15.
Bede. in v. cap. Joan.
Ps. 95,7.
Aug. Tr. xvii. c. 2.

Aug. Tr. xvii. c. 3.

1 Cor. 11.

wonder at the impotence of him, who was two less than forty? Some man was necessary for his recovery; but it was a man who was God. He found the man falling short by the number two, and therefore gave two commandments, to fill up the deficiency. For the two precepts of our Lord signify love; the love of God being first in order of command, the love of our neighbour, in order of performance. *Take up thy bed*, our Lord saith, meaning, When thou wert impotent, thy neighbour carried thee; now thou art made whole, carry thy neighbour. *And walk;* but whither, except to the Lord thy God. BEDE. What mean the words, *Arise*, and *walk;* except that thou shouldest raise thyself from thy torpor and indolence, and study to advance in good works. *Take up thy bed*, i. e. thy neighbour by which thou art carried, and bear him patiently thyself. AUG. Carry him then with whom thou walkest, that thou mayest come to Him with Whom thou desirest to abide. As yet however he wist not who Jesus was; just as we too believe in Him though we see Him not. Jesus again does not wish to be seen, but conveys Himself out of the crowd. It is in a kind of solitude of the mind, that God is seen: the crowd is noisy; this vision requires stillness.

Bede. c.v.num. 30.

Aug. Tr. xvii. c. 9.

14. Afterward Jesus findeth him in the temple, and said unto him, Behold, thou art made whole: sin no more, lest a worse thing come unto thee.

15. The man departed, and told the Jews that it was Jesus, which had made him whole.

16. And therefore did the Jews persecute Jesus, and sought to slay him, because he had done these things on the sabbath day.

17. But Jesus answered them, My Father worketh hitherto, and I work.

18. Therefore the Jews sought the more to kill him, because he not only had broken the sabbath, but said also that God was his Father, making himself equal with God.

CHRYS. The man, when healed, did not proceed to the Chrys. market place, or give himself up to pleasure or vain glory, Hom.
xxxvii. but, which was a great mark of religion, went to the temple: *Afterward Jesus findeth him in the temple.* AUG. The Lord Aug. Jesus saw him both in the crowd, and in the temple. The Tr. xvii.
c. 11. impotent man does not recognise Jesus in the crowd; but in the temple, being a sacred place, he does. ALCUIN[c]. For in loc. if we would know our Maker's grace, and attain to the sight of Him, we must avoid the crowd of evil thoughts and affections, convey ourselves out of the congregation of the wicked, and flee to the temple; in order that we may make ourselves the temple of God, souls whom God will visit, and in whom He will deign to dwell.

And (He) said unto him, *Behold, thou art made whole; sin no more, lest a worse thing come upon thee.* CHRYS. Chrys. Here we learn in the first place, that his disease was the con- Hom.
xxxviii. sequence of his sins. We are apt to bear with great indif- 1. ference the diseases of our souls; but, should the body suffer ever so little hurt, we have recourse to the most energetic remedies. Wherefore God punishes the body for the offences of the soul. Secondly, we learn, that there is really a Hell. Thirdly, that it is a place of lasting and infinite punishment. Some say indeed, Because we have corrupted ourselves for a short time, shall we be tormented eternally? But see how long this man was tormented for his sins. Sin is not to be measured by length of time, but by the nature of the sin itself. And besides this we learn, that if, after undergoing a heavy punishment for our sins, we fall into them again, we shall incur another and a heavier punishment still: and justly; for one, who has undergone punishment, and has not been made better by it, proves himself to be a hardened person, and a despiser; and, as such, deserving of still greater torments. Nor let it embolden us, that we do not see all punished for their offences here: for if men do not suffer for their offences here, it is only a sign that their punishment will be the greater hereafter. Our diseases however do not always arise from sins; but only most commonly so. For some spring from other lax habits: some are sent for the sake of trial, as Job's were. But why

---

[c] Alcuin's commentary on St. John's Gospel is the work always referred to.

does Christ make mention of this palsied man's sins? Some say, because he had been an accuser of Christ. And shall we say the same of the man afflicted with the palsy? *Matt.* 9, 2. For he too was told, *Thy sins are forgiven thee?* The truth is, Christ does not find fault with the man here for his past sins, but only warns him against future. In healing others, however, He makes no mention of sins at all: so that it would seem to be the case that the diseases of these men had arisen from their sins; whereas those of the others had come from natural causes only. Or perhaps through these, He admonishes all the rest. Or he may have admonished this man, knowing his great patience of mind, and that he would bear an admonition. It is a disclosure too of His divinity, for He implies in saying, *Sin no more,* that He *Aug.* knew what sins He had committed. AUG. Now that the *Tr. xvii.* *c. 12.* man had seen Jesus, and knew Him to be the author of his recovery, he was not slow in preaching Him to others: *The man departed, and told the Jews that it was Jesus which* *Chrys.* *had made him whole.* CHRYS. He was not so insensible to *Hom.* *xxxviii.* the benefit, and the advice he had received, as to have any *2.* malignant aim in speaking this news. Had it been done to disparage Christ, he could have concealed the cure, and put forward the offence. But he does not mention Jesus's saying, *Take up thy bed,* which was an offence in the eyes of the Jews; but *told the Jews that it was Jesus which had* *Aug.* *made him whole.* AUG. This announcement enraged them, *Tr. xviii.* *c. 13.* *And therefore did the Jews persecute Jesus, because He had done these things on the sabbath day.* A plain bodily work had been done before their eyes, distinct from the healing of the man's body, and which could not have been necessary, even if healing was; viz. the carrying of the bed. Wherefore our Lord openly says, that the sacrament of the Sabbath, the sign of observing one day out of seven, was only a temporary institution, which had attained its fulfilment in Him: *But Jesus answered them, My Father worketh hitherto, and I work:* as if He said, Do not suppose that My Father rested on the Sabbath in such a sense, as that from that time forth, He has ceased from working; for He worketh up to this time, though without labour, and so work I. God's resting means only that He made no other

creature, after the creation. The Scripture calls it rest, to
remind us of the rest we shall enjoy after a life of good
works here. And as God only when He had made man in
His own image and similitude, and finished all His works,
and seen that they were very good, rested on the seventh
day: so do thou expect no rest, except thou return to the
likeness in which thou wert made, but which thou hast lost by
sin; i. e. unless thou doest good works. AUG. It may be said ^{Aug.}
then, that the observance of the sabbath was imposed on the ^{iv. super} ^{Gen. ad}
Jews, as the shadow of something to come; viz. that spiritual ^{litteram}
rest, which God, by the figure of His own rest promised ^(c. xi.)
to all who should perform good works. AUG. There will be
a sabbath of the world, when the six ages, i. e. the six days,
as it were, of the world, have passed: then will come that
rest which is promised to the saints. AUG. The mystery of ^{Aug.}
which rest the Lord Jesus Himself sealed by His burial: for ^{iv. Gen.} ^{ad lit.}
He rested in His sepulchre on the sabbath, having on ^{c. xi.}
the sixth day finished all His work, inasmuch as He said,
It is finished. What wonder then that God, to prefigure the ^{c. 19.}
day on which Christ was to rest in the grave, rested one
day from His works, afterwards to carry on the work of
governing the world. We may consider too that God, when
He rested, rested from the work of creation simply, i. e.
made no more new kinds of creatures: but that from that time
till now, He has been carrying on the government of those
creatures. For His power, as respects the government of
heaven and earth, and all the things that He had made, did
not cease on the seventh day: they would have perished
immediately, without His government: because the power of
the Creator is that on which the existence of every creature
depends. If it ceased to govern, every species of creation
would cease to exist: and all nature would go to nothing.
For the world is not like a building, which stands after the
architect has left it; it could not stand the twinkling of an
eye, if God withdrew His governing hand. Therefore when
our Lord says, *My Father worketh hitherto,* he means the
continuation of the work; the holding together, and governing
of the creation. It might have been different, had He said,
Worketh even now. This would not have conveyed the sense
of continuing. As it is we find it, *Until now;* i. e. from the

Aug. time of the creation downwards. AUG. He says then, as it
Tr.xvii.
s. 15. were, to the Jews, Why think ye that I should not work on
the sabbath? The sabbath day was instituted as a type^d of
Me. Ye observe the works of God: by Me all things were
made. The Father made light, but He spoke, that it might
be made. If He spoke, then He made it by the Word; and
I am His Word. My Father worked when He made the
world, and He worketh until now, governing the world: and
as He made the world by Me, when He made it, so He
Chrys. governs it by Me, now He governs it. CHRYS. Christ
Hom. defended His disciples, by putting forward the example of
xxxviii.
2. their fellow-servant David: but He defends Himself by a
reference to the Father. We may observe too that He does
not defend Himself as man, nor yet purely as God, but
sometimes as one, sometimes as the other; wishing both to
be believed, both the dispensation of His humiliation, and the
dignity of His Godhead; wherefore He shews His equality
to the Father, both by calling Him His Father emphatically,
(*My* Father,) and by declaring that He doeth the same
things, that the Father doth, (*And I work.*) *Therefore*, it
follows, *the Jews sought the more to kill Him, because he
not only had broken the sabbath, but said also that God was
Aug. His Father.* AUG. i. e. not in the secondary sense in which
Tr.xviii.
s. 16. it is true of all of us, but as implying equality. For we all of
Matt. 6. us say to God, *Our Father, Which art in heaven.* And the
Isaiah Jews say, *Thou art our Father.* They were not angry then
63, 16. because He called God His Father, but because He called
Aug. Him so in a sense different from men. AUG. The words,
de Con.
Ev. l.iv. *My Father worketh hitherto, and I work*, suppose Him to
c. x. be equal to the Father. This being understood, it followed
from the Father's working, that the Son worked: inasmuch
Chrys. as the Father doth nothing without the Son. CHRYS. Were
Hom.
xxxviii. He not the Son by nature, and of the same substance, this
s. 3. defence would be worse than the former accusation made.
For no prefect could clear Himself from a transgression of
the king's law, by urging that the king broke it also. But,
on the supposition of the Son's equality to the Father, the
defence is valid. It then follows, that as the Father worked

---

^d Since our everlasting rest, which the sabbath foreshadowed, is in Him.
see Conf. fin. de Civ. D. xi. 8. &c.

on the Sabbath without doing wrong: the Son could do so
likewise. AUG. So, the Jews understood what the Arians Aug.
do not. For the Arians say that the Son is not equal to the $_{s.\ 16.}^{Tr.\ xvii.}$
Father, and hence sprang up that heresy which afflicts the
Church. CHRYS. Those however who are not well-disposed Chrys.
to this doctrine, do not admit that Christ made Himself $_{xxxviii.}^{Hom.}$
equal to the Father, but only that the Jews thought He did. 3.
But let us consider what has gone before. That the Jews
persecuted Christ, and that He broke the sabbath, and said
that God was His Father, is unquestionably true. That
which immediately follows then from these premises, viz. His
making Himself equal with God, is true also. HILARY. $_{vii.\ de}^{Hilar.}$
The Evangelist here explains why the Jews wished to kill Trin. c.
Him. CHRYS. And again, had it been that our Lord Himself 15.
did not mean this, but that the Jews misunderstood Him,
He would not have overlooked their mistake. Nor would
the Evangelist have omitted to remark upon it, as he does c. 11.
upon our Lord's speech, *Destroy this temple.* AUG. The Aug.
Jews however did not understand from our Lord that He $_{s.\ 16.}^{Tr.\ xvii.}$
was the Son of God, but only that He was equal with God;
though Christ gave this as the result of His being the Son of
God. It is from not seeing this, while they saw at the same
time that equality was asserted, that they charged Him with
making Himself equal with God: the truth being, that He
did not *make* Himself equal, but the Father had begotten
Him equal.

19. Then answered Jesus and said unto them,
Verily, verily, I say unto you, The Son can do nothing
of himself, but what he seeth the Father do: for what
things soever he doeth, these also doeth the Son likewise.

20. For the Father loveth the Son, and sheweth
him all things that himself doeth: and he will shew
him greater works than these, that ye may marvel.

HILARY. He refers to the charge of violating the sabbath, Hilar.
brought against Him. *My Father worketh hitherto, and I* $_{Trin.\ c.}^{vii.\ de}$
work; meaning that He had a precedent for claiming the 17.

right He did; and that what He did was in reality His Father's doing, who acted in the Son. And to quiet the jealousy which had been raised, because by the use of His Father's name He had made Himself equal with God, and to assert the excellency of His birth and nature, He says, *Verily, verily, I say unto you, The Son can do nothing of Himself, but what He seeth the Father do.* Aug. Some who would be thought Christians, the Arian heretics, who say that the very Son of God who took our flesh upon Him, was inferior to the Father, take advantage of these words to throw discredit upon our doctrine, and say, You see that when our Lord perceived the Jews to be indignant, because He seemed to make Himself equal with God, He gave such an answer as shewed that He was not equal. For they say, he who can do nothing but what he sees the Father do is not equal but inferior to the Father. But if there is a greater God, and a less God, (the Word being God,) we worship two Gods, and not one[e]. Hilary. Lest then that assertion of His equality, which must belong to Him, as by Name and Nature the Son, might throw doubt upon His Nativity[f], He says that the Son *can do nothing of Himself.* Aug. As if He said: Why are ye offended that I called God *My Father,* and that I make Myself equal with God? I am equal, but equal in such a sense as is consistent with His having begotten Me; with My being from Him, not Him from Me. With the Son, being and power are one and the same thing. The Substance of the Son then being of the Father, the power of the Son is of the Father also: and as the Son *is* not of Himself, so He *can* not of Himself. *The Son can do nothing of Himself, but what He seeth the Father do.—* His seeing and His being born of the Father are the same. His vision is not distinct from His Substance, but the whole

Marginal notes:
Aug. Tr.xviii. 3, 5.
Hilar. vii. de Tr.c.17.
Aug. Tr. xx. 4.
xxi. 4.

---

[e] This is the answer of the Catholic to the Arian argument, and is drawn out more fully in Augustin's text, where the Arian blasphemy, that there was a greater and a lesser God, is said to savour of Paganism. Nic.

[f] i. e. left to themselves, people would be vacillating between the thought our Lord was not equal to the Father or not the Son, and therefore our Lord at once conveys the doctrine of His Equality with the Father, and yet that He was the Son, "The Only-Begotten God operating by the operations of the power of the Father, and so He wrought that, which He knew in His own intrinsic knowledge that the Nature of God the Father, inseparable from Himself, Which He possessed through His true Nativity, could work." S. Hil. l. c.

together is of the Father. HILARY. That the wholesome Hilar.
order of our confession, i. e. that we believe in the Father $\begin{smallmatrix}vii. de\\Tr. c. 17.\end{smallmatrix}$
and the Son, might remain, He shews the nature of His birth;
viz. that He derived the power of acting not from an acces-
sion of strength supplied for each work, but by His own
knowledge in the first instance. And this knowledge He
derived not from any particular visible precedents, as if what
the Father had done, the Son could do afterwards; but that
the Son being born of the Father, and consequently conscious
of the Father's virtue and nature within Him, could do
nothing but what He saw the Father do: as he here testifies;
God does not see by bodily organs, but by the virtue of His
nature. AUG. If we understand this subordination of the Son Aug.
to arise from the human nature, it will follow that the Father $\begin{smallmatrix}ii. de Tr.\\c. 3.\end{smallmatrix}$
walked first upon the water, and did all the other things
which the Son did in the flesh, in order that the Son might do
them. Who can be so insane as to think this [d]? AUG. Yet Aug.
that walking of the flesh upon the sea was done by the Father $\begin{smallmatrix}Tr. xx.\\s. 6.\end{smallmatrix}$
through the Son. For when the flesh walked, and the
Divinity of the Son guided, the Father was not absent, as the
Son Himself saith below, *The Father that dwelleth in Me,* c. 14.
He doeth the works. He guards however against the carnal s. 9.
interpretation of the words, *The Son can do nothing of Him-* (v. 10.)
self. As if the case were like that of two artificers, master
and disciple, one of whom made a chest, and the other made
another like it, by adding, *For whatsoever things he doeth,*
these doeth the Son likewise. He does not say, Whatsoever
the Father doeth, the Son does *other* things like them, but
the very same things. The Father made the world, the Son
made the world, the Holy Ghost made the world. If the
Father, Son, and Holy Ghost are one, it follows that one
and the same world was made by the Father, through the
Son, in the Holy Ghost. Thus it is the very same thing
that the Son doeth. He adds *likewise,* to prevent another
error arising. For the body seems to do the same things
with the mind, but it does not do them in a like way, inas-

---

[d] *The Son can do nothing of Him-*
self, but what He seeth the Father do.
If this arises from His human nature,
then He must have seen in His human
nature, i. e. visibly, with the natural
eye, each several act of His done beforehand by the Father. It follows
that the subordination here mentioned
arises from the Sonship itself of the
Son's, not from His human nature.

much as the body is subject, the soul governing, the body
visible, the soul invisible. When a slave does a thing at the
command of his master, the same thing is done by both;
but is it in a like way? Now in the Father and Son there
is not this difference; they do the same things, and in a like
way. Father and Son act with the same power; so that the

Hilar. Son is equal to the Father. HILARY. Or thus; *All things*
vii. de
Tr.c.18. and *the same*, He says, to shew the virtue of His nature, its
being the same with God's. That is the same nature, which
can do all the same things. And as the Son does all the
same things in a like way, the likeness of the works excludes
the notion of the worker existing alone [g]. Thus we come to
a true idea of the Nativity, as our faith receives it: the likeness of the works bearing witness to the Nativity, their

Chrys. sameness to the Nature. CHRYS. Or thus; That *the Son*
Hom.
xxxviii. *can do nothing of Himself*, must be understood to mean, that
4. He can do nothing contrary to, or displeasing to, the Father.
And therefore He does not say that He *does* nothing contrary, but that He *can* do nothing; in order to shew His perfect
likeness, and absolute equality to the Father. Nor is this a
sign of weakness in the Son, but rather of goodness. For as
when we say that it is impossible for God to sin, we do not
charge Him with weakness, but bear witness to a certain
ineffable goodness; so when the Son says, I can do nothing
of myself, it only means, that He can do nothing contrary to

Aug. the Father. AUG. This is not a sign of failing in Him, but
contra
Serm. of His abiding in His birth from the Father. And it is as
Ariano- high an attribute of the Almighty that He does not change,
rum,c.9.
(xiv.) as it is that He does not die. The Son could do what He
had not seen the Father doing, if He could do what the
Father does not do through Him; i. e. if He could sin: a
supposition inconsistent with the immutably good nature
which was begotten from the Father. That He cannot do;
this then is to be understood of Him, not in the sense of

Chrys. deficiency, but of power. CHRYS. And this is confirmed by
Hom.
xxxviii. what follows: *For whatsoever he doeth, these also doeth the*
4. *Son likewise.* For if the Father does all things by Himself,

g " Similitudo operum solitudinem
operantis exclusit." Bened. and edd.
i. e. as before, the Son is equal to The
Father, since He doeth *all* the same
things. Yet the very expression " sameness" implies a plurality of Persons.
Nic. reads similitudinem, which does
not belong to the argument here.

so does the Son also, if this *likewise* is to stand good. You see how high a meaning these humble words bear. He gives His thoughts a humble dress purposely. For whenever He expressed Himself loftily, He was persecuted, as an enemy of God. AUG. Having said that He did the same things that the Father did, and in a like way, He adds, *For the Father loveth the Son, and sheweth Him all things that Himself doeth. And sheweth Him all things that Himself doeth:* this has a reference to the words above; *But what He seeth the Father do.* But again, our human ideas are perplexed, and one may say, So then the Father first does something, that the Son may see what He does; just as an artificer teaches his son his art, and shews him what he makes, that he may be able to make the same after him. On this supposition, when the Father does a thing, the Son does not do it; in that the Son is beholding what His Father doeth. But we hold it as a fixed and incontrovertible truth, that the Father makes all things through the Son, and therefore He must shew them to the Son, *before* He makes them. And where does the Father shew the Son what He makes, except in the Son Himself, by whom He makes them? For if the Father makes a thing for a pattern, and the Son attends to the workmanship as it goes on, where is the indivisibility of the Trinity? The Father therefore does not shew the Son what He doeth by doing it, but by shewing doeth it, through the Son. The Son seeth, and the Father sheweth, before a thing is made, and from the shewing of the Father, and the seeing of the Son, that is made which is made; made by the Father, through the Son. But thou wilt say, I shew my Son what I wish him to make, and he makes it, and I make it through him. True; but before thou doest any thing, thou shewest it to thy son, that he may do it for thy example, and thou by him; but thou speakest to thy son words which are not thyself; whereas the Son Himself is the Word of the Father; and could He speak by the Word to the Word? Or, because the Son was the great Word, were lesser words to pass between the Father and the Son, or a certain sound and temporary creation, as it were, to go out of the mouth of the Father, and strike the ear of the Son? Put away these bodily notions, and if thou art simple, see the

Aug. Tr. xxi. s. 2.

truth in simplicity. If thou canst not comprehend what God is, comprehend at least what He is not. Thou wilt have advanced no little way, if thou thinkest nothing that is untrue of God. See what I am saying exemplified in thine own mind. Thou hast memory, and thought, thy memory sheweth to thy thought Carthage: before thou perceivest what is in her, she sheweth it to thought, which is turned toward her: the memory then hath shewn, the thought hath perceived, and no words have passed between them, no outward sign been used. But whatever is in thy memory, thou receivest from without: that which the Father sheweth to the Son, He doth not receive from without; the whole goes on within; there being no creature existing without, but what the Father hath made by the Son. And the Father maketh by shewing, in that He maketh by the Son who sees. The Father's shewing begets the Son's seeing, as the Father begets the Son? Shewing begets seeing, not seeing shewing. But it would be more correct, and more spiritual, not to view the Father as distinct from His shewing, or the Son from His seeing. HILARY. It must not be supposed that the Only Begotten God needed such shewing on account of ignorance. For the shewing here is only the doctrine of the nativity [h]; the self-existing Son, from the self-existing Father. AUG. For to see the Father is to see His Son. The Father so shews all His works to the Son, that the Son sees them from the Father [i]. For the birth of the Son is in His seeing: He sees from the same source, from which He is, and is born, and remains. HILARY. Nor did the heavenly discourse lack the caution, to guard against our inferring from these words any difference in the nature of the Son and the Father. For He says that the works of the Father were shewn to Him, not that strength was supplied Him for the doing of them, in order to teach that this shewing is substantially nothing else than His birth; for that simultaneously with the Son Himself is born the Son's knowledge of the works the Father will do through Him. AUG. But now from Him whom we called coeternal with the Father, who saw

Hilar. vii. de Trin. c. 19.

Aug. Tr. xxi.

Hilar. vii. de Trin. c. 19.

Aug. Tr. xxi. s. 5.

---

[h] i. e. implying another person (who shews) who is the *author*: first in order of succession, i. e. the Father. It is explained by the Aug. following.

[i] i. e. not looking *toward* the Father, but from Him; i. e. being in the Father at the time.

the Father, and existed in that He saw, we return to the things of time, *And He will shew him greater works than these*. But if He will shew him, i. e. is about to shew him, He hath not yet shewn him: and when He does shew him, others also will see; for it follows, *That ye may believe*. It is difficult to see what the eternal Father can shew in time to the coeternal Son, Who knows all that exists within the Father's mind. *For as the Father raiseth up the dead, and quickeneth them, even so the Son quickeneth whom He will*. To raise the dead was a greater work than to heal the sick. But this is explained by consideriug that He Who a little before spoke as God, now begins to speak as man. As man, and therefore living in time, He will be shewn greater works in time. Bodies will rise again by the human dispensation by which the Son of God assumed manhood in time; but souls by virtue of the eternity of the Divine Substance. For which reason it was said before that the Father loved the Son, and shewed Him what things soever He did. For the Father shews the Son that souls are raised up; for they are raised up by the Father and the Son, even as they cannot live, except God give them life. Or the Father is about to shew this to us, not to Him; according to what follows, *That ye may believe*. This being the reason why the Father would *shew Him greater things than these*. But why did He not say, shall shew you, instead of the Son? Because we are members of the Son, and He, as it were, learns in His members, even as He suffers in us. For as He says, *Inasmuch as ye have done it unto one of the least of these My brethren, ye have done it unto Me:* so, if we ask Him, how He, the Teacher of all things, learns, He replies, When one of the least of My brethren learns, I learn.

Tr. xix.

Tr. xxi.

Matt. 25, 40.

21. For as the Father raiseth up the dead, and quickeneth them; even so the Son quickeneth whom he will.

22. For the Father judgeth no man, but hath committed all judgment unto the Son:

23. That all men should honour the Son, even as

they honour the Father.   He that honoureth not
the Son honoureth not the Father which hath sent
him.

Aug.   AUG. Having said that the Father would shew the Son
Tr. xxi.
s. 5, 6. greater works than these, He proceeds to describe these
greater works: *For as the Father raiseth up the dead, and
quickeneth them, even so the Son quickeneth whom He will.*
These are plainly greater works, for it is more of a miracle
that a dead man should rise again, than that a sick man
should recover. We must not understand from the words,
that some are raised by the Father, others by the Son; but
that the Son raises to life the same whom the Father raiseth.
And to guard against any one saying, The Father raises the
dead by the Son, the former by His own power, the latter, like
an instrument, by another power, He asserts distinctly the
power of the Son: *The Son quickeneth whom he will.* Observe
here not only the power of the Son, but also His will. Father
and Son have the same power and will.   The Father willeth
nothing distinct from the Son; but both have the same will,
Hilar. even as they have the same substance. HILARY. For to will is
de Trin.
vii.c.19. the free power of a nature, which by the act of choice, resteth
Aug. in the blessedness of perfect excellence. AUG. But who are
Tr. xxi.
s. 11. these dead, whom the Father and Son raise to life ?   He
alludes to the general resurrection which is to be; not to the
resurrection of those few, who were raised to life, that the
rest might believe; as Lazarus, who rose again, to die
afterwards.   Having said then, *For as the Father raiseth up
the dead, and quickeneth them,* to prevent our taking the
words to refer to the dead whom He raised up for the sake
of the miracle, and not to the resurrection to life eternal,
He adds, *For the Father judgeth no man;* thus shewing that
He spoke of that resurrection of the dead which would take
Tr.xxiii. place at the judgment.   Or the words, *As the Father raiseth
s. 13.
up the dead, &c.* refer to the resurrection of the soul; *For the
Father judgeth no man, but hath committed all judgment
unto the Son,* to the resurrection of the body. For the
resurrection of the soul takes place by the substance of the

Father and the Son[k], and therefore it is the work of the Father
and the Son together: but the resurrection of the body takes
place by a dispensation of the Son's humanity, which is a
temporal dispensation, and not coeternal with the Father.
But see how the Word of Christ leads the mind in different Tr. xxi.
directions, not allowing it any carnal resting place; but by [s. 12.]
variety of motion exercising it, by exercise purifying it, by
purifying enlarging its capacity, and after enlarging filling
it. He said just before that the Father shewed what things
soever He did to the Son. So I saw, as it were, the Father
working, and the Son waiting: now again I see the Son
working, the Father resting. Aug. For this, viz. that the Aug.
Father *hath given all judgment unto the Son,* does not mean de Trin.
that He *begat* the Son with this attribute, as is meant in the (xiii.)
words, *So hath He given to the Son to have life in Himself.*
For if so, it would not be said, *The Father judgeth no man,*
because, in that the Father begat the Son equal, He judgeth
with the Son. What is meant is, that in the judgment, not
the form of God but the form of the Son of man will appear;
not because He will not judge Who hath given all judgment
to the Son; since the Son says of Him below, *There is one* c. 19.
that seeketh and judgeth, but *the Father judgeth no man;*
i. e. no one will see Him in the judgment, but all will see
the Son, because He is the Son of man, even the ungodly
who *will look on Him Whom they pierced.* HILARY. Having Zech.
said that *the Son quickeneth whom He will,* in order that [12.]
we might not lose sight of the nativity, and think that He de Trin.
stood upon the ground of His own unborn power, He im- vii.c.20.
mediately adds, *For the Father judgeth no man, but hath*
given all judgment unto the Son. In that all judgment is
given to Him, both His nature, and His nativity are shewn;
because only a self-existent nature can possess all things,
and nativity cannot have any thing, except what is given it.
CHRYS. As He gave Him life, i. e. begot Him living; so He Chrys.
gave Him judgment, i. e. begot Him a judge. *Gave,* it is Hom.
said, that thou mayest not think Him unbegotten, and imagine [l.]

---

[k] For the soul becomes blessed from
partaking of God, not from partaking
of another blessed soul, nor by partaking
in any Angelic nature. For as the
soul being inferior to God gains life to
that which is inferior to itself, i. e. the
body; so the soul again cannot be
endowed with heavenly life, but by
Him who is superior to the soul, even
God.

two Fathers: *All judgment,* because He has the awarding

Hilar. vii. de Trin. c. 20. both of punishment and reward. HILARY. All judgment is given to Him, because He quickens whom He will. Nor can the judgment be looked on as taken away from the Father, inasmuch as the cause of His not judging is, that the judgment of the Son is His. For all judgment is given from the Father. And the reason for which He gives it, appears immediately after: *That all men may honour the Son even as* Chrys. Hom. xxxix. 2. *they honour the Father.* CHRYS. For, lest you should infer from hearing that the Author of His power was the Father, any difference of substance, or inequality of honour, He connects the honour of the Son with the honour of the Father, shewing that both have the same. But shall men then call Him the Father? God forbid; he who calls Him the Father, does not honour the Son equally with the Father, but confounds Aug. xxi. s. 13. both. AUG. First indeed, the Son appeared as a servant, and the Father was honoured as God. But the Son will be seen to be equal to the Father, *that all men may honour the* 1 ref. not found *Son, even as they honour the Father.* [1]But what if persons are found, who honour the Father, and do not honour the Son? It cannot be: *He that honoureth not the Son, honoureth not the Father which hath sent Him.* It is one thing to acknowledge God, as God; and another to acknowledge Him as the Father. When thou acknowledgest God the Creator, thou acknowledgest an almighty, supreme, eternal, invisible, immutable Spirit. When thou acknowledgest the Father, thou dost in reality acknowledge the Son; for He could not be the Father, had He not the Son. But if thou honour the Father as greater, the Son as less, so far as thou givest less honour to the Son, thou takest away from the honour of the Father. For thou in reality thinkest that the Father could not or would not beget the Son equal to Himself; which if He would not do, He was envious, if He Tr.xxiii. s. 13. could not, He was weak. Or, *That all men should honour the Son even as they honour the Father;* has a reference to the resurrection of souls, which is the work of the Son, as well as of the Father. But the resurrection of the body is meant in what comes after: *He that honoureth not the Son, honoureth not the Father that sent Him.* Here is no *as;* the man Christ is honoured, but not as the Father Who sent

Him, since with respect to His manhood He Himself saith,
My Father is greater than I. But some one will say, Tr. xxi.
if the Son is sent by the Father, He is inferior to the Father. s. 17.
Leave thy fleshly actions, and understand a mission, not a
separation. Human things deceive, divine things make
clear; although even human things give testimony against
thee, e. g. if a man offers marriage to a woman, and cannot
obtain her by himself, he sends a friend, greater than himself,
to urge his suit for him. But see the difference in human
things. A man does not go with him whom he sends; but
the Father Who sent the Son, never ceased to be with the
Son; as we read, *I am not alone, but the Father is with Me.* c. 21.
Aug. It is not, however, as being born of the Father, that Aug.
the Son is said to be sent, but from His appearing in this iv. de
world, as the Word made flesh; as He says, *I went forth* 28.(xx.)
from the Father, and am come into the world: or from His John 16,
being received into our minds individually, as we read[1], *Send*
her, that she may be with me, and may labour with me.
Hilary. The conclusion then stands good against all the Hilar.
fury of heretical minds. He is the Son, because He does vii. de
nothing of Himself: He is God, because, whatsoever things 21.
the Father doeth, He doeth the same; They are one, because
They are equal in honour: He is not the Father, because He
is sent.

24. Verily, verily, I say unto you, He that heareth
my word, and believeth on him that sent me, hath
everlasting life, and shall not come into condemnation;
but is passed from death unto life.

Gloss. Having said that the Son quickeneth whom He
will, He next shews that we attain to life through the Son:
Verily, verily, I say unto you, He that heareth My word, and
believeth on Him that sent Me, hath everlasting life. Aug. If Aug.
in hearing and believing is eternal life, how much more in Tr.xxii.
understanding? But the step to our piety is faith, the fruit s. 2.
of faith, understanding. It is not, Believeth on Me, but *on*
Him that sent Me. Why is one to hear His word, and believe
another? Is it not that He means to say, His word is in

---

[1] Wisd. 9, 10. The Vulgate is: Mitte illam ut mecum sit, et mecum laboret.

Me? And what is, *Heareth My word,* but heareth Me? And it is, *Believeth on Him that sent Me;* as to say, He that believeth on Him, believeth on His Word, i. e. on Me, because I am the Word of the Father. CHRYS. Or, He did not say, He that heareth My words, and believeth on Me ; as they would have thought this empty boasting and arrogance. To say, *Believeth on Him that sent Me,* was a better way of making His discourse acceptable. To this end He says two things: one, that he who hears Him, believes on the Father; the other, that he who hears and believes *shall not come into condemnation.* AUG. But who is this favoured Person? Will there be any one better than the Apostle Paul, who says, *We must all appear before the judgment-seat of Christ?* Now judgment sometimes means punishment, sometimes trial. In the sense of trial, we must all appear before the judgment-seat of Christ: in the sense of condemnation we read, some *shall not come into judgment ;* i. e. shall not be condemned. It follows, *but is passed from death into life:* not, is now passing, but hath passed from the death of unbelief, into the life of faith, from the death of sin, unto the life of righteousness. Or, it is so said perhaps, to prevent our supposing that faith would save us from bodily death, that penalty which we must pay for Adam's transgression. He, in whom we all then were, heard the divine sentence, *Thou shalt surely die ;* nor can we evade it. But when we have suffered the death of the old man, we shall receive the life of the new, and by death make a passage to life. But to what life? To life everlasting : the dead shall rise again at the end of the world, and enter into everlasting life. For this life does not deserve the name of life ; only that life is true which is eternal. AUG. We see the lovers of this present transitory life so intent on its welfare, that when in danger of death, they will take any means to delay its approach, though they can not hope to drive it off altogether. If so much care and labour then is spent on gaining a little additional length of life, how ought we to strive after life eternal ? And if they are thought wise, who endeavour in every way to put off death, though they can live but a few days longer ; how foolish are they who so live, as to lose the eternal day ?

Chrys.
Hom.
xxxix.
2.

Aug.
Tr.xxii.
s.4.et sq.

1 Cor. 6.

Gen. 2.

Tr. xix.

Tr.xxii.

Aug.
de Verb.
Dom.
Serm.
lxiv.

25. Verily, verily, I say unto you, The hour is coming, and now is, when the dead shall hear the voice of the Son of God: and they that hear shall live.

26. For as the Father hath life in himself; so hath he given to the Son to have life in himself.

AUG. Some one might ask thee, The Father quickeneth him who believes on Him; but what of thee? dost thou not quicken? Observe thou that the Son also quickens whom He will: *Verily, verily, I say unto you, The hour is coming, and now is, when the dead shall hear the voice of the Son of God; and they that hear shall live.* CHRYS. After, *The hour cometh,* He adds, *and now is;* to let us know that it will not be long before it comes. For as in the future resurrection we shall be roused by hearing His voice speaking to us, so is it now. THEOPHYL. Here He speaks with a reference to those whom He was about to raise from the dead: viz. the daughter of the ruler of the synagogue, the son of the widow, and Lazarus. AUG. Or, He means to guard against our thinking, that the being passed from death to life, refers to the future resurrection; its meaning being, that he who *believes* is passed: and therefore He says, *Verily, verily, I say unto you, The hour cometh,* (what hour?) *and now is, when the dead shall hear the voice of the Son of God, and they that hear shall live.* He saith not, because they live, they hear; but in consequence of hearing, they come to life again. But what is hearing, but obeying? For they who believe and do according to the true faith, live, and are not dead; whereas those who believe not, or, believing, live a bad life, and have not love, are rather to be accounted dead. And yet that hour is still going on, and will go on, the same hour, to the end of the world: as John says, *It is the last hour.* AUG. *When the dead,* i. e. unbelievers, *shall hear the voice of the Son of God,* i. e. the Gospel: *and they that hear,* i. e. who obey, *shall live,* i. e. be justified, and no longer remain in unbelief. AUG. But some one will ask, Hath the Son life, whence those who believe will live? Hear His own words: *As the Father hath life in Himself, so*

Aug. Tr.xxiii. s. 14.

Chrys. Hom. xxxix.2.

Aug. Tr.xxii. s. 12.

1 John 2, 13.

Aug. Tr.xxii. s. 9.

o

hath He given to the Son to have life in Himself. Life is original and absolute in Him, cometh from no other source, dependeth on no other power. He is not as if He were partaker of a life, which is not Himself; but has life in Himself: so as that He Himself is His own life. Hear, O dead soul, the Father, speaking by the Son: arise, that thou mayest receive that life which thou hast not in thyself, and enter into the first resurrection. For this life, which the Father and the Son are, pertaineth to the soul, and is not perceived by the body. The rational mind only discovers the life of wisdom. HILARY. The heretics, driven hard by Scripture proofs, are obliged to attribute to the Son at any rate a likeness, in respect of virtue, to the Father. But they do not admit a likeness of nature, not being able to see that a likeness of virtue, could not arise but from a likeness of nature; as an inferior nature can never attain to the virtue of a higher and better one. And it cannot be denied that the Son of God has the same virtue with the Father, when He says, *What things soever (the Father) doeth, the same doeth the Son likewise.* But an express mention of the likeness of nature follows: *As the Father hath life in Himself, so hath He given to the Son to have life in Himself.* In life are comprehended nature and essence. And the Son, as He hath it, so hath He it given to Him. For the same which is life in both, is essence in both; and the life, i. e. essence, which is begotten from life, is born; though not born unlike the other. For, being life from life, it remains like in nature to its origin.

Aug.
xv. de
Trin.
c. 47.
(xxvi.)
Hilar.
vii. de
Trin.
c. 27,28. AUG. The Father must be understand not to have given life to the Son, who was existing without life, but so to have begotten Him, independently of time, that the life which He gave Him in begetting, was coeternal with His own. HILARY. Living born from living, hath the perfection of nativity, without the newness of nature. For there is nothing new implied in generation from living to living, the life not coming at its birth from nothing. And the life which derives its birth from life, must by the unity of nature, and the sacrament of a perfect birth, both be in the living being, and have the being who lives it, in itself. Weak human nature indeed is made up of unequal elements, and brought to life out of inanimate matter; nor does the human offspring

live for some time after it is begotten. Neither does it
wholly live from life, since much grows up in it insensibly, and decays insensibly. But in the case of God, the
whole of what He is, lives: for God is life, and from life, can
nothing be but what is living. AUG. *Given to the Son*, then, Aug.
has the meaning of, begat the Son; for He gave Him the Tr. xxii. s. 10.
life, by begetting. As He gave Him being, so He gave Him
to have life in Himself; so that the Son did not stand in
need of life to come to Him from without; but was in Himself
the fulness of life, whence others, i. e. believers, received
their life. What then is the difference between Them?
This, that one gave, the other received. CHRYS. The like- Chrys.
ness is perfect in all but one respect, viz. that, in point of Hom. xxxix.
essence, one is the Father, the other the Son. HILARY. For 3.
the person of the receiver, is distinct from that of the giver:
it being inconceivable that one and the same person, should
give to and receive from Himself. He who lives of Himself
is one person: He who acknowledges an Author of His life
is another.

27. And hath given him authority to execute judgment also, because he is the Son of man.

28. Marvel not at this: for the hour is coming, in
the which all that are in the graves shall hear his
voice,

29. And shall come forth; they that have done
good, unto the resurrection of life; and they that have
done evil, unto the resurrection of damnation.

THEOPHYL. The Father granted the Son power not only
to give life, but also to execute judgment. *And hath given
Him authority to execute judgment.* CHRYS. But why does Chrys.
He dwell so constantly on these subjects; judgment, resur- Hom. xxxix.
rection, and life? Because these are the most powerful s. 3.
arguments for bringing men over to the faith, and the most
likely ones to prevail with obstinate hearers. For one who
is persuaded that he shall rise again, and be called by the
Son to account for his misdeeds, will, though he know
nothing more than this, be anxious to propitiate his Judge.

It follows, *Because He is the Son of man, marvel not at this.*
Paul of Samosata reads it, *Hath given Him power to execute
judgment also, because He is the Son of man.* But this connexion has no meaning; for He does not receive the power
to judge because He is man, (as, on this supposition, what
would prevent all men from being judges:) but because He
is the ineffable Son of God; therefore is He Judge. We
must read it then, *Because He is the Son of man, marvel
not at this.* As Christ's hearers thought him a mere man,
and as what He asserted of Himself was too high to be true
of men, or even angels, or any being short of God Himself,
there was a strong obstacle in the way of their believing,
which our Lord notices in order to remove it: Marvel not,
He says, that He is the Son of man: and then adds the
reason why they should not marvel: *For the hour is coming,
in the which all that are in the graves shall hear the voice
of the Son of God.* And why did He not say, Marvel not
that He is the Son of man: because in truth He is the Son
of God? Because, having given out that it was He who
should raise men from the dead, the resurrection being a
strictly divine work, He leaves His hearers to infer that He is
God, and the Son of God. Persons in arguing often do this.
When they have brought out grounds amply sufficient to
prove the conclusion they want, they do not draw that conclusion themselves; but, to make the victory greater, leave
the opponent to draw it. In referring above to the resurrection of Lazarus and the rest, he said nothing about judgment,
for Lazarus did not rise again for judgment; whereas now,
that He is speaking of the general resurrection, He brings in
the mention of the judgment: *And (they) shall come forth,* He
says, *they that have done good unto the resurrection of life,
and they that have done evil unto the resurrection of damnation.* Having said above, *He that heareth My words, and
believeth on Him that sent Me, hath everlasting life;* that
men might not suppose from this, that belief was sufficient
for salvation, He proceeds to speak of works: *And they that
have done good,—and they that have done evil.* AUG. Or
thus: Inasmuch as the Word was in the beginning with God,
the Father gave Him to have life in Himself; but inasmuch
as the Word was made flesh of the Virgin Mary, being made

man, He became the Son of man: and as the Son of man,
He received power to execute judgment at the end of the
world; at which time the bodies of the dead shall rise again.
The souls then of the dead God raises by Christ the Son of
God; their bodies by the same Christ, the Son of man.
Wherefore He adds, *Because He is the Son of man:* for, as
to the Son of God, He always had the power.   Aug. At the
judgment will appear the form of man, that form will judge,
which was judged; He will sit a Judge Who stood before the
judge; He will condemn the guilty, Who was condemned
innocent.   For it is proper that the judged should see their
Judge.   Now the judged consist of both good and bad; so
that the form of the servant will be shewn to good and bad
alike; the form of God to the good only.   *Blessed are the*
pure in heart, for they shall see God.   Aug. None if the
founders of false religious sects have been able to deny the
resurrection of the soul, but many have denied the resurrection of the body; and, unless Thou, Lord Jesus, hadst
declared it, what answer could we give the gainsayer?   To
set forth this truth, He says, *Marvel not at this;* (i. e. that
He hath given power to the Son of man to execute judgment,)
for the hour is coming, &c.   Aug. He does not add, *And*
now is, here; because this hour would be at the end of the
world.   Marvel not, i. e. marvel not, men will all be judged
by a man.   But what men? Not those only, whom He will
find alive, *For the hour cometh, in which all that are in their*
graves shall hear His voice.   Aug. What can be plainer?
Men's bodies are in their graves, not their souls.   Above
when He said, *The hour cometh,* and added, *and now is;*
He proceeds, When the dead shall hear the voice of the
Son of God.   He does not say, All the dead; for by the
dead are meant the wicked, and the wicked have not all
been brought to obey the Gospel.   But in the end of the
world all that are in their graves shall hear His voice, and
come forth.   He does not say, *Shall live,* as He said above,
when He spoke of the eternal and blessed life; which all
will not have, who shall come forth from their graves.   This
judgment was committed to Him because He was the Son
of man.   But what takes place in this judgment? *They that*
have done good shall go unto the resurrection of life, i. e. to

Aug.
de Ver.
Dom.
Ser. 64.

Matt. 5,
8.
Aug.
Tr. xix.
s. 14.

Aug.
de Ver.
Dom.
Ser. 64.

Aug.
Sup.
Joan.
Tr. xix.
s. 17,18.

live with the Angels of God; *they that have done evil unto the resurrection of judgment.* Judgment here meaning damnation.

30. I can of mine own self do nothing: as I hear, I judge: and my judgment is just; because I seek not mine own will, but the will of the Father which hath sent me.

Aug.
Tr. xix.
s. 19.
AUG. We were about to ask Christ, Thou wilt judge, and the Father not judge: wilt not Thou then judge according to the Father? He anticipates us by saying, *I can of Mine own Self do nothing.*

Chrys.
Hom.
xxxix. 4.
CHRYS. That is, nothing that is a departure from, or that is unlike to, what the Father wishes, shall ye see done by Me, but *as I hear, I judge.* He is only shewing that it was impossible He should ever wish any thing but what the Father wished. I judge, His meaning

Aug.
Tr. xxiii.
s. 15.
v. 19.
is, as if it were My Father that judged. AUG. When He spoke of the resurrection of the soul, He did not say, Hear, but, See. Hear implies a command issuing from the Father.

Aug.
Serm.
contr.
Arrian.
c. 9. (xiv.)
He speaks as man, who is inferior to the Father. AUG. *As I hear, I judge,* is said with reference either to His human subordination, as the Son of man, or to that immutable and simple nature of the Sonship derived from the Father; in which nature hearing and seeing is identical

ut sup.
c. xvii.
with being. Wherefore as He hears, He judges. The Word is begotten one with the Father, and therefore judges ac-

c. xvii.
cording to truth. It follows, *And My judgment is just, because I seek not Mine own will, but the will of the Father which hath sent Me.* This is intended to take us back to

sc. Adam.
that man who, by seeking his own will, not the will of Him who made him, did not judge himself justly, but had a just judgment pronounced upon him. He did not believe that, by doing his own will, not God's, he should die. So he did his own will, and died; because the judgment of God is just, which judgment the Son of God executes, by not seeking His own will, i. e. His will as being the Son of man. Not that He has no will in judging, but His will is not His own in such sense, as to be different from the Father's. AUG.

Aug.
Tr. xix.
319.
I seek not then Mine own will, i. e. the will of the Son of man, in opposition to God: for men do their own will, not

God's, when, to do what they wish, they violate God's commands. But when they so do what they wish, as at the
same time to follow the will of God, they do not their own
will. Or, *I seek not Mine own will:* i. e. because I am not
of myself, but of the Father. CHRYS. He shews that the Chrys.
Father's will is not a different one from His own, but one and xxxix.4.
the same, as a ground of defence. Nor marvel if being
hitherto thought no more than a mere man, He defends
Himself in a somewhat human way, and shews his judgment
to be just on the same ground which any other person would
have taken; viz. that one who has his own ends in view,
may incur suspicion of injustice, but that one who has not
cannot. AUG. The only Son says, *I seek not Mine own* Aug.
will: and yet men wish to do their own will. Let us do the Tr. xxi.
will of the Father, Christ, and Holy Ghost: for these have
one will, power, and majesty.

31. If I bear witness of myself, my witness is not
true.

32. There is another that beareth witness of me;
and I know that the witness which he witnesseth of me
is true.

33. Ye sent unto John, and he bare witness unto
the truth.

34. But I receive not testimony from man: but
these things I say, that ye might be saved.

35. He was a burning and a shining light: and ye
were willing for a season to rejoice in his light.

36. But I have greater witness than that of John:
for the works which the Father hath given me to finish,
the same works that I do, bear witness of me, that the
Father hath sent me.

37. And the Father himself, which hath sent me,
hath borne witness of me. Ye have neither heard his
voice at any time, nor seen his shape.

38. And ye have not his word abiding in you: for
whom he hath sent, him ye believe not.

39. Search the Scriptures; for in them ye think ye

have eternal life: and they are they which testify of
me.

40. And ye will not come to me, that ye might
have life.

Chrys.
Hom.
xl. 1. CHRYS. He now brings proof of those high declarations
respecting Himself. He answers an objection: *If I bear
witness of Myself, My witness is not true.* These are Christ's
own words. But does not Christ in many places bear witness
of Himself? And if all this is false, where is our hope of
salvation? Whence shall we obtain truth, when the Truth
Itself says, *My witness is not true.* We must believe then
that *true*, here, is said, not with reference to the intrinsic
value of His testimony, but to their suspicions; for the Jews
might say, We do not believe Thee, because no one who bears
witness to himself is to be depended on. In answer then,
he puts forth three clear and irrefragable proofs, three witnesses as it were, to the truth of what He had said; the works
which He had done, the testimony of the Father, and the
preaching of John: putting the least of these foremost, i. e.
the preaching of John: *There is another that beareth witness of Me: and I know that the witness which he witnesseth
of Me is true.* Aug.
de Verb.
Dom. s.
43. AUG. He knew Himself that His witness
of Himself was true, but in compassion to the weak and
unbelieving, the Sun sought for candles, that their weak sight
might not be dazzled by His full blaze. And therefore John
was brought forward to give his testimony to the truth. Not
that there is such testimony really, for whatever witnesses
bear witness to Him, it is really He who bears witness to
Himself; as it is His dwelling in the witnesses, which moves
them so to give their witness to the truth. ALCUIN. Or
thus; Christ, being both God and man, He shews the proper
existence of both, by sometimes speaking according to the
nature he took from man, sometimes according to the majesty
of the Godhead. *If I bear witness of Myself, My witness is
not true:* this is to be understood of His humanity; the sense
being, *If I,* a man, *bear witness of Myself,* i. e. without
God, *My witness is not true:* and then follows, *There is another
that beareth witness of Me.* The Father bore witness of
Christ, by the voice which was heard at the baptism, and at

the transfiguration on the mount. *And I know that His witness is true;* because He is the God of truth. How then can His witness be otherwise than true? CHRYS. But according to the former interpretation, they might say to Him, If Thy witness is not true, how sayest Thou, I know that the witness of John is true? But His answer meets the objection: *Ye sent unto John, and he bare witness of the truth:* as if to say: Ye would not have sent to John, if ye had not thought him worthy of credit. And what is more remarkable, they did send to him, not to ask Him about Christ, but about himself. For they who were sent out did not say, What sayest thou of Christ? but, *Who art thou? what sayest thou of thyself?* In so great admiration did they hold him. ALCUIN. But he bore witness not to himself, but to the truth: as the friend of the truth, he bore witness to the truth, i. e. Christ. Our Lord, on His part, does not reject the witness of John, as not being necessary, but shews only that men ought not to give such attention to John as to forget that Christ's witness was all that was necessary to Himself. *But I receive not,* He says, *testimony from men.* BEDE. Because I do not want it. John, though he bore witness, did it not that Christ might increase, but that men might be brought to the knowledge of Him. CHRYS. Even the witness of John was the witness of God: for what he said, God taught him. But to anticipate their asking how it appeared that God taught John, as if the Jews had objected that John's witness might not be true, our Lord anticipates them by saying, " Ye sought him yourselves to enquire of him; that is why I use his testimony, for I need it not." He adds, *But these things I say that ye might be saved.* As if He said, I being God, needed not this human kind of testimony. But, since ye attend more to him, and think him more worthy of credit than any one else, while ye do not believe me, though I work miracles; for this cause I remind you of his testimony. But had they not received John's testimony? Before they have time to ask this, He answers it: *He was a burning and a shining light, and ye were willing for a season to rejoice in his light.* He says this to shew, how lightly they had held by John, and how soon they had left him, thus preventing him from leading them to Christ. He calls him a candle,

Chrys. Hom. xl. 2.

c. 1, 22.

Chrys. Hom. xl. 2.

because John had not his light from himself, but from the grace of the Holy Spirit. ALCUIN. John was a candle lighted by Christ, the Light, burning with faith and love, shining in word and deed. He was sent before, to confound the enemies

Ps. 131. of Christ, according to the Psalm, *I have ordained a lantern for Mine Anointed; as for His enemies, I shall clothe them with*

Chrys. *shame*[m]. CHRYS. I therefore direct you to John, not because
Hom.
xl. 2. I want his testimony, but that ye may be saved: for *I have greater witness than that of John,* i. e. that of my works; *The works which the Father hath given Me to finish, the same works that I do bear witness of Me, that the Father hath sent Me.* ALCUIN. That He enlightens the blind, that He opens the deaf ear, looses the mouth of the dumb, casts out devils,

Hilar. raises the dead; these works bear witness of Christ. HILARY.
vi. de
Trin. c. The Only-begotten God shews Himself to be the Son, on
27. the testimony not of man only, but of His own power. The works which He does, bear witness to His being sent from the Father. Therefore the obedience of the Son and the authority of the Father are set forth in Him who was sent. But the testimony of works not being sufficient evidence, it follows, *And the Father Himself which hath sent Me, hath borne witness of Me.* Open the Evangelic volumes, and examine their whole range: no testimony of the Father to the Son is given in any of the books, other than that He is the Son. So what a calumny is it in men now saying that this is only a name of adoption: thus making God

Bede. a liar, and names unmeaning. BEDE. By His mission we
v. Joan. must understand His incarnation. Lastly, He shews that God is incorporeal, and cannot be seen by the bodily eye: *Ye have neither heard His voice at any time, nor seen His shape.* ALCUIN. The Jews might say, We heard the voice of the Lord at Sinai, and saw Him under the appearance of fire. If God then bears witness of Thee, we should know His voice. To which He replies, I have the witness of the Father, though ye understand it not; because ye never heard

Chrys. His voice, or saw His shape. CHRYS. How then says Moses,
Hom. xl.
3

---

[m] Alcuin literally, John bore witness of Christ, like a candle, not in order to heal his friends, but to confound his enemies .... John was not a candle, as if lighted from himself, but lighted by Christ. The words in the text are taken from an interlineary gloss and a sermon of St. Bernard on John. Nic.

Ask—whether there hath been any such thing as this great Deut. 4,
thing is: did ever people hear the voice of God, speaking out 32. 33.
of the midst of the fire, as thou hast heard and seen? Isaiah
too, and many others, are said to have seen Him. So what
does Christ mean here? He means to impress upon them
the philosophical doctrine, that God has neither voice,
or appearance, or shape; but is superior to such modes of
speaking of Him. For as in saying, *Ye have never heard
His voice,* He does not mean to say that He has a voice, only
not an audible one to them; so when He says, *Nor have even
His shape,* no tangible, sensible, or visible shape is implied to
belong to God: but all such mode of speaking is pronounced
inapplicable to God. ALCUIN. For it is not by the carnal
ear, but by the spiritual understanding, through the grace of
the Holy Spirit, that God is heard. And they did not hear
the spiritual voice, because they did not love or obey Him,
nor saw they His shape; inasmuch as that is not to be seen
by the outward eye, but by faith and love. CHRYS. But it Chrys.
was impossible for them to declare that they had received, Hom.xl.
3.
and obeyed God's commands: and therefore He adds, *Ye
have not His word abiding in you;* i. e. the commandments,
the law, and the prophets; though God instituted them, ye
have them not. For if the Scriptures every where tell you to
believe on Me, and ye believe not, it is manifest that His
word is gone from you: *For whom He hath sent, Him ye
believe not.* ALCUIN. Or thus; they cannot have abiding in
them the Word which was in the beginning, who came not to
keep in mind, or fulfil in practice, that word of God which
they hear. Having mentioned the testimonies of John, and
the Father, and of His works, He adds now that of the
Mosaic Law: *Search the Scriptures, for in them ye think ye
have eternal life; and they are they which testify of
Me:* as if He said, Ye think ye have eternal life in the
Scriptures, and reject Me as being opposed to Moses: but
you will find that Moses himself testifies to My being God,
if you search the Scripture carefully. All Scripture indeed
bears witness of Christ, whether by its types, or by prophets,
or by the ministering of Angels. But the Jews did not
believe these intimations of Christ, and therefore could not
obtain eternal life: *Ye will not come to Me, that ye may*

have life; meaning, The Scriptures bear witness of Me, but ye will not come to Me notwithstanding, i. e. ye will not believe on Me, and seek for salvation at My hands.

Chrys.
Hom.xl.
3. CHRYS. Or the connection may be given thus. They might say to Him, How, if we have never heard God's voice, has God borne witness to you? So He says, *Search the Scriptures;* meaning that God had borne witness of Him by the Scriptures. He had borne witness indeed at the Jordan, and on the mount. But they did not hear the voice on the mount, and did not attend to it at the Jordan. Wherefore He sends them to the Scriptures, when they would also find the Hom.
xli. 1. Father's testimony. He did not send them however to the Scriptures simply to read them, but to examine them attentively, because Scripture ever threw a shade over its own meaning, and did not display it on the surface. The treasure was, as it were, hidden from their eye. He does not say, For in them ye have eternal life, but, For in them ye *think* ye have eternal life; meaning that they did not reap much fruit from the Scriptures, thinking, as they did, that they should be saved by the mere reading of them, without faith. For which reason He adds, *Ye will not come to Me;* Bede.
in v.
Joan. i. e. ye will not believe on Me. BEDE. That coming is put for believing we know, *Come unto Him, and be lightened.* Ps. 33. He adds, *That ye might have life;* For, if the soul which sinneth dies, they were dead in soul and mind. And therefore He promises the *life* of the soul, i. e. eternal happiness.

41. I receive not honour from men.

42. But I know you, that ye have not the love of God in you.

43. I am come in my Father's name, and ye receive me not: if another shall come in his own name, him ye will receive.

44. How can ye believe, which receive honour one of another, and seek not the honour that cometh from God only?

45. Do not think that I will accuse you to the

---

[n] Vulg. They had an eye unto Him, and were lightened.

Father: there is one that accuseth you, even Moses, in whom ye trust.

46. For had ye believed Moses, ye would have believed me : for he wrote of me.

47. But if ye believe not his writings, how shall ye believe my words?

CHRYS. Our Lord having made mention of John, and the witness of God, and His own works, many, who did not see that His motive was to induce them to believe, might suspect Him of a desire for human glory, and therefore He says, *I receive not honour from men:* i. e. I do not want it. My nature is not such as to want that glory, which cometh from men. For if the Son receives no addition from the light of a candle, much more am not I in want of human glory. ALCUIN. Or, *I receive not honour from men:* i. e. I seek not human praise; for I came not to receive carnal honour *from* men, but to give spiritual honour *to* men. I do not bring forward this testimony then, because I seek my own glory; but because I compassionate your wanderings, and wish to bring you back to the way of truth. Hence what follows, *But I know you that ye have not the love of God in you.* CHRYS. As if to say, I said this to prove that it is not from your love of God, that you persecute Me; for He bears witness to Me, by My own works, and by the Scriptures. So that, if ye loved God, as ye rejected Me, thinking Me against God, so now ye would come to Me. But ye do not love Him. And He proves this, not only from what they do now, but from what they will do in time to come: *I am come in My Father's name, and ye receive Me not; if another shall come in his own name, him ye will receive.* He says plainly, *I am come in the Father's name,* that they might never be able to plead ignorance as an excuse ALCUIN. As if He said, For this cause came I into the world, that through Me the name of the Father might be glorified; for I attribute all to Him. As then they would not receive Him, Who came to do His Father's will; they had not the love of God. But Antichrist will come not in the Father's name, but in his own, to seek, not the Father's glory, but his own. And the Jews having rejected Christ, it

Chrys.
Hom.
xli. 1.

Chrys.
Hom.
xli. 1.

was a fit punishment on them, that they should receive Antichrist, and believe a lie, as they would not believe the Truth. AUG. Hear John, *As ye have heard that Antichrist shall come, even now are there many Antichrists.* But what dost thou dread in Antichrist, except that he will exalt his own name, and despise the name of the Lord? And what else does he do, who says, " I justify;" or those who say, " Unless we are good, ye must perish °?" Wherefore my life shall depend on Thee, and my salvation shall be fastened to Thee. Shall I so forget my foundation? Is not my rock Christ? CHRYS. Here is the crowning proof of their impiety. He says, as it were, If it was the love of God that made you persecute me, you would persecute Antichrist much more: for he does not profess to be sent by the Father, or to come according to His will; but, on the contrary, usurping what does not belong to him, will proclaim himself to be God over all. It is manifest that your persecution of Me is from malice and hatred of God. Then He gives the reason of their unbelief: *How can ye believe, which receive honour one of another, and seek not the honour that cometh from God only?* another proof this, that theirs was not a zeal for God, but a gratification of their own passions. ALCUIN. How faulty then is the boasting temper, and that eagerness for human praise, which likes to be thought to have what it has not, and would fain be thought to have all that it has, by its own strength. Men of such temper cannot believe; for in their hearts, they are bent solely on gaining praise, and setting themselves up above others. BEDE. The best way of guarding against this sin, is to bring to our consciences the remembrance, that we are dust, and should ascribe all the good that we have not to ourselves, but to God. And we should endeavour always to be such, as we wish to appear to others. Then, as they might ask, Wilt thou accuse us then to the Father? He anticipates this question: *Do not think that I will accuse you to the Father.* CHRYS. For I am not come to condemn, but to save. *There is one that accuseth you, even Moses, in whom you trust.* As He had said of the

Marginal notes:
Aug. de Verb. Dom. Serm. 45. a med.
I John 2, 18.
Chrys. Hom. xli. 13.
Chrys. Hom. xli. 2.

° Alluding to the Donatists, who made baptismal justification to depend on the goodness of the minister, and denied the efficacy of any but their own Baptism. Nic.

Scriptures above : *In them ye think ye have eternal life.* So now of Moses He says, *In whom ye trust,* always answering them out of their authorities. But they will say, How will he accuse us ? What hast Thou to do with Moses, Thou who hast broken the sabbath ? So He adds : *For had ye believed Moses, ye would perhaps have believed Me, for he wrote of me.* This is connected with what was said before. For where evidence that He came from God had been forced upon them by His words, by the voice of John, and the testimony of the Father, it was certain that Moses would condemn them; for he had said, If any one shall come, ^{alluding to Deut.} doing miracles, leading men to God, and foretelling the future 13, 1. with certainty, you must obey him. Christ did all this, and they did not obey Him. ALCUIN. *Perhaps,* He says, in accommodation to our way of speaking, not because there is really any doubting in God. Moses prophesied of Christ, *A Prophet shall the Lord your God raise up from among* Deut. *your brethren like unto me: Him shall ye hear.* AUG. But, ^{18, 18. Aug.} in fact, the whole that Moses wrote, was written of Christ, cont. i. e. it has reference to Him principally ; whether it point ^{Faust. l. xvi. c. 9.} to Him by figurative actions, or expression; or set forth His grace and glory.

　　But if ye believe not his writings, how shall ye believe My words. THEOPHYL. As if He said, He has even written, and has left his books among you, as a constant memento to you, lest you forget His words. And since you believe not his writings, how can ye believe My unwritten words ? ALCUIN. From this we may infer too, that he who knows the commandments against stealing, and other crimes, and neglects them, will never fulfil the more perfect and refined precepts of the Gospel. CHRYS. Indeed had they attended Chrys. to His words, they ought and would have tried to learn from ^{Hom. xli. 2.} Him, what the things were which Moses had written of Him. But they are silent. For it is the nature of wickedness to defy persuasion. Do what you will, it retains its venom to the last.

CHAP. VI.

1. After these things Jesus went over the sea of Galilee, which is the sea of Tiberias.

2. And a great multitude followed him, because they saw his miracles which he did on them that were diseased.

3. And Jesus went up into a mountain, and there he sat with his disciples.

4. And the Passover, a feast of the Jews, was nigh.

5. When Jesus then lifted up his eyes, and saw a great company come unto him, he saith unto Philip, Whence shall we buy bread, that these may eat?

6. And this he said to prove him: for he himself knew what he would do.

7. Philip answered him, Two hundred pennyworth of bread is not sufficient for them, that every one of them may take a little.

8. One of his disciples, Andrew, Simon Peter's brother, saith unto him,

9. There is a lad here, which hath five barley loaves, and two small fishes: but what are they among so many?

10. And Jesus said, Make the men sit down. Now there was much grass in the place. So the men sat down, in number about five thousand.

11. And Jesus took the loaves; and when he had given thanks, he distributed to the disciples, and the disciples to them that were set down; and likewise of the fishes as much as they would.

12. When they were filled, he said unto his disciples, Gather up the fragments that remain, that nothing be lost.

13. Therefore they gathered them together, and filled twelve baskets with the fragments of the five barley loaves, which remained over and above unto them that had eaten.

14. Then those men, when they had seen the miracle that Jesus did, said, This is of a truth that Prophet that should come into the world.

CHRYS. As missiles rebound with great force from a hard body, and fly off in all directions, whereas a softer material retains and stops them; so violent men are only excited to greater rage by violence on the side of their opponents, whereas gentleness softens them. Christ quieted the irritation of the Jews by retiring from Jerusalem. He went into Galilee, but not to Cana again, but beyond the sea: *After these things Jesus went over the sea of Galilee, which is the sea of Tiberias.* ALCUIN. This sea hath different names, from the different places with which it is connected; the sea of Galilee, from the province; the sea of Tiberias, from the city of that name. It is called a sea, though it is not salt water, that name being applied to all large pieces of water, in Hebrew. This sea our Lord often passes over, in going to preach to the people bordering on it. THEOPHYL. He goes from place to place to try the dispositions of people, and excite a desire to hear Him: *And a great multitude followed Him, because they saw His miracles which He did on them that were diseased.* ALCUIN. viz. His giving sight to the blind, and other like miracles. And it should be understood, that all, whom He healed in body, He renewed likewise in soul. CHRYS. Though favoured with such teaching, they were influenced less by it, than by the miracles; a sign of their low state of belief: for Paul says of tongues, that *they are for a sign, not to them that believe, but to them that believe not.* They were wiser of whom it is said, that *they were astonished at His doctrine.* The

Margin notes: Chrys. Hom. xlii. 1. Chrys. Hom. xlii. 1. 1 Cor. 14, 22. Matt. 7, 28.

P

Evangelist does not say what miracles He wrought, the great object of his book being to give our Lord's discourses. It follows: *And Jesus went up into a mountain, aud there sat with His disciples.* He went up into the mountain, on account of the miracle which was going to be done. That the disciples alone ascended with Him, implies that the people who stayed behind were in fault for not following. He went up to the mountain too, as a lesson to us to retire from the tumult and confusion of the world, and leave wisdom in solitude. *And the passover, a feast of the Jews, was nigh.* Observe, in a whole year, the Evangelist has told us of no miracles of Christ, except His healing the impotent man, and the nobleman's son. His object was to give not a regular history, but only a few of the principal acts of our Lord. But why did not our Lord go up to the feast? He was taking occasion, from the wickedness of the Jews, gradually to abolish the Law. THEOPHYL. The persecutions of the Jews gave Him reason for retiring, and thus setting aside the Law. The truth being now revealed, types were at an end, and He was under no obligation to keep the Jewish feasts. Observe the expression, *a feast of the Jews,* not a feast of Christ. BEDE. If we compare the accounts of the different Evangelists, we shall find very clearly, that there was an interval of a year between the beheading of John, and our Lord's Passion. For, since Matthew says that our Lord, on hearing of the death of John, withdrew into a desert place, where He fed the multitude; and John says that the Passover was nigh, when He fed the multitude; it is evident that John was beheaded shortly before the Passover. And at the same feast, the next year Christ suffered. It follows, *When Jesus then lifted up His eyes, and saw a great company come unto Him, He saith unto Philip, Whence shall we buy bread, that these may eat?* *When Jesus lifted up His eyes,* this is to shew us, that Jesus was not generally with His eyes lifted up, looking about Him, but sitting calm and attentive, surrounded by His disciples. CHRYS. Nor did He only sit with His disciples, but conversed with them familiarly, and gained possession of their minds. Then He looked, and saw a crowd advancing. But why did He ask Philip that question? Because He knew

Mat. 14, 13.

Chrys. Hom. xlii. 1.

that His disciples, and he especially, needed further teaching. For this Philip it was who said afterwards, *Shew us the* c. 14, 8. *Father, and it sufficeth us.* And if the miracle had been performed at once, without any introduction, the greatness of it would not have been seen. The disciples were made to confess their own inability, that they might see the miracle more clearly; *And this He said to prove him.* AUG. One Aug. kind of temptation leads to sin, with which God never tempts de Verb. Dom. any one; and there is another kind by which faith is tried. Serm. In this sense it is said that Christ proved His disciple. This 17. James is not meant to imply that He did not know what Philip 1, 13. Deut. would say; but is an accommodation to men's way of speak- 13, 3. ing. For as the expression, *Who searcheth the hearts of men,* does not mean the searching of ignorance, but of absolute knowledge; so here, when it is said that our Lord proved Philip, we must understand that He knew him perfectly, but that He tried him, in order to confirm his faith. The Evangelist himself guards against the mistake which this imperfect mode of speaking might occasion, by adding, *For He Himself knew what He would do.* ALCUIN. He asks him this question, not for His own information, but in order to shew His yet unformed disciple his dulness of mind, which he could not perceive of himself. THEOPHYL. Or to shew others it. He was not ignorant of His disciple's heart Himself. AUG. But if our Lord, according to John's account, Aug. de Con. on seeing the multitude, asked Philip, tempting him, whence Evang. they could buy food for them, it is difficult at first to see l. ii. c. xlvi. how it can be true, according to the other account, that the disciples first told our Lord, to send away the multitude; and that our Lord replied, *They need not depart; give ye* Matt. *them to eat.* We must understand then it was after saying 25, 16. this, that our Lord saw the multitude, and said to Philip what John had related, which has been omitted by the rest. CHRYS. Or they are two different occasions altogether. Chrys. Hom. THEOPHYL. Thus tried by our Lord, Philip was found to be xlii. s. 1. possessed with human notions, as appears from what follows, *Philip answered Him, Two hundred pennyworth of bread is not sufficient for them, that every one of them may take a little.* ALCUIN. Wherein he shews his dulness: for, had he perfect ideas of his Creator, he would not be thus doubting

Aug.
de Con.
Evan.
l. ii. c.
xlvi.

His power. AUG. The reply, which is attributed to Philip by John, Mark puts in the mouth of all the disciples, either meaning us to understand that Philip spoke for the rest, or else putting the plural number for the singular, which is often done. THEOPHYL. Andrew is in the same perplexity that Philip is; only he has rather higher notions of our Lord: *There is a lad here which hath five barley loaves and two*

Chrys.
Hom.
xlii. 11.

small fishes. CHRYS. Probably He had some reason in his mind for this speech. He would know of Elijah's miracle, by which a hundred men were fed with twenty loaves. This was a great step; but here he stopped. He did not rise any higher. For his next words are, *But what are these among so many?* He thought that less could produce less in a miracle, and more more; a great mistake; inasmuch as it was as easy for Christ to feed the multitude from a few fishes as from many. He did not really want any material to work from, but only made use of created things for this purpose in order to shew that no part of the creation was severed from His wisdom. THEOPHYL. This passage confounds the Manicheans, who say that bread and all such things were created by an evil Deity. The Son of the good God, Jesus Christ, multiplied the loaves. Therefore they could not have been naturally evil; a good God would never

Aug.
de Con.
Evang.
ii.c.xlvi.

have multiplied what was evil. AUG. Andrew's suggestion about the five loaves and two fishes, is given as coming from the disciples in general, in the other Evangelists, and the plural number is used. CHRYS. And let those of us, who

Chrys.
Hom.
xlii. 11.

are given to pleasure, observe the plain and abstemious eating of those great and wonderful men [b]. He made the men sit down before the loaves appeared, to teach us that with Him, things that are not are as things that are; as Paul

Rom.
25, 17.

says, *Who calleth those things that be not, as though they were.* The passage proceeds then: *And Jesus said, Make the men sit down.* ALCUIN. *Sit down,* i. e. lie down, as the ancient custom was, which they could do, as *there was much grass in the place.* THEOPHYL. i. e. green grass. It was the time of the Passover, which was kept the first month of the spring. *So the men sat down in number about five thousand.* The Evangelist only counts the *men,* following

[b] Alluding to the five loaves and two fishes.

the direction in the law. Moses numbered the people from twenty years old and upwards, making no mention of the women; to signify that the manly and juvenile character is especially honourable in God's eyes. *And Jesus took the loaves; and when He had given thanks, He distributed* [c] *to them that were sat down: and likewise of the fishes as much as they would.* CHRYS. But why when He is going ^{Chrys.} to heal the impotent, to raise the dead, to calm the sea, _{Hom.} _{xlii. 11.} does He *not* pray, but here does give thanks? To teach us to give thanks to God, whenever we sit down to eat. And He prays more in lesser matters, in order to shew that He does not pray from any motive of need. For had prayer been really necessary to supply His wants, His praying would have been in proportion to the importance of each particular work. But acting, as He does, on His own authority, it is evident, He only prays out of condescension to us. And, as a great multitude was collected, it was an opportunity of impressing on them, that His coming was in accordance with God's will. Accordingly, when a miracle was private, He did not pray; when numbers were present, He did. HILARY. Five loaves are then set before the _{Hilar.} multitude, and broken. The broken portions pass through _{iii. de} _{Trin.} into the hands of those who break, that from which they are _{c. 18.} broken all the time not at all diminishing. And yet there they are, the bits taken from it, in the hands of the persons breaking [d]. There is no catching by eye or touch the miraculous operation: that is, which was not, that is seen, which is not understood. It only remains for us to believe that God can do all things. AUG. He multiplied in His _{Aug.} hands the five loaves, just as He produces harvest out of a _{Tr. xxiv.} _{s. 1.} few grains. There was a power in the hands of Christ; and those five loaves were, as it were, seeds, not indeed committed to the earth, but multiplied by Him who made the earth. CHRYS. Observe the difference between the servant _{Chrys.} and the lord. The Prophets received grace, as it were, by _{Hom.} _{xlii. 3.}

---

[c] Vulgate omits, *to the disciples, and the disciples.*

[d] Hilary literally. The operation escapes the sight; whilst you follow with your eyes one hand filled with fragments, you see that the other has

not lost its portion; meantime the heap of fragments increases; those who break are engaged in supplying, those who eat in receiving, the hungry are satisfied; twelve baskets are filled with what remains. Nic.

measure, and according to that measure performed their
miracles: whereas Christ, working this by His own absolute
power, produces a kind of superabundant result. *When
they were filled, He said unto His disciples, Gather up the
fragments that remain, that nothing be lost. Therefore they
gathered them together, and filled twelve baskets with the
fragments.* This was not done for needless ostentation, but
to prevent men from thinking the whole a delusion; which
was the reason why He made use of an existing material to
work from. But why did He give the fragments to His
disciples to carry away, and not to the multitude? Because
the disciples were to be the teachers of the world, and therefore it was most important that the truth should be impressed
upon them. Wherefore I admire not only the multitude of
the loaves which were made, but the definite quantity of the
fragments; neither more nor less than twelve baskets full, and
corresponding to the number of the twelve Apostles. THE-
OPHYL. We learn too from this miracle, not to be pusillani-
mous in the greatest straits of poverty. BEDE. When the
multitude saw the miracle our Lord had done, they marvelled; as they did not know yet that He was God. *Then
those men,* the Evangelist adds, i. e. *carnal* men, whose
understanding was carnal, *when they had perceived the
miracle that Jesus did, said, This is of a truth that Prophet
that should come into the world.* ALCUIN. Their faith
being as yet weak, they only call our Lord a Prophet,
not knowing that He was God. But the miracle had produced considerable effect upon them, as it made them
call our Lord *that Prophet,* singling Him out from the
rest. They call Him a Prophet, because some of the
Prophets had worked miracles; and properly, inasmuch as
our Lord calls Himself a Prophet; *It cannot be that a
prophet perish out of Jerusalem.* AUG. Christ is a Prophet,
and the Lord of Prophets; as He is an Angel, and the Lord
of Angels. In that He came to announce something, He
was an Angel; in that He foretold the future, He was a
Prophet; in that He was the Word made flesh, He was
Lord both of Angels and Prophets; for none can be a
Prophet without the word of God. CHRYS. Their expression, *that should come into the world,* shews that they

Luke
13, 33.
Aug.
Tr.xxiv.
s. 7.

expected the arrival of some great Prophet. And this is
why they say, *This is of a truth that Prophet:* the article
being put in the Greek, to shew that He was distinct from
other Prophets. AUG. But let us reflect a little here. Forasmuch as the Divine Substance is not visible to the eye, and
the miracles of the divine government of the world, and
ordering of the whole creation, are overlooked in consequence
of their constancy; God has reserved to Himself acts,
beside the established course and order of nature, to do at
suitable times; in order that those who overlooked the daily
course of nature, might be roused to wonder by the sight of
what was different from, though not at all greater, than what
they were used to. The government of the world is a greater
miracle, than the satisfying the hunger of five thousand with
five loaves; and yet no one wonders at this: the former
excited wonder; not from any real superiority in it, but
because it was uncommon. But it would be wrong to gather
no more than this from Christ's miracles: for, the Lord
who is on the mount[e], and the Word of God which is on
high, the same is no humble person to be lightly passed
over, but we must look up to Him reverently. ALCUIN.
Mystically, the sea signifies this tumultuous world. In the
fulness of time, when Christ had entered the sea of our
mortality by His birth, trodden it by His death, passed over
it by His resurrection[f], then followed Him crowds of believers,
both from the Jews and Gentiles. BEDE. Our Lord went
up to the mountain, when He ascended to heaven, which is
signified by the mountain. ALCUIN. His leaving the multitude below, and ascending the heights with His disciples,
signifies, that lesser precepts are to be given to beginners,
higher to the more matured. His refreshing the people
shortly before the Passover signifies our refreshment by the
bread of the divine word; and the body and blood, i. e. our
spiritual passover, by which we pass over from vice to virtue.
And the Lord's eyes are spiritual gifts, which he mercifully
bestows on His Elect. He turns His eyes upon them, i. e.
has compassionate respect unto them. AUG. The five barley
loaves signify the old law; either because the law was
given to men not as yet spiritual, but carnal, i. e. under the

Side notes: Aug. Tr.xxiv. s. 1, 2.

Aug.lib. lxxxiii. Quæst. q. 61. in princ.

---

e V. 15. departed into a mountain   f V. 1. Jesus went over the sea of
Himself alone.   Galilee.

dominion of the five senses, (the multitude itself consisted
of five thousand:) or because the Law itself was given by
Moses in five books.   And the loaves being of barley is also
an allusion to the Law, which concealed the soul's vital
nourishment, under carnal ceremonies.   For in barley the
corn itself is buried under the most tenacious husk.   Or,
it alludes to the people who were not yet freed from the
husk of carnal appetite, which cling to their heart.   BEDE.
Barley is the food of cattle and slaves : and the old law was
given to slaves and cattle, i. e. to carnal men.   AUG. The
two fishes again, that gave the pleasant taste to the bread,
seem to signify the two authorities by which the people were
governed, the Royal, viz. and the Priestly; both of which
prefigure our Lord, who sustained both characters.   BEDE.
Or, by the two fishes are meant the saying or writings of
the Prophets, and the Psalmist.   And whereas the number
five refers to the five senses, a thousand stands for perfection.   But those who strive to obtain the perfect government
of their five senses, are called men, in consequence of their
superior powers : they have no womanly weaknesses ; but by
a sober and chaste life, earn the sweet refreshment of heavenly
wisdom.   AUG. The boy who had these is perhaps the
Jewish people, who, as it were, carried the loaves and fishes
after a servile fashion, and did not eat them.   That which
they carried, while shut up, was only a burden to them ;
when opened became their food.   BEDE. And well is it
said, *But what are these among so many?*   The Law was of
little avail, till He took it into His hand, i. e. fulfilled it,
and gave it a spiritual meaning.   *The Law made nothing
perfect.*   AUG. By the act of breaking He multiplied the
five loaves.   The five books of Moses, when expounded by
breaking, i. e. unfolding them, made many books.   AUG.
Our Lord by breaking, as it were, what was hard in the
Law, and opening what was shut, that time when He opened
the Scriptures to the disciples after the resurrection, brought
the Law out in its full meaning.   AUG. Our Lord's question
proved the ignorance of His disciples, i. e. the people's ignorance of the Law.   They lay on the grass, i. e. were carnally
minded, rested in carnal things, *for all flesh is grass.*   Men
are filled with the loaves, when what they hear with the ear, they
fulfil in practice.   AUG. And what are the fragments, but the

Bede.
Hom. in
Luc. c.
vi.
Aug.lib.
lxxxiv.
Quæst.
qu. 61.

Aug.
Tr.xxiv.
5.

Bede.
Aug.
xxiv. 5.

Heb. 7,
19.
Aug.
Tr.xxiv.
s. 5.
Aug.lib.
lxxxiii.
Quæst.
qu. 61.

Aug.
Tr.xxiv.
s. 5.

Isa. 40,
6.
Aug.
Tr.xxiv.
s. 6.

parts which the people could not eat? An intimation, that
those deeper truths, which the multitude cannot take in,
should be entrusted to those who are capable of receiving
them, and afterwards teaching them to others; as were the
Apostles. For which reason twelve baskets were filled with
them. ALCUIN. Baskets are used for servile work. The
baskets here are the Apostles and their followers, who,
though despised in this present life, are within filled with
the riches of spiritual sacraments. The Apostles too are
represented as baskets, because, that through them, the
doctrine of the Trinity was to be preached in the four parts
of the world. His not making new loaves, but multiplying
what there were, means that He did not reject the Old
Testament, but only developed and explained it.

15. When Jesus therefore perceived that they
would come and take him by force, to make him a
king, he departed again into a mountain himself
alone.

16. And when even was now come, his disciples
went down unto the sea,

17. And entered into a ship, and went over the sea
toward Capernaum. And it was now dark, and Jesus
was not come to them.

18. And the sea arose by reason of a great wind
that blew.

19. So when they had rowed about five and twenty
or thirty furlongs, they see Jesus walking on the sea,
and drawing nigh unto the ship: and they were
afraid.

20. But he saith unto them, It is I; be not afraid.

21. Then they willingly received him into the ship:
and immediately the ship was at the land whither they
went.

BEDE. The multitude concluding, from so great a miracle,
that He was merciful and powerful, wished to make
Him a king. For men like having a merciful king to rule
over them, and a powerful one to protect them. Our Lord

knowing this, retired to the mountain: *When Jesus therefore perceived that they would come and take Him by force to make Him a king, He departed again into a mountain Himself alone.* From this we gather, that our Lord went down from the mountain before, where He was sitting with His disciples, when He saw the multitude coming, and had fed them on the plain below. For how could He go up to the mountain again, unless He had come down from it. Aug. This is not at all inconsistent with what we read, that *He went up into a mountain apart to pray :* the object of escape being quite compatible with that of prayer. Indeed our Lord teaches us here, that whenever escape is necessary, there is great necessity for prayer. Aug. Yet He who feared to be made a king, was a king; not made king by men, (for He ever reigneth with the Father, in that He is the Son of God,) but making men kings: which kingdom of His the Prophets had foretold. Christ by being made man, made the believers in Him Christians, i. e. members of His kingdom, incorporated and purchased by His Word. And this kingdom will be made manifest, after the judgment; when the brightness of His saints shall be revealed. The disciples however, and the multitude who believed on Him, thought that He had come to reign now; and so would have taken Him by force, to make Him a king, wishing to anticipate His time, which He kept secret. CHRYS. See what the belly can do. They care no more for the violation of the Sabbath; all their zeal for God is fled, now that their bellies are filled: Christ has become a Prophet, and they wish to enthrone Him as king. But Christ makes His escape; to teach us to despise the dignities of the world. He dismisses His disciples, and goes up into the mountain.—These, when their Master had left them, went down in the evening to the sea; as we read; *And when even was now come, His disciples went down unto the sea.* They waited till evening, thinking He would come to them; and then, as He did not come, delayed no longer searching for Him, but in the ardour of love, *entered into a ship, and went over the sea toward Capernaum.* They went to Capernaum thinking they should find Him there. AUG. The Evangelist now returns to explain why they went, and

Aug.
de Con.
Ev. ii.
c. xlvii.
Mat.14,
23.

Aug.
Tr. xxv.
2.

Chrys.
Hom.
xlii. 3.

Hom.
xliii. 1.

Aug.
Tr. xxv.
s. 5.

relate what happened to them while they were crossing the lake: *And it was dark,* he says, *and Jesus was not come to them.* CHRYS. The mention of the time is not accidental, but meant to shew the strength of their love. They did not make excuses, and say, It is evening now, and night is coming on, but in the warmth of their love went into the ship. And now many things alarm them: the time, *And it was now dark;* and the weather, as we read next, *And the sea arose by reason of a great wind that blew;* their distance from land, *So when they had rowed about five and twenty or thirty furlongs.* BEDE. The way of speaking we use, when we are in doubt; about five and twenty, we say, or thirty. CHRYS. And at last He appears quite unexpectedly: *They see Jesus walking upon the sea, drawing nigh.* He reappears after His retirement, teaching them what it is to be forsaken, and stirring them to greater love; His reappearance manifesting His power. They were disturbed, *were afraid,* it is said. Our Lord comforts them: *But He saith unto them, It is I, be not afraid.* BEDE. He does not say, I am Jesus, but only *I am.* He trusts to their easily recognising a voice, which was so familiar to them, or, as is more probable, He shews that He was the same who said to Moses, *I am that I am.* CHRYS. He appeared to them in this way, to shew His power; for He immediately calmed the tempest: *Then they wished to receive Him into the ship; and immediately the ship was at the land, whither they went.* So great was the calm, He did not even enter the ship, in order to work a greater miracle, and to shew his Divinity more clearly[g]. THEOPHYL. Observe the three miracles here; the first, His walking on the sea; the second, His stilling the waves; the third, His putting them immediately on shore, which they were some distance off, when our Lord appeared. CHRYS. Jesus does not shew Himself to the crowd walking on the sea, such a miracle being too much for them to hear. Nor even to the disciples did He shew Himself long, but disappeared immediately. AUG. Mark's[1] account does not contradict this. He says indeed that our Lord told the disciples first to enter the ship, and go before Him over the sea, while He dismissed the crowds, and that when the crowd was

Marginal notes:
Chrys. Hom. xlii. 1.

Bede in v. cap.

Joan. Chrys. Hom. xliii. 1.

Bede in Matt. c. xiv.

Exod. 3, 14. Chrys. Hom. xliii.s.1.

Chrys. Hom. xliii. 1.

[1] Matthew, in Aquinas and Aug. De Con. Ev. l. ii. c. xlvii. Mark 6, 45.

[g] ἤθελον λαβεῖν αὐτὸν in the Greek: our translation, "they willingly received Him."

dismissed, He went up alone into the mountain to pray:
while John places His going up alone in the mountain first,
and then says, *And when even was now come, His disciples
went down unto the sea.* But it is easy to see that John
relates that as done *afterwards* by the disciples, which our
Lord had ordered *before* His departure to the mountain.
Chrys. CHRYS. Or take another explanation. This miracle seems
Hom.
xliii. 1. to me to be a different one, from the one given in Matthew:
for there they do not receive Him into the ship immediately,
whereas here they do[h]: and there the storm lasts for some
time, whereas here as soon as He speaks, there is a calm.
He often repeats the same miracle in order to impress it on
Aug. men's minds. AUG. There is a mystical meaning in our
Tr. xxv.
s. 3. Lord's feeding the multitude, and ascending the mountain:
et seq. for thus was it prophesied of Him, *So shall the congregation
Ps. 7. of the people come about Thee: for their sake therefore lift
up Thyself again:* i. e. that the congregation of the people
may come about Thee, lift up Thyself again. But why is it
fled; for they could not have detained Him against His
will? This fleeing has a meaning; viz. that His flight is
above our comprehension ; just as, when you do not understand a thing, you say, It escapes me. He fled alone unto
the mountain, because He is ascended from above all heavens.
But on His ascension aloft a storm came upon the disciples in
the ship, i. e. the Church, and it became dark, the light, i. e.
Jesus, having gone. As the end of the world draws nigh,
error increases, iniquity abounds. Light again is love, ac-
1 John cording to John, *He that hateth his brother is in darkness.*
2, 9.
The waves and storms and winds then that agitate the ship,
are the clamours of the evil speaking, and love waxing cold.
Howbeit the wind, and storm, and waves, and darkness were
Matt. not able to stop, and sink the vessel; *For he that endureth
10, 22. to the end, the same shall be saved.* As the number five
has reference to the Law, the books of Moses being five, the
number five and twenty, being made up of five pieces, has
the same meaning. And this law was imperfect, before the
Gospel came. Now the number of perfection is six, so
therefore five is multiplied by six, which makes thirty: i. e.

[h] So in the Catena. But Chrysostom,   to be in doubt longer in St. Matthew
Why did not they at once receive   whether it was our Lord.
this? alluding to the disciples seeming

the law is fulfilled by the Gospel. To those then who fulfil
the law Jesus comes treading on the waves, i. e. trampling
under foot all the swellings of the world, all the loftiness of
men: and yet such tribulations remain, that even they who
believe on Jesus, fear lest they should be lost. THEOPHYL.
When either men or devils try to terrify us, let us hear
Christ saying, *It is I, be not afraid,* i. e. I am ever near you,
God unchangeable, immoveable; let not any false fears
destroy your faith in Me. Observe too our Lord did not
come when the danger was beginning, but when it was
ending. He suffers us to remain in the midst of dangers
and tribulations, that we may be proved thereby, and flee for
succour to Him Who is able to give us deliverance when we
least expect it. When man's understanding can no longer
help him, then the Divine deliverance comes. If we are
willing also to receive Christ into the ship, i. e. to live in
our hearts, we shall find ourselves immediately in the place,
where we wish to be, i. e. heaven. BEDE. This ship, however,
does not carry an idle crew; they are all stout rowers; i. e.
in the Church not the idle and effeminate, but the stre-
nuous and persevering in good works, attain to the harbour
of everlasting salvation.

22. The day following, when the people which stood
on the other side of the sea saw that there was none
other boat there, save that one whereinto his disciples
were entered, and that Jesus went not with his disciples into the boat, but that his disciples were gone
away alone;

23. (Howbeit there came other boats from Tiberias
nigh unto the place where they did eat bread, after
that the Lord had given thanks:)

24. When the people therefore saw that Jesus was
not there, neither his disciples, they also took shipping,
and came to Capernaum, seeking for Jesus.

25. And when they had found him on the other
side of the sea, they said unto him, Rabbi, when
camest thou hither?

26. Jesus answered them and said, Verily, verily, I say unto you, Ye seek me, not because ye saw the miracles, but because ye did eat of the loaves, and were filled.

27. Labour not for the meat which perisheth, but for that meat which endureth unto everlasting life, which the Son of man shall give unto you: for him hath God the Father sealed.

Chrys. Hom. xliii. 2.

CHRYS. Our Lord, though He did not actually shew Himself to the multitude walking on the sea, yet gave them the opportunity of inferring what had taken place; *The day following, the people which stood on the other side of the sea saw that there was none other boat there, save that one whereinto His disciples were entered, and that Jesus went not with His disciples into the boat, but that His disciples were gone away alone.* What was this but to suspect that He had walked across the sea, on His going away? For He could not have gone over in a ship, as there was only one there, that in which His disciples had entered; and He had not gone in with them.

Aug. Tr. xxv. 8.

AUG. Knowledge of the miracle was conveyed to them indirectly. Other ships had come to the place where they had eaten bread; in these they went after Him; *Howbeit there came other boats from Tiberias, nigh unto the place where they did eat bread, after that the Lord had given thanks. When the people therefore saw that Jesus was not there, neither His disciples, they also took shipping, and came to Capernaum, seeking for Jesus.*

Chrys. Hom. xliii. 1.

CHRYS. Yet after so great a miracle, they did not ask Him how He had passed over, or shew any concern about it: as appears from what follows; *And when they had found Him on the other side of the sea, they said unto Him, Rabbi, when camest Thou hither?* Except we say that this *when* meant *how.* And observe their lightness of mind. After saying, *This is that Prophet,* and wishing to take Him by force to make Him king, when they find Him, nothing of the kind is thought of.

Aug. Tr. xxv. 8.

AUG. So He Who had fled to the mountain, mixes and converses with the multitude. Only just now they would have kept Him, and made Him king.

But after the sacrament of the miracle, He begins to discourse, and fills their souls with His word, whose bodies He had satisfied with bread. ALCUIN. [1] He who set an example of declining praise, and earthly power, sets teachers also an example of deliverance in preaching. CHRYS. Kindness and lenity are not always expedient. To the indolent or insensible disciple the spur must be applied; and this the Son of God does. For when the multitude comes with soft speeches, *Rabbi, when camest Thou hither?* He shews them that He did not desire the honour that cometh from man, by the severity of His answer, which both exposes the motive on which they acted, and rebukes it. *Jesus answered them and said, Verily, verily, I say unto you, Ye seek Me, not because ye saw the miracles, but because ye did eat of the loaves, and were filled.* AUG. As if He said, Ye seek Me to satisfy the flesh, not the spirit. CHRYS. After the rebuke, however, He proceeds to teach them: *Labour not for the meat which perisheth, but for that meat which endureth unto everlasting life;* meaning, Ye seek for temporal food, whereas I only fed your bodies, that ye might seek the more diligently for that food, which is not temporary, but contains eternal life. ALCUIN. Bodily food only supports the flesh of the outward man, and must be taken not once for all, but daily; whereas spiritual food remaineth for ever, imparting perpetual fulness, and immortality. AUG. Under the figure of food He alludes to Himself. Ye seek Me, He saith, for the sake of something else; seek Me for My own sake. CHRYS. But, inasmuch as some who wish to live in sloth, pervert this precept, *Labour not, &c.* it is well to notice what Paul says, *Let him that stole steal no more, but rather let him labour, working with his hands the thing which is good, that he may have to give to him that needeth.* And he himself too, when he resided with Aquila and Priscilla at Corinth, worked with his hand. By saying, *Labour not for the meat which perisheth,* our Lord does not mean to tell us to be idle; but to work, and give alms. This is that meat which perisheth not; to labour for the meat which perisheth, is to be devoted to the interests of this life. Our Lord saw that the multitude had no thought of believing, and only wished to fill their

Chrys. Hom. xliv. 1.

Aug. Tr. xxv. 10.

Chrys. Hom. xliv. 1.

Aug. Tr. xxv. 10.

Chrys. Hom. xliv. 1.

Ephes. 4, 28.

---

[1] Not found in Alcuin, but in a Gloss.

bellies, without working; and this He justly called the meat
which perisheth. AUG. As He told the woman of Samaria
above, *If thou knewest Who it is that saith to thee, Give me
to drink, thou wouldest have asked of Him, and He would
have given thee living water.* So He says here, *Which the
Son of man shall give unto you.* ALCUIN. When, through
the hand of the priest, thou receivest the Body of Christ,
think not of the priest which thou seest, but of the Priest
thou dost not see. The priest is the dispenser of this food,
not the author. The Son of man gives Himself to us, that
we may abide in Him, and He in us. Do not conceive that
Son of man to be the same as other sons of men: He
stands alone in abundance of grace, separate and distinct
from all the rest: for that Son of man is the Son of God, as
it follows, *For Him hath God the Father sealed.* To seal is
to put a mark upon; so the meaning is, Do not despise Me
because I am the Son of man, for I am the Son of man in
such sort, as that the Father hath sealed Me, i. e. given Me
something peculiar, to the end that I should not be confounded with the human race, but that the human race should
be delivered by Me. HILARY. A seal throws out a perfect
impression of the stamp, at the same time that it takes in
that impression. This is not a perfect illustration of the
Divine nativity: for sealing supposes matter, different kinds
of matter, the impression of harder upon softer. Yet He
who was God Only-Begotten, and the Son of man only by
the Sacrament of our salvation, makes use of it to express
the Father's fulness as stamped upon Himself. He wishes to
shew the Jews He has the power of giving the eternal meat,
because He contained in Himself the fulness of God. CHRYS.
Or sealed, i. e. sent Him for this purpose, viz. to bring us
food; or, sealed, was revealed the Gospel by means of His
witness. ALCUIN. To take the passage mystically: on the
day following, i. e. after the ascension of Christ, the multitude
standing in good works, not lying in worldly pleasures,
expects Jesus to come to them. The one ship is the one
Church: the other ships which come besides, are the conventicles of heretics, who seek their own, not the things of
Jesus Christ. Wherefore He well says, *Ye seek Me, because
ye did eat of the loaves.* AUG. How many there are who

seek Jesus, only to gain some temporary benefit. One man has a matter of business, in which he wants the assistance of the clergy; another is oppressed by a more powerful neighbour, and flies to the Church for refuge: Jesus is scarcely ever sought for Jesus' sake. GREG. In their persons too our Lord condemns all those within the holy Church, who, when brought near to God by sacred Orders, do not seek the recompense of righteousness, but the interests of this present life. To follow our Lord, when filled with bread, is to use Holy Church as a means of livelihood; and to seek our Lord not for the miracle's sake, but for the loaves, is to aspire to a religious office, not with a view to increase of grace, but to add to our worldly means. BEDE. They too seek Jesus, not for Jesus' sake, but for something else, who ask in their prayers not for eternal, but temporal blessings. The mystical meaning is, that the conventicles of heretics are without the company of Christ and His disciples. And other ships coming, is the sudden growth of heresies. By the crowd, which saw that Jesus was not there, or His disciples, are designated those who seeing the errors of heretics, leave them and turn to the true faith.

Greg. xxiii. Moral. (c. xxv.)

28. Then said they unto him, What shall we do, that we might work the works of God?

29. Jesus answered and said unto them, This is the work of God, that ye believe on him whom he hath sent.

30. They said therefore unto him, What sign shewest thou then, that we may see, and believe thee? what dost thou work?

31. Our fathers did eat manna in the desert; as it is written, He gave them bread from heaven to eat.

32. Then said Jesus unto them, Verily, verily, I say unto you, Moses gave you not that bread from heaven; but my Father giveth you the true bread from heaven.

33. For the bread of God is he which cometh down from heaven, and giveth life unto the world.

34. Then said they unto him, Lord, evermore give us this bread.

ALCUIN. They understood that the meat, which remaineth unto eternal life, was the work of God: and therefore they ask Him what to do to work the work of God, i. e. obtain the meat: *Then said they unto Him, What shall we do that we might work the works of God?* BEDE. i. e. By keeping what commandments shall we be able to fulfil the law of God?

Chrys. Hom. xlv. 1. CHRYS. But they said this, not that they might learn, and do them, but to obtain from Him another exhibition of His bounty. THEOPHYL. Christ, though He saw it would not avail, yet for the good of others afterwards, answered their question; and shewed them, or rather the whole world, what was the work of God: *Jesus answered and said unto them, This is the work of God, that ye believe on Him whom He hath sent.*

Aug. Tr. xxv. in Joan. AUG. He does not say, That ye believe Him, but, *that ye believe on Him.* For the devils believed Him, and did not believe on Him; and we believe Paul, but do not believe on Paul. To believe on Him is believing to love, believing to honour Him, believing to go unto Him, and be made members incorporate of His Body. The faith, which God requires of us, is that which worketh by love. Faith indeed is distinguished from works by the Apostle,

Rom. 3, 28. who says, *That man is justified by faith without the deeds of the law.* But the works indeed which appear good, without faith in Christ, are not really so, not being referred

Rom. 10, 4. to that end, which makes them good. *For Christ is the end of the law for righteousness to every one that believeth.* And therefore our Lord would not separate faith from works, but said that faith itself was the doing the work of God; He saith not, This is your work, but, *This is the work of God, that ye believe on Him:* in order that he that glorieth

Aug. xxv. 12. might glory in the Lord. AUG. To eat then that meat which endureth unto everlasting life, is to *believe* on Him. Why dost thou make ready thy tooth and thy belly? Only believe, and thou hast eaten already. As He called on them to believe, they still asked for miracles whereby to believe; *They said therefore unto Him, What sign shewest Thou then, that we may see and believe Thee? What dost Thou work?*

CHRYS. Nothing can be more unreasonable than their asking Chrys.
for another miracle, as if none had been given already.   And $_{xlv.\ 1.}^{Hom.}$
they do not even leave the choice of the miracle to our Lord;
but would oblige Him to give them just that sign, which was
given to their fathers: *Our fathers did eat manna in the
desert.* ALCUIN. And to exalt the miracle of the manna,
they quote the Psalm, *As it is written, He gave them bread
from heaven to eat.* CHRYS. Whereas many miracles were Chrys.
performed in Egypt, at the Red Sea, and in the desert, they $_{xlv.\ 1.}^{Hom.}$
remembered this one the best of any.   Such is the force of
appetite.   They do not mention this miracle as the work
either of God, or of Moses, in order to avoid raising Him on
the one hand to an equality with God, or lowering Him on the
other by a comparison with Moses; but they take a middle
ground, only saying, *Our fathers did eat manna in the
desert.* AUG. Or thus; Our Lord sets Himself above Moses, Aug.
who did not dare to say that He gave the meat which perisheth $_{s.\ 12.}^{Tr.\ xxv.}$
not.   The multitude therefore remembering what Moses had
done, and wishing for some greater miracle, say, as it were,
Thou promisest the meat which perisheth not, and doest not
works equal to those Moses did.   He gave us not barley
loaves, but manna from heaven. CHRYS. Our Lord might Chrys.
have replied, that He had done miracles greater than Moses: $_{xxv.\ 1.}^{Hom.}$
but it was not the time for such a declaration.   One thing
He desired, viz. to bring them to taste the spiritual meat:
then *Jesus said unto them, Verily, verily, I say unto you,
Moses gave you not that bread from heaven; but My Father
giveth you the true bread from heaven.* Did not the manna
come from heaven? True, but in what sense did it? The
same in which the birds are called, the birds of heaven[k];
and just as it is said in the Psalm, *The Lord thundered out* Ps. 17.
of heaven. He calls it the true bread, not because the
miracle of the manna was false, but because it was the
figure, not the reality.   He does not say too, Moses gave it
you not, but I: but He puts God for Moses, Himself for
the manna. AUG. As if He said, That manna was the type Aug.
of this food, of which I just now spoke; and which all my $_{31.}^{Tr.\ xxv.}$
miracles refer to.   You like my miracles, you despise what
is signified by them.   This bread which God gives, and

[k] Volucres cœli, Vulgate translation of fowls of the air.

which this manna represented, is the Lord Jesus Christ, as we read next, *For the bread of God is He which cometh down from heaven, and giveth life unto the world.* BEDE. Not to the physical world, but to men, its inhabitants. THEOPHYL. He calls Himself the true bread, because the only-begotten Son of God, made man, was principally signified by the manna. For manna means literally, what is this? The Israelites were astonished at first on finding it, and asked one another what it was. And the Son of God, made man, is in an especial sense this mysterious manna, which we ask about, saying, What is this? How can the Son of God be the Son of man? How can one person consist of two natures? ALCUIN. Who by the humanity, which was assumed, came down from heaven, and by the divinity, which assumed it, gives life to the world. THEOPHYL. But this bread, being essentially life, (for He is the Son of the living Father,) in quickening all things, does but what is natural to Him to do. For as natural bread supports our weak flesh, so Christ, by the operations of the Spirit, gives life to the soul; and even incorruption to the body, (for at the resurrection the body will be made incorruptible.) Wherefore He says, that He *giveth life unto the world.* Chrys. Hom. xlv. 1. CHRYS. Not only to the Jews, but to the whole world. The multitude, however, still attached a low meaning to His words: *Then said they unto Him, Lord, evermore give us this bread.* They say, *Give us this bread,* not, Ask Thy Father to give it us: whereas He had said that His Father gave this bread. Aug. Tr. xxv. 13. AUG. As the woman of Samaria, when our Lord told her, *Whosoever drinketh of this water shall never thirst,* thought He meant natural water, and said, *Sir, give me this water,* that she might never be in want of it again: in the same way these say, Give us this bread, which refreshes, supports, and fails not.

35. And Jesus said unto them, I am the bread of life: he that cometh to me shall never hunger; and he that believeth on me shall never thirst.

36. But I said unto you, That ye also have seen me, and believe not.

37. All that the Father giveth me shall come to me; and him that cometh to me I will in no wise cast out.

38. For I came down from heaven, not to do mine own will, but the will of him that sent me.

39. And this is the Father's will which hath sent me, that of all which he hath given me I should lose nothing, but should raise it up again at the last day.

40. And this is the will of him that sent me, that every one which seeth the Son, and believeth on him, may have everlasting life: and I will raise him up at the last day.

CHRYS. Our Lord now proceeds to set forth mysteries; and first speaks of His Divinity: *And Jesus said unto them, I am the bread of life.* He does not say this of His body, for He speaks of that at the end ; *The bread that I will give you is My flesh.* Here He is speaking of His Divinity. The *flesh* is bread, by virtue of the Word ; this bread is heavenly bread, on account of the Spirit which dwelleth in it. THEO-PHYL. He does not say, *I am the bread* of nourishment, but *of life*, for, whereas all things brought death, Christ hath quickened us by Himself. But the life here, is not our common life, but that which is not cut short by death : *He that cometh to Me shall never hunger; and He that believeth on Me shall never thirst.* AUG. *He that cometh to Me*, i. e. that believeth on Me, *shall never hunger*, has the same meaning as shall never thirst ; both signi-fying that eternal society, where there is no want. THEO-PHYL. Or, *shall never hunger or thirst*, i. e. shall never be wearied[1] of hearing the word of God, and shall never thirst as to the understanding: as though He had not the water of baptism, and the sanctification of the Spirit. AUG. Ye desire bread from heaven: but, though you have it before you, you eat it not. This is what I told you: *But I said unto you, that ye also have seen Me, and believe not.* ALCUIN. As if He said, I did not say what I did to you about the bread, because I thought you would eat it, but rather to

Chrys.
Hom.
xlv. 2.

Aug.
Tr. xxv.
14.

1 non
famem
feret ac-
cipiendi
sermo-
nem.

Aug.
Tr. xxv.
14.

convict you of unbelief. I say, that ye see Me, and believe

Chrys. Hom. xliv. 2. c. 5. not. CHRYS. Or, *I said to you*, refers to the testimony of the Scriptures, of which He said above, *They are they which testify of Me;* and again, *I am come in My Father's name, and ye receive Me not. That ye have seen Me,* is a silent

Aug. Tr. xxv. 14. allusion to His miracles. AUG. But, because ye have seen Me, and believed not, I have not therefore lost the people of God: *All that the Father giveth Me, shall come unto Me; and him that cometh to Me, I will in no wise cast out.* BEDE. *All,* He saith, absolutely, to shew the fulness of the number who should believe. These are they which the Father gives the Son, when, by His secret inspiration, He makes them believe in the Son. ALCUIN. Whomsoever therefore the Father draweth to belief in Me, he, by faith, shall come to Me, that he may be joined to Me. *And those,* who in the steps of faith and good works, *shall come to Me, I will in no wise cast out;* i. e. in the secret habitation of a pure conscience, he shall dwell with Me, and at the last I will receive him to

Aug. Tr. xxv. 14. everlasting felicity. AUG. That inner place, whence there is no casting out, is a great sanctuary, a secret chamber, where is neither weariness, or the bitterness of evil thoughts, or the

Mat. 25. cross of pain and temptation: of which it is said, *Enter thou*

Chrys. Hom. xliv. 2. *into the joy of thy Lord.* CHRYS. The expression, *that the Father giveth Me,* shews that it is no accident whether a man believes or not, and that belief is not the work of human cogitation, but requires a revelation from on high, and a mind devout enough to receive the revelation. Not that they are free from blame, whom the Father does not give, for they are deficient even in that which lies in their own power, the will to believe. This is a virtual rebuke to their unbelief, as it shews that whoever does not believe in Him, transgresses the Father's will. Paul, however, says, that He gives them

1 Cor. 15, 24. up to the Father: *When He shall have given up the kingdom to God, even the Father.* But as the Father, in giving, does not take from Himself, so neither does the Son when He gives up. The Son is said to give up to the Father, because we are brought to the Father by Him. And of the Father at

1 Cor. 1, 9. the same time we read, *By Whom ye were called unto the fellowship of His Son.* Whoever then, our Lord says, cometh to Me, shall be saved, for to save such I took up

flesh: *For I came down from heaven not to do Mine own will, but the will of Him that sent Me.* But what? Hast thou one will, He another? No, certainly. Mark what He says afterwards; *And this is the will of Him that sent Me, that every one which seeth the Son, and believeth on Him, should have everlasting life.* And this is the Son's will too; *For the Son quickeneth whom He will.* He says then, I c. 5, 21. came to do nothing but what the Father wills, for I have no will distinct from My Father's: all things that the Father hath are Mine. But this not now: He reserves these higher truths for the end of His ministry. AUG. This is the Aug. reason why He does not cast out those who come to Him. Tr. xxv. 15. *For I came down from heaven not to do Mine own will, but the will of Him that sent Me.* The soul departed from God, because it was proud. Pride casts us out, humility restores us. When a physician in the treatment of a disease, cures certain outward symptoms, but not the cause which produces them, his cure is only temporary. So long as the cause remains, the disease may return. That the cause then of all diseases, i. e. pride, might be eradicated, the Son of God humbled Himself. Why art thou proud, O man? The Son of God humbled Himself for thee. It might shame thee, perhaps, to imitate a humble man; but imitate at least a humble God. And this is the proof of His humility: *I came not to do Mine own will, but the will of Him that sent Me.* Pride does its own will; humility the will of God. HILARY. Hilar. Not that He does what He does not wish. He fulfils iii. de Trin. obediently His Father's will, wishing also Himself to fulfil c. 9. that will. AUG. For this very reason therefore, I will not cast Aug. out Him that cometh to Me; because I came not to do Mine Tr. xxv own will. I came to teach humility, by being humble in Joan. 16. Myself. He that cometh to Me, is made a member of Me, and necessarily humble, because He will not do His own will, but the will of God; and therefore is not cast out. He was cast out, as proud; he returns to Me humble, he is not sent away, except for pride again; he who keeps his humility, falleth not from the truth. And further, that He does not cast out such, because He came not to do His will, He shews when He says, *And this is the Father's will which hath sent*

Me, that of all which He hath given Me, I should lose

Mat. 18, *nothing.* Every one of an humble mind is given to Him: *It*
14. *is not the will of your Father, that one of these little ones should*
perish. The swelling ones may perish; of the little ones none

Mat. 18, can; for *except ye be as a little child, ye shall not enter into*
3. 5. *the kingdom of heaven.* AUG. They therefore who by God's
Aug.
de Cor. unerring providence are foreknown, and predestined, called,
et Gra-
tia,c.ix. justified, glorified, even before their new birth, or before
they are born at all, are already the sons of God, and cannot
possibly perish; these are they who truly come to Christ.
By Him there is given also perseverance in good unto the
end; which is given only to those who will not perish.

Chrys. Those who do not persevere will perish. CHRYS. *I should*
Hom.
xliv. 3. *lose nothing;* He lets them know, he does not desire his own
honour, but their salvation. After these declarations, *I will*
in no wise cast out, and *I should lose nothing,* He adds,
But should raise it up at the last day. In the general
resurrection the wicked will be cast out, according to Matthew,

Mat. 22, *Take him, and cast him into outer darkness.* And, *Who is*
13.
Mat. 10, *able to cast both soul and body into hell.* He often brings
23. in mention of the resurrection for this purpose: viz. to warn
men not to judge of God's providence from present events,

Aug. but to carry on their ideas to another world. AUG. See how
Tr. xxv.
19. the twofold resurrection is expressed here. He who cometh
to Me, shall forthwith rise again; by becoming humble, and
a member of Me. But then He proceeds; *But I will raise*
him up at the last day. To explain the words, *All that the*
Father hath given Me, and, *I should lose nothing,* He
adds; *And this is the will of Him that hath sent Me, that*
every one which seeth the Son, and believeth on Him, may have
everlasting life: and I will raise him up at the last day.

c. 5, 24. Above He said, *Whoso heareth My word, and believeth on Him*
that sent Me: now it is, *Every one which seeth the Son, and*
believeth on Him. He does not say, believe on the Father,
because it is the same thing to believe on the Father, and on
the Son; for *as the Father hath life in Himself, even so hath*
He given to the Son to have life in Himself; and again, *That*
whoso seeth the Son and believeth on Him, should have ever-
lasting life; i. e. by believing, by passing over to life, as at

the first resurrection. But this is only the first resurrection, He alludes to the second when He says, *And I will raise him up at the last day.*

41. The Jews then murmured at him, because he said, I am the bread which came down from heaven.

42. And they said, Is not this Jesus, the son of Joseph, whose father and mother we know? how is it then that he saith, I came down from heaven?

43. Jesus therefore answered and said unto them, Murmur not among yourselves.

44. No man can come to me, except the Father which hath sent me draw him: and I will raise him up at the last day.

45. It is written in the prophets, And they shall be all taught of God. Every man therefore that hath heard, and hath learned of the Father, cometh unto me.

46. Not that any man hath seen the Father, save he which is of God, he hath seen the Father.

CHRYS. The Jews, so long as they thought to get food for their carnal eating, had no misgivings; but when this hope was taken away, then, we read, *the Jews murmured at Him because He said, I am the bread which came down from heaven.* This was only a pretence. The real cause of their complaint was that they were disappointed in their expectation of a bodily feast. As yet however they reverenced Him, for His miracle; and only expressed their discontent by murmurs. What these were we read next: *And they said, Is not this Jesus, the Son of Joseph, whose father and mother we know? how is it then that He saith, I came down from heaven?* AUG. But they were far from being fit for that heavenly bread, and did not hunger for it. For they had not that hunger of the inner man. CHRYS. It is evident that they did not yet know of His miraculous birth: for they call Him the Son of Joseph. Nor are they blamed for this. Our Lord does not reply, I am not the Son of Joseph: for the miracle of His birth would have overpowered them.

Chrys.
Hom.
xlvi. 1.

Aug.
Tr.xxxvi.
1.

Chrys.
Hom.
xlvi. 1.

And if the birth according to the flesh were above their belief, how much more that higher and ineffable birth.

Aug.
Tr.xxvi.
AUG. He took man's flesh upon Him, but not after the manner of men; for, His Father being in heaven, He chose a mother upon earth, and was born of her without a father. The answer to the murmurers next follows: *Jesus therefore answered and said unto them, Murmur not among yourselves;* as if to say, I know why ye hunger not after this bread, and so cannot understand it, and do not seek it: *No man can come to Me except the Father who hath sent Me draw him.* This is the doctrine of grace: none cometh, except he be drawn. But whom the Father draws, and whom not, and why He draws one, and not another, presume not to decide, if thou wouldest avoid falling into error. Take the doctrine as it is given thee: and, if thou art not drawn,

Chrys.
Hom.
xlvi. 1.
pray that thou mayest be. CHRYS. But here the Manichees attack us, asserting that nothing is in our own power. Our Lord's words however do not destroy our free agency, but only shew that we need Divine assistance. For He is speaking not of one who comes without the concurrence of his own will, but one who has many hindrances in the way of his

Aug.
Tr.xxvi.
2. et sq.
coming. AUG. Now if we are drawn to Christ without our own will, we believe without our own will; the will is not exercised, but compulsion is applied. But, though a man can enter the Church involuntarily, he cannot believe other than voluntarily; *for with the heart man believeth unto righteousness.* Therefore if he who is drawn, comes without his will, he does not believe; if he does not believe, he does not come. For we do not come to Christ, by running, or walking, but by believing, not by the motion of the body, but the will of the mind. Thou art drawn by thy will. But what

Ps. 36.
is it to be drawn by the will? *Delight thou in the Lord, and He will give thee thy heart's desire.* There is a certain craving of the heart, to which that heavenly bread is pleasant. If the Poet could say, " Trahit sua quemque voluptas," how much more strongly may we speak of a man being drawn to Christ, i. e. being delighted with truth, happiness, justice, eternal life, all which is Christ? Have the bodily senses their pleasures, and has not the soul hers? Give me one who loves, who longs, who burns, who sighs for the source of

his being and his eternal home; and he will know what I
mean. But why did He say, *Except my Father draw him?*
If we are to be drawn, let us be drawn by Him to whom
His love saith, *Draw me, we will run after Thee.* But Cant. 1,
let us see what is meant by it. The Father draws to the ⁴·
Son those who believe on the Son, as thinking that He has
God for His Father. For the Father begat the Son equal to
Himself; and whoso thinks and believes really and seriously
that He on Whom He believes is equal to the Father, him the
Father draws to the Son. Arius believed Him to be a
creature; the Father drew not him. Thomas says, Christ is
only a man. Because he so believes, the Father draws him
not. He drew Peter who said, *Thou art the Christ, the Son* Mat. 16.
of the living God; to whom accordingly it was told, *For flesh*
and blood hath not revealed it unto thee, but My Father which
is in heaven. That revelation is the drawing. For if earthly
objects, when put before us, draw us; how much more shall
Christ,when revealed by the Father? For what doth the soul more
long after than truth ? But here men hunger, there they will be
filled. Wherefore He adds, *And I will raise him up at the last*
day : as if He said, He shall be filled with that, for which
he now thirsts, at the resurrection of the dead; for I will
raise him up. AUG. Or the Father draws to the Son, by the Aug. de
works which He did by Him. CHRYS. Great indeed is the Qu. Nov.
et Vet.
Son's dignity; the Father draws men, and the Son raises them Chrys.
up. This is no division of works, but an equality of power. Hom.
xlvi. 1.
He then shews the way in which the Father draws. *It is*
written in the Prophets, And they shall all be taught of
God. You see the excellence of faith; that it cannot be
learnt from men, or by the teaching of man, but only from
God Himself. The Master sits, dispensing His truth to all,
pouring out His doctrine to all. But if all are to be taught
of God, how is it that some believe not? Because all here
only means the generality, or, all that have the will. AUG. Aug.
Or thus; When a schoolmaster is the only one in a town, we de Præ-
dest.
say loosely, This man teaches all here to read; not that all Sancto-
learn of him, but that he teaches all who do learn. And in rum,
c. viii.
the same way we say that God teaches all men to come to Aug.
Christ: not that all do come, but that no one comes in any super
Joan.
other way. AUG. All the men of that kingdom shall be Tr. xxv.
7.

taught of God; they shall hear nothing from men: for, though in this world what they hear with the outward ear is from men, yet what they understand is given them from within; from within is light and revelation. I force certain sounds into your ears, but unless He is within to reveal their meaning, how, O ye Jews, can ye acknowledge Me, ye whom the Father hath not taught? BEDE. He uses the plural, *In the Prophets*, because all the Prophets being filled with one and the same spirit, their prophecies, though different, all tended to the same end; and with whatever any one of them says, all the rest agree; as with the prophecy of Joel, *All shall be taught of God.* GLOSS. These words are not found in Joel, but something like them; *Be glad then ye children of Sion, and rejoice in the Lord your God, for He hath given you a Teacher.* And more expressly in Isaiah, *And all thy children shall be taught of the Lord.* CHRYS. An important distinction. All men before learnt the things of God through men; now they learn them through the Only Son of God, and the Holy Spirit. AUG. All that are taught of God come to the Son, because they have heard and learnt from the Father of the Son: wherefore He proceeds, *Every man that hath heard, and hath learned of the Father, cometh to Me.* But if every one that hath heard and learnt of the Father cometh, every one that hath not heard of the Father hath not learnt. For beyond the reach of the bodily senses is this school, in which the Father is heard, and men taught to come to the Son. Here we have not to do with the carnal ear, but the ear of the heart; for here is the Son Himself, the Word by which the Father teacheth, and together with Him the Holy Spirit: the operations of the three Persons being inseparable from each other. This is attributed however principally to the Father, because from Him proceeds the Son, and the Holy Spirit. Therefore the grace which the Divine bounty imparts in secret to men's hearts, is rejected by none from hardness of heart: seeing it is given in the first instance, in order to take away hard-heartedness. Why then does He not teach all to come to Christ? Because those whom He teaches, He teaches in mercy; and those whom He teaches not, He teaches not in judgment. But if we say, that those, whom He teaches not, wish to learn, we

Joel 2, 23.
Quia dedit nobis lectorem justitiæ. Vulg.
Isa. 54, 13.
Chrys. Hom. xlvi. 1.
Aug. de Præ-dest. Sancto-rum, c. viii. et seq.

shall be answered, Why then is it said, *Wilt thou not turn* Ps.84,6.
again, and quicken us? If God does not make willing minds
out of unwilling, why prayeth the Church, according to our
Lord's command, for her persecutors? For no one can say,
I believed, and therefore He called me: rather the preventing mercy of God called him, that he might believe. AUG. Aug.
Behold then how the Father draweth; not by laying a neces- Tr. xxvi.
sity on man, but by teaching the truth. To draw, belongeth seq.
to God: *Every one that hath heard, and hath learned of the
Father, cometh to Me.* What then? Hath Christ taught
nothing? Not so. What if men saw not the Father teaching, but saw the Son. So then the Father taught, the Son
spoke. As I teach you by My word, so the Father teaches
by His Word. But He Himself explains the matter, if we
read on: *Not that any man hath seen the Father, save He
which is of God, He hath seen the Father;* as if He said,
Do not when I tell you, *Every man that hath heard and
learnt of the Father,* say to yourselves, We have never seen
the Father, and how then can we have learnt from Him?
Hear Him then in Me. I know the Father, and am from Him,
just as a word is from him who speaks it; i. e. not the mere
passing sound, but that which remaineth with the speaker,
and draweth the hearer. CHRYS. We are all from God. Chrys.
That which belongs peculiarly and principally to the Son, xlvi.s.1.
He omits the mention of, as being unsuitable to the weakness
of His hearers.

47. Verily, verily, I say unto you, He that believeth
on me hath everlasting life.

48. I am that bread of life.

49. Your fathers did eat manna in the wilderness,
and are dead.

50. This is the bread which cometh down from
heaven, that a man may eat thereof, and not die.

51. I am the living bread which came down from
heaven: if any man eat of this bread, he shall live for
ever.

AUG. Our Lord wishes to reveal what He is; *Verily, verily,* Aug.
Tr.xxvi.
s. 10.

I say unto you, He that believeth on Me, hath everlasting life. As if He said; He that believeth on Me hath Me: but what is it to have Me? It is to have eternal life: for the Word which was in the beginning with God is life eternal, and the life was the light of men. Life underwent death, that life might kill death. CHRYS. The multitude being urgent for bodily food, and reminding Him of that which was given to their fathers, He tells them that the manna was only a type of that spiritual food which was now to be tasted in reality, *I am that bread of life.* CHRYS. He calls Himself the bread of life, because He constitutes one life, both present, and to come. AUG. And because they had taunted Him with the manna, He adds, *Your fathers did eat manna in the wilderness, and are dead.* Your fathers they are, for ye are like them; murmuring sons of murmuring fathers. For in nothing did that people offend God more, than by their murmurs against Him. And therefore are they dead, because what they saw they believed, what they did not see they believed not, nor understood. CHRYS. The addition, *In the wilderness,* is not put in without meaning, but to remind them how short a time the manna lasted; only till the entrance into the land of promise. And because the bread which Christ gave seemed inferior to the manna, in that the latter had come down from heaven, while the former was of this world, He adds, *This is the bread which cometh down from heaven.* AUG. This was the bread the manna typified, this was the bread the altar typified. Both the one and the other were sacraments, differing in symbol, alike in the thing signified. Hear the Apostle, *They did all eat the same spiritual meat.* CHRYS. He then gives them a strong reason for believing that they were given for higher privileges than their fathers. Their fathers eat manna and were dead; whereas of this bread He says, that *a man may eat thereof, and not die.* The difference of the two is evident from the difference of their ends. By bread here is meant wholesome doctrine, and faith in Him, or His body: for these are the preservatives of the soul. AUG. But are we, who eat the bread that cometh down from heaven, relieved from death? From visible and carnal death, the death of the body, we are not: we shall die, even as they died. But from spiritual

Chrys. (Nic.)

Theoph.

Chrys. Hom. xlv. 1.

Aug. Tr.xxvi. 11.

Chrys. Hom. xlvi. 2.

Aug. Tr.xxvi. s. 12.

1 Cor. 10.
Chrys. Hom. xlvi. 2.

Aug. Tr.xxvi. 11.

death which their fathers suffered, we are delivered. Moses and many acceptable of God, eat the manna, and died not, because they understood that visible food in a spiritual sense, spiritually tasted it, and were spiritually filled with it. And we too at this day receive the visible food; but the Sacrament is one thing, the virtue of the Sacrament another. Many a one receiveth from the Altar, and perisheth in receiving; *eating and drinking his own damnation, as saith* 1 Cor. the Apostle. To eat then the heavenly bread spiritually, is 11, 29. to bring to the Altar an innocent mind. Sins, though they be daily, are not deadly. Before you go to the Altar, attend to the prayer you repeat: *Forgive us our debts, as we* Matt. 6, *forgive our debtors.* If thou forgivest, thou art forgiven: 12. approach confidently; it is bread, not poison. None then that eateth of this bread, shall die. But we speak of the virtue of the Sacrament, not the visible Sacrament itself; of the inward, not of the outward eater. ALCUIN. Therefore I say, He that eateth this bread, dieth not: *I am the living bread which came down from heaven.* THEOPHYL. By Theoph. becoming incarnate, He was not then first man, and after- in v. 83. wards assumed Divinity, as Nestorius fables. AUG. The Aug. manna too came down from heaven; but the manna was Tr.xxvi. shadow, this is substance. ALCUIN. But men must be quick- 13. ened by my life: *If any man eat of this bread, he shall live,* not only now by faith and righteousness, but *for ever.*

51. —And the bread that I will give is my flesh, which I will give for the life of the world.

AUG. Our Lord pronounces Himself to be bread, not only Gloss. in respect of that Divinity, which feeds all things, but also in (Nic.) respect of that human nature, which was assumed by the Word of God: *And the bread,* He says, *that I will give is My flesh, which I will give for the life of the world.* BEDE. This bread our Lord then gave, when He delivered to His disciple the mystery of His Body and Blood, and offered Himself to God the Father on the altar of the cross. *For the life of the world,* i. e. not for the elements, but for man- kind, who are called the world. THEOPHYL. *Which I shall give:* this shews His power; for it shews that He was not crucified as a servant, in subjection to the Father, but of his own accord; for though He is said to have been given up by the Father, yet He delivered Himself up also. And observe, the bread which is taken by us in the mysteries, is not only the sign of Christ's flesh, but is itself the very flesh of Christ; for He does not say, *The bread which I will give,* is the sign of My flesh, but, *is My flesh.* The bread is by a mystical benediction conveyed in unutterable words, and by the indwelling of the Holy Ghost, transmuted into the flesh of Christ. But why see we not the flesh? Because, if the flesh were seen, it would revolt us to such a degree, that we should be unable to partake of it. And therefore in condescension to our infirmity, the mystical food is given to us under an appearance suitable to our minds. He gave His flesh for the life of the world, in that, by dying, He destroyed death. By the life of the world too, I understand the resurrection; our Lord's death having brought about the resurrection of the whole human race. It may mean too the sanctified, beatified, spiritual life; for though all have not attained to this life, yet our Lord gave Himself for the world, and, as far as lies in Him, the whole world is sanctified.

Aug.
Tr.xxvi.
13.

Aug. But when does flesh receive the bread which He calls His flesh? The faithful know and receive the Body of Christ, if they labour to be the body of Christ. And they become the body of Christ, if they study to live by the Spirit of Christ: for that which lives by the Spirit of Christ, is the body of Christ. This bread the Apostle sets forth, where he says, *We being many are one body.* O sacrament of mercy, O sign of unity, O bond of love! Whoso wishes to live, let him draw nigh, believe, be incorporated, that he may be quickened.

1 Cor.
12, 12.

52. The Jews therefore strove among themselves, saying, How can this man give us his flesh to eat?

53. Then Jesus said unto them, Verily, verily, I say unto you, Except ye eat the flesh of the Son of man, and drink his blood, ye have no life in you.

54. Whoso eateth my flesh, and drinketh my blood, hath eternal life; and I will raise him up at the last day.

Aug. The Jews not understanding what was the bread of Aug.
peace, *strove among themselves, saying, How can this man* $^{\text{Tr.xxvi.}}_{\text{s. 14.}}$
give us His flesh to eat? Whereas they who eat the bread
strive not among themselves, for God makes them to dwell
together in unity. Bede. The Jews thought that our Lord
would divide His flesh into pieces, and give it them to eat:
and so mistaking Him, strove. Chrys. As they thought it Chrys.
impossible that He should do as He said, i. e. give them $^{\text{Hom.}}_{\text{xlvii. 1.}}$
His flesh to eat, He shews them that it was not only possible,
but necessary: *Then said Jesus unto them, Verily, verily,*
I say unto you, Except ye eat the flesh of the Son of man,
and drink His blood, ye have no life in you. Aug. As if He Aug.
said, The sense in which that bread is eaten, and the mode $^{\text{Tr.xxvi.}}_{15.}$
of eating it, ye know not; but, *Except ye eat the flesh of the*
Son of man, and drink His blood, ye have no life in you.
Bede. And that this might not seem addressed to them
alone, He declares universally, *Whoso eateth My flesh, and*
drinketh My blood, hath eternal life. Aug. And that they Aug.
might not understand him to speak of this life, and make that $^{\text{Tr.xxvi.}}_{15.}$
an occasion of striving, He adds, *Hath eternal life.* This
then he hath not who eateth not that flesh, nor drinketh that
blood. The temporal life men may have without Him, the
eternal they cannot. This is not true of material food. If we
do not take that indeed, we shall not live, neither do we live,
if we take it: for either disease, or old age, or some accident
kills us after all. Whereas this meat and drink, i. e. the
Body and Blood of Christ, is such that he that taketh it not
hath not life, and he that taketh it hath life, even life eternal.
Theophyl. For it is not the flesh of man simply, but of God: Theoph.
and it makes man divine, by inebriating him, as it were, with $^{\text{in v. 52.}}$
divinity. Aug. There are some who promise men deliverance Aug.
from eternal punishment, if they are washed in Baptism and $^{\text{de Civ.}}_{\text{Dei,lxxi.}}$
partake of Christ's Body, whatever lives they live. The c. 25.
Apostle however contradicts them, where he says, *The works* Gal. 5,
of the flesh are manifest, which are these; adultery, fornica- $^{\text{19. et}}_{\text{seq.}}$
tion, uncleanness, lasciviousness, idolatry, witchcraft, hatred,
variance, emulations, wrath, strife, seditions, heresies, envyings,
murders, drunkenness, revellings, and such like; of the which
I tell you before, as I have also told you in time past, that
they which do such things shall not inherit the kingdom of

R

God. Let us examine what is meant here. He who is in the unity of His body, (i. e. one of the Christian members,) the Sacrament of which body the faithful receive when they communicate at the Altar; he is truly said to eat the body, and drink the blood of Christ. And heretics and schismatics, who are cut off from the unity of the body, may receive the same Sacrament; but it does not profit them, nay, rather is hurtful, as tending to make their judgment heavier, or their forgiveness later. Nor ought they to feel secure in their abandoned and damnable ways, who, by the iniquity of their lives, desert righteousness, i. e. Christ; either by fornication, or other sins of the like kind. Such are not to be said to eat the body of Christ; forasmuch as they are not to be counted among the members of Christ. For, not to mention other things, men cannot be members of Christ, and at the same time members of an harlot. Aug. By this meat and drink then, He would have us understand the society of His body, and His members, which is the Church, in the predestined, and called, and justified, and glorified saints and believers. The Sacrament whereof, i. e. of the unity of the body and blood of Christ, is administered, in some places daily, in others on such and such days from the Lord's Table: and from the Lord's Table it is received by some to their salvation, by others to their condemnation. But the thing itself of which this is the Sacrament, is for our salvation to every one who partakes of it, for condemnation to none. To prevent us supposing that those who, by virtue of that meat and drink, were promised eternal life, would not die in the body, He adds, *And I will raise him up at the last day;* i. e. to that eternal life, a spiritual rest, which the spirits of the Saints enter into. But neither shall the body be defrauded of eternal life, but shall be endowed with it at the resurrection of the dead in the last day.

Aug. super Joan. c. xxvi.15.

55. For my flesh is meat indeed, and my blood is drink indeed.

56. He that eateth my flesh, and drinketh my blood, dwelleth in me, and I in him.

57. As the living Father hath sent me, and I live

by the Father: so he that eateth me, even he shall live by me.

58. This is that bread which came down from heaven: not as your fathers did eat manna, and are dead: he that eateth of this bread shall live for ever.

59. These things said he in the synagogue, as he taught in Capernaum.

BEDE. He had said above, *Whoso eateth My flesh and drinketh My blood, hath eternal life:* and now to shew the great difference between bodily meat and drink, and the spiritual mystery of His body and blood, He adds, *For My flesh is meat indeed, and My blood is drink indeed.* CHRYS. i. e. this is no enigma, or parable, but ye must really eat the body of Christ; or He means to say that the true meat was He who saved the soul. AUG. Or thus: Whereas men desire meat and drink to satisfy hunger and thirst, this effect is only really produced by that meat and drink, which makes the receivers of it immortal and incorruptible; i. e. the society of Saints, where is peace and unity, full and perfect. On which account our Lord has chosen for the types of His body and blood, things which become one out of many. Bread is a quantity of grains united into one mass, wine a quantity of grapes squeezed together. Then He explains what it is to eat His body and drink His blood: *He that eateth My flesh, and drinketh My blood, dwelleth in Me, and I in him.* So then to partake of that meat and that drink, is to dwell in Christ and Christ in thee. He that dwelleth not in Christ, and in whom Christ dwelleth not, neither eateth His flesh, nor drinketh His blood: but rather eateth and drinketh the sacrament of it to his own damnation. CHRYS. Or, having given a promise of eternal life to those that eat Him, He says this to confirm it: *He that eateth My flesh, and drinketh My blood, dwelleth in Me, and I in him.* AUG. As for those, as indeed there are many, who either eat that flesh and drink that blood hypocritically, or, who having eaten, become apostates, do they dwell in Christ, and Christ in them? Nay, but there is a certain mode of eating that flesh, and drinking that blood, in the which he that

Chrys. Hom. xlvii. 1.

Aug. Tr.xxvi. 17.

Chrys. Hom. xlvii. 1.

Aug. de Verb. Dom.

eateth and drinketh, dwelleth in Christ, and Christ in him.

Aug. de Civ. Dei, l. i. c. xxv. AUG. That is to say, such an one eateth the body and drinketh the blood of Christ not in the sacramental sense, but in reality. CHRYS. And because I live, it is manifest

Chrys. Hom. xlvi. that he will live also: *As the living Father hath sent Me, and I live by the Father, even so he that eateth Me, even he*

Aug. de Verb. Dom. (Nic.) *shall live by Me.* As if He said, As the Father liveth, so do I live; adding, lest you should think Him unbegotten, *By the Father*, meaning that He has His source in the Father. *He that eateth Me, even he shall live by Me;* the life here meant is not life simply, but the justified life: for even unbelievers live, who never eat of that flesh at all. Nor is it of the general resurrection He speaks, (for all will rise

Aug. Tr. xxvi. s. 19. again,) but of the resurrection to glory, and reward. AUG. He saith not, As I eat the Father, and live by the Father, so he that eateth Me, even he shall live by Me. For the Son does not grow better by partaking of the Father, as we do by partaking of the Son, i. e. of His one body and blood, which this eating and drinking signifies. So that His saying, *I live by the Father*, because He is from Him, must not be understood as detracting from His equality. Nor do the words, *Even he that eateth Me, the same shall live by Me*, give us the equality that He has. He does not equalize, but only mediates between God and man. If, however, we understand the words, *I live by the Father*, in

c. 14, 28. the sense of those below, *My Father is greater than I*, then it is as if He said, That I live by the Father, i. e. refer my

[1] exin- anitio life to Him, as my superior, my[1] humiliation in my incarnation is the cause; but He who lives by Me, lives by Me by virtue of partaking of My flesh.

Hilar. vii. de Trin. c. 14. HILARY. Of the truth then of the body and blood of Christ, no room for doubting remains: for, by the declaration of our Lord Himself, and by the teaching of our own faith, the flesh is really flesh, and the blood really blood. This then is our principle of life. While we are in the flesh, Christ dwelleth

c. 14, 19. in us by His flesh. And we shall live by Him, according as He liveth. If then we live naturally by partaking of Him according to the flesh, He also liveth naturally by the indwelling of the Father according to the Spirit. His birth did not give Him an alien or different nature from the

Father. AUG. That we who cannot obtain eternal life of ourselves, might live by the eating that bread, He descended from heaven: *This is the bread which cometh down from heaven.* HILARY. He calls Himself the bread, because He is the origin of His own body. And lest it should be thought that the virtue and nature of the Word had given way to the flesh, He calls the bread His flesh, that, inasmuch as the bread came down from heaven, it might be seen that His body was not of human conception, but a heavenly body. To say that the bread is His own, is to declare that the Word assumed His body Himself. THEOPHYL. For we do not eat God simply, God being impalpable and incorporeal; nor again, the flesh of man simply, which would not profit us. But God having taken flesh into union with Himself, that flesh is quickening. Not that it has changed its own for the Divine nature; but, just as heated iron remains iron, with the action of the heat in it; so our Lord's flesh is quickening, as being the flesh of the Word of God. BEDE. And to shew the wide interval between the shadow and the light, the type and the reality, He adds, *Not as your fathers did eat manna, and are dead: he that eateth of this bread shall live for ever.* AUG. The death here meant is death eternal. For even those who eat Christ are subject to natural death; but they live for ever, because Christ is everlasting life. CHRYS. For if it was possible without harvest or fruit of the earth, or any such thing, to preserve the lives of the Israelites of old for forty years, much more will He be able to do this with that spiritual food, of which the manna is the type. He knew how precious a thing life was in men's eyes, and therefore repeats His promise of life often; just as the Old Testament had done; only that it only offered length of life, He life without end. This promise was an abolition of that sentence of death, which sin had brought upon us. *These things said He in the synagogue, as He taught in Capernaum;* where many displays of His power took place. He taught in the synagogue and in the temple, with the view of attracting the multitude, and as a sign that He was not acting in opposition to the Father. BEDE. Mystically, Capernaum, which means beautiful town, stands for the world: the synagogue, for the Jewish people. The meaning is, that our

Aug. Tr.xxvi. c. 20.

Hilar. de Trin. c. 18.

Aug. Tr.xxvi. 20.

Chrys. Hom. xlvii. 1.

Exod. 20, 12. Deut. 22, 7. 1 Kings 3, 14. Ps. 21, 4; 91,16. Prov. 3, 2.

Lord hath, by the mystery of the incarnation, manifested Himself to the world, and also taught the Jewish people His doctrines.

60. Many therefore of his disciples, when they had heard this, said, This is an hard saying; who can hear it?

61. When Jesus knew in himself that his disciples murmured at it, he said unto them, Doth this offend you?

62. What and if ye shall see the Son of man ascend up where he was before?

63. It is the spirit that quickeneth; the flesh profiteth nothing: the words that I speak unto you, they are spirit, and they are life.

64. But there are some of you that believe not. For Jesus knew from the beginning who they were that believed not, and who should betray him.

65. And he said, Therefore said I unto you, that no man can come unto me, except it were given unto him of my Father.

66. From that time many of his disciples went back, and walked no more with him.

67. Then said Jesus unto the twelve, Will ye also go away?

68. Then Simon Peter answered him, Lord, to whom shall we go? thou hast the words of eternal life.

69. And we believe and are sure that thou art that Christ, the Son of the living God.

70. Jesus answered them, Have not I chosen you twelve, and one of you is a devil?

71. He spake of Judas Iscariot the son of Simon: for he it was that should betray him, being one of the twelve.

AUG. Such is our Lord's discourse. The people did not perceive that it had a deep meaning, or, that grace went along with it: but receiving the matter in their own way, and taking His words in a human sense, understood Him as if He spoke of cutting of the flesh of the Word into pieces, for distribution to those who believed on Him: *Many therefore, not of His enemies, but even of His disciples, when they heard this, said, This is an hard saying, who can hear it?* CHRYS. i. e. difficult to receive, too much for their weakness. They thought He spoke above Himself, and more loftily than He had a right to do; and so said they, *Who can bear it?* which was answering in fact for themselves, that they could not. AUG. And if His disciples thought that saying hard, what would His enemies think? Yet it was necessary to declare a thing, which would be unintelligible to men. God's mysteries should draw men's attention, not enmity. THEO-PHYL. When you hear, however, of His disciples murmuring, understand not those really such, but rather some who, as far as their air and behaviour went, seemed to be receiving instruction from Him. For among His disciples were some of the people, who were called such, because they stayed some time with His disciples. AUG. They spoke, however, so as not to be heard by Him. But He, who knew what was in them, heard within Himself: *When Jesus knew within Himself that His disciples murmured at it, He said unto them, Doth this offend you?* ALCUIN. i. e. that I said, you should eat My flesh, and drink My blood. CHRYS. The revelation however of these hidden things was a mark of His Divinity: hence the meaning of what follows; *And if ye shall see the Son of man ascend up where He was before;* supply, What will ye say? He said the same to Nathanael, *Because I said to thee, I saw thee under the fig tree, believest thou? Thou shalt see greater things than these.* He does not add difficulty to difficulty, but to convince them by the number and greatness of His doctrines. For if He had merely said that He came down from heaven, without adding any thing further, he would have offended His hearers more; but by saying that His flesh is the life of the world, and that as He was sent by the living Father, so He liveth by the Father; and at last by adding that He came down from heaven, He removed all doubt. Nor

Margin notes:
Aug. Tr. xxvii. 2.

Chrys. Hom. xlvii. 2.

Aug. Tr. xxvii. 2.

Aug. Tr. xxvii. 3.

Chrys. Hom. xlvii. 2.

does He mean to scandalize His disciples, but rather to remove their scandal. For so long as they thought Him the Son of Joseph, they could not receive His doctrines; but if they once believed that He had come down from heaven, and would ascend thither, they would be much more willing and able to admit them. AUG. Or, these words are an answer to their mistake. They supposed that He was going to distribute His body in bits: whereas He tells them now, that He should ascend to heaven whole and entire: *What and if ye shall see the Son of man ascend up where He was before?* ye will then see that He does not distribute His body in the way ye think. Again; Christ became the Son of man, of the Virgin Mary here upon earth, and took flesh upon Him: He says then, *What and if ye shall see the Son of man ascend up where He was before?* to let us know that Christ, God and man, is one person, not two; and the object of one faith, not a quaternity, but a Trinity. He was the Son of man in heaven, as He was Son of God upon earth; the Son of God upon earth by assumption of the flesh, the Son of man in heaven, by the unity of the person. THEOPHYL. Do not suppose from this that the body of Christ came down from heaven, as the heretics Marcion and Apollinarius say; but only that the Son of God and the Son of man are one and the same. CHRYS. He tries to remove their difficulties in another way, as follows, *It is the spirit that quickeneth, the flesh profiteth nothing:* that is to say, You ought to understand My words in a spiritual sense: he who understands them carnally is profited nothing. To interpret carnally is to take a proposition in its bare literal meaning, and allow no other. But we should not judge of mysteries in this way; but examine them with the inward eye; i. e. understand them spiritually. It was carnal to doubt how our Lord could give His flesh to eat. What then? Is it not real flesh? Yea, verily. In saying then that *the flesh profiteth nothing,* He does not speak of His own flesh, but that of the carnal hearer of His word. AUG. Or thus, *the flesh profiteth nothing.* They had understood by His flesh, as it were, of a carcase, that was to be cut up, and sold in the shambles, not of a body animated by the spirit. Join the spirit to the flesh, and it profiteth

Chrys. Hom. xlvii. 3.

Aug. Tract. xxvii. s. 5.

much: for if the flesh profited not, the Word would not
have become flesh, and dwelt among us. The Spirit hath
done much for our salvation, by means of the flesh. AUG.
For the flesh does not cleanse of itself, but by the Word
who assumed it: which Word, being the principle of life in
all things, having taken up soul and body, cleanseth the
souls and bodies of those that believe. *It is the spirit,* then,
that quickeneth: the flesh profiteth nothing; i. e. the flesh
as they understood it. I do not, He seems to say, give My
body to be eaten in this sense. He ought not to think of
the flesh carnally: *The words that I speak unto you, they
are spirit, and they are life.* CHRYS. i. e. are spiritual, have Chrys.
nothing carnal in them, produce no effects of the natural Hom.
xlvii. 2.
sort; not being under the dominion of that law of necessity,
and order of nature established on earth. AUG. If then Aug.
thou understandest them spiritually, they are life and spirit Tr.xxvii.
to thee: if carnally, even then they are life and spirit, but
not to thee. Our Lord declares that in eating His body, and
drinking His blood, we dwell in Him, and He in us. But
what has the power to affect this, except love? *The love of* Rom. 5,
God is shed abroad in our hearts by the Holy Spirit, which 5.
is given to us. CHRYS. Having spoken of His words being Chrys.
taken carnally, He adds, *But there are some of you that* Tr.xlvii.
2.
believe not. *Some,* He says, not including His disciples in
the number. This insight shews His high nature. AUG. He Aug.
says not, There are some among you who understand not; Tr.xxvii.
s. 7.
but gives the reason why they do not understand. The
Prophet said, *Except ye believe, ye shall not understand*ᵃ. Is. 7, 9.
For how can he who opposes be quickened? An adversary,
though he avert not his face, yet closes his mind to the ray
of light which should penetrate him. But let men believe,
and open their eyes, and they will be enlightened. CHRYS. Chrys.
To let you know that it was before these words, and not Tr.xxvii.
2.
after, that the people murmured and were offended, the
Evangelist adds, *For Jesus knew from the beginning, who
they were that believed not, and who should betray Him.*
THEOPHYL. The Evangelist wishes to shew us, that He
knew all things before the foundation of the world: which
was a proof of His divinity. AUG. And after distinguishing Aug.
Tr.xxvii.
7.

ᵃ Be established. Non permanebitis, Vulg.

those who believed from those who did not believe, our Lord gives the reason of the unbelief of the latter, *And He said, Therefore said I unto you, that no man can come unto Me, except it were given him of My Father.* CHRYS. As if He said, Men's unbelief does not disturb or astonish Me: I know to whom the Father hath given to come to Me. He mentions the Father, to shew first that He had no eye to His own glory; secondly, that God was His Father, and not Joseph. AUG. So then (our) faith is given to us: and no small gift it is. Wherefore rejoice if thou believest; but be not lifted up, for what hast thou which thou didst not receive? And that this grace is given to some, and not to others, no one can doubt, without going against the plainest declarations of Scripture. As for the question, why it is not given to all, this cannot disquiet the believer, who knows that in consequence of the sin of one man, all are justly liable to condemnation; and that no blame could attach to God, even if none were pardoned; it being of His great mercy only that so many are. And why He pardons one rather than another, rests with Him, whose judgments are unsearchable, and His ways past finding out.

And from that time many of the disciples went back, and walked no more with Him. CHRYS. He does not say, withdrew[b], but *went back*, i. e. from being good hearers, from the belief which they once had. AUG. Being cut off from the body, their life was gone. They were no longer in the body; they were created among the unbelieving. There went back not a few, but many after Satan, not after Christ; as the Apostle says of some women, *For some had already turned aside after Satan.* Our Lord says to Peter, *Get thee behind Me.* He does not tell Peter to go after Satan. CHRYS. But it may be asked, what reason was there for speaking words to them which did not edify, but might rather have injured them? It was very useful and necessary; for this reason, they had been just now urgent in petitioning for bodily food, and reminding Him of that which had been given to their fathers. So He reminds them here of spiritual food; to shew that all those miracles were typical. They ought not then to have been offended, but should have

Marginal references:
Chrys. Hom. xlvi. 2.
Aug. Tr.xxvii. 7.
1 Cor. 4, 7.
Chrys. Hom. xlvii. 3.
Aug. Tr.xxvii. 8.
1 Tim. 5, 15.
Chrys. Hom. xlvi. 2.

---

b οὐκ ἀνεχώρησαν, ἀλλ' ἀπῆλθον εἰς τὰ ὀπίσω.

enquired of Him further. The scandal was owing to their
fatuity, not to the difficulty of the truths declared by our
Lord. AUG. And perhaps this took place for our consola- Aug.
tion; since it sometimes happens that a man says what is $\frac{\text{Tr.xxvii.}}{8.}$
true, and what He says is not understood, and they which
hear are offended and go. Then the man is sorry he spoke
what was true; for he says to himself, I ought not to have
spoken it; and yet our Lord was in the same case. He
spoke the truth, and destroyed many. But He is not
disturbed at it, because He knew from the beginning which
would believe. We, if this happens to us, are disturbed.
Let us desire consolation then from our Lord's example; and
withal use caution in our speech. BEDE. Our Lord knew well
the intentions of the other disciples which stayed, as to staying
or going; but yet He put the question to them, in order to
prove their faith, and hold it up to imitation: *Then said
Jesus unto the twelve, Will ye also go away?* CHRYS. This Chrys.
was the right way to retain them. Had He praised them, $\frac{\text{Hom.}}{\text{xlvii. 3.}}$
they would naturally, as men do, have thought that they
were conferring a favour upon Christ, by not leaving Him:
by shewing, as He did, that He did not need their company,
He made them hold the more closely by Him. He does
not say, however, Go away, as this would have been to cast
them off, but asks whether they wished to go away; thus preventing their staying with Him from any feeling of shame or
necessity: for to stay from necessity would be the same as going
away. Peter, who loved his brethren, replies for the whole
number, *Lord, to whom shall we go?* AUG. As if he said, Thou Aug.
castest us from Thee: give us another to whom we shall go, $\frac{\text{Tr.xxvii.}}{\text{s. 9.}}$
if we leave Thee. CHRYS. A speech of the greatest love: Chrys.
proving that Christ was more precious to them than father $\frac{\text{Hom.}}{\text{xlvii. 3.}}$
or mother. And that it might not seem to be said, from
thinking that there was no one whose guidance they could
look to, he adds, *Thou hast the words of eternal life:*
which shewed that he remembered his Master's words,
I will raise Him up, and, *hath eternal life.* The Jews
said, *Is not this the Son of Joseph?* how differently Peter:
*We believe and are sure, that Thou art that Christ, the
Son of the living God.* AUG. For we believed, in order Aug
to know. Had we wished first to know, and then to $\frac{\text{Tr.xxvii.}}{\text{s. 9.}}$
believe, we could never have been able to believe. This

we believe, and know, *that Thou art the Christ the Son of God;* i. e. that Thou art eternal life, and that in Thy flesh and blood Thou givest what Thou art Thyself. CHRYS. Peter however having said, *We believe,* our Lord excepts Judas from the number of those who believed: *Jesus answered them, Have not I chosen you twelve, and one of you is a devil?* i. e. Do not suppose that, because you have followed Me, I shall not reprove the wicked among you. It is worth enquiring, why the disciples say nothing here, whereas afterwards they ask in fear, *Lord, is it I?* But Peter had not yet been told, *Get thee behind Me, Satan;* and therefore had as yet no fear of this sort. Our Lord however does not say here, *One of you* shall betray Me, but, *is a devil:* so that they did not know what the speech meant, and thought that it was only a case of wickedness in general, that He was reproving. The Gentiles on the subject of election blame Christ foolishly. His election does not impose any necessity upon the person with respect to the future, but leaves it in the power of His will to be saved or perish. BEDE. Or we must say, that He elected the eleven for one purpose, the twelfth for another: the eleven to fill the place of Apostles, and persevere in it unto the end; the twelfth to the service of betraying Him, which was the means of saving the human race. AUG. He was elected to be an involuntary and unconscious instrument of producing the greatest good. For as the wicked turn the good works of God to an evil use, so reversely God turns the evil works of man to good. What can be worse than what Judas did? Yet our Lord made a good use of his wickedness; allowing Himself to be betrayed, that He might redeem us. In, *Have I not chosen you twelve,* twelve seems to be a sacred number used in the case of those, who were to spread the doctrine of the Trinity through the four quarters of the world. Nor was the virtue of that number impaired, by one perishing; inasmuch as another was substituted in his room. GREG. *One of you is a devil:* the body [b] is here named after its head. CHRYS. Mark the wisdom of Christ: He neither, by exposing him, makes him shameless and contentious; nor again emboldens him, by allowing him to think himself concealed.

Marginal references:
Chrys. Hom. xlvii. 3.
Matt. 26, 22. Mat. 16, 23.
Aug. Tr. xxvii. s. 10.
Greg. Moral. l. xiii. c. xxxiv.
Chrys. Hom. xlvii. 4.

---

b i. e. the whole body of wicked. Judas, as being one of that body, is named after its head, the devil.

CHAP. VII.

1. After these things Jesus walked in Galilee: for he would not walk in Jewry, because the Jews sought to kill him.

2. Now the Jews' feast of tabernacles was at hand.

3. His brethren therefore said unto him, Depart hence, and go into Judæa, that thy disciples also may see the works that thou doest.

4. For there is no man that doeth any thing in secret, and he himself seeketh to be known openly. If thou do these things, shew thyself to the world.

5. For neither did his brethren believe in him.

6. Then Jesus said unto them, My time is not yet come: but your time is alway ready.

7. The world cannot hate you: but me it hateth, because I testify of it, that the works thereof are evil.

8. Go ye up unto this feast: I go not up yet unto this feast; for my time is not yet fully come.

AUG. As the believer in Christ would have in time to come to hide himself from persecution, that no guilt might attach to such concealment, the Head began with doing Himself, what He sanctioned in the member; *After these things Jesus walked in Galilee: for he would not walk in Jewry, because the Jews sought to kill Him.* BEDE. The connexion of this passage admits of much taking place in the interval previously. Judæa and Galilee are divisions of the province of Palestine. Judæa has its name from the tribe of Judah; but it embraces not only the territories of Judah, but of Benjamin, all of which were called Judæa, because Judah

Aug.Tr. xxviii.2.

was the royal tribe. Galilee has its name, from the milky,
i. e. white, colour of its inhabitants; Galilee being Greek for
milk. AUG. It is not meant that our Lord *could* not walk
among the Jews, and escape being killed; for He had this
power, whenever He chose to shew it: but He set the
example of so doing, as an accommodation to our weakness.
He had not lost His power, but He indulged our frailty.
CHRYS. That is to say, He displayed the attribute both of
divinity and humanity. He fled from His persecutors as
man, He remained and appeared amongst them as God;
being really both. THEOPHYL. He withdrew too now to
Galilee, because the hour of His passion was not yet come;
and He thought it useless to stay in the midst of His enemies, when the effect would only have been to irritate them
the more. The time at which this happened is then given;
Now the Jews' feast of tabernacles was at hand. AUG.
What the feast of tabernacles is, we read in the Scriptures.
They used to make tents on the festival, like those in which
they lived during their journey in the desert, after their
departure from Egypt. They celebrated this feast in commemoration of the good things the Lord had done for them;
though they were the very people who were about to slay
the Lord. It is called the day of the feast [a], though it lasted
many days. CHRYS. It appears here, that a considerable
time had passed since the last events. For when our Lord
sat upon the mount, it was near the feast of the Passover,
and now it is the feast of tabernacles: so that in the five
intermediate months the Evangelist has related nothing but
the miracle of the loaves, and the conversation with those
who ate of them. As our Lord was unceasingly working
miracles, and holding disputes with people, the Evangelists
could not relate all; but only aimed at giving those, in which
complaint or opposition had followed on the part of the Jews,
as was the case here. THEOPHYL. His brethren saw that
He was not preparing to go to the feast: *His brethren therefore
said unto him, Depart hence, and go into Judæa.* BEDE.
Meaning to say, Thou doest miracles, and only a few see
them: go to the royal city, where the rulers are, that they
may see Thy miracles, and so Thou obtain praise. And as

Marginal references:
Aug.Tr. xxviii.2.
Chrys. Hom. xlviii.1.
Aug.Tr. xxviii.3.
Chrys. Hom. xlviii.1.

[a] St. Augustine goes by the Vulgate, dies festus.

our Lord had not brought all His disciples with Him, but
left many behind in Judæa, they add, *That Thy disciples also
may see the works that Thou doest.* THEOPHYL. i. e. the
multitudes that follow Thee.   They do not mean the twelve,
but the others that had communication with Him.   AUG. Aug.Tr.
When you hear of our Lord's brethren, you must understand^{xxviii.3.}
the kindred of Mary, not her offspring after our Lord's birth.
For as the body of our Lord once only lay in the sepulchre,
and neither before, nor after that once ; so could not the
womb of Mary have possibly conceived any other mortal
offspring.   Our Lord's works did not escape His disciples,
but they escaped His brethren ; hence their suggestion,
That Thy disciples may see the works that Thou doest.   They
speak according to the wisdom of the flesh, to the Word that
was made flesh, and add, *For there is no man that doeth any
thing in secret, and he himself seeketh to be known openly.
If Thou do these things, shew Thyself to the world;* as if to
say, Thou doest miracles, do them in the eyes of the world,
that the world may honour Thee.   Their admonitions aim at
procuring glory for Him ; and this very thing, viz. aiming at
human glory, proved that they did not believe in Him, as we
next read, *For neither did His brethren believe on Him.*
They were Christ's kindred, but they were on that very
account above believing in Him.   CHRYS. It is striking to Chrys.
observe the great sincerity of the Evangelists ; that they are ^{Hom.}_{xlviii.1,}
not ashamed to mention things which appear to be to our ^{2.}
Lord's disadvantage, but take particular care to tell us of
them.   It is a considerable reflexion on our Lord, that His
brethren do not believe on Him.   The beginning of their
speech has a friendly appearance about it : but there is much
bitterness in it, thus charging Him with the motives of fear
and vain glory ; *No man,* say they, *doeth any thing in secret :*
this was reproaching Him tacitly with fear ; and was an
insinuation too that His miracles had not been real and solid
ones.   In what follows, *And he himself seeketh to be
known openly,* they taunt Him with the love of glory.
Christ however answers them mildly, teaching us not to take
the advice of people ever so inferior to ourselves angrily ;
*Then Jesus said unto them, My time is not yet come: but
your time is alway ready.*   BEDE. This is no contradiction

Gal. 4,4. to what the Apostle says, *But when the fulness of time was come, God sent forth His Son.* Our Lord referring here to Aug.Tr. the time not of His nativity, but of His glorification. AUG. xxviii.5. They gave Him advice to pursue glory, and not allow Himself to remain in concealment and obscurity; appealing altogether to worldly and secular motives. But our Lord was laying down another road to that very exaltation, viz. humility: *My time,* He says, i. e. the time of My glory, when I shall come to judge on high, *is not yet come; but your time,* i. e. the glory of the world, *is always ready.* And let us, who are the Lord's body, when insulted by the lovers of this world, say, Your time is ready: ours is not yet come. Our country is a lofty one, the way to it is low. Whoso

Chrys. rejecteth the way, why seeketh he the country? CHRYS. Hom. xlviii. 2. Or there seems to be another meaning concealed in the words; perhaps they intended to betray Him to the Jews; and therefore He says, *My time is not yet come,* i. e. the time of My cross and death: *but your time is always ready;* for though you are always with the Jews, they will not kill you, because you are of the same mind with them: *The world cannot hate you; but Me it hateth, because I testify of it, that the works thereof are evil:* as if He said, How can the world hate them who have the same wishes and aims with itself? It hateth Me, because I reprove it. I seek not then glory from men; inasmuch as I hesitate not to reprove them, though I know that I am hated in consequence, and that My life is aimed at. Here we see that the hatred of the Jews was owing to His reproofs, not to His breaking the sabbath. THEOPHYL. Our Lord brings two arguments in answer to their two charges. To the charge of fear He answers, that He reproves the deeds of the world, i. e. of those who love worldly things; which He would not do, if He were under the influence of fear; and He replies to the charge of vain glory, by sending them to the feast, *Go ye up unto this feast.* Had He been possessed at all with the desire for glory, He would have kept them with Him: for

Chrys. the vain glorious like to have many followers. CHRYS. This Hom. xlviii. 2. is to shew too, that, while He does not wish to humour them, He still allows them to observe the Jewish ordinances. Aug.Tr. xxviii. AUG. Or He seems to say, *Go ye up to this feast,* and seek 5. 8.

for human glory, and enlarge your carnal pleasures, and forget heavenly things.

I go not up unto this feast; CHRYS. i. e. not with you, for *My time is not yet full come.* It was at the next passover that He was to be crucified. AUG. Or My time, i. e. the time of My glory, is not yet come. That will be My feast day; not a day which passeth and is gone, like holidays here: but one which remaineth for ever. Then will be festivity; joy without end, eternity without stain, sunshine without a cloud. Chrys. Hom. xlviii. 2. Aug. Tract. xxviii. 8.

9. When he had said these words unto them, he abode still in Galilee.

10. But when his brethren were gone up, then went he also up unto the feast, not openly, but as it were in secret.

11. Then the Jews sought him at the feast, and said, Where is he?

12. And there was much murmuring among the people concerning him: for some said, He is a good man: others said, Nay; but he deceiveth the people.

13. Howbeit no man spake openly of him for fear of the Jews.

THEOPHYL. Our Lord at first declares that He will not go up to the feast, (*I go not up with you,*) in order not to expose Himself to the rage of the Jews; and therefore we read, that, *When He had said these words unto them, He abode still in Galilee.* Afterwards, however, He goes up; *But when His brethren were gone up, then went He also up unto the feast.* AUG. He went up, however, not to get temporary glory, but to teach wholesome doctrine, and remind men of the eternal feast. CHRYS. He goes up, not to suffer, but to teach. And He goes up secretly; because, though He could have gone openly, and kept the violence and impetuosity of the Jews in check, as He had often done before; yet to do this every time, would have disclosed His divinity; and he wished to establish the fact of His incarnation, and to teach us the way of life. And He went up privately too, to shew us what Aug. Tract. xxviii. Chrys. Hom. xlviii. s. 2.

s

we ought to do, who cannot check our persecutors. It is not said, however, in secret, but, *as it were in secret;* to shew that it was done as a kind of economy. For had He done all things as God, how should we of this world know what to do, when we fell into danger? ALCUIN. Or, He went up in secret, because He did not seek the favour of men, and took no pleasure in pomp, and being followed about with crowds. BEDE. The mystical meaning is, that to all those carnal persons who seek human glory, the Lord remains in Galilee; the meaning of which name is, " passing over;" applying to those his members who pass from vice to virtue, and make progress in the latter. And our Lord Himself delayed to go up, signifying that Christ's members seek not temporal but eternal glory. And He went up secretly, because all[b] glory is from within: that is, *from a pure heart and good conscience, and faith unfeigned.* AUG. Or the meaning is, that all the ceremonial of the ancient people was the figure of what was to be; such as the feast of tabernacles. Which figure is now unveiled to us. Our Lord went up in secret, to represent the figurative system. He concealed Himself at the feast itself, because the feast itself signified, that the members of Christ were in a strange country. For he dwells in the tents, who regards himself as a stranger in the world. The word scenopegia here means the feast of tabernacles. CHRYS. *Then the Jews sought Him at the feast, and said, Where is He?* out of hatred and enmity; for they would not call Him by His name. There was not much reverence or religion in this observance of the feast, when they wanted to make it an opportunity of seizing Christ. AUG. *And there was much murmuring in the people concerning Him.* A murmuring arising from disagreement. *For some said, He is a good man: others said, Nay; but He seduceth the people.* Whoever had any spark of grace, said, *He is a good man;* the rest, *Nay, but He seduceth the people.* That such was said of Him, Who was God, is a consolation to any Christian, of whom the same may be said. If to seduce be to decide, Christ was not a seducer, nor can any Christian be. But if by seducing be meant bringing a person by persuasion out of one way of thinking into another,

non occ.

Ps. 45, 14.
1 Tim. 1, 5.
Aug. Tract. xxviii. 9.

Chrys. Hom. xlix. 1.

Aug. Tract. xxviii. s. 11.

---

[b] The king's daughter is all glorious within.

then we must enquire from what, and to what. If from good
to evil, the seducer is an evil man; if from evil to good, a
good one. And would that we were all called, and really
were, such seducers. CHRYS. The former, I think, was the
opinion of the multitude, the one, viz. who pronounced Him
a good man; the latter the opinion of the priests and rulers;
as is shewn by their saying, *He deceiveth the people*, not, He
deceiveth us. AUG. *Howbeit no man spake openly of Him,*
for fear of the Jews; none, that is, of those who said, *He*
is a good man. They who said, *He deceiveth the people,*
proclaimed their opinion openly enough; while the former
only dared whisper theirs. CHRYS. Observe, the corruption
is in the rulers: the common people are sound in their judgment, but have not liberty of speech, as is generally their
case.

Chrys. Hom. xlix. 1.

Aug. Tract. xxviii. 12.

Chrys. Hom. xlix. 1.

14. Now about the midst of the feast Jesus went up
into the temple, and taught.

15. And the Jews marvelled, saying, How knoweth
this man letters, having never learned?

16. Jesus answered them, and said, My doctrine is
not mine, but his that sent me.

17. If any man will do his will, he shall know of the
doctrine, whether it be of God, or whether I speak of
myself.

18. He that speaketh of himself seeketh his own
glory: but he that seeketh his glory that sent him, the
same is true, and no unrighteousness is in him.

CHRYS. Our Lord delays His visit, in order to excite men's
attention, and goes up not the first day, but about the middle
of the feast: *Now about the midst of the feast Jesus went*
up into the temple, and taught. Those who had been
searching for Him, when they saw Him thus suddenly appear,
would be more attentive to His teaching, both favourers and
enemies; the one to admire and profit by it; the other to
find an opportunity of laying hands on Him. THEOPHYL.
At the commencement of the feast, men would be attending
more to the preachings of the festival itself; and afterwards

Chrys. Hom. xlix. 1.

Aug.

Aug.
Tract.
xxviii.
s. 60. would be better disposed to hear Christ. AUG. The feast seems, as far as we can judge, to have lasted several days. And therefore it is said, "about the middle of the feast day^c:" [c] i. e. when as many days of that feast had passed, as were to come. So that His assertion, *I go not up yet to this feast day*, (i. e. to the first or second day, as you would wish me,) was strictly fulfilled. For He went up afterwards, about the

Aug. de
Quæst.
Nov. et
Vet.
Test. 2.
78. middle of the feast. AUG. In going there too, He went up, not to the feast day, but to the light. They had gone to enjoy the pleasures of the festival, but Christ's feast day was that on which by His Passion He redeemed the world.

Aug.
super
Joan.
Tract.
xxix. 2 AUG. He who had before concealed Himself, taught and spoke openly, and was not laid hold on. The one was intended for an example to us, the other to testify His power. Chrys.
Hom.
xlix. 1. CHRYS. What His teaching is, the Evangelist does not say; but that it was very wonderful is shewn by its effect even upon those who had accused Him of deceiving the people, who turned round and began to admire Him: *And the Jews marvelled, saying, How knoweth this Man letters, having never learned?* See how perverse they are even in their admiration. It is not His doctrine they admire,

Aug.
Tract.
xxix. 2. but another thing altogether. AUG. All, it would appear, admired, but all were not converted. Whence then the admiration? Many knew where He was born, and how He had been educated; but had never seen Him learning letters. Yet now they heard Him disputing on the law, and bringing forward its testimonies. No one could do this, who had not read the law; no one could read who had not learnt letters; Chrys.
Hom.
xlix. 1. and this raised their wonder. CHRYS. Their wonder might have led them to infer, that our Lord became possessed of this learning in some divine way, and not by any human process. But they would not acknowledge this, and contented themselves with wondering. So our Lord repeated it to them: *Jesus answered them and said, My doctrine is not* Aug.
Tract.
xxix.
s. 3. *Mine, but His that sent Me.* AUG. *Mine is not mine,* appears a contradiction; why did He not say, This doctrine is not Mine? Because the doctrine of the Father being the Word of the Father, and Christ Himself being that Word, Christ Himself is the doctrine of the Father. And therefore He

---

c Vulgate taken as above literally.

calls the doctrine both His own, and the Father's. A word must be a word of some one's. What is so much Thine as Thou, and what is so much not Thine as Thou, if what Thou art, Thou art of another. His saying then, *My doctrine is not Mine own*, seems briefly to express the truth, that He is not from Himself; it refutes the Sabellian heresy, which dares to assert that the Son is the same as the Father, there being only two names for one thing. CHRYS. Or He calls it His Chrys. Hom. own, inasmuch as He taught it; not His own, inasmuch as xlix. 2. the doctrine was of the Father. If all things however which the Father hath are His, the doctrine for this very reason is His; i. e. because it is the Father's. Rather that He says, *Is not Mine own*, shews very strongly, that His doctrine and the Father's are one: as if He said, I differ nothing from Him; but so act, that it may be thought I say and do nothing else than doth the Father. AUG. Or thus: In one Aug. de Trin. i. sense He calls it His, in another sense not His; according c. xi. to the form of the Godhead His, according to the form of the servant not His. AUG. Should any one however not Aug. Tract. understand this, let him hear the advice which immediately xxix. follows from our Lord: *If any man will do His will, he shall* s. 6. *know of the doctrine, whether it be of God, or whether I speak of Myself.* What meaneth this, *If any man will do His will?* To do His will is to believe on Him, as He Himself says, *This is the work of God, that ye believe on Him* c. 6, 29. *whom He hath sent.* And who does not know, that to work the work of God, is to do His will? To know is to understand. Do not then seek to understand in order to believe, but believe in order to understand, for, *Except ye believe,* Is. 7, 9. Vulg. *ye shall not understand.* CHRYS. This is as much as to Chrys. say, Put away the anger, envy, and hatred which you have Hom. xlix. 1. towards Me, and there will be nothing to prevent your knowing, that the words which I speak are from God. Then He brings in an irresistible argument taken from human experience: *He that speaketh of himself, seeketh his own glory:* as if to say, He who aims at establishing some doctrine of his own, does so for no purpose, but to get glory. But I seek the glory of Him that sent. me, and wish to teach you for His, i. e. another's, sake: and then it follows, *But he that seeketh His glory that sent Him, the same is*

true, and there is no unrighteousness in Him. THEOPHYL.
As if He said, I speak the truth, because My doctrine containeth the truth : there is no unrighteousness in Me, because
I usurp not another's glory. AUG. He who seeketh his own
glory is Antichrist. But our Lord set us an example of
humility, in that being found in fashion as a man, He sought
His Father's glory, not His own. Thou, when thou doest
good, takest glory to thyself, when thou doest evil, upbraidest
God. CHRYS. Observe, the reason why He spake so humbly
of Himself, is to let men know, that He does not aim at
glory, or power; and to accommodate Himself to their
weakness, and to teach them moderation, and a humble, as
distinguished from an assuming, way of speaking of themselves.

Aug.
Tract.
xxix.
s. 8.

Chrys
Hom.
xlix 2.

19. Did not Moses give you the law, and yet none
of you keepeth the law? Why go ye about to kill me?

20. The people answered and said, Thou hast a
devil: who goeth about to kill thee?

21. Jesus answered and said unto them, I have
done one work, and ye all marvel.

22. Moses therefore gave unto you circumcision:
(not because it is of Moses, but of the fathers:) and
ye on the sabbath day circumcise a man.

23. If a man on the sabbath day receive circumcision, that the law of Moses should not be broken;
are ye angry at me, because I have made a man every
whit whole on the sabbath day?

24. Judge not according to the appearance, but
judge righteous judgment.

Chrys.
Hom.
xlix. 2.

CHRYS. The Jews brought two charges against Christ; one,
that He broke the sabbath; the other, that He said God was
His Father, making Himself equal with God. The latter
He confirmed first by shewing, that He did nothing in
opposition to God, but that both taught the same. Then
turning to the charge of breaking the sabbath, He says,
Did not Moses give you a law, and none of you keepeth the

law? as much as to say, The law says, Thou shalt not kill,
whereas ye kill.   And then, *Why go ye about to kill Me?* As
if to say, If I broke a law to heal a man, it was a transgression, but a beneficial one; whereas ye transgress for an
evil end; so you have no right to judge Me for breaking the
law.   He rebukes them then for two things; first, because they
went about to kill Him; secondly, because they were going
about to kill another, when they had not even any right to
judge Him.   AUG. Or He means to say, that if they kept Aug.
the law, they would see Him pointed to in every part of it, Tr.xxx.
and would not seek to kill Him, when He came.   The
people return an answer quite away from the subject, and
only shewing their angry feelings: *The people answered and
said, Thou hast a devil: who goeth about to kill Thee?* He
who cast out devils, was told that He had a devil.   Our
Lord however, in no way disturbed, but retaining all the
serenity of truth, returned not evil for evil, or railing for
railing.   BEDE. Wherein He left us an example to take it
patiently, whenever wrong censures are passed upon us,
and not answer them by asserting the truth, though able
to do so, but rather by some wholesome advice to the persons; as doth our Lord: *Jesus answered and said unto
them, I have done one work, and ye all marvel.* AUG. As Aug.
if He said, What if ye saw all My works?   For all that they Tr.xxx.
saw going on in the world was of His working, but they saw s. 3.
not Him Who made all things.   But He did one thing, made
a man whole on the sabbath day, and they were in commotion: as if, when any one of them recovered from a
disease on the sabbath, he who made him whole were any
other than He, who had offended them by making one man
whole on the sabbath.   CHRYS. *Ye marvel,* i. e. are dis- Chrys.
turbed, are in commotion.   Observe how well He argues with Hom.
them from the law.   He wishes to prove that this work was xlix. 3.
not a violation of the law; and shews accordingly that there
are many things more important than the law for the observance of the sabbath, by the observance of which that law is
not broken but fulfilled.   *Moses therefore,* He says, *gave
unto you circumcision, not because it is of Moses, but of the
fathers, and ye on the sabbath day circumcise a man.*
AUG. As if He said, Ye have done well to receive circum- Aug.
                                                           Tr.xxx.
                                                           s. 4.

cision from Moses, *not because it is of Moses, but of the fathers;* for Abraham first received circumcision from the Lord. *And ye circumcise on the sabbath.* Moses has convicted you: ye received a law to circumcise on the eighth day; and ye received a law to rest on the seventh day. If the eighth day after a child is born happen to be the sabbath, ye circumcise the child; because circumcision appertaineth to, is a kind of sign of, salvation; and men ought not to rest from the work of salvation on the sabbath. ALCUIN. Circumcision was given for three reasons; first, as a sign of Abraham's great faith; secondly, to distinguish the Jews from other nations; thirdly, that the receiving of it on the organ of virility, might admonish us to observe chastity both of body and mind. And circumcision then possessed the same virtue that baptism does now; only that the gate was not yet open. Our Lord concludes: *If a man on the sabbath day receive circumcision, that the law of Moses should not be broken; are ye angry at Me because I have made a man every whit whole on the sabbath day?* CHRYS. Which is as much as to tell them, The breaking of the sabbath in circumcision is a keeping of the law; and in the same way I by healing on the sabbath have kept the law. Ye, who are not the legislators, enforce the law beyond its proper bounds; whereas Moses made the law give way to the observance of a commandment, which did not come from the law, but from the fathers. His saying, *I have made a man every whit whole on the sabbath day,* implies that circumcision was a partial recovering. AUG. Circumcision also was perhaps a type of our Lord Himself. For what is circumcision but a robbing of the flesh, to signify the robbing the heart of its carnal lusts. And therefore it was not without reason that it was applied to that member by which the mortal creature is propagated: *for by one man sin entered into the world.* And therefore every one is born with the foreskin, because every one is born with the fault of his propagation. And God does not change us either from the corruption of our birth, or from that we have contracted ourselves by a bad life, except by Christ: and therefore they circumcised with knives of stone, to prefigure Christ, who is the stone; and on the eighth day, because our Lord's resurrection took place on the day after the seventh day;

Chrys. Hom. xlix. 3.

Aug. Tr.xxx. 5.

Rom. 5, 12.

vite propa- genis

which resurrection circumcises us, i. e. destroys our carnal
appetites. Regard this, saith our Lord, as a type of My
good work in making a man every whit whole on the sabbath
day: for he was healed, that he might be whole in body,
and he believed, that he might be whole in mind. Ye are
forbidden indeed to do servile work on the sabbath; but
is it a servile work to heal on the sabbath? Ye eat and
drink on the sabbath, because it is necessary for your
health : which shews that works of healing are by no means
to be omitted on the sabbath. CHRYS. He does not say, Chrys.
however, I have done a greater work than circumcision; Hom.
but only states the matter of fact, and leaves the judgment xlix. 3.
to them, saying, *Judge not according to the appearance, but
judge righteous judgment:* as if to say, Do not, because
Moses has a greater name with you than I, decide by
degree of personal eminence ; but decide by the nature of the
thing itself, for this is to judge righteously. No one however has blamed Moses for making the sabbath give place
to the commandment of circumcision, which was not derived from the law, but from another source. Moses then
commands the law to be broken to give effect to a commandment not of the law: and he is more worthy of credit
than you. AUG. What our Lord here tells us to avoid, in Aug.
judging by the person, is very difficult in this world not to Tr.xxx.
do. His admonition to the Jews is an admonition to us as s. 7.
well; for every sentence which our Lord uttered, was written
for us, and is preserved to us, and is read for our profit.
Our Lord is above; but our Lord, as the truth, is here as
well. The body with which He rose can be only in one
place, but His truth is diffused every where. Who then is
he who judges not by the person? He who loves all alike.
For it is not the paying men different degrees of honour
according to their situation, that will make us chargeable
with accepting persons. There may be a case to decide
between father and son: we should not put the son on an
equality with the father in point of honour; but, in respect
of truth, if he have the better cause, we should give him the
preference; and so give to each their due, that justice do
not destroy desert[d].

[d] ut non perdat equitas meritum.

25. Then said some of them of Jerusalem, Is not this he, whom they seek to kill?

26. But, lo, he speaketh boldly, and they say nothing unto him. Do the rulers know indeed that this is the very Christ?

27. Howbeit we know this man whence he is: but when Christ cometh, no man knoweth whence he is.

28. Then cried Jesus in the temple as he taught, saying, Ye both know me, and ye know whence I am: and I am not come of myself, but he that sent me is true, whom ye know not.

29. But I know him: for I am from him, and he hath sent me.

30. Then they sought to take him: but no man laid hands on him, because his hour was not yet come.

Aug. Tr.xxxi. 1. AUG. It was said above that our Lord went up to the feast secretly, not because He feared being taken, (for He had power to prevent it,) but to shew figuratively, that even in the very feast which the Jews celebrated, He was hid, and that it was His mystery. Now however the power appears, which was thought timidity: He spoke publicly at the feast, in so much that the multitude marvelled: *They said some of them at Jerusalem, Is not this He, whom they seek to kill? but, lo, He speaketh boldly, and they say nothing to Him.* They knew the fierceness with which He had been sought for; they marvelled at the power by which he was not taken.

Chrys. Hom. l. 1. CHRYS. The Evangelist adds, *from Jerusalem:* for there had been the greatest display of miracles, and there the people were in the worst state, seeing the strongest proofs of His divinity, and yet willing to give up all to the judgment of their corrupt rulers. Was it not a great miracle, that those who raged for His life, now that they had Him in their grasp, became on a sudden quiet? AUG. So, not fully understanding Christ's power, they supposed that it was owing to the knowledge of the rulers that He was spared: *Do the rulers know indeed that this is the very Christ?* CHRYS. But they do not follow the opinion of the rulers, but put forth another most perverse and absurd one; *Howbeit we know this Man, whence He is; but when Christ cometh, no man knoweth whence He is.* Aug. This notion did not arise Aug. without foundation. We find indeed that the Scriptures Tr.xxxi. s. 2. said of Christ, *He shall be called a Nazarene,* and thus pre- Matt. 2, dicted whence He would come. And the Jews again told 23. Herod, when he enquired, that Christ would be born in Bethlehem of Judah, and adduced the testimony of the Prophet. How then did this notion of the Jews arise, that, when Christ came, no one would know whence He was? From this reason, viz. that the Scriptures asserted both. As man, they foretold whence Christ would be; as God, He was hid from the profane, but revealed Himself to the godly. This notion they had taken from Isaiah, *Who shall declare His* Isa. 53. *generation?* Our Lord replies, that they both knew Him, and knew Him not: *Then cried Jesus in the temple as He taught, saying, Ye both know Me, and know whence I am:* that is to say, Ye both know whence I am, and do not know whence I am: ye know whence I am, that I am Jesus of Nazareth, whose parents ye know. The birth from the Virgin was the only part of the matter unknown to them: with this exception, they knew all that pertained to Jesus as man. So He well says, *Ye both know Me, and know whence I am:* i. e. according to the flesh, and the likeness of man. But in respect of His divinity, He says, *I am not come of Myself, but He that sent Me is true.* CHRYS. By which He discloses Chrys. Hom. what was in their minds. I am not, He seems to say, of the l. 1. number of those who have come without reason, but He is true that sent Me; and if He is true, He hath sent Me in truth; and therefore He who is sent must needs speak the truth. He then convicts them from their own assertions. For whereas they had said, *When Christ cometh, no man knoweth whence He is,* He shews that Christ did come from one whom they knew not, i. e. the Father. Wherefore He adds, *Whom ye know not.* HILARY. Every man, ever born in Hilar. de Trin. the flesh, is in a certain sense from God. How then could He ult. med. say that they were ignorant who He was, and whence He was[a]? Because our Lord is here referring to His own peculiar

---

[a] Because even considering Him man, He would be born of God in the common sense.

birth from God, which they were ignorant of, because they did not know that He was the Son of God. His very saying then that they did not know whence He was, was telling them whence He was. If they did not know whence He was, He could not be from nothing; for then there would be no *whence* to be ignorant of. He must therefore be from God. And then not knowing *whence* He is, was the reason that they did not know *who* He is. He does not know the Son who does not know His birth from the Father. CHRYS. Or the ignorance, He here speaks of, is the ignorance of a bad life; as Paul saith, *They profess that they know God, but in works they deny Him.* Our Lord's reproof is twofold: He first published what they were speaking secretly, crying out, in order to put them to shame. AUG. Lastly, to shew whence they could get to know Him (who had sent Him), He adds, *I know Him:* so if you would know Him, enquire of Me. *No one knoweth the Father, save the Son, and he to whom the Son will reveal Him. And if I should say, I know Him not, I should be a liar like unto you.* CHRYS. Which is impossible: for He that sent Me is true, and therefore He that is sent must be true likewise. He every where attributes the knowledge of the Father to Himself, as being from the Father: thus here, *But I know Him, for I am from Him.* HILARY. I ask however, does the being from Him express a work of creation, or a birth by generation? If a work of creation, then every thing which is created is from Him. And how then does not all creation know the Father, if the Son knows Him, because He is from Him? But if the knowledge of the Father is peculiar to Him, as being from Him, then the being from Him is peculiar to Him also; i. e. the being the true Son of God by nature. So you have then a peculiar knowledge springing from a peculiar generation. To prevent however any heresy applying the being from Him, to the time of His advent, He adds, *And He hath sent Me:* thus preserving the order of the Gospel sacrament; first announcing Himself born, and then sent. AUG. *I am from Him,* He says, i. e. as the Son from the Father: but that you see Me in the flesh is because *He hath sent Me.* Wherein understand not a difference of nature, but the authority of a father. CHRYS. His saying however, *Whom ye know not,* irritated the Jews, who

Chrys. Hom. l. 1.

Tit. 1, 16.

Aug. Tr.xxxi. 4.

c. 8, 55.

Chrys. Hom. l. 1.

Hilar. vi. de Trin. ultra med.

Aug. Tr.xxxi. 4.

Chrys. Hom. l. 2.

professed to have knowledge; and *they sought to take Him,
but no man laid hands on Him.*   Mark the invisible check
which is kept upon their fury: though the Evangelist does
not mention it, but preserves purposely a humble and
human way of speaking, in order to impress us with Christ's
humanity; and therefore only adds, *Because His hour was
not yet come.*   Aug. That is, because He was not so pleased; Aug.
for our Lord was not born subject to fate.   Thou must not $^{Tract.}_{xxxi.}$
believe this even of thyself, much less of Him by Whom thou s. 5.
wert made.   And if thine hour is in His will, is not His hour
in His own will? His home then here does not mean the time
that He was obliged to die, but the time that He deigned to
be put to death.

31. And many of the people believed on him, and
said, When Christ cometh, will he do more miracles
than these which this man hath done?

32. The Pharisees heard that the people murmured
such things concerning him; and the Pharisees and
the chief priests sent officers to take him.

33. Then said Jesus unto them, Yet a little while
am I with you, and then I go unto him that sent me.

34. Ye shall seek me, and shall not find me : and
where I am, thither ye cannot come.

35. Then said the Jews among themselves, Whither
will he go, that we shall not find him? will he go
unto the dispersed among the Gentiles, and teach the
Gentiles?

36. What manner of saying is this that he said, Ye
shall seek me, and shall not find me: and where I am,
thither ye cannot come?

Aug. *And many of the people believed on Him.*   Our Lord Aug.
brought the poor and humble to be saved.   The common $^{Tract.}_{xxxi.\,7.}$
people, who soon saw their own infirmities, received His
medicine without hesitation.   Chrys. Neither had these Chrys.
$^{Hom.\,l.}_{2.}$

however a sound faith; but took up a low way of speaking, after the manner of the multitude: *When Christ cometh, will He do more miracles than this Man hath done?* Their saying, *When Christ cometh,* shews that they were not steady in believing that He was the Christ: or rather, that they did not believe He was the Christ at all; for it is the same as if they said, that Christ, when He came, would be a superior person, and do more miracles. Minds of the grosser sort are influenced not by doctrine, but by miracles. AUG. Or they mean, If there are not to be two Christs, this is He. The rulers however, possessed with madness, not only refused to acknowledge the physician, but even wished to kill Him: *The Pharisees heard that the people murmured such things concerning Him, and the Pharisees and chief priests sent officers to take Him.* CHRYS. He had discoursed often before, but they had never so treated Him. The praises of the multitude however now irritated them; though the transgression of the sabbath still continued to be the reason put forward. Nevertheless, they were afraid of taking this step themselves, and sent officers instead. AUG. Not being able to take Him against His will, they sent men to hear Him teach. Teach what? *Then said Jesus unto them, Yet a little while I am with you.* CHRYS. He speaks with the greatest humility: as if to say, Why do ye make such haste to kill Me? Only wait a little time. AUG. That which ye wish to do now, ye shall do sometime, but not now: because it is not My will. For I wish to fulfil My mission in due course, and so to come to My passion. CHRYS. In this way He astonished the bolder part of the multitude, and made the earnest among them more eager to hear Him; so little time being now left, during which they could have the benefit of His teaching. He does not say, I am here, simply; but, *I am with you;* meaning, Though you persecute Me, I will not cease fulfilling my part towards you, teaching you the way to salvation, and admonishing you. What follows, *And I go unto Him that sent Me,* was enough to excite some fear. THEOPHYL. As if He were going to complain of them to the Father: for if they reviled Him who was sent, no doubt they did an injury to Him that sent. BEDE. *I go to Him that*

Aug. Tract. xxxi. 7.

Aug. Tract. xxxi. s. 8.

Chrys. Hom. l. 2.

Aug. Tract. xxxi. 8.

Chrys. Hom. l. 2.

sent Me: i. e. I return to My Father, at whose command I
became incarnate. He is speaking of that departure, from
which He has never returned. CHRYS. That they wanted
His presence, appears from His saying, *Ye seek Me, and
shall not find Me.* But when did the Jews seek Him? Luke
relates that the women lamented over Him: and it is probable that many others did the same. And especially, when
the city was taken, would they call Christ and His miracles
to remembrance, and desire His presence. AUG. Here He
foretels His resurrection: for the search for Him was to
take place after His resurrection, when men were conscience-
stricken. They would not acknowledge Him, when present;
afterward they sought Him, when they saw the multitude
believing on Him; and many pricked in their hearts said,
What shall we do? They perceived that Christ's death was
owing to their sin, and believed in Christ's pardon to sinners;
and so despaired of salvation, until they drank of that blood
which they shed. CHRYS. Then lest any should think that
His death would take place in the common way, He adds,
And where I am, thither ye cannot come. If He continued
in death, they would be able to go to Him: for we all are going
thitherwards. AUG. He does not say, Where I shall be, but
Where I am. For Christ was always there in that place
whither He was about to return: He returned in such a
way, as that He did not forsake us. Visibly and according
to the flesh, He was upon earth; according to His invisible
majesty, He was in heaven and earth. Nor again is it, Ye
will not be able, but, Ye are not able to come: for they were
not such at the time, as to be able. That this is not meant
to drive men to despair, is shewn by His saying the very
same thing to His disciples; *Whither I go, ye cannot come;*
and by His explanation last of all to Peter, *Whither I go, ye
cannot follow Me now, but ye shall follow Me afterwards.*
CHRYS. He wants them to think seriously how little time
longer He should be with them, and what regret they will
feel when He is gone, and they are not able to find Him.
I go unto Him that sent Me; this shews that no injury
was done Him by their plots, and that His passion was
voluntary. The words had some effect upon the Jews, who
asked each other, where they were to go, which was like

Chrys.
Hom. l.
2.

Aug.
Tract.
xxxi. 9.

Chrys.
Hom.
xlix. 3.

Aug.
Tract.
xxxi. 9.

Chrys.
Hom. l.
32.

persons desiring to be quit of Him: *Then said the Jews among themselves, Whither will He go, that we shall not find Him? Will He go to the dispersed among the Gentiles, and teach the Gentiles?* In the fulness of their self-satisfaction, they call them Gentiles, as a term of reproach; the Gentiles being dispersed every where; a reproach which they themselves underwent afterwards. Of old all the nation was united together: but now that the Jews were mixed with the Gentiles in every part of the world, our Lord would not have said, *Whither I go, ye cannot come,* in the sense of going to the Gentiles. AUG. *Whither I go,* i. e. to the bosom of the Father. This they did not at all understand: and yet even their mistake is an unwitting prophecy of our salvation; i. e. that our Lord would go to the Gentiles, not in His own person, but by His feet, i. e. His members. He sent to us those whom He had made His members, and so made us His members. CHRYS. They did not mean, that our Lord was going to the Gentiles for their hurt, but to teach them. Their anger had subsided, and they believed what He had said. Else they would not have thought of asking each other, *What manner of saying is this that He said, Ye shall seek Me, and shall not find Me: and whither I am, ye cannot come.*

Aug. Tract. xxxi. 10.

Chrys. Hom. l. 3.

37. In the last day, that great day of the feast, Jesus stood and cried, saying, If any man thirst, let him come unto me, and drink.

38. He that believeth on me, as the Scripture hath said, out of his belly shall flow rivers of living water.

39. (But this spake he of the Spirit, which they that believe on him should receive: for the Holy Ghost was not yet given; because that Jesus was not yet glorified.)

Chrys. Hom. l. 1.

CHRYS. The feast being over, and the people about to return home, our Lord gives them provisions for the way: *In the last day, that great day of the feast, Jesus stood and cried, saying, If any man thirst, let him come unto Me, and drink.* AUG. The feast was then going on, which is called scenopegia, i. e. building of tents. CHRYS. Which lasted seven days. The first and last days were the most important; *In the last day, that great day of the feast,* says the Evangelist. Those between were given chiefly to amusements. He did not then make the offer on the first day, or the second, or the third, lest amidst the excitements that were going on, people should let it slip from their minds, He *cried out,* on account of the great multitude of people present. THEOPHYL. To make Himself audible, inspire confidence in others, and shew an absence of all fear in Himself. CHRYS. *If any thirsteth:* as if to say, I use no compulsion or violence: but if any have the desire strong enough, let him come. AUG. For there is an inner thirst, because there is an inner man: and the inner man of a certainty loves more than the outer. So then if we thirst, let us go not on our feet, but on our affections, not by change of place, but by love. CHRYS. He is speaking of spiritual drink, as His next words shew: *He that believeth on Me, as the Scripture hath said, out of his belly shall flow rivers of living water.* But where does the Scripture say this? No where. What then? We should read, *He that believeth in Me, as saith the Scripture,* putting the stop here; and then, *out of his belly shall flow rivers of living water:* the meaning being, that that was a right kind of belief, which was formed on the evidence of Scripture, not of miracles. *Search the Scriptures,* He had said before. JEROME. Or this testimony is taken from the Proverbs, where it is said, *Let thy fountains be dispersed abroad, and rivers of waters in the streets.* AUG. The belly of the inner man, is the heart's conscience. Let him drink from that water, and his conscience is quickened and purified; he drinks in the whole fountain, nay, becomes the very fountain itself. But what is that fountain, and what is that river, which flows from the belly of the inner man? The love of his neighbour. If any one, who drinks of the water, thinks that it is meant to satisfy himself alone, out of his belly there doth not flow living water. But if he does good to his neighbour, the stream is not dried up, but flows. GREG. When sacred preaching floweth from the soul of the faithful, rivers of living water, as it were, run down from the

T

Marginal notes:
Aug. Tract. xxxii. 1.

Chrys. Hom. li. 1.

Aug. Tract. xxxii. 11.

Chrys. Hom. li. 1.

Hierom. in prolog. Gen. Prov. 5, 16. Aug. Tract. xxxii. 4.

Greg. super Ezech. Hom. x.

bellies of believers. For what are the entrails of the belly
but the inner part of the mind; i. e. a right intention, a holy
desire, humility towards God, mercy toward man. CHRYS.

Chrys.
Hom.
li. 1.
He says, *rivers*, not river, to shew the copious and overflow-
ing power of grace: and *living water*, i. e. always moving;
for when the grace of the Spirit has entered into and settled
in the mind, it flows freer than any fountain, and neither
fails, nor empties, nor stagnates. The wisdom of Stephen,
the tongue of Peter, the strength of Paul, are evidences of
this. Nothing hindered them; but, like impetuous torrents,
they went on, carrying every thing along with them. AUG.

Aug.
Tract.
xxxii.5.
What kind of drink it was, to which our Lord invited them, the
Evangelist next explains; *But this He spake of the Spirit,
which they that believe on Him should receive.* Whom does
the Spirit mean, but the Holy Spirit? For every man has
within him his own spirit. ALCUIN. He promised the Holy
Spirit to the Apostles before the Ascension; He gave it to
them in fiery tongues, after the Ascension. The Evangelist's
words, *Which they that believe on Him should receive*, refer

Aug.
Tract.
xxxii.6.
to this. AUG. The Spirit of God was, i. e. was with God,
before now; but was not yet given to those who believed on
Jesus; for our Lord had determined not to give them the
Spirit, till He was risen again: *The Holy Ghost was not yet

Chrys.
Hom.
li. 1.
given, because that Jesus was not yet glorified.* CHRYS. The
Apostles indeed cast out devils by the Spirit before, but only
by the power which they had from Christ. For when He
sent them, it is not said, He gave them the Holy Spirit, but,
He gave unto them power. With respect to the Prophets,
however, all agree that the Holy Spirit was given to them:

Aug.
iv. de
Trin. c.
xx.
Luke 1,
15.
but this grace had been withdrawn from the world. AUG.
Yet we read of John the Baptist, *He shall be filled with the
Holy Ghost even from his mother's womb.* And Zacharias
was filled with the Holy Ghost, and prophesied. Mary was
filled with the Holy Ghost, and prophesied of our Lord.
And so were Simeon and Anna, that they might acknowledge
the greatness of the infant Christ. We are to understand
then that the giving of the Holy Spirit was to be certain,
after Christ's exaltation, in a way in which it never was
before. It was to have a peculiarity at His coming, which
it had not before. For we no where read of men under the

influence of the Holy Spirit, speaking with tongues which
they had never known, as then took place, when it was
necessary to evidence His coming by sensible miracles.
AUG. If the Holy Spirit then is received now, why is there no
one who speaks the tongues of all nations? Because now
the Church herself speaks the tongues of all nations. Whoso
is not in her, neither doth he now receive the Holy Spirit.
But if only thou lovest unity, whoever hath any thing in her,
hath it for thee. Put away envy, and that which I have
is thine. Envy separateth, love unites: have it, and thou
hast all things: whereas without it nothing that thou canst
have, will profit thee. *The love of God is shed abroad in* Rom. 5,
our hearts by the Holy Spirit which is given to us. But ^{9.}
why did our Lord give the Holy Spirit after His resurrection?
That the flame of love might mount upwards to our own
resurrection: separating us from the world, and devoting us
wholly to God. He who said, *He that believeth in Me, out
of his belly shall flow rivers of living water,* hath promised
life eternal, free from all fear, and change, and death. Such
then being the gifts which He promised to those in whom
the Holy Spirit kindled the flame of love, He would not give
that Spirit till He was glorified: in order that in His own
person He might shew us that life, which we hope to attain
to in the resurrection. AUG. If this then is the cause why Aug.
the Holy Spirit was not yet given; viz. because Jesus was cont.
not yet glorified; doubtless, the glorification of Jesus when l. xxxii.
it took place, was the cause immediately of its being given. c. 17.
The Cataphryges, however, said that they first received the
promised Paraclete, and thus strayed from the Catholic faith.
The Manichæans too apply all the promises made respecting
the Holy Spirit to Manichæus, as if there were no Holy Spirit
given before. CHRYS. Or thus; By the glory of Christ, He Chrys.
means the cross. For, whereas we were enemies, and gifts Hom.
are not made to enemies, but to friends, it was necessary that li. 2.
the victim should be first offered up, and the enmity of the
flesh removed; that, being made friends of God, we might be
capable of receiving the gift.

40. Many of the people therefore, when they heard
this saying, said, Of a truth this is the Prophet.

41. Others said, This is the Christ. But some said, Shall Christ come out of Galilee?

42. Hath not the Scripture said, That Christ cometh of the seed of David, and out of the town of Bethlehem, where David was?

43. So there was a division among the people because of him.

44. And some of them would have taken him; but no man laid hands on him.

45. Then came the officers to the chief priests and Pharisees; and they said unto them, Why have ye not brought him?

46. The officers answered, Never man spake like this man.

47. Then answered them the Pharisees, Are ye also deceived?

48. Have any of the rulers or of the Pharisees believed on him?

49. But this people who knoweth not the law are cursed.

50. Nicodemus saith unto them, (he that came to Jesus by night, being one of them,)

51. Doth our law judge any man, before it hear him, and know what he doeth?

52. They answered and said unto him, Art thou also of Galilee? Search, and look: for out of Galilee ariseth no prophet.

53. And every man went unto his own house.

Aug. Tract. xxxiii.1. AUG. Our Lord having invited those, who believed in Him, to drink of the Holy Spirit, a dissension arose among the multitude: *Many of the people therefore, when they heard this saying, said, Of a truth this is the Prophet.* THEOPHYL. The one, that is, who was expected. *Others,* i. e. the people *said, This is the Christ.* ALCUIN. These had now begun to

[1] Nic. water   drink in that spiritual thirst [1], and had laid aside the unbe-

lieving thirst. But others still remained dried up in their unbelief: *But some said, Shall Christ come out of Galilee? Hath not the Scripture said, That Christ cometh of the seed of David, and out of the town of Bethlehem, where David was?* They knew what were the predictions of the Prophets respecting Christ, but knew not that they all were fulfilled in Him. They knew that He had been brought up at Nazareth, but the place of His birth they did not know; and did not believe that it answered to the prophecies. CHRYS. But be it so, they knew not His birth-place: were they ignorant also of His extraction? that He was of the house and family of David? Why did they ask, *Hath not the Scripture said, that Christ cometh of the seed of David?* They wished to conceal His extraction, and therefore put forward where He had been educated. For this reason, they do not go to Christ and ask, How say the Scriptures that Christ must come from Bethlehem, whereas Thou comest from Galilee? purposely and of malice prepense they do not do this. And because they were thus inattentive, and indifferent about knowing the truth, Christ did not answer them: though He had lauded Nathanael, when he said, *Can any good thing come out of Nazareth?* and called Him an Israelite indeed, as being a lover of truth, and well learned in the ancient Scriptures. Chrys. Hom. li. 11.

So there was a division among the people concerning Him. THEOPHYL. Not among the rulers; for they were resolved one way, viz. not to acknowledge Him as Christ. The more moderate of them only used malicious words, in order to oppose Christ's path to glory; but the more malignant wished to lay hands on Him: *And some of them would have taken Him.* CHRYS. The Evangelist says this to shew, that they had no concern for, and no anxiety to learn, the truth. Chrys. Hom. li. 2.

But no man laid hands on Him. ALCUIN. That is, because He Who had the power to control their designs, did not permit it. CHRYS. This were sufficient to have raised some compunction in them; but no, such malignity believes nothing; it looks only to one thing, blood. AUG. They however who were sent to take Him, returned guiltless of the offence, and full of admiration: *Then came the officers to the chief priests and Pharisees; and they said unto them,* Chrys. Hom. li. 2. Aug. Tract. xxxiii.1,

Why have ye not brought Him? ALCUIN. They who wished to take and stone Him, reprove the officers for not bringing Him. CHRYS. The Pharisees and Scribes profited nothing by seeing the miracles, and reading the Scriptures; but their officers, who had done neither, were captivated with once hearing Him; and they who went to take hold of Him, were themselves taken hold of by the miracle. Nor did they say, We could not because of the multitude: but made themselves proclaimers of Christ's wisdom: *The officers answered, Never man spake like this Man.* AUG. He spoke thus, because He was both God and man. CHRYS. Not only is their wisdom to be admired, for not wanting miracles, but being convinced by His teaching only, (for they do not say, Never man did such miracles as this Man, but, *Never man spake like this Man,*) but also their boldness, in saying this to the Pharisees, who were such enemies of Christ. They had not heard a long discourse, but minds unprepossessed against Him did not require one. AUG. The Pharisees however rejected their testimony: *Then answered them the Pharisees, Are ye also led away?* As if to say, We see that you are charmed by His discourse. ALCUIN. And so they were led away; and laudably too, for they had left the evil of unbelief, and were gone over to the faith. CHRYS. They make use of the most foolish argument against them: *Have any of the rulers or of the Pharisees believed on Him? but this people who knoweth not the law are cursed?* This then was their ground of accusation, that the people believed, but they themselves did not. AUG. They who knew not the law, believed on Him who had given the law, and they who taught the law condemned Him; thus fulfilling our Lord's words, *I am come, that they which see not might see, and that they which see might be made blind.* CHRYS. How then are they cursed, who are convinced by the law? Rather are ye cursed, who have not observed the law. THEOPHYL. The Pharisees answer the officers courteously and gently; because they are afraid of their forthwith separating from them, and joining Christ. CHRYS. As they said that none of the rulers believed on Him, the Evangelist contradicts them: *Nicodemus saith unto them, (he that came to Jesus by night, being one of them.)* AUG. He was not unbelieving, but

fearful; and therefore came by night to the light, wishing to
be enlightened, but afraid of being known to go.   He replies,
*Doth our law judge any man before it hear him, and know
what he doeth?*   He thought that, if they would only hear Him
patiently, they would be overcome, as the officers had been.
But they preferred obstinately condemning Him, to knowing
the truth.   Aug. He calls the law of God, *our law;* because
it was given to men.   Chrys. Nicodemus shews that they Chrys.
knew the law, and did not act according to the law. Hom. lii. 1, 2.
They, instead of disproving this, take to rude and angry
contradiction: *They answered and said unto him, Art thou
also of Galilee?*   Aug. i. e. led away by a Galilean.   Our Lord Aug.
was called a Galilean, because His parents were of the town Tract. xxxiii.
of Nazareth; I mean by parents, Mary.   Chrys. Then, by 2.
way of insult, they direct Him to the Scriptures, as if He were Chrys. Hom.
ignorant of them; *Search and look, for out of Galilee ariseth* lii. 11.
no prophet: as if to say, Go, learn what the Scriptures say.
Alcuin. They knew the place where He had resided, but
never thought of enquiring where He was born; and therefore
they not only denied that He was the Messiah, but even that
He was a prophet.   Aug. No prophet indeed ariseth out of Aug.
Galilee, but the Lord of prophets arose thence. Tract. xxxiii.

   And every man went unto his own house.   Alcuin. Having 11.
effected nothing, devoid of faith, and therefore incapable of
being benefited, they returned to their home of unbelief and
ungodliness.

CHAP. VIII.

1. Jesus went unto the mount of Olives.

2. And early in the morning he came again into the temple, and all the people came unto him; and he sat down, and taught them.

3. And the Scribes and Pharisees brought unto him a woman taken in adultery; and when they had set her in the midst,

4. They say unto him, Master, this woman was taken in adultery, in the very act.

5. Now Moses in the law commanded us, that such should be stoned: but what sayest thou?

6. This they said, tempting him, that they might have to accuse him. But Jesus stooped down, and with his finger wrote on the ground, as though he heard them not.

7. So when they continued asking him, he lifted up himself, and said unto them, He that is without sin among you, let him first cast a stone at her.

8. And again He stooped down, and wrote on the ground.

9. And they which heard it, being convicted by their own conscience, went out one by one, beginning at the eldest, even unto the last: and Jesus was left alone, and the woman standing in the midst.

10. When Jesus had lifted up himself, and saw none but the woman, he said unto her, Woman, where are those thine accusers? hath no man condemned thee?

11. She said, No man, Lord. And Jesus said unto her, Neither do I condemn thee: go, and sin no more.

ALCUIN. Our Lord at the time of His passion used to spend the day in Jerusalem, preaching in the temple, and performing miracles, and return in the evening to Bethany, where He lodged with the sisters of Lazarus. Thus on the last day of the feast, having, according to His wont, preached the whole day in the temple, in the evening He *went to the mount of Olives.* AUG. And where ought Christ to teach, except on the mount of Olives; on the mount of ointment, on the mount of chrism. For the name Christ is from chrism, chrism being the Greek word for unction. He has anointed us, for wrestling with the devil. ALCUIN. The anointing with oil is a relief to the limbs, when wearied and in pain. The mount of Olives also denotes the height of our Lord's pity, olive in the Greek signifying pity. The qualities of oil are such as to fit in to this mystical meaning. For it floats above all other liquids: and the Psalmist says, *Thy mercy is over all Thy works. And early in the morning, He came again into the temple:* i. e. to denote the giving and unfolding of His mercy, i. e. the now dawning light of the New Testament in the faithful, that is, in His temple. His returning *early in the morning,* signifies the new rise of grace. BEDE. And next it is signified, that after He began to dwell by grace in His temple, i. e. in the Church, men from all nations would believe in Him: *And all the people came to Him, and He sat down and taught them.* ALCUIN. The sitting down, represents the humility of His incarnation. And the people came to Him, when He sat down, i. e. after taking up human nature, and thereby becoming visible, many began to hear and believe on Him, only knowing Him as their friend and neighbour. But while these kind and simple persons are full of admiration at our Lord's discourse, the Scribes and Pharisees put questions to Him, not for the sake of instruction, but only to entangle the truth in their nets: *And the Scribes and Pharisees brought unto Him a woman taken in adultery; and when they had set her in the midst, they say unto Him, Master, this woman was taken in adultery, in the very act.* AUG. They had remarked upon Him already, as being over lenient. Of Him indeed it had been prophesied, *Ride on because of the word of truth, of meekness, and of righteousness.* So as a teacher He

Aug.
Tract.
xxxiii.
3.

Ps. 144.

Aug.
Tract.
xxxiii.
s. 4.
Ps. 44.

exhibited truth, as a deliverer meekness, as a judge righteousness. When He spoke, His truth was acknowledged; when
against His enemies He used no violence, His meekness was
praised. So they raised the scandal on the score of justice.
For they said among themselves, If He decide to let her go,
He will not do justice; for the law cannot command what is
unjust: *Now Moses in the law commanded us, that such
should be stoned:* but to maintain His meekness, which has
made Him already so acceptable to the people, He must
decide to let her go. Wherefore they demand His opinion:
And what sayest Thou? hoping to find an occasion to accuse
Him, as a transgressor of the law: *And this they said
tempting Him, that they might have to accuse Him.* But
our Lord in His answer both maintained His justice, and
departed not from meekness. *Jesus stooped down, and with
His finger wrote on the ground.* AUG. As if to signify that
such persons were to be written in earth, not in heaven,
where He told His disciples they should rejoice they were
written. Or His bowing His head (to write on the ground),
is an expression of humility; the writing on the ground
signifying that His law was written on the earth which bore
fruit, not on the barren stone, as before. ALCUIN. The
ground denotes the human heart, which yieldeth the fruit
either of good or of bad actions: the finger jointed and
flexible, discretion. He instructs us then, when we see any
faults in our neighbours, not immediately and rashly to condemn them, but after searching our own hearts to begin with,
to examine them attentively with the finger of discretion.
BEDE. His writing with His finger on the ground perhaps
shewed, that it was He who had written the law on stone.

    *So when they continued asking Him, He lifted Himself
up.* AUG. He did not say, Stone her not, lest He should
seem to speak contrary to the law. But God forbid that He
should say, Stone her; for He came not to destroy that
which He found, but to seek that which was lost. What
then did He answer? *He that is without sin among you,
let him first cast a stone at her.* This is the voice of justice.
Let the sinner be punished, but not by sinners; the law
carried into effect, but not by transgressors of the law. GREG.
For he who judges not himself first, cannot know how to

Margin notes:
Aug.
de Con.
Evang.
lib. ii.
c. 10.

Aug.
Tract.
xxxiii.
5.

judge correctly in the case of another. For though He
know what the offence is, from being told, yet He cannot
judge of another's deserts, who supposing himself innocent,
will not apply the rule of justice to himself. AUG. Having Aug.
with the weapon of justice smitten them, He deigned not Tract.
even to look on the fallen, but averted His eyes: *And again* xxxiii.
He stooped down, and wrote on the ground. ALCUIN. This 5.
is like our Lord; while His eyes are fixed, and He seems
attending to something else, He gives the bystanders an
opportunity of retiring: a tacit admonition to us to consider
always both before we condemn a brother for a sin, and
after we have punished him, whether we are not guilty
ourselves of the same fault, or others as bad. AUG. Thus Aug.
smitten then with the voice of justice, as with a weapon, Tract.
they examine themselves, find themselves guilty, and one by xxxiii.
one retire: *And they which heard it, went out one by one,* s. 5.
*beginning at the eldest*ᵃ. GLOSS. The more guilty of them,
perhaps, or those who were more conscious of their faults.
AUG. There were left however two, the pitiable[1] and the Aug.
pitiful, *And Jesus was left alone, and the woman standing* Tract.
in the midst: the woman, you may suppose, in great alarm, xxxiii.
expecting punishment from one in whom no sin could be 5, 6.
found. But He who had repelled her adversaries with the [1] miseria
word of justice, lifted on her the eyes of mercy, and asked; et mise-
When Jesus had lifted Himself up, and saw none but the ricordia.
woman, He said unto her, Woman, where are these thine
accusers? hath no man condemned thee? She said, No man,
Lord. We heard above the voice of justice; let us hear now
that of mercy: *Jesus said unto her, Neither do I condemn*
thee; I, who thou fearedst would condemn thee, because
thou foundest no fault in me. What then, Lord? Dost Thou
favour sin? No, surely. Listen to what follows, *Go, and sin*
no more. So then our Lord condemned sin, but not the
sinner. For did He favour sin, He would have said, Go,
and live as thou wilt: depend on my deliverance: howsoever
great thy sins be, it matters not: I will deliver thee from
hell, and its tormentors. But He did not say this. Let
those attend, who love the Lord's mercy, and fear His truth.
Truly, *Gracious and righteous is the Lord.*   Ps.35,7.

ᵃ Vulgate omits ὑπὸ τῆς συνιιδήσεως ἰλεγχόμενοι ἕως τῶν ἐσχάτων.

12. Then spake Jesus again unto them, saying, I am the light of the world: he that followeth me shall not walk in darkness, but shall have the light of life.

ALCUIN. Having absolved the woman from her sin, lest some should doubt, seeing that He was really man, His power to forgive sins, He deigns to give further disclosure of His divine nature; *Then spake Jesus again unto them, saying, I am the Light of the world.* BEDE. Where it is to be observed, He does not say, *I am* the light of Angels, or of heaven, but *the Light of the world,* i. e. of mankind who live in darkness, as we read, *To give light to them that sit in darkness, and in the shadow of death.* CHRYS. As they had brought Galilee as an objection against Him, and doubted His being one of the Prophets, as if that was all He claimed to be, He wished to shew that He was not one of the Prophets, but the Lord of the whole earth: *Then spake Jesus again unto them, saying, I am the Light of the world:* not of Galilee, or of Palestine, or of Judæa. AUG. The Manichæans suppose the sun of the natural world to be our Lord Christ; but the Catholic Church reprobates such a notion; for our Lord Christ was not made the sun, but the sun was made by Him: inasmuch as *all things were made by Him.* And for our sake did He come to be under the sun, being the light which made the sun: He hid Himself under the cloud of the flesh, not to obscure, but to temper His light. Speaking then through the cloud of the flesh, the Light unfailing, the Light of wisdom says to men, *I am the Light of the world.* THEOPHYL. You may bring these words against Nestorius: for our Lord does not say, In Me is the light of the world, but, *I am the Light of the world:* He who appeared man, was both the Son of God, and the Light of the world; not, as Nestorius fondly holds, the Son of God dwelling in a mere man. AUG. He withdraws you however from the eyes of the flesh, to those of the heart, in that He adds, *He that followeth Me shall not walk in darkness, but shall have the light of life.* He thinks it not enough to say, *shall have light,* but adds, *of life.* These words of our Lord agree with those of the Psalm, *In Thy light shall we see light; for with Thee is the well of life.* For bodily uses, light is one

Luke 1, 79.
Chrys. Hom. lii. 2.

Aug. Tract. xxxiv. 2.

c. 1, 3.

Aug. Tract. xxxiv. s. 5.

Ps. 35.

thing, and a well another; and a well ministers to the mouth, light to the eyes. With God the light and the well are the same. He who shines upon thee, that thou mayest see Him, the Same flows unto thee, that thou mayest drink Him. What He promises is put in the future tense; what we ought to do in the present. *He that followeth Me,* He says, *shall have;* i. e. by faith now, in sight hereafter. The visible sun accompanieth thee, only if thou goest westward, whither it goeth also; and even if thou follow it, it will forsake thee, at its setting. Thy God is every where wholly; He will not fall from thee, if thou fall not from Him. Darkness is to be feared, not that of the eyes, but that of the mind; and if of the eyes, of the inner not the outer eyes; not those by which white and black, but those by which just and unjust, are discerned. CHRYS. *Walketh not in darkness,* i. e. spiritually Chrys. abideth not in error. Here He tacitly praises Nicodemus Hom. lii. 2. and the officers, and censures those who had plotted against Him; as being in darkness and error, and unable to come to the light.

13. The Pharisees therefore said unto him, Thou bearest record of thyself; thy record is not true.

14. Jesus answered and said unto them, Though I bear record of myself, yet my record is true: for I know whence I came, and whither I go; but ye cannot tell whence I come, and whither I go.

15. Ye judge after the flesh; I judge no man.

16. And yet if I judge, my judgment is true: for I am not alone, but I and the Father that sent me.

17. It is also written in your law, that the testimony of two men is true.

18. I am one that bear witness of myself, and the Father that sent me beareth witness of me.

CHRYS. Our Lord having said, *I am the Light of the world;* Chrys. and, *he that followeth Me, walketh not in darkness,* the Hom. lii. 2. Jews wish to overthrow what He has said: *The Pharisees therefore said unto Him, Thou bearest record of Thyself, Thy record is not true.* ALCUIN. As if our Lord Himself were the only (one that bore) witness to Himself; whereas the truth was that He had, before His incarnation, sent many Chrys. Hom. lii. 2. witnesses to prophesy of His Sacraments. CHRYS. Our Lord however overthrew their argument: *Jesus answered and said, Though I bear record of Myself, yet My record is true.* This is an accommodation to those who thought Him no more than a mere man. He adds the reason, *For I know whence I come, and whither I go;* i. e. I am God, from God, and the Son of God: though this He does not say expressly, from His habit of mingling lofty and lowly words together. Now God is surely a competent witness to Himself. Aug. AUG. The wituess of light is true, whether the light Tract. xxxv. 6. shew itself, or other things. The Prophet spake the truth, but whence had he it, but by drawing from the fount of s. 5. truth? Jesus then is a competent witness to Himself. *For I know whence I come, and whither I go:* this has reference to the Father; for the Son gave glory to the Father who sent Him. How greatly then should man glorify the Creator, who made Him. He did not separate from His Father, however, when He came, or desert us when He returned: unlike that sun which in going to the west, leaves the east. And as that sun throws its light on the faces both of him who sees, and him who sees not; only the one sees with the light, the other sees not: so the Wisdom of God, the Word, is every where present, even to the minds of unbelievers; but they have not the eyes of the understanding, wherewith to see. To distinguish then between believers and enemies among the Jews, as between light and darkness, He adds, *But ye cannot tell whence I come, and whither I go.* Tract. xxxvi. 3. These Jews saw the man, and did not believe in the God, and therefore our Lord says, *Ye judge after the flesh,* i. e. in saying, *Thou bearest record of Thyself, Thy record is not true.* THEOPHYL. As if to say: Ye judge untruly, according to the flesh, thinking, because I am in the flesh, that I am flesh Aug. only, and not God. AUG. Understanding Me not as God, Tract. xxxvi. 3. in Joan. and seeing Me as man, ye think Me arrogant in bearing witness of Myself. For any man who bears high testimony to himself, is thought proud and arrogant. But men are Chrys. Hom. l. 2. frail, and may either speak the truth, or lie: the Light cannot lie. CHRYS. As to live according to the flesh is to live

amiss; so to judge according to the flesh, is to judge unjustly. They might say, however, If we judge wrongly, why
dost Thou not convict us, why dost Thou not condemn us?
So He adds, *I judge no man.* Aug. Which may be under- Aug.
stood in two ways; *I judge no man,* i. e. not now: as He $\frac{\text{Tract.}}{\text{xxxvi.}}$
says elsewhere, *God sent not His Son into the world to* s. 4.
*condemn the world, but that the world through Him might
be saved:* not that He abandons, but only defers, His justice.
Or having said, *Ye judge according to the flesh,* He says
immediately, *I judge no man,* to let you know that Christ
does not judge according to the flesh, as men judged Him.
For that Christ is a judge appears from the next words, *And
yet if I judge, My judgment is true.* Chrys. As if to say : Chrys.
In saying, *I judge no man,* I meant that I did not anticipate $\frac{\text{Hom.}}{\text{lii. 2.}}$
judgment. If I judged justly, I should condemn you, but
now is not the time for judging. He alludes however to the
future judgment, in what follows; *For I am not alone, but I
and the Father that sent Me*; which means that He will not
condemn them alone, but He and the Father together. This
is intended too to quiet suspicion, as men did not think the
Son worthy to be believed, unless He had the testimony of
the Father also. Aug. But if the Father is with Thee, how Aug.
did He send Thee ? O Lord, Thy mission is Thy incarnation. $\frac{\text{Tract.}}{\text{xxxvi.7.}}$
Christ was here according to the flesh without withdrawing
from the Father, because the Father and the Son are every
where. Blush, thou Sabellian; our Lord doth not say, I
am the Father, and I the self-same person am the Son; but,
I am not alone, because the Father is with Me. Make a
distinction then of persons, and distinction of intelligences :
acknowledge that the Father is the Father, the Son the Son :
but beware of saying, that the Father is greater, the Son less.
Theirs is one substance, one coeternity, perfect equality.
Therefore, He says, My judgment is true, because I am the
Son of God. But that thou mayest understand how that the
Father is with Me, it is not for the Son ever to leave the
Father. I have taken up the form of a servant; but I have
not lost the form of God. He had spoken of judgment:
now He speaks of witness: *It is also written in your law,
that the testimony of two men is true.* Aug. Is this made a
bad use of by the Manichæans, that our Lord does not say,

in the law of God, but, *in your law?* Who does not recognise here a manner of speaking customary in Scripture? *In your law*, i. e. the law given to you. The Apostle speaks of *his* Gospel in the same way, though he testifies to having received it not from men, but by the revelation of Jesus Christ. AUG. There is much difficulty, and a great mystery seems to be contained, in God's words, *In the mouth of two or three witnesses, let every word be established.* It is possible that two may speak false. The chaste Susannah was arraigned by two false witnesses: the whole people spake against Christ falsely. How then must we understand the word, *By the mouth of two or three witnesses shall every word be established:* except as an intimation of the mystery of the Trinity, in which is perpetual stability of truth? Receive then our testimony, lest ye feel our judgment. I delay My judgment: I delay not My testimony: *I am one that beareth witnes of Myself, and the Father that sent Me beareth witness of Me.* BEDE. In many places the Father bears witness of the Son; as, *This day have I begotten Thee;* also, *This is My beloved Son.* CHRYS. *It is written in your law, that the testimony of two men is true.* If this is to be taken literally, in what respect does our Lord differ from men? The rule has been laid down for men, on the ground that one man alone is not to be relied on: but how can this be applicable to God? These words are quoted then with another meaning. When two men bear witness, both to an indifferent matter, their witness is true: this constitutes the testimony of two men. But if one of them bear witness to himself, then they are no longer two witnesses. Thus our Lord means to shew that He is consubstantial with the Father, and does not need another witness, i. e. besides the Father's. *I and the Father that sent Me.* Again, on human principles, when a man bears witness, his honesty is supposed; he is not borne witness to; and a man is admitted as a fair and competent witness in an indifferent matter, but not in one relating to himself, unless he is supported by other testimony. But here it is quite otherwise. Our Lord, though giving testimony in His own case, and though saying that He is borne witness to by another, pronounces Himself worthy of belief; thus shewing His all-sufficiency. He says He

Marginal references:

Aug.
Tract.
xxxvi.
10.
Deut.10.

Ps. 2.

Matt. 3,
17.
Chrys.
Hom.
lii. 3.

deserves to be believed. ALCUIN. Or it is as if He said, If
your law admits the testimony of two men who may be
deceived, and testify to more than is true; on what grounds
can you reject Mine and My Father's testimony, the highest
and most sure of all?

19. Then said they unto him, Where is thy Father?
Jesus answered, Ye neither know me, nor my Father :
if ye had known me, ye should have known my Father
also.

20. These words spake Jesus in the treasury, as he
taught in the temple : and no man laid hands on him ;
for his hour was not yet come.

AUG. Those who had heard our Lord say, *Ye judge after* Aug.
the flesh, shewed that they did so; for they understood Tract.
what He said of His Father in a carnal sense: *Then said* xxxvii.
they unto Him, Where is Thy Father? meaning, We have
heard Thee say, *I am not alone, but I and the Father that
sent Me.* We see Thee alone; prove to us then that Thy
Father is with Thee. THEOPHYL. Some remark that this is
said in contumely and contempt; to insinuate either that He
is born of fornication, and knows not who His Father is ; or
as a slur on the low situation of His father, i. e. Joseph ; as
if to say, Thy father is an obscure, ignoble person ; why
dost Thou so often mention him? So because they asked the
question, to tempt Him, not to get at the truth, *Jesus
answered, Ye neither know Me, nor My Father.* AUG. As Aug.
if He said, *Ye ask where is Thy Father?* As if ye knew Tract.
Me already, and I were nothing else but what ye see. But xxxvii.
ye know Me not, and therefore I tell you nothing of My
Father. Ye think Me indeed a mere man, and therefore
among men look for My Father. But, forasmuch as I am
different altogether, according to My seen and unseen
natures, and speak of My Father in the hidden sense according to My hidden nature ; it is plain that ye must first know
Me, and then ye will know My Father ; *If ye had known
Me, ye would have known My Father also.* CHRYS. He tells Chrys.
them, it is of no avail for them to say they know the Father, Hom.
lii. 3.

U

Orig.
tom.xix.
1. in
Joan. in
princ. if they do not know the Son. ORIGEN. *Ye neither know Me, nor My Father :* this seems inconsistent with what was said above, *Ye both know Me, and know whence I am.* But the latter is spoken in reply to some from Jerusalem, who asked, *Do the rulers know indeed that this is the very Christ? Ye neither know Me,* is addressed to the Pharisees. To the former persons from Jerusalem however He said, *He that sent Me is true, Whom ye know not.* You will ask then, How is that true, *If ye know Me, ye would know My Father also?* when they of Jerusalem, to whom He said, *Ye know Me,* did not know the Father. To this we must reply, that our Saviour sometimes speaks of Himself as man, and sometimes as God. *Ye both know Me,* He says as man : *ye neither know Me,* as God. AUG. What does this mean : *If ye knew Me, ye would know My Father also,* but, *I and My Father are one?* It is a common expression, when you see one man very like another, If you have seen him, you have seen the other. You say this, because they are so like. And thus our Lord says, *If ye had known Me, ye had known My Father also;* not that the Father is the Son, but that the Son is like the Father. THEOPHYL. Let the Arian blush: for if, as he says, the Son be a creature, how does it follow that he who knows the creature, knows God? For not even by knowing the substance of Angels, does one know the Divine Substance? Forasmuch therefore as he who knows the Son, knows the Father, it is certain that the Son is consubstantial with the Father. AUG. This word perhaps[c] is used only by way of rebuke, though it seems to express doubt. As used by men indeed it is the expression of doubt, but He who knew all things could only mean by that doubt to rebuke unbelief. Nay, even we sometimes say perhaps, when they are certain of a thing, e. g. when you are angry with your slave, and say, Do not you heed me? Consider, perhaps I am your master. So our Lord's doubt is a reproof to the unbelievers, when He says, *Ye should have known perhaps My Father also.* ORIGEN. It is proper to observe, that the followers of other sects think this text proves clearly, that the God, whom the Jews worshipped, was not the Father of Christ. For if, say they, our Saviour said this to the

Aug.
Tract.
xxxvii.
7.

Aug.
Tract.
xxxviii.
s. 3.

Orig.
tom.xix.
1. in
Joan. in
princ.

---

[c] forsitan in Vulgate, before ἤδειτε ἄν.

Pharisees, who worshipped God as the Governor of the world, it is evident that the Father of Jesus, whom the Pharisees knew not, was a different person from the Creator. But they do not observe that this is a usual manner of speaking in Scripture. Though a man may know the existence of God, and have learned from the Father that He only must be worshipped, yet if his life is not good, he is said not to have the knowledge of God. Thus the sons of Eli, on account of their wickedness, are said not to have known God. And thus again the Pharisees did not know the Father; because they did not live according to their Creator's command. And there is another thing meant too by knowing God, different from merely believing in Him. It is said, *Be still then, and* Ps. 45, *know that I am God.* And this, it is certain, was written [10.] for a people that believed in the Creator. But to know by believing, and believe simply, are different things. To the Pharisees, to whom He says, *Ye neither know Me, nor My Father,* He could with right have said, Ye do not even believe in My Father; for he who denies the Son, has not the Father, either by faith or knowledge. But Scripture gives us another sense of knowing a thing, viz. being joined to that thing. Adam knew his wife, when he was joined to her. And if he who is joined to a woman knows that woman, he who is joined to the Lord is one spirit, and knows the Lord. And in this sense the Pharisees neither knew the Father, nor the Son. But may not a man know God, and yet not know the Father? Yes; these are two different conceptions. And therefore among an infinite number of prayers offered up in the Law, we do not find any one addressed to God the Father. They only pray to Him as God and Lord; in order not to anticipate the grace shed by Jesus over the whole world, calling all men to the Sonship, according to the Psalm, *I will declare Thy name unto my brethren.*

These words spake Jesus in the treasury, as He taught in the temple. ALCUIN. Treasury (Gazophylacium): Gaza is the Persian for wealth: phylattein is to keep. It was a place in the temple, where the money was kept. CHRYS. He spake Chrys. in the temple magisterially, and now He was speaking to Hom. those who railed at and accused Him, for making Himself liii. 1.

Aug.
Tract.
xxxvii.
8. equal to the Father. AUG. Great however is His confidence
and fearlessness: it not being possible that He should
undergo any suffering, but that which He voluntarily undertook. Wherefore it follows, *And no man laid hands on Him,
for His hour was not yet come.* Some, when they hear this,
think Christ to have been under the control of fate. But if
fate comes from the verb fari, to speak, as some derive it,
how can the Word of God be under the control of fate?
Where are the fates? In the heavens, you say, in the courses
and revolutions of the stars. How then can fate have power
over Him, by Whom the heavens and stars were made; when
even thy will, if thou exert it aright, transcends the stars?
Dost thou think that because the flesh of Christ was placed
beneath the heavens, that therefore His power was subjected
to the heavens? *His hour* then *had not yet come;* i. e. the
hour, not on which he should be obliged to die, but on
Orig.
tom.xix.
in Joan. which He should deign to be put to death. ORIGEN. Whenever it is added, Jesus spoke these words in such a place,
you will, if you attend, discover a meaning in the addition.
γαζοφυ
λακίῳ The treasury was a place for keeping the money, which was
given for the honour of God, and the support of the poor.
The coins are the divine words, stamped with the likeness
of the great King. In this sense then let every one contribute
to the edification of the Church, carrying into that spiritual
treasury all that he can collect, to the honour of God, and
the common good. But while all were thus contributing to
the treasury of the temple, it was especially the office of Jews
to contribute his gifts, which were the words of eternal life.
While Jesus therefore was speaking in the treasury, no one
laid hands on Him; His discourse being stronger than those
who wished to take Him; for there is no weakness in that
which the Word of God utters. BEDE. Or thus; Christ
speaks in the treasury; i. e. He had spoken in parables to
the Jews; but now that He unfolded heavenly things to His
disciples, His treasury began to be opened, which was the
meaning of the treasury being joined to the temple; all that
the Law and the Prophets had foretold in figure, appertained
to our Lord.

21. Then said Jesus again unto them, I go my way,

and ye shall seek me, and shall die in your sins : whither I go, ye cannot come.

22. Then said the Jews, Will he kill himself? because he saith, Whither I go, ye cannot come.

23. And he said unto them, Ye are from beneath ; I am from above : ye are of this world, I am not of this world.

24. I said therefore unto you, that ye shall die in your sins : for if ye believe not that I am he, ye shall die in your sins.

AUG. In accordance with what was just, He said that *no man laid hands on Him, because His hour was not yet come;* He now speaks to the Jews of His passion, as a free, and not a compulsory sacrifice on His part: *Then said Jesus again unto them, I go My way.* Death to our Lord was a return to the place whence He had come. BEDE. The connexion of these words is such, that they might have been spoken at one place and one time, or at another place and another time : as either nothing at all, or some things, or many may have intervened. ORIGEN. But some one will object: If this was spoken to men who persisted in unbelief, how is it He says, *Ye shall seek Me?* For to seek Jesus is to seek truth and wisdom. You will answer that it was said of His persecutors, that they sought to take Him. There are different ways of seeking Jesus. All do not seek Him for their health and profit: and only they who seek Him aright, find peace. And they are said to seek Him aright, who seek the Word which was in the beginning with God, in order that He may lead them to the Father. AUG. *Ye shall seek Me,* then, He says, not from compassionate regret, but from hatred: for after He had departed from the eyes of men, He was sought for both by those who hated, and those who loved Him: the one wanting to persecute, the other to have His presence. And that ye may not think that ye shall seek Me in a good sense, I tell you, *Ye shall die in your sin.* This is to seek Christ amiss, to die in one's sin: this is to hate Him, from Whom alone cometh salvation. He pronounces sentence on them prophetically, that they shall die in their

Margin notes:
Aug. Tract. xxxviii. 2.

Orig. tom. xix. in Joan. s. 3.

Aug. Tract. xxxviii. 2.

ἁμαρτία plural in our Transl.

sins. BEDE. Note: *sin* is in the singular number, *your* in the plural ; to express one and the same wickedness in all.

Orig.
tom.xix.
in Joan.
s. 3. ORIGEN. But I ask, as it is said below that many believed on Him, whether He speaks to all present, when He says, *Ye shall die in your sins?* No: He speaks to those only, whom He knew would not believe, and would therefore die in their sins, not being able to follow Him. *Whither I go,* He says, *ye cannot come;* i. e. there where truth and wisdom are, for with them Jesus dwells. They cannot, He says, because they will not: for had they wished, He could not reasonably have said, *Ye shall die in your sin.* Aug.
Tract.
xxviii.
s. 2. AUG. This He tells His disciples in another place; without saying to them, however, *Ye shall die in your sin,* He only says, *Whither I go, ye cannot follow Me now;* not preventing, but only delaying their coming. Orig.
tom.xix.
3. ORIGEN. The Word, while still present, yet threatens to depart. So long as we preserve the seeds of truth implanted in our minds, the Word of God does not depart from us. But if we fall into wickedness, then He says to us, *I go away;* and when we seek Him, we shall not find Him, but shall die in our sin, die caught in our sin. But we should not pass over without notice the expression itself: *Ye shall die in your sins.* If *ye shall die* be understood in the ordinary sense, it is manifest that sinners die in their sins, the righteous in their righteousness. But if we understand it of death in the sense of sin; then the meaning is, that not their bodies, but their souls were sick unto death. The Physician seeing them thus grievously sick, says, *Ye shall die in your sins.* And this is evidently the meaning of the words, *Whither I go ye cannot come.* For when a man dies in his sin, he cannot go where Jesus goes: no dead man Ps. 113. can follow Jesus: *The dead praise not Thee, O Lord.* AUG. Aug.
Tract.
xxxviii. They take these words, as they generally do, in a carnal sense, and ask, *Will He kill Himself, because He saith, Whither I go, ye cannot come?* A foolish question. For why? Could they not go where He went, if He killed Himself? Were they never to die themselves? *Whither I go,* then, He says; meaning not His departure at death, but where He went after death. THEOPHYL. He shews here that He will rise again in glory, and sit at the right hand of God. Orig.
tom.xix.
in Joan.
s. 4. ORIGEN. May they not however have a higher meaning in saying this?

For they had opportunities of knowing many things from their apocryphal books or from tradition. As then there was a prophetical tradition, that Christ was to be born at Bethlehem, so there may have been a tradition also respecting His death, viz. that He would depart from this life in the way which He declares, *No man taketh it from Me, but I lay it down* c.10,18. *of Myself.* So then the question, *Will He kill Himself,* is not to be taken in its obvious sense, but as referring to some Jewish tradition about Christ. For His saying, *I go My way,* shews that He had power over His own death, and departure from the body; so that these were voluntary on His part. But I think that they bring forward this tradition which had come down to them, on the death of Christ, contemptuously, and not with any view to give Him glory. *Will He kill Himself?* say they: whereas, they ought to have used a loftier way of speaking, and have said, Will His soul wait His pleasure, to depart from His body? Our Lord answers, *Ye are from beneath,* i. e. ye love earth; your hearts are not raised upwards. He speaks to them as earthly men, for their thoughts were earthly. CHRYS. As if to say, No wonder Chrys. that ye think as ye do, seeing ye are carnal, and understand Hom. liii. 1. nothing spiritually. *I am from above.* AUG. From whom Aug. above? From the Father Himself, Who is above all. *Ye are* Tract. xxxviii. *of this world, I am not of this world.* How could He be of 4. the world, by Whom the world was made? BEDE. And Who was before the world, whereas they were of the world, having been created after the world had begun to exist. CHRYS. Or He says, *I am not of this world,* with reference Chrys. to worldly and vain thoughts. THEOPHYL. I affect nothing Hom. liii. 1. worldly, nothing earthly: I could never come to such madness as to kill Myself. Apollinarius, however, falsely infers from these words, that our Lord's body was not of this world, but came down from heaven. Did the Apostles then, to whom our Lord says below, *Ye are not of this world,* derive c.15,19. all of them their bodies from heaven? In saying then, *I am not of this world,* He must be understood to mean, I am not of the number of you, who mind earthly things. ORIGEN. Orig. *Beneath,* and, *of this world,* are different things. *Beneath,* tom.xix. in Joan. refers to a particular place; this material world embraces s. 5.

different tracts[d], which all are beneath, as compared with things immaterial and invisible, but, as compared with one another, some beneath, some above. Where the treasure of each is, there is his heart also. If a man then lay up treasure upon earth, he is beneath: if any man lay up treasure in heaven, he is above; yea, ascends above all hearers, attains to a most blissful end. And again, the love of this world makes a man of this world: whereas he who loveth not the world, neither the things that are in the world, is not of the world. Yet is there beyond this world of sense, another world, in which are things invisible, the beauty of which shall the pure in heart behold, yea, the First-born of every creature may be called the world, insomuch as He is absolute wisdom, and in wisdom all things were made. In Him therefore was the whole world, differing from the material world, in so far ¹ ᵣatio as the ¹ scheme divested of the matter, differs from the subject matter itself. The soul of Christ then says, *I am not of this world;* i. e. because it has not its conversation in this world.

Aug. AUG. Our Lord expresses His meaning in the words, *Ye are*
Tract.
xxxviii. *of this world,* i. e. ye are sinners. All of us are born in sin;
6. all have added by our actions to the sin in which we were born. The misery of the Jews then was, not that they had sin, but that they would die in their sin: *I said therefore unto you, that ye shall die in your sin.* Amongst the multitude, however, who heard our Lord, there were some who were about to believe; whereas this most severe sentence had gone forth against all: *Ye shall die in your sin;* to the destruction of all hope even in those who should hereafter believe. So His next words recall the latter to hope: *For if ye believe not that I am He, ye shall die in your sin:* therefore if ye believe that I am He, ye shall not die in your
Chrys. sin. CHRYS. For if He came in order to take away sin, and
Hom.
liii. 1. a man cannot put that off, except by washing, and cannot be baptized except he believe; it follows, that he who believes not must pass out of this life, with the old man, i. e. sin, within him: not only because he believes not, but because
Aug. he departs hence, with his former sins upon him. AUG. His
Tract.
xxxviii. saying, *If ye believe not that I am,* without adding any thing,
8.

[d] e. g. earth beneath, sky above.

proves a great deal. For thus it was that God spoke to
Moses, *I am that I am.* But how do I understand, *I am* Exod. 3.
that I am, and, *If ye believe not that I am?* In this
way. All excellence, of whatever kind, if it be mutable,
cannot be said really to be, for there is no real *to be,* where there
is a *not to be.* Analyze the idea of mutability, and you will find, ·
was, and *will be;* contemplate God, and you will find, *is,*
without possibility of a past. In order to be, thou must leave
him behind thee. So then, *If ye believe not that I am,* means
in fact, If ye believe not that I am God; this being the condition, on which we shall not die in our sins. God be
thanked that He says, *If ye believe not,* not, If ye understand not; for who could understand this? ORIGEN. It is Orig.
manifest, that he, who dies in his sins, though he say that he tom.xix.
believes in Christ, does not really believe. For he who
believes in His justice does not do injustice ; he who believes
in His wisdom, does not act or speak foolishly ; in like
manner with respect to the other attributes of Christ, you
will find that he who does not believe in Christ, dies in his
sins : inasmuch as he comes to be the very contrary of what
is seen in Christ.

25. Then said they unto him, Who art thou? And
Jesus saith unto them, Even the same that I said
unto you from the beginning.

26. I have many things to say and to judge of you :
but he that sent me is true ; and I speak to the world
those things which I have heard of him.

27. They understood not that he spake to them of
the Father.

AUG. Our Lord having said, *If ye believe not that I am,* Aug.
ye shall die in your sins ; they enquire of Him, as if wishing to Tract.
xxxviii.
know in whom they are to believe, that they might not die s. 11.
in their sin *: Then said they unto Him, Who art Thou?* For
when Thou saidst, *If ye believe not that I am,* Thou didst
not add, who Thou art. But our Lord knew that these were
some who would believe, and therefore after being asked,
Who art Thou? that such might know what they should
believe Him to be, *Jesus saith unto them, The beginning,*

who also speak to you; not as if to say, *I am the beginning,* but, Believe Me to be the beginning; as is evident from the Greek, where beginning is feminine. Believe Me then to be the beginning, but ye die in your sins: for the beginning cannot be changed; it remains fixed in itself, and is the source of change to all things. But it is absurd to call the Son the beginning, and not the Father also. And yet there are not two beginnings, even as these are not two Gods. The Holy Spirit is the Spirit of the Father and the Son; not being either the Father, or the Son. Yet Father, Son, and Holy Spirit are one. God, one Light, one beginning. He adds, *Who also speak to you,* i. e. Who humbled Myself for your sakes, and condescended to those words. Therefore believe Me to be the beginning; because that ye may believe this, not only am I the beginning, but I also speak with you, that ye may believe that I am. For if the Beginning had remained with the Father in its original nature, and not taken upon it the form of a servant, how could men have believed in it? Would their weakly minds have taken in the spiritual Word, without the medium of sensible sound? BEDE. In some copies we find, *Who also speak to you;* but it is more consistent to read *for* (quia), not, *who* (qui): in which case the meaning is: Believe Me to be the beginning, for for your sakes have I condescended to these words. CHRYS. See here the madness of the Jews; asking after so long time, and after all His miracles and teaching, *Who art Thou?* What is Christ's answer? From the beginning I speak with you; as if to say, Ye do not deserve to hear any thing from Me, much less this thing, Who I am. For ye speak always, to tempt Me. But I could, if I would, confound and punish you: *I have many things to say, and to judge of you.* AUG. Above He said, *I judge no man;* but, *I judge not,* is one thing, *I have to judge,* another. *I judge not,* He says, with reference to the present time. But the other, *I have many things to say, and to judge of you,* refers to a future judgment. And I shall be true in My judgment, because I am truth, the Son of the true One. *He that sent Me is true.* My Father is true, not by partaking of, but begetting truth. Shall we say that truth is greater than one who is true? If we say this, we shall

Tract. xxxix. 1, 2.

Tract. xx, xviii. 11.

Chrys. Hom. liii. 1.

Aug. Tract. xxxix.

begin to call the Son greater than the Father. CHRYS. He says this, that they may not think that He allows them to talk against Him with impunity, from inability to punish them; or that He is not alive to their contemptuous designs. THEOPHYL. Or having said, *I have many things to say, and to judge of you*, thus reserving His judgment for a future time, He adds, But He that sent Me is true: as if to say, Though ye are unbelievers, My Father is true, Who hath appointed a day of retribution for you. CHRYS. Or thus: As My Father hath sent Me not to judge the world, but to save the world, and My Father is true, I accordingly judge no man now; but speak thus for your salvation, not your condemnation: *And I speak to the world those things that I have heard of Him.* ALCUIN. And to hear from the Father is the same as to be from the Father; He has the hearing from the same sense that He has the being. AUG. The coequal Son gives glory to the Father: as if to say, I give glory to Him whose Son I am: how proudly thou detractest from Him, whose servant Thou art. ALCUIN. They did not understand however what He meant by saying, *He is true that sent Me: they understand not that He spake to them of the Father.* For they had not the eyes of their mind yet opened, to understand the equality of the Father with the Son.

Chrys. Hom. liii. 1.

Chrys. Hom. liii. 1.

Aug. Tract. xxxix. s. 6.

28. Then said Jesus unto them, When ye have lifted up the Son of man, then shall ye know that I am he, and that I do nothing of myself; but as my Father hath taught me, I speak these things.

29. And he that sent me is with me: the Father hath not left me alone; for I do always those things that please him.

30. As he spake these words, many believed on him.

AUG. When our Lord said, He is true that sent Me, the Jews did not understand that He spake to them of the Father. But He saw some there, who, He knew, would believe on Him after His passion. *Then said Jesus unto them, When ye have lifted up the Son of man, then ye shall*

Aug. Tract. xl. 2.

Exod.
3, 14.
know that I am. Recollect the words, *I am that I am,* and ye will know why I say, *I am.* I pass over your knowledge, in order that I may fulfil My passion. In your appointed time ye will know who I am; when ye have lifted up the Son of man. He means the lifting up of the cross; for He was lifted up on the cross, when He hung thereon. This was to be accomplished by the hands of those who should afterwards believe, whom He is now speaking to; with what intent, but that no one, however great his wickedness and consciousness of guilt might despair, seeing even the mur-
Chrys.
Hom.
liii. 1, 2.
derers of our Lord forgiven. CHRYS. Or the connection is this: When His miracles and teaching had failed to convert men, He spoke of the cross; *When ye have lifted up the Son of man, then ye shall know that I am He:* as if to say, Ye think that ye have killed Me; but I say that ye shall then, by the evidence of miracles, of My resurrection, and your captivity, know most especially, that I am Christ the Son of God, and that I do not act in opposition to God; *But that as My Father hath taught Me,* I speak these things. Here He shews the likeness of His substance to the Father's; and that He says nothing beyond the Paternal intelligence. If I were contrary to God, I should not have moved His anger so much against those who did not hear Me. AUG.
Aug.
Tr. xl.
s. 3. et
seq.
Or thus: Having said, *Then shall ye know that I am,* and in this, *I am,* implied the whole Trinity: lest the Sabellian error should creep in, He immediately adds, *And I do nothing of Myself;* as if to say, I am not of Myself; the Son is God from the Father. Let not what follows, *as the Father hath taught Me, I speak these things,* suggest a carnal thought to any of you. Do not place as it were two men before your eyes, a Father speaking to his son, as you do when you speak to your sons. For what words could be spoken to the only Word? If the Father speaks in your hearts without sound, how does He speak to the Son? The Father speaks to the Son incorporeally, because He begat the Son incorporeally: nor did He teach Him, as having begotten Him untaught; rather the teaching Him, was the begetting Him knowing. For if the nature of truth be simple, to be, in the Son, is the same as to know. As then the Father gave the Son existence by begetting, so He gave Him knowledge also.

CHRYS. He gives now a humbler turn to the discourse: *And* Chrys.
He that sent Me. That this might not be thought however Hom.
to imply inferiority, He says, *Is with Me.* The former is
His dispensation, the latter His divinity. AUG. And though Aug.
both are together, yet one is sent, the other sends. For the Tr xl. 6.
mission is the incarnation; and the incarnation is of the Son
only, not of the Father. He says then, *He that sent Me,*
meaning, By whose Fatherly authority I am made incarnate. The Father however, though He sent the Son, did
not withdraw from Him, as He proceeds to say: *The Father
hath not left Me alone.* For it could not be that where He
sent the Son, there the Father was not; He who says, *I fill* Jer. 33.
heaven and earth. And He adds the reason why He did
not leave Him: *For I do always those things that please
Him;* always, i. e. not from any particular beginning, but
without beginning and without end. For the generation
from the Father hath no beginning in time. CHRYS. Or, He Chrys.
means it as an answer to those who were constantly saying that Hom.
liii. 2.
He was not from God, and that because He did not keep the
sabbath; *I do always,* He says, *do those things that please
Him;* shewing that the breaking the sabbath even was pleasing
to Him. He takes care in every way to shew that He does
nothing contrary to the Father. And as this was speaking
more after a human fashion, the Evangelist adds, *As He spake
these words, many believed on Him;* as if to say, Do not be
disturbed at hearing so humble a speech from Christ; for those
who had heard the greatest doctrines from Him, and were
not persuaded, were persuaded by these words of humility.
These then believed on Him, yet not as they ought; but
only out of joy, and approbation of His humble way of
speaking. And this the Evangelist shews in his subsequent
narration, which relates their unjust proceedings towards
Him.

31. Then said Jesus to those Jews which believed
on him, If ye continue in my word, then are ye my
disciples indeed;

32. And ye shall know the truth, and the truth
shall make you free.

33. They answered him, We be Abraham's seed, and were never in bondage to any man: how sayest thou, Ye shall be made free?

34. Jesus answered them, Verily, verily, I say unto you, Whosoever committeth sin is the servant of sin.

35. And the servant abideth not in the house for ever: but the Son abideth ever.

36. If the Son therefore shall make you free, ye shall be free indeed.

Aug. (Chrys. Nic.) Hom. liv. 1. CHRYS. Our Lord wished to try the faith of those who believed, that it might not be only a superficial belief: *Then said Jesus to those Jews which believed on Him, If ye continue in My word, then are ye My disciples indeed.* His saying, *if ye continue,* made it manifest what was in their hearts. He knew that some believed, and would not continue. And He makes them a magnificent promise, viz. that they shall become His disciples indeed; which words are a tacit rebuke to some who had believed and afterwards withdrawn.

Aug. de Verb. Dom. s. xlvii. AUG. We have all one Master, and are fellow disciples under Him. Nor because we speak with authority, are we therefore masters; but He is the Master of all, Who dwells in the hearts of all. It is a small thing for the disciple to come to Him in the first instance: he must continue in Him: if we continue not in Him, we shall fall. A little sentence this, but a great work; *if ye continue.* For what is it to continue in God's word, but to yield to no temptations? Without labour, the reward would be gratis; if with, then a great reward indeed.

Aug. Tr.xli.1. xl. 9. *And ye shall know the truth.* AUG. As if to say: Whereas ye have now belief, by continuing, ye shall have sight. For it was not their knowledge which made them believe, but rather their belief which gave them knowledge. Faith is to believe that which you see not: truth to see that which you believe? By continuing then to believe a thing, you come at last to see the thing; i. e. to the contemplation of the very truth as it is; not conveyed in words, but revealed by light. The truth is unchangeable; it is the bread of the soul, refreshing others, without diminution to itself; changing him who eats into itself, itself not changed. This truth is the Word of God, which put on flesh for our sakes, and lay hid; not meaning to bury itself, but only to defer its manifestation, till its suffering in the body, for the ransoming of the body of sin, had taken place. CHRYS. Or, *ye shall know* Chrys. *the truth*, i. e. Me: for I am the truth. The Jewish was a Hom. liv. 1. typical dispensation; the reality ye can only know from Me. Aug. Some one might say perhaps, And what does it profit Aug. me to know the truth? So our Lord adds, *And the truth* de Verb. Dom. *shall free you;* as if to say, If the truth doth not delight Serm. you, liberty will. To be freed is to be made free, as to be xlviii. ἐλευθ. healed is to be made whole. This is plainer in the Greek; ἐώσιι in the Latin we use the word free chiefly in the sense of escape of danger, relief from care, and the like. THEOPHYL. As He said to the unbelievers alone, *Ye shall die in your sin,* so now to them who continue in the faith He proclaims absolution. AUG. From what shall the truth free us, but Aug. from death, corruption, mutability, itself being immortal, iv. de Trin. c. uncorrupt, immutable? Absolute immutability is in itself 18. eternity. CHRYS. Men who really believed could have borne Chrys. to be rebuked. But these men began immediately to shew Hom. liv. 1. anger. Indeed if they had been disturbed at His former saying, they had much more reason to be so now. For they might argue; If He says we shall know the truth, He must mean that we do not know it now: so then the law is a lie, our knowledge a delusion. But their thoughts took no such direction: their grief is wholly worldly; they know of no other servitude, but that of this world: *They answered Him, We be Abraham's seed, and were never in bondage to any man. How sayest Thou then, we shall be made free?* As if to say, They of Abraham's stock are free, and ought not to be called slaves: we have never been in bondage to any one. AUG. Or it was not those who believed, but the Aug. unbelieving multitude that made this answer. But how Tr. xli.2. could they say with truth, taking only secular bondage into account, that *we have never been in bondage to any man?* Was not Joseph sold? were not the holy prophets carried into captivity? Ungrateful people! Why does God remind you so continually of His having taken you out of the house of bondage if you never were in bondage? Why do you who are now

talking, pay tribute to the Romans, if you never were in
bondage? CHRYS. Christ then, who speaks for their good,
not to gratify their vainglory, explains His meaning to have
been that they were the servants not of men, but of sin, the
hardest kind of servitude, from which God only can rescue:
Jesus answered them, Verily, verily, I say unto you, Who-
soever committeth sin is the servant of sin. AUG. This
asseveration is important: it is, if one may say so, His
oath. *Amen* means true, but is not translated. Neither the
Greek nor the Latin Translator have dared to translate it.
It is a Hebrew word; and men have abstained from trans-
lating it, in order to throw a reverential veil over so
mysterious a word: not that they wished to lock it up, but
only to prevent it from becoming despised by being exposed.
How important the word is, you may see from its being
repeated. *Verily I say unto you,* says Verity itself; which
could not be, even though it said not verily. Our Lord however has recourse to this mode of enforcing His words, in
order to rouse men from their state of sleep and indifference.
Whosoever, He saith, *committeth sin,* whether Jew or Greek,
rich or poor, king or beggar, *is the servant of sin.* GREG.
Because whoever yields to wrong desires, puts his hitherto
free soul under the yoke of the evil one, and takes him for
his master. But we oppose this master, when we struggle
against the wickedness which has laid hold upon us, when
we strongly resist habit, when we pierce sin with repentance,
and wash away the spots of filth with tears. GREG. And
the more freely men follow their perverse desires, the more
closely are they in bondage to them. AUG. O miserable
bondage! The slave of a human master when wearied with
the hardness of his tasks, sometimes takes refuge in flight.
But whither does the slave of sin flee? He takes it along
with him, wherever he goes; for his sin is within him. The
pleasure passes away, but the sin does not pass away: its
delight goes, its sting remains behind. He alone can free
from sin, who came without sin, and was made a sacrifice
for sin. And thus it follows: *The servant abideth not in the*
house for ever. The Church is the house: the servant is the
sinner; and many sinners enter into the Church. So He
does not say, *The servant* is, not in the house; but, *The*

Chrys.
Hom.
liv. 1.

Aug.
Tr. xli.
3.

Greg.
iv. Mor.
c. 42. in
Nov.
Ex. 21.

Greg.
xxv.
Moral.
c. 20.
not in
Nov.
Ex. 14.

servant abideth not in the house for ever. If a time then is
to come, when there shall be no servant in the house; who
will there be there? Who will boast that he is pure from sin?
Christ's are fearful words. But He adds, *The Son abideth
for ever.* So then Christ will live alone in His house. Or
does not the word Son, imply both the body and the head?
Christ purposely alarms us first, and then gives us hope.
He alarms us, that we may not love sin; He gives us hope,
that we may not despair of the absolution of our sin. Our
hope then is this, that we shall be freed by Him who is
free. He hath paid the price for us, not in money, but in
His own blood: *If the Son therefore shall make you free,
ye shall be free indeed.* AUG. Not from the barbarians, but Aug. de Verb. Dom.
from the devil; not from the captivity of the body, but from
the wickedness of the soul. AUG. The first stage of freedom Ser. xlvii.
is, the abstaining from sin. But that is only incipient, it is Aug.
not perfect freedom: for the flesh still lusteth against the super Joan.
spirit, so that ye do not do the things that ye would. Full Tr. xl.
and perfect freedom will only be, when the contest is over, 10. et seq.
and the last enemy, death, is destroyed. CHRYS. Or thus: Chrys. Hom.
Having said that *whosoever committeth sin, is the servant* liv. 1, 2.
of sin, He anticipates the answer that their sacrifices saved
them, by saying, *The servant abideth not in the house for
ever, but the Son abideth ever. The house,* He says, meaning the Father's house on high; in which, to draw a comparison from the world, He Himself had all the power, just
as a man has all the power in his own house. *Abideth not,*
means, has not the power of giving; which the Son, who is
the master of the house, has. The priests of the old law had
not the power of remitting sins by the sacraments of the law;
for all were sinners. Even the priests, who, as the Apostle
says, were obliged to offer up sacrifices for themselves. But
the Son has this power; and therefore our Lord concludes:
If the Son shall make you free, ye shall be free indeed;
implying that that earthly freedom, of which men boasted so
much, was not true freedom. AUG. Do not then abuse your Aug. Tr. xli. 8.
freedom, for the purpose of sinning freely; but use it in order
not to sin at all. Your will will be free, if it be merciful:
you will be free, if you become the servant of righteousness.

37. I know that ye are Abraham's seed; but ye seek to kill me, because my word hath no place in you.

38. I speak that which I have seen with my Father: and ye do that which ye have seen with your father.

39. They answered and said unto him, Abraham is our father. Jesus saith unto them, If ye were Abraham's children, ye would do the works of Abraham.

40. But now ye seek to kill me, a man that hath told you the truth, which I have heard of God: this did not Abraham.

41. Ye do the deeds of your father.

Aug.
Tr. xlii.
1.

AUG. The Jews had asserted they were free, because they were Abraham's seed. Our Lord replies, *I know that ye are Abraham's seed;* as if to say, I know that ye are the sons of Abraham, but according to the flesh, not spiritually and by faith. So He adds, *But ye seek to kill Me.* CHRYS.

Chrys.
Hom.
liv. 2.

He says this, that they might not attempt to answer, that they had no sin. He reminds them of a present sin; a sin which they had been meditating for some time past, and which was actually at this moment in their thoughts: putting out of the question their general course of life. He thus removes them by degrees out of their relationship to Abraham, teaching them not to pride themselves so much upon it: for that, as bondage and freedom were the consequences of works, so was relationship. And that they might not say, We do so justly, He adds the reason why they did so; *Because*

Aug.
Tr. xlii.
1.

My word hath no place in you. AUG. That is, hath not place in your heart [c], because your heart does not take it in. The word of God to the believing, is like the hook to the fish; it takes when it is taken: and that not to the injury of those who are caught by it. They are caught for their

Chrys.
Hom.
liv. 2.

salvation, not for their destruction. CHRYS. He does not say, Ye do not take in My word, but *My word has not room in you;* shewing the depth of His doctrines. But they might say; What if thou speakest of thyself? So He adds, *I speak that which I have seen of My Father;* for I

[c] capit Vulg. for χωρεῖ ἐν. Aug. goes off upon the Latin word.

have not only the Father's substance, but His truth. AUG. ^{Aug.}
Our Lord by His Father wishes us to understand God: as ^{Tr. xlii.} ^{11.}
if to say, I have seen the truth, I speak the truth, because I
am the truth. If our Lord then speaks the truth which He
saw with the Father, it is Himself that He saw, Himself
that He speaks; He being Himself the truth of the
Father. ORIGEN. This is proof that our Saviour was ^{Orig.}
witness to what was done with the Father: whereas men, to ^{tom. xx. in Joan.}
whom the revelation is made, were not witnesses. THE- ^{s. 7.}
OPHYL. But when you hear, *I speak that which I have seen,*
do not think it means bodily vision, but innate knowledge,
sure, and approved. For as the eyes when they see an object,
see it wholly and correctly; so I speak with certainty what I
know from My Father.

And ye do that which ye have seen with your father. ^{Orig.}
ORIGEN. As yet He has not named their father; He men- ^{tom. xx. 13.}
tioned Abraham indeed a little above, but now He is going
to mention another father, viz. the devil: whose sons they
were, in so far as they were wicked, not as being men. Our
Lord is reproaching them for their evil deeds. CHRYS.
Another reading has, *And*[1] *do ye do that which ye have seen* ^{1 ποιῆτε,}
with your father; as if to say, As I both in word and deed ^{ye do, or do.}
declare unto you the Father, so do ye by your works shew
forth Abraham. ORIGEN. Also another reading has; *And* ^{Orig.}
do ye do what ye have heard from the Father. All that was ^{tom. xx. 7.}
written in the Law and the Prophets they had heard from
the Father. He who takes this reading, may use it to prove
against them who hold otherwise, that the God who gave the
Law and the Prophets, was none other than Christ's Father.
[d]And we use it too as an answer to those who maintain two
original natures in men, and explain the words, *My word* ^{c. 8.}
hath no place in you, to mean that these were by nature
incapable of receiving the word. How could those be of an
incapable nature, who had *heard from the Father*[e]? And
how again could they be of a blessed nature, who sought to
kill our Saviour, and would not receive His words. *They*
answered and said unto Him, Abraham is our father. This
answer of the Jews is a great falling off from our Lord's

---

d This is the meaning of the original;   • The reading in Origen for, *have*
it is slightly altered in the Catena.   *seen with your father.*

meaning. He had referred to God, but they take Father in the sense of the father of their nature, Abraham. AUG. As if to say, What art thou going to say against Abraham? They seem to be inviting Him to say something in disparagement of Abraham; and so to give them an opportunity of executing their purpose. ORIGEN. Our Saviour denies that Abraham is their father: *Jesus saith unto them, If ye were Abraham's children, ye would do the works of Abraham.* AUG. And yet He says above, *I know that ye are Abraham's seed.* So He does not deny their origin, but condemns their deeds. Their flesh was from him; their life was not. ORIGEN. Or we may explain the difficulty thus. Above it is in the Greek, *I know that ye are Abraham's seed.* So let us examine whether there is not a difference between a bodily seed and a child. It is evident that a seed contains in itself all the proportions of him whose seed it is, as yet however dormant, and waiting to be developed; when the seed first has changed and moulded the material it meets with in the woman, derived nourishment from thence and gone through a process in the womb, it becomes a child, the likeness of its begetter. So then a child is formed from the seed: but the seed is not necessarily a child. Now with reference to those who are from their works judged to be the seed of Abraham, may we not conceive that they are so from certain seminal proportions implanted in their souls? All men are not the seed of Abraham, for all have not these proportions implanted in their souls. But he who is the seed of Abraham, has yet to become his child by likeness. And it is possible for him by negligence and indolence even to cease to be the seed. But those to whom these words were addressed, were not yet cut off from hope: and therefore Jesus acknowledged that they were as yet the seed of Abraham, and had still the power of becoming children of Abraham. So He says, *If ye are the children of Abraham, do the works of Abraham.* If as the seed of Abraham, they had attained to their proper sign and growth, they would have taken in our Lord's words. But not having grown to be children, they cared not; but wish to kill the Word, and as it were break it in pieces, since it was too great for them to take in. If any of you then be the seed of Abraham, and as yet do not take in the word of

Marginal notes: Aug. Tr. xlii. s. 3. — Orig. tom. xx. 9. — Aug. Tr. xlii. 4. — Orig. tom. xx. 2. et sq.

God, let him not seek to kill the word; but rather change himself into being a son of Abraham, and then he will be able to take in the Son of God.   Some select one of the works of Abraham, viz. that in Genesis, *And Abraham be-* Gen. 15, *lieved God, and it was counted to him for righteousness.* 6. But even granting to them that faith is a work, if this were so, why was it not, *Do the work of Abraham:* using the singular number, instead of the plural? The expression as it stands is, I think, equivalent to saying, Do all the works of Abraham : i. e. in the spiritual sense, interpreting Abraham's history allegorically.   For it is not incumbent on one, who would be a son of Abraham, to marry his maidservants, or after his wife's death, to marry another in his old age.

But now ye seek to kill Me, a man that hath told you the truth. CHRYS. This truth, that is, that He was equal to Chrys. the Father: for it was this that moved the Jews to kill Him. Hom. liv. 2. To shew, however, that this doctrine is not opposed to the Father, He adds, *Which I have heard from God.* ALCUIN. Because He Himself, Who is the truth, was begotten of God the Father, to hear, being in fact the same with to be from the Father.   ORIGEN. *To kill Me,* He says, *a man.*   I say Orig. nothing now of the Son of God, nothing of the Word, because tom. xx. 11. the Word cannot die; I speak only of that which ye see.   It is in your power to kill that which you see, and offend Him Whom ye see not.

This did not Abraham. ALCUIN. As if to say, By this you prove that you are not the sons of Abraham; that you do works contrary to those of Abraham.   ORIGEN. It might Orig. seem to some, that it were superfluous to say that Abraham tom. xx. 12. did not this; for it were impossible that it should be; Christ was not born at that time.   But we may remind them, that in Abraham's time there was a man born who spoke the truth, which he heard from God, and that this man's life was not sought for by Abraham.   Know too that the Saints were never without the spiritual advent of Christ.   I understand then from this passage, that every one who, after regeneration, and other divine graces bestowed upon him, commits sin, does by this return to evil incur the guilt of crucifying the Son of God, which Abraham did not do.

Ye do the works of your father.   AUG. He does not say Aug. Tr. xlii. 6.

Chrys.
Hom.
liv. 2. as yet who is their father. CHRYS. Our Lord says this with a view to put down their vain boasting of their descent; and persuade them to rest their hopes of salvation no longer on the natural relationship, but on the adoption. For this it was which prevented them from coming to Christ; viz. their thinking that their relationship to Abraham was sufficient for their salvation.

41. Then said they to him, We be not born of fornication; we have one Father, even God.

42. Jesus said unto them, If God were your Father, ye would love me: for I proceeded forth and came from God; neither came I of myself, but he sent me.

43. Why do ye not understand my speech? even because ye cannot hear my word.

Aug.
Tr. xlii.
7. AUG. The Jews had begun to understand that our Lord was not speaking of sonship according to the flesh, but of manner of life. Scripture often speaks of spiritual fornication, with many gods, and of the soul being prostituted, as it were, by paying worship to false gods. This explains what follows: *Then said they to Him, We be not born of fornication; we have one Father, even God.* THEOPHYL. As if their motive against Him was a desire to avenge God's honour. ORIGEN. Or their sonship to Abraham having been Orig.
tom. xx.
14. disproved, they reply by bitterly insinuating, that our Saviour was the offspring of adultery. But perhaps the tone of the answer is disputatious, more than any thing else. For whereas they have said shortly before, *We have Abraham for our father,* and had been told in reply, *If ye are Abraham's children, do the works of Abraham;* they declare in return that they have a greater Father than Abraham, i. e. God; and that they were not derived from fornication. For qui nihil
facit ex
se the devil, who has no power of creating any thing from himself, begets not from a spouse, but a harlot, i. e. matter, those who give themselves up to carnal things, that is, cleave to matter. CHRYS. But what say ye? Have ye God for your Chrys.
Hom.
liv. 3. Father, and do ye blame Christ for speaking thus? Yet true it was, that many of them were born of fornication, for

people then used to form unlawful connexions.   But this is
not the thing our Lord has in view.   He is bent on proving
that they are not from God.   *Jesus said unto them, If God
were your Father, ye would love Me: for I proceeded forth
and came from God.*   HILARY. It was not that the Son of
God condemned the assumption of so religious a name; that
is, condemned them for professing to be the sons of God, and
calling God their Father; but that He blamed the rash presumption of the Jews in claiming God for their Father, when
they did not love the Son.   *For I proceeded forth, and came
from God.*   To *proceed forth*, is not the same with to *come.*
When our Lord says that those who called God their Father,
ought to love Him, because He *came forth* from God, He
means that His being born of God was the reason why He
should be loved: the proceeding forth, having reference to
His incorporeal birth.   Their claim to be the sons of God,
was to be made good by their loving Christ, Who was begotten
from God.   For a true worshipper of God the Father must
love the Son, as being from God[f].   And he only can love
the Father, who believes that the Son is from Him.   AUG.
This then is the eternal procession, the proceeding forth of
the Word from God: from Him It proceeded as the Word
of the Father, and came to us: *The Word was made flesh.*
His advent is His humanity: His staying, His divinity.   Ye
call God your Father; acknowledge Me at least to be a
brother.   HILARY. In what follows, He teaches that His
origin is not in Himself; *Neither came I of Myself, but He
sent Me.*   ORIGEN. This was said, I think, in allusion to
some who came without being sent by the Father, of whom
it is said in Jeremiah, *I have not sent these prophets, yet they
ran.*   Some, however, use this passage[1] to prove the existence of two natures[g].   To these we may reply, Paul hated
Jesus when he persecuted the Church of God, at the time,
viz. that our Lord said, *Why persecutest thou Me?*   Now
if it is true, as is here said, *If God were your Father,
ye would love Me;* the converse is true, If ye do not love
Me, God is not your Father.   And Paul for some time did

Hilar.
vi. de
Trin. c.
30.

Aug.
Tr. xlii.
8.

c. 1, 14.

Hilar.
lib. v.
ibid.

Orig.
tom. xx.
15.

Jer. 23,
21.
[1] i. e. if
God
were
your
Father,
&c.
Acts 9,
4.

---

[f] The Son *is from God* not by reason
of His advent, but His nativity.
[g] Alluding to the belief that some
men were of a good nature, being the
creation of God, others evil, being
made by the devil.

not love Jesus. There was a time when God was not Paul's father. Paul therefore was not by nature the son of God, but afterwards was made so. And when does God become any one's Father, except when he keeps His commandments?

Chrys. Hom. liv. 3.

CHRYS. And because they were ever enquiring, *What is this which He saith, Whither I go ye cannot come?* He adds here, *Why do ye not understand My speech? even because ye cannot hear My word.* AUG. And they could not hear,

Aug. Tr. xlii. 9.

because they would not believe, and amend their lives.

Orig. tom. xx. 18. (Nic.)

ORIGEN. First then, that virtue must be sought after, which hears the divine word; that by degrees we may be strong enough to embrace the whole teaching of Jesus. For so long as a man has not had his hearing restored by the Word,

Mark 7, 34.

which says to the deaf ear, *Be opened:* so long he cannot hear.

44. Ye are of your father the devil, and the lusts of your father ye will do. He was a murderer from the beginning, and abode not in the truth, because there is no truth in him. When he speaketh a lie, he speaketh of his own: for he is a liar, and the father of it.

45. And because I tell you the truth, ye believe me not.

46. Which of you convinceth me of sin? And if I say the truth, why do ye not believe me?

47. He that is of God heareth God's words: ye therefore hear them not, because ye are not of God.

Chrys. Hom. liv. 3.

CHRYS. Our Lord, having already cut off the Jews from relationship to Abraham, overthrows now this far greater claim, to call God their Father, *Ye are of your father the*

Aug. Tr. xlii. 10.

devil. AUG. Here we must guard against the heresy of the Manichæans, who hold a certain original nature of evil, and a nation of darkness with princes at their head, whence the devil derives his existence. And thence they say our flesh is produced; and in this way interpret our Lord's speech,

Ye are of your father the devil: viz. to mean that they
were by nature evil, drawing their origin from the opposite
seed of darkness.   ORIGEN. And this seems to be the Orig.
same mistake, as if one said, that an eye which saw right ^{tom. xx.}
was different in kind from an eye which saw wrong.
For just as in these there is no difference of kind, only one
of them for some reason sees wrong; so, in the other case,
whether a man receives a doctrine, or whether he does not,
he is of the same nature.   AUG. The Jews then were children Aug.
of the devil by imitation, not by birth : *And the lusts of your* ^{Tr. xlii.}_{11.}
father ye will do, our Lord says.   Ye are his children then,
because ye have such lusts, not because ye are born of him :
for *ye seek to kill Me, a man that hath told you the truth :*
and he envied man, and killed him : *he was a murderer from*
the beginning ; i. e. of the first man on whom a murder
could be committed : man could not be slain, before man
was created.   The devil did not go, girt with a sword, against
man : he sowed an evil word, and slew him.   Do not suppose
therefore that you are not guilty of murder, when you suggest
evil thoughts to your brother.   The very reason why ye
rage against the flesh, is that ye cannot assault the soul.
ORIGEN. Consider too ; it was not one man only that he Orig.
killed, but the whole human race, inasmuch as in Adam ^{tom. xx.}_{21.}
all die; so that he is truly called a murderer from the be-
ginning.   CHRYS. He does not say, his works, but *his lusts* Chrys.
ye will do, meaning that both the devil and the Jews ^{Hom.}_{liv. 3.}
were bent on murder, to satisfy their envy.   *And stood*
not in the truth.   He shews whence sprang their continual
objection to Him, that He was not from God.   AUG. But Aug.
it will be objected perhaps, that if from the beginning of ^{xi. de}_{Civ.Dei,}
his existence, the devil stood not in the truth, he was never ^{c. 13.}
in a state of blessedness with the holy angels, refusing, as
he did, to be subject to his Creator, and therefore false and
deceitful; unwilling at the cost of pious subjection to hold
that which by nature he was; and attempting in his pride
and loftiness to simulate that which he was not.   This
opinion is not the same with that of the Manichæans, that
the devil has his own peculiar nature, derived as it were
from the opposite principle of evil.   This foolish sect does
not see that our Lord says not, Was alien from the truth, but

Stood not in the truth, meaning, fell from the truth. And thus they interpret John, *The devil sinneth from the beginning*, not seeing that if sin is natural, it is no sin. But what do the testimonies of the prophets reply? Isaiah, setting forth the devil under the figure of the prince of Babylon, says, *How art thou fallen from heaven, O Lucifer, son of the morning!* Ezekiel says, *Thou hast been in Eden, the garden of God.* Which passages, as they cannot be interpreted in any other way, shew that we must take the word, *He stood not in the truth*, to mean, that he was in truth, but did not remain in it; and the other, that the devil sinneth from the beginning, to mean, that he was a sinner not from the beginning of his creation, but from the beginning of sin. For sin began in him, and he was the beginning of sin.

ORIGEN. There is only one way of standing in the truth; many and various of not standing in it. Some try to stand in the truth, but their feet tremble and shake so, they cannot. Others are not come to that pass, but are in danger of it, as we read in the Psalms, *My feet were almost gone:* others fall from it. *Because the truth is not in him*, is the reason why the devil did not stand in the truth. He imagined vain things, and deceived himself; wherein He was so far worse than others, in that, while others are deceived by him, he was the author of his own deception. But farther; does *the truth is not in him*, mean that he holds no true doctrine, and that every thing he thinks is false; or that he is not a member of Christ, who says, *I am the truth?* Now it is impossible that any rational being should think falsely on every subject and never be even ever so slightly right in opinion. The devil therefore may hold a true doctrine, by the mere law of his rational nature: and therefore his nature is not contrary to truth, i. e. does not consist of simple error and ignorance; otherwise he could never have known the truth.

AUG. Or when our Lord says, *The truth is not in him*, He intends it as an index: as if we had asked Him, how it appeared that the devil stood not in the truth; and He said, *Because the truth is not in him.* For it would be in him, if he stood in it.

When he speaketh a lie, he speaketh of his own: for he is a liar, and the father of it. AUG. Some have thought from

Margin notes:
1 John 3, 8.

Ezek. 28, 13.

Orig. tom. xx. 22.

Ps. 72.

c. 14, 6.

Aug. xi. de Civ.Dei, c. xiv.

Aug. Tr. xlii. s. 12, 13.

these words that the devil had a father, and asked who was
the father of the devil. This is the error of the Manichæans.
But our Lord calls the devil the father of a lie for this reason:
Every one who lies is not the father of his own lie; for you
may tell a lie, which you have received from another; in which
case you have lied, but are not the father of the lie. But the
lie wherewith, as with a serpent's bite, the devil slew man,
had no source but himself: and therefore he is the father of
a lie, as God is the Father of the truth. THEOPHYL. For he
accused God to man, saying to Eve, But of envy He hath
forbidden you the tree: and to God he accused man, as in
Job, *Doth Job serve God for nought?* ORIGEN. Note how-Job 1, 9.
ever; this word, liar, is applied to man, as well as to the Orig.
tom. xx.
devil, who begat a lie, as we read in the Psalm, *All men are* 23.
liars. If a man is not a liar, he is not an ordinary man, Ps. 111.
but one of those, to whom it is said, *I have said, Ye are* Ps. 81.
Gods. When a man speaketh a lie, he speaketh of his
own; but the Holy Spirit speaketh the word of truth and
wisdom; as he said below, *He shall receive of Mine, and* c. 16, 15.
shall shew it unto you. AUG. Or thus: The devil is not Aug. de
a singular, but a common name. In whomsoever the works Quæst.
Nov. et
of the devil are found, he is to be called the devil. It is the Vet.
Test. 2,
name of a work, not of a nature. Here then our Lord means 90.
by the father of the Jews, Cain; whom they wished to imitate, by killing the Saviour: for he it was who set the first
example of murdering a brother. That he spoke a lie of
his own, means that no one sins but by his own will. And
inasmuch as Cain imitated the devil, and followed his works,
the devil is said to be his father. ALCUIN. Our Lord being
the truth, and the Son of the true God, spoke the truth; but
the Jews, being the sons of the devil, were averse to the truth;
and this is why our Lord says, *Because I tell you the truth,*
ye believe not. ORIGEN. But how is this said to the Jews Orig.
who believed on Him? Consider: a man may believe in one tom. xx.
24.
sense, not believe in another; e. g. that our Lord was crucified by Pontius Pilate, but not that He was born of the
Virgin Mary. In this same way, those whom He is speaking
to, believed in Him as a worker of miracles, which they saw
Him to be; but did not believe in His doctrines, which were
too deep for them. CHRYS. Ye wish to kill Me then, be-Chrys.
Hom. liv.
s. 3.

cause ye are enemies of the truth, not that ye have any fault to find in Me: for, *which of you convinceth Me of sin?* THE-OPHYL. As if to say: If ye are the sons of God, ye ought to hold sinners in hatred. If ye hate Me, when ye cannot convince Me of sin, it is evident that ye hate Me because of the truth: i. e. because I said I was the Son of God. ORIGEN.

Orig. tom. xx. in Joan. s. 25. A bold speech this; which none could have had the confidence to utter, but he Who did no sin; even our Lord.

Greg. Hom. xviii. in Evang. GREG. Observe here the condescension of God. He who by virtue of His Divinity could justify sinners, deigns to shew from reason, that He is not a sinner. It follows: *He that is of God heareth God's words; ye therefore hear them not, because ye are not of God.*

Aug. Tr. xlii. 16. AUG. Apply this not to their nature, but to their faults. They both are from God, and are not from God at the same time; their nature is from God, their fault is not from God. This was spoken too to those, who were not only faulty, by reason of sin, in the way in which all are: but who it was foreknown would never possess such faith as would free them from the bonds of sin.

Greg. ut sup. GREG. Let him then, who would understand God's words, ask himself whether he hears them with the ears of his heart. For there are some who do not deign to hear God's commands even with their bodily ears; and there are others who do this, but do not embrace them with their heart's desire; and there are others again who receive God's words readily, yea and are touched, even to tears: but who afterwards go back to their sins again; and therefore cannot be said to hear the word of God, because they neglect to practise it.

48. Then answered the Jews, and said unto him, Say we not well that thou art a Samaritan, and hast a devil?

49. Jesus answered, I have not a devil; but I honour my Father, and ye do dishonour me.

50. And I seek not mine own glory; there is one that seeketh and judgeth.

51. Verily, verily, I say unto you, If a man keep my saying, he shall never see death.

CHRYS. Whenever our Lord said any thing of lofty mean- Chrys.
ing, the Jews in their insensibility set it down madness: $\frac{\text{Hom.lv.}}{1.}$
*Then answered the Jews and said unto Him, Say we not
well that Thou art a Samaritan, and hast a devil?* ORIGEN. Orig.
But how, we may ask, when the Samaritans denied a future $\frac{\text{tom.xx.}}{28.}$
life, and the immortality of the soul, could they dare to call
our Saviour, Who had preached so much on the resurrection
and the judgment, a Samaritan? Perhaps they only mean
a general rebuke to Him for teaching, what they did not approve of. ALCUIN. The Samaritans were hated by the Jews;
they lived in the land that formerly belonged to the ten
tribes, who had been carried away. ORIGEN. It is not un- Orig.
likely too, some may have thought that He held the Sama- $\frac{\text{tom.xx.}}{28.}$
ritan opinion of there being no future state really, and only
put forth the doctrine of a resurrection and eternal life, in
order gain to the favour of the Jews. They said that He had
a devil, because His discourses were above human capacity,
those, viz. in which He asserted that God was His Father,
and that He had come down from heaven, and others of a
like kind: or perhaps from a suspicion, which many had,
that He cast out devils by Beelzebub, the prince of the devils.
THEOPHYL. Or they called Him a Samaritan, because He
transgressed the Hebrew ordinances, as that of the sabbath:
the Samaritans not being correct observers of the law. And
they suspected Him of having a devil, because He could
disclose what was in their thoughts. When it was that
they called Him a Samaritan, the Evangelist no where says:
a proof that the Evangelists left out many things. GREG. Greg.
See; when God suffers a wrong, He does not reply reproach- $\frac{\text{Hom.}}{\text{xviii. in}}$
fully: *Jesus answered, I have not a devil.* An intimation this Evang.
to us, that when reproached by our neighbours falsely, we
should not retort upon them by bringing forward their evil
deeds, however true such charges might be; lest the vehicle
of a just rebuke turn into a weapon of rage. CHRYS. Chrys.
And observe, when He had to teach them, and pull down $\frac{\text{Hom.lv.}}{1.}$
their pride, He used roughness; but now that He has to
suffer rebuke, He treats them with the utmost mildness: a
lesson to us to be severe in what concerns God, but careless
of ourselves. AUG. And to imitate His patience first, if Aug.
we would attain to His power. But though being reviled, $\frac{\text{Tr. xliv.}}{1. 2.}$

He reviled not again, it was incumbent on Him to deny the charge. Two charges had been made against Him: *Thou art a Samaritan, and hast a devil.* In reply He does not say, *I am not a Samaritan:* for Samaritan means keeper; and He knew He was a keeper: He could not redeem us, without at the same time preserving us. Lastly, He is the Samaritan, who went up to the wounded, and had compassion on him. ORIGEN. Our Lord, even more than Paul, wished to become all things to all men, that He might gain some: and therefore He did not deny being a Samaritan. *I have not a devil,* is what Jesus alone can say; as He alone can say, *The prince of this world cometh, and hath nothing in Me.* None of us are quite free from having a devil. For even lesser faults come from him. AUG. Then after being so reviled, all that He says to vindicate His glory, is, *But I honour My Father:* as if to say, That you may not think Me arrogant, I tell you, I have One, Whom I honour. THEOPHYL. He honoured the Father, by revenging Him, and not suffering murderers or liars to call themselves the true sons of God. ORIGEN. Christ alone honoured the Father perfectly. No one, who honours any thing which is not honoured by God, honours God. GREG. As all who have zeal toward God are liable to meet with dishonour from wicked men, our Lord has Himself set us an example of patience under this trial; *And ye do dishonour Me.* AUG. As if to say, I do my duty: ye do not do yours. ORIGEN. And this was not addressed to them only, but to all who by unrighteous deeds inflict injury upon Christ, who is righteousness; or by scoffing at wisdom wrong Him who is wisdom: and the like. GREG. How we are to take injuries, He shews us by His own example, when He adds, *I seek not Mine own glory, there is one that seeketh and judgeth.* CHRYS. As if to say, I have told you this[h] on account of the honour which I have for My Father; and for this ye dishonour Me. But I concern not myself for your reviling: ye are accountable to Him, for whose sake I undergo it. ORIGEN. God seeks Christ's glory, in every one of those who receive Him: which glory He finds in those who cultivate the seeds of virtue implanted in them. And those in whom He finds

Orig. tom. xx. s. 28.
s. 29.
c.14,30.
Aug. Tr.xliii. 3.
Orig. tom. xx. 29.
Greg. Hom. xliii. 3.
Aug. Tr.xliii. 3.
Orig. tom. xx. 29.
ut sup.
Chrys. Hom. lv. 1.
Orig. tom. xx. s. 30.

---

[h] i. e. that they had no right to call God their Father.

not His Son's glory, He punishes: *There is one that seeketh and judgeth.* AUG. Meaning of course the Father. But how is it then that He says in another place, *The Father judgeth no man, but hath committed all judgment unto the Son.* Judgment is sometimes put for condemnation, whereas here it only stands for trial: as if to say, There is one, even My Father, who distinguishes My glory from yours; ye glory after this world, I not after this world. The Father distinguishes the glory of the Son, from that of all men: for that He has been made man, does not bring us to a comparison with Him. We men have sin: He was without sin, even when He was in the form of a servant; for, as the Word which was in the beginning, who can speak worthily of Him? ORIGEN. Or thus; If that is true which our Saviour says below, *All men are thine,* it is manifest that the judgment itself of the Son, is the Father's. GREG. As the perversity of the wicked increases, preaching so far from giving way, ought even to become more active. Thus our Lord, after He had been accused of having a devil, imparts the treasures of preaching in a still larger degree: *Verily, verily, I say unto you, If a man keep My saying, he shall never see death.* AUG. *See* is put for experience. But since, about to die Himself, He spoke with those about to die, what means this, *If a man keep My saying, he shall never see death?* What, but that He saw another death from which He came to free us, death eternal, the death of the damned, which is shared with the devil and his angels! That is the true death: the other is a passage only. ORIGEN. We must understand Him, as it were, to say, If a man keep My light, he shall not see darkness for ever; *for ever* being taken as common to both clauses, as if the sentence were, *If a man keep My saying for ever, He shall not see death for ever:* meaning that a man does not see death, so long as he keeps Christ's word. But when a man, by becoming sluggish in the observance of His words, and negligent in the keeping of his own heart, ceases to keep them, he then sees death; he brings it upon himself. Thus taught then by our Saviour, to the prophet who asks, *What man is he that liveth, and shall not see death?* we are able to answer, He who keepeth Christ's word. CHRYS. He says, *keep,* i. e. not by faith, but

Aug.
Tr. xliii.
4.

c. 5, 22.

Orig.
tom. xx.
31.
(Nic.)
c. 17, 10.
Greg.
Hom.
xviii. in
Evang.

Aug.
Tr. xliii.
10, 11.

Orig.
tom. xx.
s. 31.

Ps. 88.

Chrys.
Hom.
lv. 1.

by purity of life. And at the same time too He means it as a
tacit intimation that they can do nothing to Him. For if
whoever keepeth His word, shall never die, much less is it
possible that He Himself should die.

52. Then said the Jews unto him, Now we know
that thou hast a devil. Abraham is dead, and the
prophets; and thou sayest, If a man keep my saying,
he shall never taste of death.

53. Art thou greater than our father Abraham,
which is dead? and the prophets are dead; whom
makest thou thyself?

54. Jesus answered, If I honour myself, my honour
is nothing; it is my Father that honoureth me; of
whom ye say, that he is your God:

55. Yet ye have not known him; but I know him:
and if I should say, I know him not, I shall be a liar
like unto you: but I know him, and keep his saying.

56. Your father Abraham rejoiced to see my day:
and he saw it, and was glad.

ut sup. GREG. As it is necessary that the good should grow better
by contumely, so are the reprobate made worse by kindness.
On hearing our Lord's words, the Jews again blaspheme:
Then said the Jews unto Him, Now we know Thou hast a
Orig. *devil.* ORIGEN. Those who believe the Holy Scriptures,
tom. xx. understand that what men do contrary to right reason, is not
32, 33. done without the operation of devils. Thus the Jews thought
that Jesus had spoken by the influence of the devil, when
He said, *If a man keep My saying, he shall never see death.*
And this idea they laboured under, because they did not know
the power of God. For here He was speaking of that death
ἐχθρὸν of enmity to reason, by which sinners perish: whereas they
τῷ λόγῳ understand Him of that death which is common to all; and
therefore blame Him for so speaking, when it was certain
that Abraham and the Prophets were dead: *Abraham is*
dead, and the Prophets; and Thou sayest, If a man keep My
saying, he shall never taste of death. Shall never taste of

death, they say, instead of, *shall not see death;* though
between tasting and seeing death there is a difference. Like
careless hearers, they mistake what our Lord said. For
as our Lord, in that He is the true bread, is good to taste;
in that He is wisdom, is beautiful to behold; in like manner
His adversary death is both to be tasted and seen. When
then a man stands by Christ's help in the spiritual place $\overset{\dot{\epsilon}\nu\ \tau\tilde{\varphi}}{\delta\iota\kappa\nu\upsilon}$.
pointed out to him, he shall not taste of death if he preserves $\mu\acute{\iota}\nu\omega$
that state: according to Matthew, *There be those standing* $\overset{\nu o\eta\tau\tilde{\varphi}}{\tau\acute{o}\pi\varphi}$
HERE, *which shall not taste of death.* But when a man hears Mat.16,
Christ's words and keeps them, he shall not see death. 28.
CHRYS. Again, they have recourse to the vainglorious Chrys.
argument of their descent: *Art Thou greater than our* $\overset{\text{Hom.}}{\text{lv. 1.}}$
father Abraham, which is dead? They might have said,
Art Thou greater than God, whose words they are dead who
heard? But they do not say this, because they thought Him
inferior even to Abraham. ORIGEN. For they do not see Orig.
that not Abraham only, but every one born of woman, is less $\overset{\text{tom. xx.}}{33.}$
than He who was born of a Virgin. Now were the Jews
right in saying that Abraham was dead? for he heard the
word of Christ, and kept it, as did also the Prophets, who,
they say, were dead. For they kept the word of the Son of
God, when the word of the Lord came to Hosea, Isaiah, or
Jeremiah; if any one else kept the word, surely those
Prophets did. They utter a lie then when they say, *We
know that Thou hast a devil;* and when they say, *Abraham
is dead, and the Prophets.* GREG. For being given over to ut sup.
eternal death, which death they saw not, and thinking only, as
they did, of the death of the body, their minds were darkened,
even while the Truth Himself was speaking. They add:
Whom makest Thou Thyself? THEOPHYL. As if to say, Thou
a person of no account, a carpenter's son of Galilee, to take
glory to Thyself! BEDE. *Whom makest Thou Thyself?* i. e.
Of what merit, of what dignity wouldest Thou be accounted?
Nevertheless, Abraham only died in the body; his soul
lived. And the death of the soul which is to live for ever,
is greater than the death of the body that must die some
time. ORIGEN. This was the speech of persons spiritually Orig.
blind. For Jesus did not make Himself what He was, but $\overset{\text{tom. xx.}}{33.}$
received it from the Father: *Jesus answered and said, If I*

Y

honour Myself, My honour is nothing. CHRYS. This is to answer their suspicions; as above, *If I bear witness of Myself, My witness is not true.* BEDE. He shews in these words that the glory of this present life is nothing. AUG. This is to answer those who said, *Whom makest Thou Thyself?* He refers His glory to the Father, from Whom He is: *It is My Father that honoureth Me.* The Arians take occasion from those words to calumniate our faith, and say, Lo, the Father is greater, for He glorifieth the Son. Heretics, have ye not read that the Son also glorifieth the Father? ALCUIN. The Father glorified the Son, at His baptism, on the mount, at the time of His passion, when a voice came to Him, in the midst of the crowd, when He raised Him up again after His passion, and placed Him at the right hand of His Majesty. CHRYS. He adds, *Of whom ye say that He is your God;* meaning to tell them that they were not only ignorant of the Father, but even of God. THEOPHYL. For had they known the Father really, they would have reverenced the Son. But they even despise God, who in the Law forbad murder, by their clamours against Christ. Wherefore He says, *Ye have not known Him.* ALCUIN. As if to say, Ye call Him your God, after a carnal manner, serving Him for temporal rewards. Ye have not known Him, as He should be known; ye are not able to serve Him spiritually. AUG. Some heretics say that the God proclaimed in the Old Testament is not the Father of Christ, but a kind of prince of bad angels. These He contradicts when He calls Him His Father, whom the Jews called their God, and knew not. For had they known Him, they would have received His Son. Of Himself however He adds, *But I know Him.* And here too, to men judging after the flesh, He might appear arrogant. But let not arrogance be so guarded against, as that truth be deserted. Therefore our Lord says, *And if I should say I know Him not, I should be a liar like unto you.* CHRYS. As if to say, As ye, saying that ye know Him, lie; so were I a liar, did I say I knew Him not. It follows, however, (which is the greatest proof of all that He was sent from God,) *But I know Him.* THEOPHYL. Having that knowledge by nature; for as I am, so is the Father also; I know Myself, and therefore I know

Chrys. Hom. liv. 1, 2. c. 5.

Aug. Tr. xliii. 14.

Chrys. Hom. lv. 2.

Aug. Tr. xliii. 15.

Chrys. Hom. lv. 2.

Him.   And He gives the proof that He knows Him: *And I
keep His saying,* i. e. His commandments.   Some understand, *I keep His saying,* to mean, I keep the nature of
His substance unchanged; for the substance of the Father
and the Son is the same, as their nature is the same; and
therefore I know the Father.   *And* here has the force of
because: *I know Him* because *I keep His saying.*   Aug.
He spoke the saying of the Father too, as being the Son;
and He was Himself that Word of the Father, which He
spoke to men.   Chrys. In answer then to their question,
Art Thou greater than our father Abraham, He shews them
that He is greater than Abraham ; *Your father Abraham
rejoiced to see My day: he saw it, and was glad;* he must
have rejoiced, because My day would benefit him, which is
to acknowledge Me greater than himself.   Theophyl. As if
to say, He regarded My day, as a day to be desired, and
full of joy; not as if I was an unimportant or common person.
Aug. He did not fear, but *rejoiced to see:* he rejoiced in
hope, believing, and so by faith *saw.*   It admits of doubt
whether He is speaking here of the temporal day of the
Lord, that, viz. of His coming in the flesh, or of that day
which knows neither rising or setting.   I doubt not however
that our father Abraham knew the whole : as he says to his
servant whom he sent, *Put thy hand under my thigh, and
swear to me by the God of heaven.*   What did that oath
signify, but that the God of heaven was to come in the flesh,
out of the stock of Abraham.   Greg. Abraham saw the day
of the Lord even then, when he entertained the three Angels,
a figure of the Trinity.   Chrys. They are aliens from
Abraham if they grieve over what he rejoiced in.   By this
day perhaps He means the day of the cross, which Abraham
prefigured by the offering up of Isaac and the ram : intimating hereby that He did not come to His passion unwillingly.   Aug. If they rejoiced to whom the Word appeared
in the flesh, what was his joy, who beheld in spiritual vision
the light ineffable, the abiding Word, the bright illumination
of pious souls, the indefectible wisdom, still abiding with
God the Father, and sometime to come in the flesh, but not
to leave the Father's bosom.

Aug. Tr.xliii. 15.

Chrys. Hom. lv. 2.

Aug. Tr.xliii. 16.

Gen. 24, 2.

Greg. Hom. xv. in Evang.

Chrys. Hom. liv. 2.

Aug. Tr.xliii. 16.

57. Then said the Jews unto him, Thou art not yet fifty years old, and hast thou seen Abraham?

58. Jesus said unto them, Verily, verily, I say unto you, Before Abraham was, I am.

59. Then took they up stones to cast at him: but Jesus hid himself, and went out of the temple, going through the midst of them, and so passed by.

Greg. Hom. xviii. in Evang. GREG. The carnal minds of the Jews are intent on the flesh only; they think only of His age in the flesh: *Then said the Jews unto Him, Thou art not fifty years old, and hast Thou seen Abraham?* that is to say, Many ages have passed since Abraham died; and how then could he see thy day? For they took His words in a carnal sense. THE- OPHYL. Christ was then thirty-three years old. Why then do they not say, Thou art not yet forty years old, instead of *fifty?* A needless question this: they simply spoke as chance led them at the time. Some however say that they mentioned the fiftieth year on account of its sacred character, as being the year of jubilee, in which they redeemed their captives, and gave up the possessions they had bought.

ut sup. GREG. Our Saviour mildly draws them away from their carnal view, to the contemplation of His Divinity; *Jesus said unto them, Verily, verily, I say unto you, Before Abraham was, I am.* *Before* is a particle of past time, *am*, of present. Divinity has no past or future, but always the present; and therefore He does not say, Before Abraham was, I was: but, Exod. 3, 14. *Before Abraham was, I am:* as it is in Exodus, *I am that I am.* *Before* and *after* might be said of Abraham with reference to different periods of his life; *to be*, in the present, is said of the truth only.

Aug. Tr. xliii. 18. AUG. Abraham being a creature, He did not say *before Abraham* was, but, *before Abraham was made.* Nor does He say, I am made; because that, *in the beginning* WAS *the* ut sup. *Word.* GREG. Their unbelieving minds, however, were unable to support these indications of eternity; and not un- derstanding Him, sought to destroy Him: *Then they took up* Aug. Tr. xliii. 18. *stones to cast at Him.* AUG. Such hardness of heart, whither was it to run, but to its truest likeness, even the

stones? But now that He had done all that He could do
as a teacher, and they in return wished to stone Him, since
they could not bear correction, He leaves them: *Jesus hid
Himself, and went out of the temple.* He did not hide
Himself in a corner of the temple, as if He was afraid, or
take refuge in a house, or run behind a wall, or a pillar ; but
by His heavenly power, making Himself invisible to His
enemies, went through the midst of them: *Jesus hid Himself, and went out of the temple.* GREG. Who, had He
chosen to exert the power of His Divinity, could, without
a word, by His mere nod, have seized them, with the very
stones in their hands, and delivered them to immediate
death. But He who came to suffer, was slow to execute
judgment. AUG. For His part was more to exhibit patience Aug.
than exercise power. ALCUIN. He fled, because His hour Tr.xliii.
was not yet come; and because He had not chosen this 18.
kind of death. AUG. So then, as a man, He flies from the Aug.
stones; but woe to them, from whose stony hearts God flies. Tr.xliii.
BEDE. Mystically, a man throws a stone at Jesus, as often as 18.
he harbours an evil thought; and if he follows it up, so far
as lies in him, he kills Jesus. GREG. What does our Lord ut sup.
mean by hiding Himself, but that the truth is hidden to
them, who despise His words. The truth flies the company
of an unhumbled soul. His example shews us, that we should
in all humility rather retreat from the wrath of the proud,
when it rises, than resist it, even though we might be able.

CHAP. IX.

1. And as Jesus passed by, he saw a man which was blind from his birth.

2. And his disciples asked him, saying, Master, who did sin, this man, or his parents, that he was born blind?

3. Jesus answered, Neither hath this man sinned, nor his parents: but that the works of God should be made manifest in him.

4. I must work the works of him that sent me, while it is day: the night cometh, when no man can work.

5. As long as I am in the world, I am the light of the world.

6. When he had thus spoken, he spat on the ground, and made clay of the spittle, and he anointed the eyes of the blind man with the clay,

7. And said unto him, Go, wash in the pool of Siloam, (which is by interpretation, Sent.) He went his way therefore, and washed, and came seeing.

Chrys.
Hom.
lvi. 1. CHRYS. The Jews having rejected Christ's words, because of their depth, He went out of the temple, and healed the blind man; that His absence might appease their fury, and the miracle soften their hard hearts, and convince their unbelief. *And as Jesus passed by, He saw a man which was blind from his birth.* It is to be remarked here that, on going out of the temple, He betook Himself intently to this manifestation of His power. He first saw the blind man, not the blind man Him: and so intently did He fix His eye upon him, that His disciples were struck, and asked, *Rabbi,*

who did sin, this man or his parents, that he was born blind? BEDE. Mystically, our Lord, after being banished from the minds of the Jews, passed over to the Gentiles. The passage or journey here is His descent from heaven to earth, where He saw the blind man, i. e. looked with compassion on the human race. AUG. For the blind man here is the human race. Blindness came upon the first man by reason of sin: and from him we all derive it: i. e. man is blind from his birth. AUG. *Rabbi* is Master. They call Him Master, because they wished to learn: they put their question to our Lord, as to a Master. THEOPHYL. This question does not seem a proper one. For the Apostles had not been taught the fond notion of the Gentiles, that the soul has sinned in a previous state of existence. It is difficult to account for their putting it. CHRYS. They were led to ask this question, by our Lord having said above, on healing the man sick of the palsy, *Lo, thou art made whole; sin no more.* Thinking from this that the man had been struck with the palsy for his sins, they ask our Lord of the blind man here, whether he *did sin, or his parents;* neither of which could have been the reason of his blindness; the former, because he had been blind from his birth; the latter, because the son does not suffer for the father.

Jesus answered, Neither hath this man sinned, nor his parents. AUG. Was he then born without original sin, or had he never added to it by actual sin? Both this man and his parents had sinned, but that sin was not the reason why he was born blind. Our Lord gives the reason; viz. *That the works of God should be made manifest in him.* CHRYS. He is not to be understood as meaning that others had become blind, in consequence of their parents' sins: for one man cannot be punished for the sin of another. But had the man therefore suffered unjustly? Rather I should say that that blindness was a benefit to him: for by it he was brought to see with the inward eye. At any rate He who brought him into being out of nothing, had the power to make him in the event no loser by it. Some too say, that the *that* here, is expressive not of the cause, but of the event, as in the passage in Romans, *The law entered that sin might abound;* the effect in this case being, that our Lord by

Margin notes:
non occ.

Aug.
Tr. xliv.
1, 2.

Aug.
Tr. xliv.
1, 2.

Chrys.
Hom.
liv. 1.
c. 5.

Aug.
Hom.
xliv. 3.

Chrys.
Hom.
lvi. 1, 2.

Rom. 5,
20.

opening the closed eye, and healing other natural infirmities,
demonstrated His own power. GREG. One stroke falls on
the sinner, for punishment only, not conversion; another for
correction; another not for correction of past sins, but pre-
vention of future; another neither for correcting past, nor
preventing future sins, but by the unexpected deliverance
following the blow, to excite more ardent love of the Saviour's
goodness. CHRYS. *That the glory of God should be made
manifest*, He saith of Himself, not of the Father; the
Father's glory was manifest already. *I must work the works
of Him that sent Me:* ·i. e. I must manifest Myself, and
shew that I do the same that My Father doeth. BEDE. For
when the Son declared that He worked the works of the
Father, He proved that His and His Father's works were the
same: which are, to heal the sick, to strengthen the weak,
and enlighten man. AUG. By His saying, *Who sent Me*,
He gives all the glory to Him from Whom He is. The
Father hath a Son Who is from Him, but hath none from
whom He Himself is. CHRYS. *While it is day*, He adds;
i. e. while men have the opportunity· of believing in Me;
while this life lasts; *The night cometh, when none can work*.
Night here means that spoken of in Matthew, *Cast him into
outer darkness*. Then will there be night, wherein none can
work, but only receive for that which he has worked. While
thou livest, do that which thou wilt do: for beyond it is
neither faith, nor labour, nor repentance. AUG. But if we work
now, now is the day· time, now is Christ present; as He
says, *As long as I am in the world, I am the light of the
world*. This then is the day. The natural day is completed
by the circuit of the sun, and contains only a few hours:
the day of Christ's presence will last to the end of the world:
for He Himself has said, *Lo, I am with you alway, even unto
the end of the world*. CHRYS. He then confirms His words
by deeds: *When He had thus spoken, He spat on the ground,
and made clay of the spittle, and anointed the eyes of the blind
man with the clay*. He who had brought greater substances
into being out of nothing, could much more have given sight
without the use of any material: but He wished to shew
that He was the Creator, Who in the beginning used clay for
the formation of man. He makes the clay with spittle, and

Greg.
in Præf.
Moral.
c. 5.

Chrys.
Hom.
liv. 2.

Aug.
Tr. xliv.
4.

Chrys.
Hom.
lvi. 2.

Mat. 22,
13.

Aug.
Tr. xliv.
5.

Mat. 28,
20.
Chrys.
Hom.
lvi. 2.

Hom.
lvii. 1.

not with water, to make it evident that it was not the pool of
Siloam, whither He was about to send him, but the virtue
proceeding from His mouth, which restored the man's
sight. And then, that the cure might not seem to be the
effect of the clay, He ordered the man to wash: *And He
said unto him, Go, wash in the pool of Siloam.* The
Evangelist gives the meaning of Siloam, *which is by interpretation, Sent,* to intimate that it was Christ's power that
cured him even there. As the Apostle says of the rock in
the wilderness, that *that Rock was Christ,* so Siloam had a
spiritual character: the sudden rise of its water being a 1 Cor.
10, 14.
silent figure of Christ's unexpected manifestation in the flesh.
But why did He not tell him to wash immediately, instead
of sending him to Siloam? That the obstinacy of the Jews
might be overcome, when they saw him going there with the
clay on his eyes. Besides which, it proved that He was
not averse to the Law, and the Old Testament. And there
was no fear of the glory of the case being given to Siloam:
as many had washed their eyes there, and received no such
benefit. And to shew the faith of the blind man, who
made no opposition, never argued with himself, that it was
the quality of clay rather to darken, than give light, that He
had often washed in Siloam, and had never been benefited;
that if our Lord had the power, He might have cured him by
His word; but simply obeyed: *he went his way therefore,
and washed, and came seeing.* Thus our Lord manifested Hom.
lvi. 2.
His glory: and no small glory it was, to be proved the Creator
of the world, as He was proved to be by this miracle. For
on the principle that the greater contains the less, this act of
creation included in it every other. Man is the most honourable of all creatures; the eye the most honourable member of
man, directing the movements, and giving him sight. The eye
is to the body, what the sun is to the universe; and therefore
it is placed aloft, as it were, upon a royal eminence. THE-
OPHYL. Some think that the clay was not laid upon the eyes,
but made into eyes. AUG. Our Lord spat upon the ground, Aug.
Tr. xlv.
and made clay of the spittle, because He was the Word made
2.
flesh. The man did not see immediately as he was anointed;
i. e. was, as it were, only made a catechumen. But he was

sent to the pool which is called Siloam, i. e. he was baptized in Christ; and then he was enlightened. The Evangelist then explains to us the name of this pool: *which is by interpretation, Sent:* for, if He had not been sent, none of us would have been delivered from our sins. GREG. Or thus: By His spittle understand the savour of inward contemplation. It runs down from the head into the mouth, and gives us the taste of revelation from the Divine splendour even in this life. The mixture of His spittle with clay is the mixture of supernatural grace, even the contemplation of Himself with our carnal knowledge, to the soul's enlightenment, and restoration of the human understanding from its original blindness.

Greg.
viii.
Moral.
c. xxx.
(49.)

8. The neighbours therefore, and they which before had seen him that he was blind, said, Is not this he that sat and begged?

9. Some said, This is he: others said, He is like him: but he said, I am he.

10. Therefore said they unto him, How were thine eyes opened?

11. He answered and said, A man that is called Jesus made clay, and anointed mine eyes, and said unto me, Go to the pool of Siloam, and wash: and I went and washed, and I received sight.

12. Then said they unto him, Where is he? He said, I know not.

13. They brought to the Pharisees him that aforetime was blind.

14. And it was the sabbath day when Jesus made the clay, and opened his eyes.

15. Then again the Pharisees also asked him how he had received his sight. He said unto them, He put clay upon mine eyes, and I washed, and do see.

16. Therefore said some of the Pharisees, This man is not of God, because he keepeth not the sabbath

day. Others said, How can a man that is a sinner
do such miracles? And there was a division among
them.

17. They say unto the blind man again, What
sayest thou of him, that he hath opened thine eyes?
He said, He is a prophet.

CHRYS. The suddenness of the miracle made men incre- Chrys.
dulous: *The neighbours therefore, and they which had seen* Hom.
lvii. s. 1.
*him that he was blind, said, Is not this he that sat and
begged?* Wonderful clemency and condescension of God!
Even the beggars He heals with so great considerateness:
thus stopping the mouths of the Jews; in that He made not
the great, illustrious, and noble, but the poorest and meanest,
the objects of His providence. Indeed He had come for
the salvation of all. *Some said, This is he.* The blind man
having been clearly recognised in the course of his long walk
to the pool; the more so, as people's attention was drawn by
the strangeness of the event; men could no longer say,
This is not he; *Others said, Nay, but he is like him.* AUG. Aug.
His eyes being opened had altered his look. *But he said,* Tr. xliv.
8.
I am he. He spoke gratefully; a denial would have convicted
Him of ingratitude. CHRYS. He was not ashamed of his Chrys.
former blindness, nor afraid of the fury of the people, nor Hom.
lvii. s. 2.
averse to shew himself, and proclaim his Benefactor. *Therefore
said they unto him, How were thine eyes opened?* How they
were, neither he nor any one knew: he only knew the fact; he
could not explain it. *He answered and said, A man that is
called Jesus made clay, and anointed mine eyes.* Mark his
exactness. He does not say how the clay was made; for he
could not see that our Lord spat on the ground; he does not say
what he does not know; but that He anointed him he could feel.
And said unto me, Go to the pool of Siloam, and wash. This
too he could declare from his own hearing; for he had heard
our Lord converse with His disciples, and so knew His
voice. Lastly, he shews how strictly he had obeyed our
Lord. He adds, *And I went, and washed, and received
sight.* AUG. Lo, he is become a proclaimer of grace, an Aug.
Tr. xliv.
evangelist, and testifies to the Jews. That blind man testi- s. 8.

fied, and the ungodly were vexed at the heart, because they had not in their heart what appeared upon his countenance. *Then said they unto him, Where is He?* CHRYS. This they said, because they were meditating His death, having already begun to conspire against Him. Christ did not appear in company with those whom He cured; having no desire for glory, or display. He always withdrew, after healing any one; in order that no suspicion might attach to the miracle. His withdrawal proved the absence of all connexion between Him and the healed; and therefore that the latter did not publish a false cure out of favour to Him. *He said, I know not.* AUG. Here he is like one anointed, but unable yet to see: he preaches, and knows not what he preaches. BEDE. Thus he represents the state of the catechumen, who believes in Jesus, but does not, strictly speaking, know Him, not being yet washed. It fell to the Pharisees to confirm or deny the miracle. CHRYS. The Jews, whom they asked, *Where is He?* were desirous of finding Him, in order to bring Him to the Pharisees; but, as they could not find Him, they bring the blind man. *They brought to the Pharisees him that afore-time was blind;* i. e. that they might examine him still more closely. The Evangelist adds, *And it was the sabbath day when Jesus made the clay, and opened his eyes;* in order to expose their real design, which was to accuse Him of a departure from the law, and thus detract from the miracle: as appears from what follows, *Then again the Pharisees also asked him how he had received his sight.* But mark the firmness of the blind man. To tell the truth to the multitude before, from whom he was in no danger, was not so great a matter: but it is remarkable, now that the danger is so much greater, to find him disavowing nothing, and not contradicting any thing that he said before: *He said unto them, He put clay upon mine eyes, and I washed, and do see.* He is more brief this time, as his interrogators were already informed of the matter: not mentioning the name of Jesus, nor His saying, *Go, and wash;* but simply, *He put clay upon mine eyes, and I washed, and do see;* the very contrary answer to what they wanted. They wanted a disavowal, and they receive a confirmation of the story.

Therefore said some of the Pharisees. AUG. *Some,* not

Chrys. Hom. lvii. 2.

Aug. Tr. xliv. 8.

Chrys. Hom. lvii. 2.

Aug. Tr. xliv. 9.

all: for some were already anointed. But they, who neither saw, nor were anointed, said, *This man is not of God, because he keepeth not the sabbath day.* Rather He kept it, in that He was without sin; for to observe the sabbath spiritually, is to have no sin. And this God admonishes us of, when He enjoins the sabbath, saying, *In it thou shalt do no ser-* Exod.20, *vile work.* What servile work is, our Lord tells us above, 10. *Whosoever committeth sin, is the servant of sin.* They c. 8, 34. observed the sabbath carnally, transgressed it spiritually. CHRYS. Passing over the miracle in silence, they give all Chrys. the prominence they can to the supposed transgression; lvii. 2. not charging Him with healing on the sabbath, but with not keeping the sabbath. *Others said, How can a man that is a sinner do such miracles?* They were impressed by His miracles, but only in a weak and unsettled way. For whereas such might have shewn them, that the sabbath was not broken; they had not yet any idea that He was God, and therefore did not know that it was the Lord of the sabbath who had worked the miracle. Nor did any of them dare to say openly what his sentiments were, but spoke ambiguously; one, because he thought the fact itself improbable; another, from his love of station. It follows, *And there was a division among them.* That is, the people were divided first, and then the rulers. AUG. It was Christ, who divided the day into light Aug. and darkness. CHRYS. Those who said, Can a man that is xliv.4,5. a sinner do such miracles? wishing to stop the others' mouths, Chrys. make the object of our Lord's goodness again come forward; lviii. 1. but without appearing to take part with Him themselves: *They say unto the blind man again, What sayest thou of Him, that He hath opened thine eyes?* THEOPHYL. See with what good intent they put the question. They do not say, What sayest thou of Him that keepeth not the sabbath, but mention the miracle, *that He hath opened thine eyes;* meaning, it would seem, to draw out the healed man himself; He hath benefited them, they seem to say, and thou oughtest to preach Him. AUG. Or they sought how they could throw reproach Aug. upon the man, and cast him out of their synagogue. He Tr. xliv. declares however openly what he thinks: *He said, He is a* 9. *Prophet.* Not being anointed yet in heart, he could not confess the Son of God; nevertheless, he is not wrong in what he

Luke 4, 24. says: for our Lord Himself says of Himself, *A prophet is not without honour, save in his own country.*

18. But the Jews did not believe concerning him, that he had been blind, and received his sight, until they called the parents of him that had received his sight.

19. And they asked them, saying, Is this your son, who ye say was born blind? how then doth he now see?

20. His parents answered them and said, We know that this is our son, and that he was born blind:

21. But by what means he now seeth, we know not; or who hath opened his eyes, we know not: he is of age; ask him: he shall speak for himself.

22. These words spake his parents, because they feared the Jews: for the Jews had agreed already, that if any man did confess that he was Christ, he should be put out of the synagogue.

23. Therefore said his parents, He is of age; ask him.

Chrys.
Hom.
lviii. 1.

CHRYS. The Pharisees being unable, by intimidation, to deter the blind man from publicly proclaiming his Benefactor, try to nullify the miracle through the parents: *But the Jews did not believe concerning him, that he had been blind, and received his sight, until they had called the parents*

Aug.
Tr. xliv.
s. 10.

of him that had received his sight. AUG. i. e. had been blind, and now saw. CHRYS. But it is the nature of truth,

Chrys.
Hom.
lviii. 3.

to be strengthened by the very snares that are laid against it. A lie is its own antagonist, and by its attempts to injure the truth, sets it off to greater advantage: as is the case now. For the argument which might otherwise have been urged, that the neighbours knew nothing for certain, but spoke from a mere resemblance, is cut off by introduction of the parents, who could of course testify to their own son. Having brought these before the assembly, they interrogate them with great sharpness, saying, *Is this your son,* (they

say not, who was born blind, but) *who ye say was born blind?*
Say. Why what father is there, that would say such things of
a son, if they were not true? Why not say at once, Whom ye
made blind? They try two ways of making them deny the
miracle: by saying, *Who ye say was born blind,* and by
adding, *How then doth he now see?* THEOPHYL. Either, say
they, it is not true that he now sees, or it is untrue that he
was blind before: but it is evident that he now sees; therefore
it is not true that he was born blind. CHRYS. Three things Chrys.
then being asked,—if he were their son, if he had been blind, Hom.
lviii. 2.
and how he saw,—they acknowledge two of them: *His*
parents answered them and said, We know that this is our
son, and that he was born blind. But the third they refuse
to speak to: *But by what means he now seeth, we know not.*
The enquiry in this way ends in confirming the truth of the
miracle, by making it rest upon the incontrovertible evidence
of the confession of the healed person himself; *He is of*
age, they say, *ask him; he can speak for himself.* AUG. As Aug.
if to say, We might justly be compelled to speak for an infant, Tr. xliv.
10.
that could not speak for itself: but he, though blind from
his birth, has been always able to speak. CHRYS. What Chrys.
Hom.
sort of gratitude is this in the parents; concealing what they lvii. 2.
knew, from fear of the Jews? as we are next told; *These*
words spake his parents, because they feared the Jews. And
then the Evangelist mentions again what the intentions and
dispositions of the Jews were: *For the Jews had agreed*
already, that if any man did confess that He was Christ, he
should be put out of the synagogue. AUG. It was no disad- Aug.
Tr. xliv.
vantage to be put out of the synagogue: whom they cast out, 10.
Christ took in.

Therefore said his parents, He is of age, ask him. ALCUIN.
The Evangelist shews that it was not from ignorance, but
fear, that they gave this answer. THEOPHYL. For they were
fainthearted; not like their son, that intrepid witness
to the truth, the eyes of whose understanding had been
enlightened by God.

24. Then again called they the man that was blind,
and said unto him, Give God the praise: we know that
this man is a sinner.

25. He answered and said, Whether he be a sinner or no, I know not: one thing I know, that, whereas I was blind, now I see.

26. Then said they to him again, What did he to thee? how opened he thine eyes?

27. He answered them, I have told you already, and ye did not hear: wherefore would ye hear it again? will ye also be his disciples?

28. Then they reviled him, and said, Thou art his disciple; but we are Moses' disciples.

29. We know that God spake unto Moses: as for this fellow, we know not from whence he is.

30. The man answered and said unto them, Why herein is a marvellous thing, that ye know not from whence he is, and yet he hath opened mine eyes.

31. Now we know that God heareth not sinners: but if any man be a worshipper of God, and doeth his will, him he heareth.

32. Since the world began was it not heard that any man opened the eyes of one that was born blind.

33. If this man were not of God, he could do nothing.

34. They answered and said unto him, Thou wast altogether born in sins, and dost thou teach us? And they cast him out.

Chrys. Hom. lviii. 2.

CHRYS. The parents having referred the Pharisees to the healed man himself, they summon him a second time: *Then again called they the man that was blind.* They do not openly say now, Deny that Christ has healed thee, but conceal their object under the pretence of religion: *Give God the praise,* i. e. confess that this man has had nothing to do with the work. AUG. Deny that thou hast received the benefit. This is not to give God the glory, but rather to blaspheme Him. ALCUIN. They wished him to give glory to God, by calling Christ a sinner, as they did: *We know that this man is a sinner.* CHRYS. Why then did ye not

Aug. Tr. xliv. s. 11.

Chrys. Hom. lviii. 2.

convict Him, when He said above, *Which of you convinceth* c. 8, 46.
Me of sin? ALCUIN. The man, that he might neither expose
himself to calumny, nor at the same time conceal the truth,
answers not that he knew Him to be righteous, but, *Whether
He be a sinner or no, I know not.* CHRYS. But how comes Chrys.
this, *whether He be a sinner, I know not,* from one who had lviii. 2.
said, *He is a Prophet?* Did the blind fear? far from it: he
only thought that our Lord's defence lay in the witness of
the fact, more than in another's pleading. And he gives
weight to his reply by the mention of the benefit he had
received: *One thing I know, that, whereas I was blind, now
I see:* as if to say, I say nothing as to whether He is a sinner; but only repeat what I know for certain. So being
unable to overturn the fact itself of the miracle, they fall
back upon former arguments, and enquire the manner of the
cure: just as dogs in hunting pursue wherever the scent
takes them: *Then said they to him again, What did He do to
thee? How opened He thine eyes?* i. e. was it by any charm?
For they do not say, How didst thou see? but, *How opened
He thine eyes?* to give the man an opportunity of detracting
from the operation. So long now as the matter wanted examining, the blind man answers gently and quietly; but, the
victory being gained, he grows bolder: *He answered them,
I have told you already, and ye did not hear: wherefore
would ye hear it again?* i. e. Ye do not attend to what is
said, and therefore I will no longer answer you vain questions, put for the sake of cavil, not to gain knowledge: *Will ye
also be His disciples?* AUG. *Will ye also?* i. e. I am already, Aug.
do ye wish to be? I see now, but do not envy. He says Tr. xliv.
this in indignation at the obstinacy of the Jews; not tole- video,
rating blindness, now that he is no longer blind himself. non
CHRYS. As then truth is strength, so falsehood is weakness: Chrys.
truth elevates and ennobles whomever it takes up, however lviii. 2.
mean before: falsehood brings even the strong to weakness
and contempt.

Then they reviled him, and said, Thou art His disciple. Aug.
AUG. A malediction only in the intention of the speakers, Tr. xliv.
not in the words themselves. May such a malediction be ελοιδ-
upon us, and upon our children! It follows: *But we are* ησαν,
Moses' disciples. We know that God spake unto Moses. But dixe-
runt,
Vulg,

z

ye should have known, that our Lord was prophesied of c. 5, 46. by Moses, after hearing what He said, *Had ye believed Moses, ye would have believed Me, for he wrote of Me.* Do ye follow then a servant, and turn your back on the Lord? Even so, for it follows: *As for this fellow, we know not whence He is.* CHRYS. Ye think sight less evidence than hearing; for what ye say, ye know, is what ye have heard from your fathers. But is not He more worthy of belief, who has certified that He comes from God, by miracles which ye have not heard only, but seen? So argues the blind man: *The man answered and said, Why herein is a marvellous thing, that ye know not whence He is, and yet He hath opened mine eyes.* He brings in the miracle every where, as evidence which they could not invalidate: and, inasmuch as they had said that a man that was a sinner could not do such miracles, he turns their own words against them; *Now we know that God heareth not sinners;* as if to say, I quite agree with you in this opinion. AUG. As yet however He speaks as one but just anointed[1], for God hears sinners too. Else in vain would the publican cry, *God be merciful to me a sinner.* By that confession he obtained[2] justification, as the blind man had his sight. THEOPHYL. Or, that God heareth not sinners, means, that God does not enable sinners to work miracles. When sinners however implore pardon for their offences, they are translated from the rank of sinners to that of penitents. CHRYS. Observe then, when he said above, *Whether He be a sinner, I know not,* it was not that he spoke in doubt; for here he not only acquits him of all sin, but holds him up as one well pleasing to God: *But if any man be a worshipper of God, and doeth His will, him He heareth.* It is not enough to know God, we must do His will. Then he extols His deed: *Since the world began, was it not heard that any man opened the eyes of one that was born blind:* as if to say, If ye confess that God heareth not sinners; and this Man has worked a miracle, such an one, as no other man has; it is manifest that the virtue whereby He has wrought it, is more than human: *If this Man were not of God, He could do nothing.* AUG. Freely, stedfastly, truly. For how could what our Lord did, be done by any other than God, or by disciples even,

c. 5, 46.

Chrys.
Hom.
lviii. s. 3.

Aug.
Tr. xliv.
s. 13.
[1] adhuc
inunctus
loquitur.
Luke
18, 13.
[2] meruit

Chrys.
Hom.
lviii. 3.

Aug.
Tr. xliv.
13.

except when their Lord dwelt in them? CHRYS. So then Chrys. Hom. viii. 3. because speaking the truth he was in nothing confounded, when they should most have admired, they condemned him: *Thou wast altogether born in sins, and dost thou teach us?* AUG. What meaneth *altogether?* That he was quite blind. Aug. Tr. xliv. 14. Yet He who opened his eyes, also saves him altogether. CHRYS. Or, *altogether*, that is to say, from thy birth thou art Chrys. Hom. lviii. 3. in sins. They reproach his blindness, and pronounce his sins to be the cause of it; most unreasonably. So long as they expected him to deny the miracle, they were willing to believe him, but now *they cast him out.* AUG. It was they Aug. Tr. xliv. 14. themselves who had made him teacher; themselves, who had asked him so many questions; and now they ungratefully cast him out for teaching. BEDE. It is commonly the way with great persons to disdain learning any thing from their inferiors.

35. Jesus heard that they had cast him out; and when he had found him, he said unto him, Dost thou believe on the Son of God?

36. He answered and said, Who is he, Lord, that I might believe on him?

37. And Jesus said unto him, Thou hast both seen him, and it is he that talketh with thee.

38. And he said, Lord, I believe. And he worshipped him.

39. And Jesus said, For judgment I am come into this world, that they which see not might see; and that they which see might be made blind.

40. And some of the Pharisees which were with him heard these words, and said unto him, Are we blind also?

41. Jesus said unto them, If ye were blind, ye should have no sin: but now ye say, We see: therefore your sin remaineth.

CHRYS. Those who suffer for the truth's sake, and con-Chrys. Hom. lix. 1. fession of Christ, come to greatest honour; as we see in the instance of the blind man. For the Jews cast him out of the temple, and the Lord of the temple found him; and received him as the judge doth the wrestler after his labours, and crowned him: *Jesus heard that they had cast him out; and when He had found him, He saith unto him, Dost thou believe on the Son of God?* The Evangelist makes it plain that Jesus came in order to say this to him. He asks him, however, not in ignorance, but wishing to reveal Himself to him, and to shew that He appreciated his faith; as if He said, The people have cast reproaches on Me, but I care not for them; one thing only I care for, that thou mayest believe. Better is he that doeth the will of God, than ten thousand of

Eilar.
vi. de
Trin.
circa
fin.

the wicked. HILARY. If any mere confession whatsoever of Christ were the perfection of faith, it would have been said, *Dost thou believe in Christ?* But inasmuch as all heretics would have had this name in their mouths, confessing Christ, and yet denying the Son, that which is true of Christ alone, is required of our faith, viz. that we should believe in the Son of God. But what availeth it to believe on the Son of God as being a creature, when we are required to have faith in Christ, not as a creature of God, but as the Son of

Chrys.
Hom.
lix. 1.

God. CHRYS. But the blind man did not yet know Christ, for before he went to Christ he was blind, and after his cure, he was taken hold of by the Jews: *He answered and said, Who is He, Lord, that I might believe on Him?* The speech this of a longing and enquiring mind. He knows not who He is for whom he had contended so much; a proof to thee of his love of truth. The Lord however says not to him, I am He who healed thee; but uses a middle way of speaking, *Thou hast both seen Him.* THEOPHYL. This He says to remind him of his cure, which had given him the power to see. And observe, He that speaks is born of Mary, and the Son is the Son of God, not two different Persons, according to the error of Nestorius: *And it is He that talketh with thee.* AUG. First, He washes the face of his heart. Then,

Aug.
Tr. xliv.
15.

his heart's face being washed, and his conscience cleansed, he acknowledges Him as not only the Son of man, which he believed before, but as the Son of God, Who had taken flesh upon Him: *And he said, Lord, I believe. I believe,* is a small thing. Wouldest thou see what he believes of Him?

And falling down, he worshipped Him. BEDE. An example Vulgate
to us, not to pray to God with uplifted neck, but prostrate
upon earth, suppliantly to implore His mercy. CHRYS. He Chrys.
adds the deed to the word, as a clear acknowledgment of Hom.
His divine power. The Lord replies in a way to confirm
His faith, and at the same time stirs up the minds of His
followers: *And Jesus said, For judgment have I come into
this world.* AUG. The day then was divided between light and Aug.
darkness. So it is rightly added, *that they which see not,* Tr.xliv.
may see; for He relieved men from darkness. But what is
that which follows: *And that they which see might be made
blind.* Hear what comes next. Some of the Pharisees
were moved by these words: *And some of the Pharisees
which were with Him heard these words, and said unto Him,
Are we blind also?* What had moved them were the words,
And that they which see might be made blind. It follows;
*Jesus saith unto them, If ye were blind, ye should have no
sin;* i. e. If ye called yourselves blind, and ran to the physician.
But now ye say, We see; therefore your sin remaineth: for
in that saying, *We see,* ye seek not a physician, ye shall
remain in your blindness. This then which He has just
before said, *I came, that they that see not might see;* i. e.
they who confess they cannot see, and seek a physician, in
order that they may see: and that they which see not may
be made blind; i. e. they which think they can see, and seek
not a physician, may remain in their blindness. This act
of division He calls judgment, saying, *For judgment have I
come into this world:* not that judgment by which He will
judge quick and dead at the end of the world. CHRYS. Or, Chrys.
for judgment, He saith; i. e. for greater punishment, shewing Hom.
that they who condemned Him, were the very ones who were
condemned. Respecting what He says, *that they which see
not might see, and that they which see might be made blind;*
it is the same which St. Paul says, *The Gentiles which* Rom. 9,
followed not after righteousness, have attained to righteous- 30. 31.
*ness, even the righteousness which is of faith. But Israel,
which followed after the law of righteousness, hath not
attained to the law of righteousness.* THEOPHYL. As if to
say, Lo, he that saw not from his birth, now sees both in body
and soul; whereas they who seem to see, have had their

Chrys.
Hom.
lix. 1.
understanding darkened. CHRYS. For there is a twofold vision, and a twofold blindness; viz. that of sense, and that of the understanding. But they were intent only on sensible things, and were ashamed only of sensible blindness: wherefore He shews them that it would be better for them to be blind, than seeing so: *If ye were blind, ye shoutd have no sin;* your punishment would be easier; *But now ye say, We see.* THEOPHYL. Overlooking the miracle wrought on the blind man, ye deserve no pardon; since even visible miracles

Chrys.
Hom.
lix. 1, 2.
make no impression on you. CHRYS. What then they thought their great praise, He shews would turn to their punishment; and at the same time consoles him who had been afflicted with bodily blindness from his birth. For it is not without reason that the Evangelist says, *And some of the Pharisees which were with him, heard these words;* but that he may remind us that those were the very persons who had first withstood Christ, and then wished to stone Him. For there were some who only followed in appearance, and were easily changed to the contrary side. THEOPHYL. Or, if ye were blind, i. e. ignorant of the Scriptures, your offence would be by no means so heavy a one, as erring out of ignorance: but now, seeing ye call yourselves wise and understanding in the law, your own selves condemn you.

CHAP. X.

1. Verily, verily, I say unto you, He that entereth not by the door into the sheepfold, but climbeth up some other way, the same is a thief and a robber.

2. But he that entereth in by the door is the shepherd of the sheep.

3. To him the porter openeth; and the sheep hear his voice: and he calleth his own sheep by name, and leadeth them out.

4. And when he putteth forth his own sheep, he goeth before them, and the sheep follow him: for they know his voice.

5. And a stranger will they not follow, but will flee from him: for they know not the voice of strangers.

CHRYS. Our Lord having reproached the Jews with blindness, they might have said, We are not blind, but we avoid Thee as a deceiver. Our Lord therefore gives the marks which distinguish a robber and deceiver from a true shepherd. First come those of the deceiver and robber: *Verily, verily, I say unto you, He that entereth not by the door into the sheepfold, but climbeth up some other way, the same is a thief and a robber.* There is an allusion here to Antichrist, and to certain false Christs who had been, and were to be. The Scriptures He calls *the door.* They admit us to the knowledge of God, they protect the sheep, they shut out the wolves, they bar the entrance to heretics. He that useth not the Scriptures, but climbeth up some other way, i. e. some self-chosen [1], some unlawful way, is a thief. Climbeth up, He says, not, enters, as if it were a thief getting over a wall, and running all risks. *Some other way,* may refer too

Chrys. Hom. lix. 2.

[1] ἑτέραν ἑαυτῷ

to the commaudments and traditions of men which the Scribes taught, to the neglect of the Law. When our Lord further on calls Himself the Door, we need not be surprised. According to the office which He bears, He is in one place the Shepherd, in another the Sheep. In that He introduces us to the Father, He is the Door; in that He takes care of us, He is the Shepherd. Aug. Or thus: Many go under the name of good men according to the standard of the world, and observe in some sort the commandments of the Law, who yet are not Christians. And these generally boast of themselves, as the Pharisees did; *Are we blind also?* But inasmuch as all that they do they do foolishly, without knowing to what end it tends, our Lord saith of them, *Verily, verily, I say unto you, He that entereth not by the door into the sheepfold, but climbeth up some other way, the same is a thief and a robber.* Let the Pagans then, the Jews, the Heretics, say, " We lead a good life;" if they enter not by the door, what availeth it? A good life only profiteth, as leading to life eternal. Indeed those cannot be said to lead a good life, who are either blindly ignorant of, or wilfully despise, the end of good living. No one can hope for eternal life, who knows not Christ, who is the life, and by that door enters into the fold. Whoso wisheth to enter into the sheepfold, let him enter by the door; let him preach Christ; let him seek Christ's glory, not his own. Christ is a lowly door, and he who enters by this door must be lowly, if he would enter with his head whole. He that doth not humble, but exalt himself, who wishes to climb up over the wall, is exalted that he may fall. Such men generally try to persuade others that they may live well, and not be Christians. Thus they climb up by some other way, that they may rob and kill. They are thieves, because they call that their own, which is not; robbers, because that which they have stolen, they kill. CHRYS. You have seen His description of a robber, now see that of the Shepherd: *But he that entereth in by the door is the shepherd of the sheep.* AUG. He enters by the door, who enters by Christ, who imitates the suffering of Christ, who is acquainted with the humility of Christ, so as to feel and know, that if God became man for us, man should not think himself God, but man. He

Aug. Tr. xlv. 2. et sq.

Chrys. Hom. lix. 2.

Aug. de Verb. Dom. Serm. xlix.

who being man wishes to appear God, does not imitate Him,
who being God, became man.   Thou art bid to think less of
thyself than thou art, but to know what thou art.

To Him the porter openeth.   CHRYS. The porter perhaps Chrys.
is Moses ; for to him the oracles of God were committed. Hom.
xlix. 2.
THEOPHYL. Or, the Holy Spirit is the porter, by whom the
Scriptures are unlocked, and reveal the truth to us.   AUG. Aug.
Or, the porter is our Lord Himself; for there is much less Tr. xlvi. 2.
difference between a door and a porter, than between a door
and a shepherd.   And He has called Himself both the door
and the shepherd.   Why then not the door and the porter?
He opens Himself, i. e. reveals[1] Himself.   If thou seek [1] expo-
another person for porter, take the Holy Spirit, of whom our nit.
Lord below saith, *He will guide you into all truth.*   The c.16, 13.
door is Christ, the Truth; who openeth the door, but He
that *will guide you into all Truth?*   Whomsoever thou
understand here, beware that thou esteem not the porter
greater than the door; for in our houses the porter ranks
above the door, not the door above the porter.   CHRYS. As Chrys.
they had called Him a deceiver, and appealed to their own Hom. lix. 2.
unbelief as the proof of it; (*Which of the rulers believeth* c. 7, 48.
on Him?) He shews here that it was because they refused to
hear Him, that they were put out of His flock.   *The sheep*
hear His voice.   The Shepherd enters by the lawful door ;
and they who follow Him are His sheep ; they who do not,
voluntarily put themselves out of His flock.

And He calleth His own sheep by name.   AUG. He knew Aug.
the names of the predestinated; as He saith to His disciples, Tr. xlv. 12.
Rejoice that your names are written in heaven.   Luke
19, 14.
And leadeth them out.   CHRYS. He led out the sheep, Chrys.
when He sent them not out of the reach of, but into the Hom. lix. 2.
midst of, the wolves.   There seems to be a secret allusion to
the blind man.   He called him out of the midst of the Jews;
and he heard His voice.   AUG. And who is He who leads Aug.
them out, but the Same who loosens the chain of their sins, Tr. xlv. 14.
that they may follow Him with free unfettered step ?   GLOSS.
And when He putteth forth His own sheep, He goeth before
them, He leadeth them out from the darkness of ignorance
into light, while He goeth before in the pillar of cloud, and Chrys.
fire.   CHRYS. Shepherds always go behind their sheep ; but Hom. lix. 2.

He, on the contrary, goes before, to shew that He would lead

Aug.
Tr. xlv.
c. 14.
Rom. 6,
9.
Infra
17, 24. all to the truth. AUG. And who is this that goeth before the sheep, but He who *being raised from the dead, dieth no more;* and who said, *Father, I will also that they, whom Thou hast given Me, be with Me where I am?*

And the sheep follow Him, for they know His voice. And a stranger will they not follow, but will flee from him; for they know not the voice of strangers. CHRYS. The strangers

Chrys.
Hom.
xlix. 3. are Theudas, and Judas, and the false apostles who came after Christ. That He might not appear one of this number, He gives many marks of difference between Him and them. First, Christ brought men to Him by teaching them out of the Scriptures; they drew men from the Scriptures. Secondly, the obedience of the sheep; for men believed on Him, not only during His life, but after death: their followers ceased, as soon as they were gone. THEOPHYL. He alludes to Antichrist, who shall deceive for a time, but

Aug.
Tr. xlv.
10. ct
seq. lose all his followers when he dies. AUG. But here is a difficulty. Sometimes they who are not sheep hear Christ's voice; for Judas heard, who was a wolf. And sometimes the sheep hear Him not; for they who crucified Christ heard not; yet some of them were His sheep. You will say, While they did not hear, they were not sheep; the voice, when they heard it, changed them from wolves to sheep. Still I am disturbed by the Lord's rebuke to the

Ezek.34,
4. shepherds in Ezekiel, *Neither have ye brought again that which strayed.* He calls it a stray sheep, but yet a sheep all the while; though, if it strayed, it could not have heard the voice of the Shepherd, but the voice of a stranger. What

2 Tim.
2, 19. I say then is this; *The Lord knoweth them that are His.* He knoweth the foreknown, he knoweth the predestinated. They are the sheep: for a time they know not themselves, but the Shepherd knows them; for many sheep are without the fold, many wolves within. He speaks then of the predestinated. And now the difficulty is solved. The sheep do hear the Shepherd's voice, and they only. When

Mat.10,
32. is that? It is when that voice saith, *He that endureth to the end shall be saved.* This speech His own hear, the alien hear not.

6. This parable spake Jesus unto them: but they understood not what things they were which he spake unto them.

Aug. Our Lord feedeth by plain words, exerciseth by obscure. For when two persons, one godly, the other ungodly, hear the words of the Gospel, and they happen to be such that neither can understand them; one says, What He saith is true and good, but we do not understand it: the other says, It is not worth attending to. The former, in faith, knocks, yea, and, if he continue to knock, it shall be opened unto him. The latter shall hear the words in Isaiah, *If ye will not believe, surely ye shall not be established*[1]. ut sup.

Isa.7,9.
[1] non intelligetis

7. Then said Jesus unto them again, Verily, verily, I say unto you, I am the door of the sheep.

Aug. non permanebitis Vulg.

8. All that ever came before me are thieves and robbers: but the sheep did not hear them.

9. I am the door: by me if any man enter in, he shall be saved, and shall go in and out, and find pasture.

10. The thief cometh not, but for to steal, and to kill, and to destroy: I am come that they might have life, and that they might have it more abundantly.

Chrys. Our Lord, to waken the attention of the Jews, unfolds the meaning of what He has said; *Then said Jesus unto them again, Verily, verily, I say unto you, I am the door of the sheep.* Aug. Lo, the very door which He had shut up, He openeth; He is the Door: let us enter, and let us enter with joy.

Chrys. Hom. lix. 3.

Aug. Tr. xlv. 8.

All that ever came before Me are thieves and robbers. Chrys. He saith not this of the Prophets, as the heretics think, but of Theudas, and Judas, and other agitators. So he adds in praise of the sheep, *The sheep heard them not;* but he no where praises those who disobeyed the prophets, but condemns them severely. Aug. Understand, All that ever came at variance with Me. The Prophets were not at variance[2] with Him. They came with Him, who came with

Chrys. Hom. lix. 3.

Aug. Tr. xlv. 8.

[2] præter.

the Word of God, who spake the truth. He, the Word, the Truth, sent heralds before Him, but the hearts of those whom He sent were His own. They came with Him, inasmuch as He is always, though He assumed the flesh in time: *In the beginning was the Word.* His humble advent in the flesh was preceded by just men, who believed on Him as about to come, as we believe on Him come. The times are different, the faith is the same. Our faith knitteth together both those who believed that He was about to come, and those who believe that He has come. All that ever came at variance with Him were thieves and robbers; i. e. they came to steal and to kill; *but the sheep did not hear them.* They had not Christ's voice; but were wanderers, dreamers, deceivers. Why He is the Door, He next explains, *I am the Door; by Me if any man enter in he shall be saved.* ALCUIN. As if to say, The sheep hear not them, but Me they hear; for I am the Door, and whoever entereth by Me not falsely but in sincerity, shall by perseverance be saved. THEOPHYL. The door admits the sheep into the pasture; *And shall go in and out, and find pasture.* What is this pasture, but the happiness to come, the rest to which our Lord brings us? AUG. What is this, *shall go in and out?* To enter into the Church by Christ the Door, is a very good thing, but to go out of the Church is not. Going in must refer to inward cogitation; going out to outward action; as in the Psalm, *Man goeth forth to his work.* THEOPHYL. Or, to *go in* is to watch over the inner man; to *go out,* to mortify the outward man, i. e. our members which are upon the earth. He that doth this shall find pasture in the life to come. CHRYS. Or, He refers to the Apostles who went in and out boldly; for they became the masters of the world, none could turn them out of their kingdom, and they found pasture. AUG. But He Himself explains it more satisfactorily to me in what follows: *The thief cometh not, but for to steal, and for to kill: I am come that they might have life, and that they might have it more abundantly.* By going in they have life; i. e. by faith, which worketh by love; by which faith they go into the fold. *The just liveth*[1] *by faith.* And by going out they will *have it more abundantly:* i. e. when true believers die, they have life more abundantly, even a

Aug. Tr. xlv. c. 15.

Ps. 103, 24.

Colos. 3.

Chrys. Hom. lix. 3.

Aug. Tr. xlv. 15.

[1] *vivit Vulg.*

Heb. 10, 38.

life which never ends. Though in this fold there is not
wanting pasture, then they will find pasture, such as will
satisfy them. *To-day shalt thou be with Me in paradise.* Luke23,
                                                                43.
GREG. *Shall go in,* i. e. to faith : *shall go out,* i. e. to sight : Greg.
and find pasture, i. e. in eternal fulness. ALCUIN. *The thief* super
                                                                    Ezek.
cometh not but for to steal, and to kill. As if He said, And well Hom.
may the sheep not hear the voice of the thief; for he cometh xiii.
not but for to steal: he usurpeth another's office, forming
his followers not on Christ's precepts, but on his own.   And
therefore it follows, *and to kill,* i. e. by drawing them from
the faith; *and to destroy,* i. e. by their eternal damnation.
CHRYS. *The thief cometh not but for to steal, and to kill,* Chrys.
                                                                Hom.
and to destroy; this was literally fulfilled in the case of those lix. 1.
movers of sedition[3], whose followers were nearly all destroyed;
deprived by the thief even of this present life.   But came,
He saith, for the salvation of the sheep; *That they might
have life, and that they might have it more abundantly,*
in the kingdom of heaven.   This is the third mark of difference between Himself, and the false prophets. THEOPHYL.
Mystically, the thief is the devil, steals by wicked thoughts,
kills by the assent of the mind to them, and destroys by
acts.

11. I am the good shepherd: the good shepherd
giveth his life for the sheep.

12. But he that is an hireling, and not the shepherd,
whose own the sheep are not, seeth the wolf coming,
and leaveth the sheep, and fleeth : and the wolf catcheth
them, and scattereth the sheep.

13. The hireling fleeth, because he is an hireling,
and careth not for the sheep.

AUG. Our Lord has acquainted us with two things which Aug.
                                                             Tr. xlvi.
were obscure before; first, that He is the Door; and now 1.
again, that He is the Shepherd: *I am the good Shepherd.*
Above He said that the shepherd entered by the door. If c. xlvii.
                                                             1.
He is the Door, how doth He enter by Himself?   Just as
He knows the Father by Himself, and we by Him; so He
enters into the fold by Himself, and we by Him.   We enter

---

[a] Theudas, Judas, mentioned above.

by the door, because we preach Christ; Christ preaches Himself. A light shews both other things, and itself too.

Tr. xliv. 5. There is but one Shepherd. For though the rulers of the Church, those who are her sons, and not hirelings, are shep- Tr.xlvii. 3. herds, they are all members of that one Shepherd. His office of Shepherd He hath permitted His members to bear. Peter is a shepherd, and all the other Apostles: all good Bishops are shepherds. But none of us calleth himself the door. He could not have added *good*, if there were not bad shepherds as well. They are thieves and robbers; or at forma bonitatis. Greg. Hom. xiv. in Evang. least mercenaries. GREG. And He adds what that goodness is, for our imitation: *The good Shepherd giveth His life for the sheep.* He did what He bade, He set the example of what He commanded: He laid down His life for the sheep, that He might convert His body and blood in our Sacrament, and feed with His flesh the sheep He had redeemed. A path is shewn us wherein to walk, despising death; a stamp is applied to us, and we must submit to the impression. Our first duty is to spend our outward possessions upon the sheep; our last, if it be necessary, is to sacrifice our life for the same sheep. Whoso doth not give his substance to the Aug. Tr.xlvii. sheep, how can he lay down his life for them? AUG. Christ was not the only one who did this. And yet if they who did it are members of Him, one and the same Christ did it always. He was able to do it without them; they were not Aug. de Verb. Dom. Serm. 1. without Him. AUG. All these however were good shepherds, not because they shed their blood, but because they did it for the sheep. For they shed it not in pride, but in love. Should any among the heretics suffer trouble in consequence of their errors and iniquities, they forthwith boast of their martyrdom; that they may be the better able to steal under so fair a cloak: for they are in reality wolves. But not all who give their bodies to be burned, are to be thought to shed their blood for the sheep; rather against the sheep; for the 1 Cor. 13, 3. Apostle saith, *Though I give my body to be burned, and have not charity, it profiteth me nothing.* And how hath he even convic- tus the smallest charity, who does not love connexion with Christians? to command which, our Lord did not mention Chrys. Hom. lx. 5. many shepherds, but one, *I am the good Shepherd.* CHRYS. Our Lord shews here that He did not undergo His passion

unwillingly; but for the salvation of the world.   He then
gives the difference between the shepherd and the hireling :
*But he that is an hireling, and not the shepherd, whose own
the sheep are not, seeth the wolf coming, and leaveth the
sheep, and fleeth.*   GREG. Some there are who love earthly Greg.
possessions more than the sheep, and do not deserve the Hom. in Evang.
name of a shepherd.   He who feeds the Lord's flock for the xiv.
sake of temporal hire, and not for love, is an hireling, not
a shepherd.   An hireling is he who holds the place of
shepherd, but seeketh not the gain of souls, who panteth
after the good things of earth, and rejoices in the pride of
station.   AUG. He seeketh therefore in the Church, not God, Aug.
but something else.   If he sought God he would be chaste; de Verb. Dom.
for the soul hath but one lawful husband, God.   Whoever Serm.
seeketh from God any thing beside God, seeketh unchastely. xlix.
GREG. But whether a man be a shepherd or an hireling, Greg.
cannot be told for certain, except in a time of trial.   In Hom. in Evang.
tranquil times, the hireling generally stands watch like the xiv.
shepherd.   But when the wolf comes, then every one shews
with what spirit he stood watch over the flock.   AUG. The Aug.
wolf is the devil, and they that follow him; according to de Verb. Dom.
Matthew, *Which come to you in sheeps' clothing, but inwardly* Serm.
they are ravening wolves.   AUG. Lo, the wolf hath seized xlix. Matt. 7,
a sheep by the throat, the devil hath enticed a man into 15.
adultery.   The sinner must be excommunicated.   But if he Aug. Tr. xlvi.
is excommunicated, he will be an enemy, he will plot, 8.
he will do as much harm as he can.   Wherefore thou
art silent, thou dost not censure, thou hast seen the wolf
coming, and fled.   Thy body has stood, thy mind has fled.
For as joy is relaxation, sorrow contraction, desire a reaching forward of the mind; so fear is the flight of the mind.
GREG. The wolf too cometh upon the sheep, whenever any Greg.
spoiler and unjust person oppresses the humble believers. Hom. in Evang.
And he who seems to be shepherd, but leaves the sheep and xiv.
flees, is he who dares not to resist his violence, from fear of
danger to himself.   He flees not by changing place, but
by withholding consolation from his flock.   The hireling
is inflamed with no zeal against this injustice.   He only
looks to outward comforts, and overlooks the internal suffering of his flock.   *The hireling fleeth, because he is an*

hireling, and careth not for the sheep. The only reason that the hireling fleeth, is *because he is an hireling;* as if to say, He cannot stand at the approach of danger, who doth not love the sheep that he is set over, but seeketh earthly gain. Such an one dares not face danger, for fear he should lose what he so much loves. AUG. But if the Apostles were shepherds, not hirelings, why did they flee in persecution? And why did our Lord say, *When they persecute you in this city, flee ye into another?* Let us knock, then will come one, who will explain. AUG. A servant of Christ, and minister of His Word and Sacraments, may flee from city to city, when he is specially aimed at by the persecutors, apart from his brethren; so that his flight does not leave the Church destitute. But when all, i. e. Bishops, Clerics, and Laics, are in danger in common, let not those who need assistance be deserted by those who should give it. Let all flee together if they can, to some place of security; but, if any are obliged to stay, let them not be forsaken by those who are bound to minister to their spiritual wants. Then, under pressing persecution, may Christ's ministers flee from the place where they are, when none of Christ's people remain to be ministered to, or when that ministry may be fulfilled by others who have not the same cause for flight. But when the people stay, and the ministers flee, and the ministry ceases, what is this but a damnable flight of hirelings, who care not for the sheep? AUG. On the good side are the door, the porter, the shepherd, and the sheep; on the bad, the thieves, the robbers, the hirelings, the wolf. AUG. We must love the shepherd, beware of the wolf, tolerate the hireling. For the hireling is useful so long as he sees not the wolf, the thief, and the robber. When he sees them, he flees. AUG. Indeed he would not be an hireling, did he not receive wages from the hirer. Sons wait patiently for the eternal inheritance of their father; the hireling looks eagerly for the temporal wages from his hirer; and yet the tongues of both speak abroad the glory of Christ. The hireling hurteth, in that he doeth wrong, not in that he speaketh right: the grape bunch hangeth amid thorns; pluck the grape, avoid the thorn. Many that seek temporal advantages in the Church, preach Christ, and through them Christ's voice is heard; and the

Aug. Tr. xlvi. 7.

Mat. 10, 23.

Aug. ad Honor. Ep. clxxx.

Aug. Tr. xlvi. 1.

Aug. de Verb. Dom. s. xlix.

Aug. Tr. xlvi. 5.

c. 6.

sheep follow not the hireling, but the voice of the Shepherd heard through the hireling.

14. I am the good shepherd, and know my sheep, and am known of mine.

15. As the Father knoweth me, even so know I the Father: and I lay down my life for the sheep.

16. And other sheep I have, which are not of this fold: them also I must bring, and they shall hear my voice; and there shall be one fold, and one shepherd.

17. Therefore doth my Father love me, because I lay down my life, that I might take it again.

18. No man taketh it from me, but I lay it down of myself. I have power to lay it down, and I have power to take it again. This commandment have I received of my Father.

19. There was a division therefore again among the Jews for these sayings.

20. And many of them said, He hath a devil, and is mad; why hear ye him?

21. Others said, These are not the words of him that hath a devil. Can a devil open the eyes of the blind?

CHRYS. Two evil persons have been mentioned, one that kills, and robs the sheep, another that doth not hinder: the one standing for those movers of seditions; the other for the rulers of the Jews, who did not take care of the sheep committed to them. Christ distinguishes Himself from both; from the one who came to do hurt by saying, *I am come that they might have life;* from those who overlook the rapine of the wolves, by saying that He giveth His life for the sheep. Wherefore He saith again, as He said before, *I am the good Shepherd.* And as He had said above that the sheep heard the voice of the Shepherd and followed Him, that no one might have occasion to ask, What sayest Thou then of those

Chrys. Hom. lx. 1.

that believe not? He adds, *And I know My sheep, and am known of Mine.* As Paul too saith, *God hath not cast away His people, whom He foreknew.* GREG. As if He said, I love My sheep, and they love and follow Me. For he who loves not the truth, is as yet very far from knowing it. THEO-PHYL. Hence the difference of the hireling and the Shepherd. The hireling does not know his sheep, because he sees them so little. The Shepherd knows His sheep, because He is so at-tractive to them. CHRYS. Then that thou mayest not attribute to the Shepherd and the sheep the same measure of knowledge, He adds, *As the Father knoweth Me, even so know I the Father:* i. e. I know Him as certainly as He knoweth Me. This then is a case of like knowledge, the other is not; as He saith, *No man knoweth who the Son is, but the Father.* GREG. *And I lay down My life for My sheep.* As if to say, This is why I know My Father, and am known by the Father, because I lay down My life for My sheep; i. e. by My love for My sheep, I shew how much I love My Father. CHRYS. He gives it too as a proof of His authority. In the same way the Apostle maintains his own commission in opposition to the false Apostles, by enumerating his dangers and suffer-ings. THEOPHYL. For the deceivers did not expose their lives for the sheep, but, like hirelings, deserted their followers. Our Lord, on the other hand, protected His disciples: *Let these go their way.* GREG. But as He came to redeem not only the Jews, but the Gentiles, He adds, *And other sheep I have, which are not of this fold.* AUG. The sheep hitherto spoken of are those of the stock of Israel according to the flesh. But there were others of the stock of Israel, accord-ing to faith, Gentiles, who were as yet out of the fold; pre-destinated, but not yet gathered together. *They are not of this fold,* because they are not of the race of Israel, but they will be of this fold: *Them also I must bring.* CHRYS. What wonder that these should hear My voice, and follow Me, when others are waiting to do the same. Both these flocks are dispersed, and without shepherds; for it follows, *And they shall hear My voice.* And then He foretells their future union: *And there shall be one fold and one Shepherd.* GREG. Of two flocks He maketh one fold, uniting the Jews and Gentiles in His faith. THEOPHYL. For there is one sign of

Margin notes (left column):

Rom. 11, 12.

Greg. Hom. in Evang. xiv.

Chrys. Hom. lx. 1.

Luke 10, 23.

Greg. Hom. in Evang. xiv.

Chrys. Hom. lx. 1.

infr. 18, 8.

Greg. Hom. xiv.

Aug. de Verb. Dom. s. 1.

Chrys. Hom. lx. 2.

Greg. Hom. Evang. xiv.

baptism for all, and one Shepherd, even the Word of God. Let the Manichean mark; there is but one fold and one Shepherd set forth both in the Old and New Testaments. AUG. What does He mean then when He says, *I am not sent but unto the lost sheep of the house of Israel?* Only, that whereas He manifested Himself personally to the Jews, He did not go Himself to the Gentiles, but sent others. CHRYS. The word *must* here (*I must bring*) does not signify necessity, but only that the thing would take place. *Therefore doth My Father love Me, because I lay down My life, that I might take it again.* They had called Him an alien from His Father. AUG. i. e. Because I die, to rise again. There is great force in, *I lay down*. Let not the Jews, He says, boast; rage they may, but if I should not choose to lay down My life, what will they do by raging? THEOPHYL. The Father does not bestow His love on the Son as a reward for the death He suffered in our behalf; but He loves Him, as beholding in the Begotten His own essence, whence proceeded such love for mankind. CHRYS. Or He says, in condescension to our weakness, Though there were nothing else which made Me love you, this would, that ye are so loved by My Father, that, by dying for you, I shall win His love. Not that He was not loved by the Father before, or that we are the cause of such love. For the same purpose He shews that He does not come to His Passion unwillingly: *No man taketh it from Me, but I lay it down of Myself.* AUG. Wherein He shewed that His natural death was not the consequence of sin in Him, but of His own simple will, which was the why, the when, and the how: *I have power to lay it down.* CHRYS. As they had often plotted to kill Him, He tells them their efforts will be useless, unless He is willing. I have such power over My own life, that no one can take it from Me, against My will. This is not true of men. We have not the power of laying down our own lives, except we put ourselves to death. Our Lord alone has this power. And this being true, it is true also that He can take it again when He pleases: *And I have power to take it again:* which words declare beyond a doubt a resurrection. That they might not think His death a sign that God had forsaken Him, He adds, *This commandment have I received from My Father;* i. e. to

Aug. Tr.xlvii. 4.

Mat. 15, 24.

Chrys. Hom. lx.

Aug. Tr.xlvii. 7.

Chrys. Hom. lx. 2.

Aug. iii. de Trin. c. xxxviii.

Chrys. Hom. lx. 2.

lay down My life, and take it again. By which we must not understand that He first waited to hear this commandment, and had to learn His work; He only shews that that work which He voluntarily undertook, was not against the Father's will. THEOPHYL. He only means His perfect agreement with His Father. ALCUIN. For the Word doth not receive a command by word, but containeth in Himself all the Father's commandments. When the Son is said to receive what He possesseth of Himself, His power is not lessened, but only His generation declared. The Father gave the Son every thing in begetting Him. He begat Him perfect. THEOPHYL. After declaring Himself the Master of His own life and death, which was a lofty assumption, He makes a more humble confession; thus wonderfully uniting both characters; shewing that He was neither inferior to or a slave of the Father on the one hand, nor an antagonist on the other; but of the same power and will. AUG. How doth our Lord lay down His own life? Christ is the Word, and man, i. e. in soul and body. Doth the Word lay down His life, and take it again; or doth the human soul, or doth the flesh? If it was the Word of God that laid down His soul[1] and took it again, that soul was at one time separated from the Word. But, though death separated the soul and body, death could not separate the Word and the soul. It is still more absurd to say that the soul laid down itself; if it could not be separated from the Word, how could it be from itself? The flesh therefore layeth down its life and taketh it again, not by its own power, but by the power of the Word which dwelleth in it. This refutes the Apollinarians, who say that Christ had not a human, rational soul. ALCUIN. But the light shined in darkness, and the darkness comprehended it not. *There was a division among the Jews for these sayings. And many of them said, He hath a devil, and is mad.* CHRYS. Because He spoke as one greater than man, they said He had a devil. But that He had not a devil, others proved from His works: *Others said, These are not the words of Him that hath a devil. Can a devil open the eyes of the blind?* As if to say, Not even the words themselves are those of one that hath a devil; but if the words do not convince you, be persuaded by the works. Our Lord having already given proof who

Aug.
Tr. xlvii.

[1] ψυχὴ, life.

Chrys.
Hom.
lx. 3.

He was by His works, was silent. They were unworthy of
an answer. Indeed, as they disagreed amongst themselves,
an answer was unnecessary. Their opposition only brought
out, for our imitation, our Lord's gentleness, and long suffering. ALCUIN. We have heard of the patience of God, and
of salvation preached amid revilings. They obstinately
preferred tempting Him to obeying Him.

22. And it was at Jerusalem the feast of the dedication, and it was winter.

23. And Jesus walked in the temple in Solomon's
porch.

24. Then came the Jews round about him, and said
unto him, How long dost thou make us to doubt? If
thou be the Christ, tell us plainly,

25. Jesus answered them, I told you, and ye believed
not: the works that I do in my Father's name, they
bear witness of me.

26. But ye believe not, because ye are not of my
sheep, as I said unto you.

27. My sheep hear my voice, and I know them, and
they follow me.

28. And I give unto them eternal life; and they
shall never perish, neither shall any man pluck them
out of my hand.

29. My Father, which gave them me, is greater than
all; and no man is able to pluck them out of my
Father's hand.

30. I and my Father are one.

AUG. *And it was at Jerusalem the feast of the dedication.* Aug.
Encænia is the feast of the dedication of the temple; from Tract.
xlviii.2.
the Greek word χαινὸν, signifying new. The dedication of
any thing new was called encænia. CHRYS. It was the feast Chrys.
of the dedication of the temple, after the return from the Hom.
lxi. 1.
Babylonish captivity. ALCUIN. Or, it was in memory of
the dedication under Judas Maccabeus. The first dedi-

cation was that of Solomon in the autumn; the second that of Zorobabel, and the priest Jesus in the spring. This was in winter time. BEDE. Judas Maccabeus instituted an annual commemoration of this dedication. THEOPHYL. The Evangelist mentions the time of winter, to shew that it was near His passion. He suffered in the following spring; for which reason He took up His abode at Jerusalem. GREG. Or because the season of cold was in keeping with the cold malicious hearts of the Jews. CHRYS. Christ was present with much zeal at this feast, and thenceforth stayed [1]in Judæa; His passion being now at hand. *And Jesus walked in the temple in Solomon's porch.* ALCUIN. It is called Solomon's porch, because Solomon went to pray there. The porches of a temple are usually named after the temple. If the Son of God walked in a temple where the flesh of brute animals was offered up, how much more will He delight to visit our house of prayer, in which His own flesh and blood are consecrated? THEOPHYL. Be thou also careful, in the winter time, i. e. while yet in this stormy wicked world, to celebrate the dedication of thy spiritual temple, by ever renewing thyself, ever rising upward in heart. Then will Jesus be present with thee in Solomon's porch, and give thee safety under His covering. But in another life no man will be able to dedicate Himself. AUG. The Jews cold in love, burning in their malevolence, approached Him not to honour, but persecute. *Then came the Jews round about Him, and said unto Him, How long dost Thou make us to doubt? If Thou be the Christ, tell us plainly.* They did not want to know the truth, but only to find ground of accusation. CHRYS. Being able to find no fault with His works, they tried to catch Him in His words. And mark their perversity. When He instructs by His discourse, they say, *What sign shewest Thou?* When He demonstrates by His works, they say, *If Thou be the Christ, tell us plainly.* Either way they are determined to oppose Him. There is great malice in that speech, *Tell us plainly.* He had spoken plainly[1], when up at the feasts, and had hid nothing. They preface however with flattery: *How long dost Thou make us[2] to doubt?* as if they were anxious to know the truth, but really only meaning to provoke Him to say something that they might

Greg.
i. Mor.
c. 11.
Chrys.
Hom.
lxi. 1.
[1] *συνεχῶς*
ἰσχυ-
ρίαζιν

τῇ σκίᾳ
αὐτοῦ

Aug.
Tract.
xlviii. 3.

Chrys.
Hom.
lxi.

[1] *παρρη-*
σία
openly
before
all
[2] V.tollis
αἰρεῖς

lay hold of. ALCUIN. They accuse Him of keeping their minds in suspense and uncertainty, who had come to save their souls[a]. AUG. They wanted our Lord to say, *I am the Christ.* Perhaps, as they had human notions of the Messiah, having failed to discern His divinity in the Prophets, they wanted Christ to confess Himself the Messiah, of the seed of David; that they might accuse Him of aspiring to the regal power. ALCUIN. And thus they intended to give Him into the hands of the Proconsul for punishment, as an usurper against the emperor. Our Lord so managed His reply as to stop the mouths of His calumniators, open those of the believers; and to those who enquired of Him as a man, reveal the mysteries of His divinity: *Jesus answered them, I told you, and ye believed not: the works that I do in My Father's name, they bear witness of Me.* CHRYS. He reproves their malice, for pretending that a single word would convince them, whom so many words had not. If you do not believe My works, He says, how will you believe My words? And He adds why they do not believe: *But ye believe not, because ye are not of My sheep.* AUG. He saw that they were persons predestinated to eternal death, and not those for whom He had bought eternal life, at the price of His blood. The sheep believe, and follow the Shepherd. THEOPHYL. After He had said, *Ye are not of My sheep,* He exhorts them to become such: *My sheep hear My voice.* ALCUIN. i. e. Obey My precepts from the heart. *And I know them, and they follow Me,* here by walking in gentleness and innocence, hereafter by entering the joys of eternal life. *And I give unto them eternal life.* AUG. This is the *pasture* of which He spoke before: *And shall find pasture.* Eternal life is called a goodly pasture: the grass thereof withereth not, all is spread with verdure. But these cavillers thought only of this present life. *And they shall not perish eternally ;* as if to say, Ye shall perish eternally, *because ye are not of My sheep.* THEOPHYL. But how then did Judas perish? Because he did not continue to the end. Christ speaks of them who persevere. If any sheep is separated from the flock, and wanders from the Shepherd, it incurs danger im-

Aug. Tract. xlviii.

Chrys. Hom. lxi. 2.

Aug. Tract. xlviii. c. 4.

Aug. Tract. xlviii. 5, 6.

ου μη

απόλλυνται

εἰς τὸν αἰῶνα

---

[a] Alc. literally, Christ did not come to make them doubt, but to give them life: they made themselves to doubt, tempting Christ, not believing in Him.

Aug.
Tract.
xlviii. 6.
2 Tim.
2, 19.

mediately. AUG. And He adds why they do not perish: *Neither shall any man pluck them out of My hand.* Of those sheep of which it is said, *The Lord knoweth them that are His,* the wolf robbeth none, the thief taketh none, the robber killeth none. Christ is confident of their safety; and He knows what He gave up for them.

Hilar.
de Trin.
vii.c.22.

HILARY. This is the speech of conscious power. Yet to shew, that though of the Divine nature He hath His nativity from God, He adds, *My Father which gave Me them is greater than all.* He does not conceal His birth from the Father, but proclaims it. For that which He received from the Father, He received in that He was born from Him. He received it in the birth itself, not after it; though He was born when He received it.

Aug.
Tract.
xlviii.

AUG. The Son, born from everlasting of the Father, God from God, has not equality with the Father by growth, but by birth. This is that greater than all which the Father gave Him [b]; viz. to be His Word, to be His Only-Begotten Son, to be the brightness of His light. Wherefore no man taketh His sheep out of His hand, any more than from His Father's hand: *And no man is able to pluck them out of My Father's hand.* If by hand we understand power, the power of the Father and the Son is one, even as Their divinity is one. If we understand the Son, the Son is the hand of the Father, not in a bodily sense, as if God the Father had limbs, but as being He by Whom all things were made. Men often call other men hands, when they make use of them for any purpose. And sometimes a man's work is itself called his hand, because made by his hand; as when a man is said to know his own hand, when he recognises his own handwriting. In this place, however, *hand* signifies power. If we take it for Son, we shall be in danger of imagining that if the Father has a hand, and that hand is His Son, the Son must have a Son too.

Hilar.
vii. de
Trin.
c. 22.

HILARY. The hand of the Son is spoken of as the hand of the Father, to let thee see, by a bodily representation, that both have the same nature, that the nature and virtue of the Father is in the Son also.

Chrys.
Hom.
lxi.

CHRYS. Then that thou mayest not suppose that the Father's power protects the sheep, while He is Himself too weak to do so, He adds, *I and My Father are*

[b] Pater meus quod dedit mihi majus omnibus est. V.

one. AUG. Mark both those words, *one* and *are*, and thou ^{Aug.} wilt be delivered from Scylla and Charybdis. In that He says, *one* the Arian, in *we are* the Sabellian, is answered. There are both Father and Son. And if *one,* then there is no difference of persons between them. AUG. *We* are *one.* What He is, that am I, in respect of essence, not of relation. HILARY. The heretics, since they cannot gainsay these words, endeavour by an impious lie to explain them away. They maintain that this unity is unanimity only; a unity of will, not of nature; i. e. that the two are one, not in that they *are* the same, but in that they will the same. But they are one, not by any economy merely, but by the nativity of the Son's nature, since there is no falling off of the Father's divinity in begetting Him. They are one whilst the sheep that are not plucked out of the Son's hand, are not plucked out of the Father's hand : whilst in Him working, the Father worketh ; whilst He is in the Father, and the Father in Him. This unity, not creation but nativity, not will but power, not unanimity but nature accomplisheth. But we deny not therefore the unanimity of the Father and Son ; for the heretics, because we refuse to admit concord in the place of unity, accuse us of making a disagreement between the Father and Son. We deny not unanimity, but we place it on the ground of unity. The Father and Son are one in respect of nature, honour, and virtue : and the same nature cannot will different things.

Margin references:
Aug. Tract. xxxvi. non occ.
Aug. vii. de Trin.
c. 2. Hilar. viii. de Trin. c. 5.

31. Then the Jews took up stones again to stone him.

32. Jesus answered them, Many good works have I shewed you from my Father; for which of those works do ye stone me?

33. The Jews answered him, saying, For a good work we stone thee not; but for blasphemy; and because that thou, being a man, makest thyself God.

34. Jesus answered them, Is it not written in your law, I said, Ye are gods?

35. If he called them gods, unto whom the word of God came, and the scripture cannot be broken ;

36. Say ye of him, whom the Father hath sanctified, and sent into the world, Thou blasphemest; because I said, I am the Son of God?

37. If I do not the works of my Father, believe me not.

38. But if I do, though ye believe not me, believe the works: that ye may know, and believe, that the Father is in me, and I in him.

Aug.
Tract.
xlviii. 8.

AUG. At this speech, *I and My Father are one*, the Jews could not restrain their rage, but ran to take up stones, after their hardhearted way: *Then the Jews took up stones again to stone Him.* HILARY. The heretics now, as unbelieving and rebellious against our Lord in heaven, shew their impious hatred by the stones, i. e. the words they cast at Him; as if they would drag Him down again from His throne to the cross. THEOPHYL. Our Lord remonstrates with them; *Many good works have I shewed you from My Father*, shewing that they had no just reason for their anger. ALCUIN. Healing of the sick, teaching, miracles. He shewed them of the Father, because He sought His Father's glory in all of them. *For which of these works do ye stone Me?* They confess, though reluctantly, the benefit they have received from Him, but charge Him at the same time with blasphemy, for asserting His equality with the Father; *For a good work we stone Thee not, but for blasphemy; and because that Thou, being a man, makest Thyself God.*

Hilar.
vii. de
Trin.
c. 23.

Aug.
Tract.
xlviii. 8.

AUG. This is their answer to the speech, *I and My Father are one.* Lo, the Jews understood what the Arians understand not. For they are angry for this very reason, that they could not conceive but that by saying, *I and My Father are one*, He meant the equality of the Father and the Son.

Hilar.
vii. de
Trin.
c. 23.

HILARY. The Jew saith, *Thou being a man*, the Arian, Thou being a creature: but both say, *Thou makest Thyself God.* The Arian supposes a God of a new and different substance, a God of another kind, or not a God at all. He saith, Thou art not Son by birth, Thou art not God of truth; Thou art a superior creature. CHRYS. Our Lord did not correct the Jews, as if they misunderstood His speech, but con-

Chrys.
Hom.
lxi. 2.

firmed and defended it, in the very sense in which they had taken it. *Jesus answered them, Is it not written in your law,* Aug. i. e. the Law given to you, *I have said, Ye are* Aug. *Gods?* God saith this by the Prophet in the Psalm. Our Tract. xlviii. Lord calls all those Scriptures the Law generally, though Ps.82,6. elsewhere He spiritually distinguishes the Law from the Prophets. *On these two commandments hang all the Law* Matt. *and the Prophets.* In another place He makes a threefold 22, 40. division of the Scriptures; *All things must be fulfilled which* Luke *were written in the Law of Moses, and in the Prophets, and* 24, 44. *in the Psalms concerning Me.* Now He calls the Psalms the Law, and thus argues from them ; *If he called them gods unto whom the word of God came, and the scripture cannot be broken, say ye of Him whom the Father hath sanctified, and sent into the world, Thou blasphemest, because I said, I am the Son of God?* HILARY. Before Hilar. proving that He and His Father are one, He answers the vii. de Trin. absurd and foolish charge brought against Him, that He c. 24. being man made Himself God.   When the Law applied this title to holy men, and the indelible word of God sanctioned this use of the incommunicable name, it could not be a crime in Him, even though He were man, to make Himself God. The Law called those who were mere men, gods; and if any man could bear the name religiously, and without arrogance, surely that man could, who was sanctified by the Father, in a sense in which none else is sanctified to the Sonship ; as the blessed Paul saith, *Declared* [1] *to be the Son* [1] predes-*of God with power, according to the Spirit of holiness.* For tinatus v. all this reply refers to Himself as man; the Son of God Rom. 1, 4. being also the Son of man.   AUG. Or *sanctified,* i. e. in Aug. begetting, gave Him holiness, begat Him holy.   If men to Tract. whom the word of God came were called gods, much more xlviii. the Word of God Himself is God.   If men by partaking of the word of God were made gods, much more is the Word of which they partake, God.   THEOPHYL. Or, *sanctified,* i.e. set apart to be sacrificed for the world: a proof that He was God in a higher sense than the rest.   To save the world is a divine work, not that of a man made divine by grace. CHRYS. Or, we must consider this a speech of humility, Chrys. Hom. lxi.

made to conciliate men. After it he leads them to higher things; *If I do not the works of My Father, believe Me not;* which is as much as to say, that He is not inferior to the Father. As they could not see His substance, He directs them to His works, as being like and equal to the Father's. For the equality of their works, proved the equality of their power. HILARY. What place hath adoption, or the mere conception of a name then, that we should not believe Him to be the Son of God by nature, when He tells us to believe Him to be the Son of God, because the Father's nature shewed itself in Him by His works? A creature is not equal and like to God: no other nature has power comparable to the divine. He declares that He is carrying on not His own work, but the Father's, lest in the greatness of the works, the nativity of His nature be forgotten. And as under the sacrament[1] of the assumption of a human body in the womb of Mary, the Son of God was not discerned, this must be gathered from His work; *But if I do, though ye believe not Me, believe the works.* Why doth the sacrament of a human birth hinder the understanding of the divine, when the divine birth accomplishes all its work by aid of the human? Then He tells them what they should gather from His works; *That ye may know and believe, that the Father is in Me, and I in Him.* The same declaration again, *I am the Son of God: I and the Father are one.* AUG. The Son doth not say, *The Father is in Me, and I in Him,* in the sense in which men who think and act aright may say the like; meaning that they partake of God's grace, and are enlightened by His Spirit. The Only-begotten Son of God is in the Father, and the Father in Him, as an equal in an equal.

Margin notes:
Hilar. vii. de Trin.26.

[1] sacramenta corporis

Aug. Tract. xlviii. 10.

39. Therefore they sought again to take him: but he escaped out of their hand,

40. And went away again beyond Jordan into the place where John at first baptized; and there he abode.

41. And many resorted unto him, and said, John

did no miracle : but all things that John spake of this
man were true.

42. And many believed on him there.

BEDE. The Jews still persist in their madness ; *Therefore*
they sought again to take Him. AUG. To lay hold of Him, Aug.
not by faith and the understanding, but with bloodthirsty Tract.
violence. Do thou so lay hold of Him, that thou mayest 11. xlviii.
have sure hold ; they would fain have laid hold on Him,
but they could not: for it follows, *But He escaped out of*
their hand. They did lay hold of Him with the hand of
faith. It was no great matter for the Word to rescue His
flesh from the hands of flesh. CHRYS. Christ, after dis- Chrys.
coursing on some high truth, commonly retires immediately, Hom.
to give time to the fury of people to abate, during His lxi. 3.
absence. Thus He did now: *He went away again beyond*
Jordan, into the place where John at first baptized. He
went there that He might recall to people's minds, what had
gone on there; John's preaching and testimony to Himself.
BEDE. He was followed there by many : *And many resorted* non occ.
unto Him, and said, John did no miracle. AUG. Did not Aug.
cast out devils, did not give sight to the blind, did not raise Tract.
the dead. CHRYS. Mark their reasoning, *John did no* c. 12. xlviii.
miracle, but this Man did; wherefore He is the superior. Chrys.
But lest the absence of miracles should lessen the weight of lxi. 3. Hom.
John's testimony, they add, *But all things that John spake*
of this Man were true. Though he did no miracle, yet
every thing he said of Christ was true, whence they conclude,
if John was to be believed, much more this Man, who has
the evidence of miracles. Thus it follows, *And many*
believed on Him. AUG. These laid hold of Him while Aug.
abiding, not, like the Jews, when departing. Let us approach Tract.
by the candle to the day. John is the candle, and gave c. 12. xlviii.
testimony to the day. THEOPHYL. We may observe that
our Lord often brings out the people into solitary places,
thus ridding them of the society of the unbelieving, for their
furtherance in the faith : just as He led the people into the
wilderness, when He gave them the old Law. Mystically,
Christ departs from Jerusalem, i. e. from the Jewish people ;

and goes to a place where are springs of water, i. e. to
the Gentile Church, that hath the waters of baptism.   And
many resort unto Him, passing over the Jordan, i. e. through
baptism.

CHAP. XI.

1. Now a certain man was sick, named Lazarus, of Bethany, the town of Mary and her sister Martha.

2. (It was that Mary which anointed the Lord with ointment, and wiped his feet with her hair, whose brother Lazarus was sick.)

3. Therefore his sisters sent unto him, saying, Lord, behold, he whom thou lovest is sick.

4. When Jesus heard that, he said, This sickness is not unto death, but for the glory of God, that the Son of God might be glorified thereby.

5. Now Jesus loved Martha, and her sister, and Lazarus.

BEDE. After our Lord had departed to the other side of Jordan, it happened that Lazarus fell sick: *A certain man was sick, named Lazarus, of Bethany.* In some copies the copulative conjunction precedes, to mark the connection with the words preceding. *Lazarus* signifies *helped.* Of all the dead which our Lord raised, he was most helped, for he had lain dead four days, when our Lord raised him to life. AUG. The resurrection of Lazarus is more spoken of than any of our Lord's miracles. But if we bear in mind who He was who wrought this miracle, we shall feel not so much of wonder, as of delight. He who made the man, raised the man; and it is a greater thing to create a man, than to revive him. Lazarus was sick at Bethany, *the town of Mary and her sister Martha.* The place was near Jerusalem. ALCUIN. And as there were many women of this name, He distinguishes her by her well-known act: *It was that Mary which anointed the Lord with ointment, and wiped His feet*

Marginal notes: non occ. ἦν δὲ τις, now a certain man. Aug. Tr.xlix. 1.

2 R

Greg. Hom. lxii. 1.

Aug. de Con. Ev. ii. lxxix. Luke 7, 38.

Aug. de Verb. Dom. s. lii.

Aug. Tr.xlix. 5.

Chrys. Hom. lxii. 1.

Aug. Tr.xlix. 6.

Chrys. Hom. lxii. 1.

with her hair, whose brother Lazarus was sick. CHRYS. First we are to observe that this was not the harlot mentioned in Luke, but an honest woman, who treated our Lord with marked reverence. AUG. John here confirms the passage in Luke, where this is said to have taken place in the house of one Simon a Pharisee: Mary had done this act therefore on a former occasion. That she did it again at Bethany is not mentioned in the narrative of Luke, but is in the other three Gospels. AUG. A cruel sickness had seized Lazarus; a wasting fever was eating away the body of the wretched man day by day: his two sisters sat sorrowful at his bedside, grieving for the sick youth continually. They sent to Jesus: *Therefore his sisters sent unto Him, saying, Lord, behold he whom Thou lovest is sick.* AUG. They did not say, Come and heal; they dared not say, Speak the word there, and it shall be done here; but only, *Behold, he whom Thou lovest is sick.* As if to say, It is enough that Thou know it, Thou art not one to love and then to desert whom Thou lovest. CHRYS. They hope to excite Christ's pity by these words, Whom as yet they thought to be a man only. Like the centurion and nobleman, they sent, not went, to Christ; partly from their great faith in Him, for they knew Him intimately, partly because their sorrow kept them at home. THEOPHYL. And because they were women, and it did not become them to leave their home if they could help it. Great devotion and faith is expressed in these words, *Behold, he whom Thou lovest is sick.* Such was their idea of our Lord's power, that they were surprised, that one, whom He loved, could be seized with sickness. AUG. *When Jesus heard that, He said, This sickness is not unto death.* For this death itself was not unto death, but to give occasion for a miracle; whereby men might be brought to believe in Christ, and so escape real death. It was *for the glory of God,* wherein observe that our Lord calls Himself God by implication, thus confounding those heretics who say that the Son of God is not God. For the glory of what God? Hear what follows, *That the Son of God might be glorified thereby,* i. e. by that sickness. CHRYS. *That* here signifies not the cause, but the event. The sickness sprang from natural causes, but He turned it to the glory of God.

Now Jesus loved Martha, and her sister, and Lazarus.

AUG. He is sick, they sorrowful, all beloved.   Wherefore they had hope, for they were beloved by Him Who is the Comforter of the sorrowful, and the Healer of the sick.   CHRYS. Wherein the Evangelist instructs us not to be sad, if sickness ever falls upon good men, and friends of God.

Aug. Tr. xlix. 7.

Chrys. Hom. lxii.

non occ. v. lxii.3.

6. When he had heard therefore that he was sick, he abode two days still in the same place where he was.

7. Then after that saith he to his disciples, Let us go into Judæa again.

8. His disciples say unto him, Master, the Jews of late sought to stone thee; and goest thou thither again?

9. Jesus answered, Are there not twelve hours in the day?   If any man walk in the day, he stumbleth not, because he seeth the light of this world.

10. But if a man walk in the night, he stumbleth, because there is no light in him.

ALCUIN. Our Lord heard of the sickness of Lazarus, but suffered four days to pass before He cured it; that the recovery might be a more wonderful one. *When He had heard therefore that he was sick, He abode two days still in the place where He was.* CHRYS. To give time for his death and burial, that they might say, *he stinketh,* and none doubt that it was death, and not a trance, from which he was raised.

Then after that saith He to His disciples, Let us go into Judæa again. AUG. Where He had just escaped being stoned; for this was the cause of His leaving. He left indeed as man: He left in weakness, but He returns in power. CHRYS. He had not as yet told His disciples where He was going; but now He tells them, in order to prepare them beforehand, for they are in great alarm, when they hear of it: *His disciples say unto Him, Master, the Jews sought to stone Thee, and goest Thou thither again?* They feared both

Chrys. Hom. lxii. 1.

Aug. Tr. xlix. 7.

Chrys. Hom. lxii. 1.

for Him, and for themselves; for they were not yet confirmed in faith.   AUG. When men presumed to give advice
to God, disciples to their Master, our Lord rebuked them:
Jesus answered, Are there not twelve hours in the day?
He shewed Himself to be the day, by appointing twelve
disciples: i. e. reckoning Matthias in the place of Judas, and
passing over the latter altogether.   The hours are lightened
by the day; that by the preaching of the hours, the world
may believe on the day.   Follow Me then, saith our Lord,
if ye wish not to stumble: *If any man walk in the day, he
stumbleth not, because he seeth the light of this world.   But
if a man walk in the night he stumbleth, because there is no
light in him.*   CHRYS. As if to say, The upright need fear no
evil: the wicked only have cause to fear.   We have done nothing
worthy of death, and therefore are in no danger.   Or, If any
one seeth this world's light, he is safe; much more he who is
with Me.   THEOPHYL. Some understand the day to be the
time preceding the Passion, the night to be the Passion.
In this sense, *while it is day,* would mean, before My Passion;
Ye will not stumble before My Passion, because the Jews
will not persecute you; but when the night, i. e. My Passion,
cometh, then shall ye be beset with darkness and difficulties.

Aug.
Tr. xlix.
8.

Chrys.
Hom.
lxii. 1.

11. These things said he: and after that he saith
unto them, Our friend Lazarus sleepeth; but I go that
I may awake him out of sleep.

12. Then said his disciples, Lord, if he sleep, he
shall do well.

13. Howbeit Jesus spake of his death: but they
thought that he had spoken of taking of rest in sleep.

14. Then said Jesus unto them plainly, Lazarus is
dead.

15. And I am glad for your sakes I was not there,
to the intent ye may believe; nevertheless let us go
unto him.

16. Then said Thomas, which is called Didymus,
unto his fellowdisciples, Let us also go, that we may
die with him.

CHRYS. After He has comforted His disciples in one way, He comforts them in another, by telling them that they were not going to Jerusalem, but to Bethany: *These things saith He: and after that He saith unto them, Our friend Lazarus sleepeth; but I go that I may awake him out of sleep:* as if to say, I am not going to dispute again with the Jews, but to awaken our friend. *Our friend,* He says, to shew how strongly they were bound to go. AUG. It was really true that He was sleeping. To our Lord, he was sleeping; to men who could not raise him again, he was dead. Our Lord awoke him with as much ease from his grave, as thou awakest a sleeper from his bed. He calls him then asleep, with reference to His own power, as the Apostle saith, *But I would not have you to be ignorant, concerning them which are asleep. Asleep,* He says, because He is speaking of their resurrection which was to be. But as it matters to those who sleep and wake again daily, what they see in their sleep, some having pleasant dreams, others painful ones, so it is in death; every one sleeps and rises again with his own account[a].

CHRYS. The disciples however wished to prevent Him going to Judæa: *Then said His disciples, Lord, if he sleep, he shall do well.* Sleep is a good sign in sickness. And therefore if he sleep, say they, what need to go and awake him. AUG. The disciples replied, as they understood Him: *Howbeit Jesus spake of his death; but they thought that He had spoken of taking rest in sleep.* CHRYS. But if any one say, that the disciples could not but have known that our Lord meant Lazarus's death, when He said, *that I may awake him;* because it would have been absurd to have gone such a distance merely to awake Lazarus out of sleep; we answer, that our Lord's words were a kind of enigma to the disciples, here as elsewhere often. AUG. He then declares His meaning openly: *Then said Jesus unto them plainly, Lazarus is dead.* CHRYS. But He does not add here, *I go that I may awake him.* He did not wish to anticipate the miracle by talking of it; a hint to us to shun vain glory, and abstain from empty promises.

AUG. He had been sent for to restore Lazarus from sick-

Side notes:
Chrys. Hom. lxii. 1.

Aug. Tr.xlix. c. 9.

1 Thess. 4, 13.

Chrys. Hom. lxii. 1.

Aug. Tr.xlix. 11.

Chrys. Hom. lxii. 11.

Aug. Tr.xlix. 11.

Chrys. Hom. lxii. 2.

Aug. Tr. xlix. 11.

---

[a] cum causâ suâ dormit, cum causâ suâ surgit.

ness, not from death. But how could the death be hid from Him, into whose hands the soul of the dead had flown?

And I am glad for your sakes that I was not there, that ye might believe; i. e. seeing My marvellous power of knowing a thing I have neither seen nor heard. The disciples already believed in Him in consequence of His miracles; so that their faith had not now to begin, but only to increase. *That ye might believe,* means, believe more deeply, more firmly. THEOPHYL. Some have understood this place thus. I rejoice, He says, for your sakes; for if I had been there, I should have only cured a sick man; which is but an inferior sign of power. But since in My absence he has died, ye will now see that I can raise even the dead putrefying body; and your faith will be strengthened. CHRYS. The disciples all dreaded the Jews; and especially Thomas; *Then said Thomas, which is called Didymus, unto his fellow-disciples, Let us also go, that we may die with him.* But he who was now the most weak and unbelieving of all the disciples, afterwards became stronger than any. And he who dared not go to Bethany, afterwards went over the whole earth, in the midst of those who wished his death, with a spirit indomitable. BEDE. The disciples, checked by our Lord's answer to them, dared no longer oppose; and Thomas, more forward than the rest, says, *Let us also go that we may die with him.* What an appearance of firmness! He speaks as if he could really do what he said; unmindful, like Peter, of his frailty.

Chrys. Hom. lxii. 2.

17. Then when Jesus came, he found that he had lain in the grave four days already.

18. Now Bethany was nigh unto Jerusalem, about fifteen furlongs off:

19. And many of the Jews came to Martha and Mary, to comfort them concerning their brother.

20. Then Martha, as soon as she heard that Jesus was coming, went and met him: but Mary sat still in the house.

21. Then said Martha unto Jesus, Lord, if thou hadst been here, my brother had not died.

22. But I know, that even now, whatsoever thou wilt ask of God, God will give it thee.

23. Jesus saith unto her, Thy brother shall rise again.

24. Martha saith unto him, I know that he shall rise again in the resurrection at the last day.

25. Jesus said unto her, I am the resurrection, and the life: he that believeth in me, though he were dead, yet shall he live:

26. And whosoever liveth and believeth in me shall never die. Believest thou this?

27. She saith unto him, Yea, Lord: I believe that thou art the Christ, the Son of God, which should come into the world.

ALCUIN. Our Lord delayed His coming for four days, that the resurrection of Lazarus might be the more glorious : *Then when Jesus came, He found that He had lain in the grave four days already.* CHRYS. Our Lord had stayed two days, and the messenger had come the day before ; the very day on which Lazarus died. This brings us to the fourth day. AUG. Of the four days many things may be said. They refer to one thing, but one thing viewed in different ways. There is one day of death which the law of our birth brings upon us. Men transgress the natural law, and this is another day of death. The written law is given to men by the hands of Moses, and that is despised—a third day of death. The Gospel comes, and men transgress it—a fourth day of death. But Christ doth not disdain to awaken even these. ALCUIN. The first sin was elation of heart, the second assent, the third act, the fourth habit.

Now Bethany was nigh unto Jerusalem, about fifteen furlongs off. CHRYS. Two miles. This is mentioned to account for so many coming from Jerusalem: *And many of the Jews came to Martha and Mary, to comfort them concerning their brother.* But how could the Jews be consoling the beloved of Christ, when they had resolved that whoever confessed Christ should be put out of the synagogue?

Chrys.
Hom.
lxii. 2.

Aug.
Hom.
xlix. 12.

Chrys.
Hom.
lxii. 2.

Perhaps the extreme affliction of the sisters excited their sympathy; or they wished to shew respect for their rank. Or perhaps they who came were of the better sort; as we find many of them believed. Their presence is mentioned to do away with all doubt of the real death of Lazarus. BEDE. Our Lord had not yet entered the town, when Martha met Him: *Then Martha, as soon as she heard that Jesus was coming, went and met Him: but Mary sat still in the house.* CHRYS. Martha does not take her sister with her, because she wants to speak with Christ alone, and tell Him what has happened. When her hopes had been raised by Him, then *she went her way, and called Mary.* THEOPHYL. At first she does not tell her sister, for fear, if she came, the Jews present might accompany her. And she did not wish them to know of our Lord's coming.

Then saith Martha unto Jesus, Lord, if Thou hadst been here, my brother had not died. CHRYS. She believed in Christ, but she believed not as she ought. She did not speak as if He were God: *If Thou hadst been here, my brother had not died.* THEOPHYL. She did not know that He could have restored her brother as well absent as present. CHRYS. Nor did she know that He wrought His miracles by His own independent power: *But I know that even now, whatsoever Thou wilt ask of God, God will give it Thee.* She only thinks Him some very gifted man. AUG. She does not say to Him, Bring my brother to life again; for how could she know that it would be good for him to come to life again; she says, I know that Thou canst do so, if Thou wilt; but what Thou wilt do is for Thy judgment, not for my presumption to determine. CHRYS. But our Lord taught her the truths which she did not know: *Jesus saith unto her, Thy brother shall rise again.* Observe, He does not say, I will ask God, that he may rise again, nor on the other hand does He say, I want no help, I do all things of Myself; a declaration which would have been too much for the woman; but something between the two, *He shall rise again.* AUG. *Shall rise again,* is ambiguous: for He does not say, now. And therefore it follows: *Martha saith unto Him, I know that he shall rise again in the resurrection at the last day:* of that resurrection I am certain; of this I am doubtful.

Chrys. Hom. xii. 2.

Chrys. Hom. lxii. 3.

Chrys. Hom. lxii. 3.

Aug. Tr.xlix. 13.

Chrys. Hom. lxii. 3.

Aug. Tr.xlix. 14.

CHRYS. She had often heard Christ speak of the resurrection. Chrys.
Jesus now declares His power more plainly: *Jesus said unto* Hom.
her, I am the resurrection and the life. He needed therefore
none to help Him; for if He did, how could He be the
resurrection. And if He is the life, He is not confined by
place, but is every where, and can heal every where. ALCUIN.
I am the resurrection, because I am the life; as through Me
he will rise at the general resurrection, through Me he may
rise now. CHRYS. To Martha's, *Whatsoever Thou shalt ask*, Chrys.
He replies, *He that believeth in Me, though he were dead*, Hom.
yet shall he live: shewing her that He is the Giver of all
good, and that we must ask of Him. Thus He leads her to
the knowledge of high truths; and whereas she had been
enquiring only about the resurrection of Lazarus, tells her of
a resurrection in which both she and all present would share.
AUG. *He that believeth in Me, though he were dead:* i. e. Aug.
though his flesh die, his soul shall live till the flesh rise Tr. xlix.
again, never to die more. For faith is the life of the soul.

And whosoever liveth, in the flesh, *and believeth in Me,*
though he die for a time in the flesh, *shall not die eternally.*
ALCUIN. Because He hath attained to the life of the Spirit,
and to an immortal resurrection. Our Lord, from Whom
nothing was hid, knew that she believed, but sought from
her a confession unto salvation: *Believest thou this? She*
saith unto Him, Yea, Lord, I believe that Thou art the Christ
the Son of God, which should come into the world. CHRYS. Chrys.
She seems not to have understood His words; i. e. she saw Hom.
that He meant something great, but did not see what that lxii. 3.
was. She is asked one thing, and answers another. AUG. Aug.
When I believed that Thou wert the Son of God, I believed Tr. xlix.
that Thou wert the resurrection, that Thou wert life[b]; and that 15.
he that believeth in Thee, though he were dead, shall live.

28. And when she had so said, she went her way,
and called Mary her sister secretly, saying, The Master
is come, and calleth for thee.

29. And as soon as she heard that, she arose quickly,
and came unto him.

---

[b] Thus this is an answer to Christ's question, *Believest thou this?* i. e. that
I am the resurrection and the life.

30. Now Jesus was not yet come into the town, but was in that place where Martha met him.

31. The Jews then which were with her in the house, and comforted her, when they saw Mary, that she rose up hastily and went out, followed her, saying, She goeth unto the grave to weep there.

32. Then when Mary was come where Jesus was, and saw him, she fell down at his feet, saying unto him, Lord, if thou hadst been here, my brother had not died.

CHRYS. Christ's words had the effect of stopping Martha's grief. In her devotion to her Master she had no time to think of her afflictions: *And when she had so said, she went her way, and called Mary her sister secretly.* AUG. Silently[1], i. e. speaking in a low voice. For she did speak, *saying, The Master is come, and calleth for thee.* CHRYS. She calls her sister secretly, in order not to let the Jews know that Christ was coming. For had they known, they would have gone, and not been witnesses of the miracle. AUG. We may observe that the Evangelist has not said, where, or when, or how, the Lord called Mary, but for brevity's sake has left it to be gathered from Martha's words. THEOPHYL. Perhaps she thought the presence of Christ in itself a call, as if it were inexcusable, when Christ came, that she should not go out to meet Him. CHRYS. While the rest sat around her in her sorrow, she did not wait for the Master to come to her, but, not letting her grief detain her, rose immediately to meet Him; *As soon as she heard that, she arose quickly, and came unto Him.* AUG. So we see, if she had known of His arrival before, she would not have let Martha go without her.

Now Jesus was not yet come into the town, but was in that place where Martha met Him. CHRYS. He went slowly, that He might not seem to catch at an occasion of working a miracle, but to have it forced upon Him by others asking. *Mary,* it is said, *arose quickly,* and thus anticipated His coming. The Jews accompanied her: *The Jews then which were with her in the house, and comforted her, when they saw Mary that she arose up hastily and went out, followed*

Chrys.
Hom.
lxii. 3.

Aug.
Tr. xlix.
16.
[1] λάθρα
silentio
V.
Chrys.
Hom.
lxii.
non occ.
Aug.
Tr. xlix.
16.

Chrys.
Hom.
lxiii. 1.

Aug.
Tr. xlix.
non occ.

Chrys.
Hom.
lxiii. 1.

her, saying, She goeth unto the grave to weep there. AUG. Aug.
The Evangelist mentions this to shew how it was that so Tr. xlix. 16.
many were present at Lazarus' resurrection, and witness of
that great miracle.

*Then when Mary was come where Jesus was, and saw
Him, she fell down at His feet.* CHRYS. She is more fervent Chrys.
than her sister. Forgetful of the crowd around her, and of Hom. lxiii. 1.
the Jews, some of whom were enemies to Christ, she threw
herself at her Master's feet. In His presence all earthly
things were nought to her; she thought of nothing but giving
Him honour. THEOPHYL. But her faith seems as yet imperfect: *Lord, if Thou hadst been here, my brother had not
died.* ALCUIN. As if to say, Lord, while Thou wert with us,
no disease, no sickness dared to shew itself, amongst those
with whom the Life deigned to take up His abode. AUG. Aug.
O faithless assembly! Whilst Thou art yet in the world, de Verb. Dom.
Lazarus Thy friend dieth! If the friend dies, what will the s. lii.
enemy suppose? Is it a small thing that they will not serve
Thee upon earth? lo, hell hath taken Thy beloved. BEDE.
Mary did not say so much as Martha, she could not bring
out what she wanted for weeping, as is usual with persons
overwhelmed with sorrow.

33. When Jesus therefore saw her weeping, and
the Jews also weeping which came with her, he groaned
in the spirit, and was troubled,

34. And said, Where have ye laid him? They
said unto him, Lord, come and see.

35. Jesus wept.

36. Then said the Jews, Behold how he loved him!

37. And some of them said, Could not this man,
which opened the eyes of the blind, have caused that
even this man should not have died?

38. Jesus therefore again groaning in himself
cometh to the grave. It was a cave, and a stone lay
upon it.

39. Jesus said, Take ye away the stone. Martha,
the sister of him that was dead, saith unto him, Lord,

by this time he stinketh: for he hath been dead four days.

40. Jesus saith unto her, Said I not unto thee, that, if thou wouldest believe, thou shouldest see the glory of God?

41. Then they took away the stone from the place where the dead was laid.

CHRYS. Christ did not answer Mary, as He had her sister, on account of the people present. In condescension to them He humbled Himself, and let His human nature be seen, in order to gain them as witnesses to the miracle: *When Jesus therefore saw her weeping, and the Jews also weeping which came with her, He groaned in His spirit, and was troubled.* AUG. For who but Himself could trouble Him? Christ was troubled, because it pleased Him to be troubled; He hungered, because it pleased Him to hunger. It was in His own power to be affected in this or that way, or not. The Word took up soul and flesh, and whole man, and fitted it to Himself in unity of person. And thus according to the nod and will of that higher nature in Him, in which the sovereign power resides, He becomes weak and troubled. THEOPHYL. To prove His human nature He sometimes gives it free vent, while at other times He commands, and restrains it by the power of the Holy Ghost. Our Lord allows His nature to be affected in these ways, both to prove that He is very Man, not Man in appearance only; and also to teach us by His own example the due measures of joy and grief. For the absence altogether of sympathy and sorrow is brutal, the excess of them is womanly.

AUG. *And said, Where have ye laid him?* He knew where, but He asked to try the faith of the people. CHRYS. He did not wish to thrust the miracle upon them, but to make them ask for it, and thus do away with all suspicions. AUG. The question has an allusion too to our hidden calling. That predestination by which we are called, is hidden; and the sign of its being so is our Lord asking the question: He being as it were in ignorance, so long as we are ignorant

Chrys. Hom. lxiii. 1.

Aug. Tr.xlix.

Aug. de Ver. Dom. s. lii.
Chrys. Hom. lxiii. 1.
Aug. lib. 83. Quæst. qu. lxv.

ourselves. Or because our Lord elsewhere shews that He knows not sinners, saying, *I know you not,* because in keeping His commandments there is no sin. Matt. 7, 23.

They said unto Him, Lord, come and see. CHRYS. He had not yet raised any one from the dead; and seemed as if He came to weep, not to raise to life. Wherefore they say to Him, *Come and see.* AUG. The Lord sees when He pities, as we read, *Look upon my adversity and misery, and forgive me all my sin.* Chrys. Hom. lxiii. 1. Aug. Tr. xlix. 20. Ps. 24, 17.

Jesus wept. ALCUIN. Because He was the fountain of pity. He wept in His human nature for him whom He was able to raise again by His divine. AUG. Wherefore did Christ weep, but to teach men to weep? BEDE. It is customary to mourn over the death of friends; and thus the Jews explained our Lord's weeping: *Then said the Jews, Behold how He loved him.* AUG. *Loved him.* Our Lord came not to call the righteous but sinners to repentance. *And some of them said, Could not this Man which opened the eyes of the blind, have caused that even this man should not have died?* He was about to do more than this, to raise him from death. CHRYS. It was His enemies who said this. The very works, which should have evidenced His power, they turn against Him, as if He had not really done them. This is the way that they speak of the miracle of opening the eyes of the man that was born blind. They even prejudge Christ before He has come to the grave, and have not the patience to wait for the issue of the matter. *Jesus therefore again groaning in Himself, cometh to the grave.* That He wept, and He groaned, are mentioned to shew us the reality of His human nature. John who enters into higher statements as to His nature than any of the other Evangelists, also descends lower than any in describing His bodily affections. AUG. And do thou too groan in thyself, if thou wouldest rise to new life. To every man is this said, who is weighed down by any vicious habit. *It was a cave, and a stone lay upon it.* The dead under the stone is the guilty under the Law. For the Law, which was given to the Jews, was graven on stone. And all the guilty are under the Law, for the Law was not made for a righteous man. BEDE. Aug. Tr. xlix. non occ. Aug. Tr. xlix. 21. Chrys. Hom. lxiii. 1. Aug. Tr. xlix.

A cave is a hollow in a rock. It is called a monument, because it reminds us of the dead.

Chrys. Hom. lxiii. 2. *Jesus said, Take ye away the stone.* CHRYS. But why did He not raise him without taking away the stone? Could not He who moved a dead body by His voice, much more have moved a stone? He purposely did not do so, in order that the miracle might take place in the sight of all; to give no room for saying, as they had said in the case of the blind man, This is not he. Now they might go into the grave, and feel and see that this was the man. AUG. *Take*

Aug. Tr.xiix. c. 22. *ye away the stone;* mystically, Take away the burden of the

Aug. lib. 83. Quæst. qu. 61. law, proclaim grace. AUG. Perhaps those are signified who wished to impose the rite of circumcision on the Gentile converts; or men in the Church of corrupt life, who offend believers. AUG. Mary and Martha, the sisters of Lazarus,

Aug. de Ver. Dom. serm.lii. though they had often seen Christ raise the dead, did not fully believe that He could raise their brother; *Martha, the sister of him that was dead, saith unto Him, Lord, by this time he stinketh, for he hath been dead four days.* THE-OPHYL. Martha said this from weakness of faith, thinking it impossible that Christ could raise her brother, so long after death. BEDE. Or, these are not words of despair, but

Bede. non occ. (Nic.) of wonder. CHRYS. Thus every thing tends to stop the

Chrys. Hom. lxiii. 2. mouths of the unbelieving. Their hands take away the stone, their ears hear Christ's voice, their eyes see Lazarus come forth, they perceive the smell of the dead body. THE-OPHYL. Christ reminds Martha of what He had told her before, which she had forgotten: *Jesus saith unto her, Said I not unto thee, that, if thou wouldest believe, thou shouldest*

Chrys. Hom. lxiii. *see the glory of God?* CHRYS. She did not remember what He said above, *He that believeth in Me, though he were dead, yet shall he live.* To the disciples He had said, *That the Son of God might be glorified thereby;* here it is the glory of the Father He speaks of. The difference is made to suit the different hearers. Our Lord could not rebuke her before such a number, but only says, *Thou shalt*

Aug. Tr.xlix. *see the glory of God.* AUG. Herein is the glory of God, that he that stinketh and hath been dead four days, is brought to life again.

Then they took away the stone. ORIGEN. The delay in taking away the stone was caused by the sister of the dead, who said, *By this time he stinketh, for he hath been dead four days.* If she had not said this, it would not be said, *Jesus said, Take away the stone.* Some delay had arisen; it is best to let nothing come between the commands of Jesus and doing them. Orig.
tom. in
Joan.
xxviii.

41. And Jesus lifted up his eyes, and said, Father, I thank thee that thou hast heard me.

42. And I knew that thou hearest me always: but because of the people which stand by I said it, that they may believe that thou hast sent me.

43. And when he thus had spoken, he cried with a loud voice, Lazarus, come forth.

44. And he that was dead came forth, bound hand and foot with graveclothes : and his face was bound about with a napkin. Jesus saith unto them, Loose him, and let him go.

45. Then many of the Jews which came to Mary, and had seen the things which Jesus did, believed on him.

46. But some of them went their ways to the Pharisees, and told them what things Jesus had done.

ALCUIN. Christ, as man, being inferior to the Father, prays to Him for Lazarus's resurrection; and declares that He is heard: *And Jesus lifted up His eyes, and said, Father, I thank Thee that Thou hast heard Me.* ORIGEN. *He lifted up His eyes;* mystically, He lifted up the human mind by prayer to the Father above. We should pray after Christ's pattern, Lift up the eyes of our heart, and raise them above present things in memory, in thought, in intention. If to them who pray worthily after this fashion is given the promise in Isaiah, *Thou shalt cry, and He shall say, Here I am;* what answer, think we, our Lord and Saviour would receive? He was about to pray for the resurrection of Lazarus. He was heard by the Father before He prayed; Orig.
tom.
xxviii. Isa. 58,
9.

His request was granted before mad . And therefore He begins with giving thanks; *I thank Thee, Father, that Thou hast heard Me.* CHRYS. i. e. There is no difference of will between Me and Thee. *Thou hast heard Me,* does not shew any lack of power in Him, or that He is inferior to the Father. It is a phrase that is used between friends and equals. That the prayer is not really necessary for Him, appears from the words that follow, *And I knew that Thou heardest Me always:* as if He said, I need not prayer to persuade Thee; for Ours is one will. He hides His meaning on account of the weak faith of His hearers. For God regards not so much His own dignity, as our salvation ; and therefore seldom speaks loftily of Himself, and, even when He does, speaks in an obscure way; whereas humble expressions abound in His discourses. HILARY. He did not therefore need to pray: He prayed for our sakes, that we might know Him to be the Son: *But because of the people which stand by I said it, that they may believe that Thou hast sent Me.* His prayer did not benefit Himself, but benefited our faith. He did not want help, but we want instruction. CHRYS. He did not say, *That they may believe* that I am inferior to Thee, in that I cannot do this without prayer, but, *that Thou hast sent Me.* He saith not, *hast sent Me* weak, acknowledging subjection, doing nothing of Myself, but *hast sent Me* in such sense, as that man may see that I am from God, not contrary to God; and that I do this miracle in accordance with His will. AUG. Christ went to the grave in which Lazarus slept, as if He were not dead, but alive and able to hear, for He forthwith called him out of his grave: *And when He had thus spoken, He cried with a loud voice, Lazarus, come forth.* He calls him by name, that He may not bring out all the dead. CHRYS. He does not say, Arise, but, *Come forth,* speaking to the dead as if he were alive. For which reason also He does not say, Come forth in My Father's name, or, Father, raise him, but throwing off the whole appearance of one praying, proceeds to shew His power by acts. This is His general way. His words shew humility, His acts power. THEOPHYL. The voice which roused Lazarus, is the symbol of that trumpet which will sound at the general resurrection. (He spoke loud, to con-

Marginal references:

Chrys. Hom. lxiv. 2.

Hilar. lib. x. in Joan.

Chrys. Hom. lxiv. 2.

Aug. de Verb. Dom. Serm. lii.

Chrys. Hom. lxiv. 2.

tradict the Gentile fable, that the soul remained in the tomb. The soul of Lazarus is called to as if it were absent, and a loud voice were necessary to summon it.) And as the general resurrection is to take place in the twinkling of an eye, so did this single one: *And he that was dead came forth, bound hand and foot with grave clothes, and his face was bound about with a napkin.* Now is accomplished what was said above, *The hour is coming, when the dead* v. 25. *shall hear the voice of the Son of God, and they that hear shall live.* ORIGEN. His cry and loud voice it was which Orig. awoke him, as Christ had said, *I go to awake him.* The t.xxviii. resurrection of Lazarus is the work of the Father also, in that He heard the prayer of the Son. It is the joint work of Father and Son, one praying, the other hearing; *for as the Father* v. 21. *raiseth up the dead and quickeneth them, even so the Son quickeneth whom He will.* CHRYS. He came forth bound, Chrys. that none might suspect that he was a mere phantom. Besides, Hom. lxiv. that this very fact, viz. of coming forth bound, was itself a miracle, as great as the resurrection. *Jesus saith unto them, Loose him,* that by going near and touching him they might be certain he was the very person. *And let him go.* His humility is shewn here; He does not take Lazarus about with Him for the sake of display. ORIGEN. Our Lord had said above, Orig. *Because of the people that stand by I said it, that they may* t.xxviii. 10. *believe that Thou hast sent Me.* It would have been ignorance of the future, if He had said this, and none believed, after all. Therefore it follows: *Then many of the Jews which came to Mary, and had seen the things which Jesus did, believed on Him. But some of them went their way to the Pharisees, and told them what things Jesus had done.* It is doubtful from these words, whether those who went to the Pharisees, were of those many who believed, and meant to conciliate the opponents of Christ; or whether they were of the unbelieving party, and wished to inflame the envy of the Pharisees against Him. The latter seems to me the true supposition; especially as the Evangelist describes those who believed as the larger party. *Many believed;* whereas it is only a few who go to the Pharisees: *Some of them went to the Pharisees, and told them what things Jesus had done.* AUG. Although according to Aug.lib. the Gospel history, we hold that Lazarus was really raised to lxxxiii. Quæst. q. 65.

life, yet I doubt not that his resurrection is an allegory as well. We do not, because we allegorize facts, lose our belief in them as facts. AUG. Every one that sinneth, dies; but God, of His great mercy, raises the soul to life again, and does not suffer it to die eternally. The three miraculous resurrections in the Gospels, I understand to testify the resurrection of the soul. GREG. The maiden is restored to life in the house, the young man outside the gate, Lazarus in his grave. She that lies dead in the house, is the sinner lying in sin: he that is carried out by the gate is the openly and notoriously wicked. AUG. Or, it is death within; when the evil thought has not come out into action. But if thou actually do the evil thing, thou hast as it were carried the dead outside the gate. GREG. And one there is who lies dead in his grave, with a load of earth upon him; i. e. who is weighed down by habits of sin. But the Divine grace has regard even unto such, and enlightens them. AUG. Or we may take Lazarus in the grave as the soul laden with earthly sins. AUG. And yet our Lord loved Lazarus. For had He not loved sinners, He would never have come down from heaven to save them. Well is it said of one of sinful habits, that *He stinketh.* He hath a bad report already, as it were the foulest odour. AUG. Well may she say, He hath been dead four days. For the earth is the last of the elements. It signifies the pit of earthly sins, i. e. carnal lusts. AUG. The Lord groaned, wept, cried with a loud voice. It is hard for Him to arise, who is bowed down with the weight of evil habits. Christ troubleth Himself, to signify to thee that thou shouldest be troubled, when thou art pressed and weighed down with such a mass of sin. Faith groaneth, he that is displeased with himself groaneth, and accuseth his own evil deeds; that so the habit of sin may yield to the violence of repentance. When thou sayest, I have done such a thing, and God has spared me; I have heard the Gospel, and despised it; what shall I do? then Christ groaneth, because faith groaneth; and in the voice of thy groaning appeareth the hope of thy rising again. GREG. Lazarus is bid to *come forth,* i. e. to come forth and condemn himself with his own mouth, without excuse or reservation: that so he that lies buried in a guilty conscience, may come forth out of himself by confession.

Aug. Tr.super Joan. xlix. 3.

Greg.iv. Moral. c. xxix.

Aug. Tr.xlix. 3.

Greg. v.Moral.

Aug.lib. lxxxii. Quæst. q. lxv. Aug. in Joan.

Tr.xlix. ¹ pessimam famam Aug.lib. lxxxiii. Quæst. q. 65. Aug. Tract. in Joan. xlix. 19.

Greg. xxii. Moral.

AUG. That Lazarus came forth from the grave, signifies the soul's deliverance from carnal sins. That he came bound up in grave clothes means, that even we who are delivered from carnal things, and serve with the mind the law of God, yet cannot, so long as we are in the body, be free from the besetments of the flesh. That his face was bound about with a napkin means, that we do not attain to full knowledge in this life. And when our Lord says, *Loose him, and let him go,* we learn that in another world all veils will be removed, and that we shall see face to face. AUG. Or thus: When thou despisest, thou liest dead; when thou confessest, thou comest forth. For what is to come forth, but to go out, as it were, of thy hiding place, and shew thyself? But thou canst not make this confession, except God move thee to it, by crying with a loud voice, i. e. calling thee with great grace. But even after the dead man has come forth, he remains bound for some time, i. e. is as yet only a penitent. Then our Lord says to His ministers, *Loose him, and let him go,* i. e. remit his sins: *Whatsoever ye shall bind on earth shall be bound in heaven, and whatsoever ye shall loose on earth shall be loosed in heaven.* ALCUIN. Christ awakes, because His power it is which quickens us inwardly: the disciples loose, because by the ministry of the priesthood, they who are quickened are absolved. BEDE. By those who went and told the Pharisees, are meant those who seeing the good works of God's servants, hate them on that very account, persecute, and calumniate them.

47. Then gathered the chief priests and the Pharisees a council, and said, What do we? for this man doeth many miracles.

48. If we let him thus alone, all men will believe on him: and the Romans shall come and take away both our place and nation.

49. And one of them, named Caiaphas, being the high priest that same year, said unto them, Ye know nothing at all,

50. Nor consider that it is expedient for us, that

one man should die for the people, and that the whole
nation perish not.

51. And this spake he not of himself: but being
high priest that year, he prophesied that Jesus should
die for that nation;

52. And not for that nation only, but that also he
should gather together in one the children of God that
were scattered abroad.

53. Then from that day forth they took counsel
together for to put him to death.

THEOPHYL. Such a miracle as this should have drawn
forth wonder and praise. But they make it a reason of
plotting against His life: *Then gathered the chief priests
and Pharisees a council, and said, What do we?* AUG.
But they had no thought of believing. The miserable men
only consulted how they might hurt and kill Him, not how
themselves might be saved from death. *What do we? for
this Man doeth many miracles.* CHRYS. Him of whose
divinity they had received such certain proofs, they call only
a man. ORIGEN. This speech is an evidence of their audacity and blindness: of their audacity, because they testified
that He had done many miracles, and yet thought that they
could contend successfully against Him, and that He would
have no power of withstanding their plots; of their blindness,
because they did not reflect that He who had wrought such
miracles could easily escape out of their hands; unless
indeed they denied that these miracles were done by Divine
power. They resolved then not to let Him go; thinking
that they should thus place an impediment in the way of
those who wished to believe in Him, and also prevent the
Romans from taking away their place and nation. *If we let
Him thus alone, all men will believe on Him, and the
Romans shall come and take away both our place and
nation.* CHRYS. They say this to alarm the people; as if
they were incurring the suspicion of setting up an usurper.
If, say they, the Romans in crowds follow Him, they will
suspect us of setting up a tyranny, and will destroy our
state. But this was wholly a fiction of their own. For what

Aug.
Tr. xlix.
c. 26.

Chrys.
Hom.
lxiv.
c. 3.
Orig.
t.xxviii.
c. 11.

Chrys.
Hom.
'xiv. 3.

was the fact? Did He take armed men about with Him,
did He go with horsemen in His train? Did He not rather
choose desert places to go to? However, that they might not
be suspected of consulting only their own interests, they
declare the whole state is in danger. Aug. Or, they were ^{Aug.}
afraid that, if all believed in Christ, none would remain to ^{Tr.xlix. 26.}
defend the city of God and the temple against the Romans:
since they thought that Christ's teaching was directed
against the temple, and their laws. They were afraid of
losing temporal things, and thought not of eternal life; and
thus they lost both. For the Romans, after our Lord had
suffered and was glorified, did come and take away their
place and nation, reducing the one by siege, and dispersing
the other. Origen. Mystically: It was fit that the Gentiles ^{Orig.}
should occupy the *place* of them of the circumcision; be- ^{t.xxviii.}
cause by their fall salvation came to the Gentiles. The ^{non occ.}
Romans represent the Gentiles, being the rulers of the Gentile
world. Their *nation* again was taken away, because they
who had been the people of God, were made not a people.
Chrys. When they hesitated, and asked, *What do we?* one ^{Chrys.}
of them gave most cruel and shameless advice, viz. *Caia-* ^{Hom. lxiv.}
phas, who was[1] *High Priest that same year.* Aug. How is [1] being
it that he is called the High Priest of that year, when God ^{Aug. Tr.xlix.}
appointed one hereditary High Priest? This was owing to
the ambition and contention of parties amongst the Jews
themselves, which had ended in the appointment of several
High Priests, who took the office in turn, year by year. And
sometimes even there seems to have been more than one in
office. Alcuin. Of this Caiaphas Josephus relates, that he
bought the priesthood for a year, for a certain sum. Origen. ^{Orig.}
[a]The character of Caiaphas is shewn by his being called *the* ^{t. xxx. c. 12.}
High Priest of that same year; the year, viz. in which our
Saviour suffered. *Being the High Priest that same year, he*
said unto them, Ye know nothing at all, nor consider that
it is expedient for us that one man should die for the
people, and that the whole nation perish not. i. e. Ye sit ^{non occ.}
still, and give no attention. Attend to me. So insignificant
a thing as the life of one man may surely be made a sacrifice

---

[a] Origen's words are, All the Evangelists describe the wickedness of Caiaphas, who was High Priest of the
year in which our Saviour suffered.

for the safety of the state. THEOPHYL. He said this with a bad intention, yet the Holy Spirit used his mouth as the vehicle of a prophecy: *And this spake he not of himself: but being high priest that year, he prophesied that Jesus should die for that nation.* ORIGEN. Not every one that prophesieth is a prophet; as not every one that does a just action is just, he, for example, that does one for vainglory. Caiaphas prophesied without being a prophet, as did Balaam. Perhaps some will deny that Caiaphas prophesied by the Holy Spirit, on the ground that evil spirits may bear witness to Christ, as the one in Luke, who says, *I know Thee who Thou art, the Holy One of God;* the intention of Caiaphas too being not to induce his hearers to believe on Him, but to excite them to kill Him. *It is expedient for us.* Is this part of his prophecy true or false? If it is true, then those who contended against Jesus in the council, since Jesus died for the people, and they participate in the advantage of His death, are saved. This you say is absurd; and thence argue that the prophecy is false, and, if false, not dictated by the Holy Spirit, since the Holy Spirit does not lie. On the other side it is argued, for the truth of the prophecy, that these words only meant that *He by the grace of God should taste death for all men;* that *He is the Saviour of all men, specially of them that believe.* And in the same way the former part of the speech, *Ye know nothing at all,* is made out to be an assertion of the truth. They knew nothing of Jesus, who did not know that He was truth, wisdom, justice, and peace. And again, *That one* MAN *should die for the people.* It was as *man* that He died for the people: in so far as He is the image of the invisible God, He was incapable of death. And He died *for the people*, in that He took upon Himself, made away with, blotted out the sins of the whole world. *And this spake he not of himself.* Hence we see, what men say sometimes proceeds from themselves, sometimes from the influence of some power upon them. In the latter case though they may not be taken quite out of themselves, and in a certain sense go along with their own words, yet they do not go along with the meaning of them. Thus Caiaphas says nothing of himself; and therefore does not interpret his own prophecy, because he does

Orig. tom. xxviii. c. 12.

Luke 4, 34.

c. 14.

Heb. 2, 9. 1 Tim. 4, 10.

c. 15.

not understand it. Thus Paul too speaks of some *teachers* 1 Tim.
of the law, who understand neither what they say, nor 1, 7.
whereof they affirm. AUG. We learn hence that even bad Aug.
men may foretell things to come by the spirit of prophecy, Tr. xlix. 37.
which power the Evangelist ascribes to a divine sacrament,
he being Pontifex, i.e. High Priest. CHRYS. See the great Chrys.
virtue of the Holy Spirit, in drawing forth a prophecy from a Hom. lxv. 1.
wicked man. And see too the virtue of the pontifical office,
which made him, though an unworthy High Priest, uncon-
sciously prophesy. Divine grace only used his mouth; it
touched not his corrupt heart. AUG. Caiaphas prophesied of Aug. Tr. xlix.
the Jewish nation alone; in which nation were the sheep, of 27.
which our Lord says, *I am not sent but unto the lost sheep* Matt.
of the house of Israel. But the Evangelist knew that there 15, 34.
were other sheep, not of this fold, which were to be brought
in, and therefore adds, *And not for that nation only, but
also that He should gather together in one the children of
God that were scattered abroad;* i. e. those who were predestined to be so: for as yet there were neither sheep, nor
children of God. GREG. His persecutors accomplished this Greg. vi.
wicked purpose, and put Him to death, thinking to ex- Moral.
tinguish the devotion of His followers; but faith grew from
the very thing which these cruel and unbelieving men
thought would destroy it. That which human cruelty had
executed against Him, He turned to the purposes of His
mercy. ORIGEN. Inflamed by the speech of Caiaphas, they Orig.
determined on killing our Lord: *Then from that day forth* tom. xxviii.
they took counsel together to put Him to death. Was this c. 17.
then the work of the Holy Spirit, as well as the former, or
was it another spirit which did both first speak by the mouth
of a wicked man, and then excite others like him to kill
Christ? Answer: It is not necessary that both should be the
work of the same spirit. As some turn the Scriptures themselves, which were given for our good, to the support of bad
doctrines; so this true prophecy respecting our Saviour was
understood in a wrong sense, as if it were a call to put Him
to death. CHRYS. They sought before to kill Him; now Chrys.
their resolution was confirmed. Hom. lxv. 1.

54. Jesus therefore walked no more openly among

the Jews; but went thence unto a country near to the wilderness, into a city called Ephraim, and there continued with his disciples.

55. And the Jews' passover was nigh at hand: and many went out of the country up to Jerusalem before the passover, to purify themselves.

56. Then sought they for Jesus, and spake among themselves, as they stood in the temple, What think ye, that he will not come to the feast?

57. Now both the chief priests and the Pharisees had given a commandment, that, if any man knew where he were, he should shew it, that they might take him.

Orig.
t.xxviii.
18. ORIGEN. After this resolution of the Chief Priests and Pharisees, Jesus was more cautious in shewing Himself among the Jews, and retired to remote parts, and avoided populous places: *Jesus therefore walked no more openly among the Jews; but went thence into a country near to the wilderness, into a city called Ephraim.* Aug.
Tr.xlix.
28. AUG. Not that His power had failed Him; for, had He pleased, He might still have walked openly among the Jews, and they done nothing to Him. But He wished to shew the disciples, by His own example, that believers did not sin by retiring out of the sight of their persecutors, and hiding themselves from the fury of the wicked, rather than inflame that fury by Orig.
t.xxviii.
18. their presence. ORIGEN. It is praiseworthy, when struggles are at hand, not to avoid confession, or refuse to suffer death for the truth's sake. And it is no less praiseworthy now to avoid giving occasion for such trial. Which we should take care to do, not only on account of the uncertainty of the event of a trial in our own case, but also not to be the occasion of increasing the impiety and guilt of others. For he who is the cause of sin in another, shall be punished. If we do not avoid our persecutor, when we have the opportunity, we make ourselves responsible for his offence. But our Lord not only retired Himself, but to remove all occasion of offence from His persecutors, took His disciples with Chrys.
Hom.
lxv. 2. Him: *And there stayed with His disciples.* CHRYS. How

must it have troubled the disciples to see Him save Himself by merely human means? While all were rejoicing and keeping the feast, they remained hid, and in danger. Yet they continued with Him; as we read in Luke, *Ye are they which have* Luke 22, *continued with Me in My temptations.* ORIGEN. Mystically, Orig. Jesus *walked openly among the Jews,* when the Word of God used to come to them by the Prophets. But this Word ceased, i. e. Jesus *went thence.* And He went to that town near the wilderness, whereof Isaiah says, *More are the* Is. 54, 1. *children of the desolate, than the children of the married wife.* Ephraim signifies fertility. Ephraim was the younger brother of Manasses: Manasses stands for the elder people forgotten; the word Manasses meaning forgotten. When the elder people were forgotten and passed over, there came an abundant harvest from the Gentiles. Our Lord left the Jews, and went forth into a country—the whole world— near the wilderness, the deserted Church[1], to Ephraim, the [1] ἐγγὺς fruitful city; and there continues with His disciples up to τῆς ἐρή- this day. AUG. He who came from heaven to suffer, wished ἐκκλη- to draw near the place of His Passion, His hour being now σίας. Aug. at hand: *And the Jews' passover was nigh at hand.* That Tr. l. 2. passover they had resolved to celebrate by shedding our Lord's blood; the blood which consecrated the Passover, the blood of the Lamb. The Law obliged every one to go up to the feast: *And many went out of the country up to Jerusalem before the passover to purify them.* But ours is the true Passover; the Jewish one was a shadow. The Jews held their passover in the dark, we in the light: their posts were stained with the blood of a slain animal, our foreheads are signed with the blood of Christ. THEOPHYL. They went up before the passover, to be purified. For whoever had sinned willingly or unwillingly could not keep the passover, unless they were first purified by washings, fastings, and shaving of the head, and also offering certain stated oblations. While engaged in these purifications, they were plotting our Lord's death: *Then sought they for Jesus, and spake among themselves, as they stood in the temple, What think ye, that He will not come to the feast?* CHRYS. They lay in wait for Chrys. Him at the passover, and made the feast time the time of Hom. lxv. His death. ORIGEN. Wherefore the Evangelist does not Orig. t. xxviii.

call it the Lord's passover, but the *Jews' passover*. For then it was that they plotted our Lord's death. ALCUIN. They sought Jesus with bad intent. We seek Him, standing in God's temple, mutually encouraging one another, and praying Him to come to our feast, and sanctify us by His presence. THEOPHYL. If the common people only had done these things, the Passion would have seemed owing to men's ignorance; but the Pharisees it is, who order Him to be taken: *Now both the chief priests and the Pharisees had given a commandment, that, if any man knew where He were, he should shew it, that they might take Him.* ORIGEN. Observe, they did not know where He was; they knew that He had gone away. Mystically, they did not know where He was, because, in the place of the divine commandments, they taught the doctrines and commandments of men. AUG. Let us at least shew the Jews where He is; O that they would hear, that they would come to the Church, and take hold of Him for themselves!

Orig. tom. xxviii.

Aug. Tr. l. 4.

CHAP. XII.

1. Then Jesus six days before the passover came to Bethany, where Lazarus was which had been dead, whom he raised from the dead.

2. There they made him a supper: and Martha served: but Lazarus was one of them that sat at the table with him.

3. Then took Mary a pound of ointment of spikenard, very costly, and anointed the feet of Jesus, and wiped his feet with her hair: and the house was filled with the odour of the ointment.

4. Then saith one of his disciples, Judas Iscariot, Simon's son, which should betray him,

5. Why was not this ointment sold for three hundred pence, and given to the poor?

6. This he said, not that he cared for the poor; but because he was a thief, and had the bag, and bare what was put therein.

7. Then said Jesus, Let her alone: against the day of my burying hath she kept this.

8. For the poor always ye have with you; but me ye have not always.

9. Much people of the Jews therefore knew that he was there: and they came not for Jesus' sake only, but that they might see Lazarus also, whom he had raised from the dead.

10. But the chief priests consulted that they might put Lazarus also to death:

11. Because that by reason of him many of the Jews went away, and believed on Jesus.

ALCUIN. As the time approached in which our Lord had resolved to suffer, He approached the place which He had chosen for the scene of His suffering: *Then Jesus six days before the passover came to Bethany.* First, He went to Bethany, then to Jerusalem; to Jerusalem to suffer, to Bethany to keep alive the recollection of the recent resurrection of Lazarus; *Where Lazarus was, which had been dead, whom He raised from the dead.* THEOPHYL. On the tenth day of the month they took the lamb which was to be sacrificed on the passover, and from that time began the preparation for the feast. Or rather the ninth day of the month, i. e. six days before the passover, was the commencement of the feast. They feasted abundantly on that day. Thus we find Jesus partook of a banquet at Bethany: *There they made Him a supper, and Martha served.* That Martha served, shews that the entertainment was in her house. See the fidelity of the woman: she does not leave the task of serving to the domestics, but takes it upon herself. The Evangelist adds, in order, it would seem, to settle Lazarus' resurrection beyond dispute, *But Lazarus was one of them that sat at the table with Him.*

Aug. Tr. l. 5. AUG. He lived, talked, feasted; the truth was established, the unbelief of the Jews confounded.

Chrys. Hom. lxv. CHRYS. Mary did not take part in serving the guests generally, but gave all her attention to our Lord, treating Him not as mere man, but as God: *Then took Mary a pound of spikenard, very costly, and anointed the feet of Jesus, and wiped His feet with her hair.*

Aug. Tr. l. 6. AUG. The word *pistici* seems to be the name of some place, from which this precious ointment came. ALCUIN. Or pistici means genuine, non-adulterated. She is the woman that was a sinner, who came to our Lord in Simon's house with the box of ointment.

Aug. de Con. Evang. ii.lxxix. AUG. That she did this on another occasion in Bethany is not mentioned in Luke's Gospel, but is in the other three. Matthew and Mark say that the ointment was poured on the head, John says, on the feet. Why not suppose that it was c.lxxviii. poured both on the head, and on the feet? Matthew and Mat 26, 6. Mark14, 3. Mark introduce the supper and the ointment out of place in the order of time. When they are some way farther on in their narration[a], they go back to the sixth day before the passover. *And the house was filled with the odour of the ointment.*

[a] within two days of the crucifixion.

Aug. Remember the Apostle's words: *To the one we are* Aug.
the savour of death unto death; and to the other the savour of Tr. l.
2 Cor.
life unto life. Aug. *Then saith one of His disciples, Judas* 11, 16.
Iscariot, Simon's son, which should betray Him, Why was Aug.
de Con.
not this ointment sold for three hundred pence, and given to Evang.
ii. lxxix.
the poor? In the other Gospels it is the disciples who (156.)
murmured at the waste of the ointment. I think myself that
Judas is put for the whole body of disciples; the singular for
the plural. But at any rate we may supply for ourselves,
that the other disciples said it, or thought it, or were persuaded by this very speech of Judas. The only difference
is, that Matthew and Mark expressly mention the concurrence
of the others, whereas John only mentions Judas, whose
habit of thieving He takes occasion to notice: *This he said,
not that he cared for the poor, but because he was a thief,
and had the bag, and bare what was put therein.* ALCUIN.
He carried it as a servant, he took it out as a thief.

Aug. Judas did not perish at the time when he received Aug.
money from the Jews to betray our Lord. He was already Tr. l. 10.
a thief, already lost, and followed our Lord in body, not in
heart; wherein we are taught the duty of tolerating wicked
men, lest we divide the body of Christ. He who robs the
Church of any thing may be compared to the lost Judas.
Tolerate the wicked, thou that art good, that thou mayest
receive the reward of the good, and not fall into the punishment
of the wicked. Follow the example of our Lord's conversation
upon earth. Wherefore had He bags, to Whom the Angels
ministered, except because His Church should afterwards
have bags? Why did He admit thieves, but to shew that His
Church should tolerate thieves, while it suffered from them.
It is not surprising that Judas, who was accustomed to steal
money from the bags, should betray our Lord for money.
CHRYS. But why was a thief entrusted with the bags of the Chrys.
poor? Perhaps it was to give him no excuse of wanting Hom.
lxv. 2.
money, for of this he had enough in the bag for all his desires.
THEOPHYL. Some suppose that Judas had the keeping of the
money, as being the lowest kind of service. For that the
ministry of money matters ranks below the ministry of doctrine,
we know from what the Apostle says in the Acts, *It is not* Acts 6,
reason that we should leave the word of God, and serve 2.

Chrys.
Hom.
lxv. 2.

tables. CHRYS. Christ, with great forbearance, does not rebuke Judas for his thieving, in order to deprive him of all excuse for betraying Him. ALCUIN. *Then said Jesus, Let her alone: against the day of My burying hath she kept this:* meaning that He was about to die, and that this ointment was suitable for His burial. So to Mary who was not able to be present, though much wishing, at the anointing of the dead body, was it given to do Him this office in His lifetime.

Chrys.
Hom.
lxv. 2.

CHRYS. Again, as if to remind His betrayer, He alludes to His burial; *For the poor ye have always with you, but Me ye have not always:* as if He said, I am a burden, a trouble

Aug.
Tr. l. 13.

to thee; but wait a little, and I shall be gone. AUG. He was speaking of His bodily presence; for in respect of His majesty, providence, ineffable and invisible grace, those

Mat. 28,
20.
c. 12.

words are fulfilled, *Lo, I am with you alway, even unto the end of the world.* Or thus: In the person of Judas are represented the wicked in the Church; for if thou art a good man, thou hast Christ now by faith, and the Sacrament, and thou shalt have Him always, for when thou hast departed

Luke 23,
43.

hence, thou shalt go to Him who said to the thief, *To-day shalt thou be with Me in paradise.* But if thou art wicked, thou seemest to have Christ, because thou art baptized with the baptism of Christ, because thou approachest to the altar of Christ: but by reason of thy wicked life, thou shalt not have Him alway. It is not thou hast, but *ye have,* the whole body of wicked men being addressed in Judas.

c. 14.

Much people of the Jews therefore knew that He was there, and they came not for Jesus' sake only, but that they might see Lazarus also, whom He had raised from the dead. Curiosity brought them, not love. THEOPHYL. They wished to see with their own eyes him who had been raised from the dead, and thought that Lazarus might bring back a report of

Aug.
Tr. l. 14.

the regions below. AUG. When the news of this great miracle had spread every where, and was supported by such clear evidence, that they could neither suppress or deny the fact, then, *The chief priests consulted that they might put Lazarus to death.* O blind rage! as if the Lord could raise

Chrys.
Hom.
lxvi. 1.

the dead, and not raise the slain. Lo, the Lord hath done both. He raised Lazarus, and He raised Himself. CHRYS.

No other miracle of Christ excited such rage as this. It
was so public, and so wonderful, to see a man walking and
talking after he had been dead four days. And the fact was
so undeniable. In the case of some other miracles they had
charged Him with breaking the sabbath, and so diverted
people's minds: but here there was nothing to find fault
with, and therefore they vent their anger upon Lazarus.
They would have done the same to the blind man, had they
not had the charge to make of breaking the sabbath. Then
again the latter was a poor man, and they cast him out
of the temple; but Lazarus was a man of rank, as is plain
from the number who came to comfort his sisters. It vexed
them to see all leaving the feast, which was now coming on,
and going to Bethany. ALCUIN. Mystically, that He came
to Bethany six days before the passover, means, that He who
made all things in six days, who created man on the sixth,
in the sixth age of the world, the sixth day, the sixth hour,
came to redeem mankind. The Lord's Supper is the faith
of the Church, working by love. Martha serveth, whenever
a believing soul devotes itself to the worship of the Lord.
Lazarus is one of them that sit at table, when those who
have been raised from the death of sin, rejoice together with
the righteous, who have been ever such, in the presence of
truth, and are fed with the gifts of heavenly grace. The
banquet is given in Bethany, which means, house of obedience, i. e. in the Church: for the Church is the house of
obedience. AUG. The ointment with which Mary anointed the Aug.
feet of Jesus was justice. It was therefore a *pound*. It was Tr. li. 6.
ointment of spikenard (pistici) too, very precious. Πίστις is Greek
for faith. Dost thou seek to do justice? *The just liveth by* Heb.10,
faith. Anoint the feet of Jesus by good living, follow the 38.
Lord's footsteps: if thou hast a superfluity, give to the poor,
and thou hast wiped the Lord's feet; for the hair is a superfluous part of the body. ALCUIN. And observe, on the first
occasion of her anointing, she anointed His feet only, but
now she anoints both His feet and head. The former denotes
the beginnings of penitence, the latter the righteousness of
souls perfected. By the head of our Lord the loftiness of
His Divine nature, by His feet the lowliness of His incarnation are signified; or by the head, Christ Himself, by the

Aug. Tr. li. 7. feet, the poor who are His members. Aug. The house was filled with the odour; the world was filled with the good fame.

12. On the next day much people that were come to the feast, when they heard that Jesus was coming to Jerusalem,

13. Took branches of palm trees, and went forth to meet him, and cried, Hosanna: Blessed is the King of Israel that cometh in the name of the Lord.

14. And Jesus, when he had found a young ass, sat thereon; as it is written,

15. Fear not, daughter of Sion: behold, thy King cometh, sitting on an ass's colt.

16. These things understood not his disciples at the first: but when Jesus was glorified, then remembered they that these things were written of him, and that they had done these things unto him.

17. The people therefore that was with him when he called Lazarus out of his grave, and raised him from the dead, bare record.

18. For this cause the people also met him, for that they heard that he had done this miracle.

19. The Pharisees therefore said among themselves, Perceive ye how ye prevail nothing? behold, the world is gone after him.

Chrys. Hom. lxiv. Chrys. The Law enjoined, that on the tenth day of the first month a lamb or a kid should be shut up in the house, and be kept to the fourteenth day of the same month, on the evening of which day it was sacrificed. In accordance with this law, the Elect Lamb, the Lamb without spot, when He went up to Jerusalem to be immolated for the sanctification of the people, went up five days before, i. e. on the tenth day. Aug. Tr. li. 1. Aug. See how great was the fruit of His preaching, and how large a flock of the lost sheep of the house of Israel heard the voice of their Shepherd: *On the next day much people that were come to the feast, when they heard that*

Jesus was coming to Jerusalem, took branches of palm trees.
The branches of palms are songs of praise, for the victory
which our Lord was about to obtain by His death over death,
and His triumph over the devil, the prince of death, by the
trophy of the cross. CHRYS. They shewed now at last that they thought Him greater than a prophet: *And went forth to meet Him, and cried, Hosanna! Blessed is the King of Israel, that cometh in the name of the Lord.* AUG. Hosanna
is a simple exclamation, rather indicating some excitement
of the mind, than having any particular meaning; like many
interjections that we have in Latin. BEDE. It is a compound of two words; *Hosi* is shortened into save; *Anna* a
mere exclamation, complete. *Blessed is He that cometh in
the name of the Lord.* The name of the Lord here is the
name of God the Father; though we may understand it as
His own name; inasmuch as He also is the Lord. But the
former sense agrees better with the text above, *I am come in
My Father's name.* He does not lose His divinity, when He
teaches us humility. CHRYS. This is what more than any
thing made men believe in Christ, viz. the assurance, that
He was not opposed to God, that He came from the Father.
The words shew us the divinity of Christ. *Hosanna* is,
Save us; and salvation in Scripture is attributed to God
alone. And *cometh*, it is said, not is brought: the former
befits a lord, the latter a servant. *In the name of the Lord*,
goes to prove the same thing. He does not come in the
name of a servant, but in the name of the Lord. AUG. It
were a small thing to the King eternal to be made a human
king. Christ was not the King of Israel, to exact tribute,
and command armies, but to direct souls, and bring them to
the kingdom of heaven. For Christ then to be King of
Israel, was a condescension, not an elevation, a sign of His pity,
not an increase of His power. For He who was called on earth
the King of the Jews, is in heaven the King of Angels. THE-
OPHYL. The Jews, when they called Him King of Israel, dreamed
of an earthly king. They expected a king to arise, of more than
human greatness, who would deliver them from the government of the Romans. But how did our Lord come? The
next words tell us; *And Jesus when He had found a young
ass, sat thereon.* AUG. John relates the matter briefly, the other

Margin notes: Chrys. Hom. lxvi. 1. — Aug. Tr. li. 2. — v. 43. — Chrys. Hom. lxvi. 1. — Aug. Tr. li. 4. — Aug. Tr. li. 5.

2 D

Evangelists are more full. The ass, we read in them, was
the foal of an ass on which no man had sat: i. e. the Gentile
world, who had not received our Lord. The other ass,
which was brought, (not the foal, for there were two,) is the
believing Jew. CHRYS. He did this prophetically, to figure
the unclean Gentiles being brought into subjection to the
Gospel; and also as a fulfilment of prophecy. AUG. This
act of our Lord's is pointed to in the Prophets, though the
malignant rulers of the Jews did not see in it any fulfilment
of prophecy: *As it is written, Fear not, daughter of Sion,
behold thy King cometh sitting on an ass's colt.* Yea, in that
nation though reprobate, though blind, there remained still
the daughter of Sion; even Jerusalem. To her it is said, Fear
not, acknowledge Him whom thou praisest, and tremble not
when He suffers. That blood it is which shall wipe away
thy sins, and redeem thy life. CHRYS. Or thus: Whereas
they had had wicked kings, who had subjected them to wars,
He saith to them, Trust Me, I am not such as they, but
gentle and mild: which He shewed by the manner of His
entrance. For He did not enter at the head of an army,
but simply riding on an ass. And observe the philosophy
of the Evangelist, who is not ashamed of confessing his
ignorance at the time of what these things meant: *These
things understood not the disciple at the first, but when
Jesus was glorified.* AUG. i. e. When He shewed the power
of His resurrection, *then they remembered that these things
were written of Him, and that they had done these things
unto Him,* i. e. *those things that were written of Him.*
CHRYS. Our Lord had not then revealed these things to
them. Indeed it would have been a scandal to them had they
known Him to be King at the time of His sufferings. Nor
would they have understood the nature of His kingdom, but
have mistaken it for a temporal one. THEOPHYL. See then
the consequences of our Lord's passion[a]. It was not to no
purpose that He had reserved His greatest miracle for the
last. For the resurrection of Lazarus it was that made the
crowd believe in Him. *The people therefore that was with Him
when He called Lazarus out of his grave, and raised him
from the dead, bare record. For this cause the people also*

Chrys.
Hom.
lxvi. 1.

Aug.
Tr. li.

Chrys.
Hom.
lxvi. 1.

φιλο-
σοφίαν

Aug.
Tr. li.

Chrys.
Hom.
lvi. 1.

non occ.

---

[a] i. e. in its effect upon the minds of the disciples, enlightening them.

met Him, for that they heard that He had done this miracle.
Hence the spite and plotting of the Pharisees: *The Pharisees
therefore said among themselves, Perceive ye how ye prevail
nothing? behold the world is gone after Him.* Aug. The
crowd was disturbed by the crowd. But why grudgeth that
blind crowd, that the world should go after Him, by Whom
the world was made? Chrys. The world means here the
crowd. This seems to be the speech of that part who were
sound in their faith, but dared not profess it. They try to
deter the rest by exposing the insuperable difficulties they
would have to contend with. Theophyl. As if they said,
The more you attack Him, the more will His power and reputation increase. What use then of these attempts?

*Aug.
Tr. li. 7.
Turba
turbavit
turbam
Chrys.
Hom.
lxvi. 2.*

20. And there were certain Greeks among them
that came up to worship at the feast.

21. The same came therefore to Philip, which was
of Bethsaida of Galilee, and desired him, saying, Sir,
we would see Jesus.

22. Philip cometh and telleth Andrew: and again
Andrew and Philip tell Jesus.

23. And Jesus answered them, saying, The hour
is come, that the Son of man should be glorified.

24. Verily, verily, I say unto you, Except a corn of
wheat fall into the ground and die, it abideth alone:
but if it die, it bringeth forth much fruit.

25. He that loveth his life shall lose it, and he
that hateth his life in this world shall keep it unto life
eternal.

26. If any man serve me, let him follow me; and
where I am, there shall also my servant be: if any man
serve me, him will my Father honour.

Bede. The temple at Jerusalem was so famous, that on
the feast days, not only the people near, but many Gentiles
from distant countries came to worship in it; as that eunuch
of Candace, Queen of the Ethiopians, mentioned in the Acts.
The Gentiles who were at Jerusalem now, had come up for

this purpose: *And there were certain Gentiles among them*

Chrys.
Hom.
lxvi. 2. *who came to worship at the feast.* CHRYS. The time being now near, when they would be made proselytes. They hear Christ talked of, and wish to see Him: *The same came therefore to Philip, which was of Bethsaida of Galilee, and*

Aug.
Tr. li. 8. *desired him, saying, Sir, we would see Jesus.* AUG. Lo! the Jews wish to kill Him, the Gentiles to see Him. But they also were of the Jews who cried, *Blessed is He that cometh in the name of the Lord.* So behold them of the circumcision, and them of the uncircumcision, once so wide apart, coming together like two walls, and meeting in one faith of Christ by the kiss of peace.

Chrys.
Hom.
lxvii. 2. *Philip cometh and telleth Andrew.* CHRYS. As being the elder disciple. He had heard our Saviour say, *Go not into*

Matt.
10, 5. *the way of the Gentiles;* and therefore he communicates with his fellow-disciple, and they refer the matter to their Lord:

Aug.
Tr. li. 8. *And again Andrew and Philip tell Jesus.* AUG. Listen we to the voice of the corner stone: *And Jesus answered them, saying, The hour is come, that the Son of man should be glorified.* Did He think Himself glorified, because the Gentiles wished to see? No. But He saw that after His passion and resurrection, the Gentiles in all lands would believe on Him; and took occasion from this request of some Gentiles to see Him, to announce the approaching fulness of the Gentiles, for that the hour of His being glorified was now at hand, and that after He was glorified in the heavens, the Gentiles would believe; according to the passage

Ps. 56,
and 107. in the Psalm, *Set up Thyself, O God, above the heavens, and Thy glory above all the earth.* But it was necessary that His exaltation and glory should be preceded by His humiliation and passion; wherefore He says, *Verily, verily, I say unto you, Except a corn of wheat fall into the ground and die, it abideth alone: but if it die, it bringeth forth much fruit.* That corn was He; to be mortified in the unbelief of the Jews, to be multiplied in the faith of the Gentiles. BEDE. He Himself, of the seed of the Patriarchs, was sown in the field of this world, that by dying, He might rise again with increase. He died alone; He rose again with

Chrys.
Hom.
lxvi. 2. many. CHRYS. He illustrates His discourse by an example from nature. A grain of corn produces fruit, after it has

died. How much more then must the Son of God? The
Gentiles were to be called after the Jews had finally offended;
i. e. after His crucifixion. Now then that the Gentiles of
their own accord offered their faith, He saw that His crucifixion could not be far off. And to console the sorrow of
His disciples, which He foresaw would arise, He tells them
that to bear patiently not only His death, but their own too,
is the only way to good: *He that loveth his life shall lose it.*
AUG. This may be understood in two ways: 1. If thou lovest Aug.
it, lose it: if thou wouldest preserve thy life in Christ, fear ^{Tr.li.10.}
not death for Christ. 2. Do not love thy life here, lest thou
lose it hereafter. The latter seems to be the more evangelical evan-
sense; for it follows, *And he that hateth his life in this* ^{gelicus}
world, shall keep it unto life eternal. CHRYS. He loveth Chrys.
his life in this world, who indulges its inordinate desires; he ^{Hom.}
hateth it, who resists them. It is not, who doth not yield ^{lxvii. 1.}
to, but, *who hateth.* For as we cannot bear to hear the
voice or see the face of them whom we hate; so when the
soul invites us to things contrary to God, we should turn
her away from them with all our might. THEOPHYL. It were
harsh to say that a man should hate his soul; so He adds,
in this world : i. e. for a particular time, not for ever. And
we shall gain in the end by so doing : shall keep it unto life
eternal. AUG. But think not for an instant, that by hating Aug.
thy soul, is meant that thou mayest kill thyself. For wicked ^{Tr.li.10.}
and perverse men have sometimes so mistaken it, and have
burnt and strangled themselves, thrown themselves from
precipices, and in other ways put an end to themselves. This
did not Christ teach; nay, when the devil tempted Him
to cast Himself down, He said, *Get thee hence, Satan*[b].
But when no other choice is given thee; when the persecutor
threatens death, and thou must either disobey God's law, or
depart out of this life, then hate thy life in this world, that
thou mayest keep it unto life eternal. CHRYS. This present Chrys.
life is sweet to them who are given up to it. But he who ^{Hom.}
looks heavenwards, and sees what good things are there, soon ^{lxvii. 1.}
despises this life. When the better life appears, the worse
is despised. This is Christ's meaning, when He says, *If
any man serve Me, let him follow Me,* i. e. imitate Me, both

[b] This the second temptation in Matthew. Get thee hence, comes after all three.

in My death, and life. For he who serves, should follow him whom he serves. AUG. But what is it to *serve* Christ? The very words explain. They serve Christ who seek not their own things, but the things of Jesus Christ, i. e. who *follow* Him, walk in His, not their own, ways, do all good works for Christ's sake, not only works of mercy to men's bodies, but all others, till at length they fulfil that great work of love, and lay down their lives for the brethren. But what fruit, what reward? you ask. The next words tell you: *And where I am, there shall also My servant be.* Love Him for His own sake, and think it a rich reward for

thy service, to be with Him. CHRYS. So then death will be followed by resurrection. *Where I am,* He says; for Christ was in heaven before His resurrection. Thither let us ascend in heart and in mind.

    If any man serve Me, him will My Father honour. This must be understood as an explanation of the preceding. *There also shall My servant be.* For what greater honour can an adopted son receive than to be where the Only Son

is? CHRYS. He says, *My Father will honour him,* not, I will honour him; because they had not yet proper notions of His nature, and thought Him inferior to the Father.

27. Now is my soul troubled; and what shall I say? Father, save me from this hour: but for this cause came I unto this hour.

28. Father, glorify thy name. Then came there a voice from heaven, saying, I have both glorified it, and will glorify it again.

29. The people therefore, that stood by, and heard it, said that it thundered: others said, An angel spake to him.

30. Jesus answered and said, This voice came not because of me, but for your sakes.

31. Now is the judgment of this world: now shall the prince of this world be cast out.

32. And I, if I be lifted up from the earth, will draw all men unto me.

33. This he said, signifying what death he should die.

CHRYS. To our Lord's exhortation to His disciples to Chrys. Hom. lxvi. endurance, they might have replied that it was easy for Him, Who was out of the reach of human pain, to talk philosophically about death, and to recommend others to bear what He is in no danger of having to bear Himself. So He lets them see that He is Himself in an agony, but that He does not intend to decline death, merely for the sake of relieving Himself: *Now is My soul troubled.* AUG. 1 hear Him say, Aug. Tr. lii. 2. *He that hateth his life in this world, shall keep it unto life eternal;* and I am ravished, I despise the world; the whole of this life, however long, is but a vapour in My sight; all temporal things are vile, in comparison with eternal. And again I hear Him say, *Now is My soul troubled.* Thou biddest my soul follow Thee; but I see Thy soul troubled. What foundation shall I seek, if the Rock gives way? Lord, I acknowledge Thy mercy. Thou of Thy love wast of Thine own will troubled, to console those who are troubled through the infirmity of nature; that the members of Thy body perish not in despair. The Head took upon Himself the affections of His members. He was not troubled by any thing, but, as was said above, *He troubled Himself.* CHRYS. c. 11, 33. Chrys. Hom. lxvii. As He draws near to the Cross, His human nature appears, a nature that did not wish to die, but cleaved to this present life. He shews that He is not quite without human feelings. For the desire of this present life is not necessarily wrong, any more than hunger. Christ had a body free from sin, but not from natural infirmities. But these attach solely to the dispensation of His humanity, not to His divinity. AUG. Aug. Hom. lii. Lastly, let the man who would follow Him, hear at what hour he should follow. A fearful hour has perhaps come: a choice is offered, either to do wrong, or suffer: the weak soul is troubled. Hear our Lord. *What shall I say?* BEDE. i. e. What but something to confirm My followers? *Father, save Me from this hour.* AUG. He teaches thee Whom thou Aug. Tr. lii. 3. shouldest call on, whose will prefer to thine own. Let Him not seem to fall from His greatness, because He wishes thee to rise from thy meanness. He took upon Him man's infirmity, that He might teach the afflicted to say, *Not what I will, but what Thou wilt.* Wherefore He adds, *But for this cause came I unto this hour. Father, glorify Thy name:*

Chrys. Hom. lxvii. 2. i. e. in My passion and resurrection. CHRYS. As if He said, I cannot say why I should ask to be saved from it; *For for this cause came I unto this hour.* However ye may be troubled and dejected at the thought of dying, do not run away from death. I am troubled, yet I ask not to be spared. I do not say, Save Me from this hour, but the contrary, *Glorify Thy name.* To die for the truth was to glorify God, as the event shewed; for after His crucifixion the whole world was to be converted to the knowledge and worship of God, both the Father and the Son. But this He is silent about.

Then came there a voice from heaven, saying, I have both glorified it, and will glorify it again. GREG. When God *Greg. Moral. xxviii.* speaks audibly, as He does here, but no visible appearance is seen, He speaks through the medium of a rational creature: i. e. by the voice of an Angel. AUG. *I have Aug. Tr. lii.4. glorified it,* i. e. before I made the world; *and will glorify it again,* i. e. when Thou shalt rise from the dead. Or, *I have glorified it,* when Thou wast born of a Virgin, didst work miracles, wast made manifest by the Holy Ghost descending in the shape of a dove; *and will glorify it again,* when Thou shalt rise from the dead, and, as God, be exalted above the heavens, and Thy glory above all the earth.

The people therefore that stood by and heard it, said that Chrys. it thundered. CHRYS. The voice though loud and distinct, *Hom. lxvii. 2.* soon passed off from their gross, carnal, and sluggish minds; only the sound remaining. Others perceived an articulate voice, but did not catch what it said: *Others said, An Angel spake to Him.*

Jesus answered and said, This voice came not because of Aug. Me, but for your sakes. AUG. i. e. It did not come to tell *Tr. lii.5.* Him what He knew already, but them what they ought to know. And as that voice did not come for His sake, but *Chrys. for theirs, so His soul was not troubled for His sake, but for Hom. lxvii. 2.* theirs. CHRYS. The voice of the Father proved what they

were so fond of denying, that He was from God. For He
must be from God, if He was glorified by God. It was not
that He needed encouragement of such a voice Himself, but
He condescended to receive it for the sake of those who were
by. *Now is the judgment of this world:* this fits on to the
preceding, as shewing the mode of His being glorified.
AUG. The judgment at the end of the world will be of
eternal rewards and punishments. But there is another Aug.
judgment, not of condemnation, but of selection, which is
the one meant here; the selection of His own redeemed, and
their deliverance from the power of the devil: *Now shall the
prince of this world be cast out.* The devil is not called the
prince of this world, in the sense of being lord over heaven
and earth; God forbid. The *world* here stands for the
wicked dispersed over all the world. In this sense the devil
is the prince of the world, i. e. of all the wicked men who live
in the world. The *world* also sometimes stands for the good
dispersed throughout the world: *God was in Christ recon-*
ciling the world unto Himself. These are they from whose
hearts the prince of this world shall be cast out. Our Lord
foresaw that after His passion and glorifying, great nations all
over the world would be converted, in whom the devil was
then, but from whose hearts, on their truly renouncing him[1], he
would be cast out. But was he not cast out of the hearts of
righteous men of old? Why is it, *Now shall be cast out?*
Because that which once took place in a very few persons,
was now to take place in whole nations. What then, does
the devil not tempt at all the minds of believers? Yea, he
never ceases to tempt them. But it is one thing to reign
within, another to lay siege from without. CHRYS. What
kind of judgment it is by which the devil is cast out, I will
explain by an example. A man demands payment from his
debtors, beats them, and sends them to prison. He treats
with the same insolence one who owes him nothing. The
latter will take vengeance both for himself and the others
too. This Christ does. He revenges what He has suffered at
the devil's hands, and with Himself He revenges us too. But
that none may say, How will he be cast out, if he overcome
thee? He adds, *And I, if I be lifted up from the earth, will*
draw all men unto Me. How can He be overcome, who

Tr. lii. 6.

2 Cor.
5, 19.

[1] ex fide
renun-
ciant

Chrys.
Hom.
lxvii. 2.

draws others unto Him? This is more than saying, I shall rise again. Had He said this, it would not have proved that He would draw all things unto Him; but, *I shall draw,*

Aug. Tr. lii. 11. includes the resurrection, and this besides. AUG. What is this *all* that He draweth, but that from which the devil is cast out? He does not say, All men, but, *All things;* for all men have not faith. He does not mean then all mankind, but the whole of a man, i. e. spirit, soul, and body; by which respectively we understand, and live, and are visible. Or, if *all* means all men, it means those who are predestined to salvation: or all kinds of men, all varieties of character,

Chrys. Hom. lxvii. 3. c. 6, 46. excepting in the article of sin. CHRYS. Why then did He say above, that the Father drew men? Because the Father draws, by the Son who draws. *I shall draw,* He says, as if men were in the grasp of some tyrant, from which they could

Aug. Tr. lii. 11. not extricate themselves. AUG. *If I be lifted up from the earth,* He says, i. e. when I shall be lifted up. He does not doubt that the work will be accomplished which He came to do. By His being lifted up, He means His passion on the cross, as the Evangelist adds: *This He said, signifying by what death He should die.*

34. The people answered him, We have heard out of the law that Christ abideth for ever : and how sayest thou, The Son of man must be lifted up? who is this Son of man?

35. Then Jesus said unto them, Yet a little while is the light with you. Walk while ye have the light, lest darkness come upon you: for he that walketh in darkness knoweth not whither he goeth.

36. While ye have light, believe in the light, that ye may be the children of light. These things spake Jesus, and departed, and did hide himself from them.

Aug. Tr. lii. 12. AUG. The Jews when they understood that our Lord spoke of His own death, asked how that could be: *The people answered Him, We have heard out of the law that Christ abideth for ever: and how sayest Thou, The Son of man must be lifted up? Who is this Son of man?* Though our Lord

did not call Himself the Son of man here, they remembered
that He often called Himself so; as He had just before:
The hour is come, that the Son of man should be glorified.
They remember this, and ask, If Christ abideth for ever,
how will He be lifted up from the earth; i. e. how will He
die upon the cross? CHRYS. Hence we see, that they Chrys.
understood many of the things that He spake in parables. Hom.
lxviii. 1.
As He had talked about death a little time before, they saw
now what was meant by His being lifted up. AUG. Or they Aug.
interpreted the word by their own intended act. It was Tr. lii.
12.
not wisdom imparted, but conscience disturbed, which disclosed its meaning to them. CHRYS. And see how maliciously Chrys.
they put the question. They do not say, *We have heard* Hom.
lxviii. 1.
out of the law, that Christ doth not suffer; for in many
places of Scripture His passion and resurrection are spoken
of together, but, *abideth for ever.* And yet His immortality
was not inconsistent with the fact of His suffering. They
thought this proved however that He was not Christ. Then
they ask, *Who is this Son of man?* another malicious question;
as if to say, Do not charge us with putting this question out
of hatred to Thee; for we simply ask for information. Christ
shews them in His answer that His passion does not prevent
Him from abiding for ever: *Then Jesus said unto them, Yet
a little while is the light with you:* as if His death were but
going away for a time, as the sun's light only sets to rise
again. AUG. *Yet a little while is the light with you.* Hence Aug.
it is that ye understand[1] that Christ abideth for ever. Where- Tr. lii.
13.
fore *walk while ye have the light,* approach, understand the [1] hinc
est quod
whole, that Christ will both die, and live for ever: do this intelli-
while ye have the light. CHRYS. He does not mean only the gitis.
Chrys.
time before His crucifixion, but the whole of their lives. Hom.
For many believed on Him after His crucifixion. *Lest* lxviii. 1.
darkness come upon you. AUG. i. e. if ye so believe in the Aug.
eternity of Christ, as to deny His humiliation and death. Tr. lii.
13.
*For he that walketh in darkness, knoweth not whither he
goeth.* CHRYS. What things do the Jews now, and know Chrys.
not what they do; thinking, like men in the dark, that they Hom.
lxviii. 1.
are going the right road, while they are taking directly the
wrong one. Wherefore He adds, *While ye have the light,
believe in the light.* AUG. i. e. While ye have any truth, Aug.
Tr. lii.

believe in the truth, that ye may be born again of the truth:

Chrys.
Hom.
lxviii.
c. 1, 13. *That ye may be the children of the light.* CHRYS. i. e. My children. In the beginning of the Gospel it is said, *Born of God,* i. e. of the Father. But here He Himself is the Begetter. The same act is the act both of Father and Son.

These things spake Jesus, and departed, and did hide

Aug.
Tr. lii. *Himself from them.* AUG. Not from those which began to believe in and love Him, but from those who saw and envied Him. When He hid Himself, He consulted our weakness,

Chrys.
Hom.
lxviii. 1. He did not derogate from His own power. CHRYS. But why did He hide Himself, when they neither took up stones to cast at Him, nor blasphemed? Because He saw into their hearts, and knew the fury they were in; and therefore did not wait till they broke out into act, but retired to give their envy time to subside.

37. But though he had done so many miracles before them, yet they believed not on him:

38. That the saying of Esaias the prophet might be fulfilled, which he spake, Lord, who hath believed our report? and to whom hath the arm of the Lord been revealed?

39. Therefore they could not believe, because that Esaias said again,

40. He hath blinded their eyes, and hardened their heart; that they should not see with their eyes, nor understand with their heart, and be converted, and I should heal them.

41. These things said Esaias, when he saw his glory, and spake of him.

42. Nevertheless among the chief rulers also many believed on him; but because of the Pharisees they did not confess him, lest they should be put out of the synagogue:

43. For they loved the praise of men more than the praise of God.

CHRYS. And thus[b] the Evangelist tacitly explains it, when *he adds, But though He had done so many miracles before them, yet they believed not on Him.* THEOPHYL. He means the miracles related above. It was no small wickedness to disbelieve against such miracles as those. CHRYS. But why then did Christ come? Did He not know that they would not believe in Him? Yes: the Prophets had prohibited this very unbelief, and He came that it might be made manifest, to their confusion and condemnation; *That the saying of Esaias the prophet might be fulfilled, which He spake, Lord, who hath believed our report? and to whom hath the arm of the Lord been revealed?* ALCUIN. *Who,* i.e. so very few believed. AUG. It is evident here that the arm of the Lord is the Son of God Himself. Not that the Father has a human fleshly form; He is called the arm of the Lord, because all things were made by Him. If a man had power of such a kind, as that without any motion of his body, what he said was forthwith done, the word of that man would be his arm. Here is no ground to justify, however, the error of those who say that the Godhead is one Person only, because the Son is the arm of the Father, and a man and his arm are not two persons, but one. These men do not understand, that the commonest things require to be explained often by applying language to them taken from other things in which there happens to be a likeness, [^and that, when we are upon things incomprehensible, and which cannot be described as they actually are, this is much more necessary. Thus one man calls another man, whom he makes great use of, his arm; and talks of having lost his arm, of having his arm taken away from him.] But some mutter, and ask, What fault was it of the Jews, if it was necessary that the sayings of Esaias should be fulfilled? We answer, that God, foreseeing the future, predicted by the Prophet the unbelief of the Jews, but did not cause it. God does not compel men to sin, because He knows they will sin. He foreknows *their* sins, not His own. The Jews committed the sin, which He who knows all things foretold they would commit. CHRYS. *That the saying of Esaias might be fulfilled: that* here is expressive not of the cause, but of the

Chrys. Hom. lxviii. 1.

Chrys. Hom. lxviii. 2.

Aug. Tr. liii. 2.

Chrys. Hom. lxviii. 2.

---

[b] Refers to the last Chrysostom. [^c] Part in brackets not in Aqu.

event. They did not disbelieve because Esaias said they would; but because they would disbelieve, Esaias said they would. AUG. But what follows involved a deeper question: *Therefore they could not believe, because that Esaias said again, He hath blinded their eyes, and hardened their hearts, that they should not see with their eyes, nor understand with their heart, and be converted, and I should heal them. That they should not believe;* but if so, what sin is there in a man doing what he cannot help doing? And what is a graver point still, the cause is assigned to God; since He it is who blinded their eyes, and hardened their heart. This is not said to be the devil's doing, but God's. Yet if any ask why they could not believe, I answer, Because they would not. For as it is to the praise of the Divine will that God cannot deny Himself, so is it the fault of the human will that they could not believe. CHRYS. This is a common form of speech among ourselves. I cannot love such a man, meaning by this necessity only a vehement will. The Evangelist says *could not,* to shew that it was impossible that the Prophet should lie, not that it was impossible that they should believe. AUG. But the Prophet, you say, mentions another cause, not their will; viz. that God had *blinded their eyes, and hardened their heart.* But I answer, that they well deserved this. For God hardens and blinds a man, by forsaking and not supporting him; and this He may by a secret sentence, by an unjust one He cannot. CHRYS. For He does not leave us, except we wish Him, as He saith in Hosea, *Seeing thou hast forgotten the law of thy God, I will also forget thy children.* Whereby it is plain that we begin to forsake first, and are the cause of our own perdition. For as it is not the fault of the sun, that it hurts weak eyes, so neither is God to blame for punishing those who do not attend to His words. AUG. *And be converted, and I should heal them.* Is *not* to be understood here, from the beginning of the sentence—that they should not see with their eyes, nor understand with their hearts, nor be converted; conversion being the free gift of God? or[d], shall we suppose that a heavenly remedy is meant; whereby those who wished to establish their own

Aug.
Tr. liii.
5.

Chrys.
Hom.
lxviii. 2.

Aug.
Tr. liii.
5.

Chrys.
Hom.
lxviii.
Hos. 4,
6.

Aug.
Tr. liii.
11.

---

[d] without putting in the *not.*

righteousness, were so far deserted and blinded, as to stumble on the stumbling stone, till, with confusion of face, they humbled themselves, and sought not their own righteousness which puffeth up the proud, but God's righteousness, which justifieth the ungodly. For many of those who put Christ to death, were afterward troubled with a sense of their guilt; which led to their believing in Him. *These things said* c. 12. *Esaias, when he saw His glory, and spake of Him.* He saw Him not really, but figuratively, in prophetic vision. Be not deceived by those who say that the Father is invisible, the Son visible, making the Son a creature. For in the form of God, in which He is equal to the Father, the Son also is invisible; though He took upon Him the form of a servant, that He might be seen by men. Before His incarnation too, He made Himself visible at times to human eyes; but visible through the medium of created matter, not visible as He is. CHRYS. His glory means the vision of Him sitting Chrys. on His lofty throne: *I saw the Lord sitting upon a throne.* Hom. lxviii. 2. *Also I heard the voice of the Lord, saying, Whom shall I* Is. 6, 1. *send, and who will go for us?* ALCUIN. *Nevertheless, among the chief rulers also many believed on Him; but because of the Pharisees they did not confess Him, lest they should be put out of the synagogue. For they loved the praise of men more than the praise of God.* The praise of God is publicly to confess Christ: the praise of men is to glory in earthly things. AUG. As their faith grew, their love of human praise Aug. grew still more, and outstripped it. Tr. liii. 13.

44. Jesus cried and said, He that believeth on me, believeth not on me, but on him that sent me.

45. And he that seeth me seeth him that sent me.

46. I am come a light into the world, that whosoever believeth on me should not abide in darkness.

47. And if any man hear my words, and believe not, I judge him not: for I came not to judge the world, but to save the world.

48. He that rejecteth me, and receiveth not my words, hath one that judgeth him: the word that I have spoken, the same shall judge him in the last day.

49. For I have not spoken of myself; but the Father which sent me, he gave me a commandment, what I should say, and what I should speak.

50. And I know that His commandment is life ever-lasting: whatsoever I speak therefore, even as the Father said unto me, so I speak.

Chrys. Hom. lxviii. 1. CHRYS. Because the love of human praise prevented the chief rulers from believing, *Jesus cried and said, He that believeth on Me, believeth not on Me, but on Him that sent Me:* as if to say, Why are ye afraid to believe on Me? Your faith through Me passes to God. AUG. He signifies

Aug. Tr. liv. 2. to them that He is more than He appears to be, (for to men He appeared but a man; His Godhead was hid.) Such as the Father is, such am I in nature and in dignity; *He that believeth on Me, believeth not on Me,* i. e. on that which He

¹ not in A. sees, *but on Him that sent Me,* i. e. on the Father. [¹ He that believes in the Father must believe in Him as the Father, i. e. must believe that He has a Son; and reversely, he who believes in the Son thereby believes in the Father.] And again, if any one thinks that God has sons by grace, but not a Son equal and coeternal with Himself, neither does he

² on not in. believe ² on the Father, who sent the Son; because what he believes on is not the Father who sent Him. And to shew

c. 3. that He is not the Son, in the sense of one out of many, a son by grace, but the Only Son equal to the Father, He adds, *And He that seeth Me, seeth Him that sent Me;* so little difference is there between Me and Him that sent Me, that He that seeth Me, seeth Him. Our Lord sent His Apostles, yet none of them dared to say, He that believeth on Me. We believe an Apostle, but we do not believe on an Apostle. Whereas the Only Begotten says, *He that believeth on Me, doth not believe on Me, but on Him that sent Me.* Wherein He does not withdraw the believer's faith from Himself, but gives him a higher object than the form of a servant, for that

Chrys. Hom. lxix. 1. faith. CHRYS. *He that believeth on Me, believeth not on Me, but on Him that sent Me:* as if He said, He that taketh water from a stream, taketh the water not of the stream, but of the fountain. Then to shew that it is not possible to

believe on the Father, if we do not believe on Him, He
says, *He that seeth Me, seeth Him that sent Me.* What
then? Is God a body? By no means; *seeing* here is the
mind's vision. What follows still further shews His union
with the Father. *I am come a light into the world.* This is
what the Father is called in many places. He calls Himself
the light, because he delivers from error, and disperses the
darkness of the understanding; *that whosoever believeth in
Me should not abide in darkness.* Aug. Whereby it is Aug.
evident, that He found all in darkness. In which darkness ⁴ᵗʳ· ˡⁱᵛ·
if they wish not to remain, they must believe in the light
which is come into the world. He says in one place to His
disciples, *Ye are the light of the world;* but He did not
say to them, Ye are come a light into the world, that whosoever believeth on you should not abide in darkness. All
saints are lights, but they are so by faith, because they
are enlightened by Him, from Whom to withdraw is darkness.
CHRYS. And to shew that He does not let His despisers go Chrys.
unpunished, from want of power, He adds, *And if any man* Hom. lxix. 1.
hear My words and believe not, I judge him not. Aug. i. e. Aug.
I judge him not now. He does not say, I judge him not at Tr. liv. 5, 6.
the last day, for that would be contrary to the sentence
above, *The Father hath committed all judgment unto the* v. 22.
Son. And the reason follows, why He does not judge now;
For I came not to judge the world, but to save the world.
Now is the time of mercy, afterward will be the time of judgment. CHRYS. But that this might not serve to encourage Chrys.
sloth, He warns men of a terrible judgment coming; *He that* Hom. lxix. 2.
*rejecteth Me, and heareth not My words, hath one that
judgeth him.* Aug. Mean time they waited to know who Aug.
this one was; so He proceeds: *The word that I have spoken,* Tr. liv. 6.
the same shall judge him at the last day. He makes it
sufficiently clear that He Himself will judge at the last day.
For the word that He speaks, is Himself. He speaks Himself, announces Himself. We gather too from these words
that those who have not heard, will be judged differently
from those who have heard and despised. Aug. *I judge* Aug.
him not; the word that I have spoken shall judge him: for I de Trin. c. xii.
have not spoken of Myself. The word which the Son speaks (26.)
judges, because the Son did not speak of Himself: *for I*

2 E

have not spoken of Myself: i. e. I was not born of Myself.
AUG. [e] I ask then how we shall understand this, *I will not judge, but the word which I have spoken will judge?* Yet He Himself is the Word of the Father which speaketh. Is it thus? I will not judge by My human power, as the Son of man, but as the word of God, because I am the Son of God.

Chrys. CHRYS. Or, *I judge him not,* i. e. I am not the cause of his
Hom. destruction, but he is himself, by despising my words. The
lxviii. 2. words that I have just said, shall be his accusers, and deprive him of all excuse; *the word that I have spoken, the same shall judge him.* And what word? This, viz. that[f] *I have not spoken of Myself, but the Father which sent Me gave Me a commandment what I should say, and what I should speak.* All these things were said on their account, that they

Aug. might have no excuse. AUG. When the Father gave the
Tr. liv. Son a commandment, He did not give Him what He had
7. not: for in the Wisdom of the Father, i. e. in the Word, are all the commandments of the Father. The commandment is said to be given, because it is not from him to whom it is said to be given. But to give the Son that which He never was without, is the same as to beget the Son who never was not. THEOPHYL. Since the Son is the Word of the Father, and reveals completely what is in the mind of the Father, He says He receives a commandment what He should say, and what He should speak: just as our word, if we say what we think, brings out what is in our minds.

And I know that His commandment is life everlasting.
Aug. AUG. If life everlasting is the Son Himself, and the com-
Tr. liv. mandment is life everlasting, what is this but saying, I am the commandment of the Father? And in the same way in the following; *Whatsoever I speak therefore, even as the Father said unto Me, so I speak,* we must not understand, *said unto Me,* as if words were spoken to the Only Word.

[e] Augustine literally: That is, He has spoken from His Father. So the sentence will run thus. I shall not judge, but the Word of the Father shall judge. But the Word of the Father is the Son of God Himself: so the sentence will run, I shall not judge, but I shall judge. How can both of these be true? In this way. I shall not judge by virtue of any human praise, in that I am the Son of man, but I shall judge by virtue of the power of the Word, in that I am the Son of God.

[f] i. e. My having said so often that I have not, &c.

The Father spoke to the Son, as He gave life to the Son ; not that the Son knew not, or had not, but that He was the Son. What is meant by, *as He said unto Me, so I speak,* but that I am the Word who speaks. The Father is true, the Son is truth: the True, begat the Truth. What then could He say to the Truth, if the Truth was perfect from the beginning, and no new truth could be added to Him? That He spake to the Truth then, means that He begat the Truth.

CHAP. XIII.

1. Now before the feast of the passover, when Jesus knew that his hour was come that he should depart out of this world unto the Father, having loved his own which were in the world, he loved them unto the end.

2. And supper being ended, the devil having now put into the heart of Judas Iscariot, Simon's son, to betray him;

3. Jesus knowing that the Father had given all things into his hands, and that he was come from God, and went to God;

4. He riseth from supper, and laid aside his garments; and took a towel, and girded himself.

5. After that he poureth water into a bason, and began to wash the disciples' feet, and to wipe them with the towel wherewith he was girded.

THEOPHYL. Our Lord being about to depart out of this life, shews His great care for His disciples: *Now before the feast of the Passover, when Jesus knew that His hour was come that He should depart out of this world unto the Father, having loved His own which were in the world, He loved them unto the end.* BEDE. The Jews had many feasts, but the principal one was the passover; and therefore it is particularly said, *Before the feast of the passover.* AUG. Pascha is not a Greek word, as some think, but Hebrew: though there is remarkable agreement of the two languages in it. The Greek word to suffer being πασχεῖν, pascha has been thought to mean passion, as being derived from the above word. But in Hebrew, pascha is a passing over; the

feast deriving its name from the passing of the people of
God over the Red Sea into Egypt. All was now to take
place in reality, of which that passover was the type. Christ
was led as a lamb to the slaughter; whose blood sprinkled
upon our door-posts, i. e. whose sign of the cross marked on
our foreheads, delivers us from the dominion of this world,
as from Egyptian bondage. And we perform a most wholesome journey or pass-over, when we pass over from the devil
to Christ, from this unstable world to His sure kingdom.
In this way the Evangelist seems to interpret the word:
*When Jesus knew that His hour was come when He should
pass over*[1] *out of this world unto the Father.* This is the $^1μεταβῇ$,
pascha, this the passing over. CHRYS. He did not know $\begin{smallmatrix}\text{transeat}\\\text{V.}\end{smallmatrix}$
then for the first time : He had known long before. By His $\begin{smallmatrix}\text{Chrys.}\\\text{Hom.}\end{smallmatrix}$
departure He means His death. Being so near leaving His lxx. 1.
disciples, He shews the more love for them : *Having loved
His own which were in the world, He loved them unto the
end;* i. e. He left nothing undone which one who greatly
loved should do. He reserved this for the last, that their
love might be increased by it, and to prepare them by such
consolation for the trials that were coming. *His own* He
calls them, in the sense of intimacy. The word was used in
another sense in the beginning of the Gospel: *His own* c. 1, 11.
received Him not. It follows, *which were in the world :*
for those were dead who were *His own,* such as Abraham,
Isaac, and Jacob, who were not in the world. These then,
His own which were in the world, He loved all along, and
at the last manifested His love in completeness : *He loved
them unto the end.* AUG. *He loved them unto the end,* i. e. Aug.
that they themselves too might pass out of this world[a], by $\begin{smallmatrix}\text{Tr. lv.}\\\text{2.}\end{smallmatrix}$
love, unto Him their head. For what is *unto the end,* but
unto Christ? *For Christ is the end of the law for righteous-* Rom.
ness to every one that believeth. But these words may be $^{10,\,4.}$
understood after a human sort, to mean that Christ loved
His own up to His death. But God forbid that He should
end His love by death, who is not ended by death : except
indeed we understand it thus: *He loved His own unto death :*
i. e. His love for them led Him to death. *And supper having
been made,* i. e. having been got ready, and laid on the table

---

[a] Referring to, *that He should depart out of this world unto the Father.*

before them; not having been consumed and finished: for it was during supper that He rose, and washed His disciples' feet; as after this He sat at table again, and gave the sop to the traitor. What follows: *The devil having now put it into the heart of Judas Iscariot, Simon's son, to betray Him,* refers to a secret suggestion, not made to the ear, but to the mind; the suggestions of the devil being part of our own thoughts. Judas then had already conceived, through diabolical instigation, the intention of betraying his Master.

Chrys. Hom. lxx. 1. CHRYS. The Evangelist inserts this as if in astonishment: our Lord being about to wash the feet of the very person who had resolved to betray Him. It shews the great wickedness too of the traitor, that even the partaking of the same table, which is a check to the worst of men, did not stop him.

Aug. Tr. lv. 6. AUG. The Evangelist being about to relate so great an instance of our Lord's humility, reminds us first of His lofty nature: *knowing that the Father had given all things into His hand,* not excepting the traitor. GREG. He knew that He had even His persecutors in His hand that He might convert them from malice to love of Him. ORIGEN.

Orig. t. xxxiv. 3. *The Father hath given all things into His hands;* i. e. into His power; for His hands hold all things [b]: or to Him, for His work; *My Father worketh hitherto, and I work.*

John 5, 17.

Chrys. Hom. lxx. 1. CHRYS. *Had given all things into His hand.* What is given Him is the salvation of the believers. Think not of this giving up in a human way. It signifies His honour for, and agreement with, the Father. For as the Father hath given up all things to Him, so hath He given up all things to the

1 Cor. 15, 24. Father. *When He shall have delivered up the kingdom to God, even the Father.*

Aug. Tr. lv. 5. AUG. Knowing too, *that He was come from God, and went to God;* not that He left God when He came, or will leave us when He returns. THEOPHYL. The Father having given up all things into His hands, i. e. having given up to Him the salvation of the faithful, He deemed it right to shew them all things that pertained to their salvation; and gave them a lesson of humility, by washing His disciples' feet. Though knowing *that He was from God, and went to God,* He thought it in no way took from His glory, to wash His disciples' feet; thus proving

---

[b] He must reign till He hath put all enemies under His feet. 1 Cor. 15, 27.

that He did not usurp His greatness. For usurpers do not
condescend, for fear of losing what they have irregularly got.
AUG. Since *the Father had given all things into His hands,* Aug.
He washed not His disciples' hands indeed, but their feet ; Tr.lv.6.
and since He knew that *He came from God, and went to
God,* He performed the work not of God and Lord, but of a
man and servant. CHRYS. It was a thing worthy of Him, Chrys.
Who *came from God, and went to God,* to trample upon all Hom.
pride; *He riseth from supper, and laid aside His garment,* lxx. 1.
*and took a towel, and girded Himself. After that He
poureth water into a bason, and began to wash His disciples'
feet, and to wipe them with the towel wherewith He was
girded.* See what humility He shews, not only in washing c. 2.
their feet, but in other things. For it was not before, but
after they had sat down, that He rose; and He not only
washed them, but laid aside His garments, and girded Himself with a towel, and filled a bason; He did not order others
to do all this, but did it Himself, teaching us that we should
be willing and ready to do such things. ORIGEN. Mys- Orig.
tically, dinner is the first meal, taken early in the spiritual t. xxxii.
day, and adapted to those who have just entered upon 2.
this day. Supper is the last meal, and is set before those
who are farther advanced. According to another sense,
dinner‧ is the understanding of the Old Testament, the
supper the understanding the mysteries hid in the New.
Yet even they who sup with Jesus, who partake of the final
meal, need a certain washing, not indeed of the top parts of
their body, i. e. the soul, but its lower parts and extremities,
which cleave necessarily to earth. It is, *And began to wash;* c. 4.
for He did not finish His washing till afterwards. The feet
of the Apostles were defiled now: *All of ye shall be offended* Matt.
because of Me this night. But afterwards He cleansed them, 26, 31.
so that they needed no more cleansing. AUG. He *laid* Aug.
aside His garments, when, being in the form of God, He Tr.lv.7.
emptied Himself; He *girded Himself with a towel,* took
upon Him the form of a servant; He *poured water into a
bason,* out of which He washed His disciples' feet. He
shed His blood on the earth, with which He washed
away the filth of their sins; *He wiped them with the towel
wherewith He was girded;* with the flesh wherewith He was

clothed, He established the steps of the Evangelists; He laid aside His garments, to gird Himself with the towel; that He might take upon Him the form of a servant, He emptied Himself, not laying aside indeed what He had, but assuming what He had not. Before He was crucified, He was stripped of His garments, and when dead was wound up in linen[a] clothes: the whole of His passion is our cleansing.

6. Then cometh he to Simon Peter: and Peter said unto him, Lord, dost thou wash my feet?

7. Jesus answered and said unto him, What I do thou knowest not now; but thou shalt know hereafter.

8. Peter saith unto him, Thou shalt never wash my feet. Jesus answered him, If I wash thee not, thou hast no part with me.

9. Simon Peter saith unto him, Lord, not my feet only, but also my hands and my head.

10. Jesus saith to him, He that is washed needeth not save to wash his feet, but is clean every whit: and ye are clean, but not all.

11. For he knew who should betray him; therefore said he, Ye are not all clean.

Orig. t. xxxii. ORIGEN. As a physician, who has many sick under his care, begins with those who want his attention most; so Christ, in washing His disciples' feet, begins with the most unclean, and so comes at last to Peter, who needed the washing less than any: *Then cometh He to Simon Peter.* Peter resisted being washed, perhaps because his feet were nearly clean: *And Peter said unto Him, Lord, dost Thou wash my feet?* AUG. What is the meaning of *Thou* and *my feet?* It is better to think than speak of this; lest one should fail in explaining adequately what might have been rightly conceived. CHRYS. Though Peter was the first of the Apostles, yet it is possible that the traitor petulantly placed himself above him; and that this may be the reason, why our Lord first *began to wash,* and then *cometh to Peter.*

Aug. Tr.lvi.1.

Chrys. Hom. lxx. 2.

[a] *ἀθονίοις.* Vulgate translates *linteis,* the same as for towel here.

THEOPHYL. It is plain that our Lord did not wash Peter first, but none other of the disciples would have attempted to be washed before him. CHRYS. Some one will ask why none of them prevented Him, except Peter, this being a sign not of want of love, but of reverence. The reason seems to be, that He washed the traitor first, and came next to Peter, and that the other disciples were checked by the reply to Peter. Any of the rest would have said what Peter did, had his turn come first. ORIGEN. Or thus: All the rest put out their feet, certain that so great a one would not want to wash them without reason: but Peter, looking only to the thing itself, and seeing nothing beyond it, refused out of reverence to let his feet be washed. He often appears in Scripture as hasty in putting forth his own ideas of what is right and expedient. AUG. Or thus: We must not suppose that Peter was afraid and refused, when the others had willingly and gladly submitted to the washing. Our Lord did not go through the others first, and to the first of the Apostles afterwards; (for who is ignorant that the most blessed Peter was the first of all the Apostles?) but began with him: and Peter being the first to whom He came, was afraid; as indeed any of the others would have been.

Jesus answered and said unto him, What I do thou knowest not now; but thou shalt know hereafter. CHRYS. i. e. How useful a lesson of humility it teaches thee, and how directly this virtue leads to God. ORIGEN. Or our Lord insinuates that this is a mystery. By washing and wiping, He made beautiful the feet of those who were to preach glad tidings, and to walk on that way of which He tells them, *I am the way.* Jesus laid aside His garments that He might make their clean feet still cleaner, or that He might receive the uncleanness of their feet unto His own body, by the towel with which alone He was girded: for *He hath borne our griefs.* Observe too, He chose for washing His disciples' feet the very time that the devil had put it into the heart of Judas to betray Him, and the dispensation for mankind was about to take place. Before this the time was not come for washing their feet. And who would have washed their feet in the interval between this and the Passion? During the Passion, there was no other Jesus to do it. And after it the

Marginal notes: Chrys. Hom. lxx. 2. — Orig. t. xxxii. 5. — Chrys. Hom. lxx. 2. — Orig. t. xxxii. — Is. 52, 7. — infr. 14, 6.

Holy Ghost came upon them, by which time they should already have had their feet washed. This mystery, our Lord says to Peter, is too great for thee to understand now, but thou shalt know it hereafter when thou art enlightened.

Aug.
Tr.lvi.2. AUG. He did not refuse, because our Lord's act was above his understanding, but he could not bear to see Him bending at his feet: *Peter saith unto Him, Thou shalt not wash my feet for ever;* i. e. I will never suffer it: not for ever is the

Orig.
t. xxxii.
5. same as never. ORIGEN. This is an instance, that a man may say a thing with a good intention, and yet ignorantly to His hurt. Peter, ignorant of our Lord's deep meaning, at first, as if in doubt, says mildly, *Lord, dost Thou wash my feet?* and then, *Thou shalt never wash my feet;* which was in reality to cut himself off from having a part with Jesus. Whence he not only blames our Lord for washing the disciples' feet, but also his fellow-disciples for giving their

c. 6. feet to be washed. As Peter then did not see his own good, our Lord did not allow His wish to be fulfilled: *Jesus answered and said unto him, If I wash thee not, thou*

Aug.
Tr.lvi.2. *hast no part with Me.* AUG. *If I wash thee not,* He says, though it was only his feet that He was going to wash, just as we say, Thou treadest on me; though it is only our foot that is trodden on. ORIGEN. Let those who refuse to allegorize these and like passages, say how it is probable that he who out of reverence for Jesus said, *Thou shalt never wash my feet,* would have had no part with the Son of God; as if not having his feet washed was a deadly wickedness. Wherefore it is our feet, i. e. the affections of our mind, that are to be given up to Jesus to be washed, that our feet may be beautiful; especially if we emulate higher gifts, and wish to be numbered with those who preach glad tidings.

Chrys.
Hom.
lxx. 2. CHRYS. He does not say on what account He performs this act of washing, but only threatens him. For Peter was not persuaded by the first answer: *Thou shalt know hereafter :* he did not say, Teach me then that I may submit. But when he was threatened with separation from Christ, then he sub-

Orig.
t. xxxii.
6. mitted. ORIGEN. This saying we may use against those who make hasty and indiscreet resolutions. By shewing them, that if they adhere to these, they will have no part with Jesus, we disengage them from such resolves; even though they

may have bound themselves by oath. AUG. But he, agitated Aug.
by fear and love, dreaded more the being denied Christ, than Tr.lvi.2.
the seeing Him at His feet: *Simon Peter saith unto Him,*
Lord, not my feet only, but also my hands and my head.
ORIGEN. Jesus was unwilling to wash hands, and despised·
what was said of Him in this respect: *Thy disciples wash* Matt.
not their hands when they eat bread. And He did not wish 15, 2.
the head to be submerged, in which was apparent the image
and glory of the Father; it was enough for Him that the feet
were given Him to wash: *Jesus answered and said, He that*
is washed needeth not save to wash his feet, but is clean
every whit: and ye are clean, but not all. AUG. Clean all Aug.
except the feet. The whole of a man is washed in baptism, Tr.lvi.4.
not excepting his feet; but living in the world afterwards,
we tread upon the earth. Those human affections then,
without which we cannot live in this world, are, as it were,
our feet, which connect us with human things, so that *if we* 1 John
say we have no sin, we deceive ourselves. But if we confess 1, 8.
our sins, He who washed the disciples' feet, forgives us our
sins even down to our feet, wherewith we hold our converse
with earth. ORIGEN. It was impossible that the lowest Orig.
parts and extremities of a soul should escape defilement, t. xxxii.
even in one perfect as far as man can be; and many, even
after baptism, are covered up to their head with the dust of
wickedness; but the real disciples of Christ only need washing for their feet. AUG. From what is here said, we under- Aug.
stand that Peter was already baptized. Indeed that He Ad. Se-
baptized by His disciples, shews that His disciples must leuc.Ep.
have been baptized, either with John's baptism, or, which c. viii.
is more probable, Christ's. He baptized by means of baptized
servants; for He did not refuse the ministry of baptizing,
Who had the humility to wash feet. AUG. *And ye are clean,* Aug.
but not all: what this means the Evangelist immediately Tr. lviii.
explains: *For He knew who should betray Him; therefore* 1.
said He, Ye are not all clean. ORIGEN. *Ye are clean,* refers Orig.
to the eleven; *but not all,* to Judas. He was unclean, first, t. xxxii.
because he cared not for the poor, but was a thief; secondly, 6.
because the devil had put it into his heart to betray Christ.
Christ washes their feet after they are clean, shewing that

Apoc.
22, 11.
Aug.
Tr.lvi.4.
grace goes beyond necessity, according to the text, *He that is holy, let him be holy still.* AUG. Or, the disciples when washed had only to have their feet washed; because while man lives in this world, he contracts himself with earth, by means of his human affections, which are as it were his feet.

Chrys.
Hom.
lxx. 2.
CHRYS. Or thus: When He calls them clean, you must not suppose that they were delivered from sin before the victim was offered. He means cleanness in respect of knowledge; for they were now delivered from Jewish error.

12. So after he had washed their feet, and had taken his garments, and was set down again, he said unto them, Know ye what I have done to you?

13. Ye call me Master and Lord: and ye say well; for so I am.

14. If I then, your Lord and Master, have washed your feet; ye also ought to wash one another's feet.

15. For I have given you an example, that ye should do as I have done to you.

16. Verily, verily, I say unto you, The servant is not greater than his lord: neither he that is sent greater than he that sent him.

17. If ye know these things, happy are ye if ye do them.

18. I speak not of you all: I know whom I have chosen: but that the Scripture may be fulfilled, He that eateth bread with me hath lifted up his heel against me.

19. Now I tell you before it come, that, when it is come to pass, ye may believe that I am he.

20. Verily, verily, I say unto you, He that receiveth whomsoever I send receiveth me; and he that receiveth me receiveth him that sent me.

Aug.
Tr.lviii.
2.
AUG. Our Lord, mindful of His promise to Peter that he should know the meaning of His act, *Thou shalt know here-*

after, now begins to teach him: *So after He had washed their feet, and had taken His garments, and was sat down again, He said unto them, Know ye what I have done to you?* ORIGEN. Know ye, is either interrogative, to shew the great-ness of the act, or imperative, to rouse their minds. ALCUIN. Mystically, when at our redemption we were changed by the shedding of His blood, He took again His garments, rising from the grave the third day, and clothed in the same body now immortal, ascended into heaven, and sitteth on the right hand of the Father, from whence He shall come to judge the world. CHRYS. He speaks now not to Peter alone, but to all: *Ye call Me Master and Lord.* He accepts their judgment; and to prevent the words being set down merely to favour on their parts, adds, *And ye say well, for so I am.* AUG. It is enjoined in the Proverbs, *Let another man praise thee, and not thine own mouth.* For it is dangerous for one to praise himself, who has to beware of pride. But He who is above all things, howsoever He praise Himself, extolleth not Himself too highly. Nor can God be called arrogant: for that we should know Him is no gain to Him, but to us. Nor can any one know Him, unless He who knows, shews Himself. So that if to avoid arrogance He did not praise Himself, He would be denying us wisdom. But why should the Truth fear arrogance? To His calling Himself Master, no one could object, even were He man only, since professors in different arts call themselves so without presumption. But what free man can bear the title of lord in a man? Yet when God speaks, height cannot exalt itself, truth cannot lie; it is for us to submit to that height, to obey that truth. Wherefore ye say well in that ye call Me Master and Lord, for so I am; but if I were not what ye say, ye would say ill. ORIGEN. They do not say well, Lord, to whom it shall be said, *Depart from Me, ye that work iniquity.* But the Apostles say well, Master and Lord, for wickedness had not dominion over them, but the Word of God.

If then I your Lord and Master have washed your feet, ye also ought to wash one another's feet. CHRYS. He shews us the greater, that we may do the less. For He was the Lord, but we, if we do it, do it to our fellow-servants: *For I*

Margin notes:
Orig. t. xxxii. 7.

Chrys. Hom. lxxi. 1.

Aug. Tr. lviii. 3.
Prov. 22, 2.

Orig. t. xxxii. 7.
Matt. 7, 23.

Chrys. Hom. lxx. 1.

have given you an example, that ye should do as I have done to you. BEDE. Our Lord first did a thing, then taught it: as it is said, *Jesus began both to do and to teach.* AUG. This is, blessed Peter, what thou wast ignorant of; this thou wert told that thou shouldest know afterwards. ORIGEN. But it is not necessary for one who wishes to do all the commandments of Jesus, literally to perform the act of washing feet. This is merely a matter of custom; and the custom is now generally dropped. AUG. This act is done literally by many[1], when they receive one another in hospitality. For it is unquestionably better that it should be done with the hands, and that the Christian disdain not to do what Christ did. For when the body is bent at the feet of a brother, the feeling of humility is made to rise in the heart, or, if it be there already, is confirmed. But besides this moral meaning, is not a brother able to change a brother from the pollution of sin? Let us confess our faults one to another, forgive one another's faults, pray for one another's faults. In this way we shall wash one another's feet. ORIGEN. Or thus: This spiritual washing of the feet is done primarily by Jesus Himself, secondarily by His disciples, in that He said to them, *Ye ought to wash one another's feet.* Jesus washed the feet of His disciples as their Master, of His servants as their Lord. But the object of the master is to make His disciples as Himself; and our Saviour beyond all other masters and lords, wished His disciples to be as their Master and Lord, not having the spirit of bondage, but the spirit of adoption, whereby they cry, *Abba, Father.* So then before they become masters and lords, they need the washing of the feet, being as yet insufficient disciples, and savouring of the spirit of bondage. But when they have attained to the state of master and lord, they then are able to imitate their Master, and to wash the disciples' feet by their doctrine. CHRYS. He continues to urge them to wash one another's feet; *Verily, verily, I say unto you, The servant is not greater than his lord, neither He that is sent greater than He that sent Him;* as if to say, If I do it, much more ought you. THEOPHYL. This was a necessary admonition to the Apostles, some of whom were about to rise

Acts 1, 1.

Aug.
Tr. lviii.
4.

Orig.
t. xxxii.
c. 7.

Aug.
Tr. lviii.
4.

[1] pleros-
que

Orig.
t. xxxii.
7.

Rom. 8,
19.

Chrys.
Hom.
lxxi. 2.

higher, others to lower degrees of eminence. That none
might exult over another, He changes the hearts of all.
BEDE. To know what is good, and not to do it, tendeth not
to happiness, but to condemnation; as James saith, *To him* James
that knoweth to do good, and doeth it not, to him it is sin. 4, 17.
Wherefore He adds, *If ye know these things, happy are ye
if yo do them.* CHRYS. For all know, but all do not do. Chrys.
He then rebukes the traitor, not openly, but covertly: *I speak* Hom.
not of you all. AUG. As if to say, There is one among you Aug.
who will not be blessed, nor doeth these things. *I know* Tr.lix.1.
whom I have chosen. Whom, but those who shall be happy
by doing His commandments? Judas therefore was not
chosen. But if so, why does He say in another place, *Have
not I chosen you twelve?* Because Judas was chosen for
that for which he was necessary, but not for that happiness
of which He says, *Happy are ye, if ye do them.* ORIGEN. Orig.
Or thus: *I speak not of you all,* does not refer to, *Happy* t.xxxii.
are ye if ye do them. For of Judas, or any other person, it
may be said, Happy is he if he do them. The words refer
to the sentence above, *The servant is not greater than his
lord, neither He that is sent greater than He that sent Him.*
For Judas, being a servant of sin, was not a servant of the
Divine Word; nor an Apostle, when the devil had entered
into him. Our Lord knew those who were His, and did not
know who were not His, and therefore says, not, I know all
present, but, *I know whom 1 have chosen,* i. e. I know My
Elect. CHRYS. Then, that He might not sadden them all, He Chrys.
adds, *But that the Scripture must be fulfilled, He that eateth* Hom.
bread with Me, hath lifted up his heel against Me: shewing
that He knew who the traitor was, an intimation that would
surely have checked him, if any thing would. He does not
say, shall betray Me, but, *shall lift up his heel against Me,*
alluding to his deceit and secret plotting. AUG. *Shall lift* Aug.
up his heel against Me, i. e. shall tread upon Me. The Tr.lix.1.
traitor Judas is meant. CHRYS. *He that eateth bread with* Chrys.
Me; i. e. who was fed by Me, who partook of My table. Hom.
So that if injured ever by our servants or inferiors, we need lxxi. 2.
not be offended. Judas had received infinite benefits, and
yet thus requited his Benefactor. AUG. They then who Aug.
were chosen ate the Lord; he ate the bread of the Lord, to Tr.lix.1.

1 Cor.
11, 27. injure the Lord; they ate life, he damnation; for *he that
eateth unworthily, eateth damnation to himself.*

*Now I tell you before it come, that when it is come, ye
may believe that I am He,* i. e. of whom that Scripture fore-
Orig.
t. xxxii.
9. told. ORIGEN. *That ye may believe,* is not said, as if the
Apostles did not believe already, but is equivalent to saying,
Do as ye believe, and persevere in your belief, seeking for
no occasion of falling away. For besides the evidences the
disciples had already seen, they had now that of the fulfil-
Chrys.
Hom.
lxxii. 3. ment of prophecy. CHRYS. As the disciples were about to
go forth and to suffer many things, He consoles them by
promising His own assistance and that of others; His own,
when He says, *Happy are ye if ye do them;* that of others,
in what follows, *Verily, verily, I say unto you, He that
receiveth whomsoever I send, receiveth Me; and he that
Orig.
t. xxxii.
10. receiveth Me receiveth Him that sent Me.* ORIGEN. For he
that receiveth him whom Jesus sends, receiveth Jesus who is
represented by him; and he that receiveth Jesus, receiveth
the Father. Therefore he that receiveth whom Jesus sends,
receiveth the Father that sent. The words may have this
meaning too: He that receiveth whom I send, had attained
unto receiving Me: he who receiveth Me not by means of
any Apostle, but by My own entrance into his soul, receiveth
the Father; so that not only I abide in him, but the Father
Aug.
Tr. xlix.
2. also. AUG. The Arians, when they hear this passage,
appeal immediately to the gradations in their system, that as
far as the Apostle is from the Lord, so far is the Son from
the Father. But our Lord hath left us no room for doubt on
supr. 10,
30. this head; for He saith, *I and My Father are one.* But
how shall we understand those words of our Lord, *He that
receiveth Me, receiveth Him that sent Me?* If we take
them to mean that the Father and the Son are of one nature,
it will seem to follow, when He says, *He that receiveth
whomsoever I send, receiveth Me,* that the Son and an
Apostle are of one nature. May not the meaning be, *He
that receiveth whosoever I send, receiveth Me,* i. e. Me as
man: But *He that receiveth Me,* i. e. as God, *receiveth Him
that sent Me.* But it is not this unity of nature, which is here
put forth, but the authority of the Sender, as represented by
Him who is sent. In Peter hear Christ, the Master of the

disciple, in the Son the Father, the Begotten of the Only Begotten.

21. When Jesus had thus said, he was troubled in spirit, and testified, and said, Verily, verily, I say unto you, that one of you shall betray me.

22. Then the disciples looked one on another, doubting of whom he spake.

23. Now there was leaning on Jesus' bosom one of his disciples, whom Jesus loved.

24. Simon Peter therefore beckoned to him, that he should ask who it should be of whom he spake.

25. He then lying on Jesus' breast saith unto him, Lord, who is it?

26. Jesus answered, He it is, to whom I shall give a sop, when I have dipped it. And when he had dipped the sop, he gave it to Judas Iscariot, the son of Simon.

27. And after the sop Satan entered into him. Then said Jesus unto him, That thou doest, do quickly.

28. Now no man at the table knew for what intent he spake this unto him.

29. For some of them thought, because Judas had the bag, that Jesus had said unto him, Buy those things that we have need of against the feast; or, that he should give something to the poor.

30. He then having received the sop went immediately out: and it was night.

CHRYS. Our Lord after His twofold promise of assistance to the Apostles in their future labours, remembers that the traitor is cut off from both, and is troubled at the thought: *When Jesus had thus said, He was troubled in spirit, and testified, and said, Verily, verily, I say unto you, that one of you shall betray Me.* AUG. This did not come into His mind then for the first time; but He was now about to make

Chrys. Hom. lxii. 1.

Aug. Tr. lx. 1.

2 F

the traitor known, and single him out from the rest, and therefore was troubled in spirit. The traitor too was now just about to go forth to execute his purpose. He was troubled at the thought of His Passion being so near at hand, at the dangers to which His faithful followers would be brought at the hand of the traitor, which were even now impending over Him. Our Lord deigned to be troubled also, to shew that false brethren cannot be cut off, even in the most urgent necessity, without the troubling of the Church. He was troubled not in flesh, but in spirit; for on occasion of scandals of this kind, the spirit is troubled, not perversely, but in love, lest in separating the tares, some of the wheat too be plucked up with them. But whether He was troubled by pity for perishing Judas, or, by the near approach of His own death, He was troubled not through weakness of mind, but power: He was not troubled because any thing compelled Him, but He troubled Himself, as was said above. And in that He was troubled, He consoles the weak members of His body, i. e. His Church, that they may not think themselves reprobate, should they be troubled at the approach of death. ORIGEN. His being troubled in spirit, was the human part, suffering under the [1]excess of the spiritual. For if every Saint lives, acts, and suffers in the spirit, how much more is this true of Jesus, the Rewarder of Saints. AUG. Away then with the reasonings of the Stoics, who deny that perturbation of mind can come upon a wise man; who, as they take vanity for truth, so make their healthy state of mind insensibility. It is good that the mind of the Christian may be perturbed, not by misery, but by pity. *One of you*, He saith, i. e. one in respect of number, not of merit, in appearance[1] not in virtue. CHRYS. As He did not mention Him by name, all began to fear: *Then the disciples looked one on another, doubting of whom He spake;* not conscious of any evil in themselves, and yet trusting to Christ's words, more than to their own thoughts. AUG. They had a devoted love for their Master, but yet so that human weakness made them doubt of one another[2].

ORIGEN. They remembered too, that, as men, before they were matured, their minds were liable to change, so as to

Tr.lxi. 1.

Tr.lx.5.

Orig. t. xxxii. 11.
[1] ab exuberantiâ spiritus.
Aug. Tr.lx.3.

lxi. 2.
[1] specie non virtute
Chrys. Hom. lxxii. 1.

Aug. Tr. lxi. 3.
[2] alterum de altero stimularet.
Orig. t. xxxii. 12.

form wishes the very opposite to what they might have had before. CHRYS. While all were trembling, and not excepting even Peter, their head, John, as the beloved disciple, lay upon Jesus' breast. *He then lying on Jesus' breast saith unto Him, Lord, who is it?* AUG. This is John, whose Gospel this is, as he afterwards declares. It is the custom of the sacred writers, when they come to any thing relating to themselves, to speak of themselves, as if they were speaking of another. For if the thing itself is related correctly, what does truth lose by the omission of boasting on the writer's part? CHRYS. If thou want to know the cause of this familiarity, it is love: *Whom Jesus loved.* Others were loved, but he was loved more than any. ORIGEN. I think this has a peculiar meaning, viz. that John was admitted to a knowledge of the more secret mysteries of the Word. CHRYS. *Whom Jesus loved.* This John says to shew his own innocence, and also why it was that Peter beckoned to him, inasmuch as he was not Peter's superior: *Simon Peter therefore beckoned to him, that he should ask who it should be of whom he spake.* Peter had been just reproved, and therefore, checking the customary vehemence of his love, he did not speak himself now, but made John speak for him. He always appears in Scripture as zealous, and an intimate friend of John's. AUG. Observe too his mode of speaking, which was not by word, but by beckoning; *Beckoned and spake,* i. e. spake by beckoning. If even thoughts speak, as when it is said, *They spake among themselves,* much more may beckonings, which are a kind of outward expression of our thoughts. ORIGEN. Or, at first he beckoned, and then not content with beckoning, spake: *Who is it of whom he speaks?*

He then lying on Jesus' breast, saith unto Him, Lord, who is it? AUG. *On Jesus' breast;* the same as *in Jesus' bosom.* Or, he lay first in Jesus' bosom, and then ascended higher, and lay upon His breast; as if, had he remained lying in His bosom, and not ascended to lie on His breast, our Lord would not have told him what Peter wanted to know. By his lying at last on Jesus' breast, is expressed that greater and more abundant grace, which made him Jesus' special disciple. BEDE. That he lay in the bosom,

Aug.
Tr. lxii.
4.

Chrys.
Hom.
lxxii. 1.

Orig.
t. xxxii.
13.

Chrys.
Hom.
lxxii. 1.

Aug.
Tr. lxi.
13.

Orig.
t. xxxii.
13.

Aug.
Tr. lx.
4.

and upon the breast, was not only an evidence of present
love, but also a sign of the future, viz. of those new
and mysterious doctrines which he was afterwards com-
missioned to reveal to the world. AUG. For by *bosom* what
else is signified but secret? Here is the hollow of the
breast, the secret[1] chamber of wisdom. CHRYS. But not
even then did our Lord expose the traitor by name; *Jesus
answered, He it is, to whom I shall give a sop when I have
dipped it.* Such a mode of declaring him, should itself
have turned him from his purpose. Even if a partaking
of the same table did not shame him, a partaking of the
same bread might have. *And when He had dipped the sop,
He gave it to Judas Iscariot, the son of Simon.* AUG. Not as
some careless readers think, that then Judas received singly
Christ's body. For our Lord had already distributed the
sacraments of His body and blood to all of them, while
Judas was there, as Luke relates; and after this He dipped the
sop, as John relates, and gave it to the traitor; the dipping
of the bread perhaps signifying the deep dye of his sin; for
some dipping cannot be washed out again; i. e. when things
are dipped, in order to receive a permanent dye. If however
this dipping meant any thing good, he was ungrateful for it,
and deserved the damnation which followed him; *And after
the sop, Satan entered into him.* ORIGEN. Observe, that at
first Satan did not enter into Judas, but only put it into his
heart to betray his Master. But after the bread, he entered
into him. Wherefore let us beware, that Satan thrust not
any of his flaming darts into our heart; for if he do, he then
watches till he gets an entrance there himself. CHRYS. So
long as he was one of the twelve, the devil did not dare to
force an entrance into him; but when he was pointed out, and
expelled, then he easily leaped into him. AUG. Or entered
into him, that he might have more full possession of him:
for he was in him, when he agreed with the Jews to betray
our Lord for a sum of money, according to Luke: *Then
entered Satan into Judas Iscariot, and he went away,
and communed with the chief priests.* In this state
he came to the supper. But after the sop the devil
entered, not to tempt him, as though he were independent, but to possess him as his own. ORIGEN. It was

non occ.

Aug.
Tr. lxi.
6.

[1] secre-
tum
Chrys.
Hom.
lxxii. 1.

Aug.
Tr. lxii.
3.

Orig.
t. xxxii.
14.

Chrys.
Hom.
lxii. 1.

Aug.
Tr. lxii.
2.

Luke 22,
3. 4.

Orig.
t. xxxii.
14.

proper that by the ceremony of the bread, that good should
be taken from him, which he thought he had: whereof being
deprived, he was laid open to admit Satan's entrance. AUG.
But some will say, was his being given up to the devil the
effect of his receiving the sop from Christ? To whom we
answer, that they may learn here the danger of receiving
amiss what is in itself good. If he is reproved who does not
discern, i. e. who does not distinguish, the Lord's body from
other food, how is he condemned who, feigning himself a
friend, comes an enemy to the Lord's table?

Then said Jesus unto him, That thou doest, do quickly.
ORIGEN. This may have been said either to Judas, or to
Satan, either to provoke the enemy to the combat, or the
traitor to do his part in bringing on that dispensation, which
was to save the world; which He wished not to be delayed
any longer, but to be as soon as possible matured. AUG.
He did not however enjoin the act, but foretold it, not from
desire for the destruction of the perfidious, but to hasten on
the salvation of the faithful. CHRYS. *That thou doest, do
quickly,* is not a command, or a recommendation, but a reproof, meant to shew too that He was not going to offer any
hindrance to His betrayal. *Now no man at the table knew
for what intent He spake this unto him.* It is not easy to
see, when the disciples had asked, *Who is he,* and He had
replied, *He it is to whom I shall give a sop,* how it was that
they did not understand Him; unless it was that He spoke
too low to be heard; and that John lay upon His breast,
when he asked the question, for that very reason, i. e. that
the traitor might not be made known. For had Christ
made him known, perhaps Peter would have killed him. So
it was then, that none at the table knew what our Lord
meant. But why not John? Because he could not conceive
how a disciple could fall into such wickedness: he was far
from such wickedness himself, and therefore did not suspect
it of others. What they thought He meant we are told in
what follows: *For some of them thought, because Judas had
the bag, that Jesus had said unto him, Buy those things that
we have need of against the feast, or, that he should give something to the poor.* AUG. Our Lord then had bags, in which
He kept the oblations of the faithful, to supply the wants of

Margin notes: Aug. Tr. lxii. — Orig. t. xxxii. 15. — Aug. Tr. lxii. 4. — Chrys. Hom. lxxii. 2. — Aug. Tr. lxii. 5.

His own followers, or the poor.   Here is the first institution
of ecclesiastical property.   Our Lord shews that His commandment not to think of the morrow, does not mean that
the Saints should never save money; but that they should not
neglect the service of God for it, or let the fear of want
tempt them to injustice.   CHRYS. None of the disciples contributed this money, but it is hinted that it was certain
women, who, it is said, ministered to Him of their means.
But how was it that He Who forbad scrip, and staff, and
money, carried bags for the relief of the poor?   It was to
shew thee, that even the very poor, those who are crucified
to this world, ought to attend to this duty.   He did many
things in order to instruct us in our duty.   ORIGEN. Our
Lord then said to Judas, *That thou doest, do quickly,* and the
traitor this once obeyed his Master.   For having received
the sop, he started immediately on his work: *He then having
received the sop, went immediately out.*   And indeed he did
go out, not only from the house in which he was, but from
Jesus altogether.   It would seem that Satan, after he had
entered into Judas, could not bear to be in the same place
with Jesus: for there is no agreement between Jesus and
Satan.   Nor is it idle enquiring why after he had *received
the sop,* it is not added, that he ate it.   Why did not Judas
eat the bread, after he received it?   Perhaps because, as
soon as he had received it, the devil, who had put it into his
heart to betray Christ, fearful that the bread, if eaten, might
drive out what he had put in, entered into him, so that he
went out immediately, before he ate it.   And it may be
serviceable to remark, that as he who eateth our Lord's bread
and drinketh His cup unworthily, eateth and drinketh to his
own damnation; so the bread which Jesus gave him was
eaten by the rest to their salvation, but by Judas to his
damnation, inasmuch as after it the devil entered into him.
CHRYS. It follows: *And it was night,* to shew the impetuosity
of Judas, in persisting in spite of the unseasonableness of the
hour.   ORIGEN. The time of night corresponded with the night
which overspread the soul of Judas.   GREG. By the time of
the day is signified the end of the action.   Judas went out
in the night to accomplish his perfidy, for which he was never
to be pardoned.

Chrys.
Hom.
lxxii. 2.

Orig.
t. xxxii.
16.

Chrys.
Hom.
lxxii. 2.
Orig.
t. xxxii.
16.
Greg.
ii. Mor.
11.

31. Therefore, when he was gone out, Jesus said, Now is the Son of man glorified, and God is glorified in him.

32. If God be glorified in him, God shall also glorify him in himself, and shall straightway glorify him.

ORIGEN. After the glory of His miracles, and His trans- Orig. figuration, the next glorifying of the Son of man began, t. xxxii. 17. when Judas went out with Satan, who had entered into him; *Therefore when he was gone out, Jesus said, Now is the Son of man glorified, and God is glorified in Him.* For it is not the eternal only-begotten Word, but the glory of the Man born of the seed of David, which is here meant. Christ at His death, in which He glorified God, *having spoiled prin-* Colos. *cipalities and powers, made a shew of them, openly triumph-* 2, 15. *ing over them.* And again, *Made peace by the blood of His* Colos. *cross, to reconcile all things unto Himself, whether they be* 1, 20. *things in earth, or things in heaven.* Thus the Son of man was glorified, and *God glorified in Him;* for Christ cannot be glorified, except the Father be glorified with Him. But whoever is glorified, is glorified by some one. By whom then is the Son of man glorified? He tells you; *If God be glorified in Him, God shall also glorify Him in Himself, and shall straightway glorify Him.* CHRYS. i. e. by Him- Chrys. self, not by any other. *And shall straightway glorify Him,* Hom. lxxii. 2. i. e. not at any distant time, but immediately, while He is yet on the very cross shall His glory appear. For the sun was darkened, rocks were rent, and many bodies of those that slept arose. In this way He restores the drooping spirits of His disciples, and persuades them, instead of sorrowing, to rejoice. AUG. Or thus: The unclean went Aug. out: the clean remained with their cleanser. Thus will it Tr.lxiii. 2. be when the tares are separated from the wheat; *The righ-* Matt. *teous shall shine forth as the sun in the kingdom of their* 13, 43. *Father.* Our Lord, foreseeing this, said, when Judas went out, as if the tares were now separated, and He left alone with the wheat, the holy Apostles, *Now is the Son of man glorified;* as if to say, Behold what will take place at My glorifying, at which none of the wicked shall be present,

none of the righteous shall perish. He does not say, Now
is the glorifying of the Son of man signified; but, *Now is the
Son of man glorified;* as it is not that rock signified Christ,
but, *That Rock was Christ.* Scripture often speaks of the
things signifying, as if they were the things signified.
But the glorifying of the Son of man, is the glorifying of
God in Him; as He adds, *And God is glorified in Him,*
which He proceeds to explain; If *God is glorified in Him—*
for He came not to do His own will, but the will of Him
that sent Him—*God shall also glorify Him in Himself,* so
that the human nature which was assumed by the eternal
Word, shall also be endowed with eternity. *And shall
straightway glorify Him.* He predicts His own resurrection,
which was to follow immediately, not at the end of the
world, like ours. Thus it is; Now *is the Son of man glorified;* the *now* referring not to His approaching Passion, but
the resurrection which was immediately to follow it: as if
that which was so very soon to be, had already taken place.
HILARY. That God is glorified in Him, refers to the glory of
the body, which glory is the glory of God, in that the body
borrows its glory from its association with the Divine nature.
Because God is glorified in Him, therefore He will
glorify Him in Himself, in that He who reigns in the glory
arising from the glory of God, He forthwith passes over into
God's glory[a], leaving the dispensation of His manhood,
wholly to abide in God. Nor is He silent as to the time:
And shall straightway glorify Him. This referring to the
glory of His resurrection which was immediately to follow
His passion, which He mentions as present, because Judas
had now gone out to betray Him; whereas that God would
glorify Him in Himself, He reserves for the future. The
glory of God was shewn in Him by the miracle of the resurrection; but He will abide in the glory of God when He has
left the dispensation of subjection. The sense of these first
words, *Now is the Son of man glorified,* is not doubtful: it
is the glory of the flesh which is meant, not that of the Word.
But what means the next, *And God is glorified in Him?*
The Son of man is not another Person from the Son of God,
for, *the Word was made flesh.* How is God glorified in this

Marginal notes: 1 Cor. 10, 4. / c. 3. / Hilar. xi. de Trin. c. 42. / John 1, 14.

Son of man, who is the Son of God? The next clause helps
us; *If God is glorified in Him, God also will glorify Him
in Himself.* A man is not glorified in himself, nor, on the
other hand, does God who is glorified in man, because He
receives glory, cease to be God. So the words, *God is
glorified in Him,* either mean that Christ is glorified in the
flesh, or that God is glorified in Christ. If *God* means
Christ, it is Christ who is glorified in the flesh; if the
Father, then it is the Sacrament of unity, the Father glorified
in the Son. Again, God glorifies in Himself God glorified
in the Son of man. This overthrows the impious doctrine
that Christ is not very God, in verity of nature. For how
can that which God glorifies in Himself be out of Himself?
He whom the Father glorifies must be confessed to be in
His glory, and He who is glorified in the glory of the
Father, must be understood to be in the same case with the
Father. ORIGEN. Or thus: The word glory is here used in Orig.
a different sense from that which some Pagans attach to it, t. xxxii.
who defined glory to be the collected praises of the many. 17.
It is evident that glory in such a sense is a different thing
from that mentioned in Exodus, where it is said, that *the* Exod.
glory of the Lord filled the tabernacle, and that the face of 40, 34.
Moses was glorified. The glory here mentioned is something visible, a certain divine appearance in the temple,
and on Moses' face; but in a higher and more spiritual
sense we are glorified, when with the eye of the understanding we penetrate into the things of God. For the
mind when it ascends above material things, and spiritually
sees God, is deified: and of this spiritual glory, the
visible glory on the face of Moses is a figure: for his
mind it was that was deified by converse with God. But
there is no comparison between the excellent glory of Christ,
and the knowledge of Moses, whereby the face of his soul
was glorified: for the whole of the Father's glory shines upon
the Son, who is *the brightness of His glory, and the express* Heb. 1,
image of His Person. Yea, and from the light of this whole 3.
glory there go forth particular glories, throughout the whole c. 18.
rational creation: though none can take in the whole of the
divine glory, except the Son. But so far as the Son was
known to the world, so far only was He glorified. And as
yet He was not fully known. But afterward the Father spread

the knowledge of Him over the whole world, and then was the Son of man glorified in those who knew Him. And of this glory He hath made all who know Him partakers: as saith the Apostle; *We all, with open face beholding as in a glass the glory of the Lord, are changed into the same image, from glory to glory,* i. e. from His glory receive glory. When He was approaching then that dispensation, by which He was to become known to the world, and to be glorified in the glory of those who glorified Him, He says, *Now is the Son of man glorified.* And because *no man knoweth the Father but the Son, and he to whomsoever the Son will reveal Him,* and the Son by the dispensation was about to reveal the Father; for this reason He saith, *And God is glorified in Him.* Or compare this with the text below: *He that hath seen Me, hath seen the Father.* The Father who begat the Word is seen in the Word, who is God, and the image of the invisible God. But the words may be taken in a larger sense. For as through some the name of God was blasphemed among the Gentiles, so through the saints whose good deeds are seen and acknowledged by the world, the name of the Father in heaven is magnified. But in whom was He so glorified as in Jesus, *Who did no sin, neither was guile found in His mouth?* Such being the Son, He is glorified, and God is glorified in Him. And if God is glorified in Him, the Father returns Him more than He gave. For the glory of the Son of man, when the Father glorifies Him, far exceeds the Father's glory, when He is glorified in the Son: it being fit that the greater should return the greater glory. And as this, viz. the glorifying of the Son of man, was just about to be accomplished, our Lord adds, *And will straightway glorify Him.*

2 Cor. 3, 18.

Matt. 11, 27.

ἐκ τῆς οἰκο- νομίας

c. 14, 9.

33. Little children, yet a little while I am with you. Ye shall seek me: and as I said unto the Jews, Whither I go, ye cannot come; so now I say to you.

34. A new commandment I give unto you, That ye love one another; as I have loved you, that ye also love one another.

35. By this shall all men know that ye are my disciples, if ye have love one to another.

AUG. After He had said, *And shall straightway glorify Him,* that they might not think that God was going to glorify Him in such a way, as that He would no longer have any converse with them on earth, He says, *Little children, yet a little while I am with you:* as if He said, I shall indeed straightway be glorified by My resurrection, but I shall not straightway ascend to heaven. For we read in the Acts of the Apostles, that He was with them forty days after His resurrection. These forty days are what He means by, *A little while I am with you.* ORIGEN. *Little children,* He Orig. says; for their souls were yet in infancy. But these little t. xxxii. children, after His death, were made brethren; as before they 19. were little children, they were servants. AUG. It may be Aug. understood too thus: I am as yet in this frail flesh, even as Tr.lxiv. ye are, until I die and rise again. He was with them after 1. His resurrection, by bodily presence, not by participation of human frailty. *These are the words which I spake unto* Luke *you, while I was yet with you,* He says to His disciples after 24, 44. His resurrection; meaning, while I was in mortal flesh, as ye are. He was in the same flesh then with them, but not subject to the same mortality. But there is another Divine Presence unknown to mortal senses, of which He saith, *Lo, I* Mat.28, *am with you alway, even unto the end of the world.* This 20. is not the presence meant by, *A little while I am with you;* for it is not a little while to the end of the world: or even if it is a little while, because that in the eye of God, a thousand years are as one day, yet what follows shews that it is not what our Lord is here alluding to; for He adds, *Whither I go ye cannot follow Me now.* At the end of the world they were to follow Him, whither He went; as He saith below; *Father, I will that they be with Me, where I* c. 17,24. *am.* ORIGEN. But may there not be a deeper meaning in Orig. the words, *yet a little while &c.* After a little while He was t. xxxii. not with them. In what sense not with them? Not because 19. He was not with them according to the flesh, in that He was taken from them, was brought before Pilate, was crucified, descended into hell: but because they all forsook Him, fulfilling His prophecy: *All ye shall be offended because of Me this night.* He was not with them, because He only dwells with those who are worthy of Him. But though they thus wandered from Jesus for a little while, it was only for a little while; they soon sought Him again. Peter wept bitterly after his denial of Jesus, and by his tears sought Him: and therefore it follows, *Ye shall seek Me, and as I said unto the Jews, whither I go, ye cannot follow Me now.* To seek Jesus, is to seek the Word, wisdom, righteousness, truth, all which is Christ. To His disciples therefore who wish to follow Him, not in a bodily sense, as the ignorant think, but in the way He ordains, *Whosoever doth not bear his cross, and come after Me, cannot be My disciple.* Our Lord saith, *Whither I go ye cannot follow Me now.* For though they wished to follow the Word, and to confess Him, they were not yet

supra c. 7. strong enough to do so; *The Spirit was not yet given to them, because that Jesus was not yet glorified.* AUG. Or He means Aug. Tr. lxiv. 4. that they were not yet fit to follow Him to death for righteousness' sake. For how could they, when they were not ripe for martyrdom? Or how could they follow our Lord to immortality, they who were to die, and not to rise again till the end of the world? Or how could they follow Him to the bosom of the Father, when none could partake of that felicity, but they whose love was perfected? When He told the Jews this, He did not add *now.* But the disciples, though they could not follow Him then, would be able to do so afterwards,

Orig. t. xxxii. 19. and therefore He adds[c], *So now I say to you.* ORIGEN. As if He said, I say it to you, but with the addition of *now.* The Jews, who He foresaw would die in their sins, would never be able to follow Him; but the disciples were unable Chrys. Hom. lxxii. 3. only for a little time. CHRYS. And therefore He said, *little children;* for He did not mean to speak to them, as He had to the Jews. *Ye cannot follow Me now,* He says, in order to rouse the love of His disciples. For the departure of loved friends kindles all our affection, and especially if they are going to a place where we cannot follow them. He purposely too speaks of His death, as a kind of translation, a happy removal to a place, where mortal bodies do not enter.

Aug. Tr. lxv. 1. AUG. And now He teaches them how to fit themselves to follow Him: *A new commandment I give unto you, that ye love one* Levit. 19, 18. *another.* But does not the old law say, *Thou shalt love thy neighbour as thyself?* Why then does He call it a new

[c] ὑμῖν λέγω ἄρτι: Vobis dico modo, V.

commandment? Is it because it strips us of the old man, and puts on us the new? That it renews the hearer, or rather the doer of it? Love does do this; but it is that love which our Lord distinguishes from the carnal affection: *As I have loved you, that ye also love one another.* Not the love with which men love one another, but that of the children of the Most High God, who would be brethren of His only-begotten Son, and therefore love one another with that love with which He loved them, and would lead them to the fulfilment of their desires. CHRYS. Or, as I have loved you: for My love has not been the payment of something owing to you, but had its beginning on My side. And ye ought in like manner to do one another good, though ye may not owe it. AUG. But do not think that that greater commandment, viz. that we should love the Lord our God, is passed by. For, if we understand the two precepts aright, each is implied in the other. He who loves God cannot despise His commandment that he should love his neighbour; and he who loves his neighbour in a heavenly spiritual way, in the neighbour loves God. That is the love which our Lord distinguishes from all human love, when He adds, *As I have loved you.* For what did He, in loving us, love, but God in us; not who was in us, but so that He might be? Wherefore let each of us so love the other, as that by this working of love, we make each other the habitations of God. CHRYS. Passing over the miracles, which they were to perform, He makes love the distinguishing mark of His followers; *By this shall all men know that ye are My disciples, if ye have love one to another.* This it is that evidences the saint or the disciple, as He calls him. AUG. As if He said, Other gifts are shared with you by those who are not mine; birth, life, sense, reason, and such good things as belong alike to man and brutes; nay, and tongues, sacraments, prophecy, knowledge, faith, bestowing of goods upon the poor, giving the body to be burned: but forasmuch as they have not charity, they are tinkling cymbals, they are nothing: nothing profits them.

36. Simon Peter said unto him, Lord, whither goest thou? Jesus answered him, Whither I go, thou

Margin notes:
Chrys. Hom. lxxii. 3.

Aug. Tr. lxiv. 2.

Chrys. Hom. lxxii. 4.

Aug. Tr. lxv. 3.

canst not follow me now; but thou shalt follow me
afterwards.

37. Peter said unto him, Lord, why cannot I follow
thee now? I will lay down my life for thy sake.

38. Jesus answered him, Wilt thou lay down thy
life for my sake? Verily, verily, I say unto thee,
The cock shall not crow, till thou hast denied me
thrice.

Chrys. CHRYS. Great is love, and stronger than fire; nothing can
Hom.
lxxiii. 3. stop its course. Peter the most ardent of all, as soon as he
hears our Lord say, *Whither I go ye cannot follow Me now*,
Aug. asks, *Lord, whither goest Thou?* AUG. The disciple asks this,
Tr. lxvi.
1. as if he were ready to follow. But our Lord saw his heart;
Jesus answered him, *Whither I go, thou canst not follow
Me now;* He checks his forwardness, but does not destroy
his hope; nay, confirms it; *But thou shalt follow Me afterwards.* Why hastenest thou, Peter? The Rock has not yet
established thee with His spirit. Be not lifted up with
presumptions, thou canst not now; be not cast down with
Chrys. despair, *thou shalt follow Me afterwards.* CHRYS. Peter, on
Hom.
lxxii. 1. receiving this answer, does not check his desire, but hastily
conceives favourable hopes from it, and having got rid of the
fear of betraying our Lord, feels secure, and becomes himself
the interrogator, while the rest are silent: *Peter said unto Him,
Lord, why cannot I follow Thee now? I will lay down my
life for Thy sake.* What sayest thou, Peter? He hath said,
thou canst not, and thou sayest, thou canst: wherefore thou
shalt know by experience, that thy love is nothing, unless
thou art enabled from above: Jesus answered him, *Will
thou lay down thy life for My sake?* BEDE. Which sentence
may be read in two ways: either as affirming, thou shalt lay
down thy life for My sake, but now through fear of the
death of the body, thou shalt incur spiritual death: or as
Aug. mocking; as if He said, AUG. Wilt thou do that for Me,
Tr. lxvi.
1. which I have not done yet for thee? Canst thou go before,
who canst not come after? Why presumest thou so? Hear
what thou art: *Verily, verily, I say unto thee, The cock shall
not crow, till thou hast denied Me thrice.* Thou who

promisest Me thy death, shall thrice deny thy life. Peter
knew his great desire, his strength he knew not: he boasted
of his will, while he was yet weak; but the Physician saw c. 2.
his weakness. Some who perversely favour Peter, excuse
him, and say that he did not deny Christ, because when
asked by the servant maid, he said he did not know Him,
as the other Evangelists witness more expressly. As if to
deny the man Christ, was not to deny Christ; yea, that in
Christ, which He was made for our sakes, that that which
He made us, might not perish. By what is He the Head of
the Church, but by His humanity? And how then is he in
the body of Christ, who denies the man Christ? But why do
I argue so long? Our Lord does not say, The cock shall
not crow till thou deniest man, or the Son of man, but *till
thou deniest Me.* What is *Me,* but that which He was? So
then whatever Peter denied, he denied Christ: it is impious
to doubt it. Christ said so, and Christ said true: beyond
a doubt, Peter denied Christ. Let us not, to defend Peter,
accuse Christ. The frailty of Peter himself, acknowledged
its sin, when he witnessed by his tears the evil he had done
in denying Christ. Nor do we say this, because we have
pleasure in blaming the first of the Apostles; but that we
may take warning from him, not to be confident of our own
strength. BEDE. Nevertheless, should any one fall, let the
example of Peter save him from despair, and teach him that
he can without delay obtain pardon from God. CHRYS. It Chrys.
is manifest that our Lord permitted Peter's fall. He might $^{Hom.}_{lxxiii.1.}$
have recalled him to begin with, but as he persisted in his
vehemence, though He did not drive him to a denial, He let
him go without assistance, that He might learn his own
weakness, and not fall into such sin again, when the superintendence of the world had come to him, but that remembering what had happened to him[d], he might know
himself. AUG. That took place in the soul of Peter, which Aug.
he offered in the body; though differently from what he $^{Tr. lxvi.}_{2.}$
meant. For before the death and resurrection of our Lord,
he both died by his denial, and lived again by his tears.
AUG. This speech, *The cock shall not crow,* occurs in Aug.
all the Evangelists, but not at the same time in all. Matthew de Con.
                                                        Evang.
                                                        iii.c.11.
[d] ὅταν τῆς οἰκουμένης τὴν οἰκονομίαν δίξηται.   (5.)

and Mark introduce it *after* they have left the house, in which they were eating; Luke and John *before.* We may suppose either that the two former are recurring to what had passed, or the two latter anticipating what is coming. Or the great difference not only of the words, but of the subjects which precede the speech, and which excite Peter to the presumption of offering to die, for or with our Lord, may lead us to conclude that he made this offer three times, and that our Lord three times replied, *Before the cock crow, thou shalt deny Me thrice.*

CHAP. XIV.

1. Let not your heart be troubled: ye believe in God, believe also in me.

2. In my Father's house are many mansions: if it were not so, I would have told you. I go to prepare a place for you.

3. And if I go and prepare a place for you, I will come again, and receive you unto myself; that where I am, there ye may be also.

4. And whither I go ye know, and the way ye know.

AUG. Our Lord consoles His disciples, who, as men, would be naturally alarmed and troubled at the idea of His death, by assuring them of His divinity: *Let not your heart be troubled: ye believe in God, believe also in Me;* as if they must believe in Him, if they believed in God; which would not follow, unless Christ were God. Ye are in fear for this form of a servant; let not your heart be troubled; the form of God shall raise it up. CHRYS. Faith too in Me, and in the Father that begat Me, is more powerful than any thing that shall come upon you; and will prevail in spite of all difficulties. He shews His divinity at the same time by discerning their inward feelings: *Let not your heart be troubled.* AUG. And as the disciples were afraid for them-selves, when Peter, the boldest and most zealous of them, had been told, *The cock shall not crow, till thou hast denied Me thrice,* He adds, *In My Father's house are many*

Aug. Tr.lxvii. 1.

Chrys. Hom. lxxiii.1.

Aug. Tr.lxvii. 2.

2 G

mansions, by way of an assurance to them in their trouble, that they might with confidence and certainty look forward, after all their trials, to dwelling together with Christ in the presence of God. For though one man is bolder, wiser, juster, holier than another, yet no one shall be removed from that house of God, but each receive a mansion suited to his deserts. The penny indeed which the householder paid to the labourers who worked in his vineyard, was the same to all; for life eternal, which this penny signifies, is of the same duration to all. But there may be many mansions, many degrees of dignity, in that life, corresponding to people's deserts. GREG. The many mansions agree with the one penny, because, though one may rejoice more than another, yet all rejoice with one and the same joy, arising from the vision of their Maker. AUG. And thus God will be all in all; that is, since God is love, love will bring it to pass, that what each has, will be common to all. That which one loves in another is one's own, though one have it not one's self. And then there will be no envy at superior grace, for in all hearts will reign the unity of love. GREG. Nor is there any sense of deficiency in consequence of such inequality; for each will feel as much as sufficeth for himself. AUG. But they are rejected by the Christians, who infer from there being many mansions that there is a place outside the kingdom of heaven, where innocent souls, that have departed this life without baptism, and could not there enter into the kingdom of heaven, remain happy. But God forbid, that when every house of every heir of the kingdom is in the kingdom, there should be a part of the regal house itself not in the kingdom. Our Lord does not say, In eternal bliss *are many mansions,* but they are *in My Father's house.* CHRYS. Or thus: Our Lord having said above to Peter, *Whither I go, thou canst not follow Me now, but thou shalt follow Me afterwards,* that they might not think that this promise was made to Peter only, He says, *In My Father's house are many mansions;* i. e. You shall be admitted into that place, as well as Peter, for it contains abundance of mansions, which are ever ready to receive you: *If it were not so, I would have told you: I go to prepare a place for you.* AUG. He means evidently that there are already many mansions, and that

Greg.
super
Ezech.
Hom.
xvi.
Aug.
Tr.lxvii.
2.

Greg.
Moral.
ult. c.
xxiv.

Aug.
Tr.lxvii.
3.

Chrys.
Hom.
lxxiii. 1.

there is no need of His preparing one. CHRYS. Having said, Chrys.
Thou canst not follow Me now, that they might not think Hom. lxxiii.1.
that they were cut off for ever, He adds: *And if I go and*
prepare a place for you, I will come again and receive you
unto Myself, that where I am, there ye may be also: a
recommendation to them to place the strongest trust in Him.
THEOPHYL. *And if not, I would have told you: I go to pre-*
pare, &c. As if He said; Either way ye should not be
troubled, whether places are prepared for you, or not. For,
if they are not prepared, I will very quickly prepare them.
AUG. But why does He go and prepare a place, if there are Aug.
many mansions already? Because these are not as yet so Tract. lxviii.1.
prepared as they will be. The same mansions that He hath
prepared by predestination, He prepares by operation. They
are prepared already in respect of predestination; if they
were not, He would have said, I will go and prepare, i. e.
predestinate, a place for you; but inasmuch as they are not
yet prepared in respect of operation, He says, *And if I go*
and prepare a place for you. And now He is preparing
mansions, by preparing occupants for them. Indeed, when
He says, *In My Father's house are many mansions,* what
think we the house of God to be but the temple of God, of
which the Apostle saith, *The temple of God is holy, which* 1 Cor.
temple ye are. This house of God then is now being built, 3, 17.
now being prepared. But why has He gone away to prepare c. 3.
it, if it is ourselves that He prepares: if He leaves us, how
can He prepare us? The meaning is, that, in order that
those mansions may be prepared, the just must live by faith:
and if thou seest, there is no faith. Let Him go away then,
that He be not seen; let Him be hid, that He be believed. Then a place is prepared, if thou live by faith: let
faith desire, that desire may enjoy. If thou rightly understandest Him, He never leaves either the place He came
from, or that He goes from. He goes, when He withdraws
from sight, He comes, when He appears. But except He
remain in power, that we may grow in goodness, no place of
happiness will be prepared for us. ALCUIN. He says then,
If I go, by the absence of the flesh, *I shall come again,*
by the presence of the Godhead; or, I shall come again to
judge the quick and dead. And as He knew that they

would ask whither He went, or by what way He went, He adds, *And whither I go ye know,* i. e. to the Father, *and the way ye know,* i. e. Myself. CHRYS. He shews them that He is aware of their curiosity to know His meaning, and thus excites them to put questions to Him.

Chrys. Hom. xxiii. 2.

5. Thomas saith unto him, Lord, we know not whither thou goest; and how can we know the way?

6. Jesus saith unto him, I am the way, the truth, and the life: no man cometh unto the Father, but by me.

7. If ye had known me, ye should have known My Father also; and from henceforth ye know him, and have seen him.

Chrys. Hom. lxxiii.2.

CHRYS. If the Jews, who wished to be separated from Christ, asked whither He was going, much more would the disciples, who wished never to be separated from Him, be anxious to know it. So with much love, and, at the same time, fear, they proceed to ask: *Thomas saith unto Him, Lord, we know not whither Thou goest; and how can we know the way?*

Aug. Tr.lxix. 1.

AUG. Our Lord had said that they knew both, Thomas says that they knew neither. Our Lord cannot lie; they knew not that they did know. Our Lord proves that they did: *Jesus saith unto Him, I am the way, the truth, and the life.*

Aug. deVerb. Dom. s. liv. capit

AUG. As if He said, *I am the way,* whereby thou wouldest go; *I am the truth,* whereto thou wouldest go; *I am the life,* in which thou wouldest abide. The truth and the life every one understands; but not every one hath found the way. Even the philosophers of the world have seen that God is the life eternal, the truth which is the end of all knowledge. And the Word of God, which is truth and life with the Father, by taking upon Him human nature, is made the way. Walk by the Man, and thou wilt arrive at God. For it is better to limp on the right way, than to walk ever so stoutly by the wrong.

Hilar. vii. de Trin.

HILARY. For He who is the way doth not lead us into devious courses out of the way; nor does He who is the truth deceive us by falsehoods; nor does He who is the life leave us in the darkness of death. THEOPHYL. When thou art engaged in the practical, He is made thy way; when in the contemplative, He is made thy truth. And to the active and the contemplative is joined *life:* for we should both act and contemplate with reference to the world to come. AUG. They knew then the way, because they knew He was the way. But what need to add, *the truth, and the life?* Because they were yet to be told whither He went. He went to the truth; He went to the life. He went then to Himself, by Himself. But didst Thou leave Thyself, O Lord, to come to us? I know that Thou tookest upon Thee the form of a servant; by the flesh Thou camest, remaining where Thou wast; by that Thou returnedst, remaining where Thou hadst come to. If by this then Thou camest, and returnedst, by this Thou wast the way, not only to us, to come to Thee, but also to Thyself to come, and to return again. And when Thou wentest to life, which is Thyself, Thou raisedst that same flesh of Thine from death to life. Christ therefore went to life, when His flesh arose from death to life. And since the Word is life, Christ went to Himself; Christ being both, in one person, i. e. Word-flesh. Again, by the flesh God came to men, the truth to liars; for God is true, but every man a liar. When then He withdrew Himself from men, and lifted up His flesh to that place in which no liar is, the same Christ, by the way, by which He being the Word became flesh, by Himself, i. e. by His flesh, by the same returned to Truth, which is Himself, which truth, even amongst the liars He maintained unto death. Behold I myself[1], if I make you understand what I say, do in a certain sense go to you, though I do not leave myself. And when I cease speaking, I return to myself, but remain with you, if ye remember what ye have heard. If the image which God hath made can do this, how much more the Image which God hath begotten? Thus He goes by Himself, to Himself and to the Father, and we by Him, to Him and to the Father. CHRYS. For if, He says, ye have Me for your guide to the Father, ye shall certainly come to Him. Nor can ye come by any other way. Whereas He had said above, *No man can come to Me, except the Father draw him,* now He says, *No man cometh unto the Father but by Me,* thus

Margin notes: Aug. Tr. lxix. 2. c. 3. [1] i. e. Augustine. Chrys. Hom. lxxiii. 2. c. 6, 44.

equalling Himself to the Father. The next words explain,
Whither I go ye know, and the way ye know. *If ye had
known Me*, He says, *ye should have known My Father also;*
i. e. If ye had known My substance and dignity, ye would
have known the Father's. They did know Him, but not as
they ought to do. Nor was it till afterwards, when the Spirit
came, that they were fully enlightened. On this account
He adds, *And from henceforth ye know Him*, know Him,
that is, spiritually. *And have seen Him*, i. e. by Me; meaning that he who had seen Him, had seen the Father. They
saw Him, however, not in His pure substance, but clothed in
flesh. BEDE. How can our Lord say, *If ye had known Me, ye
should have known My Father also;* when He has just said,
Whither I go ye know, and the way ye know? We must
suppose that some of them knew, and others not : among the
latter, Thomas. HILARY. Or thus : When it is said that the
Son is the way to the Father, is it meant that He is so by
His teaching, or by His nature? We shall be able to see
from what follows : *If ye had known Me, ye should have
known My Father also.* In His incarnation asserting His
Divinity, He maintained a certain order of sight and knowledge : separating the time of seeing from that of knowing.
For Him, who He saith must be known, He speaks of as
already seen : that henceforward they might from this revelation have knowledge of the Divine Nature which they
had all along seen in Him.

*Hilar.
vii. de
Trin.*

8. Philip saith unto him, Lord, shew us the Father,
and it sufficeth us.

9. Jesus saith unto him, Have I been so long time
with you, and yet hast thou not known me, Philip?
he that hath seen me hath seen the Father; and how
sayest thou then, Shew us the Father?

10. Believest thou not that I am in the Father, and
the Father in me? the words that I speak unto you I
speak not of myself : but the Father that dwelleth in
me, he doeth the works.

11. Believe me that I am in the Father, and the

Father in me : or else believe me for the very works' sake.

HILARY. A declaration so new startled Philip. Our Hilar. vii. de Trin. Lord is seen to be man. He confesses Himself to be the Son of God, declares that, if He were known, the Father would be known, that, if He is seen, the Father is seen. The familiarity of the Apostle therefore breaks forth into questioning our Lord, *Philip saith unto Him, Lord, shew us the Father, and it sufficeth us.* He did not deny He could be non visum nesum ne-gavit. seen, but wished to be shewn him; nor did he wish to see with his bodily eyes, but that He whom he had seen might be made manifest to his understanding. He had seen the Son in the form of man, but how through that form He saw the Father, he did not know. This he wants to be shewn him, shewn to his understanding, not set before his eyes; and then he will be satisfied : *And it sufficeth us.* AUG. Aug. i. de Trin. c. viii. For to that joy of beholding His face, nothing can be added. Philip understood this, and said, *Lord, shew us the Father, and it sufficeth us.* But he did not yet understand that he could in the same way have said, Lord, shew us Thyself, and it sufficeth us. But our Lord's answer enlightens him, *Jesus saith unto him, Have I been so long with you, and yet hast thou not known Me, Philip?* AUG. But how is this, when Aug. Tr. lxx. 1. our Lord said that they knew whither He was going, and the way, because they knew Him? The question is easily settled by supposing that some of them knew, and others not; among the latter, Philip. HILARY. He reproves the Hilar. vii. de Trin. ignorance of Philip in this respect. For whereas his actions had been strictly divine, such as walking on the water, commanding the winds, remitting sins, raising the dead, He complained that in His assumed humanity, the Divine nature was not discerned. Accordingly to Philip's request, to be shewn the Father, *Our Lord answers, He that hath seen Me, hath seen the Father.* AUG. When two persons are very Aug. Tr. lxx. like each, we say, If you have seen the one, you have seen the other. So here, *He that hath seen Me, hath seen the Father ;* not that He is both the Father, and the Son, but

Hilar.
vii. de
Trin. that the Son is an absolute likeness of the Father. HILARY.
He does not mean the sight of the bodily eye: for His
fleshly part, born of the Virgin, doth not avail towards contemplating the form and image of God in Him; but the Son
of God being known with the understanding, it follows that
the Father is known also, forasmuch as He is the image of
[1]non dif-
ferat
genere. God, not differing from but expressing His Author[1]. For
our Lord's expressions do not speak of one person solitary
and without relationship, but teach us His birth. *The
Father also* excludes the supposition of a single solitary
person, and leaves us no other doctrine but that the Father
is seen in the Son, by the incommunicable likeness of birth.
Aug.
Tr. lxx.
3. AUG. But is he to be reproved, who, when he has seen the
likeness, wishes to see the man of whom he is the likeness?
No: our Lord rebuked the question, only with reference to
the mind of the asker.   Philip asked, as if the Father were
better than the Son; and so shewed that He did not know
the Son.   Which opinion our Lord corrects: *Believest thou
not that I am in the Father, and the Father in Me?* as if He
said, If it is a great wish with thee to see the Father, at any
Hilar.
vii. de
Trin. rate believe what thou dost not see.   HILARY. For what
excuse was there for ignorance of the Father, or what necessity to shew Him, when the Father was seen in the Son by
[2]propri-
etate
naturæ. His essential nature[2], while by the identity of unity, the
Begotten and the Begetter are one: *Believest thou not that I
Aug.
i. de
Trin.
11. am in the Father and the Father in Me?* AUG. He wished him
to live by faith, before he had sight, and therefore says, *Believest
thou not?* Spiritual vision is the reward of faith, vouchsafed
Hilar.
vii. de
Trin. to minds purified by faith.   HILARY. But the Father is in the
Son, and the Son in the Father, not by a conjunction of two
[3]genera. harmonizing essences[3], nor by a nature grafted into a more
capacious substance as in material bodies, in which it is
impossible that what is within can be made external to
that which contains it; but by the birth of a nature which is
life from life; forasmuch as from God nothing but God can be
Hilar.
v. de
Trin. born.   HILARY. The unchangeable God follows, so to speak,
His own nature, by begetting unchangeable God.   Nor does
the perfect birth of unchangeable God from unchangeable
God forsake His own nature.   We understand then here

the nature of God subsisting in Him, since God is in God,
nor besides Him who is God, can any other be God.
CHRYS. Or thus: Philip, because [he thought] he had seen Chrys.
the Son with his bodily eye, wished to see the Father in the Hom.
lxxiv. 1.
same way; perhaps too remembering what the Prophet said,
I saw the Lord, and therefore he says, *Shew us the Father.* Isa.6,1.
The Jews had asked, who was His Father; and Peter and
Thomas, whither He went; and neither were told plainly.
Philip therefore, that he might not seem burdensome, after
saying, *Shew us the Father,* adds, *And it sufficeth us:* i. e.
we seek for no more. Our Lord in reply does not say, that
he asked an impossible thing, but that he had not seen the
Son to begin with, for that if he had seen Him, he would
have seen the Father: *Have I been so long time with you,
and yet hast thou not known Me?* He does not say, not
seen Me, but, *not known Me;* not known that the Son,
being what the Father is, does in Himself fitly shew the
Father. Then dividing the Persons, He says, *He that hath
seen Me hath seen the Father;* that none might maintain
that He was both the Father and the Son. The words
shew too that even the Son was not seen in a bodily sense.
So if any one takes seeing here, for *knowing,* I will not contradict him, but will take the sentence as if it was, He that
hath known Me, hath known the Father. He shews here
His consubstantiality with the Father: He that hath seen
My substance, hath seen the Father. Whence it is evident
He is not a creature: for all know and see the creature, but
not all God; Philip, for instance, who wished to see the
substance of the Father. If Christ then had been of
another substance from the Father, He would never have
said, *He that hath seen Me, hath seen the Father.* A man
cannot see the substance of gold in silver: one nature cannot be made apparent by another. AUG. He then addresses Aug.
all of them, not Philip only : *The word that I speak unto* Tr. lxx.
3. and
you, I speak not of Myself. What is, *I speak not of Myself,* lxxi. 1.
but, I that speak am not of Myself? He attributes what He
does to Him, from whom He Himself, the doer, is. HILARY. Hilar.
Wherein He neither desires Himself to be the Son, nor vii. de
Trin.
hides the existence[1] of His Father's power in Him. In that [1] natu-
ram
He speaks, it is Himself that speaks in His own person; in

that He speaks not of Himself, He witnesseth His nativity,

Chrys.
Hom.
lxxiv. 2. that He is God from God. CHRYS. Mark the abundant proof of the unity of substance. For He continues; *But the Father that dwelleth in Me, He doeth the works.* As if He said, My Father and I act together, not differently from each other; agreeing with what He said below: *If I do not the works of My Father, believe Me not.* But why does He pass from words to works? Why does He not say as we might have expected, He speaketh the words? Because He means to apply what He says both to His doctrine, and to His miracles; or because His words are themselves works.

Aug.
Tr.lxx.
1, 2. AUG. For he that edifieth his neighbour by speaking, doth a good work. These two sentences are brought against us by different sects of heretics; the Arians saying that the Son is unequal to the Father, because He does not speak of Himself; the Sabellians, that the same who is the Father is the Son. For what is meant, they ask, by, *The Father that dwelleth in Me, He doeth the works*, but, I that dwell in Myself, do these

Hilar.
vii. de
Trin. works. HILARY. That the Father dwells in the Son, shews that He is not single, or solitary; that the Father works by the Son, shews that He is not different or alien. As He is not solitary who doth not speak from Himself, so neither is He alien and separable who speaketh by Him. Having shewn then that the Father spoke and worked in Him, He formally states this union: *Believe Me that I am in the Father, and the Father in Me:* that they might not think that the Father worketh and speaketh in the Son as by a mere agent or instrument, not by the unity of nature implied

Aug.
Tr.lxxi.
2. in His Divine birth. AUG. Philip alone was reproved before. CHRYS. But if this does not suffice to shew my consub-

Chrys.
Hom.
lxxiv. 2. stantiality, at least learn it from My works: *Or else believe Me for the very works' sake.* Ye have seen My miracles, and all the proper signs of My divinity; works which the Father alone worketh, sins remitted, life restored, and the

Aug.
Tr.lxxi.
2. like. AUG. Believe then for My works' sake, *that I am in the Father, and the Father in Me;* for, were we separated, we could not be working together.

12. Verily, verily, I say unto you, He that believeth on me, the works that I do shall he do also; and

greater works than these shall he do; because I go unto my Father.

13. And whatsoever ye shall ask in my name, that will I do, that the Father may be glorified in the Son.

14. If ye shall ask any thing in my name, I will do it.

CHRYS. Having said, *Believe for the works' sake,* our Lord goes on to declare that He can do much greater than these, and what is more wonderful, give others the power of working them. *Verily, verily, I say unto you, He that believeth on Me, the works that I do, shall he do also; and greater works than these shall he do.* AUG. But what are these greater works? Is it that the shadow of the Apostles, as they passed by, healed the sick? It is indeed a greater thing that a shadow should heal, than that the border of a garment should. Nevertheless, by works here our Lord refers to His words. For when He says, *My Father that dwelleth in Me, He doeth the works,* what are these works but the words which He spoke? And the fruit of those words was their faith. But these were but few converts in comparison with what those disciples made afterwards by their preaching: they converted the Gentiles to the faith. Did not the rich man go away sorrowful from His words? And yet that which one did not do at His own exhortation, many did afterwards when He preached through the disciples. He did greater works when preached by the believing, than when speaking to men's ears. Still these greater works He did by His Apostles, whereas He includes others besides them, when He says, *He that believeth on Me.* Are we not to compute any one among the believers in Christ, who does not do greater works than Christ? This sounds harsh if not explained. The Apostle says, *To him that believeth on Him that justifieth the ungodly, his faith is counted for righteousness.* By this work then we shall do the works of Christ, the very believing in Christ being the work of Christ, for He worketh this in us, though not without us. Attend then; *He that believeth on Me, the works that I do, shall he do also.* First I do them, then he will do them: I do them, that he may do them. Do what works but this, viz. that a man,

Chrys.
Hom.
lxxiv. 2.

Aug.
Tr. lxxi.
3.

c. 2.

Rom. 4,
5.

from being a sinner, become just? which thing Christ worketh in us, though not without us. This in truth I call a greater work to do, than to create the heaven and the earth ; for heaven and earth shall pass away, but the salvation and justification of the predestinated shall remain. However, the Angels in heaven are the work of Christ; shall he who worketh with Christ for his own justification, do greater even than these? Judge any one which be the greater work, 'to create the just, or to justify the ungodly? At least, if both be of equal power, the latter hath more of mercy. But it is not necessary to understand all the works of Christ, when He says, greater works than these shall he do. *These* perhaps refers to the works He had done that hour. He had then been instructing them in the faith[1]. And surely it is a less work to preach righteousness, which He did without us, than to justify the ungodly, which He so does in us, as that we do it ourselves. Great things truly did our Lord promise His people, when He went to His Father: *Because I go unto My Father.* CHRYS. i. e. I shall not perish, but shall remain in My proper dignity, in heaven. Or He means: It is your part henceforth to work miracles, since I am going. AUG. And that no one might attribute the merit to himself, He shews, that even those greater works were His own doing: *And whatsoever ye shall ask in My name, that will I do.* Before it was, *He shall do,* now, *I will do:* as if He said, Let not this appear impossible to you. He that believeth in Me, will not be greater than I; but I shall do greater works then than now; greater by him that believeth on Me, than now by Myself; which will not be a failing, but a condescension. CHRYS. *In My name,* He says. Thus the Apostles; *In the name of Jesus of Nazareth, arise and walk.* All the miracles that they did, He did: the hand of the Lord was with them. THEOPHYL. This is an explanation of the doctrine of miracles. It is by prayer, and invocation of His name, that a man is able to work miracles. AUG. *Whatsoever ye shall ask.* Then why do we often see believers asking, and not receiving? Perhaps it is that they ask amiss. When a man would make a bad use of what he asks for, God in His mercy does not grant him it. Still if God even in kindness often refuses the requests of believers,

c. 3.

1 verba fidei faciebat

Chrys. Hom. lxxiv. 2.

Aug. Tract. lxxiii 2.

Chrys. Hom. lxxiv. 2.

Acts 3, 6.

Aug Tract. lxxii. 2.

how are we to understand, *Whatsoever ye shall ask in My name, I will do?* Was this said to the Apostles only? No. He says above, *He that believeth on Me, the works that I do shall he do also.* And if we go to the lives of the Apostles themselves, we shall find that he who laboured more than they all, prayed that the messenger of Satan might depart from him, but was not granted his request. But attend: does not our Lord lay down a certain condition? *In My name,* which is Christ Jesus. Christ signifies King, Jesus, Saviour. Therefore whatever we ask for that would hinder our salvation, we do not ask in our Saviour's name: and yet He is our Saviour, not only when He does what we ask, but also when He does not. When He sees us ask any thing to the disadvantage of our salvation, He shews Himself our Saviour by not doing it. The physician knows whether what the sick man asks for is to the advantage or disadvantage of his health; and does not allow what would be to his hurt, though the sick man himself desires it; but looks to his final cure. And some things we may even ask in His name, and He will not grant them us at the time, though He will some time. What we ask for is deferred, not denied. He adds, *that the Father may be glorified in the Son.* The Son does not do any thing without the Father, inasmuch as He does it in order that the Father may be glorified in Him. CHRYS. For when the great power of Chrys. the Son is manifested, He that begat Him is glorified. He Hom. lxxiv. 2. introduces this last, to confirm the truth of what He has said. THEOPHYL. Observe the order in which the glorifying of the ἀκολου-Father comes. In the name of Jesus miracles were done, by θίαν which men were made to believe the Apostles' preaching. This brought them to the knowledge of the Father, and thus the Father was glorified in the Son.

15. If ye love me, keep my commandments.

16. And I will pray the Father, and he shall give you another Comforter, that he may abide with you for ever;

17. Even the Spirit of truth; whom the world cannot receive, because it seeth him not, neither knoweth

him: but ye know him; for he dwelleth with you, and shall be in you.

CHRYS. Our Lord having said, *Whatsoever ye shall ask in My name, that I will do;* that they might not think simply asking would be enough, He adds, *If ye love Me, keep My commandments.* And then 1 will do what ye ask, seems to be His meaning. Or the disciples having heard Him say, *I go to the Father,* and being troubled at the thought of it, He says, To love Me, is not to be troubled, but to keep My commandments: this is love, to obey and believe in Him who is loved. And as they had been expressing a strong desire for His bodily presence, He assures them that His absence will be supplied to them in another way: *And I will pray the Father, and He will give you another Comforter.*

Aug. Tract. lxxiv. 4. AUG. Wherein He shews too that He Himself is the Comforter. Paraclete means advocate, and is applied to Christ: 1 John 2, 1. *We have an Advocate with the Father, Jesus Christ the righteous.* ALCUIN. Paraclete, i. e. Comforter. They had then one Comforter, who comforted and elevated them by Didym. the sweetness of His miracles, and His preaching. DIDYMUS. De Spiritu Sancto. But the Holy Ghost was another Comforter: differing not in nature, but in operation. For whereas our Saviour in His office 1 legati of Mediator, and of Messenger [1], and as High Priest, made supplication for our sins; the Holy Ghost is a Comforter in another sense, i. e. as consoling our griefs. But do not infer from the different operations of the Son and the Spirit, a difference of nature. For in other places we find the Holy Spirit 2 legati performing the office of intercessor [2] with the Father, as, *The* Rom. 8, 26. *Spirit Himself intercedeth for us.* And the Saviour, on the other hand, pours consolation into those hearts that need it: 1 Macc. 14, 15. as in Maccabees, *He strengthened those of the people that were* Chrys. Hom. lxxiv. 2. *brought low.* CHRYS. He says, *I will ask the Father,* to make them believe Him: which they could not have done, had He simply said, *I will send.* AUG. Yet to shew that His works are Aug. contra Serm. Arrian. c. xix. inseparable from His Father's, He says below, *When I shall go, I will send Him unto you.* CHRYS. But what had He more Chrys. Hom. lxxiv. than the Apostles, if He could only ask the Father to give others the Spirit? The Apostles did this often even without praying. ALCUIN. *I will ask*—He says, as being the inferior in respect of His humanity—*My Father*, with Whom I am equal and consubstantial in respect of My Divine nature. CHRYS. *That He may abide with you for ever.* Chrys. Hom. lxxv. 1. The Spirit does not depart even at death. He intimates too that the Holy Ghost will not suffer death, or go away, as He has done. But that the mention of the Comforter might not lead them to expect another incarnation, a Comforter to be seen with the eye, He adds, *Even the Spirit of truth, Whom the world cannot receive, because it seeth Him not, neither knoweth Him.* AUG. This is the Holy Ghost in the Aug. Trinity, Whom the Catholic faith professes to be consub- Tract. lxxiv. 1. stantial and coeternal with the Father and the Son. CHRYS. Chrys. Hom. lxxv. 1. *The Spirit of truth* He calls Him, because He unfolds the figures of the Old Testament. The *world* are the wicked, *seeing* is certain knowledge; sight being the most certain of the senses. BEDE. Note too, that when He calls the Holy Spirit the Spirit of truth, He shews that the Holy Spirit is His Spirit: then when He says He is given by the Father, He declares Him to be the Spirit of the Father also. Thus the Holy Ghost proceeds both from the Father, and from the Son. GREG. The Holy Spirit kindles in every one, in whom Greg. v. Mor. He dwells, the desire of things invisible. And since worldly minds love only things visible, this world receiveth Him not, because it rises not to the love of things invisible. In proportion as secular minds enlarge themselves by the spread of their desires, in that proportion they narrow themselves, with respect to admitting Christ. AUG. Thus the world, i. e. Aug. Tract. lxxiv. 4. the lovers of the world, cannot, He says, receive the Holy Spirit: that is to say, unrighteousness cannot be righteous. The world, i. e. the lovers of the world, cannot receive Him, because it seeth Him not. The love of the world hath not invisible eyes wherewith to see that, which can only be seen invisibly. It follows: *But ye know Him, for He dwelleth with you.* And that they might not think this manebit meant a visible dwelling, in the sense in which we use the phrase with respect to a guest, He adds, *And shall be in you.* CHRYS. As if He said, He will not dwell with you as I have Chrys. Hom. lxxv. 1. done, but will dwell in your souls. AUG. To *be* in a place is prior to *dwelling. Be in you*, is the explanation of *dwell* Aug. Tract. lxxiv. 5.

with you: i. e. shews that the latter means not that He is seen, but that He is known. He must be in us, that the knowledge of Him may be in us. We see the Holy Ghost then in us, in our consciences. GREG. But if the Holy Spirit abides in the disciples, how is it a special mark of the Mediator that He abides in Him. We shall better understand, if we distinguish between the different gifts of the Spirit. In respect of those gifts without which we cannot attain to salvation, the Holy Spirit ever abides in all the Elect: but in respect of those which do not relate to our own salvation, but to the procuring that of others, He does not always abide in them. For He sometimes withdraws His miraculous gifts, that His grace may be possessed with humility. Christ has Him without measure and always. CHRYS. This speech levels at a stroke, as it were, the opposite heresies. The word *another,* shews the distinct personality of the Spirit: the word Paraclete, His consubstantiality. AUG. Comforter, the title of the Holy Spirit, the third Person in the Trinity, the Apostle applies to God: *God that comforteth those that are cast down, comforted us.* The Holy Spirit therefore Who comforts those that are cast down, is God. Or if they will have this said by the Apostle of the Father or the Son, let them not any longer separate the Holy Spirit from the Father and the Son, in His peculiar office of comforting. AUG. But when *the love of God is shed abroad in our hearts by the Holy Ghost which is given unto us,* how shall we love and keep the commandments of Christ, so as to receive the Spirit, when we are not able to love or to keep them, unless we have received the Spirit? Does love in us go first, i. e. do we so love Christ and keep His commandments as to deserve to receive the Holy Spirit, and to have the love of God the Father shed abroad in our hearts? This is a perverse opinion. For he who does not love the Father, does not love the Son, however he may think he does. It remains for us to understand, that he who loves has the Holy Spirit, and by having Him, attains to having more of Him, and by having more of Him, to loving more. The disciples had already the Spirit which our Lord promised; but they were to be given more of Him: they had Him secretly, they were to receive Him openly. The

Greg.
ii. Mor.

supr. i.
32.
ἰτ' αὐτὸν

Chrys.
Hom.
lxxv. 1.

Aug.
contr.
Serm.
Arrian.
c. xix.
2 Cor.
7, 6.

Aug.
Tract.
lxxiv.
c. 1.
Rom. 5,
5.

c. 2.

promise is made both to him who has the Spirit, and to him who has Him not; to the former, that he shall have Him; to the latter, that He shall have more of Him. CHRYS. When He had cleansed His disciples by the sacrifice of His passion, and their sins were remitted, and they were sent forth to dangers and trials, it was necessary that they should receive the Holy Spirit abundantly. But they were made to wait some time for this gift, in order that they might feel the want of it, and so be the more grateful for it when it came.

18. I will not leave you comfortless: I will come to you.

19. Yet a little while, and the world seeth me no more: but ye see me: because I live, ye shall live also.

20. At that day ye shall know that I am in my Father, and ye in me, and I in you.

21. He that hath my commandments, and keepeth them, he it is that loveth me: and he that loveth me shall be loved of my Father, and I will love him, and will manifest myself to him.

AUG. That no one might think, because our Lord was about to give the Holy Spirit, that He would therefore not be present Himself in Him, He adds, *I will not leave you comfortless.* The Greek word ὀρφανοὶ signifies " wards." Although then the Son of God has made us the adopted sons of the Father, yet here He Himself shews the affection of a Father towards us. CHRYS. At the first He said, Whither I go ye shall come; but as this was a long time off, He promises them the Spirit in the interval. And as they knew not what that was, He promises them that they most desired, His own presence, *I will come to you:* but intimates at the same time that they are not to look for the same kind of presence over again: *Yet a little while, and the world seeth Me no more:* as if He said, I will come to you, but not to live with you every day as I did before. And, *I will come to you* alone, He says, thus preventing any inconsistency with what He had said to the Jews: *Henceforth ye shall not see Me.* AUG. For the world saw Him then with the carnal eye,

Chrys. Hom. lxxv. 1.

Aug. Tr.lxxv. 1.

Chrys. Hom. lxxv. 1.

Aug. Tr.lxxv. 2.

manifest in the flesh, though it did not see the Word hidden under the flesh. But after the resurrection He was unwilling to shew even His flesh, except to His own followers, whom He allowed to see and to handle it: *Yet a little while, and the world seeth Me no more; but ye shall see Me.* But, inasmuch as the world, by which are meant all who are aliens from His kingdom, will see Him at the last judgment, it is better perhaps to understand Him here as pointing to that time, when He will be taken for ever from the eyes of the wicked, to be seen thenceforth by those who love Him. *A little while,* He says, for that which seems a long time to men, is but a moment in the eyes of God.

Because I live, ye shall live also. THEOPHYL. As if He said, Though I shall die, I shall rise again. And ye shall live also, i. e. when ye see Me risen again, ye will rejoice, and be as dead men brought to life again. CHRYS. To me however he seems to refer not only to the present life, but to the future; as if He said, The death of the cross shall not separate you from Me for ever, but only hide Me from you for a moment. AUG. But why does He speak of life as present to Him, future to them? Because His resurrection preceded, theirs was to follow. His resurrection was about so soon to take place, that He speaks of it as present; theirs being deferred till the end of the world, He does not say ye live, but *ye shall live.* Because He lives, therefore we shall live: *As by man came death, by man came also the resurrection of the dead.* It follows: *In that day* (the day of which He saith, *ye shall live also*) *ye shall know,* i. e. whereas now ye believe, then ye shall see, *that I am in the Father, and ye in Me, and I in you.* For when we shall have attained to that life in which death is swallowed up, then shall be finished that which is now begun by Him, that He should be in us, and we in Him. CHRYS. Or, in that day, on which I shall rise again, ye shall know. For His resurrection it was that established their faith. Then the powerful teaching of the Holy Spirit began. His saying, *I am in the Father,* expresses His humility; the next, *And ye in Me, and I in you,* His humanity and God's assistance to Him. Scripture often uses the same words in different senses, as applied to God and to men.

Margin notes:
Chrys. Hom. lxxv. 2.

Aug. Tr.lxxv. 3.

1 Cor. 15, 21.

Chrys. Hom. lxxv. 2.

HILARY. Or He means by this, that whereas He was in the Father by the nature of His divinity, and we in Him by means of His birth in the flesh; He on the other hand should be believed to be in us by the mystery of the Sacrament: as He Himself testified above: *Whoso eateth My flesh, and drinketh My blood, dwelleth in Me, and I in Him.* ALCUIN. By love, and the observance of His commandments, that will be perfected in us which He has begun, viz. that we should be in Him, and He in us. And that this blessedness may be understood to be promised to all, not to the Apostles only, He adds, *He that hath My commandments and keepeth them, he it is that loveth Me.* AUG. He that hath them in mind, and keepeth them in life; he that hath them in words, and keepeth them in works; he that hath them by hearing, and keepeth them by doing; he that hath them by doing, and keepeth them by persevering, *he it is that loveth Me.* Love must be shewn by works, or it is a mere barren name. THEOPHYL. As if He said, Ye think that by sorrowing, as ye do, for my death ye prove your affection; but I esteem the keeping of My commandments the evidence of love. And then He shews the privileged state of one who loves: *And he that loveth Me shall be loved of My Father, and I will love him.* AUG. *I will love him,* as if now He did not love him. What meaneth this? He explains it in what follows: *And will manifest Myself unto him,* i. e. I love him so far as to manifest Myself to him; so that, as the reward of his faith, he will have sight. Now He only loves us so that we believe; then He will love us so that we see. And whereas we love now by believing that which we shall see, then we shall love by seeing that which we have believed. AUG. He promises to shew Himself to them that love Him as God with the Father, not in that body which He bore upon earth, and which the wicked saw. THEOPHYL. Or, as after the resurrection He was to appear to them in a body more assimilated to His divinity, that they might not take Him then for a spirit, or a phantom, He tells them now beforehand not to have misgivings upon seeing Him, but to remember that He shews Himself to them as a reward for their keeping His commandments; and that therefore

Margin notes:
Hilar. viii. de Trin.

supr. 6, 54.

Aug. Tract. lxxv. 5.

Aug. Tract. lxxv. 5.

Aug. ad Paul. de videndo Dei, Ep. cxii. c. 10.

they are bound ever to keep them, that they may ever enjoy the sight of Him.

22. Judas saith unto him, not Iscariot, Lord, how is it that thou wilt manifest thyself unto us, and not unto the world?

23. Jesus answered and said unto him, If a man love me, he will keep my words: and my Father will love him, and we will come unto him, and make our abode with him.

24. He that loveth me not keepeth not my sayings: and the word which ye hear is not mine, but the Father's which sent me.

25. These things have I spoken unto you, being yet present with you.

26. But the Comforter, which is the Holy Ghost, whom the Father will send in my name, he shall teach you all things, and bring all things to your remembrance, whatsoever I have said unto you.

27. Peace I leave with you, my peace I give unto you: not as the world giveth, give I unto you.

Aug. Tract. lxxvi. 1. AUG. Our Lord having said, *A little while, and the world seeth Me no more: but ye shall see Me:* Judas, not the traitor named Scariot, but he whose Epistle is read among the Canonical Scriptures, asks His meaning: *Judas saith unto Him, not Iscariot, Lord, how is it that Thou wilt manifest Thyself unto us, and not unto the world?* Our Lord in reply explains why He manifests Himself to His own, and not to aliens, viz. because the one love Him, the other do not. *Jesus answered and said unto him, If a man love Me, he will keep My words.* Greg. Hom. xxx. in Evang. GREG. If thou wouldest prove thy love, shew thy works. The love of God is never idle; whenever it is, it doeth great things: if it do not work, it is not. Aug. Tract. lxxvi. 2. AUG. Love distinguishes the saints from the world: it maketh men to be of one mind in an house; in which house the Father and the Son take their abode; who give that love to those, to whom in the end they will manifest themselves. For there is a certain inner manifestation of God, unknown to the ungodly, to whom there is no manifestation made of the Father and the Holy Spirit, and only could be of the Son in the flesh; which latter manifestation is not as the former, being only for a little while, not for ever, for judgment, not for joy, for punishment, not for reward. *And We will come unto him:* They come to us, in that we go to Them; They come by succouring, we go by obeying; They come by enlightening, we go by contemplating; They come by filling, we go by holding: so Their manifestation to us is not external, but inward; Their abode in us not transitory, but eternal. It follows, *And will make Our abode with him.* GREG. Into some hearts He cometh, but not to make His abode with them. For some feel compunction for a season and turn to God, but in time of temptation forget that which gave them compunction, and return to their former sins, just as if they had never lamented them. But whoso loveth God truly, into his heart the Lord both comes, and also makes His abode therein: for the love of the Godhead so penetrates him, that no temptation withdraws him from it. He truly loves, whose mind no evil pleasure overcomes, through his consent thereto. AUG. But while the Father and the Son make Their abode with the loving soul, is the Holy Spirit excluded? What meaneth that which is said of the Holy Spirit above: *He dwelleth with you, and shall be in you,* but that the Spirit makes His abode with us? Unless indeed a man be so absurd as to think that when the Father and the Son come, the Holy Spirit departs, as if to give place to His superiors. Yet even this carnal thought is met by Scripture, in that it says, *Abide with you for ever.* He will therefore be in the same abode with Them for ever. As He did not come without Them, so neither They without Him. As a consequence of the Trinity, acts are sometimes attributed to single persons in it: but the substance of the same Trinity demands, that in such acts the presence of the other Persons also be implied. GREG. In proportion as a man's love rests upon lower things, in that proportion is he removed from heavenly love: *He that loveth Me not, keepeth not My sayings.* To the love then of our Maker, let the tongue, mind, life bear

Marginal notes: Greg. Hom. xxx. — Aug. Tract. lxxvi. 4. — v. 16. — Greg. Hom. xxx.

Chrys.
Hom.
lxxv. 1,
2. witness. CHRYS. Or thus : Judas thought that he should see Him, as we see the dead in sleep : *How is it, that Thou wilt manifest Thyself unto us, and not unto the world?* meaning, Alas, as Thou art to die, Thou wilt appear to us but as one dead. To correct this mistake, He says, *I and My Father will come to him,* i. e. I shall manifest Myself, even as My Father manifests Himself. *And will make our abode with Him*; which is not like a dream. It follows, *And the word which ye hear is not Mine, but the Father's which sent Me;* i. e. He that heareth not My words, inasmuch as he loveth not Me, so loveth he not My Father. This He says to shew that He spoke nothing which was not the

Aug.
Tract.
lxxvi. 5. Father's, nothing beside what seemed good to the Father. AUG. And perhaps there is a distinction at bottom, since He speaks of His sayings, when they are His own, in the plural number; as when He says, *He that loveth Me not, keepeth not My sayings:* when they are not His own, but the Father's, in the singular, i. e. as the Word, which is Himself. For He is not His own Word, but the Father's, as He is not His own image, but the Father's, or His own Son, but the Father's.

Chrys.
Hom.
lxxv. 3. CHRYS. *These things have I spoken unto you, being yet present with you.* Some of these things were obscure, and not Aug.
Tract.
lxxvii.
1. understood by the disciples. AUG. The abode He promised them hereafter is altogether a different one from this present abode He now speaks of. The one is spiritual and inward, the other outward, and perceptible to the bodily sight and Chrys.
Hom.
lxxv. 3. hearing. CHRYS. To enable them to sustain His bodily departure more cheerfully, He promises that that departure shall be the source of great benefit; for that while He was then in the body, they could never know much, because the Spirit would not have come: *But the Comforter, which is the Holy Ghost, Whom the Father will send in My name, He shall teach you all things, and bring all things to* Greg.
Hom.
xxx. in
Evang. *your remembrance, whatsoever I have said unto you.* GREG. Paraclete is Advocate, or Comforter. The Advocate then intercedes with the Father for sinners, when by His inward power He moves the sinner to pray for himself. The Comforter relieves the sorrow of penitents, and cheers them Chrys.
Hom.
lxxv. 3. with the hope of pardon. CHRYS. He often calls Him

the Comforter, in allusion to the affliction in which they then were. DIDYMUS. The Saviour affirms that the Holy Spirit is Didym. sent by the Father, in His, the Saviour's, name; which name de Spir. Sancto, is the Son. Here an agreement of nature and propriety[1], so l.ii.inter to speak, of persons is shewn. The Son can come in the Hieron. opera Father's name only, consistently with the proper[1] relationship [1] pro- prietas of the Son to the Father, and the Father to the Son. No one else comes in the name of the Father, but in the name of God, of the Lord, of the Almighty, and the like. As servants who come in the name of their Lord, do so as being the servants of that Lord, so the Son who comes in the name of the Father, bears that name as being the acknow- ledged only-begotten Son of the Father. That the Holy Spirit then is sent in the Son's name, by the Father, shews that He is in unity with the Son: whence He is said too to be the Spirit of the Son, and to make those sons by adoption, who are willing to receive Him. The Holy Spirit then, Who cometh in the name of the Son from the Father, shall teach them, who are established in the faith of Christ, all things; all things which are spiritual, both the understanding of truth, and the sacrament of wisdom. But He will teach not like those who have acquired an art or knowledge by study and industry, but as being the very art, doctrine, knowledge itself. As being this Himself, the Spirit of truth will impart the knowledge of divine things to the mind. GREG. Unless Greg. Hom. the Spirit be present to the mind of the hearer, the word of xxx. the teacher is vain. Let none then attribute to the human teacher, the understanding which follows in consequence of his teaching: for unless there be a teacher within, the tongue of the teacher outside will labour in vain. Nay even the Maker Himself does not speak for the instruction of man, unless the Spirit by His unction speaks at the same time. AUG. So then the Son speaks, the Holy Spirit teaches: Aug. Tract. when the Son speaks we take in the words, when the Holy lxxvii.2. Spirit teaches, we understand those words. The whole Trinity indeed both speaks and teaches, but unless each person worked separately as well, the whole would be too much for human infirmity to take in. GREG. But why is it Greg. Hom. said of the Spirit, *He shall suggest[2] all things to you:* to xxx. [2] sug- suggest being the office of an inferior? The word is used geret Vulg.

here, as it is used sometimes, in the sense of supplying secretly. The invisible Spirit *suggests*, not because He takes a lower place in teaching, but because He teaches secretly. AUG. *Suggest*, i. e. bring to your remembrance. Every wholesome hint to remember that we receive is of the grace of the Spirit. THEOPHYL. The Holy Spirit then was both to teach and to bring to remembrance: to teach what Christ had forborne to tell His disciples, because they were not able to bear it; to bring to remembrance what Christ had told them, but which on account of its difficulty, or their slowness of understanding, they were unable to remember. CHRYS. *Peace I leave with you, My peace I give unto you:* He says this to console His disciples, who were now troubled at the prospect of the hatred and opposition which awaited them after His departure. AUG. He left no peace in this world; in which we conquer the enemy, and have love one to another: He will give us peace in the world to come, when we shall reign without an enemy, and where we shall be able to avoid disagreement. This peace is Himself, both when we believe that He is, and when we shall see Him as He is. But why does He say, *Peace I leave with you,* without the *My*, whereas He puts in *My* in, *My peace I give unto you?* Are we to understand *My* in the former; or is it not rather left out with a meaning? His peace is such peace as He has Himself; the peace which He left us in this world is rather our peace than His. He has nothing to fight against in Himself, because He has no sin: but ours is a peace in which we still say, *Forgive us our debts.* And in like manner we have peace between ourselves, because we mutually trust one another, that we mutually love one another. But neither is that a perfect peace; for we do not see into each other's minds. I could not deny however that these words of our Lord's may be understood as a simple repetition. He adds, *Not as the world giveth, give I unto you:* i. e. not as those men, who love the world, give. They give themselves peace, i. e. free, uninterrupted enjoyment of the world. And even when they allow the righteous peace, so far as not to persecute them, yet there cannot be true peace, where there is no true agreement, no union of heart. CHRYS. External peace is often even hurtful, rather than

Aug. Tract. xxvii.2.

Chrys. Hom. lxxiv. 3.

Aug. Tract. lxxvii 2.

Matt. 6, 12.

Chrys. Hom. lxxv. 3.

profitable to those who enjoy it.   AUG. But there is a peace Aug.
which is serenity of thought, tranquillity of mind, simplicity $^{\text{de Verb.}}_{\text{Dom.}}$
of heart, the bond of love, the fellowship of charity.   None serm. ix.
will be able to come to the inheritance of the Lord who
do not observe this testament of peace; none be friends
with Christ, who are at enmity with the Christians.

27. Let not your heart be troubled, neither let it be
afraid.

28. Ye have heard how I said unto you, I go away,
and come again unto you. If ye loved me, ye would
rejoice, because I said, I go unto the Father: for my
Father is greater than I.

29. And now I have told you before it come to
pass, that, when it is come to pass, ye might believe.

30. Hereafter I will not talk much with you: for
the prince of this world cometh, and hath nothing
in me.

31. But that the world may know that I love the
Father: and as the Father gave me commandment,
even so I do.   Arise, let us go hence.

CHRYS. After saying, *Peace I leave with you*, which was Chrys.
like taking farewell, He consoles them: *Let not your heart* $^{\text{Hom.}}_{\text{lxxv. 3.}}$
be troubled, neither let it be afraid: the two feelings of love
and fear were now the uppermost in them.   AUG. Though Aug.
He was only going for a time, their hearts would be troubled $^{\text{Tract.}}_{\text{lxxviii.}}$
and afraid for what might happen before He returned; 1.
lest in the absence of the Shepherd the wolf might attack
the flock: *Ye have heard how I said unto you, I go away,
and come again to you.*   In that He was man, He went: in
that He was God, He stayed. Why then be troubled and
afraid, when He left the eye only, not the heart?   To make
them understand that it was as man that He said, *I go away,
and come again to you;* He adds, *If ye loved Me ye would
rejoice, because I said, I go unto My Father; for My
Father is greater than I.* In that the Son then is unequal

with the Father, through that inequality He went to the Father, from Him to come again to judge the quick and dead: in that He is equal to the Father, He never goes from the Father, but is every where altogether with Him in that Godhead, which is not confined to place. Nay, the Son Himself, because that being equal to the Father in the form of God, He emptied Himself, not losing the form of God, but taking that of a servant, is greater even than Himself: the form of God which is not lost, is greater than the form of a servant which was put on. In this form of a servant, the Son of God is inferior not to the Father only, but to the Holy Ghost; in this the Child Christ was inferior even to His parents; to whom we read, He was subject. Let us acknowledge then the twofold substance of Christ, the divine, which is equal to the Father, and the human, which is inferior. But Christ is both together, not two, but one Christ: else the Godhead is a quaternity, not a Trinity. Wherefore He says, *If ye loved Me, ye would rejoice, because I said, I go to the Father;* for human nature should exult at being thus taken up by the Only Begotten Word, and made immortal in heaven; at earth being raised to heaven, and dust sitting incorruptible at the right hand of the Father. Who, that loves Christ, will not rejoice at this, seeing, as he doth, his own nature immortal in Christ, and hoping that He Himself will be so by Christ.

Hilar. de Trin. ix.

HILARY. Or thus: If the Father is greater by virtue of giving, is the Son less by confessing the gift? The giver is the greater, but He to whom unity with that giver is given, is not the less.

Chrys. Hom. lxxv. 4.

CHRYS. Or thus: The Apostles did not yet know what the resurrection was of which He spoke when He said, *I go, and come again to you:* or what they ought to think of it. They only knew the great power of the Father. So He tells them: Though ye fear I shall not be able to save Myself, and do not trust to My appearing again after My crucifixion; yet when ye hear that I go to My Father, ye should rejoice, because I go to one greater, one able to dissolve and change all things. All this is said in accommodation to their weakness: as we see from the next words; *And now I have told you before it come to pass; that when it does come to pass, ye may believe.*

Aug. Tract. lxxix. 1.

AUG. But is not the time for belief before a thing takes place? Is it not the praise of

faith, that it believes what it does not see? according to what
is said below to Thomas: *Because thou hast seen, thou hast
believed.* He saw one thing, believed another: what he saw was
man, what he believed was God. And if belief can be talked of
with reference to things seen, as when we say that we believe
our eyes; yet it is not mature faith, but is merely preparatory
to our believing what we do not see. *When it has come to
pass;* then He says, because after His death they would see
Him alive again, and ascending to His Father; which sight
would convince them that He was the Christ, the Son of
God; able as He was to do so great a thing, and to foretell
it. Which faith however would not be a new, but only an
enlarged faith; or a faith which had failed at His death,
and been renewed by His resurrection. HILARY. He next Hilar.
alludes to the approach of the time when He would resume ix. de Trin.
His glory. *Hereafter I will not talk much with you.*
BEDE. He says this because the time was now approaching
for His being taken, and given up to death: *For the Prince
of this world cometh.* AUG. i. e. the devil; the prince of Aug.
sinners, not of creatures; as the Apostle saith, *Against the* Tract. lxxix.2.
rulers of this world. Or, as He immediately adds by way Eph. 6, 12.
of explanation, *this darkness,* meaning, the ungodly. *And
hath nothing in Me.* God had no sin as God, nor had His
flesh contracted it by a sinful birth, being born of the Virgin.
But how, it might be asked, canst thou die, if thou hast no
sin: He answers, *But that the world may know that I love
the Father, and as the Father gave Me commandment, even
so I do. Arise, let us go hence.* He had been sitting at
table with them all this time. *Let us go:* i. e. to the place,
where He, Who had done nothing to deserve death, was to
be delivered to death. But He had a *commandment* from
His Father to die. AUG. That the Son is obedient to the Aug.
will and commandment of the Father, no more shews a contr. Serm.
difference in the two, than it would in a human father and Arrian. c. xi.
son. But over and above this comes the consideration that
Christ is not only God, and as such equal to the Father,
but also man, and as such inferior to the Father. CHRYS. Chrys. Hom.
Arise, let us go hence, is the beginning of the sentence which lxxvi. 1.
follows. The time and the place (they were in the midst of
a town, and it was night time) had excited the disciples'

fears to such a degree, that they could not attend to any thing that was said, but rolled their eyes about, expecting persons to enter and assault them; especially when they heard our Lord say, *Yet a little while I am with you;* and, *The prince of this world cometh.* To quiet their alarm then, He takes them to another place, where they imagine themselves safe, and would be able to attend to the great doctrines which He was going to set before them.

CHAP. XV.

1. I am the true vine, and my Father is the husbandman.

2. Every branch in me that beareth not fruit he taketh away : and every branch that beareth fruit, he purgeth it, that it may bring forth more fruit.

3. Now ye are clean through the word which I have spoken unto you.

HILARY. He rises in haste to perform the sacrament of His final passion in the flesh, (such is His desire to fulfil His Father's commandment :) and therefore takes occasion to unfold the mystery of His assumption of His flesh, whereby He supports us, as the vine doth its branches : *I am the true vine.* AUG. He says this as being the Head of the Church, of which we are the members, the Man Christ Jesus ; for the vine and the branches are of the same nature. When He says, *I am the true vine,* He does not mean really a vine ; for He is only called so metaphorically, not literally, even as He is called the Lamb, the Sheep, and the like ; but He distinguishes Himself from that vine to whom it is said, *How art thou turned into the degenerate plant of a strange vine unto me.* For how is that a true vine, which when grapes are expected from it, produces only thorns? HILARY. But He wholly separates this humiliation in the flesh from the form of the Paternal Majesty, by setting forth the Father as the diligent Husbandman of this vine : *And My Father is the Husbandman.* AUG. For we cultivate God, and God cultivates us. But our culture of God does not make Him better : our culture is that of adoration, not of ploughing : His culture of us makes us better. His culture consists in extirpating all the seeds of wickedness from our hearts, in

Hilar.
ix. de
Trin.

Aug.
Tr.lxxx.
2.

Jer. 11,
21.

Hilar.
ix. de
Trin.

Aug.
de Verb.
Dom.
serm.
lix.

opening our heart to the plough, as it were, of His word, in
sowing in us the seeds of His commandments, in waiting for
the fruits of piety. CHRYS. And forasmuch as Christ was
sufficient for Himself, but His disciples needed the help of
the Husbandman, of the vine He says nothing, but adds
concerning the branches, *Every branch in Me that beareth
not fruit, He taketh away.* By fruit is meant life, i. e. that
no one can be in Him without good works. HILARY. The
useless and deceitful branches He cuts down for burning.
CHRYS. And inasmuch as even the best of men require the
work of the husbandman, He adds, *And every branch that
beareth fruit, He purgeth it, that it may bring forth more
fruit.* He alludes here to the tribulations and trials which
were coming upon them, the effect of which would be to
purge, and so to strengthen them. By pruning the branches
we make the tree shoot out the more. AUG. And who is
there in this world so clean, that he cannot be more and
more changed? Here, *if we say that we have no sin, we
deceive ourselves.* He cleanseth then the clean, i. e. the
fruitful, that the cleaner they be, the more fruitful they
may be. Christ is the vine, in that He saith, *My Father
is greater than I;* but in that He saith, *I and My Father
are one,* He is the husbandman; not like those who carry on
an external ministry only; for He giveth increase within.
Thus He calls Himself immediately the cleanser of the
branches: *Now ye are clean through the word, which I
have spoken unto you.* He performs the part of the husbandman then, as well as of the vine. But why does He
not say, ye are clean by reason of the baptism wherewith ye
are washed? Because it is the word in the water which
cleanseth. Take away the word, and what is the water, but
water? Add the word to the element, and you have a sacrament. Whence hath the water such virtue as that by touching the body, it cleanseth the heart, but by the power of the
word, not spoken only, but believed? For in the word itself,
the passing sound is one thing, the abiding virtue another.
This word of faith is of such avail in the Church of God,
that by Him who believes, presents, blesses, sprinkles the
infant, it cleanseth that infant, though itself is unable to
believe. CHRYS. *Ye are clean through the word which I*

Chrys.
Hom.
lxxvi.

Hilar.
ix. de
Trin.

Chrys.
Hom.
lxxvi. 1.

Aug.
Tr. lxxx.
3.

1 John 1,
8.

have spoken unto you, i. e. ye have been enlightened by My doctrine, and been delivered from Jewish error.

4. Abide in me, and I in you. As the branch cannot bear fruit of itself, except it abide in the vine; no more can ye, except ye abide in me.

5. I am the vine, ye are the branches: He that abideth in me, and I in him, the same bringeth forth much fruit: for without me ye can do nothing.

6. If a man abide not in me, he is cast forth as a branch, and is withered; and men gather them, and cast them into the fire, and they are burned.

7. If ye abide in me, and my words abide in you, ye shall ask what ye will, and it shall be done unto you.

CHRYS. Having said that they were clean through the word which He had spoken unto them, He now teaches them that they must do their part. AUG. *Abide in Me, and I in you:* not they in Him, as He in them; for both are for the profit not of Him, but them. The branches do not confer any advantage upon the vine, but receive their support from it: the vine supplies nourishment to the branches, takes none from them: so that the abiding in Christ, and the having Christ abiding in them, are both for the profit of the disciples, not of Christ; according to what follows, *As the branch cannot bear fruit of itself, except it abide in the vine, no more can ye, except ye abide in Me.* Great display of grace! He strengtheneth the hearts of the humble, stoppeth the mouth of the proud. They who hold that God is not necessary for the doing of good works, the subverters, not the assertors, of free will, contradict this truth. For he who thinks that he bears fruit of himself, is not in the vine; he who is not in the vine, is not in Christ; he who is not in Christ, is not a Christian. ALCUIN. All the fruit of good works proceeds from this root. He who hath delivered us by His grace, also carries us onward by his help, so that we bring forth more fruit. Wherefore He repeats, and explains what He has said: *I am the vine, ye are the branches. He that abideth in Me,* by believing, obeying,

Margin notes: Chrys. Hom. lxxvi. — non occ. Aug. Tract. lxxxi. 1.

persevering, *and I in Him,* by enlightening, assisting, giving perseverance, *the same,* and none other, *bringeth forth much fruit.* AUG. But lest any should suppose that a branch could bring forth a little fruit of itself, He adds, *For without Me ye can do nothing.* He does not say, ye can do little. Unless the branch abides in the vine, and lives from the root, it can bear no fruit whatever. Christ, though He would not be the vine, except He were man, yet could not give this grace to the branches, except He were God. CHRYS. The Son then contributes no less than the Father to the help of the disciples. The Father changeth, but the Son keepeth them in Him, which is that which makes the branches fruitful. And again, the cleansing is attributed to the Son also, and the abiding in the root to the Father who begat the root.

It is a great loss to be able to do nothing, but He goes on to say more than this: *If a man abide not in Me, he is cast forth as a branch,* i. e. shall not benefit by the care of the husbandman, *and withereth,* i. e. shall lose all that it desires from the root, all that supports its life, and shall die. ALCUIN. *And men gather them,* i. e. the reapers, the Angels, *and cast them into the fire,* everlasting fire, *and they are burned.* AUG. For the branches of the vine are as contemptible, if they abide not in the vine, as they are glorious, if they abide. One of the two the branch must be in, either the vine, or the fire: if it is not in the vine, it will be in the fire. CHRYS. Then He shews what it is to abide in Him· *If ye abide in Me, and My words abide in you, ye shall ask what ye will, and it shall be done unto you.* It is to be shewn by their works. AUG. For then may His words be said to abide in us, when we do what He has commanded, and love what He has promised. But when His words abide in the memory, and are not found in the life, the branch is not accounted to be in the vine, because it derives no life from its root. So far as we abide in the Saviour we cannot will any thing that is foreign to our salvation. We have one will, in so far as we are in Christ, another, in so far as we are in this world. And by reason of our abode in this world, it sometimes happens that we ask for that which is not expedient, through ignorance. But never, if we abide in Christ, will He grant it us, Who does not grant except what is expedient for us.

Aug.
Tract.
lxxxi.3.

Chrys.
Hom.
lxxvi.1.

c. 2.

Aug.
Tract.
lxxxi 3.

Chrys.
Hom.
lxxvi.2.

Aug.
Tract.
lxxxi.4.

And here we are directed to the prayer, *Our Father.* Let us adhere to the words and the meaning of this prayer in our petitions, and whatever we ask will be done for us.

8. Herein is my Father glorified, that ye bear much fruit; so shall ye be my disciples.

9. As the Father hath loved me, so have I loved you: continue ye in my love.

10. If ye keep my commandments, ye shall abide in my love: even as I have kept my Father's commandments, and abide in his love.

11. These things have I spoken unto you, that my joy might remain in you, and that your joy might be full.

CHRYS. Our Lord shewed above, that those who plotted against them should be burned, inasmuch as they abode not in Christ: now He shews that they themselves would be invincible, bringing forth much fruit; *Herein is My Father glorified, that ye bear much fruit:* as if He said, If it appertains to My Father's glory that ye bring forth fruit, He will not despise His own glory. And he that bringeth forth fruit is Christ's disciple: *So shall ye be My disciples.* THEOPHYL. The fruit of the Apostles are the Gentiles, who through their teaching were converted to the faith, and brought into subjection to the glory of God. AUG. Made bright or glorified; the Greek word may be translated in either way. Δόξα signifies glory; not our own glory, we must remember, as if we had it of ourselves: it is of His grace that we have it; and therefore it is not our own but His glory. For from whom shall we derive our fruitfulness, but from His mercy preventing us. Wherefore He adds, *As My Father hath loved Me, even so love I you.* This then is the source of our good works. Our good works proceed from faith which worketh by love: but we could not love unless we were loved first: *As My Father hath loved Me, even so love I you.* This does not prove that our nature is equal to His, as His is to the Father's, but the grace, whereby He is the Mediator between God and man, the man

2 I

Chrys.
Hom.
lxxvi.2. Christ Jesus. The Father loves us, but in Him. CHRYS.
If then I love you, be of good cheer; if it is the Father's
glory that ye bring forth good fruit, bear no evil. Then to
rouse them to exertion, He adds, *Continue ye in My love;*
and then shews how this is to be done: *If ye keep My com-*
Aug.
Tract.
lxxxii.3.
et seq. *mandments, ye shall abide in My love.* AUG. Who doubts
that love precedes the observance of the commandments?
For who loves not, has not that whereby to keep the commandments. These words then do not declare whence love
arises, but how it is shewn, that no one might deceive himself
into thinking that he loved our Lord, when he did not keep
His commandments. Though the words, *Continue ye in My
love,* do not of themselves make it evident which love He
means, ours to Him, or His to us, yet the preceding words
do: *I love you,* He says: and then immediately after, *Continue ye in My love. Continue ye in My love,* then, is, continue in My grace: and, *If ye keep My commandments, ye
shall abide in My love,* is, Your keeping of My commandments, will be evidence to you that ye abide in My love.
It is not that we keep His commandments first, and that then
He loves; but that He loves us, and then we keep His commandments. This is that grace, which is revealed to the
humble, but hidden from the proud. But what means the
next words, *Even as I have kept My Father's commandments, and abide in His love:* i. e. the Father's love, wherewith He loveth the Son. Must this grace, wherewith the
Father loves the Son, be understood to be like the grace
wherewith the Son loveth us? No; for whereas we are sons
not by nature, but by grace, the Only Begotten is Son not by
grace, but by nature. We must understand this then to
refer to the manhood in the Son, even as the words themselves imply: *As My Father hath loved Me, even so love I
you.* The grace of a Mediator is expressed here; and Christ
is Mediator between God and man, not as God, but as man.
This then we may say, that since human nature does not
pertain to the nature of God, but does by grace pertain to
the Person of the Son, grace also pertains to that Person;
such grace as has nothing superior, nothing equal to it. For
no merits on man's part preceded the assumption of that
nature. ALCUIN. *Even as I have kept My Father's com-*

mandments. The Apostle explains what these commandments were: *Christ became obedient unto death, even the death of* Phil. 2, *the cross.* CHRYS. Then because the Passion was now ap-⁸· proaching to interrupt their joy, He adds, *These things have* Hom. *I spoken unto you, that my joy may remain in you:* as if lxxvii.1. He said, And if sorrow fall upon you, I will take it away; so that ye shall rejoice in the end. AUG. And what is Aug. Christ's joy in us, but that He deigns to rejoice on our Tract. account? And what is our joy, which He says shall be full, but to have fellowship with Him? He had perfect joy on our account, when He rejoiced in foreknowing, and predestinating us; but that joy was not in us, because then we did not exist: it began to be in us, when He called us And this joy we rightly call our own, this joy wherewith we shall be blessed; which is begun in the faith of them who are born again, and shall be fulfilled in the reward of them who rise again.

12. This is my commandment, That ye love one another, as I have loved you.

13. Greater love hath no man than this, that a man lay down his life for his friends.

14. Ye are my friends, if ye do whatsoever I command you.

15. Henceforth I call you not servants; for the servant knoweth not what his Lord doeth: but I have called you friends; for all things that I have heard of my Father I have made known unto you.

16. Ye have not chosen me, but I have chosen you, and ordained you, that ye should go and bring forth fruit, and that your fruit should remain: that whatsoever ye shall ask of the Father in my name, he may give it you.

THEOPHYL. Having said, *If ye keep My commandments, ye shall abide in My love,* He shews what commandments they are to keep: *This is My commandment, That ye love one* Greg. *another.* GREG. But when all our Lord's sacred discourses Hom. xxvii.in

are full of His commandments, why does He give this special
commandment respecting love, if it is not that every commandment teaches love, and all precepts are one? Love and
love only is the fulfilment of every thing that is enjoined.
As all the boughs of a tree proceed from one root, so all the
virtues are produced from one love: nor hath the branch,
i. e. the good work, any life, except it abide in the root of
love. AUG. Where then love is, what can be wanting?
where it is not, what can profit? But this love is distinguished from men's love to each other as men, by adding,
As I have loved you. To what end did Christ love us, but
that we should reign with Him? Let us therefore so love
one another, as that our love be different from that of other
men; who do not love one another, to the end that God may
be loved, because they do not really love at all. They who
love one another for the sake of having God within them, they
truly love one another. GREG. The highest, the only proof
of love, is to love our adversary; as did the Truth Himself,
who while He suffered on the cross, shewed His love for His
persecutors: *Father, forgive them, for they know not what
they do.* Of which love the consummation is given in the
next words: *Greater love hath no man than this, that a man
lay down his life for his friends.* Our Lord came to die for
His enemies, but He says that He is going to lay down His
life for His friends, to shew us that by loving, we are able to
gain over our enemies, so that they who persecute us are by
anticipation our friends. AUG. Having said, *This is My commandment, that ye love one another, even as I have loved you,*
it follows, as John saith in his Epistle, that as Christ laid
down His life for us, so we should lay down our lives for the
brethren. This the martyrs have done with ardent love.
And therefore in commemorating them at Christ's table, we
do not pray for them, as we do for others, but we rather pray
that we may follow their steps. For they have shewn the same
love for their brother, that has been shewn them at the Lord's
table. GREG. But whoso in time of tranquillity will not give
up his time to God, how in persecution will he give up his soul?
Let the virtue of love then, that it may be victorious in tribulation, be nourished in tranquillity by deeds of mercy. AUG.
From one and the same love, we love God and our neighbour;

Aug.
Tract.
lxxxiii.
3.

Greg.
Hom.
xxvii.

Luke 23,
34.

[1] lucrum
facere
de ini-
micis
Aug.
Tract.
lxxxiv.
1.
1 John 3.

Greg.
Hom.
xxvii.

Aug.
viii. de
Trin. c.
viii.

but God for His own sake, our neighbour for God's. So that, there being two precepts of love, on which hang all the Law and the Prophets, to love God, and to love our neighbour, Scripture often unites them into one precept. For if a man love God, it follows that he does what God commands, and if so, that he loves his neighbour, God having commanded this. Wherefore He proceeds: *Ye are My friends, if ye do what-soever I command you.* GREG. A friend is as it were a keeper of the soul. He who keeps God's commandments, is rightly called His friend. AUG. Great condescension! Though to keep his Lord's commandments, is only what a good servant is obliged to do, yet, if they do so, He calls them His friends. The good servant is both the servant, and the friend. But how is this? He tells us: *Henceforth I call you not servants, for the servant knoweth not what his Lord doeth.* Shall we therefore cease to be servants, as soon as ever we are good servants? And is not a good and tried servant sometimes entrusted with his master's secrets, still remaining a servant? We must understand then that there are two kinds of servitude, as there are two kinds of fear. There is a fear which perfect love casteth out; which also hath in it a servitude, which will be cast out together with the fear. And there is another, a pure fear, which remaineth for ever. It is the former state of servitude, which our Lord refers to, when He says, *Henceforth I call you not servants, for the servant knoweth not what his Lord doeth;* not the state of that servant to whom it is said, *Well done, thou good servant, enter thou into the joy of thy Lord:* but of him of whom it was said below, *The servant abideth not in the house for ever, but the Son abideth ever.* Forasmuch then as God hath given us power to become the sons of God, so that in a wonderful way, we are servants, and yet not servants, we know that it is the Lord who doth this. This that servant is ignorant of, who knoweth not what his Lord doeth, and when he doeth any good thing, is exalted in his own conceit, as if he himself did it, and not his Lord; and boasts of himself, not of his Lord.

But I have called you friends, for all things that I have heard of My Father, I have made known unto you. THE-OPHYL. As if He said, The servant knoweth not the counsels

Greg.
xxvii.
Moral.

Aug.
Tract.
lxxxv.2.

c. 3.

castus

Mat.25,
21.

of his lord; but since I esteem you friends, I have com-

municated my secrets to you. AUG. But how did He make
known to His disciples all things that He had heard from
the Father, when He forebore saying many things, because
He knew they as yet could not bear them? He made all
things known to His disciples, i. e. He knew that He should
make them known to them in that fulness of which the Apo-

stle saith, *Then we shall know, even as we are known.* For
as we look for the death of the flesh, and the salvation of the
soul ; so should we look for that knowledge of all things, which

the Only-Begotten heard from the Father. GREG. Or all
things which He heard from the Father, which He wished
to be made known to His servants; the joys of spiritual love,
the pleasures of our heavenly country, which He impresses
daily on our minds by the inspiration of His love. For while
we love the heavenly things we hear, we know them by loving,
because love is itself knowledge. He had made all things
known to them then, because being withdrawn from earthly

desires, they burned with the fire of divine love. CHRYS.
All things, i. e. all things that they ought to hear. *I have
heard*, shews that what He had taught was no strange

doctrine, but received from the Father. GREG. But let no
one who has attained to this dignity of being called the
friend of God, attribute this superhuman gift[1] to his own

merits: *Ye have not chosen Me, but I have chosen you.*

AUG. Ineffable grace! For what were we before Christ had
chosen us, but wicked, and lost? We did not believe in
Him, so as to be chosen by Him: for had He chosen us
believing, He would have chosen us choosing. This passage
refutes the vain opinion of those who say that we were chosen
before the foundation of the world, because God foreknew
that we should be good, not that He Himself would make us
good. For had He chosen us, because He foreknew that we
should be good, He would have foreknown also that we
should first choose Him, for without choosing Him we cannot be good; unless indeed he can be called good, who hath
not chosen good. What then hath He chosen in them who
are not good? Thou canst not say, I am chosen because I
believed; for hadst thou believed in Him, thou hadst chosen
Him. Nor canst thou say, Before I believed I did good

works, and therefore was chosen. For what good work is
there before faith ? What is there for us to say then, but that
we were wicked, and were chosen, that by the grace of the
chosen we might become good ? AUG. They are chosen then ^{Aug.}
before the foundation of the world, according to that pre- ^{de Prad.} ^{Sanct.}
destination by which God foreknew His future acts. They ^{c. xvii.}
are chosen out of the world by that call whereby God fulfills
what He has predestined: *whom He did predestinate, them* ^{Rom. 8,}
He also called. AUG. Observe, He does not choose the ^{30.} ^{Aug.}
good; but those, whom He hath chosen, He makes good: ^{Tract.}
And I have ordained you that ye should go, and bring forth ^{lxxxvi.} ^{3.}
fruit. This is the fruit which He meant, when He said,
Without Me ye can do nothing. He Himself is the way in ^{ἔθηκα,}
which He hath set us to go. GREG. *I have set you,* i. e. have ^{posui} ^{Greg.}
planted you by grace, *that ye should go by will;* to will ^{Hom.}
being to go in mind, *and bring forth fruit,* by works. What ^{xxvii.} ^{volendo}
kind of fruit they should bring forth He then shews: *And* ^{not in} ^{Vulg.}
that your fruit may remain: for worldly labour hardly
produces fruit to last our life: and if it does, death comes
at last, and deprives us of it all. But the fruit of our spiritual labours endures even after death ; and begins to be seen
at the very time that the results of our carnal labour begin
to disappear. Let us then produce such fruits as may
remain, and of which death, which destroys every thing, will
be the commencement. AUG. Love then is one fruit, now ^{Aug.}
existing in desire only, not yet in fulness. Yet even with ^{Tract.} ^{lxxxvi.}
this desire whatever we ask in the name of the Only-Begotten ^{3.}
Son, the Father giveth us: *That whatsoever ye shall ask*
the Father in My name, He may give it you. We ask in
the Saviour's name, whatever we ask, that will be profitable
to our salvation.

17. These things I command you, that ye love
one another.

18. If the world hate you, ye know that it hated me
before it hated you.

19. If ye were of the world, the world would love
his own: but because ye are not of the world, but I

have chosen you out of the world, therefore the world hateth you.

20. Remember the word that I said unto you, The servant is not greater than his lord. If they have persecuted me, they will also persecute you; if they have kept my saying, they will keep yours also.

21. But all these things will they do unto you for my name's sake, because they know not him that sent me.

Aug.
Tract.
lxxxvii.
1.
AUG. Our Lord had said, *I have ordained that ye should walk, and bring forth fruit.* Love is this fruit. Wherefore He proceeds: *These things I command you, that ye love one* Gal. 5, 22. *another.* Hence the Apostle saith: *The fruit of the Spirit is love;* and enumerates all other graces as springing from this source. Well then doth our Lord commend love, as if it were the only thing commanded: seeing that without it nothing can profit, with it nothing be wanting, whereby a Chrys. Hom. lxxvii. 2. man is made good. CHRYS. Or thus: I have said that I lay down My life for you, and that I first chose you. I have said this not by way of reproach, but to induce you to *love one another.* Then as they were about to suffer persecution and reproach, He bids them not to grieve, but rejoice on that account: *If the world hate you, ye know that it hated Me before it hated you:* as if to say, I know it is a hard trial, Aug. Tract. lxxxvii. 2. but ye will endure it for My sake. AUG. For why should the members exalt themselves above the head? Thou refusest to be in the body, if thou art not willing, with the head, to endure the hatred of the world. For love's sake let us be patient: the world must hate us, whom it sees hate whatever it loves; *If ye were of the world, the world would* Chrys. Hom. lxxvii. 2. *love his own.* CHRYS. As if Christ's suffering were not consolation enough, He consoles them still further by telling them, the hatred of the world would be an evidence of their goodness; so that they ought rather to grieve if they were Aug. Tract. lxxxvii. 2. loved by the world: as that would be evidence of their wickedness. AUG. He saith this to the whole Church, which is often called the world; as, *God was in Christ,* 2 Cor. 5, 19.

reconciling the world unto Himself.   The whole world then
is the Church, and the whole world hateth the Church.   The
world hateth the world, the world in enmity, the world reconciled, the defiled world, the changed world.   Here it may Tract.
be asked, If the wicked can be said to persecute the wicked; 4. lxxxviii.
e. g. if impious kings, and judges, who persecute the righteous, punish murderers and adulterers also ; how are we to
understand our Lord's words, *If ye were of the world, the
world would love his own?*   In this way ; The world is in
them who punish these offences, and the world is in them
who love them.   The world then hates its own so far as it
punishes the wicked, loves its own so far as it favours them.
Again, if it be asked how the world loves itself, when it Tract.
hates the means of its redemption, the answer is, that it loves 4. lxxxvii.
itself with a false, not a true love, loves what hurts it ; hates
nature, loves vice.   Wherefore we are forbidden to love what
it loves in itself; commanded to love what it hates in itself.
The vice in it we are forbidden, the nature in it we are
commanded, to love.   And to separate us from this lost
world, we are chosen out of it, not by merit of our own, for
we had no merits to begin with, not by nature which was
radically corrupt, but by grace : *But because ye are not of
the world, but I have chosen you out of the world, therefore
the world hateth you.*   GREG. For the dispraise of the Greg.
perverse, is our praise.   There is nothing wrong in not Hom. in
pleasing those, who do not please God.   For no one can by ix.
one and the same act please God, and the enemies of God.
He proves himself no friend to God, who pleases His enemy ;
and he whose soul is in subjection to the Truth, will have to
contend with the enemies of that Truth.   AUG. Our Lord, in Aug.
exhorting His servants to bear patiently the hatred of the Tract.
lxxxviii.
world, proposes to them an example than which there can 1.
be no better and higher one, viz. Himself : *Remember the
word that I said unto you, The servant is not greater than
his lord.   If they have persecuted Me, they will also persecute you: if they have kept My saying, they will keep
yours also.*   GLOSS. They observed[1] it in order to calumniate [1] kept—
it, as we read in the Psalms, *The ungodly seeth*[2] *the righ-* observa-
verant,
teous.   THEOPHYL. Or thus: If, He says, they have perse- Vulg.
[2] obser-
cuted your Lord, much more will they persecute you; if vabit,
Vulg.

they had persecuted Him, but kept His commandments, they would keep yours also. CHRYS. As if He said, Ye must not be disturbed at having to share My sufferings; for

Aug. Tract. lxxxviii. 1. ye are not better than I. AUG. *The servant is not greater than his Lord.* Here the servant is the one who has the purified fear, which abideth for ever. CHRYS. Then follows

Chrys. Hom. lxxvii. 2. another consolation, viz. that the Father is despised and injured with them : *But all these things will they do unto you for My name's sake, because they know not Him that sent Me.* AUG. *All these things,* viz. what He had mentioned,

Aug. Tract. lxxxviii. 2. that the world would hate them, persecute them, despise their word. *For My Name's sake,* i. e. in you they will hate Me, in you persecute Me, your word they will not keep, because it is mine. They who do these things for His name's sake are as miserable, as they who suffer them are blessed : except when they do them to the wicked as well; for then both they who do, and they who suffer, are miserable. But how do they do all these things for His name's sake, when they do nothing for Christ's name's sake, i. e. for justice sake ? We shall do away with this difficulty, if we take the words as applying to the righteous ; as if it were, All these things will ye suffer from them, for My name's sake. If, *for My name's sake,* mean this, i. e. My name which they hate in you, justice which they hate in you ; of the good, when they persecute the wicked, it may be said in the same way, that they do so both for righteousness' sake, which they love, which love is their motive in persecuting, and for unrighteousness' sake, the unrighteousness of the wicked, which they hate. *Because they know not Him that sent Me,* i. e. know

Wisd. 15, 3. not according to that knowledge of which it is said, *To know Thee is perfect righteousness.*

22. If I had not come and spoken unto them, they had not had sin: but now they have no cloke for their sin.

23. He that hateth me hateth my Father also.

24. If I had not done among them the works which none other man did, they had not had sin : but now have they both seen and hated both me and my Father.

25. But this cometh to pass, that the word might be fulfilled that is written in their law, They hated me without a cause.

CHRYS. Then by way of another consolation, He declares the injustice of these persecutions both towards Him and them: *If I had not come and spoken unto them, they had not had sin.* AUG. Christ spoke to the Jews only, not to any other nation. In them then was that world which hated Christ and His disciples; and not only in them, but in us also. Were the Jews then without sin before Christ came in the flesh, because Christ had not spoken to them? By sin here He means not every sin, but a certain great sin, which includes all, and which alone hinders the remission of other sins, viz. unbelief. They did not believe in Christ, who came that they might believe on Him. This sin then they would not have had, had not Christ come; for Christ's advent, as it was the salvation of the believing, so was the perdition of the unbelieving. *But now they have no cloke for their sin.* If those to whom Christ had not come or spoken, had not an excuse for their sin, why is it said here that these had no excuse, because Christ had come and spoken to them? If the first had excuse, did it do away with their punishment altogether, or only mitigate it? I answer, that this excuse covered, not all their sin, but only this one, viz. that they did not believe in Christ. But they are not of this number to whom Christ came by His disciples: they are not to be let off with a lighter punishment, who altogether refused to receive Christ's love, and, as far as concerned them, wished its destruction. This excuse they may have who died before they heard of Christ's Gospel ; but this will not shield them from damnation. For whoever are not saved in the Saviour, who came to seek what was lost, shall without doubt go to perdition: though some will have lighter, others severer punishments. He perishes to God, who is punished with an exclusion from that happiness which is given to the saints. But there is as great a diversity of punishments, as there is of sins: though how this is settled is a matter known to the Divine Wisdom indeed, but

Chrys.
Hom.
lxxvii.
2.

Aug.
Tract.
lxxxix.
l.

προφασιν,
excusa-
tionem
Vulg.
cloke E.
T.

too deep for human conjecture to examine or pronounce
upon. CHRYS. As the Jews persecuted Him out of professed
regard for the Father, He takes away this excuse: *He that*
hateth Me, hateth My Father also. ALCUIN. For as he who
loves the Son, loves the Father also, the love of the Father
being one with that of the Son, even as their nature is one:
so he who hateth the Son, hateth the Father also. AUG.
But He has just said, *Because they know not Him that sent*
Me. How could they hate one whom they did not know?
For if they hated God, believing Him to be something else,
and not God, this was not hatred of God. In the case of
men, it often happens that we hate or love persons whom
we have never seen, simply in consequence of what we have
heard of them. But if a man's character is known to us, he
cannot properly be said to be unknown. And a man's
character is not shewn by his face, but by his habits and
way of life: else we should not be able to know ourselves,
for we cannot see our own face. But history and fame
sometimes lie; and our faith is imposed upon. We cannot
penetrate into men's hearts; we only know that such things
are right, and others wrong; and if we escape error here, to
be mistaken in men is a venial matter. A good man may
hate a good man ignorantly, or rather love him ignorantly,
for he loves the good man, though he hates the man whom
he supposes him to be. A bad man may love a good man,
supposing him to be a bad man like himself, and therefore
not, properly speaking, loving him, but the person whom he
takes him to be. And in the same way with respect to God.
If the Jews were asked whether they loved God, they would
reply that they did love Him, not intending to lie, but only
being mistaken in so saying. For how could they who
hated the Truth, love the Father of the Truth? They did
not wish their actions to be judged, and this the Truth did.
They hated the Truth then, because they hated the punishment which He would inflict upon such as they. But at
the same time they did not know that He was the Truth,
who came to condemn them. They did not know that the
Truth was born of God the Father, and therefore they did
not know God the Father Himself. Thus they both hated,
and also knew not, the Father. CHRYS. Thus then they have

Chrys. Hom. lxxvii.2.

Aug. Tr.xc.1.

Chrys. Hom. lxxvii.2.

no excuse, He says; I gave them doctrine, I added miracles, which, according to Moses' law, should convince all if the doctrine itself is good also: *If I had not done among them the works that none other man did, they had not had sin.* Aug. The sin of not believing Him, notwithstanding His doctrine and His miracles. But why does He add, *Which none other man did?* Christ did no work greater than the raising of the dead, which we know the ancient Prophets did before Him. Is it that He did some things which no one else did? But others also did what neither He nor any one else did. True: yet none of the ancient prophets, that we read of, healed so many bodily defects, sicknesses, infirmities. For to say nothing of single cases, Mark says, that *whither-soever He entered, into villages, or cities, or country, they laid the sick in the streets, and besought Him that they might touch if it were but the border of His garment: and as many as touched Him were made whole.* Such works as these no one else had done *in them. In them,* meaning, not amongst them, or before them, but within them. But even where particular works, like some of these, had been done before, whoever worked such did not really do them; for He did them through them; whereas He performs these miracles by His own power. For even if the Father or the Holy Spirit did them, yet it was none other than He; for the Three Persons are of one substance. For these benefits then they ought to have returned Him not hatred, but love. And this He reproaches them with; *But now they have both seen and hated both Me and My Father.* Chrys. And that the disciples may not say, Why then hast Thou brought us into such difficulties? Couldest not thou foresee the resistance and hatred we should meet with, He quotes the prophecy: *But this cometh to pass, that the word might be fulfilled that is written in their law, They hated Me without a cause.* Aug. Under the name of the Law, the whole of the Old Testament is included: and therefore our Lord says here, *That is written in their law;* the passage being in the Psalms. Aug. *Their law,* He says, not as made by them, but as given to them. A man hates *without a cause,* who seeks no advantage from his hatred. Thus the ungodly hate God; the righteous love Him, i. e. looking for no other

Aug.
Tr. xci.
1.

Mark 6,
56.

Chrys.
Hom.
lxxvii.1.

Aug.
xv. de
Trin. c.
xvii.

Aug.
Tr. xci.
4.

Greg.
xxv.
Moral.

good but Him: He is their all in all.   GREG. It is one thing
not to do good, another to hate the teacher of goodness; as
there is a difference between sudden and deliberate sins.
Our state generally is that we love what is good, but from
infirmity cannot perform it.   But to sin of set purpose, is
neither to do nor to love what is good.   As then it is sometimes a heavier offence to love than to do, so is it more
wicked to hate justice than not to do it.   There are some in
the Church, who not only do not do what is good, but even
persecute it, and hate in others what they neglect to do
themselves.   The sin of these men is not that of infirmity or
ignorance, but deliberate wilful sin.

26. But when the Comforter is come, whom I will
send unto you from the Father, even the Spirit of
truth, which proceedeth from the Father, he shall
testify of me :

27. And ye also shall bear witness, because ye have
been with me from the beginning.

Chrys.
Hom.
lxxvii.
2.

CHRYS. The disciples might say, If they have heard
words from Thee, such as none other hath spoken, if they
have seen works of Him, such as none other hath done, and
yet have not been convinced, but have hated Thy Father,
and Thee with Him, why dost Thou send us to preach ?
How shall we be believed ? Such thoughts as these He
now answers: *But when the Comforter is come, Whom I will
send unto you from the Father, even the Spirit of Truth
which proceedeth from the Father, he shall testify of Me.*

Aug.
Tr. xcii.
2.

AUG. As if He said, Seeing Me, they hated and killed Me:
but the Comforter shall give such testimony concerning Me,
as shall make them believe, though they see Me not.   And
because He shall testify, ye shall testify also : *And ye also
shall bear witness:* He will inspire your hearts, and ye shall
proclaim with your voices.   And ye will preach what ye
know; *Because ye have been with Me from the beginning ;*
which now ye do not do, because ye have not yet the fulness
of the Spirit.   But the love of God shall then be shed
abroad in your hearts by the Spirit which shall be given you,

and shall make you confident witnesses to Me. The Holy
Spirit by His testimony made others testify; taking away
fear from the friends of Christ's, and converting the hatred of
His enemies into love. DIDYMUS. The Holy Spirit He Didym.
calls the Comforter, a name taken from His office, which is De Spir. Sanct.
not only to relieve the sorrows of the faithful, but to fill
them with unspeakable joy. Everlasting gladness is in
those hearts, in which the Spirit dwells. The Spirit, the
Comforter, is sent by the Son, not as Angels, or Prophets, or
Apostles, are sent, but as the Spirit must be sent which is of
one nature with the Divine wisdom and power that sends
Him. The Son when sent by the Father, is not separated
from Him, but abides in the Father, and the Father in Him.
In the same way the Holy Spirit is not sent by the Son, and
proceedeth from the Father, in the sense of change of place.
For as the Father's nature, being incorporeal, is not local, so
neither hath the Spirit of truth, Who is incorporeal also, and
superior to all created things, a local nature. CHRYS. He Chrys.
calls Him not the Holy Spirit, but the Spirit of truth, to Hom. lxxvii.
shew the perfect faith that was due to Him. He knew that 3.
He proceedeth from the Father, for He knew all things; He
knew where He Himself came from, as He says of Himself
above, *I know whence I came, and whither I go.* DIDYMUS. John 8, 14.
He does not say, from God, or, from the Almighty, but, *from* ut sup.
the Father: because though the Father and God Almighty
are the same, yet the Spirit of truth properly proceeds from
God, as the Father, the Begetter. The Father and the Son
together send the Spirit of truth: He comes by the will
both of the Father and the Son. THEOPHYL. Elsewhere He
says that the Father sends the Spirit; now He says He
does: *Whom I will send unto you;* thus declaring the
equality of the Father and the Son. That He might not be
thought however to be opposed to the Father, and to be
another and rival source, as it were, of the Spirit, He adds,
From the Father; i. e. the Father agreeing, and taking an
equal part in sending Him. When it is said that He proceedeth, do not understand His procession to be an external
mission, such as is given to ministering spirits, but a certain
peculiar, and distinct procession, such as is true of the Holy
Spirit alone. To proceed is not the same as being sent, but

is the essential nature of the Holy Ghost, as coming from
the Father. AUG. If it be asked here whether the Holy
Ghost proceeds from the Son also, we may answer thus:
The Son is the Son of the Father alone, and the Father is
the Father of the Son only; but the Holy Spirit is not the
Spirit of one, but of both; since Christ Himself saith, *The
Spirit of your Father which speaketh in you.* And the
Apostle says, *God hath sent the Spirit of His Son into your
hearts.* This indeed, I think, is the reason why He is called
peculiarly the Spirit. For both of the Father and the Son
separately we may pronounce, that each is a Spirit. But
what each is separately in a general sense, He who is not
either one separately, but the union of both, is spiritually.
But if the Holy Spirit is the Spirit of the Son, why should
we not believe that He proceeds from the Son? Indeed if
He did not proceed from the Son, Christ would not after the
resurrection have breathed on His disciples, and said, *Receive ye the Holy Ghost.* This too is what is meant by the
virtue which went out of Him, and healed all. If the Holy
Ghost then proceeds both from the Father and the Son, why
does Christ say, *Who proceedeth from the Father?* He says
it in accordance with His general way of referring all that
He has to Him from whom He is; as where He says, *My
doctrine is not Mine, but His that sent Me.* If the doctrine
was His, which He says was not His own, but the Father's,
much more does the Holy Spirit proceed from Him, consistently with His proceeding from the Father. From whom
the Son hath His Godhead, from Him He hath it that the
Holy Ghost proceedeth from Him. And this explains why
the Holy Ghost is not said to be born, but to proceed. For
if He were born, He would be the Son of both Father and
Son, an absurd supposition; for if two together have a Son,
those two must be father and mother. But to imagine any
such relation as this between God the Father, and God the
Son, is monstrous. Even the human offspring does not
proceed from father or mother at the same time; when it proceeds from the father, it does not proceed from the mother.
Whereas the Holy Spirit does not proceed from the Father
into the Son, and from the Son into the creature to be
sanctified; but proceeds from Father and Son at once. And

Aug.
Tr.xcix.
6, et sq.

Matt.
10, 20.

Gal. 4,
6.

John 20,
29.

Luke 6.

if the Father is life, and the Son is life, so the Holy
Ghost is life also.   Just then as the Father when He had life
in Himself, gave also to the Son to have life in Himself; so
He gave to the Son also that life should proceed from Him,
even as it proceeded from Himself.

CHAP. XVI.

1. These things have I spoken unto you, that ye should not be offended.

2. They shall put you out of the synagogues: yea, the time cometh, that whosoever killeth you will think that he doeth God service.

3. And these things will they do unto you, because they have not known the Father, nor me.

4. But these things have I told you, that when the time shall come, ye may remember that I told you of them. And these things I said not unto you at the beginning, because I was with you.

Aug. Tr.xcii. AUG. After the promise of the Holy Spirit, to inspire them with strength to give witness; He well adds, *These things have I spoken unto you, that ye should not be offended.* For Rom. 5, 5. when *the love of God is shed abroad in our hearts by the Holy Spirit which is given to us,* then great peace have Ps. 118. they that love God's law, and they are not offended at it. What they were about to suffer follows next: *They shall* Chrys. Hom. lxxvii. *put you out of the synagogues.* CHRYS. *For the Jews had already agreed, if any confessed that He was Christ, that he* Aug. Tr.xciii. *should be put out of the synagogue.* AUG. But what evil was it to the Apostles to be put out of the Jewish synagogues, which they would have gone out of, even if none had put them out? Our Lord wished to make known to them, that the Jews were about not to receive Him, while they on the other hand were not going to desert Him. There was no other people of God beside the seed of Abraham: if they acknowledged Christ, the Churches of Christ would be none other than the synagogues of the Jews. But inasmuch as they refused to acknowledge Him, nothing remained but that they should put out of the synagogue those who would not forsake Christ. He adds: *But the time cometh, that whoever killeth you, will think that he doeth God service.* Is this intended for a consolation, as if they would so take to heart their expulsion from the synagogues, that death would be a positive relief to them after it? God forbid that they who sought God's glory, not men's, should be so disturbed. The meaning of the words is this: They shall put you out of the synagogue, but do not be afraid of being left alone. Separated from their assemblies, ye shall assemble so many in my name, that they fearing that the temple and rites of the old law will be deserted, will kill you, and think to do God service thereby, having a zeal for God, but not according to knowledge. These who kill, are the same with those who put out of the synagogues, viz. the Jews. For Gentiles would not have thought that they were doing God service, by killing Christ's witnesses, but their own false gods; whereas every one of the Jews, who killed the preacher of Christ, thought he was doing God service, believing that whoever were converted to Christ, deserted the God of Israel. CHRYS. Then He consoles them: *And all these things will they do unto you, because they have not known the Father nor Me.* As if He said, Let this consolation content you. AUG. And He mentions these things beforehand, because trials, however soon to pass away, when they come upon men unprepared for them, are very overwhelming: *But these things have I told you, that when the hour shall come, ye may remember that I told you of them:* the hour, the hour of darkness, the hour of night. But the night of the Jews was not allowed to mix with or darken the day of the Christians. CHRYS. And He predicted these trials for another reason, viz. that they might not say that He had not foreseen them; *That ye may remember that I told you of them,* or that He had only spoken to please them, and given false hopes. And the reason is added, why He did not reveal these things sooner: *And these things I said not unto you at the beginning, because I was with you;* because, that is, ye were in My

Chrys. Hom. lxxxviii.

Aug. Tr.xciii.

Chrys. Hom. lxxxviii.

2 K 2

keeping, and might ask when you pleased, and the whole battle rested upon Me. There was no need then to tell you these things at the first, though I myself knew them. AUG. In the other three Evangelists these predictions occur before the supper; John gives them after. Still if they relate them as given very near His Passion, that is enough to explain His saying, *These things I said not unto you at the beginning.* Matthew however relates these prophecies as given long before His Passion, on the occasion of His choosing the twelve. How do we reconcile this with our Lord's words? By supposing them to apply to the promise of the Holy Spirit, and the testimony He would give amidst their suffering. This was what He had not told them at the beginning, and that because He was with them, and His presence was a sufficient consolation. But as He was about to depart, it was meet that He should tell them of His coming, by whom the love of God would be shed abroad in their hearts, to preach the word of God with boldness. CHRYS. Or, He had foretold that they should suffer scourgings, but not that their death could be thought doing God service; which was the strangest thing of all. Or, He there told them what they would suffer from the Gentiles, here what from the Jews.

Aug. Tr.xciv. 1.

Chrys. Hom. lxxviii. 1.

5. But now I go my way to him that sent me; and none of you asketh me, Whither goest thou?

6. But because I have said these things unto you, sorrow hath filled your heart.

7. Nevertheless I tell you the truth; It is expedient for you that I go away: for if I go not away, the Comforter will not come unto you; but if I depart, I will send him unto you.

8. And when he is come, he will reprove the world of sin, and of righteousness, and of judgment:

9. Of sin, because they believe not on me;

10. Of righteousness, because I go to my Father, and ye see me no more;

11. Of judgment, because the prince of this world is judged.

CHRYS. The disciples, not as yet perfected, being over- Chrys. come by sorrow, our Lord blames and corrects them, saying, Hom. lxxviii. *But now I go My way to Him that sent Me; and none of* l. *you asketh Me, Whither goest Thou?* They were so struck down at hearing that whosoever killed them would think that he was doing God service, that they could say nothing. Wherefore He adds, *But because I have said these things unto you, sorrow hath filled your hearts.* It was no small consolation to them to know, that the Lord knew their superabundant sorrow, because of His leaving them, and because of the evils which they heard they were to suffer, but knew not whether they should suffer manfully. AUG. Aug. Or whereas they had asked Him above, whither He was Tr.xciv. going, and He had replied that He was going whither they would not come; now He promises that He will go in such a way that no one will ask Him whither He goeth: *and none of you asketh Me, Whither goest Thou?* Going up to heaven, they questioned Him not in words, but followed with their eyes. But our Lord saw what effect His words would produce upon their minds. Not having yet that inward consolation which the Holy Ghost was to impart, they were afraid to lose the outward presence of Christ, and so, when they could no longer doubt from His own words that they were going to lose Him, their human affections were saddened, for the loss of their visible object. Wherefore it follows; *But because I have said these things unto you, sorrow hath filled your heart.* But He knew that it would be for their good, forasmuch as that inward sight wherewith the Holy Ghost would console them, was the better one: *Nevertheless I tell you the truth; It is expedient for you that I go away.* CHRYS. As if He said, Though your grief be ever so great, Chrys. ye must hear how that it is profitable for you that I go away. Hom. lxxviii. What the profit is He then shews: *For if I go not away, the Comforter will not come unto you.* AUG. This He says Aug. not on account of any inequality between the Word of God i. de Trin. and the Holy Ghost, but because the presence of the Son of c. 19. man amongst them would impede the coming of the latter. For the Holy Ghost did not humble Himself as did the Son, by taking upon Him the form of a servant. It was necessary therefore that the form of the servant should be removed from their eyes; for so long as they looked upon that, they thought that Christ was no more than what they saw Him to be. So it follows: *But if I depart, I will send Him unto* *you.* AUG. But could He not send Him while here, Him, Who, we know, came and abode on Him at His baptism, yea Him from Whom we know He never could be separated? What meaneth then, *If I go not away, the Comforter will not come unto you,* but, ye cannot receive the Spirit, so long as ye know Christ according to the flesh? Christ departing in the body, not the Holy Ghost only, but the Father, and the Son also came spiritually. GREG. As if He said plainly, If I withdraw not My body from your eyes, I cannot lead you to the understanding of the Invisible, through the Comforting Spirit. AUG. The Holy Ghost the Comforter brought this, that the form of a servant which our Lord had received in the womb of the Virgin, being removed from the fleshly eye, He was manifested to the purified mental vision in the very form of God in which He remained equal to the Father, even while He deigned to appear in the flesh. CHRYS. What say they here, who entertain unworthy notions of the Spirit? Is it expedient for the master to go away, and a servant to come? He then shews the good that the Spirit will do: *And when He is come, He will reprove the world of sin, of righteousness, and of judgment.* AUG. But how is it that Christ did not reprove the world? Is it because Christ spoke among the Jews only, whereas the Holy Spirit, poured into His disciples throughout the whole world, reproved not one nation only, but the world? But who would dare to say that the Holy Ghost reproved the world by Christ's disciples, and that Christ did not, when the Apostle exclaims, *Do ye seek a proof of Christ speaking in Me?* Those then whom the Holy Ghost reproves, Christ reproves also. *He shall reprove the world,* means, He shall pour love into your hearts, insomuch, that fear being cast out, ye shall be free to reprove. He then explains what He has said: *Of sin, because they believed not in Me.* He mentions this as the sin above all others, because while it remains, the others are retained, when it departs, the others are remitted. AUG. But it makes a great difference whether one believes in Christ, or only that He is

Aug.
Tr.xciv.

Greg.
viii.
Moral.
c. xvii.

Aug.
deVerb.
Dom.
Serm.
lx.

Chrys.
Hom.
xxviii.

Aug.
Tr. xcv.
1.

2 Cor.
13, 3.
Vulg.

Aug.
de Verb.
Dom. s.
lxi.

Christ. For that He was Christ, even the devils believed:
but he believes *in* Christ, who both hopes in Christ and
loves Christ. AUG. The world is reproved of sin, because Aug.
it believes not in Christ, and reproved of righteousness, the $_2^{\text{Tr. xcv.}}$
righteousness of those that believe. The very contrast of
the believing, is the censure of the unbelieving. *Of righte-*
ousness, because I go to the Father: as it is the common
objection of unbelievers, How can we believe what we do not
see? so the righteousness of believers lies in this, *Because*
I go to the Father, and ye see Me no more. For blessed are
they which see not, and believe. The faith even of those
who saw Christ is praised, not because they believed what
they saw, i. e. the Son of man, but because they believed
what they saw not, i. e. the Son of God. And when the
form of the servant was withdrawn from their sight altogether,
then only was fulfilled in completeness the text, *The just* Heb.10,
liveth by faith. It will be your righteousness then, of which $^{38.}$
the world will be reproved, that ye shall believe in Me, not
seeing Me. And when ye shall see Me, ye shall see Me
as I shall be, not as I am now with you, i. e. ye shall not see
Me mortal, but everlasting. For in saying, *Ye see Me* jam non
no more, He means that they should see Him no more for $\frac{\text{videbitis}}{\text{meVulg.}}$
ever. AUG. Or thus: They believed not, He went to the Aug.
Father. Theirs therefore was the sin, His the righteousness. de Verb.
But that He came from the Father to us, was mercy; that s. lxi.
He went to the Father, was righteousness; according to the
saying of the Apostle, *Wherefore God also hath highly* Philip.
exalted Him. But if He went to the Father alone, what $^{2, 9.}$
profit is it to us? Is He not alone rather in the sense of being
one with all His members, as the head is with the body? So
then the world is reproved of sin, in those who believe not
in Christ; and of righteousness, in those who rise again in
the members of Christ. It follows, *Of judgment, because the*
prince of this world is judged: i. e. the devil, the prince of
the wicked, who in heart dwell only in this world which they
love. He is judged in that he is cast out; and the world is s. lx.
reproved of this judgment; for it is vain for one who does
not believe in Christ to complain of the devil, whom judged,
i. e. cast out, and permitted to attack us from without, only
for our trial, not men only but women, boys and girls, have

Aug.
Tr. xcv. by martyrdom overcome. AUG. Or, *is judged*, i. e. is destined irrevocably for the punishment of eternal fire. And of this judgment is the world reproved, in that it is judged with its prince, the proud and ungodly one whom it imitates. Let men therefore believe in Christ, lest they be reproved of the sin of unbelief, by which all sins are retained; pass over to the number of the believing, lest they be reproved of the righteousness of those whom justified they do not imitate; beware of the judgment to come, lest with the prince of this

Chrys. world whom they imitate, they too be judged. CHRYS. Or
Hom.
lxxviii. thus: *Shall reprove the world of sin*, i. e. cut off all excuse, and shew that they have sinned unpardonably in not believing in Me, when they see the ineffable gift of the Holy Ghost

Aug. obtained by calling upon Me. AUG. In this way too the
de Qu.
N. et Holy Ghost reproved the world of sin, i. e. by the mighty
V. Test. works He did in the name of the Saviour, Who was con-
qu. 89. demned by the world. The Saviour, His righteousness retained, feared not to return to Him Who sent Him, and in that He returned, proved that He had come from Him:

Chrys. *Of righteousness, because I go to the Father.* CHRYS. i. e. My
Hom.
lxxviii. going to the Father will be a proof that I have led an
2. irreproachable life, so that they will not be able to say,
c. 9, 24, *This man is a sinner; this man is not from God.* Again,
16. inasmuch as I conquered the devil, (which no one who was a sinner could do,) they cannot say that I have a devil, and am a deceiver. But as he hath been condemned by Me, they shall be assured that they shall trample upon him afterwards; and My resurrection will shew that he was not

Aug. able to detain Me. AUG. The devils seeing souls go from
de Qu.
V. et hell[1] to heaven, knew that the prince of this world was judged,
N. Test. and being brought to trial in the Saviour's cause, had lost
qu. 89.
[1] inferis all right to what he held. This was seen on our Saviour's ascension, but was declared plainly and openly in the descent of the Holy Ghost on the disciples.

12 I have yet many things to say unto you, but ye cannot bear them now.

13. Howbeit when he, the Spirit of truth, is come, he will guide you into all truth: for he shall not speak

of himself: but whatsoever he shall hear, that shall he speak; and he will shew you things to come.

14. He shall glorify me: for he shall receive of mine, and shall shew it unto you.

15. All things that the Father hath are mine: therefore said I, that he shall take of mine, and shall shew it unto you.

THEOPHYL. Our Lord having said above, *It is expedient for you that I go away,* He enlarges now upon it: *I have yet many things to say unto you, but ye cannot bear them now.* AUG. All heretics, when their fables are rejected for their extravagance by the common sense of mankind, try to defend themselves by this text; as if these were the things which the disciples could not at this time bear, or as if the Holy Spirit could teach things, which even the unclean spirit is ashamed openly to teach and preach. But bad doctrines such as even natural shame cannot bear are one thing, good doctrines such as our poor natural understanding cannot bear are another. The one are allied to the shameless body, the other lie far beyond the body. But what are these things which they could not bear? I cannot mention them for this very reason; for who of us dare call himself able to receive what they could not? Some one will say indeed that many, now that the Holy Ghost has been sent, can do what Peter could not then, as earn the crown of martyrdom. But do we therefore know what those things were, which He was unwilling to communicate? For it seems most absurd to suppose that the disciples were not able to bear then the great doctrines, that we find in the Apostolical Epistles, which were written afterwards, which our Lord is not said to have spoken to them. For why could they not bear then what every one now reads and bears in their writings, even though he may not understand? Men of perverse sects indeed cannot bear what is found in Holy Scripture concerning the Catholic faith, as we cannot bear their sacrilegious vanities; for not to bear means not to acquiesce in. But what believer or even catechumen before he has been baptized and received the

Aug.
Tract.
xcvii.

Tr.xcvi.
5.

Tr.xcvi.
1.

Holy Ghost, does not acquiesce in and listen to, even if he does not understand, all that was written after our Lord's xcvii. 5. ascension? But some one will say, Do spiritual men never hold doctrines which they do not communicate to carnal xcviii.3. men, but do to spiritual? There is no necessity why any doctrines should be kept secret from the babes, and revealed to the grown up believers ª. Spiritual men ought not altogether to withhold spiritual doctrines from the carnal, seeing the Catholic faith ought to be preached to all; nor at the same time should they lower them in order to accommodate them to the understanding of persons who cannot receive them, and so make their own preaching contemptible, rather xcvii. 1. than the truth intelligible. So then we are not to understand these words of our Lord to refer to certain secret doctrines, which if the teacher revealed, the disciple would not be able to bear, but to those very things in religious doctrine which are within the comprehension of all of us. If Christ chose to communicate these to us, in the same way in which He does to the Angels, what men, yea what spiritual men, which the Apostles were not now, could bear them? For indeed every thing which can be known of the creature is xcvi. 4. inferior to the Creator; and yet who is silent about Him? While in the body we cannot know all the truth, as the Apostle 1 Cor. says, *We know in part;* but the Holy Spirit sanctifying us, 13. fits us for enjoying that fulness of which the same Apostle says, *Then face to face.* Our Lord's promise, *But when He the Spirit of truth shall come, He shall teach you all truth, or shall lead you into all truth,* does not refer to this life only, but to the life to come, for which this complete fulness is reserved. The Holy Spirit both teaches believers now all the spiritual things which they are capable of receiving, and Didym. also kindles in their hearts a desire to know more. DIDYMUS. de Sp. Or He means that His hearers had not yet attained to all Sanct. ii. ult . those things which for His name's sake they were able to bear: med. inter so revealing lesser things, He puts off the greater for a future opera time, such things as they could not understand till the Cross Hieron. itself of their crucified Head had been their instruction. As yet they were slaves to the types, and shadows, and images

---

ª For the same preaching, he argues, will be received by each according to their capacity; so that no difference need be made in the preaching.

of the Law, and could not bear the truth of which the Law was the shadow. But when the Holy Ghost came, He would lead them by His teaching and discipline in'o all truth, transferring them from the dead letter to the quickening Spirit, in Whom alone all Scripture truth resides. CHRYS. Having said then, *Ye cannot bear them now,* but then ye shall be able, and, The Holy Spirit *shall lead you into all truth;* lest this should make them suppose that the Holy Spirit was the superior, He adds, *For He shall not speak of Himself, but whatsoever He shall hear, that shall He speak.* AUG. This is like what He said of Himself above, i. e. *I can of Mine own Self do nothing; as I hear I judge.* But that may be understood of Him as man; how must we understand this of the Holy Ghost, Who never became a creature by assuming a creature? As meaning that He is not from Himself. The Son is born of the Father, and the Holy Ghost proceeds from the Father. In what the difference consists between proceeding and being born, it would require a long time to discuss, and would be rash to define. But to hear is with Him to know, to know to be. As then He is not from Himself, but from Him from Whom He proceeds, from Whom His being is, from the same is His knowledge. From the same therefore His hearing. The Holy Ghost then always hears, because He always knows; and He hath heard, hears, and will hear from Him from Whom He is. DIDYMUS. *He shall not speak of Himself,* i. e. not without Me, and Mine and the Father's will: because He is not of Himself, but from the Father and Me. That He exists, and that He speaks, He hath from the Father and Me. I speak the truth; i. e. I inspire as well as speak by Him, since He is the Spirit of Truth. To say and to speak in the Trinity must not be understood according to our usage, but according to the usage of incorporeal natures, and especially the Trinity, which implants Its will in the hearts of believers, and of those who are worthy to hear It. For the Father then to speak, and the Son to hear, is a mode of expressing the identity of their nature, and their agreement. Again, the Holy Spirit, Who is the Spirit of truth, and the Spirit of wisdom, cannot hear from the Son what He does not know, seeing He is the very thing which is produced from the Son, i. e. truth proceeding

Chrys. Chrys. Hom. lxxviii.

Aug. Aug. Tr. xlix.

Didymus. ut supr.

significatio est

from truth, Comforter from Comforter, God from God. Lastly, lest any one should separate Him from the will and society of the Father and the Son, it is written, *Whatsoever He shall hear, that shall He speak.* AUG. But it does not follow from hence that the Holy Spirit is inferior: for it is only signified that He proceeds from the Father. AUG. Nor let the use of the future tense perplex you: that hearing is eternal, because the knowledge is eternal. To that which is eternal, without beginning, and without end, a verb of any tense may be applied. For though an unchangeable nature does not admit of was, and shall be, but only is, yet it is allowable to say of It, was, and is, and shall be; was, because It never began; shall be, because It never shall end; is, because It always is.

DIDYMUS. By the Spirit of truth too the knowledge of future events hath been granted to holy men. Prophets filled with this Spirit foretold and saw things to come, as if they were present: *And He will shew you things to come.* BEDE. It is certain that many filled with the grace of the Holy Spirit have foreknown future events. But as many gifted saints have never had this power, the words, *He will shew you things to come,* may be taken to mean, bring back to your minds the joys of your heavenly country. He did however inform the Apostles of what was to come, viz. of the evils that they would have to suffer for Christ's sake, and the good things they would receive in recompense. CHRYS. In this way then He raised their spirits; for there is nothing for which mankind so long, as the knowledge of the future. He relieves them from all anxiety on this account, by shewing that dangers would not fall upon them unawares. Then to shew that He could have told them all the truth into which the Holy Spirit would lead them, He adds, *He shall glorify Me.*

AUG. By pouring love into the hearts of believers, and making them spiritual, and so able to see that the Son Whom they had known before only according to the flesh, and thought a man like themselves, was equal to the Father. Or certainly because that love filling them with boldness, and casting out fear, they proclaimed Christ to men, and so spread His fame throughout the whole world. For what they were going to do in the power of the Holy Ghost, this the Holy Ghost says He does Himself. CHRYS. And because He had said, *Ye have*

Marginal notes:

Aug. ii. de Trin. c. xiii.

Aug. Tr. xcix.

ut sup.

Chrys. Hom. lxxviii. 2.

Aug. Tr. c.

Chrys. Hom. lxxviii. 2.

Mat. 23, 8.

one Master, even Christ, that they might not be prevented by
this from admitting the Holy Ghost as well, He adds, *For He
shall receive of Mine, and shall shew it unto you.* DIDYMUS. Didym.
To *receive* must be taken here in a sense agreeable to the de Spir. Sanct.
Divine Nature. As the Son in giving is not deprived of what ut sup.
He gives, nor imparts to others with any loss of His own,
so too the Holy Ghost does not receive what before He had
not; for if He received what before He had not, the gift being
transferred to another, the giver would be thereby a loser.
We must understand then that the Holy Ghost receives
from the Son that which belonged to His nature, and that
there are not two substances implied, one giving, and the
other receiving, but one substance only. In like manner the
Son too is said to receive from the Father that wherein He
Himself subsists. For neither is the Son any thing but what
is given Him by the Father, nor the Holy Ghost any substance but that which is given Him by the Son. AUG. But Aug.
it is not true, as some heretics have thought, that because Tr. c.
the Son receives from the Father, the Holy Ghost from the
Son, as if by gradation, that therefore the Holy Ghost is
inferior to the Son. He Himself solves this difficulty, and
explains His own words: *All things that the Father hath
are Mine: therefore said I, that He shall take of Mine,
and shall shew it unto you.* DIDYMUS. As if He said, ut sup.
Although the Spirit of truth proceeds from the Father, yet all
things that the Father hath are Mine, and even the Spirit of
the Father is Mine, and receiveth of Mine. But beware,
when thou hearest this, that thou think not it is a thing or
possession which the Father and the Son have. That which
the Father hath according to His substance, i. e. His eternity,
immutability, goodness, it is this which the Son hath also.
Away with the cavils of logicians, who say, therefore the
Father is the Son. Had He said indeed, All that God hath
are Mine, impiety might have taken occasion to raise its
head; but when He saith, *All things that the Father hath
are Mine,* by using the name of the Father, He declareth
Himself the Son, and being the Son, He usurpeth not the
Paternity, though by the grace of adoption He is the Father
of many saints. HILARY. Our Lord therefore hath not left it Hilar.
uncertain whether the Paraclete be from the Father, or from viii. de
Trin.
ante
med.

the Son; for He is sent by the Son, and proceedeth from the
Father, both these He receiveth from the Son.   You ask
whether to receive from the Son and to proceed from the
Father be the same thing.   Certainly, to receive from the
Son must be thought one and the same thing with receiving
from the Father: for when He says, *All things that the
Father hath are Mine, therefore said I, that He shall
receive of Mine*, He sheweth herein that the things are
received from Him, because all things which the Father hath
are His, but that they are received from the Father also.
This unity hath no diversity; nor doth it matter from whom
the thing is received; since that which is given by the
Father, is counted also as given by the Son.

16. A little while, and ye shall not see me: and
again, a little while, and ye shall see me, because I go
to the Father.

17. Then said some of his disciples among themselves, What is this that he saith unto us, A little
while, and ye shall not see me: and again, a little
while, and ye shall see me: and, Because I go to the
Father?

18. They said therefore, What is this that he saith,
A little while? we cannot tell what he saith.

19. Now Jesus knew that they were desirous to ask
him, and said unto them, Do ye enquire among yourselves of that I said, A little while, and ye shall not
see me: and again, a little while, and ye shall see
me?

20. Verily, verily, I say unto you, That ye shall
weep and lament, but the world shall rejoice: and ye
shall be sorrowful, but your sorrow shall be turned
into joy.

21. A woman when she is in travail hath sorrow,
because her hour is come: but as soon as she is
delivered of the child, she remembereth no more the
anguish, for joy that a man is born into the world.

22. And ye now therefore have sorrow : but I will
see you again, and your heart shall rejoice, and your
joy no man taketh from you.

CHRYS. Our Lord after having relieved the spirits of the Chrys.
disciples by the promise of the Holy Spirit, again depresses Hom.
lxxix.
them : *A little while, and ye shall not see Me.* He does this
to accustom them to the mention of His departure, in order
that they may bear it well, when it does come. For nothing
so quiets the troubled mind, as the continued recurrence to
the subject of its grief. BEDE. He saith, *A little while, and* Bede.
ye shall not see Me, alluding to His going to be taken that Hom. 1.
Dom.
night by the Jews, His crucifixion the next morning, and Sec.par.
Oct.
burial in the evening, which withdrew Him from all human Pasch.
sight. CHRYS. But then, if one examines, these are words Chrys.
of consolation : *Because I go to the Father.* For they shew Hom.
lxxix.1.
that His death was only a translation : and more consolation
follows: *And again, a little while, and ye shall see Me :* an
intimation this that He would return, and after a short
separation, come and live with them for ever. AUG. The Aug.
meaning of these words however was obscure, before their Tr. c. 1.
fulfilment; *Then said some of His disciples among themselves, What is this that He saith unto us, A little while,
and ye shall not see Me : and again, a little while, and ye
shall see Me : and, Because I go to the Father.* CHRYS. Chrys.
Either sorrow had confused their minds, or the obscurity of Hom.
lxxix.1.
the words themselves prevented their understanding them,
and made them appear contradictory. If we shall see Thee,
they say, how goest Thou? If Thou goest, how shall we
see Thee? *What is this that He saith unto us, A little
while? We cannot tell what He saith.* AUG. For above, Aug.
because He did not say, *A little while,* but simply, *I go to* Tr.ci.1.
the Father, He seemed to speak plainly. But what to them
was obscure at the time, but by and by manifested, is manifest to us. For in a little while He suffered, and they did
not see Him; and again, in a little while He rose again, and
they saw Him. He says, *And ye shall see Me no more;* for
the mortal Christ they saw no more. ALCUIN. Or thus, It
will be a little time during which ye will not see Me, i. e.
the three days that He rested in the grave; and again, it

will be a little time during which ye shall see Me, i. e. the
forty days of His appearance amongst them, from His Passion
to His ascension. And ye shall see Me for that little time
only, *Because I go to the Father;* for I am not going to stay
always in the body here, but, by that humanity which I
have assumed to ascend to heaven. It follows; *Now Jesus
knew that they were desirous to ask Him, and said unto them,
Do ye enquire among yourselves of that I said, A little
while, and ye shall not see Me: and again, a little while,
and ye shall see Me? Verily, verily, I say unto you, That
ye shall weep and lament.* Their merciful Master, understanding their ignorance and doubts, replied so as to explain
what He had said. Aug. Which must be understood thus,
viz. that the disciples sorrowed at their Lord's death, and
then immediately rejoiced at His resurrection. The world
(i. e. the enemies of Christ, who put Him to death) rejoiced
just when the disciples sorrowed, i. e. at His death: *Ye shall
weep and lament, but the world shall rejoice; and ye shall
be sorrowful, but your sorrow shall be turned into joy.*
Alcuin. But this speech of our Lord's is applicable to all
believers who strive through present tears and afflictions to
attain to the joys eternal. While the righteous weep, the world
rejoiceth; for having no hope of the joys to come, all its
delight is in the present. Chrys. Then He shews that
sorrow brings forth joy, short sorrow infinite joy, by an
example from nature; *A woman when she is in travail hath
sorrow, because her hour is come; but as soon as she is
delivered of the child, she remembereth no more the anguish,
for joy that a man is born into the world.* Aug. This comparison does not seem difficult to understand. It was one
which lay near at hand, and He Himself immediately shews
its application. *And ye now therefore have sorrow; but I will
see you again, and your heart shall rejoice.* The bringing
forth is compared to sorrow, the birth to joy, which is
especially true in the birth of a boy. *And your joy no
man taketh from you:* their joy is Christ. This agrees with
what the Apostle saith, *Christ being risen from the dead
dieth no more.* Chrys. By this example He also intimates
that He loosens the chains of death, and creates men anew.
He does not say however that she should not have tribulation,

Marginal notes: Aug. Tr. ci. — Chrys. Hom. lxxix. — Aug. Tr. ci. — Rom. 6, 9. Chrys. Hom. lxxix.

but that she should not remember it; so great is the joy which
follows. And so is it with the saints. He saith not, that a boy
is born, but that *a man*, a tacit allusion to His own resurrection. Aug. To this joy it is better to refer what was said above, Aug.
A little while and ye shall not see Me, and again, a little while Tr.ci. 6.
and ye shall see Me. For the whole space of time that this
world continues is but a little while. *Because I go to the
Father,* refers to the former clause, *a little while and ye shall
not see Me,* not to the latter, *a little while and ye shall
see Me.* His going to the Father was the reason why they
would not see Him. So to them who then saw Him in
the body He says, *A little while and ye shall not see Me;*
for He was about to go to the Father, and mortals would
thenceforth never see Him again, as they saw Him now.
The next words, *A little while and ye shall see Me,* are a
promise to the whole Church. For this little while appears
long to us while it is passing, but when it is finished we shall
then see how little a time it has been. ALCUIN. The woman
is the holy Church, who is fruitful in good works, and brings
forth spiritual children unto God. This woman, while she
brings forth, i. e. while she is making her progress in the
world, amidst temptations and afflictions, hath sorrow because
her hour is come; for no one ever hated his own flesh.
Aug. Nor yet in this bringing forth of joy, are we entirely Aug.
without joy to lighten our sorrow, but, as the Apostle saith, Tr. ci.6.
we *rejoice in hope:* for even the woman, to whom we are Rom.
compared, rejoiceth more for her future offspring, than she 12, 12.
sorrows for her present pain. ALCUIN. *But as soon as she
is delivered,* i. e. when her laborious struggle is over, and
she has got the palm, *she remembereth no more her former
anguish, for joy* at reaping such a reward, *for joy that a man
is born into the world.* For as a woman rejoiceth when
a man is born into the world, so the Church is filled with
exultation when the faithful are born into life eternal. BEDE. Bede.
Nor should it appear strange, if one who departeth from this in Hom.
Dom.
life is said to be born. For as a man is said to be born Sec.post.
when he comes out of his mother's womb into the light of vet.
Pasch.
day, so may he be said to be born who from out of the
prison of the body, is raised to the light eternal. Whence
the festivals of the saints, which are the days on which

they died, are called their birthdays. ALCUIN. *I will see you again*, i. e. I will take you to Myself. Or, *I will see you again*, i. e. I shall appear again and be seen by you; *and your heart shall rejoice.* AUG. This fruit indeed the Church now yearneth for in travail, but then will enjoy in her delivery. And it is a male child, because all active duties are for the sake of devotion; for that only is free which is desired for its own sake, not for any thing else, and action is for this end. This is the end which satisfies and is eternal: for nothing can satisfy but what is itself the ultimate end. Wherefore of them it is well said, *Your joy no man taketh from you.*

Aug. Tr. ci. 5.

23. And in that day ye shall ask me nothing. Verily, verily, I say unto you, Whatsoever ye shall ask the Father in my name, he will give it you.

24. Hitherto have ye asked nothing in my name: ask, and ye shall receive, that your joy may be full.

25. These things have I spoken unto you in proverbs: but the time cometh, when I shall no more speak unto you in proverbs, but I shall shew you plainly of the Father.

26. At that day ye shall ask in my name: and I say not unto you, that I will pray the Father for you:

27. For the Father himself loveth you, because ye have loved me, and have believed that I came out from God.

28. I came forth from the Father, and am come into the world: again, I leave the world, and go to the Father.

CHRYS. Again our Lord shews that it is expedient that He should go: *And in that day shall ye ask Me nothing.* AUG. The word *ask* here means not only to seek for, but to ask a question: the Greek word from which it is translated has both meanings. CHRYS. He says, *And in that day,* i. e. when I shall have risen again, *ye shall ask Me nothing,* i. e. not say to Me, *Shew us the Father,* and, *Whither*

Chrys. Hom. lxxix.

Aug. Tr. ci. 4.

Chrys. Hom. lxxix.

goest Thou? since ye will know this by the teaching of
the Holy Ghost: or, *Ye shall ask Me nothing,* i. e. not
want Me for a Mediator to obtain your requests, as My
name will be enough, if you only call upon that: *Verily,
verily, I say unto you, Whatsoever ye shall ask the Father
in My Name, He will give it you.* Wherein He shews His
power; that neither seen, or asked, but named only to the
Father, He will do miracles. Do not think then, He saith,
that because for the future I shall not be with you, that you
are therefore forsaken: for My name will be a still greater
protection to you than My presence: *Hitherto have ye asked
nothing in My Name: ask, and ye shall receive, that your
joy may be full.* THEOPHYL. For when your prayers shall
be fully answered, then will your gladness be greatest.
CHRYS. These words being obscure, He adds, *These things* Chrys.
have I spoken to you in proverbs, but the time cometh when Hom.
I shall no more speak unto you in proverbs: for forty days
He talked with them as they were assembled, speaking of
the kingdom of God. And now, He says, ye are in too
great fear to attend to My words, but then, when you see Me
risen again, you will be able to proclaim these things openly.
THEOPHYL. He still cheers them with the promise that help adhuc.
will be given them from above in their temptations: *At that
day ye shall ask in My Name.* And ye will be so in favour with
the Father, that ye will no longer need my intervention:
*And I say not unto you that I will pray the Father for you,
for the Father Himself loveth you.* But that they might
not start back from our Lord, as though they were no longer
in need of Him, He adds, *Because ye have loved Me:* as if
to say, The Father loves you, because ye have loved Me;
when therefore ye fall from My love, ye will straightway fall
from the Father's love. AUG. But does He love us because Aug.
we love Him; or rather do not we love Him, because He Tr. cii.
loved us? This is what the Evangelist says, *Let us love* 1 John
God, because God first loved us. The Father then loves us, 4, 19.
because we love the Son, it being from the Father and the gamus
Son, that we receive the love from the Father and the Son. Deum,
He loves what He has made; but He would not make in Vulg.
us what He loved, except He loved us in the first place. Hilar.
HILARY. Perfect faith in the Son, which believes and loves Trin.

what has come forth from God, and deserveth to be heard
and loved for its own sake, this faith confessing the Son of
God, born from Him, and sent by Him, needeth not an
intercessor with the Father: wherefore it follows, *And have
believed that I came forth from God.* His nativity and
advent are signified by, *I came forth from the Father, and
am come into the world.* The one is dispensation, the other
nature. To have come from the Father, and to have come forth
from God, have not the same meaning; because it is one
thing to have come forth from God in the relation of Sonship [1],
another thing to háve come from the Father into this world
to accomplish the mystery [2] of our salvation. Since to come
forth from God is to subsist as His Son [3], what else can He be
but God. CHRYS. As it was consolatory to them to hear of
His resurrection, and how He came from God, and went to
God, He dwells again and again on these subjects: *Again
I leave the world, and go to the Father.* The one was
a proof that their faith in Him was not vain: the other that
they would still be under His protection. AUG. He came
forth from the Father, because He is of the Father; He
came into the world, because He shewed Himself in the
body to the world. He left the world by His departure in
the body, and went to the Father by the ascension of His
humanity, nor yet in respect of the government of His
presence, left the world; just as when He went forth from
the Father and came into the world, He did so in such wise
as not to leave the Father. But our Lord Jesus Christ, we
read, was asked questions, and petitioned after His resurrection: for when about to ascend to Heaven He was asked by
His disciples when He would restore the kingdom to Israel;
when in Heaven He was asked by Stephen, to receive his
spirit. And who would dare to say that as mortal He might
be asked, as immortal He might not? I think then that when
He says, *In that day ye shall ask Me nothing,* He refers not
to the time of His resurrection, but to that time when we
shall see Him as He is: which vision is not of this present
life, but of the life everlasting, when we shall ask for nothing,
ask no questions, because there will remain nothing to be
desired, nothing to be learnt. ALCUIN. This is His meaning
then: In the world to come, *ye shall ask Me nothing:* but in

[1] in sub-
stan-
tiam
nativi-
tatis.
[2] sacra-
menta.
[3] ex na-
tivitate
subsis-
tere.
Chrys.
Hom.
lxxix.
Aug.
Tr. cii.

the mean time while ye are travelling on this wearisome road, ask what ye want of the Father, and He will give it you: *Verily, verily, I say unto you, Whatsoever ye shall ask the Father in My Name, He will give it you.* AUG. The word *whatsoever,* must not be understood to mean any thing, but something which with reference to obtaining the life of blessedness is not nothing. That is not sought in the Saviour's name, which is sought to the hindering of our salvation; for by, *in My name,* must be understood not the mere sound of the letters or syllables, but that which is rightly and truly signified by that sound. He who holds any notion concerning Christ, which should not be held of the only Son of God, does not ask in His name. But he who thinks rightly of Him, asks in His name, and receives what he asks, if it be not against his eternal salvation: he receives when it is right he should receive; for some things are only denied at present in order to be granted at a more suitable time. Again, the words, *He will give it you,* only comprehend those benefits which properly appertain to the persons who ask. All saints are heard for themselves, but not for all; for it is not, *will give,* simply, but, *will give you;* what follows: *Hitherto have ye asked nothing in My name,* may be understood in two ways: either that they had not asked in His name, because they had not known it as it ought to be known; or, *Ye have asked nothing,* because with reference to obtaining the thing ye ought to ask for, what ye have asked for is to be counted nothing. That therefore they may ask in His name not for what is nothing, but for the fulness of joy, He adds, *Ask and ye shall receive, that your joy may be full.* This *full joy* is not carnal, but spiritual joy; and it will be full, when it is so great that nothing can be added to it. AUG. And this is that full joy, than which nothing can be greater, viz. to enjoy God, the Trinity, in the image of Whom we are made. AUG. Whatsoever then is asked, which appertaineth to the getting this joy, this must be asked in the name of Christ. For His saints that persevere in asking for it, He will never in His divine mercy disappoint. But whatever is asked beside this is nothing, i. e. not absolutely nothing, but nothing in comparison with so great a thing as this. It follows: *These things have I spoken unto you in proverbs: but the time cometh, when I shall no more speak unto you in proverbs,*

Aug.
Tr. cii.

Aug.
l. de
Trin. c.
11.
Aug.
Tr. cii.

compu-
tatione.

but I shall shew you plainly of the Father. The hour of
which He speaks may be understood of the future life, when
1 Cor. we shall see Him, as the Apostle saith, *face to face,* and,
13, 12. *These things have I spoken to you in proverbs,* of that which
the Apostle saith, *Now we see as in a glass darkly.* But I
will shew you that the Father shall be seen through the Son;
Mat. 11, *For no man knoweth the Father save the Son, and he to
17. *whom the Son shall reveal Him.* GREG. When He declares
Greg.
xxx. that He will shew them plainly of the Father, He alludes to
Moral.
viii. the manifestation about to take place of His own majesty,
which would both shew His own equality with the Father,
Aug. and the procession of the coeternal Spirit from both. AUG.
Tr. cii.
c. 3. But this sense seems to be interfered with by what follows:
At that day ye shall ask in My name. What shall we have
to ask for in a future life, when all our desires shall be satisfied? Asking implies the want of something. It remains
then that we understand the words of Jesus going to make
His disciples spiritual, from being carnal and natural beings.
The natural man so understands whatever he hears of God
in a bodily sense, as being unable to conceive any other.
Wherefore whatever Wisdom saith of the incorporeal, immutable substance are proverbs to him, not that he accounts
them proverbs, but understands them as if they were proverbs.
But when, become spiritual, he hath begun to discern all
things, though in this life he see but in a glass and in part,
ye doth he perceive, not by bodily sense, not by idea of the
imagination, but by most sure intelligence of the mind, perceive and hold that God is not body, but spirit: the Son
sheweth so plainly of the Father, that He who sheweth is
seen to be of the same nature with Him who is shewn. Then
they who ask, ask in His name, because by the sound of that
name they understand nothing but the thing itself which is
expressed by that name. These are able to think that our
Lord Jesus Christ, in so far as He is man, intercedes with
the Father for us, in so far as He is God, hears us together
with the Father: which I think is His meaning when He
says, *And I say not unto you that I will pray the Father
for you.* To understand this, viz. how that the Son does
not ask the Father, but Father and Son together hear those
who ask, is beyond the reach of any but the spiritual
vision.

29. His disciples said unto him, Lo, now speakest thou plainly, and speakest no proverb.

30. Now are we sure that thou knowest all things, and needest not that any man should ask thee: by this we believe that thou camest forth from God.

31. Jesus answered them, Do ye now believe?

32. Behold, the hour cometh, yea, is now come, that ye shall be scattered, every man to his own, and shall leave me alone: and yet I am not alone, because the Father is with me.

33. These things I have spoken unto you, that in me ye might have peace. In the world ye shall have tribulation: but be of good cheer; I have overcome the world.

CHRYS. The disciples were so refreshed with the thought of being in favour with the Father, that they say they are sure He knows all things: *His disciples said unto Him, Now speakest Thou plainly, and speakest no proverb.* AUG. But why do they say so, when the hour in which He was to speak without proverbs was yet future, and only promised? Because, our Lord's communications still continuing proverbs to them, they are so far from understanding them, that they do not even understand their not understanding them. CHRYS. But since His answer met what was in their minds, they add, *Now we are sure that Thou knowest all things.* See how imperfect they yet were, after so many and great things now at last to say, *Now we are sure &c.* saying it too as if they were conferring a favour. *And needest not that any man should ask thee;* i. e. Thou knowest what offends us, before we tell Thee, and Thou hast relieved us by saying that *the Father loveth us.* AUG. Why this remark? To one Who knew all things, instead of saying, *Thou needest not that any man should ask Thee;* it would have been more appropriate to have said, Thou needest not to ask any man: yet we know that both of these were done, viz. that our Lord both asked questions, and was asked. But this is soon explained; for both were for the benefit, not of Himself, but of those whom

Chrys. Hom. lxxix.

Aug. Tr. ciii.

Chrys. Hom. lxxix. 2.

Aug. Tr.ciii.2.

He asked questions of, or by whom He was asked. He asked questions of men not in order to learn Himself, but to teach them: and in the case of those who asked questions of Him, such questions were necessary to them in order to gain the knowledge they wanted; but they were not necessary to Him to tell Him what that was, because He knew the wish of the enquirer, before the question was put. Thus to know men's thoughts beforehand was no great thing for the Lord, but to the minds of babes it was a great thing: *By this we know that Thou camest forth from God.*

Hilar. vi. de Trin. c. 34.

HILARY. They believe that He came forth from God, because He does the works of God. For whereas our Lord had said both, *I came forth from the Father*, and, *I am come into the world from the Father*, they testified no wonder at the latter words, *I am come into the world*, which they had often heard before. But their reply shews a belief in and appreciation of the former, *I came forth from the Father.* And they notice this in their reply: *By this we believe that Thou camest forth from God;* not adding, and art come into the world, for they knew already that He was sent from God, but had not yet received the doctrine of His eternal generation. That unutterable doctrine they now began to see for the first time in consequence of these words, and therefore reply that He spoke no longer in parables. For God is not born from God after the manner of human birth: His is a *coming forth* from, rather than a birth from, God. He is one from one; not a portion, not a defection, not a diminution, not a derivation, not a pretension, not a passion, but the birth of living nature from living nature. He is God coming forth from God, not a creature appointed to the name of God; He did not begin to be from nothing, but manente *came forth* from an abiding nature. To *come forth*, hath the signification of birth, not of beginning. AUG. Lastly, He reminds them of their weak tender age in respect of the inner man. *Jesus answered them, Do ye now believe?* BEDE. Which can be understood in two ways, either as reproaching, or affirming. If the former, the meaning is, Ye have awaked somewhat late to belief, for *behold the hour cometh, yea is now come, that ye shall be scattered every man to his home.* If the latter, it is, That which ye believe is true, but *behold*

Aug. Tr. ciii.

the hour cometh, &c. AUG. For they did not only with their Aug. bodies leave His body, when He was taken, but with their Tr. ciii. minds the faith. CHRYS. *Ye shall be scattered;* i. e. when Chrys. I am betrayed, fear shall so possess you, that ye will not Hom. lxxix. be able even to take to flight together. But I shall suffer no harm in consequence: *And yet I am not alone, because the Father is with Me.* AUG. He wishes to advance them Aug. so far as to understand that He had not separated from Tr. ciii. the Father because He had come forth from the Father. CHRYS. *These things have I said unto you, that ye might* Chrys. *have peace:* i. e. that ye may not reject Me from your minds. Hom. lxxix.2. For not only when I am taken shall ye suffer tribulation, but so long as ye are in the world: *In the world ye shall have tribulation.* GREG. As if He said, Have Me within you Greg. to comfort you, because you will have the world withont xxvi. Moral. you. AUG. The tribulation of which He speaks was to com- c. xi. mence thus, i. e. in every one being scattered to his home, Aug. Tract. but was not to continue so. For in saying, *And leave Me* ciii. 3. *alone,* He does not mean this to apply to them in their sufferings after His ascension. They were not to desert Him then, but to abide and have peace in Him. Wherefore He adds, *Be of good cheer.* CHRYS. i. e. raise up your Chrys. spirits again: when the Master is victorious, the disciples Hom. lxxx. should not be dejected; *I have overcome the world.* AUG. When the Holy Spirit was given them, they were of good cheer, and, in His strength, victorious. For He would not have overcome the world, had the world overcome His members. When He says, *These things have I spoken to you, that in Me ye might have peace,* He refers not only to what He has just said, but to what He had said all along, either from the time that He first had disciples, or since the supper, when He began this long and wonderful discourse. He declares this to be the object of His whole discourse, viz. that in Him they might have peace. And this peace shall have no end, but is itself the end of every pious action and intention.

CHAP. XVII.

1. These words spake Jesus, and lifted up his eyes to heaven, and said, Father, the hour is come; glorify thy Son, that thy Son also may glorify thee:

2. As thou hast given him power over all flesh, that he should give eternal life to as many as thou hast given him.

3. And this is life eternal, that they might know thee the only true God, and Jesus Christ, whom thou hast sent.

4. I have glorified thee on the earth: I have finished the work which thou gavest me to do.

5. And now, O Father, glorify thou me with thine own self with the glory which I had with thee before the world was.

Chrys. Hom. lxxx. CHRYS. After having said, *In the world ye shall have tribulation,* our Lord turns from admonition to prayer; thus teaching us in our tribulations to abandon all other things, and flee to God. BEDE. *These things spake Jesus,* those things that He had said at the supper, partly sitting c.14,31. as far as the words, *Arise, let us go hence;* and thence standing, up to the end of the hymn which now commences, *And lifted up His eyes and said, Father, the hour is come;* Chrys. Hom. lxxx. 1. *glorify Thy Son.* CHRYS. He lifted up His eyes to heaven to teach us intentness in our prayers: that we should stand with uplifted eyes, not of the body only, but of the mind. Aug. Tr. civ. AUG. Our Lord, in the form of a servant, could have prayed in silence had He pleased; but He remembered that He had not only to pray, but to teach. For not only His discourse, but His prayer also, was for His disciples' edification, yea and for ours who read the same. *Father, the hour is come*, shews that all time, and every thing that He did or suffered to be done, was at His disposing, Who is not subject to time. Not that we must suppose that this hour came by any fatal necessity, but rather by God's ordering. Away with the notion, that the stars could doom to death the Creator of the stars. HILARY. He doth not say that the day, or the time, but that the hour is come. An hour contains a portion of a day. What was this hour? He was now to be spit upon, scourged, crucified. But the Father glorifies the Son. The sun failed in his course, and with him all the other elements felt that death. The earth trembled under the weight of our Lord hanging on the Cross, and testified that it had not power to hold within it Him who was dying. The Centurion proclaimed, *Truly this was the Son of God*. The event answered the prediction. Our Lord had said, *Glorify Thy Son*, testifying that He was not the Son in name only, but properly the Son. *Thy* Son, He saith. Many of us are sons of God; but not such is the Son. For He is the proper, true Son by nature, not by adoption, in truth, not in name, by birth, not by creation. Therefore after His glorifying, to the manifestation of the truth there succeeded confession. The Centurion confesses Him to be the true Son of God, that so none of His believers might doubt what one of His persecutors could not deny. AUG. But if He was glorified by His Passion, how much more by His Resurrection? For His Passion rather shewed His humility than His glory. So we must understand, *Father, the hour is come, glorify Thy Son*, to mean, the hour is come for sowing the seed, humility; defer not the fruit, glory. HILARY. But perhaps this proves weakness in the Son; His waiting to be glorified by one superior to Himself. And who does not confess that the Father is superior, seeing that He Himself saith, *The Father is greater than I?* But beware lest the honour of the Father impair the glory of the Son. It follows: *That Thy Son also may glorify Thee.* So then the Son is not weak, inasmuch as He gives back in His turn glory for the glory which He receives. This petition for glory to be given and repaid, shews the same

Margin notes: Hilar. iii. Tr. c. 10.

Matt. 27, 54.

Aug. Tr. civ.

Hilar. iii. de Trin.

Aug.
Tr. cv.

divinity to be in both. AUG. But it is justly asked, how the Son can glorify the Father, when the eternal glory of the Father never experienced abasement in the form of man, and in respect of its own Divine perfection, does not admit. of being added to. But among men this glory was less when God was only known in Judæa; and therefore the Son glorified the Father, when the Gospel of Christ spread the knowledge of the Father among the Gentiles. *Glorify Thy Son, that Thy Son also may glorify Thee;* i. e. Raise Me from the dead, that by Me Thou mayest be known to the whole world. Then He unfolds further the manner in which the Son glorifies the Father; *As Thou hast given Him power over all flesh, that He should give eternal life to as many as Thou hast given Him. All flesh* signifies all mankind, the part being put for the whole. And this power which is given to Christ by the Father over all flesh, must

Hilar.
iii. de
Trin.

be understood with reference to His human nature. HILARY. For being made flesh Himself, He was about to restore

Hilar.
ix. de
Trin.31.

eternal life to frail, corporeal, and mortal man. HILARY. If Christ be God, not begotten, but unbegotten, then let this receiving be thought weakness. But not if His receiving of power signifies His begetting, in which He received what He is. This gift cannot be counted for weakness. For the Father is such in that He gives; the Son remains God in that He hath received the power of giving eternal life.

Chrys.
Hom.
lxxx.

CHRYS. He saith, *Thou hast given Him power over all flesh,* to shew that His preaching extended not to the Jews only, but to the whole world. But what is *all flesh?* For all did not believe? So far as lay with Him, all did. If they did not attend to His words, it was not His fault who spoke, but theirs who did not receive. AUG. He saith, *As Thou*

Aug.
Tr. cv.
2.

hast given Him power over all flesh, so *the Son may glorify Thee,* i. e. make Thee known to all flesh which Thou hast given Him; for Thou hast so given it to Him, *that He should give eternal life to as many as Thou hast given Him.*

Hilar.
iii. de
Tr.c.14.

HILARY. And in what eternal life is, He then shews: *And this is life eternal, that they might know Thee, the only true God.* To know the only true God is life, but this alone does not constitute life. What else then is added? *And*

Hilar.
iv. de
Tr. c. 9.

Jesus Christ whom Thou hast sent. HILARY. The Arians

hold, that as the Father is the only true, only just, only
wise God, the Son hath no communion of these attributes;
for that which is proper to one, cannot be partaken of by
another. And as these are as they think in the Father alone,
and not in the Son, they necessarily consider the Son a false
and vain God. HILARY. But it must be clear to every one Hilar.
that the reality of any thing is evidenced by its power. For v. de Tr. 3.
that is true wheat, which when rising with grain and fenced
with ears, and shaken out by the winnowing machine, and
ground into corn, and baked into bread, and taken for food,
fulfils the nature and function of bread. I ask then wherein
the truth of Divinity is wanting to the Son, Who hath the
nature and virtue of Divinity. For He so made use of the
virtue of His nature, as to cause to be things which were
not, and to do every thing which seemed good to Him.
HILARY. Because He says, *Thee the only*, does He separate Hilar.
Himself from communion and unity with God? He doth ix. de Trin.
separate Himself, but that He adds immediately, *And Jesus
Christ Whom Thou hast sent.* For the Catholic faith confesses Christ to be true God, in that it confesses the Father
to be the only true God; for natural birth did not introduce
any change of nature into the Only-Begotten God. AUG. Aug.
Dismissing then the Arians, let us see if we are forced to vi. de Tr. c. 9.
confess, that by the words, *That they may know Thee to be
the only true God*, He means us to understand that the
Father only is the true God, in such sense as that only the
Three together, Father, Son, and Holy Ghost, are to be
called God? Does our Lord's testimony authorize us to say
that the Father is the only true God, the Son the only true
God, and the Holy Ghost the only true God, and at the
same time, that the Father, Son, and Holy Ghost together,
i. e. the Trinity, are not three Gods, but one ᵃ true God?
AUG. Or is not the order of the words, *That they may know* Aug.
Thee and Jesus Christ, Whom Thou hast sent, to be the only Tr. c. 5.
true God? the Holy Spirit being necessarily understood,
because the Spirit is only the love of the Father and the
Son, consubstantial with both. If then the Son so glorifies
Thee as Thou hast given Him power over all flesh, and
Thou hast given Him the power, *that He should give eternal*

ᵃ One and only are the same word here, unus.

life to as many as Thou hast given Him, and, *This is life eternal, to know Thee*, it follows that He glorifies Thee by making Thee known to all whom Thou hast given Him. Moreover, if the knowledge of God is life eternal, the more advance we make in this knowledge, the more we make in life eternal. But in life eternal we shall never die. Where then there is no death, there will then be perfect knowledge of God; there will God be most glorified[1], because His glory will be greatest. Glory was defined among the ancients to be fame accompanied with praise. But if man is praised in dependence on what is said of him, how will God be praised when He shall be seen? as in the Psalm, *Blessed are they who dwell in Thy house: they will be alway praising Thee.* There will be praise of God without end, where will be full knowledge of God. There then shall be heard the everlasting praise of God, for there will there be full knowledge of God, and therefore full glorifying of Him. AUG. What He said to His servant Moses, *I am that I am;* this we shall contemplate in the life eternal. AUG. For when sight has made our faith truth, then eternity shall take possession of and displace our mortality. AUG. But God is first glorified here, when He is proclaimed, made known to, and believed in, by men: *I have glorified Thee on the earth.* HILARY. This new glory with which our Lord had glorified the Father, does not imply any advancement[2] in Godhead, but refers to the honour received from those who are converted from ignorance to knowledge. CHRYS. He says, *on the earth;* for He had been glorified in heaven, both in respect of the glory of His own nature, and of the adoration of the Angels. The glory therefore here spoken of is not that which belongeth to His substance, but that which pertaineth to the worship of man: wherefore it follows, *I have finished the work which Thou gavest Me to do.* AUG. Not Thou commandest Me, but, *Thou gavest Me,* implying evidently grace. For what hath human nature, even in the Only-Begotten, what it hath not received? But how had He finished the work which had been given Him to do, when there yet remained His passion to undergo? He says He *has* finished it, i. e. He knows for certain that He *will.* CHRYS. Or, *I have finished,* i. e. He had done all His own part, or had done

[1] clarificatio

Ps.83,4.

Aug. i. de Trin. c. viii. Exod.3.

Aug. iv. de Trin. c. xviii.

Aug. Tr. cv.

Hilar. iii. de Trin.

[2] profectum Divinitatis.

Aug. Tr. cv.

Chrys. Hom. lxxx.

the chief of it, that standing for the whole; (for the root of good was planted:) or He connects Himself with the future, as if it were already present. HILAR. After which, that we may understand the reward of His obedience, and the mystery of the whole dispensation, He adds, *And now glorify Me with the glory with Thine own Self, with the glory which I had with Thee before the world was.* AUG. He had said above, *Father, the hour is come; glorify Thy Son, that Thy Son also may glorify Thee:* the order of which words shews that the Son was first to be glorified by the Father, that the Father might be glorified by the Son. But now He says, *I have glorified Thee; and now glorify Me;* as if He had first glorified the Father, and then asked to be glorified by Him. We must understand that the first is the order in which one was to succeed the other, but that He afterwards uses a past tense, to express a thing future; the meaning being, I *will* glorify Thee on the earth, by finishing the work Thou hast given Me to do: *and now, Father, glorify Me,* which is quite the same sentence with the first one, except that He adds here the mode in which He is to be glorified; *with the glory which I had before the world was, with Thee.* The order of the words is, *The glory which I had with Thee before the world was.* This has been taken by some to mean, that the human nature which was assumed by the Word, would be changed into the Word, that man would be changed into God, or, to speak more correctly, be lost in God. For no one would say that the Word of God would by that change be doubled, or even made at all greater. But we avoid this error, if we take the glory which He had with the Father before the world was, to be the glory which He predestined for Him on earth: (for if we believe Him to be the Son of man, we need not be afraid to say that He was predestinated.) This predestined time of His being glorified, He now saw was arrived, that He might now receive what had been aforetime predestined, He prayed accordingly: *And now, Father, glorify Me, &c.* i. e. that glory which I had with Thee by Thy predestination, it is now time that I should have at Thy right hand. HILAR. Or He prayed that that which was mortal, might receive the glory immortal, that the corruption of the

Margin notes: Hilar. ix. de Trin. — Aug. Tr.cv.5. — Hilar. iii. de Trin.

flesh might be transformed and absorbed into the incorruption
of the Spirit.

6. I have manifested thy name unto the men which
thou gavest me out of the world: thine they were,
and thou gavest them me; and they have kept thy
word.

7. Now they have known that all things whatsoever
thou hast given me are of thee.

8. For I have given unto them the words which
thou gavest me: and they have received them, and
have known surely that I came out from thee, and
they have believed that thou didst send me.

Chrys.
Hom.
lxxxi.

Aug.
Tr. cvi.

CHRYS. Having said, *I have finished My work*, He shews
what kind of work it was, viz. that He should make known
the name of God: *I have manifested Thy name unto the
men which Thou gavest Me out of the world.* AUG. If He
speaks of the disciples only with whom He supped, this
has nothing to do with that glorifying of which He spoke
above, wherewith the Son glorified the Father; for what
glory is it to be known to twelve or eleven men? But if by
the men which were given to Him out of the world, He
means all those who should believe in Him afterwards, this
is without doubt the glory wherewith the Son glorifies the
Father; and, *I have manifested Thy name*, is the same as
what He said before, *I have glorified Thee;* the past being
put for the future both there and here. But what follows
shews that He is speaking here of those who were already
His disciples, not of all who should afterwards believe on
Him. At the beginning of His prayer then our Lord
is speaking of all believers, all to whom He should make
known the Father, thereby glorifying Him: for after saying,
that Thy Son also may glorify Thee, in shewing how that
was to be done, He says, *As Thou hast given Him power
over all flesh.* Now let us hear what He says to the disciples:
*I have manifested Thy name to the men which Thou gavest
Me out of the world.* Had they not known the name of
God then, when they were Jews? We read in the Psalms,

In Jewry is God known; His name is great in Israel. I have Ps.76,1. *manifested Thy name,* then, must be understood not of the name of God, but of the Father's name, which name could not be manifested without the manifestation of the Son.   For God's name, as the God of the whole creation, could not have been entirely unknown to any nation.   As the Maker then of the world, He was known among all nations, even before the spread of the Gospel.   In Jewry He was known as a God, Who was not to be worshipped with the false gods: but as the Father of that Christ, by whom He took away the sins of the world, His name was unknown; which name Christ now manifesteth to those whom the Father had given Him out of the world.   But how did He manifest it, when the hour had not come of which He said above, *The hour cometh, when I shall no more speak unto you in proverbs.* We must understand the past to be put for the future. CHRYS. That He was the Son of the Father, Christ had Chrys. already manifested to them by words and deeds.   AUG. Hom. lxxxi. *Which Thou hast given Me out of the world:* i. e. who were Aug. not of the world.   But this they were by regeneration, not Tr. cvi. by nature.   What is meant by, *Thine they were, and Thou gavest them Me?*   Had ever the Father any thing without the Son?   God forbid.   But the Son of God had that sometimes, which He had not as Son of man; for He had the universe with His Father, while He was still in His mother's womb.   Wherefore by saying, *They were Thine,* the Son of God does not separate Himself from the Father; but only attributes all His power to Him, from whom He is, and hath the same.   *And Thou gavest them Me,* then, means that He had received as man the power to have them; nay, that He Himself had given them to Himself, i. e. Christ as God with the Father, to Christ as man not with the Father.   His purpose here is to shew His unanimity with the Father, and how that it was the Father's pleasure that they should believe in Him.   BEDE. *And they have kept Thy word.* He calls Himself the Word of the Father, because the Father by Him created all things, and because He contains in Himself all words: as if to say, They have committed Me to memory so well, that they never will forget Me.   Or, *They have kept Thy word,* i. e. in that they have believed in Me: as it follows,

Now they have known that all things whatsoever Thou hast given Me, are of Thee. Some read, Now I have known, &c. But this cannot be correct. For how could the Son be ignorant of what was the Father's? It is the disciples He is speaking of; as if to say, They have learnt that there is nothing in Me alien from Thee, and that whatever I teach cometh from Thee.

Aug. Tr. cvi.   AUG. The Father gave Him all things, when having all things He begat Him.

Chrys. Hom. lxxxi.   CHRYS. And whence have they learned? From My words, wherein I taught them that I came forth from Thee. For this was what He has been labouring to shew throughout the whole of the Gospel: *For I have given unto them the words which Thou gavest Me, and they have received them.*

Aug. Tr. cvi. c. 6.   AUG. i. e. have understood and remembered them. For then is a word received, when the mind apprehends it; as it follows, *And have known surely that I came out from Thee.* And that none might imagine that that knowledge was one of sight, not of faith, He adds, *And they have believed* (*surely,* is understood) *that Thou didst send Me.* What they believed surely, was what they knew surely; for, *I came out from Thee,* is the same with, *Thou didst send Me.* They believed surely, i. e.

¹ c. 16. 31, 32.   not as He said above they believed[1], but surely, i. e. as they were about to believe firmly, steadily, unwaveringly: never any more to be scattered to their own, and leave Christ. The disciples as yet were not such as He describes them to be in the past tense, meaning such as they were to be when they had received the Holy Ghost. The question how the Father gave those words to the Son, is easier to solve, if we suppose Him to have received them from the Father as Son of man. But if we understand it to be as the Begotten of the Father, let there be no time supposed previous to His having them, as if He once existed without them: for whatever God the Father gave God the Son, He gave in begetting.

9. I pray for them: I pray not for the world, but for them which thou hast given me; for they are thine.

10. And all mine are thine, and thine are mine; and I am glorified in them.

11. And now I am no more in the world, but these are in the world, and I come to thee. Holy Father, keep through thine own name those whom thou hast given me, that they may be one, as we are.

12. While I was with them in the world, I kept them in thy name: those that thou gavest me I have kept, and none of them is lost, but the son of perdition; that the scripture might be fulfilled.

13. And now come I to thee; and these things I speak in the world, that they might have my joy fulfilled in themselves.

CHRYS. As the disciples were still sad in spite of all our Lord's consolations, henceforth He addresses Himself to the Father to shew the love which He had for them; *I pray for them;* He not only gives them what He has of His own, but entreats another for them, as a still further proof of His love. AUG. When He adds, *I pray not for the world,* by the world He means those who live according to the lust of the world, and have not the lot to be chosen by grace out of the world, as those had for whom He prayed: *But for them which Thou hast given Me.* It was because the Father had given Him them, that they did not belong to the world. Nor yet had the Father, in giving them to the Son, lost what He had given: *For they are Thine.* CHRYS. He often repeats, *Thou hast given Me,* to impress on them that it was all according to the Father's will, and that He did not come to rob another, but to take unto Him His own. Then to shew them that this power [1] had not been lately received from the Father, He adds, *And all Mine are Thine, and Thine are Mine:* as if to say, Let no one, hearing Me say, *Them which Thou hast given Me,* suppose that they are separated from the Father; for Mine are His: nor because I said, *They are Thine,* suppose that they are separate from Me: *for whatever is His is Mine.* AUG. It is sufficiently apparent from hence, that all things which the Father hath, the Only-Begotten Son hath; hath in that He is God, born from the Father, and equal with the Father; not in the sense in which the

Chrys. Hom. lxxxi.

Aug. Tr. cvi.

Chrys. Hom. lxxxi. 1.

[1] ἀρχὴ

Aug. Tr. cvi. 6.

2 M 2

Luke15, elder son is told, *All that I have is thine.* For *all* there
31. means all creatures below the holy rational creature, but
here it means the very rational creature itself, which is only
subjected to God. Since this is God the Father's, it could
not at the same time be God the Son's, unless the Son were
equal to the Father. For it is impossible that saints, of
whom this is said, should be the property of any one, except
Him who created and sanctified them. When He says
c.16,15. above in speaking of the Holy Spirit, *All things that the
Father hath are Mine,* He means all things which pertain to
the divinity of the Father; for He adds, *He* (the Holy Ghost)
shall receive of Mine; and the Holy Ghost would not receive
from a creature which was subject to the Father and the
Son. CHRYS. Then He gives proof of this, *I am glorified
in them.* If they glorify Me, believing in Me and Thee, it
is certain that I have power over them: for no one is glorified by those amongst whom he has no power. AUG. He
speaks of this as already done, meaning that it was predestined, and sure to be. But is this the glorifying of which
He speaks above, *And now, O Father, glorify Thou Me with
Thine own Self?* If then *with Thyself,* what meaneth here,
In them? Perhaps that this very thing, i. e. His glory with
the Father, was made known to them, and through them to
all that believe. CHRYS. *And now I am no more in the
world:* i. e. though I no longer appear in the flesh, I am
glorified by those who die for Me, as for the Father, and
preach Me as the Father. AUG. At the time at which He
was speaking, both were still in the world. Yet we must not
understand, *I am no more in the world,* metaphorically of
the heart and life; for could there ever have been a time
when He loved the things of the world? It remains then that
He means that He was not in the world, as He had been
before; i. e. that He was soon going away. Do we not say
every day, when any one is going to leave us, or going to
die, such an one is gone? This is shewn to be the sense by
what follows; for He adds, *And now I come to Thee.* And
then He commends to His Father those whom He was about
to leave: *Holy Father, keep through Thine own name those
whom Thou hast given Me.* As man He prays God for His
disciples, whom He received from God. But mark what

Chrys.
Hom.
lxxxi.

Aug.
Tr. cvii.
3.

Chrys.
Hom.
lxxxi.

Aug.
Tr. cvii.
4.

follows: *That they may be one, as We are:* He does not say,
That they may be one with Us, as We are one; but, *that they
may be one:* that they may be one in their nature, as We are
one in Ours. For, in that He was God and man in one person, as man He prayed, as God He was one with Him to
Whom He prayed. AUG. He does not say, That I and they Aug.
may be one, though He might have said so in the sense, that iv. de Trin.
He was the head of the Church, and the Church His body; c. ix.
not one thing, but one person: the head and the body being
one Christ. But shewing something else, viz. that His
divinity is consubstantial with the Father, He prays that His
people may in like manner be one; but one in Christ, not
only by the same nature, in which mortal man is made equal to
the Angels, but also by the same will, agreeing most entirely
in the same mind, and melted into one Spirit by the fire of
love. This is the meaning of, *That they may be one as We
are:* viz. that as the Father and the Son are one not only by
equality of substance, but also in will, so they, between whom
and God the Son is Mediator, may be one not only by the
union of nature, but by the union of love. CHRYS. Again Chrys.
He speaks as man: *While I was with them in the world, I* Hom. lxxxi.
kept them in Thy name; i. e. by Thy help. He speaks in
condescension to the minds of His disciples, who thought
they were more safe in His presence. AUG. The Son as man Aug.
kept His disciples in the Father's name, being placed among Tr. cvii. 6.
them in human form: the Father again kept them in the Son's
name, in that He heard those who asked in the Son's name.
But we must not take this carnally, as if the Father and Son
kept us in turns, for the Father, Son, and Holy Ghost guard
us at the same time: but Scripture does not raise us, except
it stoop to us. Let us understand then that when our Lord
says this, He is distinguishing the persons, not dividing the
nature, so that when the Son was keeping His disciples by
His bodily presence, the Father was waiting to succeed Him
on His departure; but both kept them by spiritual power,
and when the Son withdrew His bodily presence, He still
held with the Father the spiritual keeping. For when the
Son as man received them into His keeping, He did not
take them from the Father's keeping, and when the Father
gave them into the Son's keeping, it was to the Son as man,
who at the same time was God. *Those that Thou gavest*

Me I have kept, and none of them is lost but the son of perdition: i. e. the betrayer of Christ, predestined to perdition; *that the Scripture might be fulfilled,* especially the prophecy in Psalm cviii. Chrys. He was the only one indeed who perished then, but there were many after. *None of them is lost,* i. e. as far as I am concerned; as He says above more clearly; *I will in no wise cast out.* But when they cast themselves out, I will not draw them to Myself by dint of compulsion. It follows: *And now I come to Thee.* But some one might ask, Canst Thou not keep them? I can. Then why sayest Thou this? *That they may have My joy fulfilled in them,* i. e. that they may not be alarmed in their as yet imperfect state. Aug. Or thus: That they might have the joy spoken of above: *That they may be one, as We are one.* This His joy, i. e. bestowed by Him, He says, is to be fulfilled in them: on which account He spoke thus in the world. This joy is the peace and happiness of the life to come. He says He spoke *in the world,* though He had just now said, *I am no more in the world.* For, inasmuch as He had not yet departed, He was still here; and inasmuch as He was going to depart, He was in a certain sense not here.

14. I have given them thy word; and the world hath hated them, because they are not of the world, even as I am not of the world.

15. I pray not that thou shouldest take them out of the world, but that thou shouldest keep them from the evil.

16. They are not of the world, even as I am not of the world.

17. Sanctify them through thy truth; thy word is truth.

18. As thou hast sent me into the world, even so have I also sent them into the world.

19. And for their sakes I sanctify myself, that they also might be sanctified through the truth.

Chrys. Again, our Lord gives a reason why the disciples are worthy of obtaining such favour from the Father: *I have given them Thy word; and the world hath hated them;* i. e.

Chrys.
Hom.
lxxxi.

Aug.
Tr. cvii.

Chrys.
Hom.
lxxxii.

They are had in hatred for Thy sake, and on account of Thy
word. AUG. They had not yet experienced these sufferings Aug.
which they afterwards met with; but, after His custom, He Tr.cviii.
puts the future into the past tense. Then He gives the
reason why the world hated them; viz. *Because they are
not of the world.* This was conferred upon them by regeneration; for by nature they were of the world. It was
given to them that they should not be of the world, even as
He was not of the world; as it follows; *Even as I am not of
the world.* He never was of the world; for even His birth
of the form of a servant He received from the Holy Ghost,
from Whom they were born again. But though they were
no longer of the world, it was still necessary that they should
be in the world: *I pray not that Thou shouldest take them
out of the world.* BEDE. As if to say, The time is now
at hand, when I shall be taken out of the world; and therefore it is necessary that they should be still left in the world,
in order to preach Me and Thee to the world. *But that
Thou shouldest keep them from the evil;* every evil, but
especially the evil of schism. AUG. He repeats the same Aug.
thing again; *They are not of the world, even as I am not of* Tr.cviii.
the world. CHRYS. Above, when He said, *Them whom* Chrys.
Thou gavest Me out of the world, He meant their nature; lxxxii.
here He means their actions. *They are not of the world;* [1.]
because they have nothing in common with earth, they are
made citizens of heaven. Wherein He shews His love for
them, thus praising them to the Father. The word *as* when
used with respect to Him and the Father expresses likeness of nature; but between us and Christ there is immense
distance. *Keep them from the evil,* i. e. not from dangers
only, but from falling away from the faith. AUG. *Sanctify* Aug.
them through Thy truth: for thus were they to be kept Tr.cviii.
from the evil. But it may be asked, how it was that they
were not of the world, when they were not yet sanctified in
the truth? Because the sanctified have still to grow in
sanctity, and this by the help of God's grace. The heirs of
the New Testament are sanctified in that truth, the shadows
of which were the sanctification of the Old Testament; they
are sanctified in Christ, Who said above, *I am the way, the* c. 14, 6.
truth, and the life. It follows, *Thy discourse is truth.*

The Greek is λόγος, i. e. word. The Father then sanctified them in the truth, i. e. in His Word the Only-Begotten, them, i. e. the heirs of God, and joint-heirs with Christ. CHRYS. Or thus: *Sanctify them in Thy truth;* i. e. Make them holy, by the gift of the Holy Spirit, and sound doctrines : for sound doctrines give knowledge of God, and sanctify the soul. And as He is speaking of doctrines, He adds, *Thy word is truth,* i. e. there is in it no lie, nor any thing typical, or bodily. Again, *Sanctify them in Thy truth,* may mean, Separate them for the ministry of the word, and preaching. GLOSS. *As Thou hast sent Me into the world, even so have I also sent them into the world.* For what Christ was sent into the world, for the same end were they ; as saith Paul, *God was in Christ reconciling the world unto Himself; and hath given to us the word of reconciliation. As* does not express perfect likeness between our Lord and His Apostles, but only as much as was possible in men. *Have* sent them, He says, according to His custom of putting the past for the future. AUG. It is manifest by this, that He is still speaking of the Apostles; for the very word Apostle means in the Greek, sent. But since they are His members, in that He is the Head of the Church, He says, *And for their sakes I sanctify Myself;* i. e. I in Myself sanctify them, since they are Myself. And to make it more clear that this was His meaning, He adds, *That they also might be sanctified through the truth,* i. e. in Me; inasmuch as the Word is truth, in which the Son of man was sanctified from the time that the Word was made flesh. For then He sanctified Himself in Himself, i. e. Himself as man, in Himself as the Word: the Word and man being one Christ. But of His members it is that He saith, *And for their sakes I sanctify Myself,* i. e. them in Me, since in Me both they and I are. *That they also might be sanctified in truth:* they also, i. e. even as Myself; and *in the truth,* i. e. Myself. CHRYS. Or thus: *For their sakes I sanctify Myself,* i. e. I offer Myself as a sacrifice to Thee; for all sacrifices, and things that are offered to God, are called holy. And whereas this sanctification was of old in figure, (a sheep being the sacrifice,) but now in truth, He adds, *That they also might be sanctified through the truth;* i. e. For I make them too an

Chrys. Hom. lxxxii.

2 Cor. 5, 19.

Aug. Tr.cviii.

Chrys. Hom. lxxxii.

oblation to Thee; either meaning that He who was offered up was their head, or that they would be offered up too: as the Apostle saith, *Present your bodies a living sacrifice, holy.*   Rom. 12, 1.

20. Neither pray I for these alone, but for them also which shall believe on me through their word;

21. That they all may be one; as thou, Father, art in me, and I in thee, that they also may be one in us: that the world may believe that thou hast sent me.

22. And the glory which thou gavest me I have given them; that they may be one, even as we are one:

23. I in them, and thou in me, that they may be made perfect in one: and that the world may know that thou hast sent me, and hast loved them, as thou hast loved me.

AUG. When our Lord had prayed for His disciples, whom He named also Apostles, He added a prayer for all others who should believe on Him; *Neither pray I for these alone, but for all others who shall believe on Me through their word.*   Aug. Tr. cix.
CHRYS. Another ground of consolation to them, that they were to be the cause of the salvation of others.   AUG. *All,* i. e. not only those who were then alive, but those who were to be born; not those only who heard the Apostles themselves, but us who were born long after their death.   We have all believed in Christ through their word: for they first heard that word from Christ, and then preached it to others, and so it has come down, and will go down to all posterity.   We may see that in this prayer there are some disciples whom He does not pray for; for those, i. e. who were neither with Him at the time, nor were about to believe on Him afterwards through the Apostles' word, but believed already.   Was Nathanael with Him then, or Joseph of Arimathea, and many others, who, John says, believed on Him?   I do not mention old Simeon, or Anna the prophetess, Zacharias, Elisabeth, or John the Baptist; for it might be answered that it was not necessary to pray for dead persons, such as these who departed with such rich merits.   With   Chrys. Hom. lxxxii.   Aug. Tr. cix.

respect to the former then we must understand that they did
not yet believe in Him, as He wished, but that after His
resurrection, when the Apostles were taught and strengthened
by the Holy Spirit, they attained to a right faith. The case
Gal.1,1. of Paul however still remains, *An Apostle not of men, or by
men;* and that of the robber, who believed when even the
teachers themselves of the faith fell away. We must understand then, *their word,* to mean the word of faith itself which
they preached to the world; it being called their word,
because it was preached in the first instance and principally
by them; for it was being preached by them, when Paul
received it by revelation from Jesus Christ Himself. And
in this sense the robber too believed their word. Wherefore
in this prayer the Redeemer prays for all whom He redeemed,
both present and to come. And then follows the thing itself
which He prays for, *That they all may be one.* He asks
that for all, which he asked above for the disciples; that all
Chrys. both we and they may be one. CHRYS. And with this
Hom.
lxxxii. prayer for unanimity, He concludes His prayer; and then
begins a discourse on the same subject: *A new command-
Hilar. ment I give unto you, that ye love one another.* HILARY.
vii. de
Trin. And this unity is recommended by the great example of
unity: *As Thou, Father, art in Me, and I in Thee, that they
also may be one in Us,* i. e. that as the Father is in the Son,
and the Son in the Father, so, after the likeness of this
Chrys. unity, all may be one in the Father and in the Son. CHRYS.
Hom.
lxxxii. This *as* again does not express perfect likeness, but only
likeness as far as it was possible in men; as when He saith,
Luke 6, *Be ye merciful, even as your Father, which is in heaven, is
36.
Aug. merciful.* AUG. We must particularly observe here, that our
Tr. cx. Lord did not say, that we may be all one, but *that they may
be all one, as Thou, Father, in Me, and I in Thee,* are one,
understood. For the Father is so in the Son, that They are
one, because They are of one substance; but we can be one
in Them, but not with Them; because we and They are not of
one substance. They are in us, and we in Them, so as that
They are one in Their nature, we one in ours. They are in
us, as God is in the temple; we in Them, as the creature is
in its Creator. Wherefore He adds, *in Us,* to shew, that our
being made one by charity, is to be attributed to the grace

of God, not to ourselves. AUG. Or that in ourselves we can- Aug.
not be one, severed from each other by diverse pleasures, iii. de
and lusts, and the pollution of sin, from which we must be c. ix.
cleansed by a Mediator, in order to be one in Him. HILARY. Hilar.
Heretics endeavouring to get over the words, *I and* viii. de
My Father are one, as a proving unity of nature, and to
reduce them to mean a unity simply of natural love, and
agreement of will, bring forwards these words of our Lord's
as an example of this kind of unity : *That they may be all
one, as Thou, Father, art in Me, and I in Thee.* But though
impiety can cheat its own understanding, it cannot alter the
meaning[1] of the words themselves. For they who are born [1] intelli-
again of a nature that gives unity in life eternal, they cease gentiam
to be one in will merely, acquiring the same nature by their
regeneration : but the Father and Son alone are properly
one, because God, only-begotten of God, can only exist in
that nature from which He is derived. AUG. But why does Aug.
He say, *That the world may believe that Thou hast sent Me?* Tr. cx.
Will the world believe when we shall all be one in the
Father and the Son? Is not this unity that peace eternal,
which is the reward of faith, rather than faith itself? For
though in this life all of us who hold in the same common
faith are one, yet even this unity is not a means to belief,
but the consequence of it. What means then, *That all may
be one, that the world may believe?* He prays for the
world when He says, *Neither pray I for these alone, but
for all those who shall believe on Me through their word.*
Whereby it appears that He does not make this unity the
cause of the world believing, but prays *that the world
may believe,* as He prays that *they all may be one.* The
meaning will be clearer if we always put in the word ask;
I ask that they all may be one; I ask that they may
be one in Us; I ask that the world may believe that Thou
hast sent Me. HILARY. Or, the world will believe that Hilar.
the Son is sent from the Father, for that reason, viz. because viii. de
all who believe in Him are one in the Father and the Son. Trin.
CHRYS. For there is no scandal so great as division, whereas Chrys.
unity amongst believers is a great argument for believing; as Hom.
He said at the beginning of His discourse, *By this shall all
men know that ye are My disciples, if ye have love one to*

another. For if they quarrel, they will not be looked on as the disciples of a peacemaking Master. And I, He saith, not being a peacemaker, they will not acknowledge Me as sent from God. AUG. Then our Saviour, Who, by praying to the Father, shewed Himself to be man, now shews that, being God with the Father, He doth what He prays for: *And the glory which Thou gavest Me, I have given them.* What glory, but immortality, which human nature was about to receive in Him? For that which was to be by unchangeable predestination, though future, He expresses by the past tense. That glory of immortality, which He says was given Him by the Father, we must understand He gave Himself also. For when the Son is silent of His own cooperation in the Father's work, He shews His humility: when He is silent of the Father's cooperation in His work, He shews His equality. In this way here He neither disconnects Himself with the Father's work, when He says, *The glory which Thou gavest Me,* nor the Father with His work, when He says, *I have given them.* But as He was pleased by prayer to the Father to obtain that all might be one, so now He is pleased to effect the same by His own gift; for He continues, *That all may be one, even as We are one.* CHRYS. By glory, He means miracles, and doctrines, and unity; which latter is the greater glory. For all who believed through the Apostles are one. If any separated, it was owing to men's own carelessness; not but that our Lord anticipates this happening. HILARY. By this giving and receiving of honour, then, all are one. But I do not yet apprehend in what way this makes all one. Our Lord, however, explains the gradation and order in the consummating of this unity, when He adds, *I in them, and Thou in Me;* so that inasmuch as He was in the Father by His divine nature, we in Him by His incarnation, and He again in us by the mystery of the sacrament, a perfect union by means of a Mediator was established. CHRYS. Elsewhere[1] He says of Himself and the Father, *We will come and make Our abode with Him;* by the mention of two persons, stopping the mouths of the Sabellians. Here by saying that the Father comes to the disciples through Him, He refutes the notion of the Arians. AUG. Nor is this said, however, as if to mean

Aug. Tr. cx.

Chrys. Hom. lxxxii. 2.

Hilar. viii. de Trin.

Chrys. Hom. lxxxii.

[1] supr. c.14,23.

Aug. Tr. xc. 4.

that the Father was not in us, or we in the Father. He only means to say, that He is Mediator between God and man. And what He adds, *That they may be made perfect in one*, shews that the reconciliation made by this Mediator, was carried on even to the enjoyment of everlasting blessedness. So what follows, *That the world may know that Thou hast sent Me*, must not be taken to mean the same as the words just above, *That the world may believe.* For as long as we believe what we do not see, we are not yet made perfect, as we shall be when we have merited to see what we believe. So that when He speaks of their being made perfect, we are to understand such a knowledge as shall be by sight, not such as is by faith. These that believe are the world, not a permanent enemy, but changed from an enemy to a friend; as it follows: *And hast loved them, as Thou hast loved Me.* The Father loves us in the Son, because He elected us in Him. These words do not prove that we are equal to the Only Begotten Son; for this mode of expression, as one thing so another, does not always signify equality. It sometimes only means, because one thing, therefore another. And this is its meaning here: *Thou hast loved them, as Thou hast loved Me*, i. e. Thou hast loved them, because Thou hast loved Me. There is no reason for God loving His members, but that He loves him. But since He hateth nothing that He hath made, who can adequately express how much He loves the members of His Only Begotten Son, and still more the Only Begotten Himself.

24. Father, I will that they also, whom thou hast given me, be with me where I am; that they may behold my glory, which thou hast given me: for thou lovedst me before the foundation of the world.

25. O righteous Father, the world hath not known thee: but I have known thee, and these have known that thou hast sent me.

26. And I have declared unto them thy name, and will declare it: that the love wherewith thou hast loved me may be in them, and I in them.

Chrys.
Hom.
lxxxii.
2.

CHRYS. After He has said that many should believe on Him through them, and that they should obtain great glory, He then speaks of the crowns in store for them; *Father, I will that they also whom Thou hast given Me, be with Me where I am.*

Aug.
Tr. cxi.
1.

AUG. These are they whom He has received from the Father, whom He also chose out of the world; as He saith at the beginning of this prayer, *Thou hast given Him power over all flesh,* i. e. all mankind, *That He should give eternal life to as many as Thou hast given Him.* Wherein He shews that He had received power over all men, to deliver whom He would, and to condemn whom He would. Wherefore it is to all His members that He promises this reward, that where He is, they may be also. Nor can that but be done, which the Almighty Son saith that He wishes to the Almighty Father: for the Father and the Son have one will, which, if weakness prevent us from comprehending, piety must believe. *Where I am*: so far as pertains to the creature, He was made of the seed of David according to the flesh: He might say, *Where I am,* meaning where He was shortly to be, i. e. heaven. In heaven then, He promises us, we shall be. For thither was the form of a servant raised, which He had taken from the Virgin, and there placed on the right hand of God.

Greg.
Moral.
John 3,
13.

GREG. What means then what the Truth saith above, *No man hath ascended into heaven, but He that came down from heaven, even the Son of man which is in heaven.* Yet here is no discrepancy, for our Lord being the Head of His members, the reprobates excluded, He is alone with us. And therefore, we making one with Him, whence He came alone in Himself, thither He returns alone in us.

Aug.
Tr. cxi.

AUG. But as respects the form of God, wherein He is equal to the Father, if we understand these words, *that they may be with Me where I am*, with reference to that, then away with all bodily ideas, and enquire not where the Son, Who is equal to the Father, is: for no one hath discovered where He is not. Wherefore it was not enough for Him to say, *I will that they may be where I am,* but He adds, *with Me.* For to be with Him is the great good: even the miserable can be where He is, but only the happy can be with Him. And as in the case of the visible, though very different be whatever example we take, a blind

man will serve for one, as a blind man though He is where
the light is, yet is not himself with the light, but is absent
from it in its presence, so not only the unbelieving, but the
believing, though they cannot be where Christ is not, yet are
not themselves with Christ by sight: by faith we cannot
doubt but that a believer is with Christ. But here He is
speaking of that sight wherein we shall see Him as He is;
as He adds, *That they may behold My glory, which Thou
hast given Me.* *That they may behold,* He says, not, that
they may believe. It is the reward of faith which He speaks
of, not faith itself. CHRYS. He saith not, that they may Chrys.
partake of My glory, but, *that they may behold,* intimating Hom.
lxxxii.
that the rest there is to see the Son of God. The Father
gave Him glory, when He begat Him. AUG. When then we Aug.
shall have seen the glory which the Father gave the Son, Tr. cxi.
3.
though by this glory we do not understand here, that which
He gave to the equal Son when He begat Him, but that
which He gave to the Son of man, after His crucifixion;
then shall the judgment be, then shall the wicked be taken
away, that he see not the glory of the Lord: what glory but
that whereby He is God? If then we take their words,
That they may be with Me where I am, to be spoken by
Him as Son of God, in that case they must have a higher
meaning, viz. that we shall be in the Father with Christ.
As He immediately adds, *That they may see My glory which
Thou hast given Me;* and then, *Which Thou gavest Me
before the foundation of the world.* For in Him He loved
us before the foundation of the world, and then predestined
what He should do at the end of the world. BEDE. That
which He calls *glory* then is the love wherewith He was
loved with the Father before the foundation of the world.
And in that glory He loved us too before the foundation of
the world. THEOPHYL. After then that He had prayed for
believers, and promised them so many good things, another
prayer follows worthy of His mercy and benignity: *O
righteous Father, the world hath not known Thee;* as if to
say, I would wish that all men obtained these good things,
which I have asked for the believing. But inasmuch as they
have not known Thee, they shall not obtain the glory and Chrys.
crown. CHRYS. He says this as if He were troubled at the Hom.
lxxxii.

thought, that they should be unwilling to know One so just
and good.   And whereas the Jews had said, that they knew
God, and He knew Him not: He on the contrary says, *But
I have known Thee, and these have known that Thou hast
sent Me, and I have declared unto them Thy name, and will
declare*[1] *it*, by giving them perfect knowledge through the
Holy Ghost.   When they have learned what Thou art, they
will know that I am not separate from Thee, but Thine own
Son greatly beloved, and joined to Thee.   This I have told
them, that I might receive them, and that they who believe
this aright, shall preserve their faith and love toward Me
entire; and I will abide in them: *That the love wherewith
Thou hast loved Me may be in them, and I in them.*   AUG.
Or thus; What is to know Him, but eternal life, which He
gave not to a condemned but to a reconciled world?   For
this reason the world hath not known Thee; because Thou
art just, and hast punished them with this ignorance of Thee,
in reward for their misdeeds.   And for this reason the
reconciled world knows Thee, because Thou art merciful,
and hast vouchsafed this knowledge, not in consequence of
their merits, but of thy grace.   It follows: *But I have known
Thee.*   He is God the fountain of grace by nature, man of
the Holy Ghost and Virgin by grace ineffable.   Then because
the grace of God is through Jesus Christ, He says, *And they
have known Me*, i. e. the reconciled world have known Me,
by grace, forasmuch as *Thou hast sent Me.   And I have
made known Thy name to them* by faith, and *will make it
known* by sight: *that the love wherewith Thou hast loved
Me may be in them.*   The Apostle uses a like phrase, *I have
fought a good fight, by* a good fight being the more common
form.   The love wherewith the Father loveth the Son in us,
can only be in us because we are His members, and we are
loved in Him when He is loved wholly, i. e. both head and
body.   And therefore He adds, *And I in them;* He is in
us, as in His temple, we in Him as our Head.

Margin notes:
[1] make known
Aug. Tr. cxi. 5.
2 Tim. 4, 7.

CHAP. XVIII.

1. When Jesus had spoken these words, he went forth with his disciples over the brook Cedron, where was a garden, into the which he entered, and his disciples.

2. And Judas also, which betrayed him, knew the place: for Jesus ofttimes resorted thither with his disciples.

Aug. The discourse, which our Lord had with His disciples after supper, and the prayer which followed, being now ended, the Evangelist begins the account of His Passion. *When Jesus had spoken these words, He came forth with His disciples over the brook Cedron, where was a garden, into which He entered, and His disciples.* But this did not take place immediately after the prayer was ended; there was an interval containing some things, which John omits, but which are mentioned by the other Evangelists. Aug. A contention took place between them, which of them was the greater, as Luke relates. He also said to Peter, as Luke adds in the same place, *Behold, Satan hath desired to have you, that he might sift you as wheat, &c.* And according to Matthew and Mark, they sang a hymn, and then went to Mount Olivet. Matthew lastly brings the two narratives together: *Then went Jesus with His disciples to a place which is called Gethsemane.* That is the place which John mentions here, *Where there was a garden, into the which He entered, and His disciples.* Aug. *When Jesus had spoken these words*, shews that He did not enter before He had finished speaking. Chrys. But why does not John say, When He had prayed, He entered? Because His prayer was a speaking for His disciples' sake. It is now night time; He goes and crosses the brook, and hastens to the place

Aug.
Tr. cxii.

Aug.
de Con.
Ev. iii.
c. 111.
Luke22,
31.
Mat.26,
30.
Mark14,
26.

Aug.
Tr. cxii.
Chrys.
Hom.
lxxxiii.

which was known to the traitor; thus giving no trouble to those who were lying in wait for Him, and shewing His disciples that He went voluntarily to die. ALCUIN. *Over the brook Cedron*, i. e. of cedars. It is the genitive in the Greek. He goes *over the brook*, i. e. drinks of the brook of His Passion. *Where there was a garden*, that the sin which was committed in a garden, He might blot out in a garden. Chrys. Hom. lxxxii. Paradise signifies garden of delights. CHRYS. That it might not be thought that He went into a garden to hide Himself, it is added, *But Judas who betrayed Him knew the place: for Jesus often resorted thither with His disciples.* Aug. Tr. cxii. AUG. There the wolf in sheep's clothing, permitted by the deep counsel of the Master of the flock to go among the sheep, learned in what way to disperse the Chrys. Hom. lxxxiii. flock, and ensnare the Shepherd. CHRYS. Jesus had often met and talked alone with His disciples there, on essential doctrines, such as it was lawful for others to hear. He does this on mountains, and in gardens, to be out of reach of noise and tumult. Judas however went there, because Christ had often passed the night there in the open air. He would have gone to His house, if he had thought he should find Him sleeping there. THEOPHYL. Judas knew that at the feast time our Lord was wont to teach His disciples high and mysterious doctrines, and that He taught in places like this. And as it was then a solemn season, he thought He would be found there, teaching His disciples things relating to the feast.

3. Judas then, having received a band of men and officers from the chief priests and Pharisees, cometh thither with lanterns and torches and weapons.

4. Jesus therefore, knowing all things that should come upon him, went forth, and said unto them, Whom seek ye?

5. They answered him, Jesus of Nazareth. Jesus saith unto them, I am he. And Judas also, which betrayed him, stood with them.

6. As soon then as he said unto them, I am he, they went backward, and fell to the ground.

7. Then asked he them again, Whom seek ye? And they said, Jesus of Nazareth.

8. Jesus answered, I have told you that I am he: if therefore ye seek me, let these go their way:

9. That the saying might be fulfilled, which he spake, Of them which thou gavest me have I lost none.

GLOSS. The Evangelist had shewn how Judas had found out the place where Christ was, now he relates how he went there. *Judas then, having received a band of men and officers from the chief priests and Pharisees, cometh thither with lanterns and torches and weapons.* AUG. It was a band not of Jews, but of soldiers, granted, we must understand, by the Governor, with legal authority to take the criminal, as He was considered, and crush any opposition that might be made. CHRYS. But how could they persuade the band? By hiring them; for being soldiers, they were ready to do any thing for money. THEOPHYL. They carry torches and lanterns, to guard against Christ escaping in the dark. CHRYS. They had often sent elsewhere to take Him, but had not been able. Whence it is evident that He gave Himself up voluntarily; as it follows, *Jesus therefore, knowing all things that should come upon Him, went forth, and said unto them, Whom seek ye?* THEOPHYL. He asks not because He needed to know, for He knew all things that should come upon Him; but because He wished to shew, that though present, they could not see or distinguish Him: *Jesus saith unto them, I am He.* CHRYS. He Himself had blinded their eyes. For that darkness was not the reason is clear, because the Evangelist says that they had lanterns. Though they had not lanterns, however, they should at least have recognised Him by His voice. And if they did not know Him, yet how was it that Judas, who had been with Him constantly also, did not know Him? *And Judas also which betrayed Him stood with them.* Jesus did all this to shew that they could not have taken Him, or even seen Him when He was in the midst of them, had He not permitted it. AUG. As

Marginal notes: Nihil tale in G. — Aug. Tr. cxii. — Chrys. Hom. lxxxiii. — Chrys. Hom. lxxxiii. — Chrys. Hom. lxxxiii. — Aug. Tr. cxiii.

soon then as He said unto them, I am He, they went backward. Where now is the band of soldiers, where the terror and defence of arms? Without a blow, one word struck, drove back, prostrated a crowd fierce with hatred, terrible with arms. For God was hid in the flesh, and the eternal day was so obscured by His human body, that He was sought for with lanterns and torches, to be slain in the darkness. What shall He do when He cometh to judge, Who did thus when He was going to be judged? And now even at the present time Christ saith by the Gospel, *I am He,* and an Antichrist is expected by the Jews: to the end that they may go backward, and fall to the ground; because that forsaking heavenly, they desire earthly things. GREG. Why is this, that the Elect fall on their faces, the reprobate backward? Because every one who falls back, sees not where he falls, whereas he who falls forward, sees where he falls. The wicked when they suffer loss in invisible things, are said to fall backward, because they do not see what is behind them: but the righteous, who of their own accord cast themselves down in temporal things, in order that they may rise in spiritual, fall as it were upon their faces, when with fear and repentance they humble themselves with their eyes open. CHRYS. Lastly, lest any should say that He had encouraged the Jews to kill Him, in delivering Himself into their hands, He says every thing that is possible to reclaim them. But when they persisted in their malice, and shewed themselves inexcusable, then He gave Himself up into their hands: *Then asked He them again, Whom seek ye? And they said, Jesus of Nazareth. Jesus answered, I have told you that I am He.* AUG. They had heard at the first, *I am He,* but had not understood it; because He who could do whatever He would, willed not that they should. But had He never permitted Himself to be taken by them, they would not have done indeed what they came to do; but neither would He what He came to do. So now having shewn His power to them when they wished to take Him and could not, He lets them seize Him, that they might be unconscious agents of His will; *If ye seek Me, let these go their way.* CHRYS. As if to say, Though ye seek Me, ye have nothing to do with these: lo, I give Myself up: thus even to the last

Greg.
Ezech.
Hom.ix.

Chrys.
Hom.
lxxxii.

Aug.
Tr. cxii.

Chrys.
Hom.
lxxxiv.

hour does He shew His love for His own. AUG. He com- Aug.
mands His enemies, and they do what He commands; they Tr. cxii.
permit them to go away, whom He would not have perish.
CHRYS. The Evangelist, to shew that it was not their design Chrys.
to do this, but that His power did it, adds, *That the saying* Hom.
lxxxiii.
might be fulfilled which He spoke, Of them which Thou hast
given Me, have I lost none. He had said this with reference
not to temporal, but to eternal death: the Evangelist
however understands the word of temporal death also. AUG. Aug.
But were the disciples never to die? Why then would He Tr. cxii.
4.
lose them, even if they died then? Because they did not yet
believe in Him in a saving way.

10. Then Simon Peter having a sword drew it, and
smote the high priest's servant, and cut off his right
ear. The servant's name was Malchus.

11. Then said Jesus unto Peter, Put up thy sword
into the sheath: the cup which my Father hath given
me, shall I not drink it?

CHRYS. Peter trusting to these last words of our Lord's, Chrys.
and to what He had just done, assaults those who came to Hom.
lxxxiii.
take Him: *Then Simon Peter having a sword drew it, and*
smote the high priest's servant. But how, commanded as
he had been to have neither scrip, nor two garments, had he
a sword? Perhaps he had foreseen this occasion, and provided one. THEOPHYL. Or, he had got one for sacrificing
the lamb, and carried it away with him from the Supper.
CHRYS. But how could he, who had been forbidden ever to Chrys.
strike on the cheek, be a murderer? Because what he had Hom.
lxxxiii.
been forbidden to do was to avenge himself, but here he was 2.
not avenging himself, but his Master. They were not however yet perfect: afterwards ye shall see Peter beaten with
stripes, and bearing it humbly. *And cut off his right ear:*
this seems to shew the impetuosity of the Apostle; that he
struck at the head itself. AUG. *The servant's name was* Aug.
Malchus; John is the only Evangelist who mentions the Tr. cxii.
servant's name; as Luke is the only one who mentions that
our Lord touched the ear and healed him. CHRYS. He Chrys.
Hom.
lxxxiii.

wrought this miracle both to teach us, that we ought to do good to those who suffer, and to manifest His power. The Evangelist gives the name, that those who then read it might have the opportunity of enquiring into the truth of the account. And he mentions that he was the servant of the high priest, because in addition to the miracle of the cure itself, this shews that it was performed upon one of those who came to take Him, and who shortly after struck Him on the face.

Aug.
Tr. cxii.
5.
Aug. The name Malchus signifies, about to reign. What then does the ear cut off for our Lord, and healed by our Lord, denote, but the abolition of the old, and the creating of a new, ¹auditum hearing¹ in the newness of the Spirit, and not in the oldness of the letter? To whomsoever this is given, who can doubt that he will reign with Christ? But he was a servant too, hath reference to that oldness, which generated to bondage: the cure figures liberty. Theophyl. Or, the cutting off of the high priest's servant's right ear is a type of the people's deafness, of which the chief priests partook most strongly: the restoration of the ear, of ultimate reenlightenment of the under-

Aug.
Tr. cxii.
standing of the Jews, at the coming of Elias. Aug. Our Lord condemned Peter's act, and forbad him proceeding further: *Then said Jesus unto Peter, Put up thy sword into the sheath.* He was to be admonished to have patience: and

Chrys.
Hom.
lxxxiii.
2.
this was written for our learning. Chrys. He not only restrained Him however by threats, but consoled him also at the same time: *The cup that My Father giveth Me, shall I not drink it?* Whereby He shews that it was not by their power, but by His permission, that this had been done, and that He did not oppose God, but was obedient even unto death. Theophyl. In that He calls it a cup, He shews how pleasing and acceptable death for the salvation of men was

Aug.
Tr. cxii.
Rom. 8,
32.
to Him. Aug. The cup being given Him by the Father, is the same with what the Apostle saith, *Who spared not His own Son, but delivered Him up for us all.* But the Giver of this cup and the Drinker of it are the same; as the same

Eph. 5,
2.
Apostle saith, *Christ loved us, and gave Himself for us.*

12. Then the band and the captain and officers of the Jews took Jesus, and bound him,

13. And led him away to Annas first; for he was

father in law to Caiaphas, which was the high priest
that same year.

14. Now Caiaphas was he, which gave counsel to the
Jews, that it was expedient that one man should die
for the people.

THEOPHYL. Every thing having been done that could be
to dissuade the Jews, and they refusing to take warning,
He suffered Himself to be delivered into their hands: *Then
the band and the captain and officers of the Jews took Jesus.*
AUG. They took Him Whom they did not draw nigh to; nor Aug.
understood that which is written in the Psalms, *Draw nigh* Tr. cxii.
unto Him, and be ye lightened. For had they thus drawn 5.
nigh to Him, they would have taken Him, not to kill Him, accedite
but to be in their hearts. But now that they take Him in Vulg.
the way they do, they go backward. It follows, *and bound
Him,* Him by Whom they ought to have wished to be loosed.
And perhaps there were among them some who, afterwards
delivered by Him, exclaimed, *Thou hast broken My chains* Ps. 116.
asunder. But after that they had bound Jesus, it then appears most clearly that Judas had betrayed Him not for a
good, but a most wicked purpose: *And led Him away to
Annas first.* CHRYS. In exultation, to shew what they had Chrys.
done, as if they were raising a trophy. AUG. Why they did Hom.
so, he tells us immediately after: *For he was father in law to* 2.
Caiaphas, which was the high priest that same year. Matthew, Aug.
in order to shorten the narrative, says that He was led to Tr.cxiii.
Caiaphas; because He was led to Annas first, as being the
father in law of Caiaphas. So that we must understand that
Annas wished to act Caiaphas's part. BEDE. In order that,
while our Lord was condemned by his colleague, he might
not be guiltless, though his crime was less. Or perhaps
his house lay in the way, and they were obliged to pass by
it. Or it was the design of Providence, that they who were
allied in blood, should be associated in guilt. That Caiaphas
however was high priest for that year sounds contrary to the
law, which ordained that there be only one high priest, and
made the office hereditary. But the pontificate had now
been abandoned to ambitious men. ALCUIN. Josephus re-

lates that this Caiaphas bought the high priesthood for this year. No wonder then if a wicked high priest judged wickedly. A man who was advanced to the priesthood by avarice, would keep himself there by injustice. CHRYS. That no one however might be disturbed at the sound of the chains, the Evangelist reminds them of the prophecy that His death would be the salvation of the world: *Now Caiaphas was he which gave counsel to the Jews, that it was expedient that one man should die for the people.* Such is the overpowering force of truth, that even its enemies echo it.

Chrys. Hom. lxxxiii.

15. And Simon Peter followed Jesus, and so did another disciple: that disciple was known unto the high priest, and went in with Jesus into the palace of the high priest.

16. But Peter stood at the door without. Then went out that other disciple, which was known unto the high priest, and spake unto her that kept the door, and brought in Peter.

17. Then saith the damsel that kept the door unto Peter, Art not thou also one of this man's disciples? He saith, I am not.

18. And the servants and officers stood there, who had made a fire of coals; for it was cold: and they warmed themselves: and Peter stood with them, and warmed himself.

AUG. The temptation of Peter, which took place in the midst of the contumelies offered to our Lord, is not placed by all in the same order. Matthew and Mark put the contumelies first, the temptation of Peter afterwards; Luke the temptation first, the contumelies after. John begins with the temptation: *And Simon Peter followed Jesus, and so did another disciple.* ALCUIN. He followed his Master out of devotion, though afar off, on account of fear. AUG. Who that other disciple was we cannot hastily decide, as his name is not told us. John however is wont to signify himself by this expression, with the addition of, *whom Jesus loved.*

Aug. de Con. Evang. ii. vi.

Aug. Tr.cxiii.

Perhaps therefore he is the one. CHRYS. He omits his own name out of humility: though he is relating an act of great virtue, how that he followed when the rest fled. He puts Peter before himself, and then mentions himself, in order to shew that he was inside the hall, and therefore related what took place there with more certainty than the other Evangelists could. *That disciple was known unto the high priest, and went in with Jesus into the palace of the high priest.* This he mentions not as a boast, but in order to diminish his own merit, in having been the only one who entered with Jesus. It is accounting for the act in another way, than merely by greatness of mind. Peter's love took him as far as the palace, but his fear prevented him entering in: *But Peter stood at the door without.* ALCUIN. He stood without, as being about to deny his Lord. He was not in Christ, who dared not confess Christ. CHRYS. But that Peter would Chrys. have entered the palace, if he had been permitted, appears Hom. lxxxiii. by what immediately follows: *Then went out that other disciple who was known to the high priest, and spake unto her who kept the doors, and brought in Peter.* He did not bring him in himself, because he kept near Christ. It follows: *Then saith the damsel that kept the door unto Peter, Art not thou also one of this Man's disciples? He saith, I am not.* What sayest thou, O Peter? Didst thou not say before, *I will lay down my life for thy sake?* What then Mat.26, had happened, that thou givest way even when the damsel 35. asks thee? It was not a soldier who asked thee, but a mean porteress. Nor said she, Art thou this Deceiver's disciple, but, *this Man's:* an expression of pity. *Art not thou also,* she says, because John was inside. AUG. But what wonder, if Aug. God foretold truly, man presumed falsely. Respecting this Tr.cxiii. denial of Peter we should remark, that Christ is not only denied by him, who denies that He is Christ, but by him also who denies himself to be a Christian. For the Lord did not say to Peter, Thou shalt deny that thou art My disciple, but, *Thou shalt deny Me.* He denied Him then, when Luke22, he denied that he was His disciple. And what was this but 34. to deny that he was a Christian? How many afterwards, even boys and girls, were able to despise death, confess Christ, and enter courageously into the kingdom of heaven;

which he who received the keys of the kingdom, was now unable to do? Wherein we see the reason for His saying above, *Let these go their way, for of those which Thou hast given Me, have I lost none.* If Peter had gone out of this world immediately after denying Christ, He must have been lost. CHRYS. Therefore did Divine Providence permit Peter first to fall, in order that he might be less severe to sinners from the remembrance of his own fall. Peter, the teacher and master of the whole world, sinned, and obtained pardon, that judges might thereafter have that rule to go by in dispensing pardon. For this reason I suppose the priesthood was not given to Angels; because, being without sin themselves, they would punish sinners without pity. Passible man is placed over man, in order that remembering his own weakness, he may be merciful to others. THEOPHYL. Some however foolishly favour Peter, so far as to say that he denied Christ, because he did not wish to be away from Christ, and he knew, they say, that if he confessed that he was one of Christ's disciples, he would be separated from Him, and would no longer have the liberty of following and seeing his beloved Lord; and therefore pretended to be one of the servants, that his sad countenance might not be perceived, and so exclude him: *And the servants and officers stood there, who had made a fire of coals, and warmed themselves; and Peter stood with them, and warmed himself.* AUG. It was not winter, and yet it was cold, as it often is at the vernal equinox. GREG. The fire of love was smothered in Peter's breast, and he was warming himself before the coals of the persecutors, i. e. with the love of this present life, whereby his weakness was increased.

Margin notes: Chrys. Serm. de Petro et Elia. Aug. Tr. cxiii. Greg. ii. Mor. c. 11.

19. The high priest then asked Jesus of his disciples, and of his doctrine.

20. Jesus answered him, I spake openly to the world; I ever taught in the synagogue, and in the temple, whither the Jews always resort; and in secret have I said nothing.

21. Why askest thou me? ask them which heard

me, what I have said unto them: behold, they know
what I said.

CHRYS. As they could bring no charge against Christ, Chrys. Hom. lxxxiii. 3.
they asked Him of His disciples: *The high priest then
asked Jesus of His disciples;* perhaps where they were, and
on what account He had collected them, he wished to prove
that he was a seditious and factious person whom no one
attended to, except His own disciples. THEOPHYL. He asks
Him moreover *of His doctrine,* what it was, whether opposed
to Moses and the law, that he might take occasion thereby
to put Him to death as an enemy of God. ALCUIN. He
does not ask in order to know the truth, but to find out
some charge against Him, on which to deliver Him to the
Roman Governor to be condemned. But our Lord so tempers His answer, as neither to conceal the truth, nor yet to
appear to defend Himself: *Jesus answered him, I spake
openly to the world; I ever taught in the synagogue, and in
the temple, whither the Jews always resort; and in secret
have I said nothing.* AUG. There is a difficulty here not to Aug. Tr.cxiii.
be passed over: if He did not speak openly even to His
disciples, but only promised that He would do so at some
time, how was it that He spoke openly to the world? He
spoke more openly to His disciples afterwards, when they
had withdrawn from the crowd; for He then explained His
parables, the meaning of which He concealed from the others.
When He says then, *I spake openly to the world,*
He must be understood to mean, within the hearing
of many. So in one sense He spoke openly, i. e. in that
many heard Him; in another sense not openly, i. e. in that
they did not understand Him. His speaking apart with His
disciples was not speaking in secret; for how could He speak
in secret before the multitude, especially when that small
number of His disciples were to make known what He said
to a much larger? THEOPHYL. He refers here to the prophecy
of Esaias; *I have not spoken in secret, in a dark place of* Isa. 45, 19.
the earth. CHRYS. Or, He spoke in secret, but not, as these Chrys. Hom. lxxxiii.
thought, from fear, or to excite sedition; but only when
what He said was above the understanding of the many. To
establish the matter, however, upon superabundant evidence,

He adds, *Why askest thou Me? ask them which heard Me what I said unto them; behold, they know what I said unto them:* as if He said, Thou askest Me of My disciples; ask My enemies, who lie in wait for Me. These are the words of one who was confident of the truth of what He said: for it is incontrovertible evidence, when enemies are called in as witnesses. AUG. For what they had heard and not understood, was not of such a kind, as that they could justly turn it against Him. And as often as they tried by questioning to find out some charge against Him, He so replied as to blunt all their stratagems, and refute their calumnies.

Aug.
Tr.cxiii.
3.

22. And when he had thus spoken, one of the officers which stood by struck Jesus with the palm of his hand, saying, Answerest thou the high priest so?

23. Jesus answered him, If I have spoken evil, bear witness of the evil: but if well, why smitest thou me?

24. Now Annas had sent him bound unto Caiaphas the high priest.

THEOPHYL. When Jesus had appealed to the testimony of the people by, an officer, wishing to clear himself, and shew that he was not one of those who admired our Lord, struck Him: *And when He had thus spoken, one of the officers which stood by struck Jesus with the palm of his hand, saying, Answerest Thou the high priest so?* AUG. This shews that Annas was the high priest, for this was before He was sent to Caiaphas. And Luke in the beginning of his Gospel says, that Annas and Caiaphas were both high priests. ALCUIN. Here is fulfilled the prophecy, *I gave my cheek to the smiters.* Jesus, though struck unjustly, replied gently: *Jesus answered him, If I have spoken evil, bear witness of the evil: but if well, why smitest thou Me?* THEOPHYL. As if to say, If thou hast any fault to find with what I have said, shew it; if thou hast not, why ragest thou? Or thus: If I taught any thing unadvisedly, when I taught in the synagogues, give proof of it to the high priest; but if I taught aright, so that even ye officers admired, why smitest

thou Me, Whom before thou admiredst? AUG. What can be Aug.
truer, gentler, kinder, than this answer? He Who received Tr.cxiii.
the blow on the face neither wished for him who struck it that
fire from heaven should consume him, or the earth open its
mouth and swallow him; or a devil seize him; or any other yet
more horrible kind of punishment. Yet had not He, by Whom
the world was made, power to cause any one of these things to
take place, but that He preferred teaching us that patience by
which the world is overcome? Some one will ask here, why
He did not do what He Himself commanded, i. e. not make
this answer, but give the other cheek to the smiter? But
what if He did both, both answered gently, and gave, not
His cheek only to the smiter, but His whole body to be
nailed to the Cross? And herein He shews, that those precepts of patience are to be performed not by posture of the
body, but by preparation of the heart: for it is possible that
a man might give his cheek outwardly, and yet be angry at
the same time. How much better is it to answer truly, yet
gently, and be ready to bear even harder usage patiently.
CHRYS. What should they do then but either disprove, or Chrys.
admit, what He said? Yet this they do not do: it is not a Hom.
lxxxiii.
trial they are carrying on, but a faction, a tyranny. Not
knowing what to do further, they send Him to Caiaphas:
Now Annas sent Him bound to Caiaphas the high priest.
THEOPHYL. Thinking that as he was more cunning, he might
find out something against Him worthy of death. AUG. He Aug.
was the one to whom they were taking Him from the first, as Tr.cxiii
Matthew says; he being the high priest of this year. We
must understand that the pontificate was taken between them
year by year alternately, and that it was by Caiaphas's consent that they led Him first to Annas; or that their houses
were so situated, that they could not but pass straight by that
of Annas. BEDE. *Sent Him bound,* not that He was bound
now for the first time, for they bound Him when they took
Him. They sent Him bound as they had brought Him.
Or perhaps He may have been loosed from His bonds for
that hour, in order to be examined, after which He was
bound again, and sent to Caiaphas.

25. And Simon Peter stood and warmed himself. They said therefore unto him, Art not thou also one of his disciples? He denied it, and said, I am not.

26. One of the servants of the high priest, being his kinsman whose ear Peter cut off, saith, Did not I see thee in the garden with him?

27. Peter then denied again: and immediately the cock crew.

Aug.
Tr.cxiii.

AUG. After the Evangelist has said that they sent Jesus bound from Annas to Caiaphas, he returns to Peter and his three denials, which took place in the house of Annas: *And Simon Peter stood and warmed himself.* He repeats what

Chrys.
Hom.
lxxxiii.

he had said before. CHRYS. Or, He means that the once fervid disciple was now too torpid, to move even when our Lord was carried away: shewing thereby how weak man's nature is, when God forsakes him. Asked again, he again denies: *They said therefore unto him, Art not thou also one*

Aug.
de Con.
Evang.
iii. 6.

of His disciples? He denied it, and said, I am not. AUG. Here we find Peter not at the gate, but at the fire, when he denies the second time: so that he must have returned after he had gone out of doors, where Matthew says he was. He did not go out, and another damsel see him on the outside, but another damsel saw him as he was rising to go out, and remarked him, and told those who were by, i. e. those who were standing with her at the fire inside the hall, *This fellow*

Matt.
26, 71.
72.

also was with Jesus of Nazareth. He heard this outside, and returned, and swore, *I do not know the man.* Then John continues: *They said therefore unto him, Art not thou also one of His disciples?* which words we suppose to have been said to him when he had come back, and was standing at the fire. And this explanation is confirmed by the fact, that besides the other damsel mentioned by Matthew and Mark in the second denial, there was another person, mentioned by Luke, who also questioned him. So John uses the plural: *They said therefore unto him.* And then follows the third denial: *One of the servants of the high priest, being his kinsman whose ear Peter cut off, saith, Did not I see thee in the garden with Him?* That Matthew and

Mark speak of the party who here question Peter in the plural number, whereas Luke mentions only one, and John also, adding that that one was the kinsman of him whose ear Peter cut off, is easily explained by supposing that Matthew and Mark used the plural number by a common form of speech for the singular; or that one who had observed him most strictly put the question first, and others followed it up, and pressed Peter with more. CHRYS. But neither Chrys. did the garden bring back to his memory what he had then Hom. lxxxiii. said, and the great professions of love he had made: *Peter* 3. *then denied again, and immediately the cock crew.* AUG. Aug. Lo, the prophecy of the Physician is fulfilled, the presumption Tr.cxiii. of the sick man demonstrated. That which Peter had said he would do, he had not done. *I will lay down my life for Thy sake;* but what our Lord had foretold had come to pass, *Thou shalt deny Me thrice.* CHRYS. The Evangelists have Luke22, all given the same account of the denials of Peter, not with 34. any intention of throwing blame upon him, but to teach us Hom. how hurtful it is to trust in self, and not ascribe all to God. Chrys. lxxxiii. BEDE. Mystically, by the first denial of Peter are denoted 3. those who before our Lord's Passion denied that He was God, by the second, those who did so after His resurrection. So by the first crowing of the cock His resurrection is signified; by the second, the general resurrection at the end of the world. By the first damsel, who obliged Peter to deny, is denoted lust, by the second, carnal delight: by one or more servants, the devils who persuade men to deny Christ.

28. Then led they Jesus from Caiaphas unto the hall of judgment: and it was early; and they themselves went not into the judgment hall, lest they should be defiled; but that they might eat the Passover.

29. Pilate then went out unto them, and said, What accusation bring ye against this man?

30. They answered and said unto him, If he were not a malefactor, we would not have delivered him up unto thee.

31. Then said Pilate unto them, Take ye him, and judge him according to your law. The Jews therefore said unto him, It is not lawful for us to put any man to death.

32. That the saying of Jesus might be fulfilled, which he spake, signifying what death he should die.

Aug. Tr.cxiv. AUG. The Evangelist returns to the part where he had left off, in order to relate Peter's denial: *Then led they Jesus to Caiaphas unto the hall of judgment:* to Caiaphas from his colleague and father in law Annas, as has been said. But if to Caiaphas, how to the prætorium, which was the place where the governor Pilate resided? BEDE. The prætorium is the place where the prætor sat. Prætors were called prefects and preceptors, because they issue decrees. AUG. Either then for some urgent reason Caiaphas proceeded from the house of Annas, where both had been sitting, to the prætorium of the governor, and left Jesus to the hearing of his father in law: or Pilate had established the prætorium in the house of Caiaphas, which was large enough to afford a separate lodging to its owner, and the governor at the same time. AUG. According to Matthew, *When the morning came, they led Him away, and delivered Him to Pontius Pilate.* But He was to have been led to Caiaphas at first. How is it then that He was brought to him so late? The truth is, now He was going as it were a committed criminal, Caiaphas having already determined on His death. And He was to be given up to Pilate immediately.

And it was early. CHRYS. He was led to Caiaphas before the cock crew, but *early in the morning* to Pilate. Whereby the Evangelist shews, that all that night of examination, ended in proving nothing against Him; and that He was sent to Pilate in consequence. But leaving what passed then to the other Evangelists, he goes to what followed. AUG. *And they themselves entered not into the judgment hall:* i. e. into that part of the house which Pilate occupied, supposing it to be the house of Caiaphas. Why they did not enter is next explained: *Lest they should be defiled, but that they might eat the Passover.* CHRYS. For the Jews were then celebrating

Side notes: Aug. Tr.cxiv. — a Caiapha Vulg. — Aug. Tr. cxiv. — Aug. de Con. Evang. l. iii. c. vii. Mat.27, 1. 2. — Chrys. Hom. lxxxiii. — Aug. Tr. xiv. — Chrys. Hom. lxxxiii.

the passover; He Himself celebrated it one day before, reserving His own death for the sixth day; on which day the old passover was kept. Or, perhaps, the passover means the whole season. AUG. The days of unleavened bread Aug. were beginning; during which time it was defilement to Tr.cxiv. enter the house of a stranger. ALCUIN. The passover was strictly the fourteenth day of the month, the day on which the lamb was killed in the evening: the seven days following were called the days of unleavened bread, in which nothing leavened ought to be found in their houses. Yet we find the day of the passover reckoned among the days of unleavened bread: *Now the first day of the feast of unleavened* Mat.26, *bread the disciples came to Jesus, saying unto Him, Where* 17. *wilt Thou that we prepare for Thee to eat the passover?* And here also in like manner: *That they might eat the passover;* the passover here signifying not the sacrifice of the lamb, which took place the fourteenth day at evening, but the great festival which was celebrated on the fifteenth day, after the sacrifice of the lamb. Our Lord, like the rest of the Jews, kept the passover on the fourteenth day: on the fifteenth day, when the great festival was held, He was crucified. His immolation however began on the fourteenth day, from the time that He was taken in the garden. AUG. O impious Aug. blindness! They feared to be defiled by the judgment hall Tr.cxiv. of a foreign prefect, to shed the blood of an innocent brother they feared not. For that He Whom they killed was the Lord and Giver of life, their blindness saved them from knowing. THEOPHYL. Pilate however proceeds in a more gentle way: *Pilate then went out unto them.* BEDE. It was the custom of the Jews when they condemned any one to death, to notify it to the governor, by delivering the man bound. CHRYS. Pilate however seeing Him bound, and such numbers Chrys. conducting Him, supposed that they had not unquestion- Hom. able evidence against Him, so proceeds to ask the question: 4. lxxxiii. *And said, What accusation bring ye against this Man?* For it was absurd, he said, to take the trial out of his hands, and yet give him the punishment. They in reply bring forward no positive charge but only their own conjectures: *They answered and said unto him, If He were not a malefactor, we would not have delivered Him up unto thee.*

2 O

Aug.   AUG. Ask the freed from unclean spirits, the blind who saw,
Tr.cxiv. the dead who came to life again, and, what is greater than
all, the fools who were made wise, and let them answer,
whether Jesus was a malefactor. But they spoke, of whom
Ps. 39. He had Himself prophesied in the Psalms, *They rewarded*
Aug.   *Me evil for good.* AUG. But is not this account contradic-
de Cons.
Evang. tory to Luke's, who mentions certain positive charges: *And*
iii. viii. *they began to accuse Him, saying, We found this fellow per-*
Luke 23,
2.   *verting the nation, and forbidding to give tribute to Cæsar,*
saying that He Himself is Christ a King. According to John,
the Jews seem to have been unwilling to bring actual charges,
in order that Pilate might condemn Him simply on their
authority, asking no questions, but taking it for granted
that if He was delivered up to him, He was certainly guilty.
Both accounts are however compatible. Each Evangelist
only inserts what he thinks sufficient. And John's account
implies that some charges had been made, when it comes
to Pilate's answer: *Then said Pilate unto them, Take ye Him,*
and judge Him according to your law. THEOPHYL. As if to
say, Since you will only have such a trial as will suit you,
and are proud, as if you never did any thing profane, take
ye Him, and condemn Him; I will not be made a judge for
such a purpose. ALCUIN. Or as if he said, Ye who have
the law, know what the law judgeth concerning such: do
what ye know to be just.

    The Jews therefore said unto him, It is not lawful for us
Aug.   *to put any man to death.* AUG. But did not the law com-
Tr.cxiv.
4.   mand not to spare malefactors, especially deceivers such as
they thought Him ? We must understand them however to
mean, that the holiness of the day which they were beginning
to celebrate, made it unlawful to put any man to death.
Have ye then so lost your understanding by your wickedness,
that ye think yourselves free from the pollution of innocent
Chrys. blood, because ye deliver it to be shed by another? CHRYS.
Hom.
lxxxiii. Or, they were not allowed by the Roman law to put Him to
4.   death themselves. Or, Pilate having said, *Judge Him according*
to your law, they reply, *It is not lawful for us:* His sin is
not a Jewish one, He hath not sinned according to our law:
His offence is political, He calls Himself a King. Or they
wished to have Him crucified, to add infamy to death: they

not being allowed to put to death in this way themselves. They put to death in another way, as we see in the stoning of Stephen: *That the saying of Jesus might be fulfilled, which He spake, signifying what death He should die.* Which was fulfilled in that He was crucified, or in that He was put to death by Gentiles as well as Jews. AUG. As we read in Mark, *Behold, we go up to Jerusalem; and the Son of man shall be delivered unto the chief priests, and unto the scribes; and they shall condemn Him to death, and shall deliver Him to the Gentiles.* Pilate again was a Roman, and was sent to the government of Judæa, from Rome. That this saying of Jesus then might be fulfilled, i. e. that He might be delivered unto and killed by the Gentiles, they would not accept Pilate's offer, but said, *It is not lawful for us to put any man to death.*

Aug.
Tr.cxiv.
Mark
10, 33.

33. Then Pilate entered into the judgment hall again, and called Jesus, and said unto him, Art thou the King of the Jews?

34. Jesus answered him, Sayest thou this thing of thyself, or did others tell it thee of me?

35. Pilate answered, Am I a Jew? Thine own nation and the chief priests have delivered thee unto me: what hast thou done?

36. Jesus answered, My kingdom is not of this world: if my kingdom were of this world, then would my servants fight, that I should not be delivered to the Jews: but now is my kingdom not from hence.

37. Pilate therefore said unto him, Art thou a king then? Jesus answered, Thou sayest that I am a king. To this end was I born, and for this cause came I into the world, that I should bear witness unto the truth. Every one that is of the truth heareth my voice.

38. Pilate saith unto him, What is truth?

CHRYS. Pilate, wishing to rescue Him from the hatred of the Jews, protracted[1] the trial a long time: *Then Pilate entered*

Chrys.
Hom.
lxxxiii.

2 o 2

[1] non al.

into the judgment hall, and called Jesus. THEOPHYL. i. e.
Apart, because he had a strong suspicion that He was innocent,
and thought he could examine Him more accurately, away
from the crowd: and said unto Him, *Art Thou the King of
the Jews?* ALCUIN. Wherein Pilate shews that the Jews had
charged Him with calling Himself King of the Jews. CHRYS.
Or Pilate had heard this by report; and as the Jews had no
charge to bring forward, began to examine Him himself with
respect to the things commonly reported of Him.

Chrys.
Hom.
lxxxiii.
4.

*Jesus answered him, Sayest thou this thing of thyself, or
did others tell it thee of Me?* THEOPHYL. He intimates here
that Pilate was judging blindly and indiscreetly: If thou
sayest this thing of thyself, He says, bring forward proofs of
My rebellion; if thou hast heard it from others, make regular
enquiry into it. AUG. Our Lord knew indeed both what He
Himself asked, and what Pilate would answer; but He wished
it to be written down for our sakes. CHRYS. He asks not in
ignorance, but in order to draw from Pilate himself an accusation against the Jews: Pilate answered, *Am I a Jew? Thine
own nation and the chief priests have delivered Thee unto
me.* AUG. He rejects the imputation that He could have
said it of Himself; *Thine own nation and the chief priests
have delivered Thee unto me:* adding, *what hast Thou done?*
Whereby he shews that this charge had been brought against
Him, for it is as much as to say, If Thou deniest that Thou
art a King, what hast Thou done to be delivered up to me?
As if it were no wonder that He should be delivered up, if
He called Himself a King. CHRYS. He then tries to bring
round the mind of Pilate, not a very bad man, by proving to
him, that He is not a mere man, but God, and the Son of
God; and overthrowing all suspicion of His having aimed
at a tyranny, which Pilate was afraid of, *Jesus answered, My
kingdom is not of this world.* AUG. This is what the good
Master wished to teach us. But first it was necessary to
shew the falsity of the notions of both Jews and Gentiles as
to His kingdom, which Pilate had heard of; as if it meant
that He aimed at unlawful power; a crime punishable with
death, and this kingdom were a subject of jealousy to the
ruling power, and to be guarded against as likely to be hos-
tile either to the Romans or Jews. Now if our Lord had

Aug.
Tr. cxv.

Chrys.
Hom.
lxxxiii.

Aug.
Tr. cxv.

Chrys.
Hom.
lxxxiii.

Aug.
Tr. cxv.
1.

answered immediately Pilate's question, He would have seemed
to have been answering not the Jews, but the Gentiles only.
But after Pilate's answer, what He says is an answer to both
Gentiles and Jews: as if He said, Men, i. e. Jews and Gentiles,
I hinder not your dominion in this world. What more would
ye have? Come by faith to the kingdom which is not of this
world. For what is His kingdom, but they that believe in
Him, of whom He saith, *Ye are not of the world:* although He
wished that they should be *in* the world. In the same way,
here He does not say, *My kingdom is not* in *this world;* but,
is not of this world. Of the world are all men, who created
by God are born of the corrupt race of Adam. All that are
born again in Christ, are made a kingdom not of this world.
Thus hath God taken us out of the power of darkness, and
translated us to the kingdom of His dear Son. Chrys. Or Chrys.
He means that He does not derive His kingdom from the ^Hom.^
lxxxiii.
same source that earthly kings do; but that He hath His
sovereignty from above; inasmuch as He is not mere man,
but far greater and more glorious than man: *If My kingdom
were of this world, then would My servants fight, that I
should not be delivered to the Jews.* Here He shews the
weakness of an earthly kingdom, that it has its strength from its
servants, whereas that higher kingdom is sufficient to itself,
and wanting in nothing. And if His kingdom was thus the
greater of the two, it follows that He was taken of His own
will, and delivered up Himself. Aug. After shewing that Aug.
His kingdom was not of this world, He adds, *But now My* ^Tr. cxv.^
kingdom is not from hence. He does not say, Not here, for
His kingdom is here unto the end of the world, having within
it the tares mixed with the wheat until the harvest. But yet
it is not from hence, since it is a stranger in the world. Theophyl. Or He says, *from hence,* not, here; because He reigns
in the world, and carries on the government of it, and dis-
poses all things according to His will; but His kingdom is not
from below, but from above, and before all ages. Chrys. Chrys.
Heretics infer from these words that our Lord is a different ^Hom.^
lxxxiii.
person from the Creator of the world. But when He says, ἀλλό-
My kingdom is not from hence, He does not deprive the world τριον
of His government and superintendence, but only shews that
His government is not human and corruptible. *Pilate there-*

fore said unto Him, Art Thou a King then? Jesus answered,
Aug. Tr. cxv. *Thou sayest that I am a King.* AUG. He did not fear to confess Himself a King, but so replied as neither to deny that He was, nor yet to confess Himself a King in such sense as that His kingdom should be supposed to be of this world. He says, *Thou sayest,* meaning, Thou being carnal sayest it carnally. He continues, *To this end was I born, and for this cause came I into the world, that I should bear witness to the truth.* The pronoun here, *in hoc,* must not be dwelt long on, in hâc re as if it meant, *in hâc re,* but shortened, as if it stood, *ad hoc natus sum,* as the next words are, *ad hoc veni in mundum.* Wherein it is evident He alludes to His birth in the flesh, not to that divine birth which never had beginning. THEOPHYL. Or, to Pilate's question whether He was a King, our Lord answers, *To this end was I born,* i. e. to be a King. That I am born from a King, proves that I am a King. Chrys. CHRYS. If then He was a King by birth, He hath nothing Hom. lxxxiii. 4. which He hath not received from another. *For this I came, that I should bear witness to the truth,* i. e. that I should make all men believe it. We must observe how He shews His humility here: when they accused Him as a malefactor, He bore it in silence; but when He is asked of His kingdom, then He talks with Pilate, instructs him, and raises his mind to higher things. *That I should bear witness to the truth,* Aug. shews that He had no crafty purpose in what He did. AUG. Tr. cxv. But when Christ bears witness to the truth, He bears witness c. 14, 6. to Himself; as He said above, *I am the truth.* But inasmuch as all men have not faith, He adds, *Every one that is of the truth heareth My voice:* heareth, that is, with the inward ear; obeys My voice, believes Me. *Every one that is of the truth,* hath reference to the grace by which He calleth according to His purpose. For as regards the nature in which we are created, since the truth created all, all are of the truth. But it is not all to whom it is given by the truth to obey the truth. For had He even said, Every one that heareth My voice is of the truth, it still would be thought that such were of the truth, because they obeyed the truth. But He does not say this, but, *Every one that is of the truth heareth My voice.* A man then is not of the truth, because he hears His voice, but hears His voice because he is of the truth. This grace is

conferred upon him by the truth. CHRYS. These words Chrys. have an effect upon Pilate, persuade him to become a hearer, Hom. lxxxiii. and elicit from him the short enquiry, What is truth? *Pilate said unto Him, What is truth?* THEOPHYL. For it had almost vanished from the world, and become unknown in consequence of the general unbelief.

38. And when he had said this, he went out again unto the Jews, and saith unto them, I find in him no fault at all.

39. But ye have a custom, that I should release unto you one at the passover: will ye therefore that I release unto you the King of the Jews?

40. Then cried they all again, saying, Not this man, but Barabbas. Now Barabbas was a robber.

AUG. After Pilate had asked, *What is truth?* he remem- Aug. Tr. cxv. bered a custom of the Jews, of releasing one prisoner at the passover, and did not wait for Christ's answer, for fear of losing this chance of saving Him, which he much wished to do: *And when he had said this, he went out again unto the Jews.* CHRYS. He knew that this question required time to Chrys. answer, and it was necessary immediately to rescue Him from Hom. lxxxiii. the fury of the Jews. So he went out. ALCUIN. Or, he did not wait to hear the reply, because he was unworthy to hear it.

And saith unto them, I find no fault in Him. CHRYS. Chrys. He did not say, He has sinned and is worthy of death; yet Hom. lxxxiii. release Him at the feast; but acquitting Him in the first place, he does more than he need do, and asks it as a favour, that, if they are unwilling to let Him go as innocent, they will at any rate allow Him the benefit of the season: *But ye have a custom, that I should release one unto you at the passover.* BEDE. This custom was not commanded in the law, but had been handed down by tradition from the old fathers, viz. that in remembrance of their deliverance out of Egypt, they should release a prisoner at the passover. Pilate tries to persuade them: *Will ye therefore that I release unto you the King of the Jews.* AUG. He could not dismiss the idea Aug. Tr. cxv.

from his mind, that Jesus was King of the Jews; as if the Truth itself, whom he had just asked what it was, had inscribed it there as a title. THEOPHYL. Pilate is judicious in replying that Jesus had done nothing wrong, and that there was no reason to suspect Him of aiming at a kingdom. For they might be sure that if He set Himself up as a King, and a rival of the Roman empire, a Roman prefect would not release Him. When then He says, *Will ye that I release unto you the King of the Jews?* he clears Jesus of all guilt, and mocks the Jews, as if to say, Him whom ye accuse of thinking Himself a King, the same I bid you release: He does no such thing. AUG. Upon this they cried out: *Then cried they all again, saying, Not this man, but Barabbas. Now Barabbas was a robber.* We blame you not, O Jews, for releasing a guilty man at the passover, but for killing an innocent one. Yet unless this were done, it were not the true passover. BEDE. Inasmuch then as they abandoned the Saviour, and sought out a robber, to this day the devil practises his robberies upon them. ALCUIN. The name Barabbas signifies, The son of their master, i. e. the devil; his master in his wickedness, the Jews' in their perfidy.

Aug. Tr. cxv.

CHAP. XIX.

1. Then Pilate therefore took Jesus, and scourged him.

2. And the soldiers platted a crown of thorns, and put it on his head, and they put on him a purple robe,

3. And said, Hail, King of the Jews! and they smote him with their hands.

4. Pilate therefore went forth again, and saith unto them, Behold, I bring him forth to you, that ye may know that I find no fault in him.

5. Then came Jesus forth, wearing the crown of thorns, and the purple robe. And Pilate saith unto them, Behold the man!

AUG. When the Jews had cried out that they did not wish Aug.
Tr.cxvi. Jesus to be released on account of the passover, but Barabbas, *Then Pilate therefore took Jesus, and scourged Him.* Pilate seems to have done this for no reason but to satisfy the malice of the Jews with some punishment short of death. On which account he allowed his band to do what follows, or perhaps even commanded them. The Evangelist only says however that the soldiers did so, not that Pilate commanded them: *And the soldiers platted a crown of thorns, and put it on His head, and they put on Him a purple robe, and said, Hail, King of the Jews! and they smote Him with their hands.* CHRYS. Pilate having called Him the King of Chrys.
Hom.
lxxxiii. the Jews, they put the royal dress upon Him, in mockery. BEDE. For instead of a diadem, they put upon Him a crown of thorns, and a purple robe to represent the purple robe

Mat. 27, 28. which kings wear. Matthew says, *a scarlet robe,* but scarlet[a] and purple are different names for the same colour. And though the soldiers did this in mockery, yet to us their acts have a meaning. For by the crown of thorns is signified the taking of our sins upon Him, the thorns which the earth of our body brings forth. And the purple robe signifies the flesh crucified. For our Lord is robed in purple, wherever

Chrys. Hom. xxxiv. He is glorified by the triumphs of holy martyrs. CHRYS. It was not at the command of the governor that they did this, but in order to gratify the Jews. For neither were they commanded by him to go to the garden in the night, but the Jews gave them money to go. He bore however all these insults silently. Yet do thou, when thou hearest of them, keep stedfastly in thy mind the King of the whole earth, and Lord of Angels bearing all these contumelies in silence,

Aug. Tr. cxvi. and imitate His example. AUG. Thus were fulfilled what Christ had prophesied of Himself; thus were martyrs taught to suffer all that the malice of persecutors could inflict; thus that kingdom which was not of this world conquered the proud world, not by fierce fighting, but by patient suffering.

Chrys. Hom. lxxxiv. CHRYS. That the Jews might cease from their fury, seeing Him thus insulted, Pilate brought out Jesus before them crowned : *Pilate therefore went forth again, and saith unto them, Behold, I bring Him forth to you, that ye may know*

Aug. Tr. cxvi. *that I find no fault in Him.* AUG. Hence it is apparent that these things were not done without Pilate's knowledge, whether he commanded, or only permitted them, for the reason we have mentioned, viz. that His enemies seeing the insults heaped upon Him, might not thirst any longer for His blood : *Then came Jesus forth, wearing the crown of thorns, and the purple robe:* not the insignia of empire, but the marks of ridicule. *And Pilate saith unto them, Behold the man!* as if to say, If ye envy the King, spare the outcast. Ignominy overflows, let envy subside.

6. When the chief priests therefore and officers saw him, they cried out, saying, Crucify him, crucify

---

[a] *coccinea,* from *coccula,* the shell-fish, from the blood of which the dye is made. Bede.

him. Pilate saith unto them, Take ye him, and
crucify him: for I find no fault in him.

7. The Jews answered him, We have a law, and by
our law he ought to die, because he made himself the
Son of God.

8. When Pilate therefore heard that saying, he was
the more afraid.

AUG. The envy of the Jews does not subside at Christ's Aug.
disgraces; yea, rather rises: *When the chief priests therefore* Tr.cxvi.
and officers saw Him, they cried out, saying, Crucify Him,
crucify Him. CHRYS. Pilate saw then that it was all in vain: Chrys.
Pilate saith unto them, Take ye Him, and crucify Him. This Hom.
lxxxiv.
is the speech of a man abhorring the deed, and urging others to 2.
do a deed which he abhors himself. They had brought our ἀφοσιού-
Lord indeed to him that He might be put to death by his μενον
sentence, but the very contrary was the result; the governor
acquitted Him: *For I find no fault in Him.* He clears
Him immediately from all charges: which shews that he
had only permitted the former outrages, to humour the
madness of the Jews. But nothing could shame the Jewish
hounds: *The Jews answered him, We have a law, and by our*
law He ought to die, because He made Himself the Son of
God. AUG. Lo, another greater outbreak of envy. The Aug.
former was lighter, being only to punish Him for aspiring to Tr. cxvi.
a usurpation of the royal power. Yet did Jesus make neither
claim falsely; both were true: He was both the Only-begotten
Son of God, and the King appointed by God upon the holy hill
of Sion. And He would have demonstrated His right to
both now, had He not been as patient as He was powerful.
CHRYS. While they disputed with each other, He was silent, Chrys.
fulfilling the prophecy, *He openeth not His mouth; He was* Hom.
lxxxiv.
taken from prison and from judgment. AUG. This agrees Is. 53,
with Luke's account, *We found this fellow perverting the* 7. 8.
Aug.
nation, only with the addition of, *because He made Himself* de Con.
the Son of God. CHRYS. Then Pilate begins to fear that Evang.
iii. 8.
what had been said might be true, and that he might appear Luke 23,
to be administering justice improperly: *When Pilate therefore* 2.
Chrys.
heard that saying, he was the more afraid. BEDE. It was Hom.
lxxxiv.
2.

not the law that he was afraid of, as he was a stranger: but he was more afraid, lest he should slay the Son of God. CHRYS. They were not afraid to say this, *that He made Himself the Son of God:* but they kill Him for the very reasons for which they ought to have worshipped Him.

9. And went again into the judgment hall, and saith unto Jesus, Whence art thou? But Jesus gave him no answer.

10. Then saith Pilate unto him, Speakest thou not unto me? knowest thou not that I have power to crucify thee, and have power to release thee?

11. Jesus answered, Thou couldest have no power at all against me, except it were given thee from above: therefore he that delivered me unto thee hath the greater sin.

12. And from thenceforth Pilate sought to release him.

Chrys. Hom. lxxxiv. 2.

CHRYS. Pilate, agitated with fear, begins again examining Him: *And went again into the judgment hall, and saith unto Jesus, Whence art Thou?* He no longer asks, *What hast Thou done?* But Jesus gave him no answer. For he who had heard, *To this end was I born, and for this cause came I into the world,* and, *My kingdom is not from hence,* ought to have resisted, and rescued Him, instead of which he had yielded to the fury of the Jews. Wherefore seeing that he asked questions without object, He answers him no more. Indeed at other times He was unwilling to give reasons, and defend Himself by argument, when His works testified so strongly for Him; thus shewing that He came voluntarily

Aug. Tr.cxvi. 4.

to His work. AUG. In comparing the accounts of the different Evangelists together, we find that this silence was maintained more than once; viz. before the High Priest, before

Isa. 53, 7.

Herod, and before Pilate. So that the prophecy of Him, *As a sheep before her shearers is dumb, so opened He not His mouth,* was amply fulfilled. To many indeed of the questions put to Him, He did reply, but where He did not reply, this comparison of the sheep shews us that His was not a silence of guilt, but of innocence; not of self-condemnation, but of compassion, and willingness to suffer for the sins of others. CHRYS. He remaining thus silent, *Then saith Pilate unto Him, Speakest Thou not unto me? knowest Thou not that I have power to crucify Thee, and have power to release Thee?* See how he condemns himself. If all depends upon thee, why, when thou findest no fault of offence, dost thou not acquit Him? ^{Chrys. Hom. lxxxiv. 2.}

Jesus answered, Thou couldest have no power at all against Me, except it were given thee from above: shewing that this judgment was accomplished not in the common and natural order of events, but mysteriously. But lest we should think that Pilate was altogether free from blame, He adds, *Therefore he that hath delivered Me unto thee hath the greater sin.* But if it was *given,* thou wilt say, neither he nor they were liable to blame. Thou speakest foolishly. *Given* means permitted; as if He said, He hath permitted this to be done; but ye are not on that account free from guilt. AUG. So He answers. When He was silent, He was silent not as guilty or crafty, but as a sheep: when He answered, He taught as a shepherd. Let us hear what He saith; which is that, as He teacheth by His Apostle, *There is no power but of God;* and that he that through envy delivers an innocent person to the higher power, who puts to death from fear of a greater power, still sins more than that higher power itself. God had given such power to Pilate, as that he was still under Cæsar's power: wherefore our Lord says, *Thou couldest have no power at all against Me,* i. e. no power however small, unless it, whatever it was, *was given thee from above.* And as that is not so great as to give thee complete liberty of action, *therefore he that delivered Me unto thee hath the greater sin.* He delivered Me into thy power from envy, but thou wilt exercise that power from fear. And though a man ought not to kill another even from fear, especially an innocent man, yet to do so from envy is much worse. Wherefore our Lord does not say, *He that delivered Me unto thee* hath the sin, as if the other had none, but, *hath the greater sin,* implying that the other also had some. THEOPHYL. *He that delivered Me unto thee,* ^{Aug. Tr.cxvi.} ^{Rom.13, 1.}

i. e. Judas, or the multitude. When Jesus had boldly replied, that unless He gave Himself up, and the Father consented, Pilate could have had no power over Him, Pilate was the more anxious to release Him; *And from thenceforth* Aug. *Pilate sought to release Him.* Aug. Pilate had sought from Tr.cxvi. the first to release : so we must understand, *from thence,* to mean from this cause, i. e. lest he should incur guilt by putting to death an innocent person.

12. But the Jews cried out, saying, If thou let this man go, thou art not Cæsar's friend: whosoever maketh himself a king speaketh against Cæsar.

13. When Pilate therefore heard that saying, he brought Jesus forth, and sat down in the judgment seat in a place that is called the Pavement, but in the Hebrew, Gabbatha.

14. And it was the preparation of the passover, and about the sixth hour: and he saith unto the Jews, Behold your King!

15. But they cried out, Away with him, away with him, crucify him. Pilate saith unto them, Shall I crucify your King? The chief priests answered, We have no king but Cæsar.

16. Then delivered he him therefore unto them to be crucified.

Aug.   Aug. The Jews thought they could alarm Pilate more by Tr.cxvi. the mention of Cæsar, than by telling him of their law, as they had done above; *We have a law, and by that law He ought to die, because He made Himself the Son of God.* So it follows, *But the Jews cried out, saying, If thou let this Man go, thou art not Cæsar's friend; whosoever maketh* Chrys. *himself a king speaketh against Cæsar.* CHRYS. But how Hom. can ye prove this ? By His purple, His diadem, His chariot, lxxxiv. 2.   His guards ? Did He not walk about with His twelve disciples only, and every thing mean about Him, food, dress, Aug.   and habitation ? Aug. Pilate was before afraid not of vio-Tr.cxvi. lating their law by sparing Him, but of killing the Son of

God, in killing Him. But he could not treat his master
Cæsar with the same contempt with which he treated the
law of a foreign nation: *When Pilate therefore heard that*
saying, he brought Jesus forth, and sat down in the judg-
ment seat in a place that is called the Pavement, but in
the Hebrew, Gabbatha. CHRYS. He went out to examine Chrys.
into the matter: his sitting down on the judgment seat Hom.
shews this. GLOSS. The tribunal is the seat of the judge, 2.
as the throne is the seat of the king, and the chair the seat
of the doctor. BEDE. Lithostraton, i. e. laid with stone; the
word signifies pavement. It was an elevated place.

And it was the preparation of the Passover. ALCUIN.
Parasceve, i. e. preparation. This was a name for the sixth
day, the day before the Sabbath, on which they prepared
what was necessary for the Sabbath; as we read, *On the* Exod.
sixth day they gathered twice as much bread. As man was 16, 22.
made on the sixth day, and God rested on the seventh; so
Christ suffered on the sixth day, and rested in the grave on
the seventh.

And it was about the sixth hour. AUG. Why then doth Aug.
Mark say, *And it was the third hour, and they crucified* Tract.
Him? Because on the third hour our Lord was crucified Mark
by the tongues of the Jews, on the sixth by the hands 15, 25.
of the soldiers. So that we must understand that the
fifth hour was passed, and the sixth began, when Pilate
sat down on the judgment seat, (*about the sixth hour,*
John says,) and that the crucifixion, and all that took
place in connexion with it, filled up the rest of the hour,
from which time up to the ninth hour there was darkness,
according to Matthew, Mark, and Luke. But since the Jews
tried to transfer the guilt of putting Christ to death from
themselves to the Romans, i. e. to Pilate and his soldiers,
Mark, omitting to mention the hour at which He was
crucified by the soldiers, has expressly recorded the third
hour; in order that it might be evident that not only the
soldiers who crucified Jesus on the sixth hour, but the Jews
who cried out for His death at the third, were His crucifiers.
There is another way of solving this difficulty, viz. that the
sixth hour here does not mean the sixth hour of the day; as
John does not say, It was about the sixth hour of the day,

but, *It was 'he preparation of the passover, and about the sixth hour.* Parasceve means in Latin, præparatio. For *Christ our passover,* as saith the Apostle, *is sacrificed for us.* The preparation for which passover, counting from the ninth hour of the night, which seems to have been the hour at which the chief priests pronounced upon our Lord's sacrifice, saying, *He is guilty of death,* between it and the third hour of the day, when He was crucified, according to Mark, is an interval of six hours, three of the night and three of the day. THEOPHYL. Some suppose it to be a fault of the transcriber,

Chrys.
Hom.
lxxxiv.
who for the letter y, three, put s, six. CHRYS. Pilate, despairing of moving them, did not examine Him, as he intended, but delivered Him up. And he saith unto the Jews, *Behold your King!* THEOPHYL. As if to say, See the kind of Man whom ye suspect of aspiring to the throne, a humble person,

Chrys.
Hom.
lxxxiv.
2.
who cannot have any such design. CHRYS. A speech that should have softened their rage; but they were afraid of letting Him go, lest He might draw away the multitude again. For the love of rule is a heavy crime, and sufficient to condemn a man. They cried out, *Away with Him, away with Him.* And they resolved upon the most disgraceful kind of death, *Crucify Him,* in order to prevent all memorial of Him afterwards.

Aug.
Tr.cxvi.
8.
AUG. Pilate still tries to overcome their apprehensions on Cæsar's account; *Pilate saith unto them, Shall I crucify your King?* He tries to shame them into doing what he had not been able to soften them into by putting Christ to shame.

The chief priests answered, We have no king but Cæsar.

Chrys.
Hom.
lxxxiv.
2.
CHRYS. They voluntarily brought themselves under punishment, and God gave them up to it. With one accord they denied the kingdom of God, and God suffered them to fall into their own condemnation; for they rejected the kingdom of Christ, and called down upon their own heads that of

Aug.
Tr.cxvi.
Cæsar. AUG. But Pilate is at last overcome by fear: *Then delivered he Him therefore unto them to be crucified.* For it would be taking part openly against Cæsar, if when the Jews declared that they had no king but Cæsar, he wished to put another king over them, as he would appear to do if he let go unpunished a Man whom they had delivered to him for punishment on this very ground. It is not however,

delivered Him unto them to crucify Him, but, *to be crucified,*
i. e. by the sentence and authority of the governor. The
Evangelist says, *delivered unto them,* to shew that they were
implicated in the guilt from which they tried to escape. For
Pilate would not have done this except to please them.

16. And they took Jesus, and led him away.

17. And he bearing his cross went forth into a place
called the place of a skull, which is called in the Hebrew
Golgotha:

18. Where they crucified him, and two other with
him, on either side one, and Jesus in the midst.

GLOSS. By the command of the governor, the soldiers took
Christ to be crucified. *And they took Jesus, and led Him
away.* AUG. They, i. e. the soldiers, the guards of the Aug.
governor, as appears more clearly afterwards; *Then the* Tr.cxvi.
soldiers when they had crucified Jesus; though the Evangelist
might justly have attributed the whole to the Jews, who
were really the authors of what they procured to be done.
CHRYS. They compel Jesus to bear the cross, regarding it as Chrys.
unholy, and therefore avoiding the touch of it themselves. Hom.
And He bearing His cross went forth into a place called the lxxxv.l.
*place of a skull, which is called in Hebrew Golgotha, where
they crucified Him.* The same was done typically by
Isaac, who carried the wood. But then the matter only
proceeded as far as his father's good pleasure ordered, but
now it was fully accomplished, for the reality had appeared.
THEOPHYL. But as there Isaac was let go, and a ram offered;
so here too the Divine nature remains impassible, but the
human, of which the ram was the type, the offspring of that
straying ram, was slain. But why does another Evangelist
say that they hired Simon to bear the cross? AUG. Both Aug.
bore it; first Jesus, as John says, then Simon, as the other de Con.
three Evangelists say. On first going forth, He bore His own iii. x.
cross. AUG. Great spectacle, to the profane a laughing- Aug.
stock, to the pious a mystery. Profaneness sees a King Tract.
bearing a cross instead of a sceptre; piety sees a King cxvii.
bearing a cross, thereon to nail Himself, and afterwards to
nail it on the foreheads of kings. That to profane eyes was

contemptible, which the hearts of Saints would afterwards
glory in; Christ displaying His own cross on His shoulders,
and bearing that which was not to be put under a bushel,
the candlestick of that candle which was now about to burn.
Chrys. CHRYS. He carried the badge of victory on His shoulders,
Hom.
lxxxv. as conquerors do. Some say that the *place of Calvary* was
where Adam died and was buried; so that in the very place
Hieron. where death reigned, there Jesus erected His trophy. JEROME.
super
Matt. An apt connexion, and smooth to the ear, but not true. For
c. xxvii. the place where they cut off the heads of men condemned to
death, called in consequence Calvary, was outside the city
gates, whereas we read in the book of Jesus the son of Nave,
Chrys. that Adam was buried by Hebron and Arbah. CHRYS.
Hom.
lxxxv.1. They crucified Him with the thieves: *And two others with*
Him, on either side one, and Jesus in the midst; thus ful-
Isa. 53, filling the prophecy, *And He was numbered with the trans-*
12.
gressors. What they did in wickedness, was a gain to the
truth. The devil wished to obscure what was done, but
could not. Though three were nailed on the cross, it was
evident that Jesus alone did the miracles; and the arts of
the devil were frustrated. Nay, they even added to His
glory; for to convert a thief on the cross, and bring him
into paradise, was no less a miracle than the rending of the
Aug. rocks. AUG. Yea, even the cross, if thou consider it, was a
Tr.xxxi.
in fin. judgment seat: for the Judge being the middle, one thief,
who believed, was pardoned, the other, who mocked, was
damned: a sign of what He would once do to the quick
and dead, place the one on His right hand, the other on
His left.

19. And Pilate wrote a title, and put it on the cross.
And the writing was, JESUS OF NAZARETH,
THE KING OF THE JEWS.

20. This title then read many of the Jews: for the
place where Jesus was crucified was nigh to the city:
and it was written in Hebrew, and Greek, and Latin.

21. Then said the chief priests of the Jews to Pilate,
Write not, The King of the Jews; but that he said, I
am King of the Jews.

22. Pilate answered, What I have written I have written.

CHRYS. As letters are inscribed on a trophy declaring the victory, so Pilate wrote a title on Christ's cross. *And Pilate wrote a title, and put it on the cross:* thus at once distinguishing Christ from the thieves with Him, and exposing the malice of the Jews in rising up against their King: *And the writing was, Jesus of Nazareth, the King of the Jews.* BEDE. Wherein was shewn that His kingdom was not, as they thought, destroyed, but rather strengthened. AUG. But was Christ the King of the Jews only? or of the Gentiles too? Of the Gentiles too, as we read in the Psalms, *Yet have I set My King upon My holy hill of Sion;* after which it follows, *Demand of Me, and I will give Thee the heathen for Thine inheritance.* So this title expresses a great mystery, viz. that the wild olive-tree was made partaker of the fatness of the olive-tree, not the olive-tree made partaker of the bitterness of the wild olive-tree. Christ then is King of the Jews according to the circumcision not of the flesh, but of the heart; not in the letter, but in the spirit. *This title then read many of the Jews: for the place where Jesus was crucified was nigh to the city.* CHRYS. It is probable that many Gentiles as well as Jews had come up to the feast. So the title was written in three languages, that all might read it: *And it was written in Hebrew, and Greek, and Latin.* AUG. These three were the languages most known there: the Hebrew, on account of being used in the worship of the Jews: the Greek, in consequence of the spread of Greek philosophy: the Latin, from the Roman empire being established every where. THEOPHYL. The title written in three languages signifies that our Lord was King of the whole world; practical, natural, and spiritual[1]. The Latin denotes the practical, because the Roman empire was the most powerful, and best managed one; the Greek the physical, the Greeks being the best physical philosophers; and, lastly, the Hebrew the theological, because the Jews had been made the depositaries of religious knowledge. CHRYS. But the Jews grudged our Lord this title: *Then said the chief priests of the Jews to Pilate, Write not, The King*

Margin notes:
Aug. Tract. cxviii.

Ps. 2, 6.

Aug. Tract. cxviii.

[1] practicæ, physicæ, et theologicæ.

of the Jews; but that He said, I am King of the Jews.   For
as Pilate wrote it, it was a plain and single declaration that
He was King, but the addition of, *that he said,* made it a
charge against Him of petulance and vain glory.   But Pilate
was firm: *Pilate answered, What I have written I have
written.*   AUG. O ineffable working of Divine power even in
the hearts of ignorant men! Did not some hidden voice sound
from within, and, if we may say so, with clamorous silence,
saying to Pilate in the prophetic words of the Psalm, *Alter
not the inscription of the title*[a]?   But what say ye, ye mad
priests: will the title be the less true, because Jesus said,
I am the King of the Jews?   If that which Pilate wrote cannot be altered, can that be altered which the Truth spoke?
Pilate wrote what he wrote, because our Lord said what He
said.

23. Then the soldiers, when they had crucified
Jesus, took his garments, and made four parts, to
every soldier a part; and also his coat: now the coat
was without seam, woven from the top throughout.

24. They said therefore among themselves, Let us
not rend it, but cast lots for it, whose it shall be:
that the Scripture might be fulfilled, which saith, They
parted my raiment among them, and for my vesture
they did cast lots.

On Pilate giving sentence, the soldiers under his command
crucified Jesus: *Then the soldiers, when they had crucified
Jesus, took His garments.*   And yet if we look to their intentions, their clamours, the Jews were rather the people which
crucified Him.   On the parting and casting lots for His garment, John gives more circumstances than the other Evangelists, *And made four parts, to every soldier a part:* whence
we see there were four soldiers who executed the governor's
sentence.   *And also His coat: took,* understood.   They took
His coat too.   The sentence is brought in so to shew that this
was the only garment for which they cast lots, the others

---

[a] In the LXX, the title of Ps. 56, στηλογραφίαν.   Nic.
57, 58. 1s, μὴ διαφθείρῃς τῷ Δαυὶδ εἰς

being divided. *Now the coat was without seam, woven from the top throughout.* CHRYS. The Evangelist describes the tunic, to shew that it was of an inferior kind, the tunics commonly worn in Palestine being made of two pieces. THEOPHYL. Others say that they did not weave in Palestine, as we do, the shuttle being driven upwards through the warp; so that among them the woof was not carried upwards but downwards[b]. AUG. Why they cast lots for it, next appears: *They said therefore among themselves, Let us not rend it, but cast lots for it whose it should be.* It seems then that the other garments were made up of equal parts, as it was not necessary to rend them; the tunic only having to be rent in order to give each an equal share of it; to avoid which they preferred casting lots for it, and one having it all. This answered to the prophecy: *That the Scripture might be fulfilled which saith, They parted My raiment among them, and for My vesture they did cast lots.* CHRYS. Behold the sureness of prophecy. The Prophet foretold not only what they would part, but what they would not. They parted the raiment, but cast lots for the vesture. AUG. Matthew in saying, *They parted His garments, casting lots*, means us to understand the whole division of the garments, including the tunic also for which they cast lots. Luke says the same: *They parted His raiment, and cast lots.* In parting His garments they came to the tunic, for which they cast lots. Mark is the only one that raises any question: *They parted His garments, casting upon them what every man should take;* as if they cast lots for all the garments, and not the tunic only. But it is his brevity that creates the difficulty. *Casting lots upon them:* as if it was, casting lots when they were parting the garments. *What every man should take:* i. e. who should take the tunic; as if the whole stood thus: Casting lots upon them, who should take the tunic which remained over and above the equal shares, into which the rest of the garments were divided. The fourfold division of our Lord's garment represents His Church, spread over the four quarters of the globe, and distributed equally, i. e. in concord, to all. The tunic for which they cast lots signifies the unity of all

Chrys.
Hom.
lxxxv.

Aug.
Tract.
cxviii.

Chrys.
Hom.
lxxxv.

Aug.
Tract.
cxviii.
3.
Mat.27,
35.
Luke23,
34.

Mark15,
24.

---

[b] Herodotus (ii. 3. 5.) makes the same remark of the Egyptians, who wove *downwards* also, contrary to the usual practice.

the parts, which is contained in the bond of love. And if love is the more excellent way, above knowledge, and above

Col. 3, 14. all other commandments, according to Colossians, *Above all things have charity,* the garment by which this is denoted,

desuper, is well said to be *woven from above.* *Through the whole,* is

ἄνωθεν added, because no one is void of it, who belongs to that whole, from which the Church Catholic is named. It is *without seam* again, so that it can never come unsown, and

ad unum is in one piece, i. e. brings all together into one. By the lot

provenit is signified the grace of God: for God elects not with respect to person or merits, but according to His own secret

Chrys. Hom. lxxxv. 1. counsel. CHRYS. According to some, *The tunic without seam, woven from above throughout,* is an allegory shewing that He who was crucified was not simply man, but also had Divinity from above. THEOPHYL. The garment without seam denotes the body of Christ, which was woven from above; for the Holy Ghost came upon the Virgin, and the power of the Highest overshadowed her. This holy body of Christ then is indivisible: for though it be distributed for every one to partake of, and to sanctify the soul and body of each one individually, yet it subsists in all wholly and indivisibly. The world consisting of four elements, the garments of Christ must be understood to represent the visible creation, which the devils divide amongst themselves, as often as they deliver to death the word of God which dwelleth in us, and by worldly allurements bring us over to

Aug. Tract. cxviii. their side. AUG. Nor let any one say that these things had no good signification, because they were done by wicked men; for if so, what shall we say of the cross itself? For that was made by ungodly men, and yet certainly by it were

Eph. 3, 18. signified, *What is the length, and depth, and breadth, and height,* as the Apostle saith. Its breadth consists of a cross beam, on which are stretched the hands of Him who hangs upon it. This signifies the breadth of charity, and the good works done therein. Its length consists of a cross beam going to the ground, and signifies perseverance in length of time. The height is the top which rises above the cross beam, and signifies the high end to which all things refer. The depth is that part which is fixed in the ground; there it is hidden, but the whole cross that we see rises from it.

Even so all our good works proceed from the depth of God's incomprehensible grace. But though the cross of Christ only signify what the Apostle saith, *They that are Christ's* Gal. 5, *have crucified the flesh, with the affections and lusts,* how [24.] great a good is it? Lastly, what is the sign of Christ, but the cross of Christ? Which sign must be applied to the foreheads of believers, to the water of regeneration, to the oil of chrism, to the sacrifice whereby we are nourished, or none of these is profitable for life.

24. These things therefore the soldiers did.

25. Now there stood by the cross of Jesus his mother, and his mother's sister, Mary the wife of Cleophas, and Mary Magdalene.

26. When Jesus therefore saw his mother, and the disciple standing by, whom he loved, he saith unto his mother, Woman, behold thy son!

27. Then saith he to the disciple, Behold thy mother! And from that hour that disciple took her to his own home.

THEOPHYL. While the soldiers were doing their cruel work, He was thinking anxiously of His mother: *These things therefore the soldiers did. Now there stood by the cross of Jesus His mother, and His mother's sister, Mary the wife of Cleophas, and Mary Magdalene.* AMBROSE. Mary the mother of our Lord stood before the cross of her Son. None of the Evangelists hath told me this except John. The others have related how that at our Lord's Passion the earth quaked, the heaven was overspread with darkness, the sun fled, the thief was taken into paradise after confession. John hath told us, what the others have not, how that from the cross whereon He hung, He called to His mother. He thought it a greater thing to shew Him victorious over punishment, fulfilling the offices of piety to His mother, than giving the kingdom of heaven and eternal life to the thief. For if it was religious to give life to the thief, a much richer work of piety it is for a son to honour his mother with such affection. *Behold,* He saith, *thy son; behold thy mother.* Christ made His Testament from the cross, and divided the offices of piety between the Mother and the disciples. Our Lord made not only a public, but also a domestic Testamnet. And this His Testament John sealed, a witness worthy of such a Testator. A good testament it was, not of money, but of eternal life, which was not written with ink, but with the spirit of the living God: *My tongue* Ps.45,1. *is the pen of a ready writer.* Mary, as became the mother of our Lord, stood before the cross, when the Apostles fled, and with pitiful eyes beheld the wounds of her Son. For she looked not on the death of the Hostage, but on the salvation of the world; and perhaps knowing that her Son's death would bring this salvation, she who had been the habitation of the King, thought that by her death she might add to that universal gift.

But Jesus did not need any help for saving the world, as Ps. 87. we read in the Psalm, *I have been even as a man with no help, free among the dead.* He received indeed the affection of a parent, but He did not seek another's help. Imitate her, ye holy matrons, who, as towards her only most beloved Son, hath set you an example of such virtue : for ye have not sweeter sons, nor did the Virgin seek consolation in again becoming a mother. JEROME. The Mary which in Mark and Matthew is called the mother of James and Joses, was the wife of Alpheus, and sister of Mary the mother of our Lord: which Mary John here designates *of Cleophas,* either from her father, or family, or for some other reason. She need not be thought a different person, because she is called in one place Mary the mother of James the less, and here Mary of Cleophas, for it is customary in Scripture to give Chrys. different names to the same person. CHRYS. Observe how Hom. lxxxv. the weaker sex is the stronger; standing by the cross when Aug. the disciples fly. AUG. If Matthew and Mark had not de Con. Ev. iii. mentioned by name Mary Magdalen, we should have thought 21. that there were two parties, one of which stood far off, and the other near. But how must we account for the same Mary Magdalen and the other women standing afar off, as Matthew and Mark say, and being near the cross, as John says ? By supposing that they were within such a distance as to be within sight of our Lord, and yet sufficiently far off to be out of the way of the crowd and Centurion, and soldiers who were immediately about Him. Or, we may suppose that after our Lord had commended His mother to the disciple, they retired to be out of the way of the crowd, and saw what took place afterwards at a distance: so that those Evangelists who do not mention them till after our Lord's death, describe them as standing *afar off*. That some women are mentioned by all alike, others not, makes no matter. CHRYS. Though there were other women by, He makes no mention of any of them, but only of His mother, to shew us that we should specially honour our mothers. Our parents indeed, if they actually oppose the truth, are not even to be known: but otherwise we should pay them all attention, and honour them above all the world beside: *When Jesus therefore saw His mother, and the disciple standing by, whom he loved, He saith unto His mother, Woman, behold thy son!* BEDE. By the disciple whom Jesus loved, the Evangelist means himself; not that the others were not loved, but he was loved more intimately on account of his estate of chastity; for a Virgin our Lord called him, and a Virgin he ever remained. CHRYS. Heavens! what honour does He pay to the disciple; who however conceals his name from modesty. For had he wished to boast, he would have added the reason why he was loved, for there must have been something great and wonderful to have caused that love. This is all He says to John; He does not console his grief, for this was a time for giving consolation. Yet was it no small one to be honoured with such a charge, to have the mother of our Lord, in her affliction, committed to his care by Himself on His departure: *Then saith He to the disciple, Behold thy mother!* AUG. This truly is that hour of the which Jesus, when about to change the water into wine, said, *Mother, what have I to do with thee? Mine hour is not yet come.* Then, about to act divinely, He repelled the mother of His humanity, of His infirmity, as if He knew her not: now, suffering humanly, He commends with human affection her of whom He was made man. Here is a moral lesson. The good Teacher shews us by His example how that pious sons should take care of their parents. The cross of the sufferer, is the chair

Marginal notes: Mat-thew and Mark. Chrys. Hom. lxxxv.2. Chrys. Hom. lxxxv.2. Papæ. Aug. Tr.cxix. 1.

Chrys.
Hom.
lxxxv.2.
of the Master. CHRYS. The shameless doctrine of Marcion is refuted here. For if our Lord were not born according to the flesh, and had not a mother, why did He make such provision for her? Observe how imperturbable He is during His crucifixion, talking to the disciple of His mother, fulfilling prophecies, giving good hope to the thief; whereas before His crucifixion, He seemed in fear. The weakness of His nature was shewn there, the exceeding greatness of His power here. He teaches us too herein, not to turn back, because we may feel disturbed at the difficulties before us; for when we are once actually under the trial, all will be light and easy for us. AUG. He does this to provide as it were another son for His mother in his place; *And from that hour that disciple took her unto his own.* Unto his own what? Was not John one of those who said, *Lo, we have left all, and followed Thee?* He took her then to his own, i. e. not to his farm, for he had none, but to his care, for of this he was master. BEDE. Another reading is, *Accepit eam discipulus in suam,* his own mother some understand, but to his own care seems better.

Aug.
Tr.cxix.
2.

Mat.19,
27.

28. After this, Jesus knowing that all things were now accomplished, that the Scripture might be fulfilled, saith, I thirst.

29. Now there was set a vessel full of vinegar: and they filled a spunge with vinegar, and put it upon hyssop, and put it to his mouth.

30. When Jesus therefore had received the vinegar, he said, It is finished: and he bowed his head, and gave up the ghost.

Aug.
Tr. xix.

Ps. 68.

minus

AUG. He who appeared man, suffered all these things; He who was God, ordered them: *After this Jesus knowing that all things were now accomplished;* i. e. knowing the prophecy in the Psalms, *And when I was thirsty, they gave me vinegar to drink,* said, *I thirst:* As if to say, ye have not done all: give me yourselves: for the Jews were themselves vinegar, having degenerated from the wine of the Patriarchs and the Prophets. *Now there was a vessel full of vinegar:* they had drunk from the wickedness of the world, as from a full vessel, and their heart was deceitful, as it were a spunge full of caves and crooked hiding places: *And they filled a spunge with vinegar, and put it upon hyssop, and put it to his mouth.* CHRYS. They were not softened at all by what they saw, but were the more enraged, and gave Him the cup to drink, as they did to criminals, i. e. with a hyssop. AUG. The hyssop around which they put the spunge full of vinegar, being a mean herb, taken to purge the breast, represents the humility of Christ, which they hemmed in and thought they had circumvented. For we are made clean by Christ's humility. Nor let it perplex you that they were able to reach His mouth when He was such a height above the ground: for we read in the other Evangelists, what John omits to mention, that the spunge was put upon a reed. THEOPHYL. Some say that the hyssop is put here for reed, its leaves being like a reed.

Chrys. Hom. lxxxv.

ὑσσώπῳ περι- θέντες

When Jesus therefore had received the vinegar, He said, It is finished. AUG. viz. what prophecy had foretold so long before. BEDE. It may be asked here, why it is said, *When Jesus had received the vinegar,* when another Evangelists says, *He would not drink.* But this is easily settled. He did not receive the vinegar, to drink it, but fulfil the prophecy. AUG. Then as there was nothing left Him to do before He died, it follows, *And He bowed His head, and gave up the ghost,* only dying when He had nothing more to do, like Him who had to lay down His life, and to take it up again. GREG. Ghost is put here for soul: for had the Evangelist meant any thing else by it, though the ghost departed, the soul might still have remained. CHRYS. He did not bow His head because He gave up the ghost, but He gave up the ghost because at that moment He bowed His head. Whereby the Evangelist intimates that He was Lord of all. AUG. For who ever had such power to sleep when he wished, as our Lord had to die when He wished? What power must He have, for our good or evil, Who had such power dying? THEOPHYL. Our Lord gave up His ghost to God the Father, shewing that the souls of the saints do not remain in the tomb, but go into the hand of the Father of all; while sinners are reserved for the place of punishment, i. e. hell.

Aug. Tr.cxix.

Mat.27, 34.

Aug. Tr.cxix.

Greg. xi. Mor. iii.

Chrys. Hom. lxxxv.

Aug. Tr.cxix.

31. The Jews therefore, because it was the preparation, that the bodies should not remain upon the cross on the sabbath day, (for that sabbath day was an high day,) besought Pilate that their legs might be broken, and that they might be taken away.

32. Then came the soldiers, and brake the legs of the first, and of the other which was crucified with him.

33. But when they came to Jesus, and saw that he was dead already, they brake not his legs:

34. But one of the soldiers with a spear pierced his side, and forthwith came there out blood and water.

35. And he that saw it bare record, and his record is true: and he knoweth that he saith true, that ye might believe.

36. For these things were done, that the Scripture should be fulfilled, A bone of him shall not be broken.

37. And again another Scripture saith, They shall look on him whom they pierced.

Chrys. Hom. lxxxv. CHRYS. The Jews who strained at a gnat and swallowed a camel, after their audacious wickedness, reason scrupulously about the day: *The Jews therefore because it was the preparation, that the bodies should not remain upon the cross on the sabbath.* BEDE. Parasceue, i. e. preparation: the sixth day was so called because the children of Israel prepared twice the number of loaves on that day. For that sabbath day was an high day, i. e. on account of the feast of the passover.

Aug. Tr. cxx. *Besought Pilate that their legs might be broken.* AUG. Not in order to take away the legs, but to cause death, that they might be taken down from the cross, and the feast day not be defiled by the sight of such horrid torments. THEOPHYL. For it was commanded in the Law that the sun should not set on the punishment of any one; or they were unwilling to appear tormentors and homicides on a feast day.

Chrys. Hom. lxxxv.3. CHRYS. How forcible is truth: their own devices it is that accomplish the fulfilment of prophecy: *Then came the soldiers and brake the legs of the first, and of the other which was crucified with Him. But when they came to Jesus, and saw that He was dead already, they brake not His legs: but one of the soldiers with a spear pierced His side.* THEOPHYL. To please the Jews, they pierce Christ, thus insulting even His lifeless body. But the insult issues in a miracle: for a miracle it is that blood should flow from a dead body. AUG. The Evangelist has expressed himself cautiously; not struck, or wounded, but *opened His side:* whereby was opened the gate of life, from whence the sacraments of the Church flowed, without which we cannot enter into that life which is the true life: *And forthwith came thereout blood and water.* That blood was shed for the remission of sins, that water tempers the cup of salvation. This it was which was prefigured when Noah was commanded to make a door in the side of the ark, by which the animals that were not to perish by the deluge entered; which animals prefigured the Church. To shadow forth this, the woman was made out of the side of the sleeping man; for this second Adam bowed His head, and slept on the cross, that out of that which came therefrom, there might be formed a wife for Him. O death, by which the dead are quickened, what can be purer than that blood, what more salutary than that wound! CHRYS. This being the source whence the holy mysteries are derived, when thou approachest the awful cup, approach it as if thou wert about to drink out of Christ's side. THEOPHYL. Shame then upon them who mix not water with the wine in the holy mysteries: they seem as if they believed not that the water flowed from the side. Had blood flowed only, a man might have said that there was some life left in the body, and that that was why the blood flowed. But the water flowing is an irresistible miracle, and therefore the Evangelist adds, *And he that saw it bare record.* CHRYS. As if to say, I did not hear it from others, but saw it with mine own eyes. *And his record is true,* he adds, not as if he had mentioned something so wonderful that his account would be suspected, but to stop the mouths of heretics, and in contemplation of the deep value of those mysteries which he announces.

And he knoweth that he saith true, that ye might believe.

Marginal notes:
Aug.
Tr. cxx.
ἰνύξι,
aperuit
V.

Chrys.
Hom.
lxxxv.

Chrys.
Hom.
lxxxv.
3.

Aug.
Tr. cxx.

AUG. He that saw it knoweth; let him that saw not believe his testimony. He gives testimonies from the Scriptures to each of these two things he relates. After, *they brake not His legs*, He adds, *For these things were done, that the Scripture should be fulfilled, A bone of Him shall not be broken*, a commandment which applied to the sacrifice of the paschal lamb under the old law, which sacrifice foreshadowed our Lord's. Also after, *One of the soldiers with a spear opened His side*, then follows another Scripture

Zech.
12, 10.

testimony; *And again another Scripture saith, They shall look on Him whom they pierced*, a prophecy which implies that Christ will come in the very flesh in which He was

Hieron.
Pref. ad
Pentet.

crucified. JEROME. This testimony is taken from Zacharias.

38. And after this Joseph of Arimathæa, being a disciple of Jesus, but secretly for fear of the Jews, besought Pilate that he might take away the body of Jesus: and Pilate gave him leave. He came therefore, and took the body of Jesus.

39. And there came also Nicodemus, which at the first came to Jesus by night, and brought a mixture of myrrh and aloes, about an hundred pound weight.

40. Then took they the body of Jesus, and wound it in linen clothes with the spices, as the manner of the Jews is to bury.

41. Now in the place where he was crucified there was a garden, and in the garden a new sepulchre, wherein was never man yet laid.

42. There laid they Jesus therefore because of the Jews' preparation day; for the sepulchre was nigh at hand.

Chrys.
Hom.
lxxxv.

CHRYS. Joseph thinking that the hatred of the Jews would be appeased by His crucifixion, went with confidence to ask permission to take charge of His burial: *And after this, Joseph of Arimathea besought Pilate*. BEDE. Arimathea is the same as Ramatha, the city of Elkanah, and Samuel. It was providentially ordered that he should be rich, in·

order that he might have access to the governor, and just, in
order that he might merit the charge of our Lord's body:
That he might take the body of Jesus, because he was His
disciple. CHRYS. He was not of the twelve, but of the Chrys.
seventy, for none of the twelve came near. Not that their Hom.
lxxxv.
fear kept them back, for Joseph was a disciple, *secretly for* 3.
fear of the Jews. But Joseph was a person of rank, and
known to Pilate; so he went to him, and the favour was
granted, and afterwards believed Him, not as a condemned
man, but as a great and wonderful Person: *He came there-*
fore, and took the body of Jesus. AUG. In performing this Aug.
last office to our Lord, he shewed a bold indifference to the de Con.
Evang.
Jews, though he had avoided our Lord's company when iii. xxii.
alive, for fear of incurring their hatred. BEDE. Their ferocity
being appeased for the time by their success, he sought the
body of Christ. He did not come as a disciple, but simply
to perform a work of mercy, which is due to the evil as well
as to the good. Nicodemus joined him: *And there came*
also Nicodemus, which at the first came to Jesus by night,
and brought a mixture of myrrh and aloes, about an hundred
pound weight. AUG. We must not read the words, *at the* Aug.
first, first bringing a mixture of myrrh, but attach the *first* Tr. cxx.
to the former clause. For Nicodemus at the first came to
Jesus by night, as John relates in the former part of the
Gospel. From these words then we are to infer that that
was not the only time that Nicodemus went to our Lord, but
simply the first time; and that he came afterwards and heard
Christ's discourses, and became a disciple. CHRYS. They Chrys.
bring the spices most efficacious for preserving the body Hom.
lxxxv.
from corruption, treating Him as a mere man. Yet this
shews great love. BEDE. We must observe however that it
was simple ointment; for they were not allowed to mix many Exod.
ingredients together. *Then took they the body of Jesus, and* 30, 34.
38.
wound it in linen clothes with the spices, as the manner of
the Jews is to bury. AUG. Wherein the Evangelist intimates, Aug.
that in paying the last offices of the dead, the custom of the Tr. cxx.
nation is to be followed. It was the custom of the Jewish
nation to embalm their dead bodies, in order that they might Aug.
de Con.
keep the longer. AUG. Nor does John here contradict the Evang.
iii. xxiii.

other Evangelists, who, though they are silent about Nicodemus, yet do not affirm that our Lord was buried by Joseph
alone. Nor because they say that our Lord was wrapped in
a linen cloth by Joseph, do they say that other linen cloths
may not have been brought by Nicodemus in addition; so
that John may be right in saying, not, in a single cloth,
but, *in linen cloths.* Nay more, the napkin which was
about His head and the bands which were tied round His
body being all of linen, though there were but one *linen
cloth*, He may yet be said to have been wrapped up *in
linen cloths:* linen cloths being taken in a general sense, as
comprehending all that was made of linen. BEDE. Hence
hath come down the custom of the Church, of consecrating
the Lord's body not on silk or gold cloth, but in a clean
Chrys. linen cloth. CHRYS. But as they were pressed for time, for
Hom.
lxxxv. Christ died at the ninth hour, and after that they had gone
4. to Pilate, and taken away the body, so that the evening was
now near, they lay Him in the nearest tomb : *Now in the
place where He was crucified there was a garden; and in
the garden a new sepulchre, wherein was never man yet laid.*
A providential design, to make it certain that it was His
resurrection, and not any other person's that lay with Him.
Aug.   AUG. As no one before or after Him was conceived in the
Tr.cxx.
womb of the Virgin Mary, so in this grave was there none
buried before or after Him. THEOPHYL. In that it was a
new sepulchre, we are given to understand, that we are all
renewed by Christ's death, and death and corruption destroyed. Mark too the exceeding poverty that He took up
for our sakes. He had no house in His lifetime, and now
He is laid in another's sepulchre at His death, and His
nakedness covered by Joseph. *There laid they Jesus therefore because of the Jews' preparation day; for the sepulchre*
Aug.   *was nigh at hand.* AUG. Implying that the burial was
Tr.cxx.
5. hastened, in order to finish it before the evening, when, on
account of the preparation, which the Jews with us call more
commonly in the Latin, Cæna pura, it was unlawful to do
Chrys. any such thing. CHRYS. The sepulchre was near, that the
Hom.
lxxxv. disciples might approach it more easily, and be better witnesses of what took place there, and that even enemies might

be made the witnesses of the burial, being placed there as guards, and the story of His being stolen away shewed to be false. BEDE. Mystically, the name Joseph means, apt for the receiving of a good work ; whereby we are admonished that we·should make ourselves worthy of our Lord's body, before we receive it. THEOPHYL. Even now in a certain sense Christ is put to death by the avaritious, in the person of the poor man suffering famine. Be therefore a Joseph, and cover Christ's nakedness, and, not once, but continually by contemplation, embalm Him in thy spiritual tomb, cover Him, and mix myrrh and bitter aloes ; considering that bitterest sentence of all, *Depart, ye cursed, into everlasting* Matt *fire.* 25, 41.

CHAP. XX.

1. The first day of the week cometh Mary Magdalene early, when it was yet dark, unto the sepulchre, and seeth the stone taken away from the sepulchre.

2. Then she runneth, and cometh to Simon Peter, and to the other disciple, whom Jesus loved, and saith unto them, They have taken away the Lord out of the sepulchre, and we know not where they have laid him.

3. Peter therefore went forth, and that other disciple, and came to the sepulchre.

4. So they ran both together: and the other disciple did outrun Peter, and came first to the sepulchre.

5. And he stooping down, and looking in, saw the linen clothes lying: yet went he not in.

6. Then cometh Simon Peter following him, and went into the sepulchre, and seeing the linen clothes lie,

7. And the napkin, that was about his head, not lying with the linen clothes, but wrapped together in a place by itself.

8. Then went in also that other disciple, which came first to the sepulchre, and he saw, and believed.

9. For as yet they knew not the Scripture, that he must rise again from the dead.

Chrys. Hom. lxxxv. CHRYS. The Sabbath being now over, during which it was unlawful to be there, Mary Magdalene could rest no longer,

but came very early in the morning, to seek consolation at
the grave: *The first day of the week cometh Mary Magdalene early, when it was yet dark, unto the sepulchre.* AUG. Aug.
Mary Magdalene, undoubtedly the most fervent in love, of de Con.
Evang.
all the women that ministered to our Lord; so that John iii. 24.
deservedly mentions her only, and says nothing of the others
who were with her, as we know from the other Evangelists.
AUG. *Una sabbati* is the day which Christians call the Aug.
Lord's day, after our Lord's resurrection. Matthew calls it Tr. cxx.
prima sabbati. BEDE. *Una sabbati,* i. e. one day after the
sabbath. THEOPHYL. Or thus: The Jews called the days
of the week sabbath, and the first day, *one of the sabbaths,*
which day is a type of the life to come; for that life will be
one day not cut short by any night, since God is the sun
there, a sun which never sets. On this day then our Lord
rose again, with an incorruptible body, even as we in the life
to come shall put on incorruption. AUG. What Mark says, Aug.
Very early in the morning, at the rising of the sun, does not de Con.
Evang.
contradict John's words, *when it was yet dark.* At the iii. 24.
dawn of day, there are yet remains of darkness, which dis- Mark
16, 1.
appear as the light breaks in. We must not understand
Mark's words, *Very early in the morning, at the rising of* ἡλίου
the sun, to mean that the sun was above the horizon, but ἀνατεί-
λαντος
rather what we ourselves ordinarily mean by the phrase,
when we want any thing to be done very early, we say at
the rising of the sun, i. e. some time before the sun is risen.
GREG. It is well said, *When it was yet dark:* Mary was Greg.
seeking the Creator of all things in the tomb, and because Hom.
in Ev.
she found Him not, thought He was stolen. Truly it was xxii.
yet dark when she came to the sepulchre.

And seeth the stone taken away from the sepulchre. AUG. Aug.
Con.
Now took place what Matthew only relates, the earthquake, Evang.
and rolling away of the stone, and fright of the guards. iii. 24.
CHRYS. Our Lord rose while the stone and seal were still Chrys.
on the sepulchre. But as it was necessary that others should Hom.
lxxxv.
be certified of this, the sepulchre is opened after the resurrec- 4.
tion, and so the fact confirmed. This it was which roused
Mary. For when she saw the stone taken away, she entered
not nor looked in, but ran to the disciples with all the speed
of love. But as yet she knew nothing for certain about the

resurrection, but thought that His body had been carried off. GLOSS. And therefore she ran to tell the disciples, that they might seek Him with her, or grieve with her: *Then she runneth, and cometh to Simon Peter, and to the other disciple, whom Jesus loved.* AUG. This is the way in which he usually mentions himself. Jesus loved all, but him in an especial and familiar way. *And saith unto them, They have taken away the Lord out of the sepulchre, and we know not where they have laid Him.* GREG. She puts the part for the whole; she had come only to seek for the body of our Lord, and now she laments that our Lord, the whole of Him, is taken away. AUG. Some of the Greek copies have, *taken away my Lord,* which is more expressive of love, and of the feeling of an handmaiden. But only a few have this reading. CHRYS. The Evangelist does not deprive the woman of this praise, nor leaves out from shame, that they had the news first from her. As soon as they hear it, they hasten to the sepulchre. GREG. But Peter and John before the others, for they loved most; *Peter therefore went forth, and that other disciple, and came to the sepulchre.* THEOPHYL. But how came they to the sepulchre, while the soldiers were guarding it? an easy question to answer. After our Lord's resurrection and the earthquake, and the appearance of the angel at the sepulchre, the guards withdrew, and told the Pharisees what had happened. AUG. After saying, *came to the sepulchre,* he goes back and tells us how they came: *So they ran both together: and the other disciple did outrun Peter, and came first to the sepulchre;* meaning himself, but he always speaks of himself, as if he were speaking of another person. CHRYS. On coming he sees the linen clothes set aside: *And he stooping down, and looking in, saw the linen clothes lying.* But he makes no further search: *yet went he not in.* Peter on the other hand, being of a more fervid temper, pursued the search, and examined every thing: *Then cometh Simon Peter following him, and went into the sepulchre, and seeth the linen clothes lie, and the napkin, that was about His head, not lying with the linen clothes, but wrapped together in a place by itself.* Which circumstances were proof of His resurrection. For had they carried Him away, they would

Marginal notes:
Aug. Tr. cxx.
Greg. iii. Mor. ix.
Aug. Tr. cxx.
Chrys. Hom. lxxxv.
Greg. xxii. in Evang.
Aug. Tr. cxx.
Chrys. Hom. lxxxv.

not have stripped Him; nor, if any had stolen Him, would
they have taken the trouble to wrap up the napkin, and put
it in a place by itself, apart from the linen clothes; but
would have taken away the body as it was. John mentioned
the myrrh first of all, for this reason, i. e. to shew you that
He could not have been stolen away. For myrrh would
make the linen adhere to the body, and so caused trouble to
the thieves, and they would never have been so senseless as
to have taken this unnecessary pains about the matter. After
Peter however, John entered: *Then went in also that other
disciple, which came first to the sepulchre, and he saw, and
believed.* AUG. i. e. That Jesus had risen again, some think: Aug.
but what follows contradicts this notion. He saw the Tract.
cxxii.
sepulchre empty, and believed what the woman had said:
*For as yet they knew not the Scripture, that He must rise
again from the dead.* If he did not yet know that He must
rise again from the dead, he could not believe that He had
risen. They had heard as much indeed from our Lord, and
very openly, but they were so accustomed to hear parables
from Him, that they took this for a parable, and thought He
meant something else. GREG. But this account of the Greg.
Hom.
Evangelist[1] must not be thought to be without some mystical xxii. in
meaning. By John, the younger of the two, the synagogue; Evang.
1 tam
by Peter, the elder, the Gentile Church is represented: for subtilis
though the synagogue was before the Gentile Church as
regards the worship of God, as regards time the Gentile
world was before the synagogue. They ran together, because
the Gentile world ran side by side with the synagogue from
first to last, in respect of purity and community of life, though
a purity and community of understanding[2] they had not. The 2 pari
synagogue came first to the sepulchre, but entered not: it knew sensu
the commandments of the law, and had heard the prophecies
of our Lord's incarnation and death, but would not believe in
Him who died. *Then cometh Simon Peter, and entered into the
sepulchre:* the Gentile Church both knew Jesus Christ as
dead man, and believed in Him as living God. The napkin
about our Lord's head is not found with the linen clothes,
i. e. God, the Head of Christ, and the incomprehensible
mysteries of the Godhead are removed from our poor knowledge; His power transcends the nature of the creature.

And it is found not only apart, but also *wrapped* together ; because of the linen wrapped together, neither beginning nor end is seen ; and the height of the Divine nature had neither beginning nor end. And it is *into one place :* for where there is division, God is not; and they merit His grace, who do not occasion scandal by dividing themselves into sects. But as a napkin is what is used in labouring to wipe the sweat of the brow, by the napkin here we may understand the labour of God : which napkin is found *apart*, because the suffering of our Redeemer is far removed from ours ; inasmuch as He suffered innocently, that which we suffer justly ; He submitted Himself to death voluntarily, we by necessity. But after Peter entered, John entered too ; for at the end of the world even Judæa shall be gathered in to the true faith. THEOPHYL. Or thus: Peter is practical and prompt, John contemplative and intelligent, and learned in divine things. Now the contemplative man is generally beforehand in knowledge and intelligence, but the practical by his fervour and activity gets the advance of the other's perception, and sees first into the divine mystery.

10. Then the disciples went away again unto their own home.

11. But Mary stood without at the sepulchre weeping : and as she wept, she stooped down, and looked into the sepulchre,

12. And seeth two angels in white sitting, the one at the head, and the other at the feet, where the body of Jesus had lain.

13. And they say unto her, Woman, why weepest thou? She saith unto them, Because they have taken away my Lord, and I know not where they have laid him.

14. And when she had thus said, she turned herself back, and saw Jesus standing, and knew not that it was Jesus.

15. Jesus saith unto her, Woman, why weepest thou? whom seekest thou? She, supposing him to

be the gardener, saith unto him, Sir, if thou have borne him hence, tell me where thou hast laid him, and I will take him away.

16. Jesus saith unto her, Mary. She turned herself, and saith unto him, Rabboni; which is to say, Master.

17. Jesus saith unto her, Touch me not; for I am not yet ascended to my Father: but go to my brethren, and say unto them, I ascend unto my Father, and your Father; and to my God, and your God.

18. Mary Magdalene came and told the disciples that she had seen the Lord, and that he had spoken these things unto her.

GREG. Mary Magdalene, who had been the sinner in the city, and who had washed out the spots of her sins by her tears, whose soul burned with love, did not retire from the sepulchre when the others did: *Then the disciples went away again unto their own home.* AUG. i. e. To the place where they were lodging, and from which they had ran to the sepulchre. But though the men returned, the stronger love of the woman fixed her to the spot. *But Mary stood without at the sepulchre weeping.* AUG. i. e. Outside of the place where the stone sepulchre was, but yet within the garden. CHRYS. Be not astonished that Mary wept for love at the sepulchre, and Peter did not; for the female sex is naturally tender, and inclined to weep. AUG. The eyes then which had sought our Lord, and found Him not, now wept without interruption; more for grief that our Lord had been removed, than for His death upon the cross. For now even all memorial of Him was taken away. AUG. She then saw, with the other women, the Angel sitting on the right, on the stone which had been rolled away from the sepulchre, at whose words it was that she looked into the sepulchre. CHRYS. The sight of the sepulchre itself was some consolation. Nay, behold her, to console herself still more, stooping down, to see the very place where the body lay: *And as she wept, she stooped down, and looked into the sepulchre.* GREG. For to have looked

Greg.
Hom.
xxv. in
Evang.

Aug.
Tr. cxxi.
1.

Aug.
de Con.
Ev. iii.
xxiv. 69.
Chrys.
Hom.
lxxxvi.

Aug.
Tr. cxxi.
l.

Aug.
de Con.
Ev. iii.
xxiv. 69.
Mat. 28,
5.
Chrys.
Hom.
lxxxvi.
Greg.
Hom.
xxv. ut
supr.

once is not enough for love.   Love makes one desire to look

Aug. over and over again.   AUG. In her too great grief she could
Tr.cxxi. believe neither her own eyes, nor the disciples'.   Or was it

Greg. a divine impulse which caused her to look in?   GREG. She
Hom.
xxv, sought the body, and found it not; she persevered in seeking; and so it came to pass that she found.   Her longings,
growing the stronger, the more they were disappointed, at last
found and laid hold on their object.   For holy longings
ever gain strength by delay; did they not, they would not
be longings.   Mary so loved, that not content with seeing
the sepulchre, she stooped down and looked in: let us see
the fruit which came of this persevering love: *And seeth two
Angels in white sitting, the one at the head, and the other at*

Chrys. *the feet, where the body of Jesus had lain.*   CHRYS. As her
Hom.
lxxxvi. understanding was not so raised as to be able to gather from
1. the napkins the fact of the resurrection, she is given the
sight of Angels in bright apparel, who sooth her sorrow.

Aug, AUG. But why did one sit at the head, the other at the feet?
Tr.cxxi. To signify that the glad tidings of Christ's Gospel was to
be delivered from the head to the feet, from the beginning
to the end.   The Greek word Angel means one who delivers

Greg. news.   GREG. The Angel sits at the head when the Apostles
Hom.
xxv. in preach that *in the beginning was the Word:* he sits, as it
Evang. were, at the feet, when it is said, *The Word was made flesh.*
c. 1, 14. By the two Angels too we may understand the two testaments; both of which proclaim alike the incarnation,
death, and resurrection of our Lord.   The Old seems to sit

Chrys. at the head, the New at the feet.   CHRYS. The Angels who
Hom.
lxxxvi. appear say nothing about the resurrection; but by degrees
the subject is entered on.   First of all they address her
compassionately, to prevent her from being overpowered by
a spectacle of such extraordinary brightness: *And they say
unto her, Woman, why weepest thou?*   The Angels forbad
tears, and announced, as it were, the joy that was at hand:

Greg. *Why weepest thou?*   As if to say, Weep not.   GREG. The
Hom.
fin. very declarations of Scripture which excite our tears of love,
wipe away those very tears, by promising us the sight of our

Aug. Redeemer again.   AUG. But she, thinking that they wanted
Tr.cxxi. to know why she wept, tells them the reason: *She saith unto
them, Because they have taken away my Lord.*   The lifeless

body of her Lord, she calls her Lord, putting the part for the whole; just as we confess that Jesus Christ the Son of God was buried, when only His flesh was buried. *And I know not where they have placed Him :* it was a still greater grief, that she did not know where to go to console her grief. CHRYS. As yet she knew nothing of the resurrection, but thought the body had been taken away. AUG. Here the Angels must be understood to rise up, for Luke describes them as seen standing. AUG. The hour was now come, which the Angels announced, when sorrow should be succeeded by joy: *And when she had thus said, she turned herself back.* CHRYS. But why, when she is talking to the Angels, and before she has heard any thing from them, does she turn back? It seems to me that while she was speaking, Christ appeared behind her, and that the Angels by their posture, look, and motion, shewed that they saw our Lord, and that thus it was that she turned back. GREG. We must observe that Mary, who as yet doubted our Lord's resurrection, turned back to see Jesus. By her doubting she turned her back, as it were, upon our Lord. Yet inasmuch as she loved, she saw Him. She loved and doubted: she saw, and did not recognise Him: *And saw Jesus standing, and knew not that it was Jesus.* CHRYS. To the Angels He appeared as their Lord, but not so to the woman, for the sight coming upon her all at once, would have stupified her. She was not to be lifted suddenly, but gradually to high things. GREG. *Jesus saith unto her, Woman, why weepest thou?* He asks the cause of her grief, to set her longing still more. For the mere mentioning His name whom she sought would inflame her love for Him. CHRYS. Because He appeared as a common person, she thought Him the gardener: *She, supposing Him to be the gardener, saith unto Him, Sir, if Thou have borne Him hence, tell me where Thou hast laid Him, and I will take Him away.* i. e. If thou hast taken Him away from fear of the Jews, tell me, and I will take Him again. THEOPHYL. She was afraid that the Jews might vent their rage even on the lifeless body, and therefore wished to remove it to some secret place. GREG. Perhaps, however, the woman was right in believing Jesus to be the gardener. Was not He the spiritual Gardener, who by the power of His love had sown strong

Chrys. Hom. lxxxvi.

Aug. de Con. Evang. iii. xxiv.

Aug. Tr.cxxi.

Chrys. Hom. l.

Greg. Hom. xxv.

Chrys. Hom. lxxxvi.

Greg. Hom. xxv.

Chrys. Hom. lxxxvi. l.

Greg. Hom. xxv.

seeds of virtue in her breast? But how is it that, as soon as she sees the gardener, as she supposes Him to be, she says, without having told Him who it was she was seeking, *Sir, if Thou hast borne Him hence?* It arises from her love; when one loves a person, one never thinks that any one else can be ignorant of him. Our Lord, after calling her by the common name of her sex, and not being recognised, calls her by her own name: *Jesus saith unto her, Mary;* as if to say, Recognise Him, who recognises thee. Mary, being called by name, recognises Him; that it was He whom she sought externally, and He who taught her internally to seek: *She turned herself, and saith unto Him, Rabboni; which is to say, Master.* CHRYS. Just as He was sometimes in the midst of the Jews, and they did not know Him till He pleased to make Himself known. But why does she turn herself, when she had turned herself before? It seems to me that when she said, *Where thou hast laid Him,* she turned to the Angels, to ask why they were astonished. Then Christ, calling her, discovered Himself by His voice, and made her turn to Him again. AUG. Or she first turned her body, but thought Him what He was not; now she was turned in heart, and knew who He was. Let no one however blame her, because she called the gardener, Lord, and Jesus, Master. The one was a title of courtesy to a person from whom she was asking a favour; the other of respect to a Teacher from whom she was used to learn to distinguish the divine from the human. The word Lord is used in different senses, when she says, *They have taken away my Lord,* and when she says, *Lord, if Thou have borne Him away.* GREG. The Evangelist does not add what she did upon recognising Him, but we know from what our Lord said to her: *Jesus saith unto her, Touch Me not.* Mary then had tried to embrace His feet, but was not allowed. Why not? The reason follows: *For I am not yet ascended to My Father.* AUG. But if standing upon the earth, He is not touched, how shall He be touched sitting in heaven? And did He not before His ascension offer Himself to the touch of the disciples: *Handle Me and see, for a spirit hath not flesh and bones?* Who can be so absurd as to suppose that He was willing that disciples should touch Him before He

Chrys.
Hom.
lxxxvi.
1.

Aug.
Tr.cxxi.

Greg.
Hom.
xxv.

Aug.
Tr.cxxi.
3.

Luke
24, 39.

ascended to His Father, and unwilling that women should till after? Nay, we read of women after the resurrection, and before He ascended to His Father, touching Him, one of whom was Mary Magdalene herself, according to Matthew. Either then Mary here is a type of the Gentile Church, which did not believe in Christ till after His ascension: or the meaning is that Jesus is to be believed in, i. e. spiritually touched, in no other way, but as being one with the Father. He ascends to the Father mystically, as it were, in the mind of him who hath so far advanced as to acknowledge that He is equal to the Father. But how could Mary believe in Him otherwise than carnally, when she wept for Him as a man? AUG. Touch is as it were the end of knowledge[1]; and He was unwilling that a soul intent upon Him should have its end, in thinking Him only what He seemed to be. CHRYS. Mary wished to be as familiar with Christ now, as she was before His Passion; forgetting, in her joy, that His body was made much more holy by its resurrection. So, *Touch Me not*, He says, to remind her of this, and make her feel awe in talking with Him. For which reason too He no longer keeps company with His disciples, viz. that they might look upon Him with the greater awe. Again, by saying I have not yet ascended, He shews that He is hastening there. And He who was going to depart and live no more with men, ought not to be regarded with the same feeling that He was before: *But go to My brethren, and say unto them, I ascend unto My Father, and your Father; and to My God, and your God.* HILARY. Heretics, among their other impieties, misinterpret these words of our Lord's, and say, that if His Father is their Father, His God their God, He cannot be God Himself. But though He remained in the form of God, He took upon Him the form of a servant; and Christ says this in the form of a servant to men. And we cannot doubt that in so far as He is man, the Father is His Father in the same sense in which He is of other men, and God His God in like manner. Indeed He begins with saying, *Go to My brethren.* But God can only have brethren according to the flesh; the Only-Begotten God, being Only-Begotten, is without brethren. AUG. He does not say, Our Father, but, *My Father and your Father:*

Aug. i. de Trin.

[1]*notionis*

Chrys. Hom. lxxxvi. 2.

Hilar. de Trin.

Aug. Tr.cxxi.

Mine therefore and *yours* in a different sense ; Mine by nature, yours by grace. Nor does He say, *Our God,* but, *My God*—under Him I am man—*and your God;* between you and Him I am Mediator. AUG. She then went away from the sepulchre, i. e. from that part of the garden before the rock which had been hollowed out, and with her the other women. But these, according to Mark, were seized with trembling and amazement, and said nothing to any man : *Mary Magdalene came and told the disciples that she had seen the Lord, and that He had spoken these things unto her.* GREG. So the sin of mankind is buried in the very place whence it came forth. For whereas in Paradise the woman gave the man the deadly fruit, a woman from the sepulchre announced life to men ; a woman delivers the message of Him who raises us from the dead, as a woman had delivered the words of the serpent who slew us. AUG. While she was going with the other women, according to Matthew, *Jesus met them, saying, All hail.* So we gather that there were two visions of Angels; and that our Lord too was seen twice, once when Mary took Him for the gardener, and again, when He met them by the way, and by this repeating His presence confirmed their faith. And so Mary Magdalen came and told the disciples, not alone, but with the other women whom Luke mentions. BEDE. Mystically, Mary, which name signifies, mistress, enlightened, enlightener, star of the sea, stands for the Church, which is also Magdalen, i. e. towered, (Magdalen being Greek for tower,) as we read in the Psalms, *Thou hast been a strong tower for me.* In that she announced Christ's resurrection to the disciples, all, especially those to whom the office of preaching is committed, are admonished to be zealous in setting forth to others whatever is revealed from above.

Aug.
de Con.
Evang.
iii. xxiv.
69.

Greg.
Hom.
xxv.

Aug.
de Con.
Evang.
iii. 25.
Matt.
28, 9.

Ps.61,3.

19. Then the same day at evening, being the first day of the week, when the doors were shut where the disciples were assembled for fear of the Jews, came Jesus and stood in the midst, and saith unto them, Peace be unto you.

20. And when he had so said, he shewed unto

them his hands and his side. Then were the disciples glad, when they saw the Lord.

21. Then said Jesus to them again, Peace be unto you : as my Father hath sent me, even so send I you.

22. And when he had said this, he breathed on them, and saith unto them, Receive ye the Holy Ghost :

23. Whose soever sins ye remit, they are remitted unto them; and whose soever sins ye retain, they are retained.

24. But Thomas, one of the twelve, called Didymus, was not with them when Jesus came.

25. The other disciples therefore said unto him, We have seen the Lord. But he said unto them, Except I shall see in his hands the print of the nails, and put my finger into the print of the nails, and thrust my hand into his side, I will not believe.

CHRYS. The disciples, when they heard what Mary told them, were obliged either to disbelieve, or, if they believed, to grieve that He did not count them worthy to have the sight of Him. He did not let them however pass a whole day in such reflections, but in the midst of their longing trembling desires to see Him, presented Himself to them : *Then the same day at evening, being the first day of the week, when the doors were shut where the disciples were assembled for fear of the Jews.* BEDE. Wherein is shewn the infirmity of the Apostles. They assembled with doors shut, through that same fear of the Jews, which had before scattered them : *Came Jesus, and stood in the midst.* He came in the evening, because they would be the most afraid at that time. THEOPHYL. Or because He waited till all were assembled : and with shut doors, that he might shew how that in the very same way he had risen again, i. e. with the stone lying on the sepulchre. AUG. Some are strongly indisposed to believe this miracle, and argue thus : If the same body rose again, which hung upon the Cross, how could that body enter through shut doors? But if thou comprehendest the

Chrys. Hom. lxxxvi.

Aug. Serm. cx. et cl. Pasch. aliquid simile.

mode, it is no miracle: when reason fails, then is faith
Aug.
Tr. cxx. edified. AUG. The shut door did not hinder the body,
wherein Divinity resided. He could enter without open
doors, who was born without a violation of His mother's
Chrys. virginity. CHRYS. It is wonderful that they did not think
Hom.
lxxxvi. him a phantom. But Mary had provided against this, by
the faith she had wrought in them. And He Himself too
shewed Himself so openly, and strengthened their wavering
minds by His voice: *And saith unto them, Peace be unto
you*, i. e. Be not disturbed. Wherein too He reminds them
c.14,27; of what He had said before His crucifixion; *My peace I*
16, 33.
Greg. *give to you;* and again, *In Me ye shall have peace.* GREG.
Hom.
xxvi. in And because their faith wavered even with the material body
Evang. before them, He shewed them His hands and side: *And
when He had said this, He shewed them His hands and His
Aug. side.* AUG. The nails had pierced His hands, the lance had
Tr.cxxi.
pierced His side. For the healing of doubting hearts, the
Chrys. marks of the wounds were still preserved. CHRYS. And
Hom.
lxxxvi. what He had promised before the crucifixion, *I shall see
you again, and your heart shall rejoice*, is now fulfilled:
Aug. *Then were the disciples glad when they saw the Lord.* AUG.
de Civ.
Dei. The glory, wherewith the righteous shall shine like the sun
in the kingdom of their Father, i. e. in Christ's body, we
must believe to have been rather veiled than not to have
been there at all. He accommodated His presence to man's
weak sight, and presented Himself in such form, as that His
Chrys. disciple could look at and recognise Him. CHRYS. All
Hom.
lxxxvi. these things brought them to a most confident faith. As
they were in endless war with the Jews, He says again,
Then said Jesus unto them again, Peace be unto you.
BEDE. A repetition is a confirmation: whether He repeats
it because the grace of love is twofold, or because He it is
Chrys. who made of twain one. CHRYS. At the same time He
Hom.
lxxxvi. shews the efficacy of the cross, by which He undoes all
3.
evil things, and gives all good things; which is peace.
Gen. 3, To the women above there was announced joy; for that
16. sex was in sorrow, and had received the curse, *In sorrow
κατωρ-
θωται. *shalt thou bring forth.* All hindrances then being removed,
Greg. and every thing made straight, he adds, *As My Father hath
Hom.
xxii. in *sent Me, even so send I you.* GREG. The Father sent the
Evang.

Son, appointed Him to the work of redemption. He says therefore, *As My Father hath sent Me, even so send I you;* i. e. I love you, now that I send you to persecution, with the same love wherewith My Father loved Me, when He sent Me to My sufferings. AUG. We have learnt that the Son is equal to the Father: here He shews Himself Mediator; *He Me,* and *I you.* CHRYS. Having then given them confidence by His own miracles, and appealing to Him who sent Him, He uses a prayer to the Father, but of His own authority gives them power: *And when He had said thus, He breathed on them, and saith unto them, Receive ye the Holy Ghost.* AUG. That corporeal breath was not the substance of the Holy Ghost, but to shew, by meet symbol, that the Holy Ghost proceeded not only from the Father, but the Son. For who would be so mad as to say, that it was one Spirit which He gave by breathing, and another which He sent after His ascension? GREG. But why is He first given to the disciples on earth, and afterwards sent from heaven? Because there are two commandments of love, to love God, and to love our neighbour. The spirit to love our neighbour is given on earth, the spirit to love God is given from heaven. As then love is one, and there are two commandments; so the Spirit is one, and there are two gifts of the Spirit. And the first is given by our Lord while yet upon earth, the second from heaven, because by the love of our neighbour we learn how to arrive at the love of God. CHRYS. Some say that by breathing He did not give them the Spirit, but made them meet to receive the Spirit. For if Daniel's senses were so overpowered by the sight of the Angel, how would they have been overwhelmed in receiving that unutterable gift, if He had not first prepared them for it! It would not be wrong however to say that they received then the gift of a certain spiritual power, not to raise the dead and do miracles, but to remit sins: *Whosoever sins ye remit, they are remitted unto them, and whosoever sins ye retain, they are retained.* AUG. The love of the Church, which is shed abroad in our hearts by the Holy Spirit, remits the sins of those who partake of it; but retains the sins of those who do not. Where then He has said, *Receive ye the Holy Ghost,* He instantly makes mention of the remission and retaining of

Aug.
Tr.cxxi.

Chrys.
Hom.
lxxxvi.
2.

Aug.
iv. de
Trin.
c. xx.

Greg.
Hom.
xxvi.

Chrys.
Hom.
lxxxvi.

Aug.
Tr.cxxi.
3.

Greg.
Hom.
xxvi.
sins. GREG. We must understand that those who first received the Holy Ghost, for innocence of life in themselves, and preaching to a few others, received it openly after the resurrection, that they might profit not a few only, but many. The disciples who were called to such works of humility, to what a height of glory are they led! Lo, not ¹ʰsortiun-
tur
only have they salvation for themselves, but are admitted ¹ to the powers of the supreme Judgment-seat; so that, in the place of God, they retain some men's sins, and remit others. Their place in the Church, the Bishops now hold; who receive the authority to bind, when they are admitted to the rank of government. Great the honour, but heavy the burden of the place. It is ill if one who knows not how to govern his own life, shall be judge of another's.

Chrys.
Hom.
lxxxvi.
4.
CHRYS. A priest though he may have ordered well his own life, yet, if he have not exercised proper vigilance over others, is sent to hell with the evil doers. Wherefore, knowing the greatness of their danger, pay them all respect, even though they be not men of notable goodness. For they who are in rule, should not be judged by those who are under them. And their incorrectness of life will not at all invalidate what they do by commission from God. For not only cannot a priest, but not even angel or archangel, do any thing of themselves; the Father, Son, and Holy Ghost do all. The priest only furnishes the tongue, and the hand. For it were not just that the salvation of those who come to the Sacraments in faith, should be endangered by another's wickedness.

Hom.
lxxxvii.
1.
At the assembly of the disciples all were present but Thomas, who probably had not returned from the dispersion: *But Thomas, one of the twelve, called Didymus, was not with them when Jesus came.* ALCUIN. Didymus, double or doubtful, because he doubted in believing: Thomas, depth, because with most sure faith he penetrated into the depth of our Lord's divinity.

Greg.
Hom.
xxvi.
GREG. It was not an accident that that particular disciple was not present. The Divine mercy ordained that a doubting disciple should, by feeling in his Master the wounds of the flesh, heal in us the wounds of unbelief. The unbelief of Thomas is more profitable to our faith, than the belief of the other disciples; for, the touch by which he is brought to believe, con-

firming our minds in belief, beyond all question. BEDE.
But why does this Evangelist say that Thomas was absent,
when Luke writes that two disciples on their return from
Emmaus found the eleven assembled? We must understand
that Thomas had gone out, and that in the interval of his
absence, Jesus came and stood in the midst. CHRYS. As Chrys.
to believe directly, and any how, is the mark of too easy lxxxvii.
a mind, so is too much enquiring of a gross one: and this [1.]
is Thomas's fault. For when the Apostle said, *We have*
seen the Lord, he did not believe, not because he discredited
them, but from an idea of the impossibility of the thing
itself: *The other disciples therefore said unto him, We have*
seen the Lord. But he said unto them, Except I shall see
in His hands the print of the nails, and put my finger into
the print of the nails, and thrust my hand into His side,
I will not believe. Being the grossest of all, he required the
evidence of the grossest sense, viz. the touch, and would not
even believe his eyes: for he does not say only, *Except*
I shall see, but adds, *and put my finger into the print of the*
nails, and thrust my hand into His side.

26. And after eight days again his disciples were
within, and Thomas with them : then came Jesus, the
doors being shut, and stood in the midst, and said,
Peace be unto you.

27. Then saith he to Thomas, Reach hither thy
finger, and behold my hands; and reach hither thy
hand, and thrust it into my side: and be not faithless,
but believing.

28. And Thomas answered and said unto him, My
Lord and my God.

29. Jesus saith unto him, Thomas, because thou
hast seen me, thou hast believed: blessed are they
that have not seen, and yet have believed.

30. And many other signs truly did Jesus in the
presence of his disciples, which are not written in this
book :

31. But these are written, that ye might believe

2 R

that Jesus is the Christ, the Son of God; and that believing ye might have life through his name.

Chrys. Hom. lxxxvii. **CHRYS.** Consider the mercy of the Lord, how for the sake of one soul, He exhibits His wounds. And yet the disciples deserved credit, and He had Himself foretold the event. Notwithstanding, because one person, Thomas, would examine Him, Christ allowed him. But He did not appear to him immediately, but waited till the eighth day, in order that the admonition being given in the presence of the disciples, might kindle in him greater desire, and strengthen his faith for the future. *And after eight days again His disciples were within, and Thomas with them: then came Jesus, the doors being shut, and stood in the midst, and said,*

Aug. in Serm. Tap. ad Cat. ii.8. ubi est modus corporis. *Peace be unto you.* **AUG.** You ask; If He entered by the shut door, where is the nature of His body? And I reply; If He walked on the sea, where is the weight of His body? The Lord did that as the Lord; and did He, after His resurrection, cease to be the Lord?

Chrys. Hom. lxxxvii. 1. **CHRYS.** Jesus then comes Himself, and does not wait till Thomas interrogates Him. But to shew that He heard what Thomas said to the disciples, He uses the same words. And first He rebukes him; *Then saith He to Thomas, Reach hither thy finger, and behold My hands; and reach hither thy hand, and thrust it into My side:* secondly, He admonishes him; *And be not faithless, but believing.* Note how that before they receive the Holy Ghost faith wavers, but afterward is firm. We may wonder how an incorruptible body could retain the marks of the nails. But it was done in condescension; in order that they might be sure that it was the very person Who was crucified.

Aug. deSymb. ad Cat. ii. 8. **AUG.** He might, had He pleased, have wiped all spot and trace of wound from His glorified body; but He had reasons for retaining them. He shewed them to Thomas, who would not believe except he saw and touched; and He will shew them to His enemies, not to say, as He did to Thomas, *Because thou hast seen, thou hast believed,* but to convict them: Behold the Man whom ye crucified, see the wounds which ye inflicted, recognise the side which ye pierced, that it was by you, and for you, that it was opened, and

Aug. xxii.Civ. Dei,xix. yet ye cannot enter there. **AUG.** We are, as I know not

how, afflicted with such love for the blessed martyrs, that
we would wish in that kingdom to see on their bodies the marks
of those wounds which they have borne for Christ's sake.
And perhaps we shall see them; for they will not have
deformity, but dignity, and, though on the body, shine
forth not with bodily, but with spiritual beauty. Nor yet, if virtutis
any of the limbs of martyrs have been cut off, shall they
therefore appear without them in the resurrection of the
dead; for it is said, *There shall not an hair of your head
perish.* But if it be fit that in that new world, the traces of
glorious wounds should still be preserved on the immortal
flesh, in the places where the limbs were cut off there, though
those same limbs withal be not lost but restored, shall the
wounds appear. For though all the blemishes of the
body shall then be no more, yet the evidences of virtue are
not to be called blemishes. GREG. Our Lord gave that Greg.
flesh to be touched which He had introduced through shut ${}^{\text{Hom.}}_{\text{xxvi.}}$
doors: wherein two wonderful, and, according to human
reason, contradictory things appear, viz. that after the resurrection He had a body incorruptible, and yet palpable. For
that which is palpable must be corruptible, and that which is
incorruptible must be impalpable. But He shewed Himself
incorruptible and yet palpable, to prove that His body after
His resurrection was the same in nature as before, but
different in glory. GREG. Our body also in that resurrec- Greg.
tion to glory will be subtle by means of the action of the ${}^{\text{Mor.}}_{\text{xii. 31.}}$
Spirit, but palpable by its true nature, not, as Eutychius
says, impalpable, and subtler than the winds and the air.
AUG. Thomas saw and touched the man, and confessed the Aug.
God whom he neither saw nor touched. By means of the ${}^{\text{Tr.cxxi.}}$
one he believed the other undoubtingly: *Thomas answered
and said unto Him, My Lord and my God.* THEOPHYL.
He who had been before unbelieving, after touching the
body shewed himself the best divine; for he asserted the
twofold nature and one Person of Christ; by saying, *My
Lord*, the human nature, by saying, *My God*, the divine,
and by joining them both, confessed that one and the same
Person was Lord and God.

*Jesus saith unto him, Because thou hast seen Me, thou
hast believed.* AUG. He saith not, Hast touched me, but, Aug.

hast seen me; the sight being a kind of general sense, and put in the place often of the other four senses; as when we say, Hear, and see how well it sounds; smell, and see how sweet it smells; taste, and see how well it tastes; touch, and see how warm it is. Wherefore also our Lord says, *Reach hither thy finger, and behold My hands.* What is this but, Touch and see? And yet he had not eyes in his finger. He refers them both to seeing and to touching, when He says, *Because thou hast seen, thou hast believed.* Although it might be said, that the disciple did not dare to touch, what was offered to be touched. GREG. But when the Apostle says, *Faith is the substance of things hoped for, the evidence of things not seen,* it is plain that things which are seen, are objects not of faith, but of knowledge. Why then is it said to Thomas who saw and touched, *Because thou hast seen Me, thou hast believed?* Because he saw one thing, believed another; saw the man, confessed the God. But what follows is very gladdening; *Blessed are they that have not seen, and yet have believed.* In which sentence we are specially included, who have not seen Him with the eye, but retain Him in the mind, provided we only develope our faith in good works. For he only really believes, who practises what he believes. AUG. He uses the past tense, the future to His knowledge having already taken place by His own predestination. CHRYS. If any one then says, Would that I had lived in those times, and seen Christ doing miracles! let him reflect, *Blessed are they that have not seen, and yet have believed.* THEOPHYL. Here He means the disciples who had believed without seeing the print of the nails, and His side. CHRYS. John having related less than the other Evangelists, adds, *And many other signs truly did Jesus in the presence of His disciples, which are not written in this book.* Yet neither did the others relate all, but only what was sufficient for the purpose of convincing men. He probably here refers to the miracles which our Lord did after His resurrection, and therefore says, *In the presence of His disciples,* and they being the only persons with whom He conversed after His resurrection. Then to let you understand, that the miracles were not done for the sake of the disciples only, He adds, *But these are written, that ye might*

Greg.
Hom.
xxvi.

Heb.11,
1.

Aug.
Tr.cxxi.

Chrys.
Hom.
lxxxvii.

Chrys.
Hom.
lxxxvii.

believe that Jesus is the Christ, the Son of God; addressing Himself to mankind generally.   And, this belief, he then says, profits ourselves, not Him in Whom we believe.   *And that believing ye might have life through His name,* i. e. through Jesus, which is life.

CHAP. XXI.

1. After these things Jesus shewed himself again to the disciples at the sea of Tiberias; and on this wise shewed he himself.

2. There were together Simon Peter, and Thomas called Didymus, and Nathanael of Cana in Galilee, and the sons of Zebedee, and two other of his disciples.

3. Simon Peter saith unto them, I go a fishing. They say unto him, We also go with thee. They went forth, and entered into a ship immediately; and that night they caught nothing.

4. But when the morning was now come, Jesus stood on the shore: but the disciples knew not that it was Jesus.

5. Then Jesus saith unto them, Children, have ye any meat? They answered him, No.

6. And he said unto them, Cast the net on the right side of the ship, and ye shall find. They cast therefore, and now they were not able to draw it for the multitude of fishes.

7. Therefore that disciple whom Jesus loved saith unto Peter, It is the Lord. Now when Simon Peter heard that it was the Lord, he girt his fisher's coat unto him, (for he was naked,) and did cast himself into the sea.

8. And the other disciples came in a little ship; (for they were not far from land, but as it were two hundred cubits,) dragging the net with fishes.

9. As soon then as they were come to land, they saw a fire of coals there, and fish laid thereon, and bread.

10. Jesus saith unto them, Bring of the fish which ye have now caught.

11. Simon Peter went up, and drew the net to land full of great fishes, an hundred and fifty and three: and for all there were so many, yet was not the net broken.

AUG. The preceding words of the Evangelist seem to indicate the end of the book; but He goes on farther to give an account of our Lord's appearance by the sea of Tiberias: *After these things Jesus shewed Himself again to the disciples at the sea of Tiberias.* CHRYS. He says, *Afterwards,* because He did not go continually with His disciples as before; and, *manifested Himself,* because His body being incorruptible, it was a condescension to allow Himself to be seen. He mentions the place, to shew that our Lord had taken away a good deal of their fear, and that they no longer kept within doors, though they had gone to Galilee to avoid the persecution of the Jews. BEDE. The Evangelist, after his wont, first states the thing itself, and then says how it took place: *And on this wise shewed He Himself.* CHRYS. As our Lord was not with them regularly, and the Spirit was not given them, and they had received no commission, and had nothing to do, they followed the trade of fishermen: *And on this wise shewed He Himself. There were together Simon Peter, and Thomas called Didymus, and Nathanael of Cana in Galilee;* he who was called by Philip, *and the sons of Zebedee,* i. e. James and John, *and two other of His disciples. Simon Peter saith unto them, I go a fishing.* GREG. It may be asked, why Peter, who was a fisherman before his conversion, returned to fishing, when it is said, *No man putting his hand to the plough, and looking back, is fit for the kingdom of God.* AUG. If the disciples had done this after the death of Jesus, and before His resurrection, we should have imagined that they did it in despair. But now after that He has risen from the grave, after seeing the marks of His wounds, after receiving, by means of His

Aug. Tract. cxxii.

Chrys. Hom. lxxxvii.

Chrys. Hom. lxxxvii.

Greg. Hom.

Luke 9, 62.

Aug. Tract. cxxii.

breathing, the Holy Ghost, all at once they become what they were before, fishers, not of men, but of fishes. We must remember then that they were not forbidden by their Apostleship from earning their livelihood by a lawful craft, provided they had no other means of living. For if the blessed Paul used not that power which he had with the rest of the preachers of the Gospel, as they did, but went a warfare upon his own resources, lest the Gentiles, who were aliens from the name of Christ, might be offended at a doctrine apparently venal; if, educated in another way, he learnt a craft he never knew before, that, while the teacher worked with his own hands, the hearer might not be burdened; much more might Peter, who had been a fisherman, work at what he knew, if he had nothing else to live upon at the time. But how had he not, some one will ask, when our Lord promises, *Seek ye first the kingdom of God and His righteousness, and all these things shall be added unto you?* Our Lord, we answer, fulfilled this promise, by bringing them the fishes to catch: for who else brought them? He did not bring upon them that poverty which obliged them to go fishing, except in order to exhibit a miracle[1]. GREG. The craft which was exercised without sin before conversion, was no sin after it. Wherefore after his conversion Peter returned to fishing; but Matthew sat not down again for the receipt of custom. For there are some businesses which cannot or can hardly be carried on without sin; and these cannot be returned to after conversion. CHRYS. The other disciples followed Peter: *They say unto him, We also go with thee;* for from this time they were all bound together; and they wished too to see the fishing: *They went forth and entered into a ship immediately. And that night they caught nothing.* They fished in the night, from fear. GREG. The fishing was made to be very unlucky, in order to raise their astonishment at the miracle after: *And that night they caught nothing.* CHRYS. In the midst of their labour and distress, Jesus presented Himself to them: *But when the morning was now come, Jesus stood on the shore: but the disciples knew not that it was Jesus.* He did not make Himself known to them immediately, but entered into conversation; and first He speaks after human fashion: *Then Jesus saith unto them,*

Matt. 6, 33.

[1] dispositum miraculum
Greg.
Hom.
lxxxiv.
ad telonii negotium resedit
Chrys.
Hom.
lxxxvii.

Greg.
Hom.

Chrys.
Hom.
lxxxvii.

Children, have ye any meat? as if He wished to beg some of them. *They answered, No.* He then gives them a sign to know Him by: *And He said unto them, Cast the net on the right side of the ship, and ye shall find.* *They cast therefore, and now they were not able to draw it for the multitude of fishes.* The recognition of Him brings out Peter and John in their different tempers of mind; the one fervid, the other sublime; the one ready, the other penetrating. John is the first to recognise our Lord: *Therefore that disciple whom Jesus loved saith unto Peter, It is the Lord;* Peter is the first to come to Him: *Now when Simon Peter heard that it was the Lord, he girt his fisher's coat unto Him, for he was naked.* BEDE. The Evangelist alludes to himself here the same way he always does. He recognised our Lord either by the miracle, or by the sound of His voice, or the association of former occasions on which He found them fishing. Peter was naked in comparison with the usual dress he wore, in the sense in which we say to a person whom we meet thinly clad, You are quite bare. Peter was bare for convenience sake, as fishermen are in fishing. THEOPHYL. Peter's girding himself is a sign of modesty. He girt himself with a linen coat, such as Thamian and Tyrian fishermen throw over them, when they have nothing else on, or even over their other clothes. BEDE. He went to Jesus with the ardour with which he did every thing: *And did cast himself into the sea.* *And the other disciples came in a little ship.* We must not understand here that Peter walked on the top of the water, but either swam, or walked through the water, being very near the land: *For they were not far from land, but as it were about two hundred cubits.* GLOSS. A parenthesis; for it follows, *dragging the net with fishes.* The order is, *The other disciples came in a little ship, dragging the net with fishes.* CHRYS. Another miracle follows: *As soon then as they were come to land, they saw a fire of coals there, and fish laid thereon, and bread.* He no longer works upon already existing materials, but in a still more wonderful way; shewing that it was only in condescension[1] that He wrought His miracles upon existing matter before His crucifixion. AUG. We must not understand that the bread was laid on the coals, but read it as if it stood, They saw a fire of coals there, and fish laid on the coals; and they saw bread.

Chrys. Hom. lxxxvii

[1] dispensationem

Aug. Tract. cxxii.

THEOPHYL. To shew that it was no vision, He bade them take of the fish they had caught. *Jesus saith unto them, Bring of the fish which ye have now caught.* Another miracle follows; viz. that the net was not broken by the number of fish: *Simon Peter went up, and drew the net to land full of great fishes, an hundred and fifty and three: and for all there were so many, yet was not the net broken.* AUG. Mystically, in the draught of fishes He signified the mystery[1] of the Church, such as it will be at the final resurrection of the dead. And to make this clearer, it is put near the end of the book. The number seven, which is the number of the disciples who were fishing, signifies the end of time; for time is counted by periods of seven days. THEOPHYL. In the night time before the presence of the sun, Christ, the Prophets took nothing; for though they endeavoured to correct the people, yet these often fell into idolatry. GREG. It may be asked, why after His resurrection He stood on the shore to receive the disciples, whereas before He walked on the sea? The sea signifies the world, which is tossed about with various causes of tumults, and the waves of this corruptible life; the shore by its solidity figures the rest eternal. The disciples then, inasmuch as they were still upon the waves of this mortal life, were labouring on the sea; but the Redeemer having by His resurrection thrown off the corruption of the flesh, stood upon the shore. AUG. The shore is the end of the sea, and therefore signifies the end of the world. The Church is here typified as she will be at the end of the world, just as other draughts of fishes typified her as she is now. Jesus before did not stand on the shore, but went into a ship which was Simon's, and asked him to put out a little from the land. In a former draught the nets are not thrown to the right, or to the left, so that the good or the bad should be typified alone, but indifferently: *Let down your nets for a draught*, meaning that the good and bad were mixed together. But here it is, *Cast the net on the right side of the ship;* to signify those who should stand on the right hand, the good. The one our Lord did at the beginning of His ministry, the other after His resurrection, shewing therein that the former draught of fishes signified the mixture of bad and good, which composes the Church at present;

Margin notes:

Aug. Tract. cxxii.

[1] sacramentum

Greg. Hom. xxiv.

Aug. Tract. cxxii.

Luke 5, 4.

the latter the good alone, which it will contain in eternity, when the world is ended, and the resurrection of the dead completed. But they who belong to the resurrection of life, i. e. to the right hand, and are caught within the net of the Christian name, shall only appear on the shore, i. e. at the end of the world, after the resurrection: wherefore they were not able to draw the net into the ship, and unload the fishes, as they were before. The Church keeps these of the right hand, after death, in the sleep of peace, as it were in the deep, till the net come to shore. That the first draught was taken in two little ships, the last two hundred cubits from land, a hundred and a hundred, typifies, I think, the two classes of elect, circumcised and uncircumcised. BEDE. By the two hundred cubits is signified the twofold grace of love; the love of God and the love of our neighbour; for by them we approach to Christ. The fish broiled is Christ Who suffered. He deigned to be hid in the waters of human nature, and to be taken in the net of our night; and having become a fish by the taking of humanity, became bread to refresh us by His divinity. GREG. To Peter was the holy Church committed; to him is it specially said, *Feed My sheep.* That then which is afterwards declared by word, is now signified by act. He it is who draws the fishes to the firm shore, because he it was who pointed out the stability of the eternal country to the faithful. This he did by word of mouth, by epistles; this he does daily by signs and miracles. After saying that the net was full of great fishes, the number follows: *Full of great fishes, an hundred and fifty and three.* AUG. In the draught Aug. before, the number of the fishes is not mentioned, as if in Tract. cxxii. fulfilment of the prophecy in the Psalm, *If I should declare* Ps.41,7. *them, and speak of them, they should be more than I am able to express;* but here there is a certain number mentioned, which we must explain. The number which signifies the law is ten, from the ten Commandments. But when to the law is joined grace, to the letter spirit, the number seven is brought in, that being the number which represents the Holy Spirit, to Whom sanctification properly belongs. For sanctification was first heard of in the law, with respect to the seventh day; and Isaiah praises the Holy Spirit for His sevenfold work and office. The seven of the

Spirit added to the ten of the law make seventeen; and the
numbers from one up to seventeen when added together,
Greg. make a hundred and fifty-three. GREG. Seven and ten mul-
Hom. xxiv. tiplied by three make fifty-one. The fiftieth year was a year
of rest to the whole people from all their work. In unity
Aug. is true rest; for where division is, true rest cannot be. AUG.
Tract. cxxii. It is not then signified that only a hundred and fifty-three
saints are to rise again to eternal life, but this number represents all who partake of the grace of the Holy Spirit: which
number too contains three fifties, and three over, with reference
to the mystery of the Trinity. And the number fifty is made
up of seven sevens, and one in addition, signifying that those
sevens are one. That they were *great* fishes too, is not
without meaning. For when our Lord says, *I came not to
destroy the law, but to fulfil,* by giving, that is, the Holy
Spirit through Whom the law can be fulfilled, He says almost
immediately after, *Whosoever shall do and teach them, the
same shall be called great in the kingdom of heaven.* In
the first draught the net was broken, to signify schisms; but
here to shew that in that perfect peace of the blessed there
would be no schisms, the Evangelist continues: *And for all*
[1] τοσού-
των
tanti *they were so great* [1], *yet was not the net broken;* as if alluding
to the case before, in which it was broken, and making a
favourable comparison.

12. Jesus saith unto them, Come and dine. And
none of the disciples durst ask him, Who art thou?
knowing that it was the Lord.

13. Jesus then cometh, and taketh bread, and giveth
them, and fish likewise.

14. This is now the third time that Jesus shewed
himself to his disciples, after that he was risen from
the dead.

Aug. Tract. cxxiii. Chrys. Hom. lxxxvi. Aug. xiii. de Civ.Dei, c. xxii. AUG. The fishing being over, our Lord invites them to dine:
Jesus saith unto them, Come and dine. CHRYS. John does
not say that He ate with them, but Luke does. He ate
however not to satisfy the wants of nature, but to shew the
reality of His resurrection. AUG. The bodies of the just,

when they rise again, shall need neither the word of life that they die not of disease, or old age, nor any bodily nourishment to prevent hunger and thirst. For they shall be endowed with a sure and inviolable gift of immortality, that they shall not eat of necessity, but only be able to eat if they will. Not the power, but the need of eating and drinking shall be taken away from them; in like manner as our Saviour after His resurrection took meat and drink with His disciples, with spiritual but still real flesh, not for the sake of nourishment, but in exercise of a power.

And none of His disciples durst ask Him, who art Thou? knowing that it was the Lord. AUG. No one dared to doubt that it was He, much less deny it; so evident was it. Had any one doubted, he would have asked. CHRYS. He means that they had not confidence to talk to Him, as before, but sat looking at Him in silence and awe, absorbed in regarding His altered and now supernatural form, and unwilling to ask any question. Knowing that it was the Lord, they were in fear, and only ate what, in exercise of His great power, He had created. He again does not look up to heaven, or do any thing after a human sort, thus shewing that His former acts of that kind were done only in condescension: *Jesus then cometh, and taketh bread, and giveth them, and fish likewise.* AUG. Mystically, the fried fish is Christ Who suffered. And He is the bread that came down from heaven. To Him the Church is united to His body for participation of eternal bliss. Wherefore He says, *Bring of the fishes which ye have now caught;* to signify that all of us who have this hope, and are in that septenary number of disciples, which represents the universal Church here, partake of this great sacrament, and are admitted to this bliss. GREG. By holding this last feast with seven disciples, he declares that they only who are full of the sevenfold grace of the Holy Spirit, shall be with Him in the eternal feast. Time also is reckoned by periods of seven days, and perfection is often designated by the number seven. They therefore feast upon the presence of the Truth in that last banquet, who now strive for perfection. CHRYS. Inasmuch, however, as He did not converse with them regularly, or in the same way as before, the Evangelist adds, *This is now the third time that*

Aug.
Tract.
cxxii.

Chrys.
Hom.
lxxxvii.

Aug.
Tract.
cxxiii.2.

Greg.
Hom.
xxiv.

Chrys.
Hom.
lxxxvii.

Jesus shewed Himself to His disciples, after that He was
Aug. *risen from the dead.* Aug. Which has reference not to
Tract.
cxxiii.3. manifestations, but to days; i. e. the first day after He had
risen, eight days after that, when Thomas saw and believed,
and this day at the draught of fishes; and thenceforward as
Aug. often as He saw them, up to the time of His ascension. Aug.
de Con.
Evang. We find in the four Evangelists ten occasions mentioned,
iii. 26. on which our Lord was seen after His resurrection: one at
the sepulchre by the women; a second by the women
returning from the sepulchre; a third by Peter; a fourth by
1 in cas- the two going to[1] Emmaus; a fifth in Jerusalem, when Thomas
tellum
was not present; a sixth when Thomas saw Him; a seventh
at the sea of Tiberias; an eighth by all the eleven on a mountain of Galilee, mentioned by Matthew; a ninth when for the
last time He sat at meat with the disciples; a tenth when
He was seen no longer upon earth, but high up on a cloud.

15. So when they had dined, Jesus saith to Simon
Peter, Simon, son of Jonas, lovest thou me more
than these? He saith unto him, Yea, Lord; thou
knowest that I love thee. He saith unto him, Feed
my lambs.

16. He saith to him again the second time, Simon,
son of Jonas, lovest thou me? He saith unto him,
Yea, Lord; thou knowest that I love thee. He saith
unto him, Feed my sheep.

17. He saith unto him the third time, Simon, son
of Jonas, lovest thou me? Peter was grieved because
he said unto him the third time, Lovest thou me?
And he said unto him, Lord, thou knowest all things;
thou knowest that I love thee. Jesus saith unto him,
Feed my sheep.

Theophyl. The dinner being ended, He commits to
Peter the superintendence over the sheep of the world, not
to the others: *So when they had dined, Jesus saith to
Simon Peter, Simon, son of Jonas, lovest thou Me more*

than these? AUG. Our Lord asked this, knowing it: He knew that Peter not only loved Him, but loved Him more than all the rest. ALCUIN. He is called Simon, son of John, John being his natural father. But mystically, Simon is obedience, John grace, a name well befitting him who was so obedient to God's grace, that he loved our Lord more ardently than any of the others. Such virtue arising from divine gift, not mere human will. AUG. While our Lord was being condemned to death, he feared, and denied Him. But by His resurrection Christ implanted love in his heart, and drove away fear. Peter denied, because he feared to die: but when our Lord was risen from the dead, and by His death destroyed death, what should he fear? *He saith unto Him, Yea, Lord; Thou knowest that I love Thee.* On this confession of his love, our Lord commends His sheep to him: *He saith unto him, Feed My lambs:* as if there were no way of Peter's shewing his love for Him, but by being a faithful shepherd, under the chief Shepherd. CHRYS. That which most of all attracts the Divine love is care and love for our neighbour. Our Lord passing by the rest, addresses this command to Peter: he being the chief of the Apostles, the mouth of the disciples, and head of the college. Our Lord remembers no more his sin in denying Him, or brings that as a charge against him, but commits to him at once the superintendence over his brethren. If thou lovest Me, have rule over thy brethren, shew forth that love which thou hast evidenced throughout, and that life which thou saidst thou wouldest lay down for Me, lay down for the sheep. *Chrys. Hom. lxxxviii. 1.*

　　He saith to him again the second time, Simon, son of Jonas, lovest thou Me? He saith unto Him, Yea, Lord; Thou knowest that I love Thee. Well doth He say to Peter, *Lovest thou Me,* and Peter answer, *Amo Te,* and our Lord replies again, *Feed My lambs.* Whereby, it appears that *amor* and *dilectio* are the same thing: especially as our Lord the third time He speaks does not say, *Diligis Me,* but *Amas Me. He saith unto him the third time, Simon, son of Jonas, lovest thou Me?* A third time our Lord asks Peter whether he loves Him. Three confessions are made to answer to the three denials; that the tongue might shew as *Tract. cxxii. ἀγαπᾷς diligis φιλῶ, amo.*

much love as it had fear, and life gained draw out the voice

Chrys. Hom. lxxxviii. as much as death threatened. CHRYS. A third time He asks the same question, and gives the same command; to shew of what importance He esteems the superintendence of His own sheep, and how He regards it as the greatest proof of love to Him. THEOPHYL. Thence is taken the custom Chrys. Hom. lxxxviii. of threefold confession in baptism. CHRYS. The question asked for the third time disturbed him: *Peter was grieved because He said unto him the third time, Lovest thou Me?* He was afraid perhaps of receiving a reproof again for professing to love more than he did. So he appeals to Christ Himself: *And he said unto Him, Lord, Thou knowest all things,* i. e. the secrets of the heart, present and to come. Aug. de Verb. Dom. serm. 50. AUG. He was grieved because he was asked so often by Him Who knew what He asked, and gave the answer. He replies therefore from his inmost heart; *Thou knowest that I love* Aug. Tract. cxxiv. *Thee.* AUG. He says no more, He only replies what he knew himself; he knew *he* loved Him; whether any else non occ. loved Him he could not tell, as he could not see into another's heart: *Jesus saith unto him, Feed My sheep;* as if to say, Be it the office of love to feed the Lord's flock, as it was the resolution of fear to deny the Shepherd. THEOPHYL. There is a difference perhaps between lambs and sheep. The lambs are those just initiated, the sheep are the perfected. ALCUIN. To feed the sheep is to support the believers in Christ from falling from the faith, to provide earthly sustenance for those under us, to preach and exemplify withal our preaching by our lives, to resist adversaries, to correct Aug. Tract. cxxiii. wanderers. AUG. They who feed Christ's sheep, as if they were their own, not Christ's, shew plainly that they love themselves, not Christ; that they are moved by lust of glory, power, gain, not by the love of obeying, ministering, pleasing God. Let us love therefore, not ourselves, but Him, and in feeding His sheep, seek not our own, but the things which are His. For whoso loveth himself, not God, loveth not himself: man that cannot live of himself, must die by loving himself; and he cannot love himself, who loves himself to his own destruction. Whereas when He by Whom we live is loved, we love ourselves the more, because we do not love ourselves; because we do not love ourselves in order that we may love Him by Whom we live. AUG. But unfaithful Aug.
Serm.
Pass. servants arose, who divided Christ's flock, and handed down the division to their successors: and you hear them say, Those sheep are mine, what seekest thou with my sheep, I will not let thee come to my sheep. If we call our sheep ours, as they call them theirs, Christ hath lost His sheep.

18. Verily, verily, I say unto thee, When thou wast young, thou girdedst thyself, and walkedst whither thou wouldest: but when thou shalt be old, thou shalt stretch forth thy hands, and another shall gird thee, and carry thee whither thou wouldest not.

19. This spake he, signifying by what death he should glorify God.

CHRYS. Our Lord having made Peter declare his love, Chrys.
Hom.
lxxxvii. informs him of his future martyrdom; an intimation to us how we should love: *Verily, verily, I say unto thee, When thou wast young, thou girdedst thyself, and walkedst whither thou wouldest.* He reminds him of his former life, because, whereas in worldly matters a young man has powers, an old man none; in spiritual things, on the contrary, virtue is brighter, manliness stronger, in old age; age is no hindrance to grace. Peter had all along desired to share Christ's dangers; so Christ tells him, Be of good cheer; I will fulfil thy desire in such a way, that what thou hast not suffered when young, thou shalt suffer when old: *But when thou art old.* Whence it appears, that he was then neither a young nor an old man, but in the prime of life. ORIGEN. It is not Orig.
super.
Matt. easy to find any ready to pass at once from this life ; and so he says to Peter, *When thou art old, thou shalt stretch forth thy hand.* AUG. That is, shalt be crucified. And to come Aug.
Tract.
cxxiii.
5. to this end, *Another shall gird thee, and carry thee whither thou wouldest not.* First He said what would come to pass, secondly, how it would come to pass. For it was not when crucified, but when about to be crucified, that he was led whither he would not. He wished to be released from the body, and be with Christ; but, if it were possible, he wished to attain to eternal life without the pains of death ; to

2 s

which he went against his will, but conquered by the force
of his will, and triumphing over the human feeling, so
natural a one, that even old age could not deprive Peter of
it. But whatever be the pain of death, it ought to be
conquered by the strength of love for Him, Who being our
life, voluntarily also underwent death for us. For if there is
no pain in death, or very little, the glory of martyrdom would
Chrys. not be great. CHRYS. He says, *Whither thou wouldest not,*
Hom.
lxxxviii. with reference to the natural reluctance of the soul to be
separated from the body; an instinct implanted by God to
prevent men putting an end to themselves. Then raising
the subject, the Evangelist says, *This spake He, signifying
by what death he should glorify God:* not, should die: he
expresses himself so, to intimate that to suffer for Christ was
non occ. the glory of the sufferer. But unless the mind is persuaded
that He is very God, the sight of Him can in no way enable
us to endure death. Wherefore the death of the saints is
Aug. certainty of divine glory. AUG. He who denied and loved,
Tract.
cxxiii. died in perfect love for Him, for Whom he had promised to
die with wrong haste. It was necessary that Christ should
first die for Peter's salvation, and then Peter die for Christ's
Gospel.

19. And when he had spoken this, he saith unto
him, Follow me.

20. Then Peter, turning about, seeth the disciple
whom Jesus loved following; which also leaned on his
breast at supper, and said, Lord, which is he that
betrayeth thee?

21. Peter seeing him saith to Jesus, Lord, and what
shall this man do?

22. Jesus saith unto him, If I will that he tarry till
I come, what is that to thee? follow thou me.

23. Then went this saying abroad among the
brethren, that that disciple should not die: yet Jesus
said not unto him, He shall not die; but, If I will that
he tarry till I come, what is that to thee?

Aug. Our Lord having foretold to Peter by what death he *Aug.* should glorify God, bids him follow Him. *And when He* *Tract.* *cxxiv.* *had spoken this, He saith unto him, Follow Me.* Why does He say, *Follow Me,* to Peter, and not to the others who were present, who as disciples were following their Master? Or if we understand it of his martyrdom, was Peter the only one who died for the Christian truth? Was not James put to death by Herod? Some one will say that James was not crucified, and that this was fitly addressed to Peter, because he not only died, but suffered the death of the cross, as Christ did. Theophyl. Peter hearing that he was to suffer death for Christ, asks whether John was to die: *Then Peter, turning about, seeth the disciple whom Jesus loved following; which also leaned on His breast at supper, and said, Lord, which is he that betrayeth Thee? Peter seeing him saith to Jesus, Lord, and what shall this man do?* Aug. He calls himself *Aug.* *the disciple whom Jesus loved,* because Jesus had a greater *Tract.* *cxxiv.* and more familiar love for him, than for the rest; so that He made him lie on His breast at supper. In this way John the more commends the divine excellency of that Gospel which he preached. Some think, and they no contemptible commentators upon Scripture, that the reason why John was loved more than the rest, was, because he had lived in perfect chastity from his youth up. *Then went this saying abroad among the brethren, that that disciple should not die: yet Jesus said not unto him, He shall not die; but, If I will that he tarry till I come, what is that to thee?* Theophyl. i. e. Shall he not die? Aug. *Jesus saith unto him,* *Aug.* *What is that to thee?* and He then repeats, *Follow thou Me,* *Tract.* *cxxiv.* as if John would not follow Him, because he wished to remain till He came; *Then went this saying abroad among the disciples, that that disciple should not die.* Was it not a natural inference of the disciple's? But John himself does away with such a notion: *Yet Jesus said not unto him, He shall not die; but, If I will that he tarry till I come, what is that to thee?* But if any so will, let him contradict, and say that what John says is true, viz. that our Lord did not *say* that that disciple should not die, but that nevertheless this was signified by using such words as John records. Theophyl. Or let him say, Christ did not deny that John was to die, for whatever is born dies; but said, *I will that he tarry till I come*, i. e. to live to the end of the world, and then he shall suffer martyrdom for Me. And therefore they confess that he still lives, but will be killed by Antichrist, and will preach Christ's name with Elias. But if his sepulchre be objected, then they say that he entered in alive, and went out of it after-

Aug.
Tract.
cxxiv.

wards. AUG. Or perhaps he will allow that John still lies in his sepulchre at Ephesus, but asleep, not dead; and will give us a proof, that the soil over his grave is moist and watery, owing to his respiration. But why should our Lord grant it as a great privilege to the disciple whom He loved, that he should sleep this long time in the body, when he released Peter from the burden of the flesh by a glorious martyrdom, and gave him what Paul had longed for, when he said, *I have a desire to depart and be with Christ?* If there really takes place at John's grave that which report says, it is either done to commend his precious death, since that had not martyrdom to commend it, or for some other cause not known to us. Yet the question remains, Why did our Lord say of one who was about to die, *I will that he tarry till I come?* It may be asked too why our Lord loved John the most, when Peter loved our Lord the most? I might easily reply, that the one who loved Christ the more, was the better man, and the one whom Christ loved the more, the more blessed; only this would not be a defence of our Lord's justice. This important question then I will endeavour to answer. The Church acknowledges two modes of life, as divinely revealed, that by faith, and that by sight. The one is represented by the Apostle Peter, in respect of the primacy of his Apostleship; the other by John: wherefore to the one it is said, *Follow Me*, i. e. imitate Me in enduring temporal sufferings; of the other it is said, *I will that he tarry till I come:* as if to say, Do thou follow Me, by the endurance of temporal sufferings, let him remain till I come to give everlasting bliss; or to open out the meaning more, Let action be perfected by following the example of My Passion, but let contemplation wait inchoate till at My coming it be completed: *wait*, not simply remain, continue, but wait for its completion at Christ's coming. Now in this life of action it is true, the

more we love Christ, the more we are freed from sin; but He
does not love us as we are, He frees us from sin, that we may
not always remain as we are, but He loves us heretofore
rather, because hereafter we shall not have that which dis-
pleases Him, and which He frees us from. So then let Peter
love Him, that we may be freed from this mortality; let John
be loved by Him, that we may be preserved in that immortality.
John loved less than Peter, because, as he represented that
life in which we are much more loved, our Lord said, *I will
that he remain* (i. e. wait) *till I come;* seeing that that
greater love we have not yet, but wait till we have it at His
coming. And this intermediate state is represented by Peter
who loves, but is loved less, for Christ loves us in our misery
less than in our blessedness: and we again love the contemplation of truth such as it will be then, less in our present
state, because as yet we neither know nor have it. But let
none separate those illustrious Apostles; that which Peter
represented, and that which John represented, both were
sometime to be. GLOSS. *I will that he tarry,* i. e. I will not
that he suffer martyrdom, but wait for the quiet dissolution
of the flesh, when I shall come and receive him into eternal
blessedness. THEOPHYL. When our Lord says to Peter,
Follow Me, He confers upon him the superintendence over
all the faithful, and at the same time bids him imitate Him in
every thing, word and work. He shews too His affection
for Peter; for those who are most dear to us, we bid follow
us. CHRYS. But if it be asked, How then did James assume Chrys.
the see of Jerusalem? I answer, that our Lord enthroned Hom.
Peter, not as Bishop of this see, but as Doctor of the whole lxxxviii.
world: *Then Peter, turning about, seeth the disciple whom* 2.
*Jesus loved following, which also leaned on his breast at
supper.* It is not without meaning that that circumstance
of leaning on His breast is mentioned, but to shew what confidence Peter had after his denial. For he who at the supper
dared not ask himself, but gave his question to John to put,
has the superintendence over his brethren committed to him,
and whereas before he gave a question which concerned
himself to another to put, he now asks questions himself of
his Master concerning others. Our Lord then having foretold
such great things of him, and committed the world to him, and

prophesied his martyrdom, and made known his greater love, Peter wishing to have John admitted to a share of this calling, says, *And what shall this man do?* as if to say, Will he not go the same way with us? For Peter had great love for John, as appears from the Gospels and Acts of the Apostles, which give many proofs of their close friendship. So Peter does John the same turn, that John had done him; thinking that he wanted to ask about himself, but was afraid, he puts the question for him. However, inasmuch as they were now going to have the care of the world committed to them, and could not remain together without injury to their charge, our Lord says, *If I will that he tarry till I come, what is that to thee?* as if to say, Attend to the work committed to thee, and do it: if I will that he abide here, what is that to thee? THEOPHYL. Some have understood, *Till I come,* to mean, Till I come to punish the Jews who have crucified Me, and strike them with the Roman rod. For they say that this Apostle lived up to the time of Vespasian, who took Jerusalem, and dwelt near when it was taken. Or, *Till I come,* i. e. till I give him the commission to preach, for to you I commit now the pontificate of the world: and in this follow Me, but let him remain till I come and call him, as I do thee now. CHRYS. The Evangelist then corrects the opinion taken up by the disciples.

Chrys. Hom. lxxxviii.

24. This is the disciple which testifieth of these things, and wrote these things: and we know that his testimony is true.

25. And there are also many other things which Jesus did, the which, if they should be written every one, I suppose that even the world itself could not contain the books that should be written. Amen.

Chrys. Hom. lxxxviii. 2.

Acts 2, 32.

CHRYS. John appeals to his own knowledge of these events, having been witness of them: *This is the disciple which testifieth of these things.* When we assert any un-doubted fact in common life, we do not withhold our testi-mony: much less would he, who wrote by the inspiration of the Holy Ghost. And thus the other Apostles, *And we*

are witnesses of these things, and wrote these things.
John is only one who appeals to his own testimony ; and he
does so, because he was the last who wrote. And for this
reason he often mentions Christ's love for him, i. e. to shew
the motive which led him to write, and to give weight to his
history. *And we know that his testimony is true.* He was
present at every event, even at the crucifixion, when our
Lord committed His mother to him; circumstances which
both shew Christ's love, and his own importance as a witness.
But if any believe not, let him consider what follows: *And
there are also many other things which Jesus did.* If, when
there were so many things to relate, I have not said so much
as the other, and have selected often reproaches and contumelies in preference to other things, it is evident that I
have not written partially. One who wants to shew another
off to advantage does the very contrary, omits the disho-
nourable parts. AUG. *The which, if they should be written* Aug.
every one, I suppose that even the world itself could not con- Tract.
tain the books that should be written ; meaning not the cxxiv.8.
world had not space for them, but that the capacity of readers
was not large enough to hold them : though sometimes words
themselves may exceed the truth, and yet the thing they
express be true ; a mode of speech which is used not
to explain an obscure and doubtful, but to magnify or
estimate a plain, thing : nor does it involve any departure
from the path of truth ; inasmuch as the excess of the word
over the truth is evidently only a figure of speech, and not a
deception. This way of speaking the Greeks call hyperbole,
and it is found in other parts of Scripture. CHRYS. This is Chrys.
said to shew the power of Him Who did the miracles ; i. e. Hom.
that it was as easy for Him to do them, as it is for us to speak lxxxviii.
of them, seeing He is God over all, blessed for ever.

THE END.